2018

BUSINESS REFERENCE GUIDE

The Essential Guide to Pricing Businesses and Franchises

Important Note to the Reader
This publication is designed to provide accurate and authoritative information with regard to the subject matter covered. It is sold with the understanding that the authors, editors and publisher are not engaged in rendering legal, accounting or other professional advice. If legal advice or other expert assistance is required, the services of a competent professional should be sought.

Notes to the *2018 Business Reference Guide*

Just a few explanations concerning the information in this year's Guide.

- Some quotes may be grammatically incorrect or some words improperly capitalized. We attempt to remain true to the original source and make changes only to improve readability.

- Due to space requirements, some information such as General Information, Advantages, and Disadvantages are not included in the hard copy Guide but are available in the online edition.

- Some formatting has been changed to improve readability. Except for material from a cited source like a newspaper or website, there are no quotation marks. Most of the information we present comes from our Industry Experts. Go to http://industryexpert.net/expert-directory/ to see who these valuable contributors are.

- Data for Statistics, Products and Services Segmentation, Major Market Segmentation, Industry Costs, Market Share, and Employment Size comes from IBISWorld and is used with their permission. Go to https://www.ibisworld.com to learn more about this valued resource.

Pricing Methods

Pricing methods such as multiples of Sellers Discretionary Earnings (SDE), Earnings Before Interest and Taxes (EBIT) and Earnings before Interest, Taxes, Depreciation, Amortization (EBITDA), all have two things in common: each requires that the actual earnings be calculated, and then a multiple based on many factors relating to the business must also be calculated. Multiplying the two should then produce the price for that business. Unfortunately, these methods are based on the figures being calculated and by the person doing the pricing.

The other method calls for a multiple of sales. The big advantage to this method is that it doesn't call for calculating the figures as other methods require. One simply takes the total annual sales (less sales taxes) and multiplies it by a percentage that "people in the know" are comfortable with, based on their knowledge and experience. In many cases there is a universal rule of thumb for the multiple, based on many transactions. The annual sales of a business are usually a provable figure; although an argument could be made, especially in very small businesses, that the owner could be "taking money off the top," thus reducing sales. However, unless the owner is really stealing from the business, small amounts shouldn't influence the price dramatically.

The purpose of the above information is to show that, although multipliers may stay about the same, the final result is based on figures that do reflect the impact of the economy. Sales are down and costs go up, especially in relation to sales. Therefore, we are comfortable with the final pricing results. As we keep saying, rules of thumb are just that. The purpose in supplying other information and data is so the user can adjust the rule of thumb up or down based on such information.

The pricing of a business is based on the sales and earnings, for the most part. However, another major factor in pricing a business is whether the seller will finance a portion of the selling price. If the seller won't finance a portion of the selling price, the price will generally be lower than if the seller will provide some financing. The rule is usually the lower the down payment, the higher the full price; and the seller who demands an all-cash transaction will receive, in most cases, a lower full price.

The price of a business is ultimately what someone will pay for it—it is market driven. Or, as the old saying goes, the price is what a buyer will pay and the seller will accept.

Using the Rules of Thumb

Despite all the caveats about using rules of thumb in pricing businesses, they are commonly used to do just that. The answer is quite simple—the rules are very easy to use and almost seem too simplistic. But how accurate are they? A lot more accurate than many people think. They may supply a quick fix, but if used properly, rules of thumb can come pretty close to what the business will ultimately sell for.

Rules of thumb usually come in two formats. The most commonly used rule of thumb is simply a percentage of the annual sales, or, better yet, the last 12 months of sales/revenues. For example, if the total sales were $100,000 for last year, and the multiple for the particular business is 40 percent of annual sales, then the price based on the rule of thumb would be $40,000.

Quite a few experts have said that revenue multiples are likely to be more reliable than earnings multiples. The reason is that most multiples of earnings are based on add-backs to the earnings, which can be a judgment call, as can the multiple. Sales or revenues are essentially a fixed figure. One might want to subtract sales taxes if they have not been deducted, but the sales are the sales. The only judgment then is the percentage. When it is supplied by an expert, the percentage multiplier becomes much more reliable.

The second rule of thumb used is a multiple of earnings. In small businesses, the multiple is used against what is termed Seller's Discretionary Earnings (SDE).

SDE is also called Seller's or Owner's Cash Flow and similar names. It is usually based on a multiple (generally between 1 and 5), and this number is then used as a multiple against the earnings of the business. Many of the entries also contain a multiple of EBIT and/or EBITDA.

Seller's Discretionary Earnings (SDE): The earnings of a business prior to the following items:

- income taxes
- non-recurring income and expenses
- non-operating income and expenses
- depreciation and amortization
- interest expense or income
- owner's total compensation for one owner/operator, after adjusting the total compensation of all owners to market value.

The above definition of Seller's Discretionary Earnings, although accurate, is a bit confusing. If you change the words "prior to the" and substitute the word "plus," it may be easier to understand. We would also suggest that the highest salary be used in the calculation of SDE. The reason is that we must assume that the buyer will replace the highest compensated employee or owner—at least for the SDE calculation.

Keep in mind that the multiples for the different earnings acronyms mentioned above will be different than the multiple of SDE, which, as mentioned, generally is a number between 0 and 5. The rules contained in the Guide are specific about what is being used. It will say 2.5 times SDE or 4 times EBIT, etc.

The Basics

The businesses are arranged alphabetically. In some cases, the business may go by two name descriptions, for example, gas stations and service stations. We use the one that we feel is the most common, and we try to cross-reference them. If you can't find what you are looking for, see if it is listed under another name. If there is a particular franchise you are working on and it's not in the rules, check the type of business for more information. For example, if the franchise is an ice cream shop, check the name of the franchise; and if it's not there, go to ice cream shops and other ice cream franchises. If the business is not listed, find a similar business and start there.

The Number of Businesses/Units is the approximate number of businesses of that type in the U.S. Where there is an IBISWorld report, we generally use that number. IBISWorld provides excellent reports on many, many different businesses: www.ibisworld.com. Most of these reports are well over 20 pages and are not only extensive, but most informative. They are well worth the price.

We have also provided the Standard Industrial Classification code (SIC) and the North American Industry Classification System (NAICS). For NAICS and SIC codes, go to www.naics.com.

The Rules of Thumb

The price, based on the rule of thumb, does not include inventory (unless it specifically states that it does), or real estate, and other balance-sheet items such as cash and accounts receivable. We have noticed an increase in Industry Experts telling us that inventory is included in the multiples. The price derived from the rule of thumb is for the operating assets of the business plus goodwill. It also assumes that the business will be delivered free and clear of any debt. If any debt is to be assumed by a purchaser, it is subtracted from the price based on the rule of thumb method.

In other words, the rules, unless mentioned otherwise, create a price that includes goodwill; furniture, fixtures & equipment (FF&E); and leasehold improvements, less outstanding debt, including accounts payable, loans on FF&E, bank loans, etc. The business, unless otherwise mentioned, is assumed delivered to a purchaser free and clear of any debt or encumbrances.

Accounts receivable are not included as they are generally handled outside of any transaction and also almost always belong to the seller. Work in progress, prepaid memberships, etc. also normally belong to the seller. Items such as these may be divided between buyer and seller. For example, in a dry cleaning business, the seller may have taken in a customer's clothing for dry cleaning, but the buyer may take over the business before the work has been completed and delivered back to the customer. This is generally handled outside the transaction and does not usually figure in a pricing or valuation.

Pricing Tips

These provide information from industry experts and other sources. They are intended to amplify the rules themselves. We include lots of new information every year, while maintaining important information from prior years.

Benchmark Data

This is a valuable section. We feel it is very important, in analyzing and pricing a business, that you compare it to similar businesses, or benchmarks that are unique to this type of business. One common benchmark unique to each business is the expenses. We have included as many of these as we could find. Many have been contributed by Industry Experts. If no source is mentioned, then you can assume that an Industry Expert(s) has supplied them. In many cases we have used a breakdown of expenses from IBISWorld.

The figures in Expenses (% of Annual Sales) may not always add up to 100 percent. We provide only the major categories, and there may be other expense items not included which would make up any difference. Also, in many cases, we have had to meld the figures from several different Industry Experts or sources. This may also cause some totals to slightly exceed 100 percent.

We mentioned, at the beginning of this section, that if the rule of thumb was used properly, the price derived could be more accurate than simply multiplying the sales by the percentage rule or the SDE multiple. Reviewing market-driven data, one can reasonably assume that a 10 percent swing (that's our number; yours may be higher or lower) on either side of the percentage multiple would allow for the additions or subtractions to arrive at a more accurate multiple of annual sales. Using our example above, the 40 percent figure, and then using available benchmark data could lower or raise that percentage by 10 percent. The multiple then might be more accurate.

Critics of rules of thumb claim that a rule is simply an average and doesn't allow for the variables of each individual business. Comparing the business under review with industry standards—benchmarks—can allow one to raise or lower the percentage accordingly. A 40-percent figure then could be as low as 30 percent, or as high as 50 percent.

The Benchmark section can help you look at the vital signs of the business and compare them to similar businesses. Looking at the expenses as a percentage of annual sales can be a good start. For example, if the business under review has an occupancy percentage of 12 percent against an average 8 percent benchmark, perhaps the price then should be reduced to compensate for the higher rent. The rent is pretty much a fixed expense; but the higher the rent, the lower the profit. Certainly, a new owner could lower some of the expenses, but a trained labor force, for example, is hard to replace. Obviously, reducing the percentage multiple is a judgment call; but let's face it, even business valuation is not a science, but an art—and judgment plays a large part in it.

Industry Experts' Comments

This section allows our Industry Experts to add their own personal comments about this type of business. These comments may amplify a particular area or provide additional pricing information. Many times, these Industry Experts provide information or data that can't be found anywhere else. We should add that some Industry Experts, who own or manage an office with associates, list themselves under more than one business. It may just mean that one or more agents in that office are experts in that industry.

Resources

This section includes websites of companies, publications, and trade associations related to the particular types of businesses. Some are very informative; others are really only for members.   However, many of the associations offer books or pamphlets or studies that can be informative. Every year, we find that more and more associations are charging non-members a high price for research materials that members can receive free or at a much lower price. Nation's Restaurant News, Franchise Times, AutoLaundry News, and ConvenienceStore News are examples of excellent resources, providing surveys and up-to-the-minute news about their industries. Don't forget that IBISWorld has great reports on many, many different businesses including franchises and many "mom and pop" type businesses.

Franchises

This edition contains more franchise data than any previous one. For a quick rule for many franchises, go to the Franchise entry. Additional information can be found under the entries for the specific franchise.

If you can't find the one you are looking for, see if there is a similar type of franchise that has one. If that fails, go to the particular type of business that the franchise represents. You may add to or subtract from that rule of thumb based on your assessment of the value of the franchise—is it a plus or a minus? Even if there is a rule of thumb, it is always wise to refer to the type of business for more information.

Some Final Notes

Some associations conduct their studies and surveys only every other year or even less frequently. In some cases, we have completed a particular section prior to the new data becoming available; however, we attempt to keep the information as current as possible.

We know that some of the information may be contradictory, but since we get it from those whom we believe to be experts, we still include it. The more information you have to sort through, the better your final conclusion. We think the information and data are reliable, but occasionally we find an error after the book has been printed.

Also, keep in mind that rules of thumb can vary by area and even by location. For example, businesses on the West Coast tend to sell for a higher price than the East Coast businesses, which sell for a higher price than the Midwest ones.

Thanks to our Industry Experts

We want to thank all who contributed rules of thumb, industry data, and information. It is a tribute to them that they are willing to contribute not only a rule of thumb, but also their knowledge on pricing.

We are focusing on the Industry Experts and are offering to put them on our website, provide BBP industry logos and anything else we can do to set them apart, in gratitude for their contribution. And, we also give them a complimentary copy of the current copy of the Business Reference Guide. If you're interested and feel that you are qualified, go to www.businessbrokeragepress.com and click on Services/Industry Experts.

And When All Else Fails

Keep in mind that if it's not in the Guide, we really don't have a rule of thumb for that business. We get calls from people asking for a rule of thumb for some oddball type of business like Elephant Training Schools (not really). Honestly, if we knew of one, it would be in the Guide. We're always happy to help if we can, but unless there is sufficient sales data, there generally isn't a rule of thumb available. Here are some suggestions if you can't find what you need.

- Call a similar business in your area and see if they are aware of one.

- Check with a vendor, distributor, or equipment manufacturer and see if someone there can help.

- Call a trade association for that particular industry and see if they can direct you to someone who can help. Don't do it by email or fax, but call and speak to someone. Trade associations really don't want to get involved, but an individual might get you to the next step.

If none of the above helps, then we're afraid you have to accept the fact that there just may not be one for the business you are checking on.

Thanks to our Sponsors

(For more information on any of the resources below, please see the colored pages in the center of the Guide.)

AICPA

BizComps

Business Valuation Resources

BusinessBroker.net

Deal Studio

Diamond Financial

GCF Valuation

International Business Brokers Association

International Franchise Professionals Group

International Society of Business Appraisers

Nation-List International

Nationwide Valuations

Open Escrow

PeerComps

Toons 'N Tips

Transworld

Businesses in the 2018 Guide

Introduction

28th Edition

Business Reference Guide **2018**

Introduction

	Franchise

AAMCO Transmission

Approx. Total Investment	$227,400–$333,000
Estimated Annual Sales/Unit	$645,000

SIC 7537-01	NAICS 811113	Number of Businesses/Units 671

Rules of Thumb

➢ 40–42% Annual Sales includes inventory
➢ 2–3x per room

Pricing Tips

- "In 2015, the average annual gross sales of all Operating Centers were $669,607."
  Source: http://aamcoFranchises.com/research/how-have-aamco-centers-performed-financially/
- One observation is that Franchised shops that are following the model with a good manager are successful. The typical shop has three technicians, a rebuilder and two mechanics, and a manager.
- Most of the Franchised shops have an owner who oversees but might be considered absentee.
- The better way to analyze a business is from a well-defined proforma as opposed to tax returns and financial statements. Looking at the top line on the tax return, I sell from a proforma using market values for parts, cost and labor.
- Detailed weekly reports provided to the franchisor are more important documents for analyzing historical performance than financial statements and tax returns, as these reports will reveal the prices charged ratio of major/minor repairs and warranty repairs.

Benchmark Data

Expenses as a percentage of annual sales

Production labor costs	20%
Sales/Labor	08% to 10%
Occupancy	06% to 10%
Profit (estimated pretax)	10% to 20%

Cost of Sales

Parts & Fluids	22%
Production Labor (All Technical Employees)	20%
Towing	01%
Misc. Production Supplies	03%
Total Cost of Sales	46%

Sales & Administration Expenses

Salaries (Center Mgr. & Office)	10%
Rent	08%
Insurance	03%
Utilities	01%
Advertising-Yellow Pages	08%
Telephone	01%
Legal/Accounting	01%
Bank Fees/Bad Debt	01%
Training	01%
Total Sales & Administration Expenses	34%
Net Profit	20%

A

Questions
- Following are some suggested questions:
  - ✓ Does the shop meet AAMCO standards?
  - ✓ Historic sales and change in demographics?
  - ✓ What is ratio of major to minor repairs?
  - ✓ Ratio of general auto to transmission repair?
  - ✓ Ratio of "Fleet" (commercial) vs. Retail?
  - ✓ Percentage of "Comebacks" warranty repairs?
  - ✓ Is the manager following the AAMCO 'Spiel'?

Expert Comments

Typically a buyer assumes responsibility for warranty repairs. In my analysis, I look at this very carefully and at the compensation to the rebuilder to see if it is too low.

The Internet has changed the marketing and advertising model—lowering cost but making it more difficult for the small independent to compete with the Franchises in the major market areas.

Seller Financing
- 50 percent down—five (5) years

Resources
- AAMCO Franchises: http://www.aamcoFranchises.com

Accounting Firms/CPAs		
SIC 8721-01	NAICS 541211	Number of Businesses/Units 97,680

Rules of Thumb
- ➤ 2x EBIT
- ➤ 2.2x EBITDA
- ➤ 100–125% annual revenues plus inventory
- ➤ 1.8–3x SDE plus inventory

Pricing Tips
- CPA and Accounting Practices on average sell for .6 to 1.2 times Gross Annual Revenue.
- CPA and accounting firms sell as a multiple of gross revenue. They trade between .75 and 1.5 times gross "recurring" collected revenue. Considering supply and demand is critical in pricing. Rural or low-population rural cities will not have the same kind of demand that a metropolitan area would have. For this reason, metropolitan CPA firms typically carry a multiple greater than rural or low-population practices. Size also matters, and firms that have at least $150,000 of gross recurring income in metro areas receive multiples in excess of 1. Net income margin and seller discretionary earnings margin play the most significant role in pricing firms within the range mentioned earlier. We see firms range in SDE margin from 25% on the low side to 70% on the

Business Reference Guide **2018**

high side. Firms with lower cash flow margins receive a multiple in the lower part of the range. Firms with high levels of cash flow margin are assigned multiples in the higher portion of the range. There are many other determinants in pricing, such as business to 1040 mix and level of bookkeeping vs. tax, specialties, concentration, human capital, and general infrastructure and operational efficiency. There is a high level of demand in this industry, as we have seen private equity move into this market as well as wealth management companies and other PEO related companies over the past 5 years. The wealth management and accounting industries are blending, which increases demand. More companies are diversifying into other key professional service areas, and we have seen companies carry legal and wealth management business lines alongside the traditional tax and accounting world.

- Accounting and CPA firm selling prices are a function of Gross Revenue, Customer Profile, (business client versus individuals), mix of revenue by type. What is being sold is the customer list, goodwill and the revenue stream from the customers.
- Most accounting and tax practices will sell based on a multiple of gross billings. This multiple will typically include a client retention clause. If no retention clause, the multiple will be reduced significantly.
- Small accounting and tax practices and CPA firms tend to sell for a multiple of gross revenue equal to 100%–130%. Deals are structured basically one of three ways. The first way deals are structured is the earnout. This is where a buyer pays a % of the revenue he/she collects post closing. If terms agreed were 100% of revenue, the buyer might pay the seller 20% of what they collect from the seller's client list each year for 5 years. Because this structure puts the majority, if not all, of the risk on the seller's shoulders, the multiples can be higher, sometimes as high as 200%. The second way deals are structured is a fixed price. This structure is fairly self explanatory. Buyer and seller agree to a price and there are no post closing adjustments. The buyer assumes the majority of the risk in this structure. The third way deals in this industry are put together is a combination of the two, call it a modified earnout structure. A buyer offers to pay a multiple of gross revenue for the seller's clients based on the first year following closing. This structure gives buyers the confidence to pay a little higher multiple while at the same time giving a seller the security that the buyer will not be able to cherry pick the clients. We see deals in this industry put together every day using all three deal structures.
- Product mix and any special areas of practice can affect selling price to the right buyer. There is always the possibility to split up a practice among two or more buyers if specialty work is involved.
- Revenue composition is important; retail tax, writeup, monthly accounting, review work, audit, consulting, types of revenue streams—all have an effect on sale's price.
- Biggest factor is the terms and whether seller will guarantee part or all of the income.
- The composition of billings is important. The split between recurring/one time. The split among taxes/accounting/audit/consulting/other is important in determining staff composition. Labor costs are extremely important in bottom line. Accounts receivable levels may indicate problems with billings and/or clients.

A

Benchmark Data

Statistics (Accounting Services)

Number of Establishments	97,348
Average Profit Margin	17.4%
Revenue per Employee	$198,000
Average Number of Employees	5.6
Average Wages per Employee	$72,748

Products and Services Segmentation

Financial auditing services	30.2%
Other services	21.9%
Corporate tax preparation and representative services	16.8%
Individual tax preparation and representative services	11.2%
Tax planning and consulting services	8.1%
General accounting services	5.7%
Financial statement review services	3.2%
Other financial assurance services	2.9%

Major Market Segmentation

Finance sector	22.5%
Individuals	15.6%
Manufacturing sector	13.6%
Retail sector	12.7%
Other businesses	12.3%
Utilities and mining sector	10.7%
Public sector	7.5%
Nonprofit organizations	5.1%

Industry Costs

Profit	17.4%
Wages	36.9%
Purchases	2.7%
Depreciation	1.4%
Marketing	0.8%
Rent & Utilities	6.0%
Other	34.8%

Market Share

Deloitte Touche Tohmatsu	9.2%
PricewaterhouseCoopers	9.1%
Ernst & Young	8.9%
KPMG International	5.5%

- Accounting and CPA firms with more than 60% of revenue from tax preparation are not as profitable as firms with less than 60%. As a rule of thumb, the more revenue coming from monthly accounting versus tax preparation the more profitable.
- Employee should bill out $100k per year.
- Small one-owner firms tend to show 40-60% SDE. Larger firms with more than one partner/owner show lower SDE but still typically remain in the 30-40% range.

Expenses (% of Annual Sales)

Cost of Goods...0% to 05%
Occupancy Costs... 10% to 20%
Payroll/Labor Costs .... 25% to 35%
Profit (pretax)... 35% to 45%

Questions

- Concentration questions are very good to ask and not just individual concentration but group concentration. Relatives and related entities should all be grouped together as one client because if one leaves, they all likely leave. Human capital questions are also very important to understand as well as the seasonality of cash flows, both of which can cause production or production capacity issues. I would also request to review some files for work papers as you want to have a good understanding of how they handle the gray areas, and you need to make sure you can understand the work papers as they relate to client nuances.
- Buyers should determine a seller's true motivation for selling and find out what their plans are post closing. Buyers should make sure they understand the work being performed in the seller's practice and that they have the skill set to manage the client's needs.
- Access to 3 years of financials and tax returns for review. Non-compete agreement? Seller financing?
- How long will you help me with transitioning the clients?
- How is your staff? What are the terms of the lease? How close are the clients to the office?
- What period of time will they guarantee the billings?
- Any client concentrations, risks of client losses.
- Why are you selling? Is any individual client fee over 10% of the Gross Revenue? Is any single industry over 10% of Gross Revenue? How much of Revenue is earned from tax return preparation and how much from accounting or auditing? What percent are corporate returns or individual returns? What type of client audits? What type of work does your staff do? What tax and accounting software do you use? What is the billing rate per hour? Do you bill by hour or project? How long have your clients been with this firm? How long have the employees been with this firm?
- Do you do any audit work? Are your licenses current? How many hours do you personally bill per year?
- The quality of the fees should be investigated both by looking at the cash flow percentages and investigating the billing rates of the personnel and the owner. Post-sale competition is a major risk factor so this possibility should be investigated carefully.

Industry Trend

- Providing there are no significant political changes that disrupt the industry, we see increasing demand in the next few years but also increasing supply. Demographically, accountants have held on to their practices longer than a typical entrepreneur but now have reached an age where we should see an increase in exit among accountants over the next 5 to 10 years. Current tax proposals in Congress could significantly affect the 1040 (individual taxes) if they are successful at a one-page 1040 return that can be completed by the

taxpayer. This could affect value of accounting firms, as the 1040 customers opt for a free one-page return.
- I don't see much change in the current demand for accounting firms in the next several years. Major metro areas continue to provide a seller's market for these firms.
- "6 accounting trends to watch in 2016:
  - ✓ Accountants are about to get hit by the collaboration wave
  - ✓ Technology is doing more of the heavy lifting
  - ✓ Fixed pricing can't be ignored
  - ✓ More services are becoming commercially viable
  - ✓ Accounting is working in a very small, global world
  - ✓ The big end of town is after small business"

    Source: "6 Accounting Trends to Watch in 2016" by James Solomons,
    https://www.digitalfirst.com/6-accounting-trends-watch-2016/

- Due to the baby boomer curve there will be an increase in the number of firms being offered for sale or merger.
- Aging accountants will be selling off. New regulations have also moved more people towards the sell side.
- More sellers with the baby boomers retiring. There are different opinions as to the liquidity of small accounting firms with more sellers entering the marketplace. I believe practices in major metro areas will continue to be in high demand while practices in more rural areas will struggle to find buyers at times.
- Industry trend is upward due to increased tax and government regulations on businesses and individuals.
- Still a seller's market
- Industry regulation makes entry difficult yet demand for services continually increase.
- An increase in the number of small single-owner firms billing $100K or less as laid-off industry CPAs open their own firms.
- Expert Comments
- Price is important but terms are more important (use an attorney and an established broker to protect yourself). Make sure to have both buyer and seller commitment to a written transition plan.
- Buyers are advised to move quickly when looking at firms in major metro areas as they do not tend to stay on the market long when represented by a business broker that specializes in selling accounting firms. Sellers should know that their firms have significant value that can be realized when using a professional process to identify and screen buyers. Sellers generally do not have to sell their firms for low down payments and an earnout payment structure.
- The marketability of accounting firms has been and seems to continue to be very good, especially for firms located in major metro areas. Financing available to buyers in abundance, which also adds to the marketability.
- Have a strategy. It is a long process from both the seller and buyer perspective. Be prepared as this will not happen overnight.
- We have encountered all of these scenarios over the years. When a seller meets two prospective qualified buyers, he or she will sell the practice to the one that feels right. The wise buyer will be sensitive to the feelings and emotions of the seller, and the wise seller will be sensitive to the feelings and emotions of the buyer.

- Buyers like consistency. Having a consistent 3-year revenue pattern without significant influxes shows the buyer stability in the practice and client base. Obviously with the shape of the economy over the last few years, a 5–10% decrease would not be too alarming. On the contrary, if revenues have spiked greatly over the years, you as a seller should be ready to explain this pattern. Increasing to stable revenue patterns will show the buyer that your practice is on solid financial ground.
- Buyers that are looking to buy your CPA or accounting practice are looking long-term. They are not buying your client base with the expectations that clients will turnover or leave after a tax season or two. They want your client base to adapt and become clients over the long haul. Practices that have a good reputation in the area and have been well established in the area will yield a higher market demand.
- The higher the average fees per client, the more value the buyer will find in the practice. Below-average individual tax returns fees is not always a negative. If you are charging $100 per return, but this return only takes 15 minutes to complete, then your average billing rate would be $400, not bad. However, the problem is that some buyers will not dig deep enough to understand this point and dismiss the practice right off the bat because their firm's minimum 1040 is $200. They may be doing more complicated and difficult returns for $250 and it may take them 30 minutes to complete. The key is to explain to the buyer why your fee structure is what it is and how they too can make this a profitable business.
- Buyer will need to be a CPA or have an accounting background in order to buy the business. It is a specialized and niche field. Buyers will need this education and background in order to retain the existing client base. Not everyone who wants to buy a business will be able to buy an accounting or tax practice.

Seller Financing
- The deals we do have a minimum requirement of 50% down. We see the retention risk as a balanced risk with both the seller and the buyer. Both have substantial impact on retention, and contracts need to be written with that in mind. Larger firms typically use a financing vehicle. Many have acquisitions financing already set up with their bank but many use SBA and other conventional sources. For smaller firms, bank financing is usually not used and seller financing is the preferred method.
- Most of the practice sales we are involved with utilize a combination of bank and seller financing. A typical deal structure is as follows: the buyer puts in 10% of the purchase price, the bank provides 70–80% and the seller provides a promissory note for 10–20% of the purchase price.
  Majority of funding from buyer and outside funding. Average term 2 to 3 years. Past experience has shown the seller getting 100% of selling price at closing.
- Buyer 10–25%, seller 10–25%, bank the balance.
- The transactions I've participated in were based on notes based on client retention, or earnouts over a 1- to 3-year period. Most commonly through 2 tax seasons. Heaviest weight of earnout based on first tax season.

Resources
- accountingTODAY: http://www.accountingtoday.com
- American Institute of CPAs: http://www.aicpa.org

A

- Arizona Society of CPAS (ASCPA): https://www.ascpa.com/
- Entrepreneurial CPA Network (ECPAN): http://www.ecpan.org/
- Arizona Board of Accountancy: https://www.azaccountancy.gov/
- Arizona Society of Practicing Accountants: http://www.aztaxandaccounting.org/
- IBISWorld, January 2017: http://ibisworld.com

Accounting Firms/Practices		
SIC 8721-01	NAICS 541219	Number of Businesses/Units 140,000

Rules of Thumb

➢ 2.5–3.5x SDE plus inventory (if any)

➢ 1–1.25x annual revenues (non-CPA) plus inventory

➢ 45% x EBIT

Pricing Tips

- Rural area practices will sell for a lower multiple than urban areas. The more profitable the practice; the higher the multiple.
- Accounting firms generally sell for a multiple of revenue from 1 to 1.3 times revenue. Firms in major metro areas tend to sell faster than firms located in more rural areas and also tend to sell on the higher side of market value.
- Typically I do it in 3 phases to be discussed on a confidential basis, but it includes down payment, negotiated hourly rate and a retention bonus.
- Age of practice; makeup of the gross income; who is staying behind to do the work; will seller stay the first tax season and what's the cost for them to stay.
- "Net profit margins for the average company in the accounting category rose to 22 percent in 2015, up from 18 percent in 2014. Over the past five years, the margin was 16.2 percent. Profit growth, however, dropped to 19.5 percent from 2014's 23.8 percent. But 2015's profit growth indicated improvement over the 17.6 percent overall average for the last five years."
  Source: http://www.accountingweb.com/practice/growth/accounting-firms-saw-solid-sales-growth-in-2015
- Almost all of the deals will be subject to attrition and retention clauses. But it is equally important for the deal to also include a clause for the growth within the portfolio.
  Fee structure, client complexity, location and overall staffing requirements affect practice desirability.

Benchmark Data

- Employee should bill out $100k per year.
- Labor at less than 33% is best.
- Each employee should generate around $100k–$150k in annual billings. Owners/Partners—$200k–$250k.
- Generally revenue based on employee costs.
- Not moving the office will help retain the client base.
- Number of repeat clients on the book; it usually takes at least 250–350 to break even and above that to be profitable.

Expenses (% of Annual Sales)

Cost of Goods .... n/a
Occupancy Costs .... 08% to 15%
Payroll/Labor Costs .... 30% to 35%
Profit (pretax) .... 30% to 45%

Questions

- How is the staff? Last 3 years of financial records. Breakdown of the revenue mix. What are the seller's plans for after the sale? How will they assist post sale?
- Buyers should determine a seller's true motivation for selling and find out what their plans are post closing. Buyers should make sure they understand the work being performed in the seller's practice and that they have the skill set to manage the client's needs.
- How much retainage can you predict and will you price the business with that as a factor?
- Why are you leaving?
- What do you plan to do after you sell the practice? How often do clients come in to the office to meet with you? How many personal taxes do you do a year vs. corporate tax returns? What percentage of your work includes 'specialty' consulting work? Does your practice also provide bookkeeping services?
- Demographic of the client base. Number of years average client has been with the firm.
- Gross revenue, revenue type, number of clients, fees generated from each client, employee compensation and experience, lease on facilities, type of software used, net income.
- Will clients likely stay with new owner?
- Break down the composition of fees on an annual basis (percent from tax, bookkeeping, payroll, accounting, auditing, technology, consulting, etc.). Also ask if fee structure is based on hourly or fixed-fee arrangements. What is the effective percent of production hours (total firm hours billed/total firm hours spent)? What are the rate realizations (total fees billed/standard rates x hours billed)? Clients making up over 10% of annual fees? Any major clients coming to end of service agreements, and details? Answers indicating poor production and rate realizations have a negative impact on pricing, while positive statistics have positive impacts on pricing.

Industry Trend

- Baby boomers are getting older so more practices are coming available.
- I don't see much change in the current demand for accounting firms in the next several years. Major metro areas continue to provide a seller's market for these firms.
- Continuing to be solid; even if President Trump reduces FIT, the loyal customers will continue to utilize the professional services of a CPA.
- Continuing to grow at a rapid rate as the economy improves.
- Steady to upward
- Consolidation and firms sending work offshore

A

Expert Comments

Communicate with the client base to ensure client retention.

Buyers are advised to move quickly when looking at firms in major metro areas as they do not tend to stay on the market long when represented by a business broker that specializes in selling accounting firms. Sellers should know that their firms have significant value that can be realized when using a professional process to identify and screen buyers. Sellers generally do not have to sell their firms for low down payments and an earnout payment structure.

The marketability of accounting firms has been and seems to continue to be very good, especially for firms located in major metro areas. Financing available to buyers in abundance, which also adds to the marketability.

Don't wait too long to buy or to sell. The D's can get you: death, disability, divorce, disinterest.

Retention is the key and the first tax season is the key to that.

Locate well-established practice with experienced staff, great fee structure, and growing location.

As taxes get more complicated the need for good accountants keeps increasing. There is lots of consolidation in this industry as the older accountants start to retire and the newer ones know that to grow their practice faster, they need to acquire.

There seem to be plenty of buyers for a good accounting practice.

With technology today, accountants can process the client's work from anywhere. Office location is not as important unless it is an all-1040 tax practice.

Seller Financing

- Combination of bank and seller financing, 10-year terms on the bank loans, 1–5 on seller note.
- Most of the practice sales we are involved with utilize a combination of bank and seller financing. A typical deal structure is as follows: the buyer puts in 10% of the purchase price, the bank provides 70–80% and the seller provides a promissory note for 10–20% of the purchase price.
- Seller financing in the 3- to 4-year range.
- We are continuing to see more practices sold with outside financing. Generally, buyers are being required to pay 70 to 80% upfront at closing with minimal seller financing. Very strong seller's market.
- 5-year financing period
- Typical seller financed over 2 to 3 years and it is tied to the retention of the clients.
- Earnouts are very typically between one and two years.
- 30 percent down payment, 70 percent seller carry back, five years, 8 to 10 percent
- 20 to 40 percent down, financing three to five years for small practices; seven to 10 years for larger ones

Resources

- American Institute of Certified Public Accountants (AICPA): http://www.aicpa.org
- National Society of Accountants: http://www.nsacct.org
- *Buying a Practice* by Leon Faris and Vance Wingo: http://www.cpasales.com

Accounting/Tax Practices		
SIC 7291-01	NAICS 541213	

Rules of Thumb

➤ 1–1.35 x annual revenues plus inventory

➤ 2–3 x SDE plus inventory

➤ 5–7 x EBIT

➤ 4–6 x EBITDA

Pricing Tips

- Accounting firms generally sell for a multiple of revenue from 1 to 1.3 times revenue. Firms in major metro areas tend to sell faster than firms located in more rural areas and also tend to sell on the higher side of market value.
- Many factors may add a premium or discount to the 'rule of thumb' multiple: years established, billing rates, net earnings, reputations, location, type of work performed, established clientele, trained staff, etc.
- Diversification of client industry and no client over 20% of the practice gross revenue. Should have a good mix of accounting and tax.
- Practices in urban areas are priced higher. Practice prices do not include equipment or inventory.
- Most practices are sold on a multiple of the gross billings. This is typically anywhere from 1.0 to 1.30.
- Even distribution of revenue from tax return preparation and accounting fees is better.
- Buyers generally want earnouts, sellers want cash.
- Repeat clients, accounting vs. tax preparation work.
- Tax related revenues are priced at 1 to 1.25 times annual revenues. Monthly write-up revenues are priced at 1.25 to 1.5 times annual revenues. Other revenues priced at one times annual revenue.
- National franchises can hurt sale price due to franchise, royalty, and advertising fees charged.
- Higher average price per return results in higher asking price.
- Higher end practices will net 40%
- Dependent on type of clients; 1040 clients result in lower pricing; monthly and retainer clients result in higher pricing. Audit only preferred by a minority of firms.
- Typically practices sell for multiples of revenue from 1x to 1.75x based on location and demand in area and type of practice.

Benchmark Data

Statistics (Tax Preparation Services)

Number of Establishments... 134,066
Average Profit Margin 15.1%
Revenue per Employee $31,500
Average Number of Employees... 2.4
Average Wages per Employee $10,659

Products and Services Segmentation

Standard tax preparation services 57.0%
Basic tax preparation services.. 23.0%
Full-service tax preparation services 14.0%
Tax-related financial products 6.0%

Industry Costs

Profit 15.1%
Wages.. 33.9%
Purchases.. 4.3%
Depreciation... 3.0%
Marketing 1.9%
Rent & Utilities 7.4%
Other.. 34.4%

Market Share

H&R Block Inc.. 22.8%
Intuit Inc. 21.4%

- $100,000 billings per staff person
- A successful accounting practice should have Seller's Discretionary Earnings of 45% to 60% of revenue. The larger firm will earn 40% to 50% of revenue and the smaller firm should be 50% to 60% of revenue.
- Well-run practices have profits of 30% to 45% of revenues.
- Write-up work and monthly payroll preparation should provide approximately 75% of total revenues. Taxes should provide the remaining 25%.
- Taxpayers may also benefit by obtaining tax preparation estimates from more than one preparer from different size companies. For example, the survey found that tax preparation fees for an itemized Form 1040 with Schedule A and a state tax return averaged only $217 at one-person firms, and rose to an average of $245 for firms with three or more staff.

Expenses (% of Annual Sales)

Cost of Goods... 02%
Occupancy Costs..05% to 10%
Payroll/Labor Costs ....25% to 30%
Profit (pretax)..30% to 45%

Questions

- Buyers should determine a seller's true motivation for selling and find out what their plans are post closing. Buyers should make sure they understand the work being performed in the seller's practice and that they have the skill set to manage the clients' needs.

- Why are you selling? Is any individual client fee over 10% of the Gross Revenue? Is any single industry over 10% of Gross Revenue? How much of revenue is earned from tax return preparation and how much from accounting or bookkeeping? What type of work does your staff do? What tax and accounting software do you use? What is the billing rate per hour? Do you bill by hour or project? How long have your clients been with this firm? How long have the employees been with this firm?
- Repeat clients, accounting vs. tax preparation work
- Strengths and weaknesses of the firm. Information about the area.
- What is the breakdown between tax, write-up, consulting and audit revenues? Also, who else in the firm can do the tax and write-up work? Who reviews the work?
- How long has the firm been in business? List of clients that have left within the past 3 years. List of new clients within the last 3 years. Does the owner plan on being available after the sale? Review sample returns and work papers to get a feel for the amount of work that is done for each client.
- Why are you selling? Are the clients leaving because of location or other reason? What type of software is used now? If the clients are not walk-in, how long have they been tax clients? What industry are most of the clients? What % of clients are personal returns or business returns? Are bookkeeping services included with any client?
- Fee structure, number of clients, services performed, employee costs, Franchise fees paid, licenses required.
- Any clients not in the local service area?

Industry Trend

- I don't see much change in the current demand for accounting firms in the next several years. Major metro areas continue to provide a seller's market for these firms.
- Up and possibly up sharply depending on the IRS Tax Code changes and effects of the Affordable Care Act
- Any new tax laws would greatly affect the accounting and tax industry.
- Growth...consistent growth due to regulations
- Continued demand for acquisitions and continued exiting by aging population of CPAs

Expert Comments

Buyers are advised to move quickly when looking at firms in major metro areas as they do not tend to stay on the market long when represented by a business broker that specializes in selling accounting firms. Sellers should know that their firms have significant value that can be realized when using a professional process to identify and screen buyers. Sellers generally do not have to sell their firms for low down payments and an earnout payment structure.

The marketability of accounting firms has been and seems to continue to be very good, especially for firms located in major metro areas. Financing available to buyers in abundance, which also adds to the marketability.

While there are lots of accountants and tax preparers, satisfied clients are very loyal. Small businesses need help and often look for help from their accountant.

Accounting work growing due to outsourcing

The profit trend and industry trend is upward due to increased tax and government regulations on businesses and individuals. There is a greater need of business bookkeeping and records for proof of compliance with government regulations. Location and facilities are located in office or retail locations. A profitable, well balanced practice is highly marketable to those entering the profession from corporate and established firms to expand their client base. Replication or opening a practice is not difficult. Establishing a client base is the challenge for a new accounting practice.

Historically profitable practices will sell for a higher price.

Tax preparation has become a commodity. Anyone with $5,000, a PC, and software can easily open a tax prep office. A number of recent national Franchises have over-saturated the market.

Industry is in need of personnel and has no lack of new regulations which necessitate new audit or forensic work.

High risk, as it is easy to duplicate this type of business. Customer loyalty is not as strong in this business as in a CPA practice.

Seller Financing
- Most of the practice sales we are involved with utilize a combination of bank and seller financing. A typical deal structure is as follows: the buyer puts in 10% of the purchase price, the bank provides 70–80% and the seller provides a promissory note for 10–20% of the purchase price.
- Generally seeing more outside financing, with a combination of owner and bank financing in place.

Resources
- IBISWorld, October 2016: http://ibisworld.com
- National Association of Enrolled Agents: http://www.naea.org
- Association of International Certified Professional Accountants: http://www.aicpa.org
- National Association of Tax Professionals: http://www.natptax.com/Pages/default.aspx

Ace Cash Express		
SIC 6099-03	NAICS 522390	Number of Businesses/Units 1,750

Rules of Thumb
➤ 1.25 x annual sales plus inventory

Pricing Tips
- This company is publicly held, and their annual report is available online and is an excellent resource.

Resources

- Ace Cash Express: http://www.acecashexpress.com

Ace Hardware	Franchise
Approx. Total Investment	$650,000–$1,100,000

SIC 5251-04	NAICS 444130	Number of Businesses/Units 4,166

Rules of Thumb

➢ 45% of annual sales plus inventory

Pricing Tips

- "Sales seem to indicate that smaller sales bring a higher multiple (50%+) than stores with sales over $1 million, which seem to bring lower multiples. Price is plus inventory, and that may be the reason for lower multiples for larger stores."

Resources

- Investing In The Ace Hardware Store Franchise: http://www.myace.com

Adam & Eve Stores	Franchise
Approx. Total Investment	$172,000–$350,000

	NAICS 451120	Number of Businesses/Units 55

Rules of Thumb

➢ 35% of annual sales plus inventory

Resources

- Adam & Eve stores: http://www.adamevestores.com

Advertising Agencies		
SIC 7311-01	NAICS 541810	Number of Businesses/Units 69,685

Rules of Thumb

➢ 50% of annual revenues (billings) plus inventory.

Pricing Tips

- "What are agencies worth? This is a tough one, but typical agencies are valued at 2–5 times EBITDA (I mean realistic EBITDA that includes having the CEO actually paying himself and other agency mangers what they are worth). Digital firms have higher multiples at 8 plus. The digital sweet spot is a firm with technological prowess, owned IP, strategic vision and industry-leading expertise in a hot category like mobile, social, etc.

A - Rules of Thumb

"A good start is to take a look at what kinds of agencies or digital media companies have been purchased in the past couple of years." – Peter Levitan

Source: https://www.linkedin.com/pulse/8-tips-how-sell-your-ad-agency-wpp-peter-levitan

Benchmark Data

Statistics (Advertising Agencies)

Number of Establishments	69,685
Average Profit Margin	7.7%
Revenue per Employee	$172,000
Average Number of Employees	3.8
Average Wages per Employee	$72,425

Products and Services Segmentation

Advertising services	64.1%
Creative services	19.5%
Other	8.0%
Media planning, buying & representation	6.3%
Public relations services	2.1%

Major Market Segmentation

Retail sector	21.0%
TMT	22.0%
Automotive sector	12.0%
Financial services	13.0%
Travel & entertainment	12.0%
Other	9.0%
Consumer packaged goods	6.0%
Pharmaceutical & Healthcare sector	5.0%

Industry Costs

Profit	7.7%
Wages	41.8%
Purchases	42.1%
Depreciation	0.7%
Marketing	2.6%
Rent & Utilities	1.5%
Other	3.6%

Market Share

Omnicom Group Inc.	15.0%
Interpublic Group of Companies Inc.	8.4%
WPP PLC	6.5%

Industry Trend

- "The blockbuster $4.8 billion sale of Yahoo's core assets to Verizon communications, announced on Monday, could generate deep shifts on the global advertising industry's playing field. Verizon plans to merge the Yahoo assets with AOL, which the company bought in 2015. AOL head Tim Armstrong will spearhead the integration of the two companies along with Verizon EVP Marni Walden, a process that is sure to be tedious and lengthy. The newly bolstered telecom giant hopes to compete with Google and Facebook in an industry where 'scale is imperative.'"

Source: "Verizon, Yahoo could Reshape the Advertising Industry," by Tobi Elkin and Philip Rosenstein, July 26, 2016, www.mediapost.com/publications/article/281071/verizon-yahoo-could-reshape-the-advertisingindus.html?

- Yahoo brings with it an audience of 1 billion active worldwide users -- including 600 million active mobile users, a host of influential consumer brand partnerships, a powerful programmatic advertising and data platform and a robust editorial team.

Resources
- IBISWorld, December 2016: http://ibisworld.com
- American Association of Advertising Agencies: http://www.aaaa.org

	Franchise
Aero Colours, Inc.	
Approx. Total Investment	$49,000–$174,000

SIC 7532-02	NAICS 811121	Number of Businesses/Units 200

Rules of Thumb
➤ 70% of annual sales

Resources
- Drive N Style: http://www.drivenstyle.com/

Aircraft Cleaning		
SIC 4581-04	NAICS 561720	Number of Businesses/Units 3,807

Rules of Thumb
➤ 100% of annual sales plus inventory

➤ 3 x SDE plus inventory

Pricing Tips
- Minimum 3 yrs. in business, 2.5 x net if owner operated, as much as 4x net if work is performed by a crew or crews.

Benchmark Data
- Labor should run approximately 25% of sales.
- Corporate aircraft cleaning is a very specialized service; if it survived the first 18 months, chances are it will do well.
- All services are mobile.

Expenses (% of Annual Sales)

Cost of Goods	05% to 10%
Occupancy Costs	10%
Payroll/Labor Costs	25% to 35%
Profit (pretax)	55% to 60%

Questions

- Number of accounts, how long servicing those accounts, percentage of sales from which accounts
- How many aircraft do you service per week, per month? Number of employees? The buyer is going to need to keep the employees.
- Transition period is very important.

Industry Trend

- Increase in demand
- Private aviation is a rapidly growing industry.

Expert Comments

- "Cleaning an airplane after the passengers leave is no easy job—it's messy, sometimes disgusting, and can even be downright dangerous, employees told ABC News. 'We encounter human feces, sometimes blood, most of the time vomit from passengers that get motion sick' said Joel Castillo, who works for Air Serv, a company that handles the cabin cleaning for commercial flights. Castillo's job is to empty the blue liquid that's in the toilets on airplanes. Cabin cleaners are also responsible for sweeping the plane to see what passengers left behind, and they say they often find dirty diapers and half-eaten food stuffed into the seat pockets."

  Source: http://abcnews.go.com/Health/airplane-cabin-cleaners-demanding-protection/story?id=26075813

- Strong barrier to entry; quality equipment is a must; high profit; labor intense; and a current downturn in general aviation
- Aviation is a very difficult industry as a startup business.

Resources

- National Business Aviation Association: http://www.nbaa.org

Aircraft Manufacturing—Parts, Supplies, Engines, etc. (Kit-built & Ultralight aircraft industry)		
SIC 3724	NAICS 336412	

Rules of Thumb

➤ 40–70% of annual sales includes value of equipment

➤ 4 x EBIT

Pricing Tips

- Add for any FAA approvals and for high-value equipment.
- FAA approvals and/or contracts with major OEM's very important.
- Each business varies so greatly from the next. It takes someone who knows the industry to know the exact business being described before a price can be established.
- When very specialized equipment is needed, add some if a good business. Add value of real estate.

Benchmark Data

- Revenue per employee should be at least $100,000 per annum.

Expenses (% of Annual Sales)

Cost of Goods	35%
Occupancy Costs	20%
Payroll/Labor Costs	35%
Profit (pretax)	10%

Questions

- Approvals and contracts
- What is the reputation of the aircraft or related product being sold? What is the reputation of the company? Is business up or down? What about accidents—any deaths? A company with a great reputation may be worth little because of their product—or, vice versa.
- Where are sales today in comparison to one, two . . . years ago? Why are they up or down?" Have there been any structural failures or successful liability suits against them? Is it movable or must buyer move?

Industry Trend

- "This industry remains the healthiest industrial segment of the world economy. We forecast production of 52,673 turbine-powered aircraft worth $1.999 trillion between 2016 and 2025. The military component of this market is worth $484.5 billion, while the civil sector is worth $1.45 trillion. These numbers are all in 2016 dollars. Over half of the new build market—$1.095 trillion—comprises commercial transports (including regional aircraft). Business aircraft are second, worth $269.7 billion. Fighters are third, worth $242.1 billion.

  "The world aircraft industry is still growing. That's the good news. The bad news is that the industry's growth rate downshifted significantly last year. Meanwhile, the sluggish level of growth that remains is threatened by several looming macroeconomic trends. Most of all, the jetliner primes' lofty production goals appear out of line with economic reality.

  "Several market segments have already been impacted. The result was a weak 2% growth rate for 2015 over 2014, measured in value of deliveries. This compares with the strong 7.1% compound annual growth rate (CAGR) the industry enjoyed in 2010–2014."

  Source: "Trends and Themes in the Aircraft Market" by Richard Aboulafia, October 10, 2016, http://advancedmanufacturing.org/trends-and-themes-in-the-aircraft-market/

- "Another reason why the aircraft market has become less cyclical—and now less likely to crash—is the advent of no-frills airlines. Because they are prepared to vary prices to ride out the ups and downs of demand for flights, their demand for planes is smoother. The rise of budget carriers in emerging markets is also helping. Budget airlines account for around 60% of seat capacity in India and South-East Asia; in Europe, the figure is around 40%, according to CAPA, an aviation-consulting firm."

  Source: http://www.economist.com/blogs/economist-explains/2016/01/economist-explains-10?zid=293&ah= e50f636873b42369614615ba3c16df4a

- Highly cyclical with the economy and military spending

Expert Comments

Sales and profits are declining due to technological factors such as increased time between overhauls.

Low competition based on high barriers to entry.

Seller Financing

- 3 years max, 1 year least
- We've never sold a 'seller-financed' ultralight aircraft business. It is always a cash deal.

Airport Operations		
SIC 4581-06	NAICS 488119	Number of Businesses/Units 2,385

Rules of Thumb

➢ 90–100% of annual sales includes inventory

➢ 4 x EBIT

➢ 5 x EBITDA

➢ 4–5 x SDE includes inventory

Pricing Tips

- Pricing would be highly dependent on the sector. In certain segments there is lot of personal goodwill. A prospective buyer should separate the personal goodwill from the business goodwill in calculating a purchase price. Many smaller businesses are highly dependent upon the owner's talent or specialty. These businesses should be valued with consideration to an earnout or employment contact to ensure ongoing stability.
- FBOs and MROs are about real estate. Revenues per square foot can be a good metric, but most transactions above $3MM use a multiple of EBITDA plus inventory.
- The FBO business is really a real-estate play. Take a careful look at the city leasehold agreements and the fuel farm, as EPA regulations can be costly to implement. Most fuel farms now must be built above ground. For air charter companies, take a close look at the age/condition of the aircraft used and existing contracts.
- First, if a fixed base operator, perform due diligence on EPA regulation adherence (e.g., fuel farm) and hangar leases with city or county.

Benchmark Data

Statistics (Airport Operations)

Number of Establishments	2,385
Average Profit Margin	7.5%
Revenue per Employee	$86,500
Average Number of Employees	44.3
Average Wages per Employee	$30,811

Products and Services Segmentation

Aeronautical services	51.2%
Parking and ground transportation services	19.5%
Retail stores and hospitality services	11.6%
Car rental services	9.8%
Other services	7.9%

Major Market Segmentation

Individual consumers	48.8%
Passenger airlines	45.3%
Other	5.9%

Industry Costs

Profit	7.5%
Wages	35.4%
Purchases	5.6%
Depreciation	36.6%
Marketing	0.9%
Rent & Utilities	4.1%
Other	9.9%

Market Share

The Port Authority of New York and New Jersey	13.4%

- For FBO, labor costs should be 20–35%. Occupancy could be variable depending on the airport and real estate costs. Rent+utilities 14%.
- Standard & Poor's benchmarks are a good starting place. Premiums placed on location, e.g., Van Nuys, CA or major cities.
- High private-jet-traffic airports. Jet fuel sales a plus. General aviation service only and/or airports with less than 5,000-foot runways sell at a discount.

Expenses (% of Annual Sales)

Cost of Goods	30% to 40%
Occupancy Costs	05% to 10%
Payroll/Labor Costs	25% to 35%
Profit (pretax)	05% to 15%

Questions

- Why sell? How long is lease with city? Any renewable lease clauses? If so, at what rate?
- Insurance can be a major cost component. What is the company's safety record? Does the business operate under any FAA certificates (IE 135 charter or 141 flight school)? Is maintenance involved with the FBO? How many IAs and A&Ps are employed? Are they contract workers? Is it an FAA certified repair station? Is it an authorized repair station for an OEM? What is the hangar occupancy rate? Is there a waiting list? How long? What are the average rates per square foot?

A - Rules of Thumb

Industry Trend

- Industry consolidation expected as smaller operators are displaced from the market. Improving economic conditions expected to result in revenue growth.
- "The airport operations industry will continue to expand over the next five years as the U.S. economy continues to improve and travel rates grow. Several airports will invest in new infrastructure to expand capacity and ease congestion. The federal government, through its airports improvement program, has budgeted more than $3.0 billion annually over the five years to 2020 to assist airports with capital improvements to improve safety and capacity as well as to alleviate environmental concerns. Despite this projected investment, capacity constraints at airports are expected to suppress revenue growth to some degree. Industry revenue is expected to increase 1.9% per year on average over the next five years, totaling $26.6 billion in 2020. "The total number of domestic trips is forecast to increase 1.6% per year on average through 2020. Likewise, the number of inbound international trips by foreigners is anticipated to grow an annualized 4.2% over the same period. Lower ticket prices resulting from increased competition among airlines, especially those offering budget fares, will assist this growth."
  Source: http://clients1.ibisworld.com/reports/us/industry/industryoutlook.aspx?entid=1194
- "Although the slow growth of the U.S. economy and the European recession has dampened the near- term prospects for general aviation, the long-term outlook remains favorable. We see growth in business aviation demand over the long term driven by a growing U.S. and world economy especially in the turbo jet, turboprop and turbine rotorcraft markets. As the fleet grows, the number of general aviation hours flown is projected to increase an average of 1.5 percent a year through 2033."
  Source: FAA Aerospace Forecast Fiscal Years 2013-2033
- Private jet aviation is the main driver of many of these airport businesses; how the business jet industry goes is how these services will go.
- Major research firms are showing a delivery of over 10,000 private jets in the next 10 years, implying a need for more airport service providers, including FBOs. City governments are now taking ownership of some FBOs, which is a threat to entrepreneurship. The inability of FBO owners to get more than a 25-year lease from a city is also a threat to profitability.

Expert Comments

An operator's location is the primary determinant of volume and marketability.

A major source of income is from fuel sales. Margins vary greatly depending on competition. Location is a key factor that affects the amount of traffic at an airport and thus the volume of business. Smaller FBOs are harder to market because most require owner operators with a passion for aviation. After a long down period, the industry is tending up. FBOs are difficult to duplicate as the property is generally owned and controlled by some government entity. The number of operators allowed at any given airfield in limited.

Seller Financing

- Outside and partial seller financing. Depends on the particular sale
- 3–5 years

Resources

- International Air Transport Association (IATA): http://www.iata.org
- Aeronautical Repair Station Association (ARSA): http://www.arsa.org
- Professional Aviation Maintenance Association (PAMA): http://pama. wildapricot.org/
- Federal Aviation Administration: http://www.faa.gov/
- Aircraft Electronics Association (AEA): http://www.aea.net
- Aviation Suppliers Association (ASA): http://www.aviationsuppliers.org
- National Air Transportation Association (NATA): http://www.nata.aero
- Aircraft Owner's and Pilot's Association (AOPA): http://www.aopa.org
- Aviation International News: http://ainonline.com
- General Aviation Manufacturers Association: http://www.gama.aero/
- IBISWorld May 2017: http://ibisworld.com

Allegra Marketing-Print-Mail		Franchise
Approx. Total Investment		$162,464–$516,949
	NAICS 323114	Number of Businesses/Units 280

Rules of Thumb

➤ 60–65% of annual sales plus inventory

Resources

- Allegra Network: http://www.allegranetwork.com

All Tune and Lube		Franchise
Approx. Total Investment		$125,000
SIC 7549-03	NAICS 81191	Number of Businesses/Units 150

Rules of Thumb

➤ 20–25% of annual sales

Resources

- All Tune and Lube: http://www.alltuneandlube.com

AlphaGraphics		Franchise
Approx. Total Investment		$247,800–385,400
SIC 7336-02	NAICS 541430	Number of Businesses/Units 284

Rules of Thumb

➤ 60–65% of annual sales plus inventory

Resources

- AlphaGraphics Franchise Opportunity: http://alphagraphicsfranchise.com/

Aluminum Smelting Machinery		
	NAICS 331316	

Rules of Thumb

➢ 70% annual sales plus inventory

➢ 5x EBITDA

Pricing Tips

- If balance sheet is sound, business is worth an average between twice net assets and 5 times EBITDA.

Benchmark Data

- $250,000 per employee

Expenses (% of Annual Sales)

Cost of Goods	70%
Occupancy Costs	05%
Payroll/Labor Costs	25%
Profit (pretax)	10%

Questions

- Indebtedness? Officers' loan or debt? Backlog and list of references.

Industry Trend

- The aluminum market is growing fast. New smelters are being built. Older are being extended or revamped. Market for machinery will be excellent for next 5 years at least.

Expert Comments

Highly specialized market. Vendor must establish himself on short list of major EPCMs through references. Spare parts market captive and profitable.

Ambulance Services		
SIC 4119-02	NAICS 62191	Number of Businesses/Units 5,269

Rules of Thumb

➢ 40% of annual revenues plus inventory

➢ 2–4.0 x SDE includes inventory

➢ 2.7–5.2 x EBITDA

Pricing Tips

- Business owners need to have a well-experienced advisor who has sold at least 10+ ambulance companies, otherwise the pricing will be off significantly and they would have little chances of closing a transaction.
- There is a very wide range of value for these businesses as there are 12–14 different characteristics that affect the pricing and multiples paid. EBITDA multiples range from 2.75 to 7.5 X EBITDA depending on company size, EBITDA, call mix and 10-12 other major factors, all of which affect value and risk, etc.
- Owner's level of involvement is definitely a major contributor to a multiplier. Revenue per vehicle is a very top-level gauge of company's performance. Revenue per vehicle varies with geography. For example, in No. California revenue per vehicle is 20% higher than in So. California. Two major expenses to watch after are payroll and cost of fuel.
- Large pricing range due to a larger number of key variables that affect valuation. Transition period with seller is critical (should be at least 6 months to a year, even on smaller businesses).
- Payer mix & breakdowns very important; breakdowns on advanced life support (ALS) vs. basic life support (BLS) transports; reimbursements; rural vs. urban mix; wheelchair transports diminish profitability.

Benchmark Data

Statistics (Ambulance Services)

Number of Establishments	5,269
Average Profit Margin	7.5%
Revenue per Employee	$91,200
Average Number of Employees	34.1
Average Wages per Employee	$36,948

Products and Services Segmentation

Emergency surface ambulance	53.3%
Nonemergency surface ambulance	19.5%
Emergency air ambulance (rotary wing)	16.9%
Other	5.3%
Emergency air ambulance (fixed wing)	3.2%
Nonemergency air ambulance	1.1%
Standby ambulance and/or first-aid services	0.7%

Major Market Segmentation

Sprains or strains of neck and back	21.9%
Contusion with intact skin surface	21.5%
Open wounds	16.5%
Fractures	13.4%
Sprains or strains excluding neck and back	13.2%
Spinal disorders	8.8%
Other	4.7%

Industry Costs

Profit	7.5%
Wages	40.4%
Purchases	8.2%
Depreciation	4.1%
Marketing	1.0%
Rent & Utilities	2.8%
Other	36.0%

Market Share

Envision Healthcare 13.2%
Air Methods 6.6%

- EBITDA as a percentage of cash deposits (not gross or net revenues) can vary greatly; industry average is 8–11%, but strong operators can achieve 18–25% EBITDA margins consistently if they are strong operators.
- Industry average EBITDA is 7–8% of net cash sales per year; well-run operations generate 18–25% EBITDA margins and these companies sell for a premium compared to equally sized companies in the market. Keeping total payroll costs down and having a good billing process/dept. are keys to drive profitability.

Expenses (% of Annual Sales)

Cost of Goods .... 02% to 12%
Occupancy Costs .... 01% to 03%
Payroll/Labor Costs .... 45% to 58%
Profit (pretax) .... 07% to 22%

Questions

- Payor mix, market share, patient demographic data.
- Knowledge of medical billing; logistics management; attention to details.
- Except regular financial due diligence, buyers should be watching for lawsuits against the company and traffic tickets. High level of lawsuits and traffic tickets indicates that the business doesn't have good driver education and discipline in place.
- Lots—There are a lot of fraudulent practices and brokers need to understand the industry and billing guidelines or they should avoid taking a listing/ representing the owner; need to know the quantity of dialysis patients; businesses with a high percentage of dialysis runs get discounted in valuation/ pricing.
- Who does billing: in-house or sub out to 3rd party? What software is used? What systems do you have in place & utilize for billing and for logistics? Do you prescreen your transports/patients?

Industry Trend

- It will become much tougher for the small operator with 5 to 15 ambulances to operate, and their margins will likely shrink, unless they invest heavily in technology and unless they know how to implement and integrate these systems and are good at managing their efficiencies, logistics and billing.
- Heavy competition, strong growth, consolidation expected to continue.
- "During the next five years, ambulance providers will exhibit revenue growth as healthcare reform bolsters the number of insured individuals, thereby lowering the occurrence of bad debt. Nevertheless, to cut healthcare costs, the federal government will likely lower reimbursement rates, causing the industry to grapple with rates that may not cover the cost of care. However, the burgeoning elderly population requires more physician care, personnel and medical equipment than any other age demographic, which will provide need-based demand for both nonemergency and emergency ambulance services."

Source: http://clients1.ibisworld.com/reports/us/industry/industryoutlook.aspx?entid=1581

- "GIA announces the release of a comprehensive global report on Ambulance Services. The global market for Ambulance Services is projected to exceed US$63 billion by 2020, driven by the growing demand for emergency and non-emergency medical care by the elderly."

Source: http://www.strategyr.com/pressMCP-6103.asp

Expert Comments

Level of service drives volume and the recurring revenues stream; billing and collections and logistics management play key roles in driving EBITDA.

Most ambulance services have high recurring revenue business model; high fragmentation. Most owners are former medics and lack skill sets required to grow these businesses beyond $2–5 MM in sales and maintain margins and maximize utilization and effectively manage payroll costs.

Very few companies consistently provide a high level of service and generate solid EBITDA margins in the 18–25% range. The industry is very fragmented, with companies over $10 MM in net cash sales and solid earnings securing premium pricing.

Amount of competition varies by region. Some areas in California are very densely populated and the density is connected to a number of medical facilities in the area. Location of the office is irrelevant to the business, however parking availability for the fleet is definitely a benefit. Government cut rates several times, therefore profits suffered and owners had to streamline their businesses and cut expenses in order to maintain profit margins. Threshold of entry in the industry is pretty high, especially if company wants to get paid by the government. The approval process is quite lengthy.

Growing number of transports, but tougher for the smaller provider (all under $5–$7 million in sales) to compete effectively against the mid-sized players; trend is to sell, merge or acquire; knowledge of ambulance billing is very important.

Seller Financing

- Most transactions involve a seller note; the size (dollar amount/percent of price) and term are variable based on numerous factors.
- Outside financing
- All across the board; typically 50–80% cash at close, with 5–10% held in escrow for repairs & warranties. Working capital is true'd up within 60–90 days post close and is normally included in the purchase price, based on historical average.
- Although we use both (outside financing and seller financing), seller financing is more typical lately.
- 3–5 years

Resources

- EMSWorld: http://www.emsworld.com/
- American Ambulance Association—primarily for members: www.the-aaa.org
- IBISWorld, January 2017: http://ibisworld.com

Ambulatory Surgery Centers

	NAICS 621493

Rules of Thumb

➢ 78% of annual sales plus inventory

➢ 2.7 x SDE plus inventory

➢ 6.3 x EBIT

➢ 5.6 x EBITDA

Benchmark Data

Expenses (% of Annual Sales)

Cost of Goods	11%
Payroll/Labor Costs	05%
Profit (pretax)	27%

Franchise

American Poolplayers Association (APA)

Approx. Total Investment	$16,695–$19,865	
SIC 7999-12	NAICS 713990	Number of Businesses/Units 297

Rules of Thumb

➢ 1.4 x annual sales

Pricing Tips

- These franchises are purchased by areas. Pricing is normally based on the number of teams in the area. The general rule of thumb is $2,000 per team in a well-managed area.

Expenses (% of Annual Sales)

Cost of Goods	n/a
Occupancy Costs	n/a
Payroll/Labor Costs	n/a
Profit (pretax)	35%

Industry Trend

- Increase in popularity and participation in recreational billiards

Resources

- American Poolplayers Association: http://www.poolplayers.com

Franchise

ANDY OnCall

	NAICS 236118	Number of Businesses/Units 34

Rules of Thumb
> 25% of annual sales

Benchmark Data

Statistics (Handyman Service Franchises)

Number of Establishments	1,449
Average Profit Margin	4.6%
Revenue per Employee	$220,700
Average Number of Employees	14.7
Average Wages per Employee	$64,760

Products and Services Segmentation

Maintenance services	63.1%
Plumbing	8.6%
Electrical	7.5%
Others	7.3%
Decks and Fences	5.1%
Painting	5.1%
Flooring	3.3%

Major Market Segmentation

Households	68.2%
Property owners and managers	14.8%
Commercial clients	10.0%
Other	7.0%

Industry Costs

Profit	4.6%
Wages	29.6%
Purchases	42.5%
Depreciation	1.0%
Marketing	0.5%
Rent & Utilities	1.1%
Other	20.7%

Resources
- ANDY OnCall: http://www.andyoncall.com
- IBISWorld, March 2017: http://ibisworld.com

Antique Malls

Rules of Thumb
> 2–4 x EBITDA

Resources

- National Association of Antique Malls (NAAM): http://www.antiqueandcollectible.com

Antique Shops/Dealers		
SIC 5932-02	NAICS 453310	

Rules of Thumb

➤ 20% of annual sales plus inventory

Resources

- Art and Antique Dealers League of America: http://aadla.com/

		Franchise
Anytime Fitness		
Approx. Total Investment		$71,559–$353,900
	NAICS 713940	Number of Businesses/Units 2,094

Rules of Thumb

➤ 2.5 x SDE plus inventory

Pricing Tips

- Multiples of SDE vary based on size of the owner benefit. SDE less than $75k, typically we see multiples in the 1 range. $75–$150k, we see multiples in the 1.8 to 2.5 range. Greater than $150k multiples may be higher.

Questions

- How much in prepaid memberships?

Expert Comments

"'We've never had any major incidents in our 12 years. I think people love getting their own key and going anytime they want. I should mention that we're not completely unstaffed; a franchise owner will likely work 30 to 50 hours a week, depending on the time of year. In January they're going to work longer, and in the summer months less.'

"'When we came up with the concept, it was a new category in the fitness industry. There was no such thing as a nonstaffed club. By using technology, we dramatically minimized overhead—taxes, utilities, rent, payroll. So-called industry experts said it would never work. They felt there was no way people would join if they didn't get hands-on service with every single visit.'"

Source: "Anytime Fitness," quotes from Chuck Runyon and Dave Mortensen, edited by Cristina Lindblad & Dimitra Kessenides, *Businessweek*

Seller Financing

- 2 years

Resources

- Anytime Fitness: http://www.anytimefitness.com

Apartment Rental		
SIC 6531-11	NAICS 531110	Number of Businesses/Units 520,336

Rules of Thumb

➢ 80% of annual revenues

Pricing Tips

- This is generally a secondary revenue source to real estate sales
- Note: A real estate license is required for the operation of this business in many states.

Benchmark Data

Statistics (Apartment Rental)

Number of Establishments	520,336
Average Profit Margin	31.6%
Revenue per Employee	$209,000
Average Number of Employees	1.5
Average Wages per Employee	$24,844

Products and Services Segmentation

Rental of one-unit structures	39.8%
Rental of two- to four-unit structures	17.3%
Rental of five- to nine-unit structures	10.9%
Rental of 50- or more unit structures	10.2%
Rental of 20- to 49-unit structures	8.0%
Rental of manufactured homes, mobile homes or trailers	3.9%

Major Market Segmentation

1 person	36.3%
2 persons	27.6%
4 or more persons	20.4%
3 persons	15.7%

Industry Costs

Profit	31.6%
Wages	11.9%
Purchases	9.2%
Depreciation	19.8%
Marketing	1.2%
Rent & Utilities	6.6%
Other	19.7%

- Fees are most often paid by the apartment owner, usually about 10% to 15% or one month's rent.

Questions

- "How long have they been in business? How do they locate apartments? Do they have an online database? How many apartment communities do they work with?"

Source: www.austinapartmentfinder.com

Resources

- IBISWorld, March 2017: http://ibisworld.com

Appliance Stores		
SIC 5064	NAICS 443111	

Rules of Thumb

➢ 2 x monthly sales plus inventory

Benchmark Data

- Markup is about 27 percent with some discounters working on a 25 percent markup.

Resources

- North American Retail Dealers Association: http://www.narda.com
- Association of Home Appliance Manufacturers: http://www.aham.org

Appraisal (Valuation Services)		
SIC 7389	NAICS 541990	

Pricing Tips

- Most of the deals are where there is a merger of firms or a buyout by a CPA firm wanting to get into the appraisal business. They usually want the seller to manage the operation for several years.

Benchmark Data

Statistics (Real Estate Appraisal)

Number of Establishments	45,955
Average Profit Margin	14.3%
Revenue per Employee	$112,300
Average Number of Employees	1.5
Average Wages per Employee	$38,248

Products and Services Segmentation

Real estate appraisal—commercial	54.4%
Real estate appraisal—residential	35.6%
Real estate consulting	1%
Appraisal management	6.6%
Real estate brokerage and other services	2.4%

Major Market Segmentation

Financial institutions & brokers	58.0%
Law offices	15.0%
Private owners	13.0%
Government and other	8.0%
Accountants	6.0%

Industry Costs

Profit	14.3%
Wages	34.4%
Purchases	9.8%
Depreciation	1.3%
Marketing	1.6%
Rent & Utilities	4.7%
Other	33.9%

Market Share

CBRE Group Inc.	9.3%

Statistics (Business Valuation Firms)

Number of Establishments	81,835
Average Profit Margin	10.2%
Revenue per Employee	$81,835
Average Number of Employees	1.0
Average Wages per Employee	$19,775

Products and Services Segmentation

Capitalization of income valuation	34.8%
Asset valuation	31.4%
Owner benefit valuation	22.1%
Market valuation	11.7%

Major Market Segmentation

Private firms	58.6%
Government institutions	30.8%
Other	6.9%
Individuals and households	3.7%

Industry Costs

Profit	10.2%
Wages	38.4%
Purchases	10.9%
Depreciation	1.0%
Marketing	1.7%
Rent & Utilities	4.2%
Other	33.6%

Resources
- Institute of Business Appraisers (IBA): http://instbusapp.org

- National Association of Certified Valuators and Analysts (NACVA): http://www.nacva.com
- American Society of Appraisers: http://www.appraisers.org
- IBISWorld, September 2016: http://ibisworld.com
- IBISWorld, July 2016: http://ibisworld.com

Arcade, Food & Entertainment Complexes		
SIC 7993-03	NAICS 713120	

Rules of Thumb

➤ 25% of annual sales includes inventory

➤ 3 x SDE includes inventory

➤ 3–3.5 x EBITDA plus vehicle value (over 15 vehicles)

Pricing Tips

- Make sure the equipment is either owned and is in current, 'fashionable' condition, or make sure there is an attractive lease arrangement that enables simple trade-in for more current gaming. These games are only as valuable as the current trend. There are 'stability' games such as air hockey, certain pinball games and redemption games where you can win toy prizes straight from the machine. The store must have a mix of current trend equipment and the stability games. Stability games are the work horses but the trendy games are very expensive to stay on top of.
- This industry is not for everyone! Although, if you are an experienced retailer and have a stomach for high rent-to-gross sales percentages, this could be a great opportunity for you to enter into a fun and rewarding industry! It is a simple business model and can be improved significantly by introducing customer promotions combining game tokens with redemption prize incentives and local food retailers.

Benchmark Data

Statistics (Arcade, Food & Entertainment Complexes)

Number of Establishments	6,284
Average Profit Margin	17.7%
Revenue per Employee	$45,000
Average Number of Employees	6.9
Average Wages per Employee	$12,315

Products and Services Segmentation

Debit-card and coin-operated games and rides	45.1%
Food and beverages	35.9%
Admissions	14.2%
Corporate and party event services	4.2%
Other	0.6%

Industry Costs

Profit	17.7%
Wages	27.2%
Purchases	26.6%
Depreciation	5.4%
Marketing	2.7%
Rent & Utilities	9.4%
Other	11.0%

Market Share

Dave & Buster's Entertainment Inc.	37.7%
CEC Entertainment Inc.	29.8%

Statistics (Golf Driving Ranges and Family Fun Centers)

Number of Establishments	55,313
Average Profit Margin	4.9%
Revenue per Employee	$71.1
Average Number of Employees	2.9
Average Wages per Employee	$18,802

Products and Services Segmentation

Other	31.9%
Amusement and recreation services	31.3%
Coin operated games and rides	12.9%
Amateur sports teams and club services	6.9%
Meals and beverages	5.4%
Fitness and recreational sport center services	5.3%
Registration for sports tournaments and matches	3.8%
Golf course and country club services and memberships	2.5%

Industry Costs

Profit	13.2%
Wages	26.3%
Purchases	21.3%
Depreciation	5.8%
Marketing	3.9%
Rent & Utilities	6.0%
Other	23.5%

- Game costs range from $2,500 to $15,000 per new machine. You do not have to buy new machinery! Sell older technology online and buy new circuitry for new games and put them In your existing game machines. It will save tremendous operating capital and the customer will not know the difference.

Expenses (% of Annual Sales)

Cost of Goods	05% to 10%
Occupancy Costs	40% to 50%
Payroll/Labor Costs	15%
Profit (pretax)	15% to 20%

Expert Comments

Games must also be attractive/specific to area demographics. Interestingly, my clients that owned a chain of stores in and around New York City found that the Asian neighborhoods demand more high-tech, challenging games and they will correspondingly pay a higher price per use. This is not a business that a client should jump into ill-informed or insufficiently researched. Only buy tried and true locations. Don't build new locations unless on a massive scale like Dave & Busters. They are a one-stop entertainment supercenter including food, bowling and usually booze. The smaller locations in malls and plazas are way too risky given the fact that kids don't need to leave the home anymore to get the most current and challenging gaming. So, if there is a location that has withstood the transition to home-based gaming through the 80s, 90s and up to now, it is likely a winner. These arcade formats only now work in certain neighborhoods, need high volume given the price of commercial real estate, etc. Get a long lease.

Location is key. This is a capital-intensive industry but a proven location is a very valuable semi-absentee opportunity. If you are buying existing units, you can use the assets in the purchase to back part of the financing.

Resources

- Coaster Grotto: http://www.coastergrotto.com/theme-park-attendance.jsp
- IBISWorld, May 2017: http://ibisworld.com
- IBISWorld, October 2016: http://ibisworld.com

Architectural Firms		
SIC 8712-02	NAICS 541310	Number of Businesses/Units 73,169

Rules of Thumb

➢ 40% of annual sales plus inventory

Pricing Tips

- "Larger Firm: Value = Earnings X Multiple Earnings = $1,200,000 Market Multiple Range: Three (3) to Five (5)
  Smaller Firm: Value = Earnings X Multiple Earnings = $100,000 Market Multiple Range: One (1) to Three (3)"
  Source: http://www.aianewmexico.org/aianmprograms/d.arne3.23.07.pdf
- "Consulting firms that specialize in ownership transitions develop a fair-market value based on a handful of factors including adjusted net worth (book value), weighted net income, weighted net fees, projected fees, and backlog of unearned fees.
  "These factors produce a range of a firm's value. For example, some consultants value a firm at between 1 and 1.5 times adjusted net worth for an internal transition or between 2 and 3 times for an external sale. Other consultants value a firm at between 3 and 5 times weighted net income or apply a percentage of their average earnings to their backlog of unearned fees."
  Source: "How Much Is Your Firm Really Worth?" excerpted and adapted from an AIA Architect article by Michael Strogoff

- Goodwill is at a minimum due to the non-repetitiveness of the clients. It is also a personal service business. The stature, reputation and contacts of the principal(s)are generally not transferable, especially in a smaller firm.

Benchmark Data

Statistics (Architects)

Number of Establishments	73,169
Average Profit Margin	12.7%
Revenue per Employee	$190,000
Average Number of Employees	3.2
Average Wages per Employee	$72,303

Products and Services Segmentation

New project architectural services	55.0%
Renovation and rehabilitation architectural service	45.0%

Major Market Segmentation

Institutional construction	52.0%
Commercial and industrial construction	27.3%
Residential construction	16.8%
Other	3.9%

Industry Costs

Profit	12.7%
Wages	38.2%
Purchases	9.5%
Depreciation	0.7%
Marketing	1.3%
Rent & Utilities	4.8%
Other	32.8%

Industry Trend

- "Profitability will also improve over the next five years, driven by an increase in demand for new construction projects. As a result, IBISWorld expects that average industry profit will marginally increase from 11.8% of revenue in 2015 to 11.9% in 2020. Growth in industry revenue and high profit margins will bring more operators to the industry, especially small companies and sole proprietors that left as a result of poor business conditions after the recession. Consequently, the number of industry operators is forecast to increase at an average rate of 1.6% per year to 77,150 companies during the five years to 2020."

Source: http://clients1.ibisworld.com/reports/us/industry/industryoutlook.aspx?entid=1401

Expert Comments

"Tools for Small Firms: Simple Business Practices that Reduce Risk
- ✓ Not documenting advice given or decisions made during conversations with the client.
- ✓ Not using a written agreement.
- ✓ Beginning work before having a signed written agreement.
- ✓ Not following the written agreement once it is in place.

✓ Taking any job that walks through the door."

Source: Rena M. Klein, FAIA, principal of R.M. Klein Consulting, in Seattle, Washington, a member of the Soloso Editorial Content Review Board who serves as the Subject Matter Expert for Practice.

Resources

- IBISWorld, June 2017: http://ibisworld.com
- AIA: http://www.aia.org

Art Galleries and Dealers		
SIC 5999-69	NAICS 453920	Number of Businesses/Units 23,135

Rules of Thumb

➢ 30% of annual revenues plus inventory

Pricing Tips

- In some galleries, much of the art work may be on consignment.
- "A surprising number of people search for answers to these and similar questions in attempts to quantify the art market. The art market, however, is not quantifiable, and the answers to these questions don't exist. To begin with, art is not a commodity that can be regulated. Anyone can call him or herself an artist, anyone can call anything that they create 'art,' and anyone can be an art dealer. Anyone can sell art wherever, whenever and under whatever circumstances they please, and price or sell whatever they call 'art' for whatever amounts of money they feel like selling it for, as long as that art is offered without fraud or misrepresentation."

Source: www.artbusiness.com

Benchmark Data

Statistics (Art Dealers)

Number of Establishments	23,135
Average Profit Margin	7.7%
Revenue per Employee	$246,100
Average Number of Employees	1.5
Average Wages per Employee	$30,441

Products and Services Segmentation

Paintings	42.0%
Drawings	29.0%
Prints	18.0%
Sculptures	6.0%
Photography and other media	5.0%

Major Market Segmentation

Modern art	47.0%
Post-war art	25.0%
19th century art	12.0%
Contemporary art	11.0%
Old masters	5.0%

Industry Costs

Profit	7.7%
Wages	12.4%
Purchases	49.3%
Depreciation	0.8%
Marketing	2.9%
Rent & Utilities	9.5%
Other	17.4%

Market Share

Christie's International	5.4%
Sotheby's Holdings Inc.	4.4%

Industry Trend

- "The Art Dealers industry is in the mature phase of its life cycle because of the industry's market acceptance and relatively low technological change. This indicates that the industry is outperforming the general economy."

  Source: http://clients1.ibisworld.com/reports/us/industry/industryoutlook.aspx?entid=1104

Expert Comments

"5 tips to building your own art business:
- ✓ Find your niche
- ✓ Know and understand basic business principles and essentials
- ✓ Build and maintain a network of professionals already running their own successful art business
- ✓ Learn to brand yourself, and start with social media and a functioning Website
- ✓ Don't get down on yourself and don't give up."

  Source: http://theartcareerproject.com

Resources

- Art Dealers Association of America: http://www.artdealers.org
- IBISWorld, January 2017: http://ibisworld.com

Arts & Crafts/Retail Stores		
SIC 5085	NAICS 45113	

Rules of Thumb

➤ 35% of annual sales plus inventory

➤ 2 x SDE plus inventory

Pricing Tips

- Inventory should be priced separately and should include any costs associated with shipping the inventory to the place of business. Also, any needed labor required to re-package product should be part of COGS and not part of labor. As with most other business valuations, look hard at attractors and detractors to the 36% rule of thumb.
- You should be able to tell if a crafter is operating the business, as opposed to a

business person, by their financials.

- Note: The people who actually create the finished arts and crafts (craftspeople) are unique and their business might be difficult to sell because of the very nature of what they produce. Their skill is usually not transferable.

Benchmark Data

Statistics (Fabric, Craft & Sewing Supplies Stores)

Number of Establishments	23,594
Average Profit Margin	14.6%
Revenue per Employee	$73,600
Average Number of Employees	2.6
Average Wages per Employee	$10,651

Products and Services Segmentation

Fabrics	60.3%
Sewing and craft supplies	37.0%
Other	2.7%

Industry Costs

Profit	4.7%
Wages	14.5%
Purchases	44.4%
Depreciation	0.9%
Marketing	1.8%
Rent & Utilities	9.2%
Other	24.5%

Market Share

Michaels Stores Inc.	27.0%
Jo-Ann Stores Inc.	25.0%
Hobby Lobby Stores Inc.	14.0%

- Rent at 10% of GAS (Gross Annual Sales). Sales per square foot at $150–$175. Sales per employee at $75,000–$125,000. Advertising at 3%–4% of GAS.

Expenses (% of Annual Sales)

Cost of Goods	50%
Occupancy Costs	15%
Payroll/Labor Costs	15%
Profit (pretax)	20%

Industry Trend

- "Locating wholesalers and distributors for products won't be difficult, and the profit potential is tremendous as product markups can be 100 percent or more."

Source: http://www.entrepreneur.com/businessideas/craft-supply-store

Resources

- Handmade Business magazine: http://handmade-business.com/
- IBISWorld, February 2017: http://ibisworld.com
- Association for Creative Industries (AFCI): http://www.afci.global

Art Supplies		
SIC 5999-65	NAICS 453998	

Rules of Thumb

➢ 25–30% annual sales plus inventory

Pricing Tips

- Many hobby stores and related businesses may carry a line of art supplies. A store specializing in just art supplies requires an owner with the appropriate knowledge.

Benchmark Data

- For Benchmark Information see Retail Stores—Small Specialty

Assisted Living Facilities/Retirement Communities (with Nursing Care)		
SIC 8361-05	NAICS 623311	

Rules of Thumb

➢ 75%–78% annual sales
➢ 2.7x SDE

Pricing Tips

- Real-estate-intensive business. SBA pays extra attention to this industry to ensure that the buyers are not acting as passive real-estate investors, but rather as small-business owners.
- Capitalization of income for going concern value including real estate
- Occupancy in market area. Going cap rates at that specific time. Whether Medicaid or private pay?
- This business is based on net operating income divided by a capitalization rate of 10% to 14%

Benchmark Data

Statistics (Nursing Care)

Number of Establishments	31,801
Average Profit Margin	7.2%
Revenue per Employee	$78,400
Average Number of Employees	55.9
Average Wages per Employee	$29,863

Products and Services Segmentation

For-profit skilled nursing facilities	43.6%
For-profit nursing homes	33.0%
Nonprofit skilled nursing facilities	10.3%
Nonprofit nursing homes	7.8%
Government nursing homes and skilled nursing facilities	4.7%
Hospice centers	0.6%

Industry Costs

Profit	6.9%
Wages	38.3%
Purchases	18.4%
Depreciation	2.4%
Marketing	0.3%
Rent & Utilities	6.6%
Other	27.1%

- "Long-Term Care Spending by Payer:
  Medicaid: 42%
  Medicare: 25%
  Out of Pocket: 22%
  Private Insurance and Other Sources: 11%"

  Source: www.leadingage.org/facts

- "The average assisted living center resident is an 85-year-old female who pays close to $3,000 a month—though many needing greater care pay closer to $4,000 or $5,000. While the assisted living industry is currently strong, experts said a major shift in demographics and the looming threat of federal regulation could transform the industry over the next two decades."

  Source: "Assisted Living Centers Are Costing the Elderly a Pretty Penny" www.foxbusiness.com

- Total expenses excluding debt service should average 68 percent.
- Operating expense ratio—65 to 70 percent

Industry Trend

- "Assisted living regulations, statutes, and policies in 23 states were changed this year, according to the National Center for Assisted Living. Over time, states are generally increasing the regulatory requirements for assisted living communities.
  - ✓ Eight states reported changes to requirements for staffing and training: Calif., Fla., Iowa, Idaho, La., Mass., Minn., and S.C.
  - ✓ While the level and types of changes varied, five states reported changes to requirements for units that serve individuals with Alzheimer's or other dementias: Iowa, La., Mass., Neb., and Ore.
  - ✓ Three states reported different kinds of changes to requirements related to medication management: Del., S.C., and Tenn.
  - ✓ Nine states reported that proposed regulations for assisted living communities are being reviewed for an update: Calif., Fla., Hawaii, Md., N.Y., N.C., Va., and Wyo. California and Florida's regulations are being updated to reflect legislative changes that have already been enacted.

  "The report also provides contact information for state agencies that oversee assisted living. The full report along with each state's summary is available online at www.ncal.org."

  Source: "NCAL Report: Nearly Half of States Modified Assisted Living Regulations in 2016"
by Rachel Reeves, October 13, 2016,
https://www.ahcancal.org/ncal/news/releases/Pages/NCAL-Report-Nearly-Half-of-States-Modified-.aspx

- "Boomers require age-sensitive language and customized amenities in assisted living."

  Source: "How Baby Boomers Are Redefining Assisted Living,"
  http://www.assistedliving.com/1-19-17-baby-boomers-are-redefining-assisted-living/

- "Between 2007 and 2015, the number of Americans ages 85 and older is expected to increase by 40 percent. By 2020, 12 million older Americans will need long-term health care."

  Source: HIAA, "A Guide to Long-Term Care Insurance"

Seller Financing

- 5 to 10 years

Resources

- Argentum: http://www.alfa.org
- Leading Age: http://www.leadingage.org
- A Place for Mom: http://www.aplaceformom.com
- IBISWorld, November 2016: http://ibisworld.com
- National Center for Assisted Living: https://www.ahcancal.org/ncal/Pages/index.aspx
- The American Seniors Housing Association: http://www.seniorshousing.org

Assisted Living Facilities/Retirement Communities (without Nursing Care)		
	NAICS 623312	Number of Businesses/Units 47,741

Benchmark Data

Statistics (Retirement Communities)

Number of Establishments	47,741
Average Profit Margin	7.6%
Revenue per Employee	$67,400
Average Number of Employees	21.5
Average Wages per Employee	$25,231

Products and Services Segmentation

Continuing care retirement communities	49.7%
Assisted living facilities and homes for the elderly	33.9%
Other	16.4%

Industry Costs

Profit	7.6%
Wages	37.3%
Purchases	6.8%
Depreciation	10.8%
Marketing	0.6%
Rent & Utilities	7.4%
Other	29.5%

Market Share

Brookdale Senior Living Inc.	7.6%

Resources

- American Senior Housing Association: http://www.seniorhousing.org
- IBISWorld, June 2017: http://ibisworld.com

	Franchise
Atlanta Bread Company	
Approx. Total Investment	$650,000–$1,000,000
Estimated Annual Sales/Unit	$1 million
SIC 5812-08 NAICS 722211	Number of Businesses/Units 167

Rules of Thumb

➢ 25–30% of annual sales plus inventory

Audio and Film Companies		
	NAICS 512120	

Rules of Thumb

➢ 4–6 x EBITDA

Pricing Tips

- Ownership of the intellectual property is key to value. Companies that provide work-for-hire services are not as valuable as those that own the final production. Since this medium ages quickly, the economic life span of the films/videos is critical.

Benchmark Data

Statistics (Audio Production Studios)

Number of Establishments	1,731
Average Profit Margin	5.9%
Revenue per Employee	$204,300
Average Number of Employees	3.3
Average Wages per Employee	$56,237

Products and Services Segmentation

Postproduction, sound editing and design	41.5%
Music recording services	27.3%
Other sound editing and production services	19.2%
Radio recording services	7.0%
Spoken word recording services	5.0%

Major Market Segmentation

Television and film clients	51.4%
Music industry clients	33.8%
Advertising clients	7.6%
Spoken word clients	6.2%
Radio programming clients	1.0%

Industry Costs

Profit	5.9%
Wages	27.5%
Purchases	25.4%
Depreciation	3.8%
Marketing	2.6%
Rent & Utilities	9.2%
Other	25.6%

Statistics (Movie & Video Production)

Number of Establishments	10,460
Average Profit Margin	13.0%
Revenue per Employee	$478,200
Average Number of Employees	9.0
Average Wages per Employee	$86,337

Products and Services Segmentation

Action and adventure	39.2%
Comedy	24.6%
Drama	15.9%
Thriller/Suspense	8.1%
Other genres	7.9%
Other	4.3%

Major Market Segmentation

Foreign distribution	39.5%
Other domestic distribution	37.0%
Domestic box office	23.5%

Industry Costs

Profit	13.0%
Wages	18.1%
Purchases	52.4%
Depreciation	3.5%
Marketing	1.7%
Rent & Utilities	3.6%
Other	7.7%

Market Share

The Walt Disney Company	20.0%
NBCUniversal Media LLC	18.4%
21st Century Fox	14.5%
Time Warner Inc.	12.8%
Sony Corporation	9.4%

Seller Financing

- 3 to 7 years

Resources

- IBISWorld, June 2017: http://ibisworld.com
- IBISWorld, May 2017: http://ibisworld.com

Audio/Video Conferencing

SIC 4822-06	NAICS 518210	

Rules of Thumb

➢ 3–4 x EBITDA

Questions
- How long are the contracts? What services are being provided?

Industry Trend
- New technology is outdating old. Tele-presence is the new upgrade name.

Expert Comments

Cost of setting up public centers is substantial. Industry is upgrading services and equipment.

Auto Body Repair

SIC 7532-01	NAICS 811121	Number of Businesses/Units 123,847

Rules of Thumb

➢ 3 x EBIT

➢ 1.5–2.3 x SDE plus inventory

➢ 2–4 x EBITDA

➢ 25–35% of Annual Sales includes inventory

Pricing Tips
- "Initial Questions to Ask the Seller of an Auto Body Shop—By compiling the following information, a buyer should be able to get a full picture of the auto body shop they are looking at:
  A. Size of the building
  B. Size of the total lot
  C. Monthly rent, including the CAM (Common Area Maintenance). If business is owned by seller: What rental amount does the seller want from a buyer? What rent does the seller currently charge himself on his company books?
  D. Number of spray booths? How many are heated and what type of heated spray booths? (downdrafts and side drafts are the two main types of heated spray booths.)
  E. Number of frame machines and the make and model number, if the seller knows.
  F. Does the business have any DRP (Direct Repair Program) contracts? If yes, what are the names of each insurance company?
  G. What % of the volume is DRP business?
  H. What is the annual gross income of the business?
  I. What is the real owner's take home earnings from the business, regardless of the form that it is received (salary, personal expenses written off by the business and cash income not reported)."

Source: http://www.businessbuyingservices.com/what-you-need-to-know-in-order-to-value-an-auto-body-shop/

- Annual volume is critical. Low volume (below $600K) shops are difficult to sell. The higher the volume the higher the multiple. Franchises sell for lower multiples. Lease terms are very important.

Benchmark Data

Statistics (Car Body Shops)

Number of Establishments	123,847
Average Profit Margin	6.2%
Revenue per Employee	$125,600
Average Number of Employees	2.7
Average Wages per Employee	$36,940

Products and Services Segmentation

Body repair services	59.7%
Painting services	20.7%
Glass replacement and repair	11.6%
Merchandise sales	3.0%
Detailing services and body conversions	1.7%
Upholstery and interior repair	1.7%
Other services	1.6%

Industry Costs

Profit	6.3%
Wages	29.4%
Purchases	51.7%
Depreciation	1.4%
Marketing	2.3%
Rent & Utilities	4.5%
Other	4.4%

Expenses (% of Annual Sales)

Cost of Goods	35% to 40%
Occupancy Costs	05% to 10%
Payroll/Labor Costs	20%
Profit (pretax)	15% to 20%

Questions

- How much of their time does the owner work on cars? When does your paint supplier contract expire? Lease terms. Employee census. Worker's comp mode rate. Reason for selling. Upside potential.
- Percentage of volume that is DRP Contracts? (Insurance Contracts) Percentage of rent to gross sales? How much space is there indoors for car storage?
- Do you supply loan cars? If so, do you get rebates from rental companies for the loaners? When will a job be booked as a sale? Do you have steady referrals from dealerships? When are initial assessments made? Is any charge made for them? After the initial estimate is made, how are contacts made with the insurance company?
- What is your real sales volume? How many DRP contracts do you have?

Which insurance companies are your DRP contracts with? What is the labor rate paid by the insurance companies? How many employees do you have? Are your employees paid a salary or a percentage of the production they produce? How many frame machines do you have? is your spray booth heated?

- Show me your profit & loss statements, tax returns, environmental compliance & OSHA documents.

Industry Trend

- Upward for established, quality-oriented operations with DRP relationships with clients, mainly insurance companies.

Expert Comments

The industry is dominated by insurance companies. Contracts are not assumable by buyers. Without a contract, your volume is going to be very small. Regardless of how well the current owner is doing, when the business is transferred, the contracts are cancelled.

Insurance referrals can go away very easily with ownership changes.

Seller Financing

- 3 to 5 years
- 5 years
- Sellers carry for three to five years with SBA requiring the seller not to receive payments for the first two years.

Resources

- Automotive Service Association, (ASA)—Great site with lots of information: http://www.asashop.org
- AutoInc.org—great, great site: http://autoinc.org
- Body Shop Business is an excellent publication and website; it also offers back issues: http://www.bodyshopbusiness.com
- fenderbender: https://www.fenderbender.com/
- IBISWorld, January 2017: http://ibisworld.com

Auto Brake Services		
SIC 7539-14	NAICS 811118	

Rules of Thumb

➤ 30% of annual sales plus inventory

➤ 4 x monthly sales plus inventory

Auto Dealers—New Cars		
SIC 5511-02	NAICS 441110	Number of Businesses/Units 21,185

Rules of Thumb

➤ Depending on the franchise, it's three to six times EBITDA plus real estate and hard assets

> Blue Sky—two to four times EBIT Earnings

> Total transaction value in the industry currently ranges from two to four times pretax earnings

> Blue Sky—two to three times net profit or new unit sales (most recent year) times average front-end gross profit per unit

> Hard assets at cost—new parts, FF&E– Book + 50 percent depreciation,

> Blue Sky—3 times recast earnings

> The goodwill component of the sale price of an auto dealership (franchised only) normally falls within the range of two to six percent of gross revenues. Where added to the assets or book value of the business, this is a reliable method of determining price.

Pricing Tips

- EBIT or EBITDA is, of course, included in the add-backs, but due to the amount of personal expense activity, we just add it back and don't separate them.

- Be aware of rental cost paid to owners of dealerships. Be aware of compensation to owners, family members, and general managers.

- Automobile dealerships should have net income of around 2% of total revenue if domestic and higher if import. Service department customer pay labor, gross profit should be between 65% and 70%, parts GP between 35% and 40%. A multiple of 4 to 6 times net income is typical. Imports bring a higher multiple than domestics. Larger stores in a mid-size or large market bring a higher multiple than smaller, rural stores.

- New auto dealerships usually have 4 profit centers, parts, used cars, F&I, and service. New car sales typically have very little margin. Ask the dealer about their absorption ratio (an industry term that indicates how much of their back-end is absorbing their overhead). Any new buyer would have to be approved by the manufacturer (Ford, GM, Toyota, etc.) Key people: used car manager, parts manager, service manager.

- The current value is two to four times net profit of the most recent year. However, the new car franchises that are bringing up to five times net profit are Honda, Toyota and Mercedes Benz.

Benchmark Data

- "Expenses in 2016
Advertising $587,787
Rent & Equivalent $724,207
Selling, General & Administrative (S, G, & A) Expense $5,970,593"

Source: NADA 2017

Statistics (New Car Dealers)

Number of Establishments	21,185
Average Profit Margin	0.4%
Revenue per Employee	$791,100
Average Number of Employees	54.2
Average Wages per Employee	$56,147

Products and Services Segmentation

New vehicles	56.4%
Used vehicles	27.0%
Parts and repair services	13.6%
Finance and insurance	3.0%

Industry Costs

Profit	0.4%
Wages	7.1%
Purchases	85.5%
Depreciation	0.2%
Marketing	1.0%
Rent & Utilities	2.3%
Other	3.5%

Market Share

AutoNation Inc.	2.4%
Penske Automotive Group Inc.	1.3%

Average Dealership Profile—2016

Total Dealership Sales	$59,590891
Total Dealership Gross	$6,771,320
Total Dealership Expense	$6,495,666
Net Profit before Taxes	$1,466,799

Source: 2017 National Auto Dealers Association (NADA) Data.
We can't say enough about how valuable this site is for anyone doing their homework on the retail auto sales industry. It is one of the very best sites we have seen.

Share of total dealership sales dollars in 2016

New Vehicle	57.97%
Used Vehicle	30.4%
Service and Parts	11.7%

Expenses (% of Annual Sales)

Cost of Goods	75% to 80%
Occupancy Costs	10% gross profit
Payroll/Labor Costs	08% to 10%
Profit (pretax)	01.5% to 03%

Questions

- How many cars per month do they sell? How is their CSI rating? Is the manufacturer requiring upgrades to the facility? If so when?
- What is your motivation for selling? Any family members part of your succession plan? Are you retiring or moving to a different location/life structure? What is your ideal deal? Are you interested in holding the real property—or selling with a carry back note? What tax attributes are associated with your business (LIFO, Goodwill, etc.)?
- Staff that will stay on? Building lease if not owned. Franchise ratings and CSI ratings.
- Are you ready to sell for market value?

- Is financing in place for new and used sales? Do you have a floor plan? Does the factory have any future plans for your facility—new or larger?
- Age of key personnel? What is the absorption ratio? Can I see your claims history? Who finances the new and used inventory? If this is a multiple-franchise operation under one roof, discover if the manufacturers are pushing for the dealership to split the franchise out into separate facilities.

Industry Trend

- Over the past two years, I've noticed a shortage of available buildings, so demand is growing and supply shrinking. This is a stable, but not a growing, industry.
- "A forecast developed by J.D. Power and LMC Automotive notes that new vehicle sales will slow down for January, but the overall outlook for the year remains positive. U.S. new-vehicle retail sales in January are expected to reach 874,400 units, a 2 percent decline compared to last year, while total light-vehicle sales are expected to reach 1,125,900 units, a 1.8 percent decline, according to the report. '"We expect 2017 to be another record year in U.S. auto sales,' said Jeff Schuster, senior vice president of forecasting at LMC Automotive."

  Source: "Report: 2017 Auto Industry Outlook Positive, Despite Slow Start," https://www.fenderbender.com/articles/8508-report-2017-auto-industry-outlook-positive-despite-slow-start

- "Following President-elect Donald Trump's pointed remarks toward Ford Motor Company and Fiat Chrysler and his proposition to revise or exit the North American Free-Trade Agreement (NAFTA), the Ann Arbor-based Center for Automotive Research (CAR) released a study that analyzed the impact of these choices, according to a report from the Detroit News. The study found that at least 31,000 jobs in the U.S. automotive and parts industries would be lost.

  "CAR'S study warns that a U.S. withdrawal from NAFTA or the application of Trump's 'big border tax' would have adverse effects on the automotive industry. The study also states that the U.S.'s withdrawal from NAFTA or further restrictions being put on 'vehicles, parts and components trade within North America will result in higher costs to producers, lower returns to investors, fewer choices for consumers and a less competitive U.S. automotive and supplier industry.' CAR predicts that Detroit's three major automakers would be hit the hardest because of their reliance on free-trade with Mexico."

  Source: "NAFTA Exit Could Cost 31,000 Jobs," https://www.fenderbender.com/articles/8436-nafta-exit-could-cost-31000-jobs

- "In recent years, auto dealerships have seen a wave of new-investor interest. High-profile buyers such as Warren Buffett and Bill Gates have joined a host of family offices and private equity investors to take part in an industry that proved its merit by emerging relatively unscathed from the Great Recession. The entry of a new set of buyers, combined with changing sales dynamics enabled by the Internet and an aging generation of dealership owners, has fueled a consolidation trend."

  Source: "You've Bought a Car Dealership? Now What?" by Ed Reinhard, January 20, 2017, http://wardsauto.com/dealer/you-ve-bought-car-dealership-now-what

- "Toyota officials say they aren't having second thoughts about plans to build a new assembly plant in Mexico for Corolla small-car production, despite U.S. government threats of a 20% border tax on Mexican imports. Output of larger passenger vehicles such as the Camry, Highlander, Sienna and some Lexus models will be concentrated at Toyota's Midwest operations in Kentucky and

Indiana, as well as in Canada. Truck output will come from the automaker's plant in Texas and in Mexico, Lentz (Toyota North America CEO Jim Lentz) says.

"A 20% border adjustment tax would raise the cost of a U.S.-built Camry—the vehicle with the highest U.S. content at 75%—by about $1,000 per unit, he says by way of example. 'If that's the base level of what everything else goes up, that's a pretty big hit to the consumer,' Lentz says. 'Manufacturers don't have the margins to absorb that. (It's a) global industry, global supply chain,' he says. 'The time it takes to shift that supply chain is really the lifecycle of a vehicle. It's difficult for the industry to move that rapidly to turn that supply chain around.'

"Ford CEO Mark Fields said here earlier this week that he, General Motors CEO Mary Barra and Fiat Chrysler Automobiles CEO Sergio Marchionne floated the idea of a 50-state standard in a recent meeting with Trump."

Source: "Toyota: No Regrets on Mexico Sourcing Plans" by David E. Zoia, January 29, 2017,
http://wardsauto.com/nada-convention-and-exposition/toyota-no-regrets-mexico-sourcing-plans

- Stable to declining

Seller Financing

- Our larger clients do not require financing. Business with property usually is lender financed. Smaller deals are mixed 50/50 or 80/20 buyer/seller financed.
- 60% working capital in cash.
- Can be a mixture of both seller and outside financing.
- 3 years—very small percentage of selling price is carried.

Resources

- Business Valuation Resources: http://www.BVResources.com
- National Automobile Dealers Association: http://www.nada.org
- Automotive News: http://www.autonews.com
- Ward's Auto: http://www.wardsauto.com
- IBISWorld, May 2017: http://ibisworld.com
- American International Auto Dealers Association: http://www.aiada.org

Auto Dealers—Used Cars		
SIC 5511-03	NAICS 441120	Number of Businesses/Units 140,809

Rules of Thumb

➢ Wholesale book value of cars; no goodwill; add parts, fixtures and equipment

Benchmark Data

Statistics (Used Car Dealers)

Number of Establishments	140,809
Average Profit Margin	2.8%
Revenue per Employee	$452,600
Average Number of Employees	2.0
Average Wages per Employee	$28,090

Products and Services Segmentation

Used vehicles 58.6%
Parts and services 30.9%
Financing and insurance.. 10.5%

Industry Costs

Profit 2.8%
Wages... 6.2%
Purchases.. 85.9%
Depreciation... 0.2%
Marketing 0.9%
Rent & Utilities 2.5%
Other.. 1.5%

Market Share

CarMax Business Services LLC 11.4%

Dealer Operating Information:

Average units sold per dealer (BHPH deals only) 610
Average cash in deal per vehicle sold $4,926
Average ACV per vehicle sold (includes recon) $5,487
Average reconditioning cost per vehicle sold $1.026
Average gross profit per vehicle sold $4.509
Average cash down payment $1,134
Average amount financed $9.664
Average term of loan (in weeks) 143

Questions

- General Questions What types of sales transactions did you have for the year under examination?

    a. Any sales at auctions? If yes, which?

    b. Any sales to wholesalers? If yes, which?

    c. Any sales to other dealers? If yes, which?

    d. Any consignment sales? If yes, describe.

    e. Any scrap sales? If yes, describe.

    f. Any in-house dealer financing sales?

    g. Any third-party financing sales?

    h. Did you have any other types of sales transactions?

    i. Did you have any sales that resulted in a loss on the sale? If yes, describe the nature of these sales.

    j. What sales did you have to relatives or family friends during the year? Identify.

Industry Trend

- "The economy looks solid, but auto industry economists and analysts are concerned a softening used-vehicle market and rising incentives on new cars and trucks could send the industry into an unwanted spiral. . . . Szakaly (Steven Szakaly, chief economist for the National Automobile Dealers Assn.) is forecasting a decline in light-vehicle sales this year to 17.1 million units, a drop from 17.5 million in 2016 and continued slide to 16.7 million vehicles in 2020. That contrasts with a J.D. Power forecast issued yesterday that calls for sales this year to slightly top 2016's record volume.

"But Banks (Jonathan Banks, vice president for consultant J.D. Power Valuation Services) worries the slowly shrinking new-vehicle market will encourage automakers to offer even higher sales incentives already averaging a record $4,000 per unit. That in turn is lowering values on used cars and trucks, and Banks fears the industry could be headed down a dangerous path. Szakaly says there's been a shift of about 300,000-400,000 buyers from new to used."

Source: "Incentives, Used-Car Market Trends Worry Analysts" by David E. Zoia, January 27, 2017
http://wardsauto.com/nada-convention-and-exposition/incentives-used-car-market-trends-worry-analysts

Resources

- Used Car News: http://www.usedcarnews.com
- National Independent Automobile Dealers Association (NIADA): http://www.niada.com
- IBISWorld, June 2017: http://ibisworld.com

Auto Detailing

SIC 7542-03	NAICS 811192	

Rules of Thumb

➢ 40–45% of annual sales plus inventory

Benchmark Data

Detailer Type

Freestanding Detail Shop	44%
Full-Service Conveyor Car Wash	28%
Mobile Detailing	12%
Self-Service Car Wash	07%
Exterior-only Car Wash	02%
Oil Change/Lube	05%
In-Bay Automatic	07%
Gas Station	09%
C-Store	05%

Operating Costs as Percentage of Revenue

Rent	13.4%
Equipment/Supplies/Maintenance	8.9%
Chemicals (incl. soap, wax, compound, etc.)	4.3%
Labor	36.7%
Utilities (incl. water/sewer)	5.4%
Advertising & Promotion	2.8%
Insurance	5.6%
Customer Claims	0.3%

Average Number of Cars Detailed Annually

Freestanding	1,310
Car Wash Combo	1,157
Mobile Service	1,560

Average Package Price Retail—Free-Standing

Complete Interior/Exterior Detail	$200.77
Interior Detail Only	$114.23
Exterior Detail Only	$135.83

Average Gross Revenue Per Car (Car Wash Sales Only)

Average Number of Cars Washed Per Month	2,907
Average Monthly Gross Income (Detail Services Only)	Gross Income
Freestanding	$12,333
Car Wash Combo	$14,200

Source for the above 5 charts: "Detailing Survey 2016—Results from Auto Laundry News," www.carwashmag.com. This is a very informative site—and publication—for Car Washes and Auto Detail; all sites should be this good.

- "A skilled detailer, who is working hard but not rushing, can probably complete a car in about 4 to 4.5 hours and make it look great. The average car would be only a few years old, be a mid-size, and be in average cosmetic condition with no major scratches or blemishes, and no major stains or excessive dirt on the interior."

Source: www.dealermarkclicks.com

Resources

- AutoLaundry News: http://www.carwashmag.com
- Auto Detailing: http://www.autodetailingnetwork.com

Auto Glass Repair/Replacement

SIC 5231-10	NAICS 811122	

Rules of Thumb

➢ 1.8 x SDE plus inventory

➢ 45–50% of annual sales plus inventory

Benchmark Data

Statistics (Auto Glass Repair & Replacement Franchises)

Number of Establishments	252
Average Profit Margin	5.4%
Revenue per Employee	$120,300
Average Number of Employees	5.1
Average Wages per Employee	$32,456

Products and Services Segmentation

Windshield repair	61.2%

Windshield replacement 18.8%
Window repair 15.3%
Window replacement 4.7%

Industry Costs

Profit 7.0%
Wages 27.1%
Purchases 39.0%
Depreciation 1.8%
Marketing 2.5%
Rent & Utilities 6.3%
Other 16.3%

Market Share

Glass Doctor 35.3%

Industry Trend

- "A number of factors are impairing the ability of independent auto-glass-replacement shops to compete with large chains. Johnson Auto Glass and Trim Shop Vice President Dan Johnson said those factors include rising prices for replacement auto glass, lower reimbursements from insurance companies and efforts to steer insured parties away from independent auto-glass-replacement companies."

    Source: "Business Tougher for Independent Auto-Glass-Replacement Companies" by Dan Heath,
    www.pressrepublican.com

Resources

- National Glass Association (NGA): http://www.glass.org
- Glass Magazine—an informative site with archived articles of past issues: http://www.glassmagazine.com
- National Windshield Repair Association: http://www.nwrassn.org/
- IBISWorld, January 2017: http://ibisworld.com

Auto Lube/Oil Change		
SIC 7549-03	NAICS 811191	Number of Businesses/Units 34,502

Rules of Thumb

➢ 40% of annual sales (tune-up) plus inventory

➢ 3 x EBIT (tune-up)

➢ 45% of annual sales (only auto lube businesses) plus inventory

➢ 1.5–2.25 x SDE plus inventory

Pricing Tips

- There are two different service and working environments applicable to this business. The first being an oil and lube facility only, no service work is performed. The second being a tune-up business, performs oil and lube, in addition to service work, brakes, tune-ups, smog inspection, etc.
- The first auto lube business generally shows a greater multiple, 2.5 SDE, while the auto tune-up business described above normally shows a 2.0 SDE.

- The reasoning for the difference in the multiples above is the first business described is generally in a low-tech environment, with non-specialized training and employee wages are lower in comparison to specialized standards in this industry. In addition, most owners have multiple locations. The owner is mostly absentee in this operation and a manager is trained to perform all facets of operation and office functions as required. Demand is also higher.
- The second business described above requires a higher skilled employee (usually certified) and in most states the employees need to be tested. In addition, the owner needs to be involved in the everyday functions of the operation, if only as an administrator. Most have a manager in place as well.
- Critical factors affecting business value are as follows: franchise vs. independent, manager and staff, customer base and vehicle count per day, average ticket per day, lease terms, equipment leased, owner's participation and location.

Benchmark Data

Statistics (Oil Change Services)

Number of Establishments	34,502
Average Profit Margin	11.6%
Revenue per Employee	$76,800
Average Number of Employees	2.6
Average Wages per Employee	$23,333

Products and Services Segmentation

Oil changes	47.6%
Cabin air filters	20.2%
Tire rotations	19.9%
Transmission flush services	8.9%
Other	3.4%

Industry Costs

Profit	11.6%
Wages	30.3%
Purchases	38.9%
Depreciation	3.1%
Marketing	2.0%
Rent & Utilities	7.5%
Other	6.6%

Market Share

Royal Dutch/Shell Group	9.4%

Seller Financing

- 4 years

Resources

- AutoInc.: http://www.autoinc.org
- National Oil & Lube News: http://www.noln.net
- Automotive Service Association: http://www.asashop.org
- IBISWorld, May 2017: http://ibisworld.com

Auto Mufflers

SIC 7533-01	NAICS 811112	

Rules of Thumb

➤ 35–40% of annual sales plus inventory

➤ 1–1.5 x SDE plus inventory

Auto Parts and Accessories—Retail Stores

SIC 5531-11	NAICS 441310	Number of Businesses/Units 64,251

Rules of Thumb

➤ 40% of annual sales plus inventory

Pricing Tips

- New cost of fixtures and equipment plus inventory at wholesale cost, nothing for goodwill. The inventory should turn over 4-6 times per year.

Benchmark Data

Statistics (Auto Parts Stores)

Number of Establishments	64,251
Average Profit Margin	4.1%
Revenue per Employee	$153,800
Average Number of Employees	6.0
Average Wages per Employee	$26,068

Products and Services Segmentation

Critical parts (new)	60.4%
Accessories	21.5%
Maintenance parts	8.3%
Critical parts (used)	7.4%
Performance parts	2.4%

Major Market Segmentation

Household and individuals	61.5%
Repair shops	23.7%
Other	8.1%
Retailers and Wholesalers for resale	6.7%

Industry Costs

Profit	4.1%
Wages	17.0%
Purchases	60.4%
Depreciation	0.9%
Marketing	1.3%
Rent & Utilities	4.5%
Other	11.8%

Market Share

AutoZone Inc. 16.6%
Advance Auto Parts Inc. 15.8%
O'Reilly Automotive Inc. 15.3%
Genuine Parts Company 12.1%

Miscellaneous Sales Information

Average store size .... 6,350 sq. ft.
Average per store sales $1,573,000
Inventory turnover 1.81
Average net sales per store sq. ft. $248

Expenses (% of Annual Sales)

Cost of Goods 61.3%
Occupancy Costs 03.4%
Payroll/Labor Costs 19.9%
Profit (pretax) 05.3%

Resources

Automotive Aftermarket Industry Association: http://www.aftermarket.org
IBISWorld, February 2017: http://ibisworld.com

Auto Rental

SIC 7514-01	NAICS 532111	Number of Businesses/Units 10,968

Rules of Thumb

➤ 45% of annual sales plus inventory

Pricing Tips

- Reservation system, and national sales efforts, are critical. Many airport locations receive 70% or more of their business from this source. Off-airport locations are different; they can survive on local advertising as well as national.

Benchmark Data

Statistics (Car Rental)

Number of Establishments 10,968
Average Profit Margin 11.4%
Revenue per Employee $270,400
Average Number of Employees 13.0
Average Wages per Employee $26,389

Products and Services Segmentation

Leisure car rental 44.9%
Business car rental 31.8%
Car leasing 20.6%
Car sharing 2.7%

Major Market Segmentation

Off-airport market	46.2%
Airport leisure customers	31.4%
Airport business customers	22.4%

Industry Costs

Profit	11.4%
Wages	9.8%
Purchases	32.5%
Depreciation	25.9%
Marketing	0.7%
Rent & Utilities	2.2%
Other	17.5%

Market Share

Enterprise Rent-A-Car Company	36.8%
Hertz Global Holdings Inc.	15.3%
Avis Budget Group Inc.	14.9%

2016 U.S. CAR RENTAL MARKET FLEET, LOCATIONS AND REVENUE

Company	U.S. Cars In Service (Avg.) 2016	# U.S. Locations	2016 U.S. Revenue Est. (in millions)
Enterprise Holdings (Includes Alamo Rent A Car, Enterprise Rent-A-Car, National Car Rental)	1,293,027	6,400	$15,314
Hertz (includes Dollar and Thrifty)	489,800	4,435	$6,100
Avis Budget Group (includes Payless, not Zipcar)	375,000	3,400	$5,550
Fox Rent A Car	19,000	20	$240
Advantage Rent-A-Car	30,000	73	$325
ACE Rent A Car	12,000	59	$100
U-Save Auto Rental System (owned by FSNA)	12,000	141	$123
International Franchise Systems (Rent-A-Wreck of America, Priceless & Nextcar)	5,500	151	$46
Affordable/Sensible	3,720	190	$32
Independents	73,000	5,600	$595
Total	2,313,027	20,469	$28,425

Source: "Auto Rental News Fact Book 2017"
http://www.autorentalnews.com/fileviewer/2451.aspx

Expenses (% of Annual Sales)

Cost of Goods	82%
Occupancy Costs	04%
Payroll/Labor Costs	08% to 10%
Profit (pretax)	06%

Questions
- Relationships with franchisor; license agreement and royalty rate

Industry Trend
- "Five business model trends for 2017:
  - ✓ Rise of auto manufacturers as mobility providers
  - ✓ Renting fleet to Lyft and Uber drivers
  - ✓ Blending of peer-to-peer and rental fleets
  - ✓ On-demand rentals take first steps
  - ✓ Opening of new online marketplaces"

  Source: "Five Business Model Trends for 2017" by Chris Brown, December 28, 2016,
http://www.autorentalnews.com/blog/auto-focus/story/2016/12/five-business-model-trends-for-2017.aspx

- Increasing transparency of pricing with Internet travel sites. Increasing use of 'yield management' in pricing. Regulatory scrutiny of merged entities.

Resources
- Auto Rental News: http://www.autorentalnews.com
- IBISWorld, November 2016: http://ibisworld.com

Auto Repair (Auto Service Centers)		
SIC 7514-01	NAICS 811111	Number of Businesses/Units 260,080

Rules of Thumb
➢ 3 x SDE plus inventory ($150,000 + SDE)

➢ 1–2.5 x SDE plus inventory, ($75,000 to $100,000 SDE)

➢ 3–3.5 x EBITDA

➢ 25–30% of annual sales plus inventory

➢ 3 x EBIT

Pricing Tips
- Key factors that affect the value or pricing of this industry are as follows: employees and management in place, lease, yelp rating, database of clients, software program, role the owner has in the business, number of service bays, equipment condition, location, services provided, family members involved, franchise vs. non-franchise.
- Size matters. Shops with sales over $1,000,000 and/or an SDE of over $200,000 will sometimes fetch a higher multiple.
- Most auto repair shops/service centers for pricing should be based on SDE and not on EBITDA. The multiple for an average shop is 2x and this would normally increase to 2.5x if the business is showing an SDE of $200k or higher. This business is not priced on revenues due to the fact there are too many variables between the sales, gross profit and expenses that overall affect the bottom line. Too many CPA's who try to value this business for their clients look at the revenues as a benchmark to determine value and this is wrong.
- Most buyers of shops need to work in the front of the shop doing estimates and customer service. There is a lot of information for people coming from different industries to get schooled on how to run a profitable shop. Also feedback I am

getting in 2016 is that the amount shop owners need to pay good technicians is going up by 20% or more.

- 3.0 to 3.5 SDE for SDE $150,000 and up to about $500,000; around 3.0 for $100,000-$150,000 and about 2.0-2.5 for under $100,000.

- "The reason it is important to understand whether the business sale is an asset sale or stock sale is that the categories for the purchase price allocation are a bit different. For stock sales, the entire purchase price may be allocated to the value of the stock. The seller pays the capital gains rate for stocks held more than one year, and the buyer does not get a write-off and must accept assets at the current book value. Occasionally, the parties may agree to allocate a portion of the purchase price to the non-compete agreement and/or the training/consulting agreement. For the portion allocated to the non-compete agreement, it is ordinary income to the seller and the buyer gets to amortize it over 15 years. For the portion allocated to the training/consulting agreement, it is ordinary income to the seller and the buyer gets to expense it out as paid."

  Source: http://www.acbrokersinc.com/blogs/purchase_price_allocation_business_sale.html

- Inventory on hand is usually small. Most parts can be delivered in a few hours. Must be a great mechanic. Small shops make a small return. Need a busy shop to make any real money.

- Lack of owner dependence is very important. Auto repair is a customer service oriented business with many owners working the front counter. Buyers often ask themselves what will happen to the customer base if the owner is not there to greet them. Advise sellers to distance themselves from the front desk and hire a service writer. One-man shows almost never sell. Tire stores grossing over $1 million are very desirable, despite low margins, and are fetching a 3-3.5 multiple. Employee costs should be around 25%; oftentimes an owner can trim some fat to boost SDE to justify a higher asking price.

- A business with fleet and commercial customers is worth a higher multiple than a full retail business. Having more than one bay and one lift per technician is important, since many times a vehicle is waiting on parts after being torn down so it's important for the technicians to have more than one work space to move from job to job. Shops that do heavy line work, such as power train and transmission repairs, also are worth a higher multiple than shops that just do light duty work only.

- Typically, when pricing a shop location is a large part of the valuation and marketability of the business. If a shop has $1 million plus in revenues the multiplier can be higher vs. a shop that does a few hundred thousand in revenues. If a shop has too much equipment the owner may believe his business is worth more, but we let them know that is just 'stuff' that helps you generate your revenues. For example, if a shop's value is $200,000 based on SDE and they have $400,000 in assets I may have the client not include every tool they own in the deal. I let them know to sell that equipment another way because they will never get paid for it on the transaction.

- Large volume shops tend to get a larger multiple percentage. If inventory is valued at less than 15% of selling price, it is often included. Shops with a high tire volume may have larger inventories and these inventories would not be included.

- Length of lease is very important. Percentage of tire sales if significant can reduce SDE and sales ratio and affect price. Condition of equipment, cleanliness of shop and brand or banner will affect local desirability and price. Reputation is also very important.

Benchmark Data

Auto Repair (Auto Mechanics)

Number of Establishments	260,080
Average Profit Margin	7.1%
Revenue per Employee	$113,200
Average Number of Employees	2.2
Average Wages per Employee	$32,114

Products and Services Segmentation

Powertrain repair services	24.9%
Scheduled and preventive repair and maintenance services	23.4%
Brake repair services	16.2%
Other repair and maintenance services	9.5%
Electrical system repair services	8.8%
Heating repair services	6.7%
Wheel alignment and repair services	5.6%
Muffler and exhaust repair services	4.9%

Industry Costs

Profit	7.1%
Wages	28.4%
Purchases	43.4%
Depreciation	1.5%
Marketing	1.1%
Rent & Utilities	6.7%
Other	11.8%

- Here are some of the benchmarks for this industry. If an auto center has six bays, each bay per month could, on average, generate $20k to $25k in revenue, and this would be a top producing center. Each tech (mechanic) should produce in parts and labor $24k per month. If the business has two techs, the center should be generating $50k per month in sales, etc. The average work order or ticket should be no less than $225/vehicle; this does vary if the auto center does tires or major repairs like transmissions or engine replacement.

- The common denominator in this industry is that sales should average $20k per each tech per service bay. So if you have five bays with four techs, the shop should average $80k per month as a minimum. Other critical elements you should look for when listing this business are: at least one mgr., three techs-at least two techs being certified, a reasonable lease and terms going forward. However, you will find franchise auto centers with higher rent factors for the most part. Lastly, go to yelp.com to see the rating the business has; it should be at least three stars or higher.

- 68% gross on labor sales and 35%–40% on parts. $100,000–$125,000 sales per employee. Need two bays per technician. Quick lube or quick service lane is a plus. Need plenty of lifts.

- Rent per bay not to exceed $1500.00; sales per bay over $150,000 minimum, with $250,000 per bay reaching capacity.

- Mechanics must generate revenue of at least $1500 to $2000 per week to cover their own salary.

- Many mechanics learn the business then leave and open their own shop. Customers are easy to find, but hard to keep.
- Average ticket should be between $400 and $550 per car. A very busy and well-staffed shop can produce on a regular basis $35K per month per technician. Cost of parts and labor should not exceed 20% of total revenues.
- $100,000 to $150,000 in annual sales per bay is typical. Any shop that is on the high side of this scale is likely to be significantly more profitable if costs are controlled. I like to see gross rent under Estimated average annual sales is $475,000.

Expenses (% of Annual Sales)

Cost of Goods	30% to 40%
Occupancy Costs	08% to 15%
Payroll/Labor Costs	20% to 35%
Profit (pretax)	10% to 18%

Questions

- Buyer should ask for two months of invoices and those invoices should match the sales for those months, three years tax returns, EDD and state tax reports for two years, copy of lease, files on the employees, owner's manual if applicable. Of course this is after an offer has been made and accepted. Once all contingencies have been satisfied and possession is within 48 hours or less, ask for list of all customers in the database, their vendors and suppliers. The buyer should be shown all the pluses and minuses of the business, from the full-time commitment to the strength of the business, current staff in place, what requirements per the state, and federal regulations in that state.
- What is the percentage of your customer base that visits at least twice a year? What is the staff turnover like.? A high percentage of repeat customers and low employee turnover usually indicate a solid business.
- The norm of three years' books and records, tax returns. List of staff and their positions and tenure. Have they been fined by the state or county for overselling? What is their car count and average ticket per customer? What software are they utilizing and how many customers are active in their database? Does the owner work within the business as a tech or hopefully as the administrator and PR person?
- Ask the seller when his last shop labor rate increase was. Ask the seller how long his top techs have been with him. See if the techs are on commission or salary.
- Average hours per repair order; average dollars per repair order; average repair orders per day; how may bays; how many lifts; how many techs; do you repair transmissions; do you sell tires or provide wheel and tire services? What do you not sell that you think should be added to the product or service line?
- Are customers in a computer base? Amount of advertising needed to keep customers. Promotions used to generate new business.
- How many technicians, how many bays, how many lifts do you have? What are your hours per RO, dollars per RO? Do you do fleet or commercial repairs? How many repair orders per month do you average?
- Price your business according to these terms or it will just sit on the market and not sell. If you are buying a business in this market try and buy one that has at least $500,000 in revenues and has a location with drive by traffic. Ask

how many cars per week do they work on (should be minimum 25). What is the average RO (should be minimum $450). What is your mark up on parts (should be 60% but if it's not, don't be too concerned; you will have room for better profits).

- Ask the seller if he is an active mechanic in the business. If not, what are his daily functions? Are there any family members in the business? Is there a good mgr. in place who will stay on after the sale? Will the key mechanics stay after the sale? Does the owner have a good software program in place and does the owner have all his customers in the database? Any hazardous waste issues in the last five years? Does the owner pay all his employees on a W-2? Are any employees paid under the table?

Industry Trend

- I see the trend slowly increasing as more drivers from their teens purchase mainly used vehicles. Even increases in gas prices has not slowed the top auto centers from increasing in sales.
- Quality customer-service-oriented shops that invest in technology-friendly technicians, tools, and training will hold their own. The smaller players will slowly shrink in numbers as the costs to keep up with technology becomes more prohibitive.
- This industry is being segmented by large dealerships and therefore the Mom and Pop auto repair shops are slowly diminishing. Auto centers doing over $750k annually in revenues should survive however. Moving forward, shops that do not bring in state-of-the-art equipment and do not change from their own ways will not survive in the next five years.
- Wages for good technicians are going to continue going up as less and less people want to go into the industry. In more rural areas shops are pressured to allow customers to bring in their own parts thus reducing profits that the shop would enjoy if they sourced the parts. Labor rates are 20-30 percent lower than in large cities because of competition from 'back yard mechanics.'
- Trend is more volume for shops with good employees. Population keeping cars longer and having them repaired instead of replaced.
- The trend that we are seeing is that shops are having to invest in original equipment manufacturers' diagnostic equipment and tools. This leads to additional costs for an independent or franchised auto repair shop. The upside is that those shops that are willing to make that investment are taking customers and jobs from other shops. Technician wages and ongoing training requirements are on the rise.
- Fewer cars entering a shop because of the quality of newer cars and the high cost of used cars. Newer cars on the road, but when they do come in, the average ticket seems to be increasing

Expert Comments

If an auto repair center owner is ready to sale their business, I suggest they search for a broker who is very familiar with the industry and knows the nuances of the operation and the right questions to ask. Make sure the shop is in compliance with all mandates per state and federal laws, keep your shop clean, and have your waiting room so clean that mothers with children will feel welcome. Make sure the broker can also relate properly to a potential buyer about the business and the industry in general.

The same holds true for someone looking to buy this business. The buyer should be shown all the pluses and minuses of the business: the full-time commitment, the strength of the business, the staff in place, and the state and federal regulations required.

The risk factor for a buyer who does not have previous experience can be challenging; the learning curve for this industry averages one to two years or more. The industry trend shows those who have weathered the storm after 2008 and have added services to their format continue to grow in revenues. To replicate a business like this from scratch can be daunting if the business owner does not have the know-how or a good game plan. Franchises continue to grow in this sector, and most first-time buyers would look at a franchise over a non-franchise auto center. Midas and Meineke are the first two franchises that continue to populate the market place.

Clean up, throw out old equipment and parts (especially old used parts), paint and, in general, brighten up the shop as much as possible. This will increase sales, employee motivation. and resale value.

Sales of automotive parts and service can be generally flat unless there is significant traffic or competition change in the immediate vicinity of the shop.

For most customers proximity to either work, home, or transit is key, as they may have to leave their wheels behind for part of a day or a whole day. If a shop is in an area with new construction, the market could grow as long as there are no new shops opened to suck up the demand. In many areas it is difficult to build new shops, as the startup costs of a new shop with all new equipment is very prohibitive. Also getting the zoning for a new automotive location is often difficult. If there are shops closing for redevelopment as land prices go up, then the remaining shops will be able to benefit from their market share.

This industry has shown a good steady growth over the last twenty years, however many smaller shops have closed their doors due to more competition from the dealerships and larger auto repair centers. The ratings reflect this going forward.

It helps if the shop has been in the community for a few years and has developed a reputation of being honest and doing good work. Shops used to carry significant amounts of inventory 10 or more years ago. Now shops have virtually zero inventory because parts are delivered quickly.

Make your employees a priority. In this sometimes fast-paced and always super-competitive industry, most owners put all of their emphasis on taking care of their customers and not their employees. Take care of your employees and they'll take care of your customers. Set realistic expectations and monitor where you are versus where you need to be; spend time to help your employees learn and earn; because the happier they are, the more you'll make.

Profit trend is up as people keep vehicles longer. Location and facilities are very important. Auto repair has been primarily a recession-proof industry so the trend is favorable. Replication takes space, technicians and specialized equipment.

It is becoming extremely difficult in many places to get permits to construct new automotive repair shops and the cost of entry is difficult. If you have a decent lease or own a building in a good traffic area that is reasonably solid with adequate parking, there is a lot of demand. However, the returns are very sensitive to the cost of occupancy and if occupancy is above 15% of sales it is usually not viable.

Although competition is extremely high, most customers will be loyal to an auto repair center that provides reliable service in a reasonable amount of time. People like knowing who they're trusting their vehicle to, and repair shops that can provide that personal touch should always be in demand.

The risk in getting into this industry usually has to do with location. If the location is hidden away it may be harder to build the business. If the location is in a prime spot the rent may become too expensive. A good technician is hard to come by and that makes it difficult, but with a good shop and location the good techs are always available. Buyers are always intrigued by this industry and see the potential in a sound investment by purchasing a shop. An owner does not need to be a mechanic, which drives the demand.

In this marketplace there is competition, however you will see a good number of auto centers come and go if they fail to provide honesty and quality service to their customers. Many smaller auto centers have gone out of business; those shops that are underachievers normally have sales under $300k annually and are not profitable. If you list a shop with sales over $500k annually you'll have a good chance of selling that business; the key is to have a good staff in place with management that will stay.

Seller Financing

- Most all auto centers I've sold post 2008 have had seller financing, normally for a three- to five-year note at 5 to 6% interest. The norm for a seller carry-back note is about 30 to 35% of the purchase price.
  In this business, outside financing is common, as there is usually a fair portion of furniture, fixtures, equipment, and leasehold improvements.
  With 25% to 30% cash down, deals are often doable.
- Typically, there is some seller financing involved in the sale of auto repair businesses. Outside financing is more typical but many lenders would require some sort of seller financing along with buyer cash. I would think you could expect about 10% to 20% down, and about 10% to 20% in seller financing with the rest outside financing.
- A portion of seller financing tied to a longer transition period is important in a non-franchised business where the seller's reputation is the basis of the client following. Bank financing is easier to get for most reputable franchised shops.
  Mostly sold at a discounted level for heavy cash down. It is impossible to find bank financing for business only shops without real estate as collateral.
- Seller financing is a must for an automotive repair business.
- Banks will fund these deals with 25% down. The banks do like to see the seller carry minimum of 10% of the purchase price.

Resources

- The Automotive Maintenance & Repair Association (AMRA): http://www.amra.org

- Automotive Service Association—an excellent site for both auto services/collision businesses: http://www.asashop.org
- AutoInc: http://www.autoinc.org
- National Institute for Automotive Service Excellence: http://www.ase.com
- IBISWorld, April 2017: http://ibisworld.com

Auto Transmission Centers	
SIC 7537-01	NAICS 811113

Rules of Thumb

➢ 3 x EBITDA

➢ 35–45% of annual sales includes inventory

➢ 1.5–2 x SDE includes inventory

Pricing Tips

- Look at present staffing and labor cost; focus on developing a pro forma with present and realistic data for each expense. Ratio of general repair vs. transmission. Are they using remanufactured units?
- Parts cost for classic shop focused on rebuilding transmission ranging from 18%, increasing as added general repair increases to 25%-28% of sales. Lower parts cost indicates use of used parts, which sh1.3ould be cause to examine warranty repair issues. If the owner is the manager or the manager will be leaving, an examination of personal versus business goodwill should be looked at, as the one dealing with the customers is a good barometer to determine how the business can be improved or affected by an ownership change. Considering that the industry is changing where general auto repair becomes a major factor, an analysis of the ratio of retail versus business from referrals from auto repair shops should be analyzed. Ask if the shop has plans to incorporate 'remanufactured units' to avoid high priced labor.
- Shop labor target is about 20% of sales and typically there are three employees. Parts cost lower than 18% is indicative of using used parts. If bottom line EBITDA is higher than 20% of sales.

Benchmark Data

- This industry is changing. Going forward, general auto repair is a significant part as well as using remanufactured parts as an alternative to rebuilding. Independent shops in major markets have a hard time competing with established franchises, and in some markets finding experienced technical employees is hard.
- Keep the Gross Profit at or below 50%, which includes parts cost and shop labor. Maintain a ratio of 80% retail, not to exceed 20%. Fleet/commercial with low concentration of accounts. Address the issues concerning a changing market regarding labor pricing methods where historically transmission shops paid hourly rates and general auto repair by 'flag' hours as percent of shop rate.
- Rules of Thumb for shop labor is 20% of sales, maintaining gross profit of 50%. Typical breakeven is $12,000 per week.

Expenses (% of Annual Sales)

Cost of Goods	18% to 24%
Occupancy Costs	08% to 15%
Payroll/Labor Costs	20% to 25%
Profit (pretax)	10% to 20%

Questions

- Why are you selling? What is the ratio of transmission to general auto? What are the demographics and tenure of employees?
- What is your job function?
- None until he has signed a confidentially agreement. Ratio of retail to commercial sale. Ratio of major to minor repairs. Are there concentrations at any account? Seasonality of the business. How many and job description of employees. Discuss the manager.
- Who is your competition?

Industry Trend

- Franchises will dominate and small shops revert to general auto repair. Long term, with improved quality the industry will change.
- The industry does not seem to be consolidating as is the body shop arena. High cost of Internet advertising is affecting the small independents; in major market areas the ones doing much better are part of a franchised group with co-op advertising.
- Manufacturers are providing longer warranties. Competition from general auto repair shops has forced migration into general auto repair. Smaller shops with less than $500,000 sales in a major market might not be in business. The costs of real estate and zoning are a problem. Many locations desired will be too expensive to justify any auto repair shop. Transmission services are considered by many cities to be heavy auto repair and often require special use permits. Attracting and keeping a highly skilled workforce.

Expert Comments

Build a proforma alternative to trying to analyze historic records.

Advertising online is important; parts cost should be in the 20% for transmission only.

Visiting with an owner of a shop that looks busy in a different market place will be much more helpful, as he will tend to be more open. Contact a good business broker who has sold these type businesses.

This is a recession resistant segment that is changing. Technology is affecting the industry in a positive way, but also negatively, as the quality of new automobile transmissions, extended warranties and high cost encourage trading up rather than repairing, especially if the shop is in an affluent area.

The industry has competition from general auto repair shops using aftermarket transmissions and from dealerships, especially on high-end automobiles. Transmissions have become very reliable. High cost of advertising makes it hard to compete for small independent shops in major markets.

Seller Financing

- Seller financing 50% down, 5 years
- Typically, all sellers want cash but end up having to address financing to sell with half down, balance paid over five years. Outside financing typically involves the buyer providing outside collateral to add to real estate loan at a conventional lender. SBA loans for a franchise without real estate is an option to get by the industry experience required.
- Seller financing unless real estate is included

Resources

- Automatic Transmission Rebuilders Association (ATRA): http://www.atra.com
- Gears Magazine: http://www.gearsmagazine.com
- Transmission Digest: http://www.transmissiondigest.com

Auto Wrecking/Recyclers/Dismantlers/Scrap/Salvage Yards (Auto Parts—Used & Rebuilt)

SIC 5015-02	NAICS 441310	

Rules of Thumb

➢ 100% of annual gross sales including inventory

➢ 25 x EBITDA

Benchmark Data

Statistics (Used Car Parts Wholesaling)

Number of Establishments	2,828
Average Profit Margin	2.2%
Revenue per Employee	$297,700
Average Number of Employees	6.4
Average Wages per Employee	$37,827

Products and Services Segmentation

General auto recycling	60.3%
Specialized motor vehicle dismantling and parts sales	39.7%

Major Market Segmentation

Automotive mechanics and repair shops	42.0%
General auto parts wholesalers	19.2%
Auto parts rebuilders and remanufacturers	14.5%
Other	11.3%
Do-it-yourself customers	6.7%
Auto parts retailers	6.3%

Industry Costs

Profit	2.2%
Wages	12.7%
Purchases	63.6%
Depreciation	1.1%
Marketing	1.0%
Rent & Utilities	3.4%
Other	16.0%

Market Share

LKQ Corporation Inc. 12.9%

Expenses (% of Annual Sales)

Cost of Goods .... 40% to 50%
Occupancy Costs 14%
Payroll/Labor Costs 10%
Profit (pretax) 25%

Questions

- Are they able to pitch the sale of their yard to at least ten potential buyers?

Industry Trend

- "Another key area of growth for the recycling industry is plastics recycling. Plastics are all around us, from the beverage container we drink out of, to the dashboard in our car, to the clothes on our back. Our modern society would be lost without the performance and utility that plastics provides. Plastics recycling is the fastest growing segment of the recycling industry, with more than 3.5 million tons of post-industrial and post-consumer plastics scrap recycled in the U.S. last year.

  "But as with all down cycles, this one is coming to an end, leaving recyclers in an even better position to benefit our economy and society in the months and years ahead."

  Source: "State of the recycling industry today" by Robin Wiener, January 18, 2017,
  http://johnstonsunrise.net/stories/the-state-of-the-recycling-industry-today,121209

- Consolidation is a trend that will continue. Smart operators will have to manage their businesses better every year.
- Wrecking yards do well in good and bad economies.

Expert Comments

Sellers should expose their opportunity to several potential buyers.

Self-service auto recycling is the trend, due to lower personnel costs.

Seller Financing

- Quality buyers pay in cash, or lease facilities long term. Some seller financing takes place, usually when involving a first-time buyer.
- 6 years for self-service yards, and 12 years for full-service yards.

Resources

- Automotive Recyclers Association of New York: http://www.arany.com
- Automotive Recyclers Association: http://www.a-r-a.org
- Institute of Scrap Recycling Industries: http://www.isri.org
- IBISWorld, March 2017: http://ibisworld.com

Aviation and Aerospace

Rules of Thumb

➤ 80% of annual sales
➤ 4–5 x EBIT
➤ 5–6 x EBITDA
➤ 3.8–6.0 x SDE

A - Rules of Thumb

Pricing Tips

- The days of Macquarie buying the Trajen FBO network for 14x EBITDA are over. The recent purchase of Landmark by Signature was about 8x EBITDA. Some large MROs (Maintenance, Repair, Overhaul) are turning away 9x EBITDA offers. Bottom line EBITDA Rules of Thumb (due to maximum leverage ratio of 5x for financial buyers): Sales under $10MM: 3x–4x EBITDA; sales $10MM–$20MM: 4x–6x EBITDA; sales over $20MM: 6x–9x EBITDA.
- To provide a rule of thumb for the industry as a whole would be misleading. A regional airlines SDE multiple will vary greatly from an avionics supplier or repair shop.
- Type of aircraft, market served, age of aircraft, revenue per flight hour and asset utilization.
- Must use both inventory and sales.

Benchmark Data

- Most FBOs and MROs are sold as a percentage of EBITDA. Please see metrics above. Breakeven cash flow on a new aircraft hangar is typically 17 years. Variable costs for fuel are about 28 cents per gallon, reflecting inclusion of general, sales, and administrative expenses.
  Revenue per flight hour

Expenses (% of Annual Sales)

Cost of Goods	20%
Occupancy Costs	10% to 15%
Payroll/Labor Costs	50%
Profit (pretax)	10% to 20%

Questions

- Current lease situation? Top 5 clients? Labor situation? Regulatory environment?
- Age of aircraft, maintenance costs, revenue flights per hour, % of utilization of assets, marketing and sales

Industry Trend

- Signature was just denied their request to extend their lease at Orange County, CA (John Wayne airport). Demand for a quality FBO and MRO continue, as value is put on excellence in customer service. Falcon Jet just announced a 5% workforce reduction at its Little Rock maintenance facility, reflecting a macroeconomic market slowdown. FAA mandates aircraft maintenance on a calendar basis, so macroeconomic factors do not necessarily infer a reason not to buy a MRO. For FBOs, many large chains are buying properties at 1st- and 2nd-tier airports, with 1 million gallons pumped annually as a minimum level metric.
- "Following years of decreased defense revenues, the aerospace industry is poised for positive growth. Due to rising passenger traffic, accelerated equipment replacement cycles, decreasing crude oil prices, and an increase in defense spending, aerospace manufacturers are on pace for record production levels of next-generation aircraft.
  "Global aerospace and defense industry revenues are expected to grow at 3.0% in 2016. The 2016 FAA forecast predicts that U.S. carrier passenger

growth will average 2.1% per year for the next 20 years. In 2016, an estimated 1,420 large commercial aircraft will be produced—40.5% more than five years ago."

Source: https://ewi.org/eto/wp-content/uploads/2016/06/16_5_18_Aerospace_Trends_eBook_FINAL.pdf

Expert Comments

The customer base is the key to success. Try not to have a customer concentration exceeding 20%.

Most FBOs need local government or county-level oversight. As an FBO is really a real estate rental and fuel sales play, EPA federal oversight is necessary. There are horror stories of FBOs being restricted by local governmental authority from selling fuel for up to the first two years of operation. MROs are under the oversight of the FAA as a Part 145 repair station. The business model is to be awarded the contract at X $/hour, but subcontract the labor at 80% of X. Skilled labor shortages exist, as there are fewer entrants into the workforce. Local governmental authorities are now awarding FBOs leases for 20 years, with up to two 5-year options to extend. In previous years, it was a 30-year lease. Break-even analysis shows true profit for CAPEX at about 17 years.

Aviation is a closed community—relationships are easily verified and confirmed. New entrants—unless they have an unheard-of capability—are generally short lived.

Aviation has always been a "darling" industry. Buyers aren't hard to find if you're making money.

Seller Financing

- Mostly 80% outside financing (equity or bank) and 20% seller financing. Clawback or earnout scenarios are known to exist, up to two years after the sale.
- Outside financing

Resources

- Helicopter Association International: http://rotor.com
- National Business Aviation Association: http://www.nbaa.org
- National Air Transportation Association: http://www.nata.org

A&W Restaurants (A&W Root Beer)		Franchise
Approx. Total Investment		$181,000–$1,468,000
Estimated Annual Sales/Unit		$350,000
SIC 5812-06	NAICS 722513	Number of Businesses/Units 630

Rules of Thumb

➢ 45% of annual sales plus inventory

Benchmark Data

- Recommended square footage is between 1,500 and 2,000 square feet.

Resources

- A&W Restaurants: http://www.awrestaurants.com

Bagel Shops		
SIC 546101	NAICS 722513	

Rules of Thumb

➢ 30–35% of annual sales plus inventory

➢ 2.5x SDE plus Inventory

Pricing Tips

- Generally worth 1/3 of gross sales volume, with a decent rent. Higher rent or upcoming increase will lower price.
- Rent a large factor; hand-rolled or frozen product?

Benchmark Data

- For additional Benchmark Information see also Restaurants-Limited Service
- Rent and payroll are the most important factors.

Expenses (% of Annual Sales)

Cost of Goods	10%
Occupancy Costs	20%
Payroll/Labor Costs	25%
Profit (pretax)	20%

Industry Trend

- "It has been a busy month for Bruegger's Bagel Bakery. No sooner was a plan approved to get two dozen franchised stores out of bankruptcy and fold them into company-owned operations than a deal was made to sell the company itself, adding another name to a growing coffee empire that also includes food purveyors Krispy Kreme and Panera.

  "The franchised stores, stretching from Albany to Rochester and including the first Bruegger's site in Troy, were owned by Flour City Bagels of suburban Rochester. Flour City, the largest U.S. franchisee of Dallas-based Bruegger's Enterprises, filed for Chapter 11 bankruptcy protection in early 2016, setting off a fight between the company and a lender over the future of the upstate stores.

  "Finally, on Aug. 16, a bankruptcy judge in Rochester approved the sale of the stores to Bruegger's Enterprises, which has more than 250 company-owned locations nationwide. Then, a week later, Le Duff America, the U.S. operator of French-themed bakery-cafes that also owns Bruegger's Enterprises, announced it would sell the bagel chain to Caribou Coffee, a Minneapolis-based coffee retailer.

  "Caribou is part of JAB Holding, the investment arm of a wealthy German family. JAB's website says it focuses on "long-term investments in companies with premium brands, attractive growth and strong margin dynamics."

  "JAB began acquiring American coffee brands in 2012, including Peet's, Caribou and Keurig Green Mountain. It then moved into complementary restaurant brands: Einstein Bros. Bagels, Krispy Kreme and Panera Bread."

  Source: "Kennedy: Bruegger's Bagel Bakery Being Sold," by Marlene Kennedy, August 30, 2107, https://dailygazette.com/article/2017/08/30/kennedy-bruegger-s-bagel-bakery-being-sold-again

Expert Comments

Easy to duplicate. Setup cost expensive. Most shopping centers already have a bagel shop.

Resources

- National Bagel Association: http://bagels.org/

Bait and Tackle Shops

| SIC 5941-01 | NAICS 451110 | |

Rules of Thumb

➢ 30% of annual sales plus inventory

Benchmark Data

- For Benchmark Information see Sporting Goods Stores

Bakeries

| SIC 5461-02 | NAICS 445291 | |

Rules of Thumb

➢ 2 x SDE plus inventory

➢ 40–45% of annual sales plus inventory

Pricing Tips

- Receivables; years in business; scope of market; new state-of-art equipment vs. old.

Benchmark Data

Statistics (Bakery Cafes)

Number of Establishments	5,012
Average Profit Margin	6.4%
Revenue per Employee	$81,500
Average Number of Employees	20.0
Average Wages per Employee	$19,256

Products and Services Segmentation

Bread and sandwiches	50.2%
Other	29.4%
Beverages	20.4%

Industry Costs

Profit	6.4%
Purchases	23.3%
Wages	38.4%
Depreciation	3.0%
Marketing	2.3%
Rent & Utilities	12.1%
Other	14.5%

Market Share

Panera Bread Company	66.2%
Einstein Noah Restaurant Group	7.8%

Expenses (% of Annual Sales)

Cost of goods sold (Food)	05% to 10%
Payroll/Labor Costs	30% to 35%
Occupancy Cost	06% to 08%
Other Overhead	10% to 15%
Profit (estimated)	20%+

- Percentage of full-line retail bakery operators offering the following items:
  1. Sodas, juices, teas ... 61%
  2. Conventional coffee service ... 56%
  3. Sandwiches ... 45%
  4. On-site dining ... 31%
  5. Espresso, other gourmet coffee ... 30%
  6. Other deli (salads, cheeses, etc.) ... 30%

  Note: Figures above are approximate.
- For additional Benchmark Information see Food Stores—Specialty

Industry Trend

- "According to the report, the global bakery market is anticipated to grow at a Compound Annual Growth Rate (CAGR) of 7.04% between 2014 and 2019. Key trends:
  - ✓ Increase in demand for gluten-free products
  - ✓ Increase in demand for organic products
  - ✓ Constant product innovations increasing revenue
  - ✓ Price fluctuations around commodities used to produce bakery products"

  Source: Global Bakery Market 2015-2019 report from Research and Markets

Resources

- Modern Baking: http://supermarketnews.com/product-categories/bakery
- Independent Bakers Association: http://www.ibabaker.com/
- IBISWorld, February 2017: http://ibisworld.com

Bakeries—Commercial		
SIC 5149-02	NAICS 311812	

Rules of Thumb

- ➢ 65–70% of annual sales plus inventory
- ➢ 3–5 x EBITDA
- ➢ 2–2.5 x SDE plus inventory

Pricing Tips

- Location of bakery: is it in a good traffic area to afford/promote retail trade or in a commercial area that makes it totally dependent on wholesale trade? This usually provides you with an indication of business split between retail and commercial, a reliable monitor of establishing value. Need to see age and condition of equipment. Is there a conveyor system in-house for receiving loose flour, rather than the more costly and time-consuming way of receiving bagged flour?

- The following table illustrates the relationship between two price multiples and company revenues, using data from a study of thousands of sales of small and very small businesses across all industries:

Size of Company	Sale Price/Revenue	Sale Price/ Discretionary Earnings
Up to $1 million revenue	0.51	2.2
$1 to $5 million revenue	0.62	2.9

Gross sales in retail & wholesale; operating hours; location.

- The above price/earnings Rules of Thumb assume a "minimal asset sale," meaning fixed assets, inventory and intangibles only. Assumes the buyer replaces all other elements of working capital, and that the assets are transferred free of liabilities. Typical light manufacturing value drivers and risk factors apply (customer concentration, brand, product differentiation, growth prospects, distribution channel, longevity in the market, condition and capacity of equipment, management depth, etc.)
- Age & sophistication of equipment; convenience of bakery to major transportation hubs allowing for plentiful pool of employees. Gross sales . . . what portion is from retail sales and how much from wholesale; inquire as to the amount of bags of flour purchased weekly; loaves of bread sold weekly.
- The SDE multiplier is subject to increase or decrease based on the age and type of equipment. Further, large commercial bakeries require specialized human resources which may be the seller(s) whose expertise will need to be replaced. Oftentimes sellers minimize the difficulty in replacing their expertise, but this should be carefully evaluated and valuation adjustments made accordingly.
- Be careful to check if one or two customers comprise a high percentage of the bakery's revenues.
- Don't be fooled by the owner's overstatement of the value of the equipment. Most bakery equipment is valued at between 10% and 25% of replacement cost new. The larger equipment requires riggers to move it. The dismantling and re-installation of ovens requires specialized skill and knowledge.
- Price will vary greatly depending on the volume and types of labor-saving equipment. This is an industry where payroll can be significantly reduced by machinery. Commercial contracts with restaurants, hotels, etc. are also a source of value.

Benchmark Data

- Pounds of flour used; # of loaves of bread baked/sold
- Cost of goods should be no more than 20% tops, just as rent should be no more than 10% of sales.
- 22%-25% cost of goods
- Direct cost of goods varies significantly from product to product. There is no little commonality between a bread bakery and a cake and pastry bakery. A well-run facility with reasonable market share should result in an SDE of 15%–20% of Gross Revenues.

Expenses (% of Annual Sales)

Cost of Goods	25% to 30%
Occupancy Costs	15% to 20%
Payroll/Labor Costs	30% to 40%
Profit (pretax)	15% to 18%

Questions

- Determine the geographic scope and customer type of its customer base.
- Ask for flour and water bills, cost/price list of major items carried, aging of receivables and payables; see gas/electric bills; determine age and condition of equipment.
- Is location of any importance to sales? If so, how long is lease?
- Review and interview key customers; evaluate equipment carefully; check for expansion opportunity.

Industry Trend

- There will be less and less small bakeries, with the larger ones of each regional area dictating market price.
- Down, as the major bakers take over the industry.
- Fewer and fewer competitors . . . with a growing trend toward baking artisan products.

Expert Comments

Overall commercial bakeries are generally a high-risk/high-competition industry.

Fastest growing market segments are functional foods, organic, low calorie, all natural, gluten free.

Receivables are very important since they determine the amount of start-up capital needed. It was the cause of the demise of many a big wholesaler in New York.

Price will vary greatly depending on the volume and types of labor-saving equipment. This is an industry where payroll can be significantly reduced by machinery. Commercial contracts with restaurants, hotels, etc. are also a source of value.

Seller Financing

- If it is a high-asset business with relatively new baking equipment, equipment loans may be available to finance the purchase. Otherwise seller financing must be in place.
- Mostly seller financing, but if equipment is modern (which most are not) then outside financing can be arranged.
- 5 to 7 years or the length of the lease if building is not owned

Banks—Commercial		
SIC 6021-01	NAICS 522110	Number of Businesses/Units 81,897

Rules of Thumb

- ➤ 350% of annual gross sales includes inventory
- ➤ 15 x SDE includes inventory
- ➤ 15 x EBIT
- ➤ 1–2 x Book Value

Benchmark Data

Statistics (Commercial Banking)

Number of Establishments	81,897
Average Profit Margin	21.2%
Revenue per Employee	$344,200
Average Number of Employees	20.0
Average Wages per Employee	$79,297

Products and Services Segmentation

Depository services and other noninterest-income generating pro	34.8%
Real estate loans	31.3%
Commercial and industrial loans	14.2%
Other	8.8%
Loans to individuals excluding credit cards	5.6%
Credit card loans	5.3%

Major Market Segmentation

Corporate clients	49.0%
Retail customers	48.0%
Other clients	3.0%

Industry Costs

Profit	21.2%
Wages	23.1%
Depreciation	3.4%
Marketing	3.1%
Rent & Utilities	9.7%
Other	38.5%
Purchases	1.0%

Market Share

Wells Fargo & Company	13.3%
JPMorgan Chase & Co.	9.6%
Bank of America Corporation	6.9%

Expenses (% of Annual Sales)

Cost of Goods	25%
Occupancy Costs	05% to 10%
Payroll/Labor Costs	35%
Profit (pretax)	25%

Questions

- Are you now or have you ever been involved in banking? How much liquid capital do you have to invest? Have you spoken with any bank regulatory authorities about your plans to acquire a bank?

Industry Trend

- "Initial market reactions to the unexpected election outcome in the United States have indicated improved prospects for banks and capital markets firms in 2017. However, ongoing structural changes are likely to continue in the form of new operating models and investments in emerging technologies for greater efficiencies and competitiveness. Meanwhile, banks and capital markets firms are expected to deepen their engagement with the fintech ecosystem as the trend towards digitization accelerates. In this fluid environment marked by policy uncertainty, how will banks and capital market firms respond?"

Source: "Banking and Securities key trends for 2017,"
https://www2.deloitte.com/us/en/pages/financial-services/articles/banking-industry-outlook.html

- "The financial and sovereign debt crises jolted the global banking industry from a period of relative calm and prosperity into one of great uncertainty. We outline below eight major trends that are likely to shape banking to 2030 and beyond.
    - ✓ Nationalism vs. globalism: limits on the global banking model
    - ✓ State capitalism: a new force in global banking
    - ✓ Trade flows: opportunity and volatility
    - ✓ New markets: the emerging will have emerged
    - ✓ Demographics: an older, more urban generation
    - ✓ Customer relationships: more personal, greater trust
    - ✓ Payments: new markets and new models
    - ✓ Energy: challenging the old order"

Source: "Building the Bank of 2030: top eight global trends"
www.ey.com/gl/en/industries/financial-services/banking---capital-markets/8-trends-shaping-the-bank-of-2030

Expert Comments

The post-recession regulatory environment has burdened smaller community banks with compliance issues that are forcing many of them to consolidate in order to achieve the necessary economies of scale required to enable compliance.

Resources

- IBISWorld, January 2017: http://ibisworld.com

Barber Shops

SIC 7241-01	NAICS 812111	

Rules of Thumb

➢ 10–25% of SDE plus inventory; add $1500 per chair

Benchmark Data

- For Benchmark Data see Hair Salons

Bars

SIC 5813-01	NAICS 722410	

Rules of Thumb

➢ 4 x monthly sales + game revenue (net) plus inventory

➢ 4 x monthly sales + liquor license and inventory

➢ 35–45% of annual sales-business only plus inventory

➢ 2–2.5 x SDE plus inventory

➢ 1.5–2.5 x EBIT

➢ 2–2.5 x EBITDA

Pricing Tips

- You have to understand how the licenses and permits impact value.
- A bar serving alcohol only should have a higher profit margin than one selling food. It is a cash business. A lot of due diligence is necessary to verify cash expenses and receipts.
- Competition, number of available licenses in town, previous violations
- Top-line method is used due to the perception of a cash business. This is changing and it is much more difficult to sell bars without documented earnings.
- Main variable is the fair market value of the liquor permit, as some areas have a high number of available permits which results in the permit having no, or limited, additional value, while in other areas limited number of available permits may cause the permit to have a substantial value. One will need to research type of permit and its availability and if in fact a market exists for the permit itself. I have seen liquor permits being sold for as high as $150,000, which obviously impacts the value of the business.
- The location, lease rate, and restrictions on the conditional use permit or liquor license will largely impact any given operation's value. As some licenses are valued at $75K plus, there is always some 'floor' value regardless of profitability.

Benchmark Data

Statistics (Bars & Nightclubs)

Number of Establishments	68,562
Average Profit Margin	5.6%
Revenue per Employee	$59,800
Average Number of Employees	5.9
Average Wages per Employee	$15,149

Products and Services Segmentation

Sale of beer and ale	35.4%
Sale of distilled spirit drinks	33.6%
Sale of meals and nonalcoholic beverages	14.1%
Sale of wine drinks	7.7%
Admissions to special events and nightclubs, including cover charge	2.6%
Other	6.6%

Industry Costs

Profit	5.6%
Wages	25.3%
Purchases	44.5%
Depreciation	2.3%
Marketing	3.2%
Rent & Utilities	6.5%
Other	12.6%

- Liquor pouring costs should be at 25% or less, beer and wine at 33%.
- Food costs under 34% helpful.
- High rents have been the cause of many failures.

- Small easily operated bars are the most desirable. Rent at 10%–12% (or less) of sales helps.
- Benchmarks vary widely with markets and types of establishments; food costs tend to be 25%-33%; however, productivity per square foot is a function of size and location (and subsequent lease rate).

Expenses (% of Annual Sales)

Cost of Goods	20% to 30%
Occupancy Costs	06% to 10%
Payroll/Labor Costs	20% to 28%
Profit (pretax)	10% to 20%

Questions

- How much do you pay the help? Are you paying any of the help in cash? Are your ASCAP BMI fees paid and current?
- Length of time employees have been at work, number of employees, tax audits? Recent violations?
- Please provide me with a copy of the permit or conditional use permit, as provided by the city and the state Alcohol Control Board.
- What conditions have been placed on the license restricting the hours, use, or entertainment associated with the license?
- Scrutinize happy hour, comps, etc. Many buyers think they can increase sales by eliminating giveaways which usually does not work. Ask to see all liquor invoices and cash receipts from liquor purchases.
- For the tax returns, why they are selling? Cooperation is key in this business. Bars are difficult to sell when there are unreported sales, weak returns. Many of the sellers in our market will not hold notes.
- Discretionary Cash Flow should be evaluated very carefully. There can be a huge difference from deal to deal.

Industry Trend

- Very strong with more creative bartenders coming on the scene and people seeing this as a career and job
- More alcohol-only bars with leased space for food trucks
- With the amount of new products emerging from the market with flavored wines, vodka, whisky...one has to stay up on what is in.
- Increasing cost inflation and changing consumer tastes, e.g., craft beer, local foods, etc.
- Smoking blue collar sports bars on the decline.
- Most bars are improving on their food to drive more bar business.
- Increasing costs and increasing competition from chains

Expert Comments

Classic cocktail and other drink trends are in, making bars more popular with millennials.

For a buyer-work in a bar first and make sure you understand the business. Do your homework about cash receipts and where the money really goes.

Location seems to be a driving factor here. Young people going out to a bar seem to prefer going to an area with a cluster of bars which allows for bar hopping.

All of the reality shows glamorizing the industry have popularized the business.

Having practical work experience in the industry is a definite plus. Avoid a 'bad' lease situation. Be comfortable with customers. Sellers should make the place look presentable and not have a bunch of broken equipment around. Police runs and bad health department inspections drive down value.

Seller Financing
- Mostly cash or buyer supplied financing
- All cash or some element of owner financing is usually necessary to make a deal happen.
- Bank financing very difficult
- 3 to 7 years

Resources
- BarProducts.com: http://www.barproducts.com
- IBISWorld, January 2017: http://ibisworld.com

Bars/Adult Clubs/Nightclubs		
SIC 5813-01	NAICS 722410	

Rules of Thumb
- ➢ 3.5 x SDE includes inventory
- ➢ 100–120% of annual sales includes inventory

Pricing Tips
- Real estate typically will lease out at a 12%–20% premium to market. Alcohol licenses may have intrinsic value to be added to cost of purchase.
- A recasted, SDC Flow is the best starting point. Be sure to examine either property or rental costs to make sure they are in line with area...Typically rental costs show a premium of 10%-20% above comparable market rates. FFE is a consideration related to its age.
- The industry has experienced a shake-out of weaker performing clubs being swallowed by larger operators as they become available. Although we have experienced recessionary forces, as the entire industry has, the Adult Club industry by and large has been more resilient than mainstream bars and nightclubs to the effects of discretionary dollar competition and distribution. The more troubling aspects are more related to legal issues of Independent Contractor Status and the efforts of the Citizens for Community Values (CCV).
- Adult clubs are of course cash-heavy operations. Verifying internal ratios of cost can lead to a back-ended method of providing gross cash flow.
- A true EBITDA + owner's compensation recast is a necessity . . .
- The best thumbnail is SDE. It stands up well to real-world numbers on the sales prices. Real estate, inventory, FFE all should be considered separately

as add backs to total sale price. Some states allow the sale of inventory alcohol to the buyer, some do not. MAI appraisals do well for real estate. FFE is a "swag" and over 3 years old stuff ought to write down to 10%-20% of initial cost.

Benchmark Data

Statistics (Strip Clubs)

Number of Establishments	4,025
Average Profit Margin	19.8%
Revenue per Employee	$115,100
Average Number of Employees	14.5
Average Wages per Employee	$24,073

Products and Services Segmentation

Alcohol	41.5%
Service revenue	39.5%
Food and merchandise	13.1%
Other services	5.9%

Industry Costs

Profit	19.8%
Wages	20.8%
Purchases	19.3%
Depreciation	3.2%
Marketing	3.9%
Rent & Utilities	5.9%
Other	27.1%

- Liquor cost should be in the range of 18%-22%; rent: optimally in the 8%–10% range of gross sales.
- SDE x 2.5-3.5 = possible sale price.
- Should be reporting an SDE in neighborhood of 23%–26% or higher.
- There are basically three revenue streams, in addition to the fees from dancers: cover charges, which can top $20; food and drinks; and services, which include the renting of private rooms. A customer may pay the club $400 to $500 for a spell in one of those rooms.
- Rent: 10%; liquor cost: 15%

Expenses (% of Annual Sales)

Cost of Goods	20%
Occupancy Costs	<10%
Payroll/Labor Costs	n/a
Profit (pretax)	25%

Questions

- What is the legal status of licenses and permits: alcohol, privilege, local?
- Detailed explanation of all income sources. Current political atmosphere. Security of license.
- What violations have been charged? Is the owner aware of any pending litigation or legislation (either local or state) which will have a negative impact? There are others, but the rest are more site specific.

Industry Trend

- Continue to maintain growth with more mainstream investments in the industry and more robust economy

Expert Comments

Industry is vital, and succeeding; the average club life can be measured almost in decades.

Major risk is from legislative actions. Operator chooses location and level of sophistication and markets accordingly.

Seller Financing

- Usually 2–4 years
- Usually all cash

Resources

- ED Publications: http://www.edpublications.com
- Association of Club Executives: http://www.acenational.org
- IBISWorld, March 2017: http://ibisworld.com

Bars/Nightclubs		
	NAICS 722410	

Rules of Thumb

➢ 40% of annual sales

➢ 2.5 x SDE plus inventory

➢ 3 x EBIT

➢ 2 x EBITDA

Pricing Tips

- The conditions or potential restrictions on the liquor license are paramount. Are there abbreviated hours, are happy hours or door fees allowed, what is the security-guard-to-patron ratio, does a significant percentage of sales need to be derived by food sales, etc.
- Buyers of nightclubs are generally going to implement their own concept and theme. Sellers rarely seek to sell when they are at the peak of their game, but when revenues begin to slide. The lifespan of a 'hot' club rarely lasts beyond 3 to 4 years, so at that point an owner may need to give the business a 'face lift' or sell it to a new owner who will implement a new theme. That in mind, value based on cash flow becomes less relevant since a new owner's investment will be the same regardless.

Benchmark Data

- See charts under Bars
- "Of the Top 100 survey participants, 42.8% identified their venues as nightclubs; 70.6% of them described their hotspots as dance clubs. Of those identifying their venue as bars, 31.7% are sports bars and 29.3% are traditional

bar/taverns. DJs and live entertainment are featured by 88.3% and 73.6% of total respondents, respectively. Nearly 80% offer a dance floor, 70.1% provide VIP areas, and 65% offer bottle service.

"Drinks generate the lion's share of venue revenues-56% of sales from alcohol is the mean among Top 100 survey participants. While in the venues, partyers favored spirits, which generate 44% of alcohol sales. Beer contributes 25% and wine 9%. A full food menu is offered by 68% of survey respondents' venues. Gaming, such as pool tables, video games systems and jukeboxes, are available at 42% of respondents' venues. Nearly three quarters (73%) have outdoor patio, terrace or rooftop space, which is an increase from 63% a year ago.

"Small companies can compete effectively by serving a local market, offering unique products or entertainment, or providing superior customer service. The industry is extremely labor-intensive: average annual revenue per worker is $60.000.

"Size varies greatly, from small corner taverns to warehouse-sized dance clubs. The majority of nightclubs range from 3,500 to 7,000 square feet, according to nightclubbiz.com. Experienced owners tend to run the largest nightclubs, which range from 10,000 to 30,000 square feet. A 3,000-square-foot club can gross between $24,000 and $64,000 per month. A 15,000-square-foot club can gross between $100,000 and $260,000 per month."

Source: National Club Industry Association of America, www.nciaa.com

Expenses (% of Annual Sales)

Cost of Goods	25%
Occupancy Costs	15%
Payroll/Labor Costs	30%
Profit (pretax)	20%

Questions
- Original invoices for liquor sales, and, with your fingers crossed, door counts per night.

Industry Trend
- There will always be a market for such venues, and buyers willing to pay premiums to A+ locations for venues.

Expert Comments
This industry is highly volatile as trends are constantly changing. Also, clubs on the Strip in Las Vegas, in Hollywood or in South Beach are significantly different from main street America.

Resources
- Nightclub & Bar: http://www.nightclub.com/
- National Club Industry Association of America, NCIAA: http://www.nciaa.com

Bars with Slot Machines

| | NAICS 722410 | |

Rules of Thumb

> ➢ 3 x SDE plus inventory

Pricing Tips

- Drinks are free to slot players. Pay close attention to only the net, providing other operating costs are in line.

Expenses (% of Annual Sales)

Cost of Goods 32%
Occupancy Costs 10%
Payroll/Labor Costs 30%
Profit (pretax) .... 17% (estimated)

Seller Financing

- Where the debt service does not exceed 35 percent of the SDE

		Franchise
Baskin-Robbins Ice Cream		
Approx. Total Investment		$94,350–$402,200
Estimated Annual Sales/Unit		$237,000
SIC 2024-98	NAICS 722515	Number of Businesses/Units 7,800

Rules of Thumb

> ➢ 46–56% of annual sales plus inventory

Resources

- Baskin Robbins: http://www.baskinrobbins.com

		Franchise
Batteries Plus Bulbs		
Approx. Total Investment		$208,450–$385,750
Estimated annual sales/Unit		$1,347,376 (for the top 25% of stores)
	NAICS 441310	Number of Businesses/Units 730

Rules of Thumb

> ➢ 30–35% of annual sales plus inventory

Resources

- Batteries Plus: http://www.batteriesplus.com

Beauty Salons		
SIC 7231-06	NAICS 812112	

Rules of Thumb

➤ 35% of annual revenues; add fixtures, equipment & inventory

➤ 2 x SDE plus inventory

➤ 4 x monthly sales plus inventory

➤ 2.5 x EBIT

➤ 4 x EBITDA

Pricing Tips

- Multiples vary significantly based on size of the company. The multiples above are for product businesses, not service based businesses like hair salons. Product businesses command significantly higher multiples than service based businesses. Growth and distribution channels are the primary drivers of value. Online direct to consumer distribution is attractive, given the higher margins, although retail distribution brings larger scale. Distribution through spas and salons is less attractive given the likely margins that need to be shared with distributors in these industries. Strength of brand is important.
- In the larger full-service salons, you may sometimes have more equipment value to consider such as skin care, facial. Some salons may still owe money; these leases can also sometimes be assumed by the buyer decreasing the sales price.
- Take into consideration the working owner and how much of the sales belong to their work performed. Will they stay on and pay commission or rent, or will they slowly flow their customers to the buyer?
- The larger the gross sales, the higher the multiples. For instance, if I have a salon that is doing $1 million in sales annually, my high number will be $500,000, then I look at the true owner benefits.
- 25% to 35% of annual sales
- Whether the operators are W-2 or #1099-and also how the chemical product costs are debited.
- What percentage of the gross sales is generated by a service generating owner and how may the change in ownership shift the owner's income? The most effective pricing point is utilizing the SDE.

Benchmark Data

Statistics (Hair & Nail Salons)

Number of Establishments	1,337,404
Average Profit Margin	7.8%
Revenue per Employee	$33,000
Average Number of Employees	1.3
Average Wages per Employee	$14,258

Products and Services Segmentation

Haircutting services 45.5%
Hair coloring and tinting services 17.1%
Nail care services 15.9%
Merchandise sales 7.2%
Other beauty care services 6.1%
Other hair care services 4.7%
Skin care services 3.5%

Industry Costs

Profit 7.8%
Wages 43.0%
Purchases 14.1%
Depreciation 1.8%
Marketing 1.6%
Rent & Utilities 15.5%
Other 16.2%

Economic Trends: Percent of Gross Revenue by Category

Hair Color Service Sales 34%
Hair Cutting Service Sales 31%
Retail Sales 17%
Skin Care, Body Care, Spa-type Service Sales 08%
Nail Service Sales 04%
Chemical Service Sales 03%
Other 03%

Expenses (% of Annual Sales)

Cost of Goods .... 06% to 12%
Occupancy Costs .... 10% to 20%
Payroll/Labor Costs .... 50% to 60%
Profit (pretax) .... 07% to 15%

Questions

- How much of the sales belong to your performance? Will you stay on? If the buyer is a stylist and so is the seller, will the clientele slowly flow to the buyer? You cannot make a client stay with you. They are yours to lose or gain. Honesty is the best policy. How long have the employees been with you? What is the turnover of technicians and why? Commission or rental? What type of products do you use and how old is the product on your shelf and why? How often and where do you advertise? Who does your website, Facebook page? Where do you find your employees? How often do you offer education classes and what company"?

Industry Trend

- Wellness products. Business Focus: Wellness + Technology + Science, the New Beauty Market.
- "The demand for organic and natural-based salon products is sky rocketing! Not only is the organic salon product market growing, but so are the salons that have chosen to be a part of the movement. 'Organic salons' are popping up all over the nation, leaving a trail of closed-down, traditional salons in its path. While the number of traditional salons is still greater than organic salons,

the organic salon growth rate suggests things are, in fact, greener on the other side. Now, with the ingredient lists of salon products available at the push of a button, it comes as no surprise that clients are demanding safer products that still perform. In fact, the organic personal care market is projected to grow an astounding 10% a year, totaling $25.1 billion by 2025."

Source: "Salon Industry Trends 2017," March 15, 2017,hubpages.com/style/Salon-Industry-Trends-2014

Expert Comments

Significant number of acquisitions of indie beauty brands, at high multiples, by large strategics and PEGS.

Do not tell your staff or clientele that you are selling until you have closed on the transaction. Then seller will take buyer to the salon and have all employees or staff there for an introduction to the new owner. Take lots of food and drink (no alcohol) and buyer should speak to each of the staff individually and openly. Listen to the concerns of the people and tell them how you will not change anything for at least 3 to 6 months so you can learn more about the needs and desires of both the staff and the clientele. Suggestion box is great.

It is very expensive to start a beauty salon from scratch with all of the build-out, equipment, impact fees from the county government, not to mention the time it takes from signing the lease, construction. You will be out approximately $250,000 from the start. Purchasing a salon that has good equipment, location, technicians and clientele in place will be far more appealing at the end of the first 12 months. Buyers always change the looks in some way that appeals to them whether it is major cleanup or paint and new floors depending on the salon itself.

The beauty industry is as old as mankind and essentially a replenishment industry; the resale possibilities are endless; rebranding is the next frontier. Location and marketing are big factors in the success of a salon.

Seller Financing

- Seller financing is suggested in this industry as most banks do not lend money on the majority of these businesses. Never take less than 50% down payment. I typically see 75% down payment or all cash balance over 2 to 3 years.
- 3 to 5 years

Resources

- Modern Salon: http://www.modernsalon.com
- IBISWorld, July 2017: http://ibisworld.com
- Salon Today: http://salontoday.com

Bed & Breakfasts		
SIC 7011-07	NAICS 721191	Number of Businesses/Units 7,843

Rules of Thumb

➢ 8–9 x SDE includes inventory and real estate

➢ 400% to 450% of annual sales includes inventory and real estate

Pricing Tips

- B&B buyers must make both a lifestyle and financial purchase decision. Innkeeping is one of the few businesses in which you want to live where you work! For the past 15+ years, we have had smaller B&Bs sold/converted back to homes than we've had homes being converted to inns! Startups are more difficult to accomplish today versus the mid-1980s primarily due to rising real estate values, high conversion cost, zoning restrictions, tougher lending practices, and a lack of market demand for innkeeping (during a strong economy). Some of the smaller inns in less popular areas were converted to alternative uses and a minority of inns closed for avoidance of taxes from capital gains and depreciation recapture.
- Smaller B&Bs (fewer than 8 rooms) are usually real-estate driven.
- 5 times gross room income; gross room income minus the net operating expenses (no debt service or management costs) = net operating income times 11 percent.

Benchmark Data

Statistics (Bed & Breakfast & Hostel Accommodations)

Number of Establishments	7,843
Average Profit Margin	16.6%
Revenue per Employee	$112,800
Average Number of Employees	3.5
Average Wages per Employee	$20,830

Products and Services Segmentation

Bed & Breakfast	69.0%
Other—including Hostels	31.0%

Major Market Segmentation

Vacation travelers	58.2%
Family travelers	21.8%
Business travelers	12.0%
Other—including meetings	8.0%

Industry Costs

Profit	16.6%
Wages	18.5%
Purchases	21.2%
Depreciation	8.5%
Marketing	2.2%
Rent & Utilities	11.3%
Other	21.7%

- Many of the of the larger inns in the Midwest are selling at about $100K/room.
- The larger inns are selling for 8 (w/o seller financing) to 10 times (w/seller financing) adjusted net operating income. The base real estate value of the smaller B&B contributes to a large part of the value. In small, supplemental income B&Bs, their value is typically $25,000 to $50,000 more than the base real estate value as a house or other real estate use. There are probably more supplemental income B&Bs than cash flow inns of the $20K+ U.S. B&Bs.

28th Edition

- Profit (estimated) 40% to 45% of sales
- Bed and Breakfast/Country Inn Statistics The data below is from Studies and Surveys done by www.innkeeping.org—a very informative site.
  - ✓ Occupancy Rate   43.7%
  - ✓ Average Daily Rate $150
  - ✓ Revenue per Available Room $58
- About the Inns—Some interesting data from an Industry Study of Innkeeping Operations and Finance from the Professional Association of Innkeepers International (PAII).
  - ✓ 72% of B&Bs are run by couples
  - ✓ 79% of innkeepers live on premises
  - ✓ The typical B&B has between 4 and 11 rooms, with 6 guest rooms or suites being the average
  - ✓ The average B&B has been open for 15 years
  - ✓ The average age of the oldest part of a B&B building is 107 years
  - ✓ 29% of B&Bs were in rural locations, 23% were urban, 5% suburban, and 43% were village
  - ✓ 94% of rooms have private baths
  - ✓ 36% have achieved an "historical designation" by a local, state or national historic preservation organization
  - ✓ 5,700 square feet is the average size for a B&B
  - ✓ 93% offer free high-speed wireless Internet
  - ✓ Most B&Bs provide the following in common areas: Internet, magazines, hot/cold beverages, board games, fireplace, refrigerator, newspapers, telephone, cookies/cakes/candies/fruit, fresh flowers and televisions.
  - ✓ Most B&Bs provide the following in guest rooms: Internet, television, luxury bed/linens, premium branded toiletries, robes, fireplaces, magazines and jetted tubs.

Expenses (% of Annual Sales)

Cost of Goods	15%
Occupancy Costs	10%
Payroll/Labor Costs	10%
Profit (pretax)	10%

Questions

- Can you show me how your B&B will work for me financially and in lifestyle?

Industry Trend

- B&Bs primarily cater to affluent travelers and getaway couples. That market appears to be growing. This is also the market that the next generation of innkeepers is coming from.

Expert Comments

Unless the B&B is in a high-occupancy area, it is difficult to cash flow with fewer than 6 rooms.

Buyers should have their home sold prior to buying a B&B. Contingent sale of a buyer home is not a very compelling offer. Sellers should have a thorough understanding of the inns for sale market. They should also realistically deal w/deal killers such as needing a new roof, windows, etc.

Many of the larger inns have been selling in the 8 to 10 capitalization rate of net income, less any needed repairs and up to a 20% discount if seller financing is not involved. In the middle part of U.S., B&Bs are selling for $80K-$100K/guestroom on avg. The popular East & West Coast locations could be up to twice that amt. The larger the inn, the less value/guestroom. Values & Expenses vary greatly due to the non-standardized structure of the bldgs. & locale.

Seller Financing

- The typical $1M+ inn sale would typically have a buyer w/$200K down and the seller would typically offer a 2nd mortgage for the gap between that amount and 70% of the sale/appraised price. Conventional commercial lending would provide up to 70% of the sale. Recently, we've seen sellers doing all the financing for inn buyers. It's a better return on the loan than alternative investments. Additionally, the seller can receive a higher price by offering attractive, below-market loan terms.
- Inns that are < $700K, conventional commercial financing is available. Over $700K, the seller and the SBA is usually involved. Typically, it's buyer 10%, seller 25% and lender 65%.
- 7 years

Resources

- Michigan Lake to Lake Bed & Breakfast Association: http://www.laketolake.com
- BedandBreakfast.com: http://www.bedandbreakfast.com
- Inns for Sale—This site has Inns and B&Bs for sale and also offers educational programs: http://www.innsforsale.com
- IBISWorld, March 2017: http://ibisworld.com
- Professional Association of Innkeepers International: http://paii.com

Bedding and Mattress Shops (Retail)		
SIC 5712-09	NAICS 442110	Number of Businesses/Units 16,728

Rules of Thumb

➢ 35% of annual sales plus inventory

Pricing Tips

- More retail locations equal more favorable manufacturer pricing.

Benchmark Data

Statistics (Bed and Mattress Stores)

Number of Establishments	16,728
Average Profit Margin	4.6%
Revenue per Employee	$175,800
Average Number of Employees	4.9
Average Wages per Employee	$23,471

Industry Costs

Profit	4.6%
Wages	13.3%
Purchases	57.8%
Depreciation	0.8%
Marketing	3.3%
Rent & Utilities	8.0%
Other	12.2%

Market Share

Mattress Firm	27.1%
Select Comfort Corporation	8.5%

Expenses (% of Annual Sales)

Cost of Goods	25%
Occupancy Costs	20%
Payroll/Labor Costs	10%
Profit (pretax)	45%

Questions
- What is the reason for selling? Where do you stand in terms of your relationships with the major bedding suppliers? What customer service issues might be pending?

Industry Trend
- "Furniture and bedding retail sales increased an estimated 3.9% this year, reaching $102 billion. This is the first time sales have topped the $100 billion mark since before the housing collapse and the Great Recession began in 2007. Looking ahead, Furniture/Today and the statisticians from Easy Analytic Software Inc. predict overall furniture and bedding sales will grow by 19.6% over the next five years to a total of $122 billion in 2020."

Source: "Furniture and bedding sales projected to grow 19.6% by 2020," by Dana French, *Furniture Today*, February 16, 2016

Expert Comments
Bedding continues to be a needed product and the consumer now has a perceived need for enhanced comfort and a better night's rest.

Resources
- Bedding Today: http://www.furnituretoday.com/
- IBISWorld, September 2016: http://ibisworld.com

Franchise	
Beef 'O' Brady's Family Sports Pubs	
Approx. Total Investment	$668,000–$1,157,000
Estimated Annual Sales/Unit	$1,066,800
NAICS 722410	Number of Businesses/Units 183

Rules of Thumb

➢ 25% of annual sales plus inventory

Resources

- Beef 'O'Brady's: http://www.beefobradys.com

Beer Distributorships/Wholesalers

SIC 5181-01	NAICS 422810	Number of Businesses/Units 4,779

Pricing Tips

- The two most important characteristics are (1) the brands carried, and (2) the territory.
- Brands vary considerably in market sales, and also vary regionally. Territories that are densely populated tend to be serviced more efficiently.
- 1 U.S. BBL (beer barrel) = 31 U.S. gallons = 13.778 = 24/12-oz. cases

Benchmark Data

Statistics (Beer Wholesaling)

Number of Establishments	4,779
Average Profit Margin	4.4%
Revenue per Employee	$572,900
Average Number of Employees	24.7
Average Wages per Employee	$52,051

Products and Services Segmentation

Cans of beer and ale	42.2%
Bottles of beer and ale	35.9%
Other malt beverages and brewing products	11.9%
Barrels and kegs of beer and ale	10.0%

Major Market Segmentation

Retail liquor stores	51.4%
Grocery stores and supermarkets	25.7%
Downstream wholesalers	13.4%
Restaurants, drinking establishments and hotels	7.6%
Other	1.9%

Industry Costs

Profit	4.4%
Wages	9.1%
Purchases	72.1%
Depreciation	1.0%
Marketing	1.3%
Rent & Utilities	0.9%
Other	11.2%

Enterprises by Employment Size

Number of Employees	Percentage
0 to 4	22.8%
5 to 9	7.2%
10 to 19	7.7%
20 to 99	28.0%
100 to 499	22.9%
500+	11.4%

Industry Trend

- "Data from the U.S. TTB on the number of permitted breweries hit another all-time high for 2016 with 7,190 total permits as of December 31, 2016. The new permit count means the TTB issued 1,110 new permits in 2016. While this count is slightly below the 1,142 new permits issued in 2015, it is still strong and is the third straight year the country added more than 1,000 newly permitted breweries. The brewery expansions parallel the business cycle expansion from 2010 to 2016 and stand out in an economy that has been sluggish and subpar relative to past business cycles. Despite all the negative rhetoric of the past six years, new breweries have continued to find growth opportunities in the beer market."

Source: https://www.nbwa.org/resources/permitted-breweries-hit-another-record-2016-7190

Expert Comments

Franchise restrictions are important constraints on resale.

Resources

- The National Beer Wholesalers Association (NBWA)—an informative website: http://www.nbwa.org
- Beer Institute: http://www.beerinstitute.org
- Beer Marketer's Insights: http://www.beerinsights.com
- IBISWorld, March 2017: http://ibisworld.com

Beer Taverns—Beer & Wine		
	NAICS 722410	

Rules of Thumb

➢ 6 x monthly sales plus inventory
➢ 55% of annual sales plus inventory
➢ 1–1.5 x annual EBIT

Pricing Tips

- There are 1,980 ounces in a keg, less 10 percent waste, about 1,700 net ounces per keg. If there are 12 ounces (net) in a glass of beer, divide 12 ounces into 1,700 net ounces per keg to determine cost and number of glasses that should be poured from that keg. Determine what a 12-ounce glass of beer is selling for, then multiply that times the number of glasses that is poured from the keg. This will give you the total gross per keg.

Resources

- Beer Institute—an excellent site: http://www.beerinstitute.org

Beer & Wine Stores—Retail

SIC 5921-04	NAICS 445310	

Rules of Thumb

➤ 4 x monthly sales plus inventory

Benchmark Data

- For Benchmark Data see Liquor Stores

	Franchise
Ben & Jerry's Homemade, Inc	

Approx. Total Investment	$164,485–$485,800
Estimated Annual Sales/Unit	$300,000

SIC 2024-98	NAICS 722515	Number of Businesses/Units 554

Rules of Thumb
35–40% of annual sales plus inventory

	Franchise
Between Rounds Bakery Sandwich Café	

Approx. Total Investment	$1,000,000 net worth
Estimated Annual Sales/Unit	$600,000

SIC 5461-01	NAICS 722513	Number of Businesses/Units 4

Rules of Thumb

➤ 40–45% of annual sales plus inventory

Resources

- Between Rounds: http://www.betweenroundsbagels.com

Bicycle Shops

SIC 5941-41	NAICS 451110	

Rules of Thumb

➤ 20% of annual sales plus inventory

➤ 1.5 x SDE plus inventory

Pricing Tips

- Gross profit should be at a minimum in the 40–45% range. Inventory turns should 2.4x–2.7x. Check whether the business is over-inventoried. This is a common problem with bike shops. Also check to see that the inventory is current and saleable. How much inventory is left over from last year? Will the buyer be able to retain the relationships with the manufacturers, ensuring a steady stream of product? Single brand shops have difficulty surviving in our market.

Benchmark Data

Statistics (Bicycle Dealership and Repair)

Number of Establishments	1,744
Average Profit Margin	3.2%
Revenue per Employee	$103,600
Average Number of Employees	1.9
Average Wages per Employee	$13,684

Products and Services Segmentation

Hybrid/cross bicycles	32.0%
Mountain bicycles	29.0%
Road bicycles	22.0%
Other bicycles	17.0%

Industry Costs

Profit	3.2%
Wages	13.2%
Purchases	64.5%
Depreciation	0.9%
Marketing	1.6%
Rent & Utilities	5.7%
Other	10.9%

Expenses (% of Annual Sales)

Cost of Goods	55%
Occupancy Costs	08%
Profit (pretax)	08%

Industry Trend

- "Since 2000, about 40 percent of bike shops have closed or have been consolidated by larger chains. Bike sales have remained essentially flat over the same time."

  Source: "When the Bike Shop Comes to You," *New York Times*, January 29, 2017

- An emerging trend is the web-based, direct sale to consumer business model that has emerged in the past five years. It's the trickle down of the Amazon style of online selling that is being adopted by specific industries, such as bicycling, and it is a direct threat to the retail model. Shop owners have to be alert to this threat and need to be prepared to challenge it with excellent customer service and customer engagement.

  "The number of independent bicycle dealers is dropping, from a high of about 8,000 in the early 1980s to about 5,000 in early 2004. The bicycle retail industry typically loses about 1,000 bicycle dealers each year, mostly start-ups, but gains that many back because of even more start-ups. However, the overall number of storefronts has been declining in the last few years. Many people have lost their lives' savings in the retail bicycle business because they loved bikes but didn't have a similar zest for the art of retailing. Bike shops run by people who are only bicycle hobbyists, and not business people, typically find the going tough in today's competitive market.

  "Add all that to the overall slim profitability in the bicycle industry, and you can really get depressed. NBDA studies show the typical bicycle dealer needs about a 36% profit margin to cover the costs of doing business and break even financially. Studies also show the average realized profit margin on bicycles to be around 36%, which is a break-even proposition devoid of profit. Fortunately, accessories products generally carry a higher profit margin than bicycles. Still, the average bike dealer's profit is less than 5% at year's end-about $25,000 for an average size store of $500,000 in annual sales.

"The level of innovation and diversity has never been higher in 'dealer-quality' bicycle products. The number of entrepreneurial companies designing and manufacturing appealing products for the public is high, both in bicycles and accessories items. There isn't any part on a bicycle which hasn't been improved in the last five or so years. The bicycle is tied to health, vitality, fun and exercise. The bicycle is one of the least expensive transportation choices available, as well as a wonderful tool for fitness and fun. The bicycle affects people's lives in very positive ways, and its use contributes to the betterment of the environment.

"Cycling participation is solid. There are approximately 45 million adult 'cyclists' today, and cycling ranks fifth on the list of most popular outdoor recreational activities."

Source: NBDA

Expert Comments

Success or failure of bicycle shops is directly tied to the owner/operator. While brands and location can be a factor, it is the dedication of the owner to the bicycling industry and his/her participation in community events, industry shows, and local business organizations that makes a difference. In many ways, owners are subject to the whims of manufacturers and the changing tastes of the public. Inventory control is key and owners have to be quick on their feet and be able to respond to a constantly changing environment in the cycling industry.

Seller Financing

- Outside financing via the SBA is common, with some seller financing involved. Most buyers have to finance the purchase, since the value of inventory can be very high.

Resources

- National Bicycle Dealers Association (NBDA): http://www.nbda.com
- Bicycle Product Suppliers Association—excellent site, well worth visiting: http://www.bpsa.org
- Bicycle Retailer & Industry News—an informative site: http://www.bicycleretailer.com
- People For Bikes: http://www.peopleforbikes.org
- IBISWorld, May 2017: http://ibisworld.com

Big Apple Bagels	Franchise
Approx. Total Investment	$294,700–$398,100
Estimated Annual Sales/Unit	$350,000
NAICS 722513	Number of Businesses/Units 84

Rules of Thumb

➢ 35–40% of annual sales plus inventory

Resources

- BAB Systems, Inc.: http://www.babcorp.com

Big City Burrito		Franchise
	NAICS 722513	Number of Businesses/Units 9

Rules of Thumb

➢ 50–55% of annual sales plus inventory

Resources

- Big City Burrito: http://www.bigcityburrito.com

Big O Tires		Franchise
Approx. Total Investment		$242,500–$1,023,300
	NAICS 441320	Number of Businesses/Units 393

Rules of Thumb

➢ 35% of annual sales plus inventory

Resources

- Big O Tires: http://www.bigotires.com

Billboard Advertising Companies (Outdoor Advertising)		
SIC 7312-01	NAICS 541850	Number of Businesses/Units 14,599

Rules of Thumb

➢ 12 x EBITDA

➢ 500% of annual sales

Pricing Tips

- Billboards are bought and sold based on multiples of Net Revenue and Cash Flow, so these are the most common methods of valuation.
- EBITDA is normally 45% to 50%. Cap rates tend to be very low, usually more like real estate than an operating business. Acquirers prefer long-term leases at low rates for existing billboard locations.
- "Billboard companies are usually worth surprisingly high prices in the market. Buyers and sellers rely almost exclusively on market multiples that are widely recognized as the best measures of fair market value. Discount rates and capitalization rates in this industry are more closely aligned with real estate yields than returns on operating businesses."

  Source: "Appraising Billboard Companies" by Jeffrey P. Wright, ASA, CFA, Business Valuation Review

Benchmark Data

Statistics (Billboard & Outdoor Advertising)

Number of Establishments	14,599
Average Profit Margin	16.3%
Revenue per Employee	$195,300
Average Number of Employees	3.0
Average Wages per Employee	$42,506

Products and Services Segmentation

Billboards: bulletin	50.9%
Billboards: poster	14.4%
Transit displays	12.9%
Street furniture and other urban fixture displays	12.5%
Alternative and other leased displays	12.5%

Major Market Segmentation

Other	22.7%
Miscellaneous retailers	14.5%
Financial, professional and real estate services	13.2%
Media and other entertainment companies	11.5%
Food and drink, including restaurants	11.1%
Nonemploying businesses and individuals	11.0%
Government and nonprofit advertisers	8.3%
Healthcare and pharmaceutical companies	7.7%

Industry Costs

Profit	16.3%
Wages	21.8%
Purchases	28.5%
Depreciation	13.0%
Marketing	2.9%
Rent & Utilities	15.4%
Other	2.1%

Market Share

Lamar Advertising Company	18.4%
Outfront Media Inc.	16.9%
Clear Channel Outdoor Holdings	14.9%

Expenses (% of Annual Sales)

Cost of Goods	05%
Occupancy Costs	10%
Payroll/Labor Costs	05%
Profit (pretax)	45%

Questions
- Net revenue, cash flow, lease costs and occupancy levels

B - Rules of Thumb

Industry Trend

- "Out of home (OOH) advertising revenue rose 4.1 percent in the second quarter of 2016 compared to the previous year, accounting for $2.35 billion, based on figures released by the Outdoor Advertising Association of America (OAAA). Year-to-date 2016 the OOH industry is up 3.8 percent, and is outperforming the local media sector, which was down the first half of 2016, according to an OAAA analysis of Kantar Media data."

  Source:http://oaaa.org/StayConnected/NewsArticles/IndustryRevenue/tabid/322/id/4616/Default.aspx
  August 22, 2016

- "'OOH's ability to augment mobile, online, and social media efforts is one of the many reasons the industry posted strong growth with both local and national advertisers in 2015,' said Stephen Freitas, OAAA chief marketing officer. 'The expansion of digital OOH formats provides advertisers with broader opportunities to engage with today's mobile consumers. These factors are the foundation for the positive outlook media analysts are projecting for OOH over the next few years.'"

  Source:https://www.oaaa.org/NewsEvents/PressReleases/tabid/327/id/4437/Default.aspx

Expert Comments

Industry growing, difficult to build new billboards

Seller Financing

- 5 years

Resources

- BPS Outdoor: http://www.bpsoutdoor.com
- Outdoor Advertising Association of America: http://www.oaaa.org
- IBISWorld, June 2017: http://ibisworld.com

Billiards		
SIC 7999-12	NAICS 339920	

Rules of Thumb

➤ 50% of annual sales plus inventory

Industry Trend

- The Pool and Billiard Halls industry is anticipated to continue declining over the next five years, despite improving macroeconomic conditions across the board. Indeed, the US economy is projected to steadily improve over the coming years as unemployment falls and business activity picks up. Income is projected to rise as unemployment falls, which will bolster discretionary spending on leisure and recreational activities. Nevertheless, pool halls are projected to further contract over the next five years, as negative participation trends will likely continue. In particular, pool halls will continue to have difficulty attracting younger customers, who will likely have even more entertainment options available in the coming years. As a result, IBISWorld forecasts industry revenue to fall at an annualized rate of 3.6% to $1.4 billion over the five years to 2022.

  Source: IBISWorld, August 2017

Resources
- Billiard Congress of America: http://home.bca-pool.com/

Blackjack Pizza		Franchise
SIC 5812-22	NAICS 722513	Number of Businesses/Units 45

Rules of Thumb
- ➢ 3–4 x SDE (15% discount for cash) plus inventory
- ➢ 40% of annual sales plus inventory

Resources
- Blackjack Pizza: http://www.blackjackpizza.com

Blimpie—America's Sub Shop		Franchise
Approx. Total Investment		$138,150–$395,050
Estimated Annual Sales/Unit		$185,000
SIC 5812-19	NAICS 722513	Number of Businesses/Units 358

Rules of Thumb
- ➢ 45–50% of annual sales plus inventory

Benchmark Data
- For Benchmark Data see Sandwich Shops

Resources
- Blimpie: http://www.kahalamgmt.com

Blood and Organ Banks		
	NAICS 621991	

Rules of Thumb
- ➢ 3 x EBIT
- ➢ 2.9 x EBITDA
- ➢ 78% of annual sales includes inventory
- ➢ 2.7 x SDE includes inventory

Benchmark Data

Expenses (% of Annual Sales)

Cost of Goods	13%
Payroll/Labor Costs	01%
Profit (pretax)	11%

Questions
- Payor mix, market share, patient demographic data

Industry Trend
- Profit expected to shrink, revenue is expected to grow, demand continues to grow.

Seller Financing
- Outside financing

Resources
American Association of Blood Banks: http://www.aabb.org
America's Blood Centers: http://www.americasblood.org

Boat Dealers

SIC 5551-04	NAICS 441222	Number of Businesses/Units 118,210

Rules of Thumb
➢ 2–3 x SDE includes used boat inventory, parts and FF&E

Pricing Tips
- Boat dealerships in the Pacific Northwest typically sell for 2–3 times SDE which includes used boat inventory, parts and FF&E.

Benchmark Data

Statistics (Boat Dealership and Repair)
Number of Establishments	118,210
Average Profit Margin	5.6%
Revenue per Employee	$125,900
Average Number of Employees	1.3
Average Wages per Employee	$17,518

Products and Services Segmentation
New boats	56.7%
Parts and repair services	29.4%
Used boats	13.9%

Industry Costs
Profit	5.9%
Wages	13.8%
Purchases	63.6%
Depreciation	0.9%
Marketing	1.3%
Rent & Utilities	3.6%
Other	11.2%

Market Share
MarineMax Inc.	6.6%

Industry Trend

- "The National Marine Manufacturers Association said advance data show that new powerboat registrations were up 6.3 percent last year and that nearly all segments were higher. The NMMA said the tow boat, pontoon, saltwater fishing boat and personal watercraft segments had the highest rates of growth last year, up 11.8 percent, 9.2 percent, 7.9 percent and 7.4 percent, respectively.

  "Outboards boats were up 6.2 percent on a rolling 12-month basis and inboard boats were up 11.8 percent. Boats 27 feet and larger were up 10.7 percent through December on a rolling 12-month basis. The NMMA said sterndrive boats continue to lag other categories; they were down 1.5 percent for the year, according to advance estimates."

  Source: "NMMA: New powerboat registrations rose 6.3 percent in 2016," February 24, 2017, http://www. tradeonlytoday.com/2017/02/nmma-new-powerboat-registrations-rose-6-3-percent-in-2016/

Resources

- National Marine Manufacturers Association (NMMA): http://www.nmma.org
- IBISWorld, March 2017: http://ibisworld.com
- Boating Industry: http://boatingindustry.com/
- Trade Only Today: http://www.tradeonlytoday.com/

		Franchise
Boba Loca Specialty Drinks		
	NAICS 722515	Number of Businesses/Units 23

Rules of Thumb

➤ 30% of annual sales plus inventory

Resources

- Boba Loca Specialty Drinks: http://www.bobaloca.com

Book Stores—Adult		
SIC 5942-01	NAICS 451211	

Rules of Thumb

➤ 100% of annual sales includes inventory

Pricing Tips

- Half down at closing; other half financed and used to prove gross sales (a kind of earnout schedule)

Benchmark Data

Expenses (% of Annual Sales)

Cost of Goods	20%
Occupancy Costs	12%
Payroll/Labor Costs	n/a
Profit (pretax)	40%

Industry Trend

- Slight drop but steady in some markets

Expert Comments

Internet retail is driving down profits.

Book Stores—New Books		
SIC 5942-01	NAICS 451211	Number of Businesses/Units 21,198

Rules of Thumb

➤ 15–20% of annual sales plus inventory

➤ 1.5–2 x SDE plus Inventory

Pricing Tips

- The underlying lease is very important. The inventory turns should be between 4 and 5 times. It is important that the store is diligently returning new book inventory as allowed.
- We don't use EBIT or EBITDA because the owner pretty much always works in the business. Normalizing for an industry standard expense would drive EBIT or EBITDA towards zero, making the multiple unrealistic. One note is that gift certificates outstanding need to be accounted for and treated as a liability. Lots of negotiation around this point.

Benchmark Data

Statistics (Book Stores)

Number of Establishments	21,198
Average Profit Margin	1.0%
Revenue per Employee	$110,300
Average Number of Employees	5.1
Average Wages per Employee	$13,729

Products and Services Segmentation

Other merchandise	29.4%
Textbooks	32.4%
Trade books	30.3%
Religious goods (including books)	5.4%
Magazines and newspapers	2.5%

Industry Costs

Profit	1.0%
Wages	12.6%
Purchases	60.1%
Depreciation	1.1%
Marketing	1.3%
Rent & Utilities	8.0%
Other	15.9%

Market Share

Barnes & Noble Inc.	30.1%
Follett Higher Education Group	6.1%
Barnes & Noble Education Inc.	17.3%

- One would like to see sales over $200 psf. Occupancy needs to be less than 10%. Cost of goods sold should approach 50%, unless it is a discounter, in which case it may be lower.
- Inventory turns of 3–4 times should be realized. Non-book sales should be at least 20% of overall sales. Store should be doing at least one event per week.

Expenses (% of Annual Sales)

Cost of Goods	30% to 35%
Occupancy Costs	06% to 10%
Payroll/Labor Costs	20% to 25%
Profit (pretax)	02% to 04%

Questions

- Sales trends, community standing, online sales, Website condition, staffing quality

  Tenure of staff, number of events, social media exposure, program of inventory returns, seasonality and is there a frequent buyer program in place.

Industry Trend

- "On Thursday, Amazon will open a store — its seventh — in the Time Warner Center at Columbus Circle. The 4,000 square-foot space, near the site of a now-shuttered Borders store, is just a few blocks from Penguin Random House, and walking distance from Simon & Schuster and Hachette's Midtown headquarters. This summer, the company plans to open another store on 34th Street. Amazon is planning to open six more stores this year, including outlets in Bellevue, Wash.; Paramus, N.J.; and San Jose, Calif."

  Source: "Amazon Sets Up Shop in the Heart of the Publishing Industry" by Alexandra Alter, May 24, 2017, https://www.nytimes.com/2017/05/24/business/media/amazon-new-bookstore-manhattan.html?mabReward= ACTM2&recp=2&module=WelcomeBackModal&contentCollection=Art%20%26%20Design&region=FixedCe nter&action=click&src=recg&pgtype=article

- "Sales of adult trade books fell 1.6% in the first nine months of 2016, compared to the same period in 2015, according to figures released this morning by the Association of American Publishers as part of its StatShot program. Sales of children's and young adult books increased 4.9% in the same period."

  Source: "Adult Trade Sales Slipped in First Nine Months of 2016," by Jim Milliot, February 24, 2017, http://www.publishersweekly.com/pw/by-topic/industry-news/financial-reporting/article/72872-adult-trade-sales-slipped-in-first-nine-months-of-2016.html

- Gradual growth in the number of independent bookstores, but the ones coming in are small. Owners of larger bookstores are aging out, but being replaced with relatively old owners (70+ selling to 50+). Competition will continue to increase from online sources, so the store has to be a community gathering spot to be successful.

Expert Comments

An independent bookstore doing over $2,000,000 in an affluent, highly educated community can be sold.

Seller Financing

- Usually, these stores are sold to wealthy buyers for cash. If there is any financing, it is typically from the sellers. Due to the high risk in the industry, seller financing is limited.

Resources

- American Booksellers Association: http://www.bookweb.org
- Publishers Weekly: http://www.publishersweekly.com
- Paz & Associates: http://www.pazbookbiz.com
- IBISWorld, June 2017: http://ibisworld.com

Book Stores—Rare and Used		
SIC 5932-01	NAICS 453310	

Rules of Thumb

> 10 to 15 percent of annual sales plus inventory. In the case of rare books, the cost of the inventory would be based on some form of wholesale value or less the bookseller's standard markup.

Pricing Tips

- Used book stores seem to be a vanishing business. Many owners of these stores have closed them and now offer their books online. Rare book stores would have the same multiple as used stores, perhaps a bit higher. The real value is the inventory.

Book Stores—Religious		
SIC 5942-11	NAICS 451211	

Rules of Thumb

> 15% of annual sales plus inventory

Industry Trend

- "Family Christian Stores, the largest retailer of Christian books and merchandise in the country, is closing all of its outlets. The chain, which went through a bankruptcy proceeding in 2015, cited changing consumer behavior and declining sales when it announced its decision to shutter on Thursday. FCS operates 240 stores in 36 states."

    Source: "Family Christian Stores to Close," by Emma Koonse and Jim Milliot, February 23, 2017, http://www.publishersweekly.com/pw/by-topic/industry-news/religion/article/72865-family-christian-stores-to-close-all-stores.html

Resources

- The Association for Christian Retail: http://www.cbaonline.org

Bowling Centers		
SIC 7933-01	NAICS 713950	Number of Businesses/Units 3,574

Rules of Thumb

➤ Maybe 2 x annual sales in highly exceptional situation

➤ 160–180% of annual sales plus inventory

➤ 5–6.5 x SDE plus inventory

➤ 5–6.5 x EBITDA

Pricing Tips

- Going rate for sales of centers including the real estate is 1.6 to 2.0 times gross revenues and/or 5.5 to 6.0 times EBITDA. EBITDA runs about 25% to 30% of revenues depending on volume, product mix, etc.
- Location, age of equipment, physical condition of facility and additional amenities are important factors.
- All multiples if real estate included. If leased, 4-5 times EBITDA after lease expense.
- Needed capital expenditures are a deduction.

Benchmark Data

Statistics (Bowling Alleys)

Number of Establishments	3,574
Average Profit Margin	5.2%
Revenue per Employee	$54,800
Average Number of Employees	19.3
Average Wages per Employee	$15,376

Products and Services Segmentation

Restaurant	27.9%
Other	18.7%
Bowling - open play	13.3%
Bar/lounge	11.8%
Laser tag	9.7%
Bowling - league play	8.4%
Snack bar	7.2%
Shoe rental	3.0%

Industry Costs

Profit	5.2%
Wages	28.2%
Purchases	19.9%
Depreciation	5.9%
Marketing	2.2%
Rent & Utilities	17.4%
Other	21.2%

Market Share

Bowlmor AMFF	12.8%

- Sales over $35,000 per lane
- Traditional sales per sq. ft. $60 BEC sales per sq. ft. $75

28th Edition

Expenses (% of Annual Sales)

Cost of Goods	20% to 30%
Occupancy Costs	10% to 20%
Payroll/Labor Costs	25% to 30%
Profit (pretax)	20% to 30%

Questions

- Stability of leagues; need for capital improvements and repairs
- Why selling; review each key staff.
- Time commitment, general business and management skills. Keep the facility in good shape, accurate accounting.
- Makeup of local market, history of facility and equipment repairs and upgrades, league schedules.
- Physical condition, necessary cap x, condition of equipment, life of lanes

Industry Trend

- More traditional centers will be converted to family entertainment centers or bowling entertainment centers with more amenities and upscale food.
- "As of January 2017, approximately 4,700 bowling centers with about 100,000 lanes were operating in the United States. Of that group, over 4,200 facilities were commercial centers; the others were operated by the military, colleges, fraternal organizations and private clubs. Approximately 25% of the commercial centers are 32 lanes or larger in size. In addition, the industry also has about 210 duckpin and candlepin centers with approximately 2,870 lanes in the United States, mostly along the east coast.

  "During the past ten years, the makeup of the industry has changed. In general, as older and smaller centers closed, they were replaced by new, larger and more diversified operations. Indeed, between 30 and 50 new facilities featuring bowling have been built annually in this country over the past few years, many in vacant big-box store buildings.

  "The majority of newly-constructed establishments combine bowling with a range of other recreational activities such as laser tag, go-karts, bumper cars, expanded video game arcades, climbing walls, redemption, bocce, glow miniature golf and similar activities to create family entertainment centers. Meanwhile, a growing number of existing centers are being converted into bowling-based entertainment centers by removing a small number of lanes and replacing them with amenities of that type.

  "Bowling lanes also have been added to many non-traditional venues such as movie theaters, adult communities, hotels and resorts, gambling casinos (commercial and Indian), churches and young-adult oriented entertainment centers such as Dave and Busters, Hooters and Gameworks.

  "In addition, a number of upscale nightclub-type complexes known as 'bowling lounges' or 'boutiques' have opened in urban areas featuring bowling lanes, plush restaurants, intimate lounges, stylish furnishings, private party rooms and high-tech video presentations enabling them to cater to large numbers of young adults, corporate parties and charitable fund-raisers.

  "Many bowling centers were built years ago in under-developed areas in the path of growth. As those locations experienced intense commercial development, many bowling buildings were converted to other uses, most often retail and other commercial uses. In some situations, the underlying land has been used for new residential or commercial development. Frequently, the size, layout and structure of the bowling buildings, together with large parking lots and strong locations facing major arteries, make conversion an attractive alternative to refurbishing an older facility."

Source: "Overview of the Bowling Industry" by Sandy Hansell and Associates

Expert Comments

If selling, analyze taxes first. If buying, check market demographics.

Owner needs attention to detail, focus on superior customer service, cater to specific demographics in local market.

Location is critical factor. Demographics, access, size of population base are important.

Seller Financing

- Mostly bank and occasional SBA financing
- Typically financed outside, many sales financed by SBA.
- In few cases with seller financing, loans are short-term (3 to 5 years) with balloon

Resources

- Bowling Proprietors Association of America: http://www.bpaa.com
- International Bowling Industry magazine: http://www.bowlingindustry.com
- Sandy Hansell & Associates: http://www.sandyhansell.com
- IBISWorld, February 2017: http://ibisworld.com

Brew Pubs

	NAICS 722410	Number of Businesses/Units 4,346

Rules of Thumb

➤ 40% of annual sales plus inventory

Benchmark Data

Statistics (Craft Beer Production)

Number of Establishments	4,346
Average Profit Margin	9.4%
Revenue Per Employee	$642,900
Average Number of Employees	2.2
Average Wages per Employee	$35,300

Products and Services Segmentation

IPA	20.4%
Seasonal	19.1%
Other	16.5%
Pale ale	13.9%
Lager	13.0%
Amber ale	8.8%
Wheat	5.5%
Fruit beer	2.8%

Industry Costs

Profit	9.4%
Wages	5.5%
Purchases	39.7%
Depreciation	4.7%
Marketing	5.2%
Rent & Utilities	6.9%
Other	28.6%

Market Share

D.G. Yuengling & Son Inc.	21.6%
Boston Beer Company	16.6%

- "It's worth noting up front that some of the advantages of brewpubs stem from their ability as the manufacturer to sell a high-value-added product (aka beer) at better margins than a typical restaurant. In the latest Brewery Operations and Benchmarking Survey, smaller brewpubs (fewer than 1,000 barrels) derived 26.8 percent of their sales from house beers, and larger brewpubs (more than 1,000 barrels) derived 46.3 percent of their sales from house beers. In 2010, those percentages were closer to 35 percent for both groups. Regardless of the specific percentage, that means roughly a third of sales stems from a product that averages gross margins that can reach more than $800 per barrel depending on the business model and beer style.

  "These benefits don't come without risk. Brewpubs are betting heavily on their ability to sell their own beers, and not surprisingly, typically have a much lower percentage of their sales come from guest beers and other bar sales. Most people come to brewpubs looking to try the house beers, so if those beers don't meet the ever-increasing quality standards, there may be challenges.

  In addition, running a brewery inside a restaurant requires additional capital, expertise, staff, and more. So brewpubs are a step beyond the average restaurant on the classic risk-reward scale, with more invested, but greater potential benefits. Given this basic tradeoff, what are the additional advantages that have allowed so many brewpubs to keep that balance firmly pointed toward reward?

  Source: "The Brewpub Advantage," by Bart Watson, February 17, 2016, https://www.brewersassociation.org/articles/the-brewpub-advantage/

Industry Trend

- "'Anyone who does want to sell, should be selling right now,' Hindy (Steve Hindy, founder of Brooklyn Brewery) told Reuters. 'Valuations are out of this world. There are people swarming all of us wanting to give us money.'

  "Merger & acquisition activity amongst top 50 craft breweries has accelerated considerably in the last two years and the list of prominent craft players that have sold all or parts of their companies is growing."

  Source: http://www.brewbound.com/news/reuters-dozens-of-craft-breweries-for-sale

- "From the buy side, the craft beer business has never been hotter, with market share now approaching 8 percent by volume in the U.S. and margins that have gotten the attention of both big brewers and non-U.S. brewers alike."

  Source: http://www.mwe.com/files/Uploads/Documents/Pubs/JFtnb15_GvtAffairs.pdf

Resources

- Brewers Association: https://www.brewersassociation.org
- IBISWorld, August 2016: http://ibisworld.com
- The Brewpub Advantage:
  https://www.brewersassociation.org/articles/the-brewpub-advantage/

Bridal Shops		
SIC 5621-04	NAICS 448190	

Rules of Thumb

➤ 10–15% of annual sales plus inventory

Pricing Tips

- Special-order gowns require deposits. Many bridal stores don't put the deposits aside but co-mingle funds during the normal course of operations (a liability issue that could be deadly for a new buyer unless appropriate safeguards are in place). A bridal store's inventory is made of samples and the samples should be considered amortized over the ordering life of the gown style.

Benchmark Data

Statistics (Lingerie, Swimwear & Bridal Stores)

Number of Establishments	47,827
Average Profit Margin	4.9%
Revenue per Employee	$110,400
Average Number of Employees	3.2
Average Wages per Employee	$16,286

Products and Services Segmentation

Lingerie	43.7%
Swimwear	23.0%
Bridal gowns	14.1%
Uniforms	6.3%
Hosiery	5.6%
Costumes	3.9%
Furs and Leather Goods	2.6%
Custom-made Garments	0.8%

Industry Costs

Profit	4.9%
Wages	14.8%
Purchases	60.6%
Depreciation	1.4%
Marketing	2.4%
Rent & Utilities	10.7%
Other	5.2%

Market Share

L Brands Inc.	39.4%

- "The average wedding cost in the United States is $25,200. Couples typically spend between $18,900 and $31,500 but, most couples spend less than $10,000. This does not include cost for a honeymoon."

Source: www.costofwedding.com

Resources

- IBISWorld, May 2017: http://ibisworld.com
- Costofwedding.com: http://costofwedding.com

Bruster's Real Ice Cream		Franchise
Approx. Total Investment		$180,000–$1,200,000
Estimated Annual Sales/Unit		$375,000
	NAICS 722515	Number of Businesses/Units 190

Rules of Thumb

> 40–45% of annual sales plus inventory

Resources

- Bruster's Ice Cream: http://www.brusters.com

Budget Blinds		Franchise
Approx. Total Investment		$89,240–$187,070
Estimated Annual Sales/Unit		$700,000
	NAICS 442291	Number of Businesses/Units 687

Rules of Thumb

> 2 x annual EBIT plus inventory & equipment
> 50–55% of annual sales plus inventory

Resources

- Budget Blinds: http://www.budget-blinds-franchise.com

Burger King		Franchise
Approx. Total Investment		$1,305,000
	NAICS 722513	Number of Businesses/Units 13,615

Rules of Thumb

> 35% of annual sales plus inventory

Resources

- Burger King: http://www.bk.com

Bus Companies (Charter, School & Scheduled)

SIC 4142-01	NAICS 485510	Number of Businesses/Units 19,293

Rules of Thumb

➤ 35% of revenues plus asset value of buses plus inventory

Benchmark Data

Statistics (Scheduled and Charter Bus Services)

Number of Establishments 7,892
Average Profit Margin 9.9%
Revenue per Employee $94,800
Average Number of Employees 6.8
Average Wages per Employee $29,515

Products and Services Segmentation

Scheduled bus services—interurban transit 26.7%
Long-distance and local charter bus services 66.1%
Other services including scheduled bus services—rural transit 7.2%

Major Market Segmentation

Private consumers—local 30.4%
Private consumers—long-distance 62.6%
All other including business travel 7.0%

Industry Costs

Profit 9.9%
Wages 31.3%
Purchases 16.1%
Depreciation 9.5%
Marketing 1.0%
Rent & Utilities 9.9%
Other 22.3%

Market Share

FirstGroup PLC 12.5%
Stagecoach Group plc 9.5%

Statistics (Public School Bus Services)

Number of Establishments 11,401
Average Profit Margin 7.2%
Revenue per Employee $49,700
Average Number of Employees 21.8
Average Wages per Employee $22,332

Products and Services Segmentation

School busing for public schools 89.9%
School busing for private schools 6.6%
Employee bus services 1.3%
Other transportation and services 2.2%

Major Market Segmentation

Public schools	89.9%
Private schools	6.6%
Other	3.5%

Industry Costs

Profit	7.2%
Wages	44.9%
Purchases	29.0%
Depreciation	9.5%
Marketing	0.5%
Rent & Utilities	3.6%
Other	5.3%

Market Share

FirstGroup PLC	20.1%
National Express Group PLC	10.4%
Student Transportation Inc.	5.0%

- "The motorcoach industry continues to be a small-business success story, with small and medium-sized operators representing more than 98% of the total industry," observed Peter Pantuso, President and CEO of the American Bus Association.
- It is important to note that the motorcoach industry provides an average of 745 million passenger trips annually which is comparable to the domestic airlines and 25 times more than Amtrak.

Industry Trend

- "Today the American Bus Association Foundation (ABAF) released the 2016 fourth quarter results of the quarterly Coach Builder Survey. Based on surveys of the major motorcoach manufacturers who sell vehicles in the United States and Canada, motorcoach sales from the participating manufacturers rose by 6.5 percent over the prior year to a total of 3,620 units (2,407 new coaches and 1,213 pre-owned coaches).
- "'2016 was a stellar year for motorcoach manufacturers,' said ABA Foundation President Peter Pantuso. 'Last year showed a 3 percent growth in new motorcoach sales and a 14.3 percent growth in pre-owned coaches. As the industry continues to grow, operators are reinvesting their profits back into the comfort for their passengers.'"

    Source: "ABA Foundation Report Says Motorcoach Manufacturing Continues to See Growth in Sales," by Melanie Hilton January 25, 2017, www.buses.org/news/article/aba-foundation-report-says-motorcoach-manufacturing-continues-to-see-growth

Seller Financing

- 3 years

Resources

- United Motorcoach Association—an informative site: http://www.uma.org
- Bus Ride Magazine—another interesting site: http://www.busride.com
- IBISWorld, December 2016: http://ibisworld.com
- IBISWorld, July 2017: http://ibisworld.com
- American Bus Association: https://www.buses.org/aba-foundation

Business Brokerage Offices

SIC 7389-22	NAICS 531210	Number of Businesses/Units 4,286

Rules of Thumb

➤ 50% of annual commissions

➤ 2 x SDE plus inventory

➤ 3–5 x EBITDA

➤ 60% of annual sales

➤ If you were to sell your business brokerage business, what multiple of SDE would you expect to sell it for?

   ✓ Average 2.8 for 2014

   ✓ Average 2.4 for 2016

Source: *Business Brokerage Press Survey* of the Business Brokerage Profession

Pricing Tips

- Usually 1 times earnings. Most industry franchise fees are from $25,000 to $45,000, plus a royalty (3–5%)
- Look at cash flow not annual gross sales. Bottom line is what the business is making: EBITDA.
- There have been sales reported at 2 times SDE. If owner is active in production, then his or her production must be subtracted, unless they will be staying for a period of time. Even then, some discount must be applied to his or her sales, because after selling, their production will most likely drop off.

Benchmark Data

Statistics (Business Brokers)

Number of Establishments	4,286
Average Profit Margin	13.0%
Revenue per Employee	$193,800
Average Number of Employees	1.6
Average Wages per Employee	$79,548

Products and Services Segmentation

Valuation	47.2%
Due diligence	22.8%
Other services	17.4%
Advertising	12.6%

Major Market Segmentation

Other	33.0%
Restaurants	17.0%
Personal Services	16.0%
Retail	14.0%
Business Services	12.0%
Manufacturing	8.0%

Industry Costs

Profit	13.0%
Wages	40.6%
Purchases	10.9%
Depreciation	0.4%
Marketing	1.7%
Rent & Utilities	3.2%
Other	30.2%

Market Share

Murphy Business & Financial Corp.	5.8%
Sunbelt	4.6%

- Although approximately 50% of business brokers operate as a single-broker office, you can leverage your market position and volume of listings, buyers, and transactions by hiring, training, and motivating additional business brokers for your office. The additional costs are minimal (you do not have to provide each broker an office or even a desk). It also gives the sellers a feeling of market presence when they are dealing with a multiple-broker office.

Expenses (% of Annual Sales)

Cost of Goods	20%
Payroll/Labor Costs	10%
Occupancy Costs	05%
Profit (pretax)	60%

Questions

- Why are you selling? Will you train me and work with me for a while? Will you help me to build this office and opportunity, provided we structure a deal that works based on your past history?

Industry Trend

- There needs to be continued marketing of the business brokerage field as a solution for business sellers and buyers and for the expansion of the industry through business brokerage education that equips business brokers to help folks locate, value, negotiate, finance, and do due diligence. Buy and close on businesses.
- Increased business transactions with boomers nearing retirement or being laid off from corporate jobs.

Expert Comments

Get as much business broker education as possible. Join and participate in industry trade groups, the International Business Brokers Association (IBBA), and any local/regional affiliate, and take advantage of the education and relationships provided. Obtain the industry standard designation of professional business brokers, the Certified Business Intermediary (CBI).

Main Street business brokerage is a rewarding and challenging business. Although badly needed when a seller wants and/or needs to sell, or a buyer wants and/or needs to buy, business brokerage has not expanded greatly because of the confidentiality of our business and the lack of absolutes. Whereas the rules follow a somewhat regular pattern, each business deal is a different buyer and a different seller and a different deal.

There seems to be a falling out of the part-time business broker, leaving the space open to full-time professionals.

Seller Financing

- Normally, a business brokerage office will sell for 1 times the owner's benefit for the most recent year. Usually, the seller is the source of any financing of the transaction, which may also have a "working together" agreement for a year or more to close any pending transactions.

Resources

- International Business Brokers Association (IBBA): http://www.ibba.org
- IBISWorld, March 2017: http://ibisworld.com
- Carolina/Virginia Business Brokers Association: http://cvbba.com/CVBBA/
- Texas Association of Business Brokers (TABB): http://tabb.org
- Sunbelt Business Brokers: http://www.sunbeltnetwork.com
- Business Buyers University: http://www.businessbuyersuniversity.com

Call Centers

SIC 7389-12	NAICS 561421	Number of Businesses/Units 27,250

Rules of Thumb

➤ 10–12 x current monthly billings for larger services; may require earnout

➤ 5–7 x current monthly billings for smaller services; may require earnout

Pricing Tips

- "Buyers are interested in businesses with a good profit margin of at least 25% or better, that have advanced equipment with updated software, management in place and a history of growth. One of the first items buyers ask for after reviewing your listing information is a current financial statement along with at least one previous year's financials. Financials show historical growth as well as future potential.

"A telemessaging service with minimal profit and technology can sell for around 2.5 to 2.8 times annual net, whereas a highly profitable operation with the latest in technology, management in place, and located in a major market could sell for as high as four times annual net. If a hypothetical $30k per month business is averaging a 25% EBITDA, then it would most likely sell for between 3 and 3.5 times yearly net. For the sake of this particular example, let's assume that it is a 3.2 yearly net, which means the selling price would be $90,000 x 3.2, or $288,000 (which equals 9.6 times monthly billing)."

Source: Steve Michaels, TAS Marketing, tas@tasmarketing.com, an excellent site with lots of information on call centers. TAS Marketing is probably the nation's largest business brokerage firm specializing in answering services, call centers, etc.

C

Benchmark Data

Statistics (Telemarketing & Call Centers)

Number of Establishments	27,250
Average Profit Margin	15.3%
Revenue per Employee	$44,600
Average Number of Employees	18.1
Average Wages per Employee	$26,970

Products and Services Segmentation

Customer service	48.0%
Technical support	16.9%
Telemarketing	18.3%
Other	8.8%
Debt collection	8.0%

Major Market Segmentation

Telecommunications and IT	47.4%
Other	21.7%
Retail	19.8%
Banking and finance	11.1%

Industry Costs

Profit	15.3%
Wages	60.3%
Purchases	13.3%
Depreciation	1.8%
Marketing	1.7%
Rent & Utilities	5.9%
Other	1.7%

Market Share

West Corporation	9.9%
Convergys Corporation	7.5%

Industry Trend

- "What does 2017 hold for the contact center? A number of key trends currently are dominating the conversation, and started to infiltrate the market well before this year.
    - ✓ Analytics
    - ✓ Call recording
    - ✓ Chat
    - ✓ Cloud
    - ✓ Compliance
    - ✓ Customer satisfaction
    - ✓ Data integration
    - ✓ Omnichannel
    - ✓ Performance management
    - ✓ Remote employment

✓ Self-service

✓ Social media

✓ Suites over standalone tools"

Source: "The Top 13 Call Center Technology Trends for 2017" by Mckay Bird November 29, 2016 https://www.tcnp3.com/home/call-centers/the-top-13-call-center-technology-trends-for-2017/

- "Telephone answering services are evolving into the contact centers of tomorrow by offering a multitude of services including: telephone answering, voice mail, fax-on-demand, text messaging, order taking, customer service and support, product fulfillment, appointment making, referral locator, credit processing, and more."

Source: Steve Michaels, TAS Marketing, tas@tasmarketing.com

Expert Comments

"Equipment—If you are six months away from selling your service then don't purchase new equipment or upgrade your software. You will not recoup your investment in that short period of time. If you sell, the buyer may also prefer a different brand of equipment or may buy only your accounts. You would then have to sell your equipment on the used market, which usually brings only pennies on the dollar. If you are two to three years from selling and have old equipment, then by all means consider either hosting or buying newer equipment. This enables you to keep up with technology and your competition by offering the same or more enhanced services.

"Automate—The biggest expense in the telephone answering service business is labor. Automating some of the functions required in the taking/delivering process can ultimately reduce your costs. Automating the messages delivery via email, fax, voice mail, text or cell phone will free up labor. You might also want to consider offering an automated attendant to increase call efficiency.

"Financial Record Keeping—Buyers are interested in businesses with a good profit margin of at least 25% or better, that have advanced equipment with updated software, management in place and a history of growth. One of the first items buyers ask for after reviewing your listing information is a current financial statement along with at least one previous year's financials. Financials show historical growth as well as future potential."

Source: Steve Michaels, TAS Marketing, tas@tasmarketing.com

Resources

- TAS Marketing, Inc.—a telephone answering service brokerage firm: http://tasmarketing.com
- International Customer Management Institute: http://www.icmi.com
- ContactCenterWorld: http://www.contactcenterworld.com
- IBISWorld, October 2016: http://ibisworld.com

Camera Stores		
SIC 5946-01	NAICS 443130	Number of Businesses/Units 1,934

Rules of Thumb

➤ 10–15% of annual revenues plus fixtures, equipment & inventory

C

Benchmark Data

Statistics (Camera Stores)

Number of Establishments	1,934
Average Profit Margin	1.7%
Revenue per Employee	$286,900
Average Number of Employees	4.0
Average Wages per Employee	$28,284

Industry Costs

Profit	1.7%
Wages	9.9%
Purchases	59.2%
Depreciation	1.2%
Marketing	1.5%
Rent & Utilities	7.3%
Other	19.2%

Industry Trend

- "The latest numbers from the Camera and Imaging Products Association continue to show that the camera industry is stabilizing after years of decline. The latest data shows that camera sales overall have started to straighten out in 2017, with the numbers for January through April, the latest available, showing between a 1.7-percent decline to a 7.1 percent growth over the previous year's sales. In 2016, data from the same time period ranged from a 31.7-percent decline to a 14-percent decline.

  "The total numbers have over 8.2 million cameras shipping out, including both fixed lens and interchangeable cameras. The data is only from CIPA members — that includes most of the major players in the market including Canon, Sony, Nikon, Fujifilm and Panasonic but doesn't include every manufacturer, most notably, Leica and medium-format companies Hasselblad and Phase One. The 2017 numbers show the industry beginning to stabilize and show slight growth for the first time since sales started falling five years ago."

  Source: "Camera sales are continuing to pick up in 2017 after years of decline" by Hillary Grigonis, June 12, 2017, https://www.digitaltrends.com/photography/camera-industry-cipa-april-2017/

Resources

- IBISWorld, September 2017: http://ibisworld.com
- The Imaging Alliance—good site: https://www.theimagingalliance.com/

Campgrounds

SIC 7033-01	NAICS 721211	Number of Businesses/Units 14,571

Rules of Thumb

- ➢ 8.5 x EBITDA
- ➢ 8.5–8.9 x SDE; add store inventory

Pricing Tips

- Often owners feel they need a lot of negotiating room. This is not necessary. The astute prospective buyer will immediately recognize the value being

---

correct, and may likely assume if they don't jump on this quickly, someone else will. Another common feeling is "we can always come down in price, but we cannot go up." Although this sounds very logical, with an unrealistic price tag you could be missing many qualified and cash buyers even viewing your business. Another negative could be the possibility of becoming market stale and having prospective buyers wondering "Why has this campground been for sale so long?"

- Typically, 3-4 times SDE + value of Real Estate. 9-13% cap rates (depending on physical condition and location).
- "Amenities sought after in both RV parks and campgrounds include large sites (nearly 50%), high ratings in a national camping directory, attractive landscaping and cooking areas, and quick check-in."

Source: National Association of RV Parks (ARVC)

- You also need to be very careful about zoning and how well accepted the park is with neighbors. If they are operating on agricultural land with a special use permit and the area is surrounded by residences . . . look out! If they are on leased land, it might be impossible to expand or continue to lease if it expires.

Benchmark Data

Statistics (Campgrounds & RV Parks)

Number of Establishments	14,571
Average Profit Margin	17.5%
Revenue per Employee	$123,300
Average Number of Employees	3.5
Average Wages per Employee	$30,412

Products and Services Segmentation

Other unit accommodations and service fees	21.2%
Campground membership, tuition and long-term fees	44.2%
RV and tent sites for travelers and others	34.6%

Industry Costs

Profit	16.8%
Wages	24.7%
Purchases	13.1%
Depreciation	8.8%
Marketing	2.1%
Rent & Utilities	9.4%
Other	24.4%

- A successful business will have operating expenses at 30% of GOI.
- It is difficult to provide percentages for expenses because of the tremendous variety of operations. Cost of Goods for store sales should run 65% if they have a mix of groceries and souvenirs. Some facilities are much more labor intensive due to extensive landscaping and cabin cleaning. Food service can be a great amenity and help to separate yourself from the competition.

Expenses (% of Annual Sales)

Cost of Goods	10%
Occupancy Costs	40%
Payroll/Labor Costs	10%
Profit (pretax)	40%

C

Questions

- Will you carry a contract? Do you have a data base of customers? Age and condition of all utilities. We always would ask about: roof, sewer, property lines and permits.

Industry Trend

- "New York state's parks, historic sites and campgrounds saw a substantial increase in attendance last year, up more than 3.9 million more visitors from 2015. According to Gov. Andrew Cuomo, New York's parks, historic sites and campgrounds hosted 69.3 million visitors in 2016, an increase of 6 percent from 2015. The number of visitors has increased by 21 percent from the 57.2 million visitors in 2011 when Cuomo took office."

  Source: "N.Y.: State park attendance up nearly 4 million visitors," February 22, 2017
  http://rvdailyreport.com/campground/n-y-state-park-attendance-up-nearly-4-million-visitors/

Expert Comments

Start 3 years with planning before selling. The price is directly tied to cash flow.

Difficult start-up business due to lake shore and PCA regulations. Typically seasonal businesses.

Sellers: Buyers are more sophisticated now and want to see credible valuation information to support the asking price and a business plan that shows the future. Have documentation about repairs and maintenance, permits and zoning and other issues that could limit the future. If you have a bank loan now, talk with your banker to see what they will require for a new owner.

Buyers: You will need to work hard for the first few years but at a realistic pace. If the current owner is completely worn out, you may want to watch their labor costs and deferred maintenance. Financing can take time and the bankers will need to see plenty of working capital in addition to the down payment. Take time up-front to understand valuation before you get caught up in negotiating based on feelings. Leased property has a far lower value. The great locations will cost more but will also provide a much better future. Different campgrounds will have a different type of customer too. Look for a location that caters to customers that you can relate to.

We are seeing an increase in people wanting to own real estate based business that they can understand. It is very difficult and expensive to get permitting to build a new facility so replication is hard. The next 20 years should be good for the business as baby boomers retire and travel.

Campgrounds are no more risky than a main street business. The one thing that gives them stability is the difficulty in building a new one, both from a cost standpoint and a land use standpoint.

Seller Financing

- The majority of campgrounds are sold with a combination of owner and bank financing. When the closing date is set as it relates to their season can complicate things. If the closing is in the fall and the campground is closed for the winter, it could mean several months of payments without income. We often see delayed closings to make it realistic.
- 20 years

C

Resources
- National Association of RV Parks and Campgrounds (ARVC): http://www.arvc.org
- IBISWorld, January 2017: http://ibisworld.com

Camps		
SIC 7032-03	NAICS 721214	Number of Businesses/Units 3,085

Rules of Thumb
➤ 2 x annual sales plus inventory

➤ 5–8 x SDE plus inventory

Pricing Tips
- Children's overnight camps use a multiple of earnings of 4.5.
- Years in business—more years, the higher the multiple.

Benchmark Data

Statistics (Summer Camps)
Number of Establishments	3,085
Average Profit Margin	10.8%
Revenue per Employee	$110,700
Average Number of Employees	8.2
Average Wages per Employee	$39,081

Major Market Segmentation
Adolescents aged 10 to 17	62.1%
Children aged 9 years and younger	34.0%
Adults 18 and older	3.9%

Industry Costs
Profit	10.8%
Wages	35.3%
Purchases	34.0%
Depreciation	6.0%
Marketing	2.2%
Rent & Utilities	8.6%
Other	3.1%

Expenses (% of Annual Sales)
Cost of Goods	15%
Occupancy Costs	30%
Payroll/Labor Costs	45%
Profit (pretax)	10

Questions
- What percentage of your campers renew from year to year? Get the figures for each of the last three years.

C

Industry Trend
- Increased need

Expert Comments

There are many more choices for parents today for their children to attend summer camp—day camps, sleepover camps, general recreational camps, specialty sports camps, computer camps, camps for the arts, for-profit and not-for-profit camps.

More and more moms and dads have to work today and that creates a need for child care in the summer months when the kids are out of school.

Seller Financing
- Seller financing, 50% down

Resources
- American Camp Association: http://www.acacamps.org
- IBISWorld, November 2016: http://ibisworld.com

Candy Stores		
SIC 5441-01	NAICS 445292	

Rules of Thumb
➢ 1.7 x SDE plus inventory

➢ 30–35% of annual sales plus inventory

Benchmark Data
- See Food Stores—Specialty for additional Benchmark Information

Expenses (% of Annual Sales)
Payroll/Labor Costs 55.6%

Industry Trend
- "See's Candies is one retailer that isn't fretting about how the surge of e-commerce is affecting foot traffic at its conventional stores. See's has been selling fresh chocolates and other candies for nearly a century in its stores with the checkerboard motif—and the company is still opening new locations. A licensee also opened the first See's in New York in March.

  "There are now 250 See's locations in 17 states, including about 150 in California. But See's, which will sell between $400 million and $450 million of candy this year, also is tapping into the growth of online shopping; customers can order most of its products on See's revamped website."

  Source: "See's Candies finds that brick-and-mortar stores are still a sweet spot" by James F. Peltz August 24, 2017, http://www.latimes.com/business/la-fi-qa-sees-candies-stores-20170824-htmlstory.html

Resources
- National Confectioners Association: http://www.candyusa.com
- Candy Industry magazine—an excellent and informative site: http://www.candyindustry.com

Card Shops

SIC 5947-10	NAICS 453220	

Benchmark Data

Statistics (Gift Shops & Card Stores)

Number of Establishments	66,612
Average Profit Margin	6.2%
Revenue per Employee	$19,700
Average Number of Employees	3.2
Average Wages per Employee	$14,263

Products and Services Segmentation

Souvenirs and novelty items	26.9%
Other	24.1%
Clothes, jewelry and costumes	17.4%
Seasonal decorations	15.0%
Greeting cards	8.8%
Kitchenware and home furnishings	7.8%

Industry Costs

Profit	6.1%
Wages	14.5%
Purchases	48.1%
Depreciation	0.9%
Marketing	0.7%
Rent & Utilities	12.3%
Other	17.3%

Market Share

Party City Holdings Inc.	7.0%

Industry Trend

- "From 2010–2015, Hallmark slashed its workforce from 22,000 FTEs to 10,500 FTEs worldwide. According to the Greeting Card Association, the sales of greeting cards has actually held steady for the last several years. This means about 6.5 billion greeting cards are purchased in the United States every year. The annual retail sales of greeting cards is estimated to be between $7 to $8 billion in total.

"If twice as many people plan to purchase cards next year, but the industry itself is expecting a 5% decrease, then the customers the industry is losing are its biggest spenders. Add in the fact that Millennials are the most tech-savvy generation to date and the potential for growth becomes even more dismal. Birthdays are acknowledged more today than ever before, but that's because people can send a simple message over Facebook instead of sending a greeting card in the mail.

"The global sales of greeting cards is expected to decline to $21 billion in total by the year 2020. Compounded annual growth in greeting card sales in the APAC region are expected to top 3.3% through 2020. Growing postal rates and increasing levels of DIY greeting cards will add to the pressure that e-cards have placed on the industry today."

Source: "35 Astonishing Greeting Card Industry Trends," June 6, 2016, http://brandongaille.com/35-astonishing-greeting-card-industry-trends/

C

Resources

- IBISWorld, October 2016: http://ibisworld.com

Carl's Jr. Restaurants

Approx. Total Investment	$1,300,000
Estimated Annual Sales/Unit	$1,364,000

SIC 5812-06	NAICS 722513	Number of Businesses/Units 674

Rules of Thumb

➢ 40% of annual sales plus inventory

Resources

- Carl's Jr. Restaurants: http://www.CKEfranchise.com

Carpet Cleaning

SIC 7217-04	NAICS 561740	Number of Businesses/Units 38,917

Rules of Thumb

➢ 60% of annual revenue plus inventory

➢ 1.5 x SDE plus inventory

Pricing Tips

- "It's also helpful to purchase a business that already has a presence among consumers in the area, which is why many people decide to buy a franchise. Franchising fees are fairly high in the industry, though, ranging from $20,000 to $50,000 on average."

  Source: http://www.iicrc.org/how-prepared-with-carpet-cleaning-business-for-sale-a-194.html

Benchmark Data

Statistics (Carpet Cleaning)

Number of Establishments	39,194
Average Profit Margin	10.7%
Revenue per Employee	$67,200
Average Number of Employees	1.8
Average Wages per Employee	$22,019

Products and Services Segmentation

Residential carpet and upholstery cleaning	44.1%
Commercial carpet and upholstery cleaning	28.1%
Other	16.7%
Offsite cleaning services	11.1%

Industry Costs

Profit	10.7%
Wages	32.9%
Purchases	22.6%
Depreciation	1.2%
Marketing	3.5%
Rent & Utilities	5.5%
Other	23.6%

Market Share

Chem-Dry Inc.	4.5%

Resources

- The Carpet and Rug Institute: http://www.carpet-rug.org
- Restoration Industry Association: http://www.restorationindustry.org
- IBISWorld, January 2017: http://ibisworld.com

Carpet/Floor Coverings

SIC 5713-05	NAICS 442210	Number of Businesses/Units 19,032

Rules of Thumb

➤ 20% of annual sales plus inventory

Benchmark Data

Statistics (Floor Covering Stores)

Number of Establishments	19,032
Average Profit Margin	3.5%
Revenue per Employee	$264,400
Average Number of Employees	3.8
Average Wages per Employee	$36,304

Products and Services Segmentation

Carpets and other soft-surface floor coverings	43.7%
Other hard-surface floor coverings	31.9%
Hardwood flooring	16.0%
Other services	8.4%

Major Market Segmentation

Do-it-for-me customers	38.3%
Do-it-yourself customers	25.6%
Building contractors	18.4%
All other establishments for resale	10.4%
Businesses for end use in their own operation	7.3%

Industry Costs

Profit	3.5%
Wages	13.9%
Purchases	60.8%
Depreciation	0.7%
Utilities	2.0%
Rent	5.1%
Other	14.0%

C

Industry Trend

- "Homeowner spending on remodeling is expected to see healthy growth through 2025, according to Demographic Change and the Remodeling Outlook, the latest biennial report in the Improving America's Housing series released today by the Harvard Joint Center for Housing Studies. Demographically based projections suggest that older owners will account for the majority of spending gains over the coming years as they adapt their homes to changing accessibility needs. Although slower to move into homeownership than previous generations, millennials are poised to enter the remodeling market in greater force, buying up older, more affordable homes in need of renovations.

  "Expenditures by homeowners age 55 and over are expected to grow by nearly 33% by 2025, accounting for more than three-quarters of total gains over the decade. The share of market spending by homeowners age 55 and over is projected to reach 56% by 2025, up from only 31% in 2005."

  Source: "Remodeling Spending Should Grow, Driven by Aging Homeowners," February 28, 2017, http://www.floordaily.net/flooring-news/remodeling-spending-should-grow-driven-by-aging-homeowners

Resources

- Floor Covering Weekly: http://www.floorcoveringweekly.com
- Floor Covering News: http://www.fcnews.net/
- Floor Daily: http://www.floordaily.net
- IBISWorld, December 2016: http://ibisworld.com

		Franchise
Cartridge World		
Approx. Total Investment		$87,300–$203,650
	NAICS 424120	Number of Businesses/Units 1,000

Rules of Thumb

➢ 30–35% of annual sales plus inventory

Resources

- Cartridge World: http://www.cartridgeworld.com

		Franchise
Carvel Ice Cream		
Approx. Total Investment		$35,100–$354,550
SIC 2024-98	NAICS 722515	Number of Businesses/Units 434

Rules of Thumb

➢ 55 percent of annual sales or 20–25 x the number of gallons of liquid ice cream mix purchased plus inventory

➢ 2.25–2.5 x SDE plus inventory

Pricing Tips

- Typically [priced] at $30 per gallon of ice cream mix used. Therefore, a 5,000-gallon store, which grosses approximately $250,000 would sell for $150,000 to $160,000 with SDE at about $65,000. The $150,000-$175,000 equates to approximately 60% of gross. Stores with disproportionate rental expense would be closer to 50% of gross or 2 times SDE. The exception is for the very few higher volume stores, above 8,000. These would sell for closer to $40 per gallon with SDE of 2.5.

- Some franchised ice cream businesses with a positive history, updated facilities and verifiable sales numbers will move to 2.5 SDE. Conversely, a short lease and less than five years on franchise agreement will result in less than 2 times SDE.
- Location drives price higher and typically has higher returns on product usage, therefore more profit. Free-standing buildings with volume in excess of 10,000 gallons, rule of thumb would be 60 percent of annual sales, with average lease of 7 years remaining.

Benchmark Data
- Food cost percentage typically is equal to SDE unless rent is above $25 per sq. ft.

Expenses (% of Annual Sales)

Cost of Goods	26%
Occupancy Costs	11%
Payroll/Labor Costs	21%
Profit (pretax)	25%

Seller Financing
- 3 to 5 years

Resources
- Carvel Ice Cream: http://www.carvelicecream.com

Car Washes—Coin Operated/Self-Service		
SIC 7542-05	NAICS 811192	

Rules of Thumb
> 4 x annual gross sales—a good place to start
> 2–3 x cap rate

Pricing Tips
- "Self-service value is derived by using a multiplier of 3 to 5 times the gross sales. Be advised the real estate is included in these basic values, and each wash has to be in business for at least three continuous years."
Source: Roger Pencek, BRG Industry Expert
- "Identify the location by looking at the visibility and characteristics of the site, says the International Carwash Association. In terms of visibility, can the customer see the car wash easily while driving by? Does the car wash have pleasing architecture, good lighting and landscaping, and appropriate signage? As to characteristics, does the facility have wide, well-maintained driveways and sidewalks? Is the car wash in good shape? If it is not, you'll have the pay for renovations or, at least, negotiate a discount on the price based on expected repairs that will be needed."

C

"Study the traffic pattern, says the International Carwash Association, including traffic speed-the slower the better in front of the car wash-and whether turns are easy or difficult to make. Also, look at the potential capture rate-the percent of cars driving by that are actually 'captured,' or stop to use the car wash.

"According to a survey by 'Professional Carwashing & Detailing' magazine, capture rates range from 0.45 percent for exterior-only conveyor washes to 0.52 percent for full-service washes. If 20,000 cars drive by the wash each day, that translates to 90 cars a day for a self-service wash (20,000 cars a day X .0045 capture rate = 90 cars). That may not sound like much, but over the course of 365 days in the year, that would translate to nearly 33,000 customers-if the car wash attracts that number each day.

"Also, ask the owner of the car wash you are considering purchasing for financial statements for the last three years. If the owner offers to provide only the past three months or so, that might not offer an accurate representation-as weather, for example, can greatly affect the number of customers who visit the car wash business. Only several years of financial statements will give you a full picture."

Source: http://smallbusiness.chron.com/buy-car-wash-business-44936.html

Benchmark Data

Miscellaneous Data

Average gross revenue per car	$8.69
Average purchase price of the new property (land only)	$642,000
Average cost of improvements (bldg., landscaping etc.)	$1,417,000
Average cost of equipment	$550,000

Expenses (Operating Costs as Percentage of Total Monthly revenues)

Electricity	6.3%
Fuel (Gas, Oil, Etc.)	5.1%
Water	5.6%
Sewer	5.6%
Chemicals	6.5%
Vending Products	1.1%
Softener Salt	1.2%
Collection	1.6%
Attendant Labor	13.2%
Bookkeeping	2.3%
Replacement Parts (Normal Wear and Tear)	5.1%
Replacement Parts (Vandalism)	1.8%
Refunds	0.5%
Pit Pumping	2.4%
Advertising & Promo	2.0%

Self-Serve Statistics for a single operation (Wand or Coin-op Style)

Average monthly gross income per bay	$1,652
Average monthly gross income per vacuum	$263
Average monthly gross income for vending	$25

Source: Auto Laundry News 2016 Self-Service Survey

Industry Trend

- "Overall, 43 percent of respondents report income growth over the previous year. Seventy percent of express-exterior participants report growth; none reports declining revenue. Twenty-two percent of exterior-only and 29 percent of express exterior respondents plan to build a new wash in the coming year—every one an express exterior."

Source: AutoLaundry News 2017 Exterior Conveyor Survey

Resources

- International Carwash Association: http://www.carwash.org
- AutoLaundry News 2017 Exterior Conveyor Survey: http://carwashmag.com
- Auto Laundry News 2016 Self-Service Survey: http://carwashmag.com

Car Washes—Full-Service/Exterior

SIC 7542-01	NAICS 811192	Number of Businesses/Units 65,685

Rules of Thumb

➤ 32% of annual sales includes inventory

➤ 3 x SDE includes inventory

➤ 23 x EBIT

➤ .80–1 x annual sales plus inventory

➤ 3.75–4.75 x EBITDA

➤ 4–6 x owner's provable net income includes income

Pricing Tips

- "Full service is more complicated since there often are several profit centers that have differing profit margins. In general, however, full-service value is calculated by taking the EBIDTA (Earnings Before Interest, Depreciation, Taxes, and Amortization) and multiplying by between 5.8 and 6.8. Be advised the real estate is included in these basic values, and each wash has to be in business for at least three continuous years."

Source: Roger Pencek, BRG Industry Expert

- Car Wash Industry in a 'Free Fall' past few years, 90% of our sales are with real estate, and that is almost the value of the transaction. I have just closed on two washes: Self Service bought for $990,000./7SS-3 Automatic. Bought in 2006....Closing Price today $330,000. Full Service Conveyor bought for $850,000.00 now sold for $130,000. Both operations sold with real estate. Most car washes are 'under water' with their financing.
- Mostly sold with real estate and is a cash business and not easy to verify income numbers.
- Tax returns are not easily available and estimating is generally the rule; therefore using water bills, etc. to figure out the sales is one common method.
- Key factors include current market conditions, owner salary, benefits, condition of equipment… these are just some of the typical costs and items buyers and sellers negotiate over.

C

Benchmark Data

Statistics (Car Wash & Auto Detailing)

Number of Establishments	65,685
Average Profit Margin	17.1%
Revenue per Employee	$50,500
Average Number of Employees	3.2
Average Wages per Employee	$18,100

Products and Services Segmentation

Conveyor car washes	49.7%
Detailing	17.7%
In-bay automatic car washes	11.4%
Self-service bays	10.8%
Hand washing	10.4%

Industry Costs

Profit	17.1%
Wages	35.8%
Purchases	21.3%
Depreciation	9.3%
Marketing	1.3%
Rent & Utilities	13.1%
Other	2.1%

Operating Costs (As a percentage of total revenues)

Rent	10.6%
Equipment & Bldg. Maintenance	3.6%
Chemicals	7.1%
Labor	35%
Utilities	6.6%
Insurance	2.6%
Advertising & Promotion	2.3%
Equipment on Lease	0%
Customer Claims	0.7%

Expenses (% of Annual Sales)

Cost of Goods	05% to 10%
Occupancy Costs	10% to 20%
Payroll/Labor Costs	42.5%
Profit (pretax)	25%

Questions

- How many vehicles per month do they do, summer vs. winter, and the average ticket on each vehicle. Any environmental issues? The length of the lease and the rent factor. Is there at least one manager?
- You need to ask the seller the name of the equipment, the age of the equipment. Is the car wash brush or brushless, any problems with the system?
- Provable Gross and Net. Is all labor on the books. What percentage of gross income is cash. Average monthly car count and ticket price, all sources of income.
- Are you clear with employees and are they all registered? Is there ground contamination? How are the tax records?

Industry Trend

- "Over the five years to 2022, revenue for the Car Wash and Auto Detailing industry is forecast to rise at an annualized rate of 1.8% to $11.5 billion. Industry operators will benefit from rising per capita disposable income, which will fuel increased spending on discretionary services, including car washing and auto detailing."

Source: IBISWorld Industry Outlook

Expert Comments

Good weather brings forth more sales; summer is generally a better season than winter. There is some seasonality in this business; best time to purchase is early summer or late spring. Have working capital and cash flow in reserve for the winter months.

Location, marketing, management, and visual appeal

In some areas replication is easy, and in others it's difficult due to the local restrictions on the usability of water and recycling it, plus the traffic problems.

Seller Financing

- Virtually no outside financing or SBA available because of figures, and lack of bookkeeping.
- Seller will generally carry 30-35% over five to seven years at 6% interest per annum.
- 20 percent down, 80 percent financing, 20-year amortization

Resources

- International Carwash Association: http://www.carwash.org
- IBISWorld, August 2017: http://ibisworld.com
- AutoLaundry News 2017 Full/Flex Survey: http://carwashmag.com
- Wash Trends Magazine: http://www.washtrends.com/site/

Car X Auto Service		Franchise
Approx. Total Investment		$214,000–326,000
Estimated Annual Sales/Unit		$750,000
	NAICS 811111	Number of Businesses/Units 164

Rules of Thumb

➤ 35–40% of annual sales plus inventory

Resources

- Car X: http://www.carx.com

Casinos/Casino Hotels		
SIC 7993-02	NAICS 713210	Number of Businesses/Units 767

C

Rules of Thumb

➤ Las Vegas Strip average: 8.1x EBITDA

➤ Indian Gaming management contracts:

  ✓ 30–40 percent net (this is pulled from the top in "Operating Income" and should be calculated before debt service

  ✓ 5–7 percent of gross used to be standard for Indian Gaming contracts

  ✓ The NIGC must approve all contracts and agreements between management and tribal nations. The NIGC (National Indian Gaming Commission) is an independent federal regulatory agency of the United States.

  ✓ Management cannot own any part of the Indian casino.

  ✓ Contracts are typically five years with options to renew.

  ✓ The tribe will be responsible for paying down the debt service.

Pricing Tips

■ Casinos Only: Annual Revenue less than $3,000,000: 2.25 to 2.75 times verifiable annual cash flow (I would use a weighted average of the past three time periods). If the 'casino' doesn't own the slot machines, then the multiple would be less.

Annual Revenue $3,000,000 to $10,000,000: 2.75 to 3.25 times verifiable annual cash flow (I would use a weighted average of the past three time periods). If the 'casino' doesn't own the slot machines, then the multiple would be less.

Annual revenue over $10,000,000 (but not over $25,000,000): 3.00 to 4.00 times verifiable annual cash flow (I would use a weighted average of the past three time periods). If the 'casino' doesn't own the slot machines, then the multiple would be less.

Benchmark Data

Statistics (Casino Hotels)

Number of Establishments	418
Average Profit Margin	18.2%
Revenue per Employee	$143,000
Average Number of Employees	1,023
Average Wages per Employee	$34,964

Products and Services Segmentation

Gambling machines	52.7%
Other	16.3%
Gaming tables	12.8%
Accommodations	11.9%
Alcoholic beverages	4.3%
Admissions to live performances	2.0%

Industry Costs

Profit	18.2%
Wages	24.4%
Purchases	19.6%
Depreciation	6.8%
Utilities	3.5%
Rent	7.9%
Other	19.6%

Market Share

MGM Resorts International	12.2%
Caesars Entertainment Corporation	5.8%

Statistics (Non-Hotel Casinos)

Number of Establishments	349
Average Profit Margin	16.5%
Revenue per Employee	$194,100
Average Number of Employees	383.4
Average Wages per Employee	$36,054

Products and Services Segmentation

On-premises gaming (riverboat and barge casinos)	69.3%
Off-track betting (riverboat and barge casinos)	14.7%
Cruise casinos	7.0%
Food and non-alcoholic beverages (riverboat and barge casinos)	4.8%
Alcoholic beverages (riverboat and barge casinos)	2.2%
Arcades and video games (riverboat and barge casinos)	2.0%

Industry Costs

Profit	16.5%
Wages	18.7%
Purchases	5.0%
Depreciation	5.4%
Marketing	8.5%
Rent & Utilities	3.4%
Other	42.5%

Market Share

Caesars Entertainment Corporation	2.9%
Penn National Gaming Inc.	6.7%

Industry Trend

- "U.S. Consumer Spending on Commercial Casino Gaming, 2003–2015: Total consumer spending at commercial casinos increased nearly 2.5 percent in 2015 when compared with the prior year, reaching a record total of $38.54 billion. The growth was due to several factors including lower gas prices and increased consumer confidence, particularly among high-end casino patrons. It also reflected the impact of new casino openings in Louisiana, Maryland, Massachusetts and Ohio."

  Source: "2016 AGA Survey of the Casino Industry State of the States"
  https://www.americangaming.org/sites/default/files/2016%20State%20of%20the%20States_FINAL.pdf

- "In order of prominence, the Top 10 Trends for 2017 are:

  1. Significant expansion opportunities are expected to arise as legislation is crafted in Brazil, India and Japan.

  2. Lotteries and casinos will both seek online opportunities — sometimes with competing efforts in the same states and countries, creating competitive challenges that legislators and regulators must sort out.

  3. Casinos will leverage their under-utilized square footage to create special attractions for Millennials, including lounges, entertainment, and skill-based gaming options.

4. States will attempt to overcome stagnating gaming receipts by proposing new forms of, or locations for, gaming such as retail gaming (i.e., a limited number of electronic gaming devices in liquor-licensed establishments), satellite casinos, and slots at airports.

5. Proponents of legalized sports betting — including the American Gaming Association, state associations and individual operators — will push their agenda more forcefully as state budgets continue to be strained, and as major sports leagues seek to capture a substantial new revenue stream.

6. Macau will again become a growth story, as gross gaming revenues continue to climb and new integrated resorts open. The mass market will dominate and VIP play will decline to less than 50 percent of GGR for the first time since Macau reverted back to China.

7. The trend toward private management and, in some instances, private ownership of lotteries will accelerate in various countries and US states.

8. State legislatures will face pressure to reduce gaming tax rates, as well as to amend or streamline regulations, in response to increasing competition and the potential for saturation in various markets.

9. More casinos in Las Vegas and Atlantic City will stage eSports events and contests, while Atlantic City will attempt to reposition itself as an eSports hub.

10. The South will be a focus of casino opportunities, as the potential for legalization and expansion is debated in Alabama, Florida, Georgia, and Louisiana."

Source: "Top 10 casino industry trends for 2017 identified by Spectrum Gaming Group," by K. Morrison, December 14, 2016 https://news.worldcasinodirectory.com/top-10-casino-industry-trends-for-2017-identi-fied-by-spectrum-gaming-group-39051

Resources

- North American Association of State & Provincial Lotteries: http://www.naspl.org
- American Gaming Association: http://www.americangaming.org
- World Casino News: https://news.worldcasinodirectory.com/
- National Indian Gaming Association: http://www.indiangaming.org
- Indian Gaming: http://www.indiangaming.com
- IBISWorld, July 2017: http://ibisworld.com
- IBISWorld, May 2017: http://ibisworld.com
- Global Gaming Business Magazine: http://ggbmagazine.com

Caterers/Catering

SIC 5812-12	NAICS 722320	Number of Businesses/Units 125,574

Rules of Thumb

➢ 35–40% of annual sales plus inventory

Benchmark Data

Statistics (Caterers)

Number of Establishments	125,574
Average Profit Margin	7.8%
Revenue per Employee	$44,000
Average Number of Employees	2.1
Average Wages per Employee	$15,096

C

Products and Services Segmentation

Food served at events on customer's premises 37.3%
Food served at events on caterer's premises... 31.4%
Other services... 10.0%
Food dropped off at the customer's event 8.6%
Food prepared for immediate consumption 8.0%
Alcoholic and nonalcoholic beverages.. 2.6%
Food prepared for customer pick-up.. 2.1%

Industry Costs

Profit 7.8%
Wages... 34.2%
Purchases... 45.9%
Depreciation... 2.0%
Marketing... 1.1%
Rent & Utilities 5.4%
Other... 3.6%

Resources

- Cater Source Journal: http://www.catersource.com
- The National Association for Catering and Events (NACE): http://www.nace.net
- IBISWorld, February 2017: http://ibisworld.com
- International Caterers Association: http://www.internationalcaterers.org

Catering Trucks		
	NAICS 722330	Number of Businesses/Units 66,860

Rules of Thumb

➢ 40% of annual sales plus inventory

Benchmark Data

Statistics (Street Vendors)

Number of Establishments.. 66,860
Average Profit Margin 6.0%
Revenue per Employee $33,700
Average Number of Employees.. 1.1
Average Wages per Employee $12,938

Industry Costs

Profit 6.0%
Wages... 38.6%
Purchases... 40.6%
Depreciation... 2.6%
Marketing... 1.3%
Rent & Utilities 6.6%
Other... 4.3%

Resources

- IBISWorld, June 2017: http://ibisworld.com

C

Cellular Telephone Stores

	NAICS 443112	

Rules of Thumb

➤ 40% of annual revenues plus inventory

Resources

- Cellular Telecommunications & Internet Association (CTIA): http://www.ctia.org

Cemeteries

SIC 6553-02	NAICS 812220	Number of Businesses/Units 8,261

Rules of Thumb

➤ 6 x SDE includes real estate

➤ 8 x EBIT includes real estate

➤ 6 x EBITDA includes real estate

Pricing Tips

- Valuations will vary depending on the strategic fit of the buyer. A local funeral home is generally the best strategic fit and should, therefore, be willing to pay the most.

Benchmark Data

Statistics (Cemetery Services)

Number of Establishments	8,261
Average Profit Margin	10.6%
Revenue per Employee	$114,400
Average Number of Employees	4.4
Average Wages per Employee	$39,122

Products and Services Segmentation

Sale of graves, plots and other spaces	28.0%
Interment services	24.8%
Sales of funeral goods	22.5%
Cemetery maintenance services	10.1%
Cremation services	7.1%
Pre-burial services	6.7%
Other	0.8%

Industry Costs

Profit	10.6%
Wages	34.4%
Purchases	21.5%
Depreciation	3.3%
Marketing	2.0%
Rent & Utilities	6.1%
Other	22.1%

Market Share

Service Corporation International	16.5%
StoneMor Partners LP	5.1%

- "Funerals are expensive. Today, the average funeral costs over $8,000 but often exceed $10,000. By comparison, funeral costs averaged $708 in 1960, which in today's dollars would be about $5,600. Opting for cremation can lower a funeral cost to around $3,500, which is one reason why cremations are becoming more popular.

"Cremation rates in the United States:

2000	26%
2005	32%
2012	43%
2020	55%
2030	70%"

Source: http://foresthill.williamcronon.net/geography-of-death/an-overview-of-the-death-careindustry/

Questions

- Trust fund information is critical. What are the liabilities? Are they properly funded? Is there a successful sales organization/program in place?

Resources

- IBISWorld, February 2017: http://ibisworld.com
- Forest Hill: http://foresthill.williamcronon.net/geography-of-death/an-overview-of-the-death-care-industry/

CertaPro Painters		Franchise
Approx. Total Investment		$129,000–$161,500
Estimated Annual Sales/Unit		$741,000
SIC 1721-01	NAICS 238320	Number of Businesses/Units 420

Rules of Thumb

➢ 45% of annual sales plus inventory

Resources

- CertaPro: http://www.certapro-franchise.com

Check Cashing Services		
SIC 6099-03	NAICS 522390	

Rules of Thumb

➢ 75% of annual revenues

➢ 2 x SDE

Pricing Tips

- The check cashing business is growing; every state has its own rules and regulations. Lease terms and whether a franchise or independent will affect pricing.

C

Benchmark Data
- See Payday Loans for additional Benchmark Data.

Services/Products Offerings & Volumes

Check Cashing	96%
Money Orders	96%
Money Transfers	96%
Bill Payments	96%
Prepaid Debit Cards	88%
Payday Advances	58%
Travelers Checks	4%
Installment Loans	25%
Other Financial Products	63%

- Check cashing should provide the owner with 1% of total gross sales as owner's discretionary income.

Expenses (% of Annual Sales)

Cost of Goods	99%
Occupancy Costs	01%
Payroll/Labor Costs	01%
Profit (pretax)	01%

Resources
- Financial Service Centers of America—an excellent site with lots of information: https://www.fisca.org/

	Franchise
Cheeburger Cheeburger Restaurants	
Approx. Total Investment	$230,000–$585,000
SIC 5812-19 NAICS 722513	Number of Businesses/Units 69

Rules of Thumb
➢ 35–40% of annual aales includes inventory

Resources
- Cheeburger: http://www.cheeburger.com

	Franchise
Chick-fil-A	
Estimated Annual Sales/Unit	$3,890,000
SIC 5812-06 NAICS 722513	Number of Businesses/Units 1,750

Rules of Thumb
➢ 60–70% of annual sales plus inventory

Resources
- Chick-Fil-A: http://www.chick-fil-a.com

Children's and Infants' Clothing Stores

	NAICS 448130	Number of Businesses/Units 17,175

Rules of Thumb

➢ 25–30% of annual sales plus inventory

Benchmark Data

Statistics (Children's & Infants' Clothing Stores)

Number of Establishments	17,175
Average Profit Margin	4.8%
Revenue per Employee	$105,800
Average Number of Employees	5.2
Average Wages per Employee	$13,312

Products and Services Segmentation

Girls' clothing	58.3%
Boys' clothing	22.2%
Infants' and toddlers' clothing	15.1%
Other	4.4%

Industry Costs

Profit	4.8%
Wages	12.6%
Purchases	63.4%
Depreciation	1.4%
Marketing	2.2%
Rent & Utilities	11.8%
Other	3.8%

Market Share

Carter's Inc.	16.7%
The Children's Place Retail Stores Inc.	12.7%
The Gymboree Corp.	12.1%
Ascena Retail Group Inc.	9.8%

- "The average family spends $107.28 on children's clothing—$123.79 for each girl, $90.77 for each boy. Spending varies dramatically depending on household income and age of the primary householders. Households with an income under $10,000 spend an average of $24.67 on boys' clothes and $49.75 on girls' clothes, while households that earn $70,000 or more spend an average of $167.04 on boys' clothes and $216.57 on girls' clothes."
Source: http://www.companiesandmarkets.com/News/Textiles-and-Clothing/Children-s-wear-market-value-to-hit-173-6-billion-by-2017/NI3785

Industry Trend

- "The global children's wear mark is estimated to hit a value of US $173.6 billion by 2017. Developed regions within Europe and North America are considered traditional leaders and account for a principal share of the global children's wear market. Asia-Pacific, spurred by rapidly escalating markets in India, China, Korea, Thailand, Taiwan and others is poised to deliver the fastest growth rate of 5.3% through to 2017."
Source: "Children's wear market value to hit $173.6 billion by 2017," by Matt Bodimeade, http://www.companiesandmarkets.com/News/Textiles-and-Clothing/Children-s-wear-market-value-to-hit-173-6-billion-by-2017/NI3785

C

Resources
- IBISWorld, June 2017: http://ibisworld.com
- Companies and Markets:
  http://www.companiesandmarkets.com/News/Textiles-and-Clothing/Children-s-wear-market-value-to-hit-173-6-billion-by-2017/NI3785

Children's Educational Franchises

Rules of Thumb
➢ 2.5 x SDE

➢ 2 x EBIT

➢ 2 x EBITDA

Pricing Tips
- The typical learning center with sales of up to $300k and EBITDA of $85k will sell at approximately a 2.5 multiple. While deals are done for more than that, it should not be the expectation of the seller.

Benchmark Data
- $250/square foot

Expenses (% of Annual Sales)
Cost of Goods	20%
Occupancy Costs	20%
Payroll/Labor Costs	25%
Profit (pretax)	25%

Questions
- Buyer needs to know the retention rate of the business, the demographics of the area, the average length of stay for the clients. How often has franchisor changed the royalty structure in the past.

Industry Trend
- Demand is increasing as schools are having a difficult time keeping up with the curriculum changes mandated by the states. As a result, the perception of parents is that they need to invest in their children's supplemental education in order to help them succeed in school.

Seller Financing
- Seller financing is common but with the more recent loosening of the lending practices by the banks outside financing is also becoming more prevalent.

Chiropractic Practices

SIC 8041-01	NAICS 621310	Number of Businesses/Units 68,625

Rules of Thumb
➢ 55–60% of annual sales includes inventory

➢ 1–2.5 x SDE includes inventory

➢ 1.5–2 x EBITDA

Pricing Tips

- Most chiropractic practices are small. Most of the practices have only one or two doctors. The average partnership has two doctors, and the typical chiropractic medical group has three chiropractors. Services rendered can vary widely, and often include product sales. Payments may be on a per-visit or per-month basis. Most chiropractic practice sales do not include the real estate, accounts receivable, debt, or cash. Most are asset rather than entity sales, so that the buyer does not take on the historic malpractice liability of the entity.

- The value of chiropractic practices is generally at an all-time low. Decisions regarding what, where, when, and how to practice are influenced by numerous factors, including personal preferences, market forces, state and federal policies and programs, and institutions that constitute the health care system. Increasing retirement, plus the trend toward shorter working hours, increases the supply of practices for sale, and decreases the available FTE workforce available as buyers. The increasing rate of boomer retirement contributes to a reduction of value of practices for sale. Of particular concern when determining value of a chiropractic practice accepting Medicare payments is ensuring not only that the purchase price is Fair Market Value but also that the valuation method does not take into account the volume or value of referrals that the selling chiropractor has made or may make to the purchaser, such that the purchase price could be challenged as a kickback or inducement. The OIG has provided guidance on the question of how to value a practice. The ailing economy is leading many Americans to skip doctor visits and put off X-rays. The results of the Income Approach of valuation identifying "dividends" [(SDE minus market rate compensation of one working owner) x 1.5-1.7 (i.e., 65-75% Cap rate)] is becoming more important. "Percentage of annual gross sales" and "SDE multiplier" as valuation Rules of Thumb are obsolete, if ever valid. Growth rates are available through the Congressional Budget Office reports, rarely above 2% historically. Chiropractic practice is riskier—and demands higher Cap rates—than other professional practices like accounting, law, architecture, and engineering, which are not subject to clinical malpractice risks, or subject to Medicare or insurance companies changing reimbursement limitations or denials. The impact of FTE work schedule and leverage of employed licensed providers is profound. Medicare is continually reducing reimbursement, which impacts other insurances which often base their payment on a percent of Medicare (i.e., 80-120% of Medicare), so dependence on insurance reimbursement is an important consideration in value. In addition, changes to Workers' Compensation laws have further reduced reimbursement and profits during the past decade. Cash practices are usually worth more since there is a higher profit for less work, and often provide a better lifestyle. You may hear from sellers or buyers that chiropractic practices sell—or sold—for a lot more than that, which is true. There was a flurry of sales of practices in the 1990s–2000s wherein the buyers then later failed, and defaulted on their loans, because they paid more than the business income could sustain. My practice-purchase lenders tell me that many banks have quit lending—or now require much bigger down payments—to chiropractors because of that.

- Patient records are not a true asset of the practice since they can't be put on the balance sheet as an asset using the Asset Approach valuation methodology. Patient record valuation is only used to specifically allocate intangibles, assuming they exist at the time of the valuation. The doctor has the physical record but usually cannot legally sell or dispose of it without the patient's consent (per state statutes), only transfer custodianship. So the doctor is basically a custodian of the record rather than an owner of an asset with independent value. When paper charts are involved, I have come

C

to the opinion that the value of the chart is zero because of the attendant custodianship liability costs. With EMR, a digital record may need to be converted from one digital platform to another either by custodianship transfer or technology succession, in which case a printout and re-entry may be required, probably exceeding in labor costs any physical value to the original digital chart.

- The library in a smaller practice—as opposed to a university or a "super group"—is presumed to not include historical or rare publications, be organized with bibliographic cataloging, nor represent a complete or unique collection for the specialty. Materials are presumed to be of mixed currency and technological validity. No value is therefore assigned to the practice library.
- Accounts receivable represent past gross charges for services rendered and as yet uncollected or adjusted-off. These receivables must be discounted to reflect both insurance company reimbursement disallowances, plus the decreasing value over time due to difficulty in collections of past due accounts. In other words, the historic collection ratio of the practice does not yet include the "standing wave" of uncollectible accounts at practice end, or at a particular point in time, as in a valuation at a particular date.
- Congress passed Health System Reform Legislation (H.R. 3590) that makes it against the law for insurance companies to discriminate against doctors of chiropractic and other providers relative to their participation and coverage in health plans. The legislation establishes a National Health Care Workforce Commission to review needs in the healthcare workforce, and specifically includes doctors of chiropractic by defining them as part of the healthcare workforce and including them in the definition of health professionals. A number of states quickly filed lawsuits seeking to block it, the outcome of which will not be known for some time. Even so, as hospitals are taking more control of local markets—and those hospitals often have orthopedists on the board—narrowing networks excluding chiropractors is a problem. The future of chiropractic economics is still unclear.
- Don't try to use boilerplate broker contracts to sell chiropractic practices, as it is easy to violate state or federal regulations; have all the paperwork and terms done by a medical practice transaction specialist attorney.

Benchmark Data

Statistics (Chiropractors)

Number of Establishments	68,625
Average Profit Margin	18.1%
Revenue per Employee	$88,700
Average Number of Employees	2.5
Average Wages per Employee	$29,982

Products and Services Segmentation

General chiropractic care	58.2%
Sports and rehabilitation chiropractic care	9.4%
Family chiropractic care	11.4%
Retail	7.8%
Diagnostics	7.9%
Other patient care	2.2%
Other	3.1%

Major Market Segmentation

Private health insurance	32.4%
Patients paying out-of-pocket	31.4%
Medicare and Medicaid	15.6%
Auto insurance	11.8%
Workers' comp	4.9%
Other	3.9%

Industry Costs

Profit	18.1%
Wages	33.8%
Purchases	11.4%
Depreciation	2.1%
Marketing	1.3%
Rent & Utilities	6.8%
Other	26.5%

- High variability in practice settings, from solo docs with no staff, to highly leveraged multi-specialty institutions.
- There are many subspecialty modalities, often described by chiropractors as 'straights' versus 'mixers', i.e., straights do just spinal manipulation, mixed add other modalities; so benchmarks vary.
- 65%–75% overhead

Components of Chiropractic Practice

Direct patient care	52.9%
Documentation	18.9%
Patient education	15.1%
Business management	13.2%

Reimbursement Categories, Managed Care, and Referral

Private Insurance	21.5%
Private pay/cash	21.2%
Managed care	19.4%
Personal injury	13.6%
Medicare	10.8%
Workers' Comp	07.8%
Pro Bono	03.9%
Medicaid	01.8%

Expenses (% of Annual Sales)

Cost of Goods	05% to 14%
Occupancy Costs	04% to 08%
Payroll/Labor Costs	05% to 15%
Profit (pretax)	25% to 50%

Questions

- State and federal law compliance, mix of patients, and type of services rendered
- If the buyer is not a licensed chiropractor, the buyer should inquire of the state if a non-chiropractor is allowed to own a chiropractic practice or employ a chiropractor in that state.

C

Industry Trend

- Competition continues to increase; consolidation has slowed the growth of business entities; increased demand, lower profitability.
- "Fast Company, Forbes, Career Cast, and other organizations repeatedly name chiropractic as a top job. Aside from the personal satisfaction of helping people, a chiropractic career is in demand; the Bureau of Labor Statistics has reported that the employment of chiropractors is expected to increase faster than the average for all occupations through the year 2022. Because chiropractors emphasize the importance of healthy lifestyles, chiropractic care is appealing to many health-conscious Americans. Projected job growth for the chiropractic profession stems from increasing consumer demand for a more natural approach to health care."

  Source: "Chiropractic profession has the best job security, according to Market Watch, April 3, 2015
- High exit of boomers increases practices for sale. Lousy insurance reimbursement and control of patient referrals under PPACA ACOs is a big concern.
- Ancillary product revenue is increasing trend (nutrition, pillows, ointments, orthotics, exercise, etc.).

Expert Comments

Working one more year will commonly net more income than selling.

Most states limit ownership to chiropractors or physicians. Don't try to use boilerplate broker contracts to sell chiropractic practices, as it is easy to violate state or federal regulations; have all the paperwork and terms done by a medical practice transaction specialist attorney.

It's easier to become a chiropractor than an MD or DO, so competition is often higher, and compensation lower.

Insured practices subject to more risk

Seller Financing

- Outside financing
- Bank financing up to 80% is pretty common.
- 75% SBA guaranteed financing is generally available.
- 2–5 years

Resources

- Medical Group Management Association: http://www.mgma.com
- American Chiropractic Association: http://www.acatoday.org
- National Society of Certified Healthcare Business Consultants: http://www.nschbc.org
- Chiropractic Economics: http://www.chiroeco.com
- National Board of Chiropractic Examiners—an excellent site: http://www.nbce.org
- IBISWorld, January 2017: http://ibisworld.com

Closet Factory	Franchise
Approx. Total Investment	$182,500–$310,000

	NAICS 238390	Number of Businesses/Units 60

Rules of Thumb
➢ 45–50% of annual sales plus inventory

Resources
▪ Closet Factory: http://www.closetfactory.com

Closets by Design	Franchise
Approx. Total Investment	$124,900–$278,400

SIC 1521-20	NAICS 238390	Number of Businesses/Units 52

Rules of Thumb
➢ 45% of annual sales plus inventory

Resources
▪ Closets by Design: http://www.closetsbydesign.com

Clothing Stores—Used		
SIC 5932-05	NAICS 453310	

Rules of Thumb
➢ 20% of annual sales plus inventory unless it is on consignment

Benchmark Data
▪ "The online clothing resale industry is a $34 billion opportunity, created by the quantity of unworn clothing and accessories in American closets and the rate at which people add to their wardrobes every year.
  "More Americans will visit a resale store than an outlet mall this year. Where Are Americans Shopping?
  - ✓ Thrift Store: 16–18%
  - ✓ Consignment Shop: 12–15%
  - ✓ Factory Outlet Mall: 11.4%
  - ✓ Apparel Store: 19.6%
  - ✓ Major Department Store: 21.3%"

Source: https://www.thredup.com/resale

Industry Trend
▪ "This is not your grandma's thrift store anymore. High-quality resale is a multi-billion dollar industry and is among the fastest growing segments in retail. With the emergence of online and mobile players, resale is attracting consumers

C

from all economic levels. And with resale penetration still relatively low, this should lead to outsized growth for many years to come.

"Growth in the resale market is expected to outpace all e-commerce and retail sectors over the next 10 years. Furthermore, consumers who shop off-price, outlets, discounters and department stores are making resale a regular part of their wardrobes. Consider this: by some estimates, over $8 billion of clothing in American closets is unused and ignored. As the success of online resellers continues, a growing portion of this hidden treasure will be unlocked. 68% of resale activity is on mobile."

Source: "ThredUP 2016 retail report, $25 billion Total resale market in 2025" https://www.thredup.com/resale

- "Every week, there is another news item about an online consignment company gaining funding. Last month, online luxury consignment seller The Real Real announced that it had raised another $40 million in its fifth round of funding. Now, the company says an IPO is next on the horizon. But with so many players in the space, how will it hold up?

"Online consignment is estimated to be a $34 billion industry, according to ThredUP, and SnobSwap says it is growing at 10% annually. Venture capital is fueling the sector's growth, and investors poured hundreds of millions of dollars into fashion resale in 2015 alone. Total funding over the past five years has passed the $500 million mark."

Source: "Online Consignment Platforms Bring New Ideas To Old Clothing," by Deborah Weinswig, June 2, 2016, https://www.forbes.com/sites/deborahweinswig/2016/06/02/online-consignment-platforms-bring-new-ideas-to-old-clothing/#79210da36eae

Resources

- The Association of Resale Professionals (NARTS)—a good site: http://www.narts.org
- Thred Up: https://www.thredup.com/resale

Cocktail Lounges

SIC 5813-03	NAICS 722410	

Rules of Thumb

➢ 40% of annual sales plus inventory

➢ $ for $ of gross sales if property is incorporated.; 40% annual sales for business only plus inventory

➢ 3–4 x monthly sales; add license (where applicable) and plus inventory

➢ 1.5–2 x SDE; add fixtures, equipment and inventory

Benchmark Data

- Sales price 2½ to 3 times the annual liquor sales. Rent should never exceed 6 percent of the gross sales.
- "When buying liquor, only purchase what you can sell. Ignoring this simple rule has put many bars out of business...The only way to maintain a profitable operation is to establish a firm system of liquor control, and usage, that lets you know, to the penny, exactly how much each drink costs, and how much liquor is poured...Each dollar tied up in inventory is a dollar not working for you. And cash flow is the name of the game. So keep your inventory lean.... If you sell one-ounce drinks for $2 each, a quart bottle can generate 32 drinks,

and $64 in revenues. If the quart bottle costs you $12, your gross profit will be $52. Subtract about $15 to cover labor and overhead, and you should clear $37.... However, if your bartender 'free pours' liquor, and his shots average 1 1/2 ounces, the number of drinks you get from a quart will be cut from 32 to 21. This will cut your revenue from $64 to $42. And your gross profit will fall from $52 to $30. And, if your bartender also gives away 4 free drinks out of the same bottle, your gross profit will drop to $22, minus your $15 in labor and overhead, which will leave you with just $7. That's why your liquor should be guarded like cash."

Source: "Eleven Tips to Owning a Profitable Bar," Specialty Group, Pittsburgh, PA

Expenses (% of Annual Sales)

Cost of Goods—Food 30%–40%
Cost of Goods—Beverages 18%–22%
Occupancy 08%
Payroll/Labor 25%
Profit (pretax) 10%

Industry Trend
- Demand for this type of business seems to be declining.

Coffee Shops		
SIC 5812-28	NAICS 722515	Number of Businesses/Units 79,398

Rules of Thumb
➢ 3.5–4 x monthly sales plus inventory

➢ 35–40% of annual sales plus inventory

➢ 2–2.2 x SDE plus inventory

Pricing Tips
- Trend of sales; owner's compensation including benefits, net profit, lease terms

Benchmark Data

Statistics (Coffee and Snack Shops)

Number of Establishments 79,398
Average Profit Margin 7.0%
Revenue per Employee $58,200
Average Number of Employees 9.1
Average Wages per Employee $15,113

Products and Services Segmentation

Coffee beverages 51.0%
Food 36.0%
Other beverages 9.0%
Other 4.0%

C

Industry Costs

Profit	7.0%
Wages	25.8%
Purchases	38.5%
Depreciation	3.6%
Marketing	3.5%
Rent & Utilities	11.1%
Other	10.5%

Market Share

Starbucks Corporation	43.3%
Dunkin' Brands Inc.	22.1%

- "Whether you're buying or selling, your rent shouldn't be more than 10% to 15% of your monthly gross sales. If it is, it has to be renegotiated or you'll be working to pay the landlord."

  Source: http://www.bizben.com/blog/posts/coffee-shop-tips-christina-lazuric-110209.php

Expenses (% of Annual Sales)

Cost of Goods	28% to 32%
Occupancy Costs	08% to 12%
Payroll/Labor Costs	25%
Profit (pretax)	16% to 20%

Questions

- Why are you selling? What problems have you had with employees, landlord, vendors, municipal officials, etc.? Do company records show all income? (unlikely).

Industry Trend

- "5 Coffee Industry Trends You Can't Miss in 2017:
  - ✓ New generation, new measure of value
  - ✓ Ready-to-drink coffee takes off
  - ✓ Morning coffee on tap
  - ✓ Out with iced coffee, in with cold brew
  - ✓ A shift toward specialty"

  Source: "5 Coffee Industry Trends You Can't Miss in 2017," by Tyler Hubbell, December 29, 2016
  https://nationalcoffeeblog.org/2016/12/29/5-coffee-industry-trends-you-cant-miss-in-2017/

- "While 82 percent of coffee drinkers nationwide report having at least one cup a day, according to Zagat's Third Annual Coffee Drinking Survey, coffee culture and drinking protocol have changed. Some consumers are seeking out boutique coffee shops with painstaking preparation methods, while others are focused on expanding their coffee experiences—trying new brewing or dispensing methods."

  Source: "Category Spotlight: The New Coffee Culture," by Nicole Potenza Denis, January 11, 2016,
  https://www.specialtyfood.com/news/article/category-spotlight-new-coffee-culture/

Expert Comments

Ease of entry; unsophisticated owner/operators; personal use of products

Resources

- IBISWorld, February 2017: http://ibisworld.com
- BizBen:
  http://www.bizben.com/blog/posts/coffee-shop-tips-christina-lazuric-110209.php

Coffee Shops (Specialty)		
SIC 5812-28	NAICS 722515	

Rules of Thumb

➤ 3 x EBIT

➤ 2.5 x EBITDA

➤ 40% of annual sales includes inventory

➤ 2.2 x SDE includes inventory

Pricing Tips

- The value of a coffee house is repeat business from a loyal customer base. Ensure that all vendor contracts will convey or transfer.
- Recognize that profitability is key to determining overall value of the operation. A well-run, mature coffee house can net to the owner in excess of 20 percent of gross revenue.

Benchmark Data

Expenses (% of Annual Sales)

Cost of Goods	28%
Occupancy Costs	10%
Payroll/Labor Costs	25%
Profit (pretax)	20%

Questions

- What is your average ticket sale? What marketing efforts are currently in place? Have you measured customer loyalty? Are your employees cross trained?

Industry Trend

- "More and more consumers are learning about coffee, and getting into specialty coffee. The industry keeps growing and growing."

  Source: "Where is the coffee industry going next? Insights from WOC 2017," June 19, 2017, https://www.perfectdailygrind.com/2017/06/coffee-industry-going-next-insights-woc-2017/

Expert Comments

While it is relatively easy to start a coffee house business, especially in relation to other types of food establishments, it can be a higher risk type of business due to the perceived simplicity of the business. Historically, specialty coffee establishments have participated in a high-growth industry segment and consequently have greater than average interest from potential buyers who are looking for a business.

C

Seller Financing

- 3 years

Resources

- National Coffee Association of USA: http://www.ncausa.org
- Specialty Coffee Association of America: http://www.sca.coffee

Coin Laundries		
SIC 7215-01	NAICS 812310	Number of Businesses/Units 22,507

Rules of Thumb

➤ 100%–125% of annual sales plus inventory

➤ 1–1½ x annual sales plus inventory

➤ 3–5 x SDE includes inventory (higher multiple for newer equipment and long lease)

➤ 4–5 x SDE plus inventory-assumes long-term lease (10+ years) and newer equipment (3-5 years old).

➤ 3–6 x EBIT

➤ 3–6 x EBITDA

Pricing Tips

- "You must buy value; which means you need to understand exactly what you are buying, being very careful not to pay too much. One of several major keys to price is gross sales. In fact, it is fair to say that a 10% misrepresentation as to gross sales can impact the overall value of a coin-laundry business by some 20%, and maybe considerably more; therefore, you must ask the right questions, and be able to assess the accuracy of the answers."

  Source: http://laundromatadvisor.com/

- "The average-size laundromat will cost you in the neighborhood of $200,000 to $500,000-whether you choose to purchase an existing laundry or build one in a retail space."

  Source: http://www.entrepreneur.com/article/190424

- "A laundry is not a re-locatable asset. These factors require a strong lease. When possible, it is always better to purchase the property. That said it is obvious that the length, quality and terms of the lease must be looked at carefully before entering into any laundry purchase. It is often necessary to re-negotiate the lease during a transaction. In many cases there are some issues that need to be modified, extensions required and rental rates or terms adjusted. It is recommended that you have an Industry Expert look at the lease; as well as your attorney.

  "The equipment, condition and age all have considerable value to the purchase decision; but not as much as you might think. In a new laundry, the cost of equipment is typically only about 55% of the total price, less in many cases. The cost of providing the services (sewer, water, mechanical work, fees, plans, permits and construction) accounts for the rest. In a laundry with equipment that is 7 years or older, you should anticipate making equipment changes as a part of your acquisition planning."

  Source: http://www.bizben.com/blog/posts/buying-a-coin-laundry-051209.php

- "One ill-advised means of independent verification, which is commonly promoted by coin-laundry touts (both on-line and as half-learned authors of books on the subject), is the comparison of claimed revenue to water usage. "I consider it ill-advised for several reasons. Firstly, it is a relatively inexpensive method by which a seller can perpetrate a fraud by simply running-off water. Secondly, issues such as leaking water and mineral deposits within water meter mechanisms (water meter maintenance tends to be neglected by water providers) can significantly affect the accuracy of an analysis. Thirdly, many commercial washers now offer surreptitious programing which can significantly impact water usage (e.g., Wascomat 'Generation 6' washer can be adjusted to utilize 1.2 to 1.9 gallons of water per lb. of laundry - a maximum differential of 58.3%!)."

  Source: An excellent article by Gary Ruff, an industry consultant who is also an attorney. Gary Ruff can be reached via his informative Web site: www.laundromatadvisor.com or at (212) 696-8502 or (631) 389-280, He maintains two offices; if you need advice or legal services in the coin laundry business-he knows his stuff.

- "Coin laundries normally sell for a multiple of their net earnings. The multiple may vary between three and five times the net cash flow, depending on several valuation factors. The following primary factors establish market value:
  - ✓ The net earnings before debt service, after adjustments for depreciation and any other nonstandard items including owner salary or payroll costs in services
  - ✓ The terms and conditions of the real estate interest (lease), particularly length, frequency and amount of increases; expense provisions; and overall ratio of rent to gross income
  - ✓ The age, condition, and utilization of the equipment, and leasehold improvements; the physical attributes of the real property in which the coin laundry is located, particularly entrances/exits, street visibility and parking
  - ✓ Existing conditions, including vend price structure in the local marketplace
  - ✓ The demographic profile in the general area or region
  - ✓ Replacement cost and land usage issues
- "This resale market standard assumes an owner/operator scenario, with no allocation for outside management fees. Marketing time for store sales averages 60 to 90 days, depending on price, financing terms and the quality and quantity of stores available at the time of sale. Coin laundry listings are generally offered by business brokers who charge a sales commission of 8 percent to 10 percent. Many coin laundry distributors also act as brokers. The accepted standard of useful life for commercial coin laundry equipment is as follows:

  Topload Washers (12 lbs. to 14 lbs.)..5–8 years
  Frontload Washers (18 lbs. to 50 lbs)..10–15 years
  Dryers (30 lbs. to 60 lbs.)..15–20 years
  Heating Systems...10–15 years
  Coin Changers.. 10–15 years"

  Source: Laundry Industry Overview, Coin Laundry Association, www.coinlaundry.org, an excellent and informative site.

- Location and demographics. It's important to study the surrounding area for city planned changes or housing changes that may affect business performance.
- Larger multiplier number used for newer equipment & long-term lease

C

Benchmark Data

Statistics (Laundromats)

Number of Establishments	22,507
Average Profit Margin	8.8%
Revenue per Employee	$96,500
Average Number of Employees	2.3
Average Wages per Employee	$17,221

Products and Services Segmentation

Washer services	53.0%
Dryer services	34.0%
Other	6.8%
Self-service dry cleaning	4.8%
Commercial laundry services	1.4%

Major Market Segmentation

Renters using laundromats	38.6%
Renters using on-site laundry facilities	22.4%
Commercial, industrial, service industries and routes	16.9%
Colleges and universities	13.4%
Homeowners	8.7%

Industry Costs

Profit	8.8%
Wages	17.9%
Purchases	20.4%
Depreciation	10.2%
Marketing	0.9%
Rent & Utilities	21.7%
Other	20.1%

Market Share

CSC ServiceWorks	20.7%

Enterprises by Employment Size

Number of Employees	Share
0-4	89.7%
10-19	1.9%
20-99	0.6%
100+	0.01%

- "Self Service Laundry Basic Info:
    - ✓ The cost of buying an existing vended-laundry ranges from less than $100,000 to over $1 million, depending on size, age, and net income.
    - ✓ Laundries typically occupy between 1,500 and 4,000 square feet of retail space, however, some go up to 6,000 square feet, depending on market size, the density of the trade area, and the quality and number of competitors.
    - ✓ Most laundries occupy retail space that is rented on a long-term lease (10-25 years). Negotiating a satisfactory lease is the single most important part of developing a new laundry, or purchasing an existing one.

PWS is an expert in this area and handles lease negotiations for all new stores we develop."

Source: http://www.pwslaundrywest.com/p-12525-industry-overview.html

- A self service laundry that is well laid out and with equipment to handle most garments should create a gross revenue of $70 per square foot per year.
- "The amount of money you can make from a laundry varies tremendously. According to the Coin Laundry Association's Brian Wallace, the annual gross income from one store can range from $30,000 to $1 million. The expenses incurred while running a store range between 65 and 115 percent of the gross income. That means that for a store grossing $30,000 per year, at best it nets $10,500 and at worst it loses $4,500. For a store grossing $1 million per year, the profit could be as high as $350,000, or there could be a loss of up to $150,000, depending on expenses. Wallace says these profit margins have less to do with the size of the store than with its owner. An owner who runs his or her store well-who keeps it clean, repairs its equipment quickly, uses energy-efficient systems and offers good customer service-will see profit margins of about 35 percent."

Source: www.entrepreneur.com

- Varies a lot depending if it's attended or unattended and what type of location it's in.
- Cleanliness tops all; working equipment; neighborhood business (quarter to half mile needs 15,000–20,000 population, predominance of renters and incomes from $15,000-$49,000 per annum.)

Expenses (% of Annual Sales)

Cost of Goods	0%
Occupancy Costs	14% to 25%
Payroll/Labor Costs	09% to 12%
Profit (pretax)	25% to 35%

Questions

- Books and records: are they available?
- What is the percentage of utility cost to your represented income?
- Occupational license? Water and sewer impact (connection) fees? Organizational skills?
- Area crime rate. Review utility bills. New development in trade area. New competition in trade area.
- I would request copies of utility bills for at least 12 months. Request model numbers and age of washers and dryers, and ask for maintenance records. Especially request information on water heating systems, as this is probably the one single point of failure that can easily be the most costly repair item.

Industry Trend

- The trend for housing is smaller as opposed to what we had experienced in the past. More and more families will enjoy the convenience of self-service laundries.
- I see these businesses becoming more in demand, as many people are retiring but still want something to do that makes a good income without a full-time work load.
- As more and more people become renters, the industry should prosper.

C

- The trend will continue to pace or follow history. The need or demand for the industry is not changing, so I would conclude a bright future.
- Large facilities will drive out smaller facilities. Successful operations will provide a wide range of services and customer assistance including pickup and delivery.

Expert Comments

The establishment of a new facility to compete with an existing store is very expensive. An existing store is established and for the most part a better investment than building a new competing facility.

Review the utility bills and match those up to the monthly sales. Review the lease rate and terms, especially future increases upcoming.

Obtaining permits to build can be quite challenging

Resources

- Coin-Op Magazine: http://www.americancoinop.com
- Laundry and Cleaning News International: http://www.laundryandcleaningnews.com/
- American Laundry News: http://www.americanlaundrynews.com
- Coin Laundry Association: http://www.coinlaundry.org
- IBISWorld, April 2017: http://ibisworld.com
- PWS Laundry West: http://www.pwslaundrywest.com/p-12525-industry-overview.html
- Entrepreneur: http://www.entrepreneur.com
- Drycleaning & Laundry Institute International: http://www.dlionline.org

Cold Stone Creamery	Franchise
Approx. Total Investment	$261,125–$404,525
Estimated Annual Sales/Unit	$421,400
SIC 2024-98 NAICS 722515	Number of Businesses/Units 925

Rules of Thumb

➢ 30% of annual sales plus inventory

➢ 1.5–2 x SDE plus inventory

Benchmark Data

- Food cost is low at 20%, rent is typically above 10% since it is location dependent.
- Leases must be at least 15 years to provide value and time for ROI long term.

Expenses (% of Annual Sales)

Cost of Goods	20%
Occupancy Costs	12%
Payroll/Labor Costs	22%
Profit (pretax)	22%

Questions

- Will you finance, how is the store managed, do you have a production staff, separate from your counter staff? Are there any wholesale or outside accounts?

Expert Comments

Product is unique; large machinery investment is required, thus difficult to duplicate without industry knowledge and sizeable investment ($250,000) in equipment.

Resources

- Kahala Management: http://www.kahalamgmt.com

Collectibles Stores		
SIC 5947-05	NAICS 453220	

Rules of Thumb

➢ 20% of annual sales plus inventory

Benchmark Data

- For Benchmark Information see Retail Stores—Small Specialty

Industry Trend

- The growth of websites competing with retail shops has forced many retail shop owners to close their doors and offer their inventory just on the Web.
- "Although hard sales data have been difficult to come by, the general consensus in the industry is that after a down period, sales of collectibles are slowly on the upswing."
  Source: "Crazy About Collectibles" by Randall G. Mielke, www.giftshopmag.com

Collection Agencies		
SIC 7322-01	NAICS 561440	Number of Businesses/Units 8,957

Rules of Thumb

➢ 2.5 x SDE plus Inventory

➢ 100% of annual revenues includes inventory

➢ Revenue of $1MM+: 75%–125% of annual revenues

➢ 4–6 x EBIDTA

Pricing Tips

- Consumer debt is a higher risk exposure than business debt collections in terms of regulatory oversight.
- Collection agencies are typically priced on a recast EBITDA income stream which includes earnings before interest, taxes, depreciation, and amortization and should add shareholders' salaries, perks and non-recurring expenses and

C

then subtract a replacement salary for the shareholders. The valuation multiple typically ranges between 4 and 6 times EBITDA. The primary determinant of the multiple is the size of the company.

Benchmark Data

Statistics (Debt Collection Agencies)

Number of Establishments	8,957
Average Profit Margin	10.2%
Revenue per Employee	$91,200
Average Number of Employees	13.7
Average Wages per Employee	$39,619

Products and Services Segmentation

Contingent-fee servicing	54.5%
Portfolio acquisition	32.0%
Fixed-fee servicing	5.9%
Other	4.0%
Collateral recovery and repossession services	3.6%

Major Market Segmentation

Financial services	34.5%
Telecommunications	22.1%
Other	14.0%
Healthcare	10.6%
Retail and commercial	10.2%
Government	8.6%

Industry Costs

Profit	10.2%
Wages	43.5%
Purchases	4.4%
Depreciation	0.9%
Marketing	1.4%
Rent & Utilities	7.5%
Other	32.1%

Market Share

Expert Global Solutions	12.6%
Portfolio Recovery Associates Inc.	5.5%
Encore Capital Group	5.1%

Expenses (% of Annual Sales)

Cost of Goods	10%
Occupancy Costs	05% to 10%
Payroll/Labor Costs	40% to 50%
Profit (pretax)	15% to 20%

Questions
- Do you have any long-term contracts with your clients or can they cancel at any time?

- Do you have any open lawsuits?
- Have you had any CFPB complaints filed against you? How were they resolved?
- Do you use an Auto Dialer?
- Tenure of existing clients, percent of revenues from clients, any change in commission rates and placement volumes, tenure of the collection staff and management, pipeline of business opportunities.

Industry Trend

- Continued consolidation as a result of the heavy regulatory environment and retirement of the baby boom generation.

Expert Comments

For a buyer this is a litigious industry with many government agencies overseeing the consumer collection process. Unfortunately, even with great care and diligence, it is easy to make a minor error that results in a fine or lawsuit.

Sustainability of profits is important.

Collection agencies typically have 30-day contracts with clients, whereby a client can pull back accounts in 30 days if performance is not meeting expectations.

Seller Financing

- Seller financing is not very common in this industry.

Resources

- Collection Advisor: http://www.collectionadvisor.com
- International Association of Commercial Collectors: http://www.commercialcollector.com
- IBISWorld, December 2016: http://ibisworld.com
- insideARM: http://www.insidearm.com/
- ACA International: http://www.acainternational.org/default

Comic Book Stores		
SIC 5942-05	NAICS 451211	

Rules of Thumb

➢ 12–15% of annual sales plus inventory

Benchmark Data

- It's difficult to say what average sales are because very few stock only comics. We would guess that the average store turns $150,000 to $200,000 in comics, but again, that is not likely to be all that any of them sell.

Industry Trend

- "According to leading comic-book sales analyst John Jackson Miller, who runs ComiChron, a blog on comic sales, unit sales of the top 300 comics were down for 15 years — some years significantly — after a high in 1997. Dovetailing unsurprisingly with the rise in movies, though, comic books have seen an increase in sales during each of the past five years. As a fitting cap, recently released sales numbers show that June was the industry's best-selling month since December 1997.

"Much of the increase comes from the releases of the first issues of two major comics — Marvel's 'Civil War II No. 1' and DC's 'Batman No. 1.' Retailers bought 381,737 copies of the former and 280,360 copies of the latter, IGN reported. These high-profile releases certainly boosted sales numbers, but there are likely many factors in play in the increased popularity in comics. For one, comic books are more accessible than ever before, partially because of the Internet. Comics, previously purchased at newsstands or in dedicated comic-book stores, can easily be bought and, in some cases, even read digitally — a trend that digital giants have noticed. In 2014, Amazon bought ComiXology, the largest digital comics platform, which sold more than 4 billion pages of comics in 2013, Wired reported. In fact, from 2012 to 2013, digital comic sales rose from $70 million to $90 million, according to the New York Times.

"Meanwhile, the number of brick-and-mortar comic-book shops has also risen in recent years, their numbers growing by 4 percent in 2013, according to Publishers Weekly. . . comic-book fans can breathe a bit more easily knowing the trend of rising sales from the past five years appears to be continuing."

Source: "The resurgence of comic books: The industry has its best-selling month in nearly two decades" by Travis M. Andrews, July 12, 2016, https://www.washingtonpost.com/news/morning-mix/wp/2016/07/12/the-resurgence-of-comic-books-the-industry-has-its-best-selling-month-in-nearly-two-decades/?utm_term=.2eb3b1fd16ce

Computer Consulting

SIC 7379-05	NAICS 541512	Number of Businesses/Units 478,018

Rules of Thumb

➢ 50–65% of annual sales plus inventory

Pricing Tips

- Note: Many consulting businesses are one-man operations or are headed by someone who has the contacts and may basically be "the business." This person may be the goodwill, and without his or her presence the business may not be worth much. If this person stays while the business is slowly being transferred and an earnout is in place, the value may still be there.

Benchmark Data

Statistics (IT Consulting)

Number of Establishments	478,018
Average Profit Margin	7.3%
Revenue per Employee	$195,100
Average Number of Employees	4.6
Average Wages per Employee	$91,595

Products and Services Segmentation

Custom application design, development and integration 25.1%
IT infrastructure and network design services 19.0%
Other services.. 22.8%
Computer systems design, development, and integration................................. 12.4%
IT technical support services 10.7%
IT technical consulting services 10.0%

Major Market Segmentation

Financial services 19.6%
Public Sector and non-profit organizations 18.8%
Manufacturing and retail 17.3%
Communications and technical.. 11.2%
Healthcare 10.9%
Other sectors 22.2%

Industry Costs

Profit 7.3%
Wages.. 46.9%
Purchases.. 13.4%
Depreciation.. 0.6%
Marketing 2.2%
Rent & Utilities 4.5%
Other.. 25.1%

Market Share

International Business Machines Corporation 2.6%
Accenture PLC... 3.5%

- "Of those that run multi-person businesses, most have fewer than three owners. Corporations have two to three non-owner employees. Almost 90% of firms earned $500,000 or less, while 4.4% earned a million or more. 75% of ICCA Consultants have over 15 years of experience in their field."

Source: Independent Computer Consultants Association, (ICCA), www.icca.org

Industry Trend

- "The number of IT jobs grew 0.2 percent sequentially last month to 5,074,900, according to TechServe Alliance, the national trade association of the IT & Engineering Staffing and Solutions industry. On a year-over-year basis, IT employment grew by 3.8% since February 2015 adding 186,500 IT workers. "Engineering employment was essentially flat up only 0.02 percent sequentially to 2,530,500. On a year-over-year basis, engineering employment grew by an anemic 0.6% since February 2015 adding 15,700 engineering workers-continuing to underperform the overall workforce."

Source: http://tsa.prod2.classfive.com//files/Index%20Release%20March.%202016MBR.pdf

Resources

- TechServe Alliance: http://www.techservealliance.org/
- IBISWorld, August 2017: http://ibisworld.com

C

Computer Programming Services

SIC 7371-02	NAICS 541511	

Pricing Tips

- Traditional methods use some multiple of revenues for valuation; however, this is fraught with problems. Growth in revenues is a key aspect, prized in establishing higher value. Earnings are not unimportant, although high-growth companies may be more attractive even without earnings. Look for stability or managed growth in operations.
- Because software companies must be nimble to respond to market actions, and are vulnerable to loss of key persons, control premiums (and lack of control discounts) and discounts for illiquidity are typically enhanced in this industry.

Questions

- 1) Productivity of current workforce 2) Projects ongoing and anticipated 3) Strategic advantages of this business over the competition.

Industry Trend

- Dow—-foreign competition at lower hourly rates is moving programming services jobs overseas.

Computer Services

SIC 7378-01	NAICS 811212	Number of Businesses/Units 56,967

Rules of Thumb

➢ 55% of annual sales, plus fixtures, equipment and inventory

Benchmark Data

Statistics (Electronic & Computer Repair Services)

Number of Establishments	56,967
Average Profit Margin	7.6%
Revenue per Employee	$129,800
Average Number of Employees	2.4
Average Wages per Employee	$41,241

Products and Services Segmentation

Other electronic equipment (including medical equipment) repair	42.3%
Computer and office machine repairs	29.3%
Communications equipment repairs	18.6%
Consumer electronics (including radio, TV and VCR) repairs	9.8%

Major Market Segmentation

Small and medium businesses	48.9%
Large companies	23.0%
Households	12.1%
Federal government	6.4%
Nonprofit organizations	4.8%
State and local governments	4.8%

Industry Costs

Profit	7.6%
Wages	31.7%
Purchases	16.5%
Depreciation	1.4%
Utilities	1.5%
Rent	5.7%
Other	35.6%

Resources

- IBISWorld, June 2017: http://ibisworld.com

Computer Stores

SIC 5734-07	NAICS 443120	Number of Businesses/Units 18,095

Rules of Thumb

➢ 30% of annual sales plus inventory

Benchmark Data

Statistics (Computer Stores)

Number of Establishments	18,095
Average Profit Margin	4.5%
Revenue per Employee	$297,900
Average Number of Employees	5.5
Average Wages per Employee	$42,855

Products and Services Segmentation

Computers	44.0%
Printers and Peripherals	32.5%
Software	23.5%

Major Market Segmentation

Consumers Aged 65 and Older	34.1%
Consumers Under the Age of 45	32.2%
Consumers Aged 45-64	26.9%
Businesses	4.7%
Other	1.6%
Government	0.5%

Industry Costs

Profit	4.5%
Wages	14.5%
Purchases	66.5%
Depreciation	0.1%
Marketing	2.1%
Rent & Utilities	4.0%
Other	8.3%

Resources

- IBISWorld, June 2017: http://ibisworld.com

C

Computer Systems Design

SIC 7373-98	NAICS 541512	

Rules of Thumb

➢ 50% of annual sales plus inventory

➢ 2–4 x SDE plus inventory

➢ 3–6 x EBIT

➢ 3–7 x EBITDA

Pricing Tips

- Very work-force intensive. Make sure the business can prosper without the owner. Contracts are important.
- System design firms are often classified as 'programming' firms. More work is being done by temporary employment firms, renting IT professional staff.
- Highly variable valuations. Biggest component of valuation is the management structure. Midmarket companies with excellent management structure can get very good multiples but a small operation which is highly owner driven may get very little. Having contracts with large customers can improve valuation significantly.

Benchmark Data

- $100,000 or more in revenues per technician and $200,000 or more per engineer
- Revenue and profit growth is more important than stability of earnings. Sales per employee is a key metric.

Expenses (% of Annual Sales)

Cost of Goods	20%
Occupancy Costs	05%
Payroll/Labor Costs	50% to 55%
Profit (pretax)	20%

Questions

- Reasons for the exit. Strategic growth plans. Customer retention plans. Employee specific compensation issues.
- Who is (are) the key employee(s) who drives the sales? Are there any critical technical roles?

Industry Trend

- Continuing growth as technology and tools become indispensable for businesses and individuals.

Expert Comments

Talented people can easily leave and start their own gig. Contracts with a very wide customer base can be very important. Corporate clients are more valuable than consumer clients.

Design firms are being acquired by the large consulting houses. May be attractive for strategic reasons, such as industry niches and/or package familiarity.

Highly knowledge driven industry. Risk can be very high depending on the importance of the role played by the current owner. If the owner's role is non-critical, then the business can be very lucrative.

Concrete Bulk Plants (Ready-Mix)

SIC 5032-30	NAICS 32732	Number of Businesses/Units 5,510

Rules of Thumb

➤ 30–35% of SDE plus fixtures, equipment and inventory

Benchmark Data

Statistics (Ready-Mix Concrete Manufacturing)

Number of Establishments.. 5,510
Average Profit Margin 6.8%
Revenue per Employee $407,900
Average Number of Employees 13.9
Average Wages per Employee $55,302

Major Market Segmentation

Public Works and Infrastructure Construction.................................... 39.0%
Residential Construction... 22.0%
Street and Highway Construction and Paving 22.0%
Commercial and Industrial Construction 17.0%

Industry Costs

Profit 6.8%
Wages.. 13.6%
Purchases... 50.1%
Depreciation.. 3.0%
Marketing 0.1%
Rent & Utilities 2.7%
Other... 23.7%

Market Share

Cemex SAB de CV 5.1%

Resources

- IBISWorld, July 2017: http://ibisworld.com

Consignment Shops

SIC 5932-04	NAICS 453310	

Rules of Thumb

➤ 15–20% of annual sales

➤ Note: Consignment shops are just that. They very seldom purchase inventory; rather, they place it on the sales floor and have agreements with the owner regarding price, and generally a schedule in which the price is reduced every month or so for a set period of time. After this period, the goods are usually returned to the owner. The shop works on essentially a commission or fee only if the goods sell.

C

Benchmark Data
- For additional Benchmark Data see Used Goods
- "What sells: clothing, bookcases, cookbooks. costume jewelry, kitchen gadgets, golf clubs. What doesn't sell: collectible dolls, fur coats, large paintings, vintage dinnerware, needlepoint art."

Source: The Association of Resale Professionals, NARTS

Industry Trend
- "Resale or retail? Can you tell the difference? Probably not! Today's resale shops look the same as mainstream retailers... except for one big difference - they sell high quality goods at lower prices! The resale industry offers 'Quality at a Savings'!

"While many businesses close their doors every day, resale remains healthy and continues to be one of the fastest growing segments of retail. With new stores entering the industry and current establishments opening additional locations, the industry has experienced a growth-in number of stores-of approximately 7% a year for the past two years. This percentage reflects the estimated number of new stores opening each year, minus the businesses that close. NARTS is proud to say that future owners who look to the Association for education prior to opening, then continue their education through NARTS membership, are very successful. Many resale shops don't survive that critical first year because the owners did not do their 'homework' and had no idea where to begin or what expect. There are currently more than 25,000 resale, consignment and Not For Profit resale shops in the United States.

"Resale is a multi-billion dollar a year industry. First Research estimates the resale industry in the U.S. to have annual revenues of approximately $17 billion including revenue from antique stores which are 13% of their statistics. Goodwill Industries alone generated $5.37 billion in retail sales from more than 2,000 Not For Profit resale stores and online sales in 2014. Longtime NARTS member, Crossroads Trading Co., based in Berkeley, CA, rang up over $20 million in sales 2012. They have 32 locations, 375 employees and plans to add additional locations. Add to this the many thousands of single location shops, hundreds of multi-location chains, franchises and Not For Profit stores and you begin to realize the vast scope of this growing industry."

Source: 2017 NARTS: The Association of Resale Professionals

Resources
- The Association of Resale Professionals: http://www.narts.org

Construction—Buildings		
	NAICS 236	

Rules of Thumb
➢ 20–30% of annual sales plus inventory

➢ 1–2 x SDE plus inventory

➢ 1–3 x EBITDA

Pricing Tips
- With very small companies with 1 or 2 employees the norm lately has been to

look at FMV of assets as bottom line for pricing purposes.

- Value in construction trades business is dependent on many factors not normally associated with small business valuation.

Benchmark Data

Statistics (Home Builders)

Number of Establishments	366,782
Average Profit Margin	6.3%
Revenue per Employee	$139,500
Average Number of Employees	1.8
Average Wages per Employee	$27,035

Products and Services Segmentation

Vinyl siding exterior homes	28.1%
Brick exterior homes	23.9%
Stucco exterior homes	25.3%
Other exterior homes	16.7%
Wood exterior homes	5.5%
Aluminum siding exterior homes	0.5%

Major Market Segmentation

Private-sector clients—property developers	81.0%
Private-sector clients—households	16.7%
State or locally funded projects	1.2%
Federally funded projects	1.1%

Industry Costs

Profit	6.3%
Wages	19.5%
Purchases	72.1%
Depreciation	0.5%
Marketing	0.4%
Rent & Utilities	1.1%
Other	0.1%

Market Share

NVR, Inc.	7.5%

- In the final analysis, a construction business should always be worth the FMV of its hard assets.

Expenses (% of Annual Sales)

Cost of Goods	20% to 30%
Occupancy Costs	05% to 10%
Payroll/Labor Costs	25%
Profit (pretax)	25% to 45%

Questions

- What would happen to this company if we plucked you out of here today for 1-3 months? Would the business operate effectively?

C

Industry Trend

- "Several factors, including the pace of economic recovery, export activity, cost of financing and technological advances will influence the Industrial Building Construction industry's performance over the next five years. Though the Federal Reserve is expected to continue gradually tightening monetary policy, interest rates are expected to remain relatively low, encouraging investments in new industrial structures. However, with the US dollar expected to continue appreciating amid global economic uncertainty, demand for the industry's services is expected to moderate as manufactures in key export markets reduce production. Consequently, industry revenue growth is expected to slow. Over the five years to 2022, IBISWorld estimates industry revenue will grow an annualized 4.2% to $50.5 billion, including a projected 3.7% increase in 2018 alone."

Source: IBISWorld Industry Outlook

Expert Comments

Make sure you understand the sales and marketing side of the business and how feasible it will be to remove the owner from the business without a serious decline in new and referral business.

Resources

- IBISWorld, February 2017: http://ibisworld.com

Construction—Excavation (Site Preparation)	
NAICS 238910	Number of Businesses/Units 46,536

Rules of Thumb

- ➤ 25% of annual sales plus inventory
- ➤ 2.2 x SDE plus inventory
- ➤ 1.8 x EBIT
- ➤ 2 x EBITDA

Pricing Tips

- Adjust for age/condition of equipment.

Benchmark Data

Statistics (Excavation Contractors)

Number of Establishments	46,536
Average Profit Margin	6.5%
Revenue per Employee	$189,000
Average Number of Employees	6.2
Average Wages per Employee	$49,399

Products and Services Segmentation

Earthmoving, excavation work, land clearing (Non-Residential Building)	41.0%
Earthmoving, excavation work, land clearing (Residential Building)	32.5%
Foundation Digging	10.6%
Nonbuilding construction excavation	8.7%
Trenching contractor	7.2%

Major Market Segmentation

Nonresidential building market	41.0%
Residential building market	32.5%
Nonbuilding construction market	26.5%

Industry Costs

Profit	6.5%
Wages	26.1%
Purchases	37.5%
Depreciation	3.6%
Marketing	0.2%
Rent & Utilities	6.9%
Other	19.2%

Expenses (% of Annual Sales)

Cost of Goods	25%
Occupancy Costs	10%
Payroll/Labor Costs	40%
Profit (pretax)	25%

Questions

- Customer lists, future contracts, condition of equipment and any lawsuits?

Industry Trend

- The construction industry is tied to the economic recovery.

Resources

- IBISWorld, May 2017: http://ibisworld.com

Construction—In General

Rules of Thumb

➢ 20–30% of annual sales plus inventory

➢ 1.5–2.5 x SDE plus inventory

➢ 2–3.5 x EBIT

➢ 2–4 x EBITDA

➢ Note: Some construction firms own significant equipment and some are run from storefronts, so Rules of Thumb are misleading. The business history is very important, as is the value of signed contracts to be completed, and understanding how a company bills its work in progress. Accounts receivable can average over 45 days, increasing the working capital required and decreasing the business value. Rules of Thumb are not very useful.

Pricing Tips

- Pricing is generally based on assets (fair market value), not including cash, receivables or investments. The best time to sell a construction business is, naturally, when it can command the highest price. Companies are worth more when they have been trading well and increasing profit in recent years, as well as demonstrating the potential for further growth.

C

External factors can also affect the price, such as low interest rates, which mean a buyer has easier access to finance, and the number of rival businesses on the market.

In other cases, you may have your own reasons for selling, such as impending retirement, or the need to free up some cash, or maybe you just don't enjoy turning up to work in the mornings any more.

Whatever has led to your decision to sell, try to avoid a rushed sale. With time on your side, you can market to a wider number of buyers, negotiate with more strength, and arrange your financial affairs in the most tax efficient way.

- Pricing a construction company is tough for several reasons. The involvement of the current owner (seller) is a key issue; if the owner is crucial to the getting of new jobs and maintaining levels of revenue, then this will decrease the price of the business. The buyer would have to discount the business relative to the loss of earning potential. Further, if there is a problem in transferring the existing or establishing a new license, such as occurs when the buyer is not qualified to obtain a license, and the seller must remain in the business in order to continue as usual, this may affect the buyer's ability to afford the business. In addition, there are significant differences in the various types of construction firms or license classifications. Therefore, Pricing Tips here are very general in nature and may not apply to all types of construction companies.

- Rule of thumb on gross revenues is very difficult as the gross profit and net profit range wildly for this industry. Consideration for the following must also be taken: revenue that is recurring by long-term contracts vs. repeat clients that still require quotes vs. amount of business that is quoted fresh to new clients.

Benchmark Data

Statistics (Municipal Building Construction)

Number of Establishments	43,158
Average Profit Margin	3.5%
Revenue per Employee	$1,266,600
Average Number of Employees	3.5
Average Wages per Employee	$60,111

Products and Services Segmentation

General contracting services	52.5%
Construction management services	20.7%
Remodeling contracting services	15.6%
Other construction activities	11.2%

Major Market Segmentation

Education sector	54.0%
Healthcare sector	25.5%
Recreation sector	13.2%
Public safety sector	5.0%
Religion sector	2.3%

Industry Costs

Profit	3.5%
Wages	4.7%
Purchases	54.4%
Depreciation	1.2%
Marketing	0.4%
Rent & Utilities	4.2%
Other	31.6%

- 1. Sales per square foot: $170. 2. $500k revenue per employee
- Specialty contractor has much higher margins than a general contractor
- Many service-related contracting businesses will charge at least 2 times their direct costs as their hourly fee for service.

Expenses (% of Annual Sales)

Cost of Goods	25%
Occupancy Costs	05% to 10%
Payroll/Labor Costs	30% to 40%
Profit (pretax)	18% to 25%

Questions

- Do you engage directly with the clients or customers, or do you have someone (manager, superintendent, etc.) do that for you?
- What is the longest vacation you took from the business and how did the business fare while you were gone?
- What profit margin do you usually see on your typical jobs?
- What is your quick ratio? What is the percent complete of each job? What amount of working capital does the business have in cash? Who are your major clients?
- Why are you getting out? Sources of your business? Is there any repeat business?
- How involved are you in the business? Does the business rely on your presence to keep new jobs coming in? How much work do you currently have on the books? Is this business influenced heavily by season changes?

Industry Trend

- Construction should continue to increase at a moderate rate. Economy is stronger, real estate values are increasing, and confidence is growing. But the days of rapid, "hockey-stick" type growth and the ease of obtaining financing are probably gone. Banks and investors are the wiser for having gone through the meltdown of 2007–2008 and won't likely let that happen again.
- The trend is fascinating because in the near future the US will revamp its infrastructure, including affordable housing. This hasn't been done since the Eisenhower years in the 1950's; it's past overdue and it will bring one of the largest contributions to the GDP. Many established construction companies will be sold by the baby boomers to the millennials. In addition, six of the 10 fastest growing industries among small businesses are tied to construction – including contractors, real estate agents and architects.
- "With 2016 in the rearview mirror, construction professionals are turning their attention to the year ahead. While construction spending failed to meet analyst expectations last year, economists predict 5% growth in the value of starts in 2017, according to Dodge Data & Analytics.
"Here are the top 10 trends to watch in 2017:
    - ✓ Collaborative project delivery methods will become more popular
    - ✓ The labor shortage will continue to plague the industry
    - ✓ The feeling of uncertainty will linger under the new administration
    - ✓ Offsite/modular construction will gain a stronger foothold in the market
    - ✓ Construction firms are cautiously optimistic for a future infrastructure

C

spending boost
- ✓ IoT holds the potential to revolutionize the job site
- ✓ Construction costs will rise due to materials and labor
- ✓ VR/AR tech will pick up steam
- ✓ The sustainable construction movement will consider changing its message
- ✓ Construction firms will face increased scrutiny and prosecution of safety and fraud incidents"

Source: "10 construction industry trends to watch in 2017," by Emily Peiffer, January 3, 2017 http://www.constructiondive.com/news/construction-industry-trends-2017/433151/

- "ConstructConnect's forecast for total construction put in place for 2017 is $1,234.5 billion, a 6.3% increase over 2016. The improved growth is expected to carry over into 2018 where construction spending will improve another 7.2%. Total residential construction spending is expected to grow 7.4% in 2017 to $501.7 billion and total nonresidential is forecast to increase 5.5% this year to $732.8 billion."

Source:" Five Commercial Construction Trends to Watch in 2017" by Kendall Jones, January 6, 2017 http://www.constructconnect.com/blog/operating-insights/five-commercial-construction-trends-watch-2017/

- I see a steady increase in jobs and sales over the next few years. This is partly due to the general lift in the economy, plus the gradual increase in home values, making better economic sense to build new homes. Home remodeling has seen a significant uptick in recent months. Of course, all the specialty trades follow the growth path of general building.
- The industry in general seems to be doing a repeat of 15 years or so ago. Companies start small and as the economy grows, so do they. Lots of small startups in the market place right now; these businesses struggle more than their high revenue, big outfit competitors.
- Most construction and specialty contracting firms were founded by skilled technicians, not by general business managers... they had to learn their trade first then become managers. Because the values of their businesses are so high, a typical technician would not be in a financial position nor the mindset to purchase the business. Hence, new owners are business managers that can run the business, but need skilled technicians as managers or supervisors. The current owners are still so heavily involved in the day-to-day operations that they must be replaced when they exit the business. Most buyers recognize this and ask the seller to stay on board for up to a year- which is not preferred by the seller. I advise sellers to start replacing themselves sooner in the selling cycle-they must start training a manager to cover their operational duties. The trend in this industry will be that more buyers will appear with less knowledge in the industry-so middle to upper managers will be in higher demand.

Expert Comments

Know where your dollars are going, and control it. A portion of profits must be re-invested into the operation for it to sustain itself. Money must be channeled into marketing and equipment upkeep to be successful.

Hire slow, fire fast. Get rid of bad employees as quickly as possible and take excellent care of your good ones. For your best employees, treat them like your son or daughter - your business is largely dependent upon them.

The construction industry as a whole rides up and down with the economy. Real estate, home building, and building in general move together, with some exceptions. The gradual recovery from the Great Recession has seen an increase in construction and related industries, but it's moved at a more steady and systematic pace (versus the construction craze of 11-12 years ago).

Historically, as the economy falls the little guys start to disappear quickly, and more of the big guys hang on. Then as the economy improves, little 1–2 man operations start popping up everywhere again, while the big outfits doing $1M+ just get bigger again. It's a cycle that keeps repeating. So there's always competition, but the way undulations in the economy affect a company varies greatly according to the company's size.

Buying: Verify solvency and liquidity, plus ongoing and future contracts. Acid Test.

Selling: Prepare your company books, tax returns and a good brochure with construction job historical.

The construction sector is very fragmented, with very poor contribution to research and development. It's very easy to enter due to the low initial investment but very difficult to get out of due to many legal and judicial implications. It's a sector of high bankruptcy rates due to poor working capital management. But the industry does offer great sources of statistics both public and private. The sector is very tied to government spending.

Be ready for earnouts to play a part in the price negotiations.

Keep the books solid and up-to-date. Contractors are notorious for not keeping good books and letting things slip. Again, this is much more common in the smaller operations. Make sure the equipment is in good working condition, including vehicles.

The competition follows the profitability, and vice versa. As one goes up, so goes the other. The industry is definitely stronger and more predictable in recent months than it was a few years ago. Construction tends to follow the economy very closely, so there's not much immunity from the inevitable rise and fall.

Seller Financing

- Seller financing is the norm for construction-related industries. Construction has all the aspects that most banks don't like: reliance upon the owner (for smaller firms), inconsistent profits, fluctuations with the economy, and license issues. Because it is very common for someone already in the trades to buy a construction company, seller financing seems a good fit. Seller financing provides confidence to the buyer (because the seller is willing to back his claims with a loan) and helps with license transfer problems - for example, sellers can "qualify" for the buyer license for a time until he obtains his own license. This way, the seller remains involved, both financially and operationally, for a period of time. And this tends to be good for business sales.
- Usually a seller requires about 30% down and will carry for a term of 3–5 years. 2 or 3 points above prime rate is typical for interest.
- Seller financing, 5-year term loan, prevailing market interest rates.
- Most typical is outside financing of 50 to 75% with approximately 10 to 25% seller financing (per each deal). Less than 10% of the companies sold would be cash down payment and seller financing of approximately 50%.

C

Resources
- National Association of Home Builders: http://www.nahb.com
- IBISWorld, February 2017: http://ibisworld.com

Construction—Specialty Trades		
SIC 1799-99		

Rules of Thumb
➢ 2–3 x EBITDA

➢ 2.5–3.5 x EBIT

➢ 2–2.5 x SDE plus inventory

➢ 50–55% of annual gross Sales plus inventory

Pricing Tips
- Specialty contractor companies tend to have higher profit margins than general construction companies. This is especially true of the service companies, versus new-install companies. So the SDE multiples are a little higher and there is less risk.
- Like most services businesses, the key is in the existing relationships. Two times SDE is fair as long as there is evidence that the relationships will transfer smoothly to the buyer.

Benchmark Data
- Service businesses will set hourly rates at 2 to 3 times their direct cost per employee per hour to cover overhead and markups.

Expenses (% of Annual Sales)
Cost of Goods	25%
Occupancy Costs	10%
Payroll/Labor Costs	40%
Profit (pretax)	25%

Questions
- How many hours a week are you involved in the business?
- Reason for selling. What he/she does on a daily basis. Employee census. Worker's comp mode rate. Upside potential.
- How do you get new jobs? Do you have a sales and marketing plan that generates new work on a consistent basis?

Industry Trend
- There appears to be a steady increase in work for the specialty contractor over the next few years. Real estate is strong, building is up, and specialty trades follow building. As more and more businesses (in every industry) move away from generalization and toward specialization, specialty construction businesses will feel this shift.

Expert Comments

Keep good books when you're planning to sell. Require good books when you're looking to buy.

Replication of a specialty contractor businesses is more difficult than general construction because there is less standardization. The competition is fierce, and every outfit seems to have their own "secret sauce" of how to make the best money in this industry.

Seller Financing

- Seller financing works well in this business; outside or conventional financing is very difficult
- 2 years

Contract Manufacturing		
SIC 3999-06	NAICS 332710	

Rules of Thumb

➤ 95% of annual sales includes inventory

➤ 4–7 x EBIT

➤ 3–5 x EBITDA plus reasonable owner's compensation

➤ 2–4 x SDE plus inventory

Pricing Tips

- Discounts for high sales concentration in a few customers; discounts for old equipment.
- Mark down for concentration of majority of revenues coming from one to three customers. Mark down for old equipment. Mark down if owner is key production or engineering employee. Smaller shops get lower multiples. Premium for larger shop with many customers—especially large company customers, newer equipment of high quality brands, ISO9000, management team, outside sales employees, current IT technology, online ordering, automated QC department. Also premium price if all contract manufacturing services are integrated under one company: metal fab, machining, painting, plating, PCB assembly, cable & harness assembly, box build, testing, fulfillment.

Benchmark Data

- $300,000 revenue per employee

Expenses (% of Annual Sales)

Cost of Goods	45% to 60%
Occupancy Costs	5% to 15%
Payroll/Labor Costs	15% to 20%
Profit (pretax)	10% to 20%

Questions

- Ask about the relationships with the present customers and any communications from them about the volume of future business. Ask about his growth vision. Ask about upcoming capital equipment purchase needs.

- Customer concentration and who has technical skill to operate
- Discuss the outlook for the company. What opportunities exist for the buyer and why the seller isn't pursuing them.

Industry Trend

- Increase in defense spending, increase in CPI and growth of GDP will all contribute to growth for this industry.
- Work presently contracted offshore is moving back to the U.S. As costs rise in Asia, the U.S. becomes more competitive.

Expert Comments

Get professional help to sell while you focus on keeping the business growing and profitable. When buying, use a team to advise you: broker, equipment appraiser, CPA, etc.; don't try to do it alone.

Cost of capital equipment and availability of skilled labor are barriers to entry.

Most contract manufacturing businesses are capital intensive and require a crew of skilled and semi-skilled employees. On the business side, the company needs professional organization and infrastructure with current enterprise management software and systems, ISO9000 and Mil Spec certifications plus an experienced management team. You can't just rent an industrial space and get this sort of business up and running in a few months. It takes years to develop the infrastructure, employees and management team, build customer relations, obtain the needed certifications and manage the operation profitably. This creates goodwill when achieved so that the business is worth much more than the value of the tangible assets.

Competition is high and the key to gross profit margins is using technology to be low-cost manufacturer.

Seller Financing

- Bank financing is typical.
- Outside financing is readily available for profitable, well-established contract manufacturing businesses. Also, the business equipment is usually valuable collateral. It is critical that the buyer have industry experience.

Resources

- Fabricators & Manufacturers Association, International: https://www.fmanet.org/

Contractors—Masonry		
SIC 1741-01	NAICS 238140	Number of Businesses/Units 86,867

Rules of Thumb

➢ 27% of annual sales includes inventory

➢ 1–2 x SDE includes inventory

Pricing Tips
- Commercial masonry is worth more than residential masonry.
- Home masonry will go for 1X SDE, and B-2-B will go for 1.5X SDE.

Benchmark Data

Statistics (Masonry)

Number of Establishments	86,867
Average Profit Margin	5.9%
Revenue per Employee	$132,500
Average Number of Employees	2.5
Average Wages per Employee	$39,531

Products and Services Segmentation

Masonry contracting using brick, block or concrete	68.4%
Other (including work with slate, marble and granite)	12.0%
Pointing, cleaning, and caulking	9.2%
Stucco contracting	6.6%
Stone contracting	3.8%

Major Market Segmentation

Residential construction market	41.2%
Commercial construction market	28.0%
Municipal construction market	23.8%
Other	7.0%

Industry Costs

Profit	5.9%
Wages	29.9%
Purchases	39.8%
Depreciation	0.7%
Marketing	0.2%
Rent & Utilities	4.4%
Other	19.1%

Expenses (% of Annual Sales)

Cost of Goods	20%
Occupancy Costs	10% to15%
Payroll/Labor Costs	50%
Profit (pretax)	15 to 20%

Questions
- What % of bids do they get?
- Union or non-union labor?
- Relationships to the customers, are the contracts assignable, and when will you introduce the buyer to customers before closing?
- Make sure they have good foremen in place to run the crews going forward with a new buyer.
- Understand the builders' contracts in place.

C

Industry Trend

- "The Masonry industry is forecast to experience steady, but slowing, growth over the next five years as revenue begins to return to its prerecessionary levels. Over the five years to 2022, IBISWorld expects industry revenue to grow at an annualized rate of 1.8% to $30.7 billion. This slowing growth is the result of stabilizing key downstream construction markets, which had ballooned from their recessionary lows over the five years to 2017; the one major exception being the municipal construction market, which is set to improve more robustly over the five-year period."

Source: IBISWorld Industry Outlook

Expert Comments

Relationships with your builders help getting the contracts for work.

Resources

- IBISWorld, March 2017: http://ibisworld.com

Convenience Stores		
SIC 5411-03	NAICS 445120	Number of Businesses/Units 124,374

Rules of Thumb

➢ 5 x EBITDA less cosmetic renovation to receive a national brand of fuel; inventory is separate and above

➢ 10–20% of annual sales plus inventory

➢ 2–2.5 x SDE plus inventory

➢ 2–3 x EBITDA plus inventory-C-store only

➢ 6–8 x EBITDA plus inventory-real estate + business

Pricing Tips

- Additional revenue sources such as: ATM machines, game machines, fresh fruits and increased deli items, Lotto sales, money orders and even check cashing have become increasingly more important to convenience store retailers with the industry trending toward lower margins and increased competition over the past several years. Many stores are also offering petroleum product discounts to their customers if paying cash rather than using credit cards. This helps the retailer with cash flow as well as saving approx. 2% (or more in some cases) in credit card processing fees which is substantial especially in high-volume gasoline sales locations selling millions of gallons of petroleum products annually.

Benchmark Data

Statistics (Convenience Stores)

Number of Establishments	42,252
Average Profit Margin	1.1%
Revenue per Employee	$187,500
Average Number of Employees	3.4
Average Wages per Employee	$16,501

Products and Services Segmentation

Tobacco products	35.9%
Food service	19.4%
Packaged beverages	15.4%
Other	11.4%
Candy and snacks	10.6%
Beer	7.3%

Industry Costs

Profit	1.1%
Wages	8.8%
Purchases	78.7%
Depreciation	0.9%
Marketing	1.1%
Rent & Utilities	3.4%
Other	6.0%

Market Share

7-Eleven Inc.	33.9%

- Overall, 80.7 percent of convenience stores (124,374 locations) sell motor fuels.
- "The average convenience store is 2,744 square feet. New stores are bigger, with 3,590 square feet, with about 2,582 square feet of sales area and about 1,008 square feet of non-sales area.

  "An average store selling fuel has around 1,100 customers per day, or more than 400,000 per year. Cumulatively, the U.S. convenience store industry alone serves nearly 160 million customers per day, and 58 billion customers every year."

  Source: nacsonline.com

Convenience Channel Market Share by Category

Cigarettes	88.43%
Packaged beverages	52.93%
Other tobacco products	91.60%
Liquor	15.60%
Packaged ice cream/frozen novelties	15.52%
Salty snacks	25.81%
Candy and gum	38.89%
Wine	7.17%
Health & beauty care	5.89%
Beer/malt beverages	60.59%
Fluid milk products	14.92%

Expenses (% of Annual Sales)

Cost of Goods	60% or less
Occupancy Costs	07% to 15% +/-
Payroll/Labor Costs	20% +/-
Profit (pretax)	10% to 15%

Questions

- Have your margins been shrinking over the past five years?

C

- Do you have accurate books so I can go to a bank for a loan?
- Any previous environmental issue, current leak test result, 3 years' tax return, lease agreement. Do you want to sell or test the market?
- Amount of gross that's tobacco related. Lottery sales, any employee or customer thefts?

Industry Trend

- "Over the five years to 2022, revenue for the Convenience Stores industry is forecast to increase at an annualized rate of 1.1% to $28.5 billion as the industry continues to strengthen due to improving economic conditions. However, sustained pressure from mass merchandisers and emerging competition from online operators will likely restrain revenue growth over the next five years. Nevertheless, increasing demand for convenience, improving personal disposable income and mild industry consolidation are expected to boost sales and lower costs.

  "Consumers are expected to shop at convenience stores more frequently as incomes increase. Higher income levels will enable consumers to pay higher prices for convenience store accessibility. In addition, per capita disposable income is forecast to grow in 2018 as unemployment remains relatively low and economic growth strengthens. These increases will further drive industry growth as consumers increasingly feel more confident about the overall economy."

  Source: IBISWorld Industry Outlook

- "With $34.5 billion in sales in 2016, the convenience store foodservice market is not only strong, but seeing continued solid growth. Prepared food accounts for the lion's share of the pie at $23.4 billion. Hot dispensed beverages comes in second at $7.3 billion, according to Mintel research shared during the 2017 Convenience Store News Convenience Foodservice & Beverage Exchange event, taking place this week in Rosemont, Illinois."

  Source: "The Future of Convenience Foodservice: iGen" by Melissa Kress, September 13, 2017, https://csnews.com/future-convenience-foodservice-igen

Expert Comments

Inside profit margins are not as sensitive as in other food operations. Folks shop for convenience, not price.

The fact that this is mostly a cash business, relatively less risky, easy to learn and replicate make this business appealing to many people. Some areas are obviously saturated and avoidable. In general, the industry is very marketable if and only if: seller has substantiating books and records for current 3 years and that daily inside sales are minimum $1,000-$1,500 (excluding extraneous revenues). Importance of location, traffic count and trading area demographic to this industry is no different than to any other retail business. Industry growth has been very stable.

Seller Financing

- Seller financing for businesses is usually limited to 5 years. If real estate is involved, seller financing is usually limited to 10 years.
- 5 years all due and payable with 15-year amortization
- 5 to 7 years

Resources
- CS News Online: http://www.csnews.com
- IBISWorld, March 2017: http://ibisworld.com
- Association for Convenience & Fuel Retailing (NACS): http://www.nacsonline.com

Cost Cutters Family Hair Care	Franchise
Approx. Total Investment	$94,495–$210,295

SIC 7241-01	NAICS 812112	Number of Businesses/Units 480

Rules of Thumb
➤ 55–60% of annual sales plus inventory

Resources
- Cost Cutters: http://www.costcutters.com

Country/General Stores		
SIC 5399-02	NAICS 452990	

Rules of Thumb
➤ 20% of annual sales plus inventory

Coupon Books		
	NAICS 541870	

Rules of Thumb
➤ 2–4 x EBITDA

Seller Financing
- Not usually seller financed. If financed, 2 to 3 years.

Court Reporting Services		
SIC 7338-01	NAICS 561492	

Rules of Thumb
➤ 30–35% of annual revenues includes inventory

Benchmark Data
- There are no major players in this industry.

Industry Trend
- Of the more than 50,000 court reporters in the United States, more than 70 percent work outside of the courtroom, according to the National Court Reporters Association.

- Statistics project that jobs in this field will grow more than 18 percent between 2008 and 2018—a good deal faster than the average for all occupations.

Resources
- The U.S. Court Reporters Association: http://www.uscra.org
- American Association of Electronic Reporters and Transcribers: http://www.aaert.org
- National Court Reporters Association: http://www.ncraonline.org
- The JCR.com: http://thejcr.com/
- Court Reporting Insider: http://www.courtreportinginsider.com/

Franchise

Coverall Health-Based Cleaning Systems (Commercial Cleaning)

Approx. Total Investment		$16,839–$49,505
	NAICS 561720	Number of Businesses/Units 8,871

Rules of Thumb
➢ 4 x EBITDA

➢ 2–3 x monthly volume

➢ Master/Area developer—sell for 3–5 x earnings plus some blue sky for size and potential of market (some cases).

Pricing Tips
- The four basic components of determining the value and price of a Master Franchise of Coverall include the collective principal amount of Franchisee Notes outstanding, the value of the exclusive rights to the population territory inclusive of the number of businesses with 5 or more employees, the value of the business structure (number of commercial accounts serviced and the number of franchisees) and the cash flow of the territory.

Expenses (% of Annual Sales)
Cost of Goods	80%
Occupancy Costs	01%
Payroll/Labor Costs	04%
Profit (pretax)	10%

Resources
- Coverall: http://www.coverall.com

Franchise

Culligan International

	NAICS 422490	Number of Businesses/Units 586

Rules of Thumb
➢ 80–120% of gross annual sales-dependent on several things: market size, current penetration rental base, water

Seller Financing

- Frequently 7 to 10 years.

Resources

- Culligan: http://www.culligan.com

	Franchise
Curves—Jenny Craig	
SIC 7299-06	NAICS 713940	Number of Businesses/Units 4,870

Rules of Thumb

➤ 1.5–2 x SDE includes inventory

➤ 30% of annual sales includes inventory

Pricing Tips

- 1.5 to 2 times SDE. The number of monthly check drafts and club size and location are important value factors along with membership trends.
- Most clubs need 175–200 members to break even. 90% EFT is typical.

Benchmark Data

- 1.5 employees per $100K sales
- It takes about 125 members to break even.
- Usually owner-operated facilities are run at minimal expenses.

Expenses (% of Annual Sales)

Cost of Goods	05%
Occupancy Costs	10% to 15%
Payroll/Labor Costs	20% to 25%
Profit (pretax)	25% to 30%

Questions

- What was your highest membership number? Review monthly membership history for last 3–5 years. Why do members join your club? Why do/don't they renew yearly membership? Explain club safety/parking lot issues if any. Review lease. Any complaints from adjoining tenants concerning music/noise issues? What are the nearest Curves Clubs to you? Other competing franchise clubs?

Expert Comments

Acquisitions of existing franchises are generally excellent investments as a result of expected return on investment, market potential, and ongoing franchisor investment and research in the fitness industry.

Other franchisors using the '30-minute-circuit' program have entered the marketplace with very mixed results. Current Curves locations have closed in market areas which were saturated.

Seller Financing

- 3 years

D

Dairy Drive-Thru

	NAICS 722515	

Rules of Thumb

➤ 25% annual sales plus inventory

Benchmark Data

- See Food Stores— Specialty

Dairy Queen

		Franchise
Approx. Total Investment		$1,083,525–$1,835,825
Estimated Annual Sales/Unit		$809,000
SIC 2024-98	NAICS 722513	Number of Businesses/Units 6,671

Rules of Thumb

➤ Price = .45 x sales for leased facility. Rent = variable item

➤ Walk-up—two windows with real estate—1.24 (+/-) x of annual sales

➤ Without real estate—.5 (+/-) x of annual sales

➤ Full Brazier—with real estate—1.15 (+/-) x of annual sales

➤ Price = 1.1–1.2 x of annual sales for stores w/real estate

Benchmark Data

Expenses (% of Annual Sales)

Cost of Goods	31%
Occupancy Costs	08%
Payroll/Labor Costs	25%
Profit (pretax)	15%

Questions

- Questions to ask seller: Leased facility—rent important; owned facility—loan & taxes important

Expert Comments

Many players in this market

Seller Financing

- Rarely seller financed.
- 5 years with balloon payment
- SBA financing—17 to 18 years with real estate; 7 to 10 years without real estate.

Resources

- Dairy Queen: http://www.dairyqueen.com

Data Processing Services

SIC 7374-01	NAICS 518210	Number of Businesses/Units 65,848

Rules of Thumb

➢ 15% of annual sales plus inventory

➢ 2.2 x SDE plus inventory

➢ 2 x EBIT

➢ 2.2 x EBITDA

Pricing Tips

- A proprietary software component could raise the multiple to as much as 10 x.

Benchmark Data

Statistics (Data Processing & Hosting Services)

Number of Establishments	65,848
Average Profit Margin	7.2%
Revenue per Employee	$251,700
Average Number of Employees	9.9
Average Wages per Employee	$96,713

Products and Services Segmentation

Application service provisioning	23.8%
Other services	22.2%
Business process management and data processing	18.4%
Data storage and management services	11.1%
Website hosting services	10.1%
IT technical support services	9.1%
IT computer network and network management services	5.3%

Major Market Segmentation

Non-financial enterprises	38.4%
Resellers	25.6%
Financial firms	15.8%
Government organizations	13.3%
Content providers	6.9%

Industry Costs

Profit	7.2%
Wages	38.6%
Purchases	17.7%
Depreciation	2.5%
Marketing	3.6%
Rent and Utilities	8.3%
Other	22.1%

Market Share

Hewlett-Packard Enterprise Company LP	10.8%
Amazon.com Inc.	6.5%

Expenses (% of Annual Sales)

Cost of Goods	n/a
Occupancy Costs	n/a
Payroll/Labor Costs	35%
Profit (pretax)	40%

Questions
- Ask for resumes of employees and meeting with a few top customers during due diligence.

Industry Trend
- "Over the five years to 2022, the Data Processing and Hosting Services industry is expected to experience strong growth, primarily due to nonindustry companies' continued outsourcing of information technology (IT) to third parties. Efforts to improve operational efficiencies, coupled with the rising costs of handing IT internally, will drive outsourcing by large companies. Moreover, the continued shift to online services will drive additional demand for industry services. As a result, IBISWorld expects industry revenue to grow at an annualized rate of 6.6% to $212.9 billion over the five years to 2022."

Source: IBISWorld Industry Outlook

Resources
- IBISWorld, August 2017: http://ibisworld.com

Dating Services

SIC 7299-26	NAICS 812990	Number of Businesses/Units 7,195

Rules of Thumb
➢ 30–35% of annual sales

Benchmark Data

Statistics (Dating Services)

Number of Establishments	7,195
Average Profit Margin	10.4%
Revenue per Employee	$277,800
Average Number of Employees	1.4
Average Wages per Employee	$84,552

Products and Services Segmentation

Online dating	49.0%
Mobile dating	26.0%
Matchmakers	14.0%
Singles events	7.0%
Other	4.0%

Major Market Segmentation

Consumers 18 to 29 years old	45.0%
Consumers 30 to 49 years old	29.0%
Consumers 50 to 64 years old	20.0%
Consumers 65 years old and up	6.0%

Industry Costs

Profit	10.4%
Wages	30.2%
Purchases	18.4%
Depreciation	2.2%
Marketing	17.1%
Rent & Utilities	8.3%
Other	13.4%

Market Share

Match Group Inc.	34.4%
eHarmony Inc.	11.3%

Industry Trend

- "Once considered taboo, online dating is now a socially accepted and booming multibillion dollar business that continues to grow. More than half, or 53 percent, of single people have created a dating profile, according to Match's recent Singles in America study, which polled over 5,000 single men and women in December. Today, 40 percent of singles have dated someone they met online, while only 25 percent met a first date through a friend."

Source: "How to land a date for Valentine's Day" by Jessica Dickler, February 14, 2017, http://www.cnbc.com/2017/02/08/the-best-and-worst-online-dating-sites.html

Resources

- Online Dating Magazine: http://www.onlinedatingmagazine.com
- IBISWorld, February 2017: http://ibisworld.com

Day Care Centers/Adult

SIC 8322-10	NAICS 624120	Number of Businesses/Units 11,085

Rules of Thumb

➢ 2.5 x SDE plus inventory

➢ 70–75% of annual sales

Pricing Tips

- The mix of payers is important. What is the % of private pay vs. Medicaid vs. VA vs. County programs... the higher the private pay component, the higher the value, as the business is not subject to governmental pricing changes. If an adult day care center also provides in-home non-medical care for their clients, this adds to the value of the enterprise. If an adult day care center has their own transportation available to clients, this adds to the value of the enterprise.

Benchmark Data

Statistics (Adult Day Care)

Number of Establishments	11,085
Average Profit Margin	6.2%
Revenue per Employee	$38,200
Average Number of Employees	17.5
Average Wages per Employee	$18,882

D

Products and Services Segmentation

Social and medical model	44.0%
Social model	33.0%
Medical model	23.0%

Industry Costs

Profit	6.2%
Wages	48.9%
Purchases	11.7%
Depreciation	2.3%
Marketing	0.6%
Rent & Utilities	5.4%
Other	24.9%

Expenses (% of Annual Sales)

Occupancy Costs	12% to 20%
Payroll/Labor Costs	25% to 35%
Profit (pretax)	20% to 25%

Questions

- What is your mix of payors? What is your employee to participant ratio? Should be 1 to 5 or less to ensure good service is provided... How do clients get to the center? Your own transportation, regional senior transport, adult children or spouses dropping participants off at the center?

Industry Trend

- With the portion of the population 65 and older growing significantly, the demand for adult day care will rise well above the overall GDP growth rate for at least another decade. This is a superior alternative to the only other option for seniors to stay in their home: the non-medical in-home care providers.

Expert Comments

This is a great industry to invest in as the growth trendline is positive and the margins are solid if the operation is run properly. Not unlike any other Main Street business.

The major risk is similar to any other business-under capitalization. It takes a long time to reach breakeven, as it takes time to bring clients into the program and keep up with those leaving the program (inevitable due to aging...) at the same time as they need higher levels of care at assisted living facilities or nursing homes.

Seller Financing

- Similar to other Main Street businesses, there is a mix of outside financing and seller financing.
- Typically, sellers will carry a small percentage (10–20%) of the transaction value.

Resources

- National Adult Day Services Association: http://www.nadsa.org
- IBISWorld, November 2016: http://ibisworld.com

Day Care Centers/Children

SIC 8351-01	NAICS 624410	Number of Businesses/Units 780,080

Rules of Thumb

➤ 2 x SDE includes inventory. Most childcare centers are acquired with the real estate.

➤ 55–60% of annual sales includes inventory

➤ 3–4 x EBIT

➤ 3.5–4.5 x EBITDA

Pricing Tips

- Pay attention to roster, curriculum, and demographics.
- The size of the center can determine the multiple of SDE. For example, I sold a center of approximately 85 students for 2.13xSDE, and a center of approximately 130 for 2.61xSDE. Typically, a center can sell for 2.5–3.0xSDE if licensed for over 200 students. In this case, it is the licensed amount that matters rather than the actual capacity; thus any center licensed for 200 or more students should list at 3xSDE.
  The same concept applies if using a percentage of annual sales. Typical Rules of Thumb will say a child care facility should sell for 50%–55% (includes inventory) of annual sales. I have sold one center licensed for approximately 130 at 66.4% of annual sales, and currently have another under contract licensed for approximately 125 students at 68% of annual sales. I sold a smaller center licensed for 85 students at 53.6% of annual sales. I would suggest using a rule of thumb closer to 60% of annual sales depending on the size of the center and the cash flow.
- If the center owns the real estate, the real estate value is figured in separately and then added to the value of the business itself. The center should have a recent real estate appraisal in place prior to listing in order to have a verified value for the property and improvements.
- Rent including CAM needs to be below 20%.
- Licensed capacity is key; centers over 125 sell for higher multiples.
- Facility layout is important, as room size dictates staff:child ratio efficiency.
- Staffing is key to profitability/value. Staff costs need to be under 50%, preferably under 40%.
- State regulations significantly impact value.
- National or large regional operators will pay 3–5X EBITDA for centers licensed for 125+. Smaller centers will sell to owner-operators for 2.5–3X SDE.
  Inventory is typically not an issue. Quality of the center facility is very important to achieve higher multiples.
- Percentage of Annual Revenue—30% to 45% of annual revenue for the business value only;
  Percentage of Annual Revenue—140% to 300% of annual revenue for the value of the real estate and business together
- Businesses with EBITDA of less than $100,000 will generally sell at a much lower multiple say 2-3 times, where an EBITDA of $300,000 will be 3.5-4 times. Building type, location, occupancy levels play a more important role in sale price than just the profit; centers with daily fees of under $60 per day per child will struggle to sell at any price; centers with a license of 50-80 children are the most; sort out sizes.

D

Benchmark Data

Statistics (Day Care)

Number of Establishments	780,080
Average Profit Margin	9.9%
Revenue per Employee	$29,400
Average Number of employees	2.1
Average Wages per Employee	$15,634

Products and Services Segmentation

Child day-care services	50.2%
Preschool programs	39.9%
Other services and receipts	5.9%
Government contributions	4.0%

Industry Costs

Profit	9.9%
Wages	53.3%
Purchases	9.5%
Depreciation	2.4%
Marketing	0.5%
Rent & Utilities	6.3%
Other	18.1%

- Dollars per enrolled student
- Revenues in this industry can be attained through a couple of different ways. Some centers focus only on low-income families, thus rely heavily on state subsidized tuition vouchers and the USDA food program. These centers typically focus only on low-income families thus have few, if any, private pay individuals. Other centers focus on middle to high income families, thus do not participate in state tuition vouchers and the USDA food program. And yet others implement a combination of private pay families, and low-income families on state vouchers. These centers also participate in the USDA food program. Thus benchmarks are hard to determine as the business model plays an important part of this equation. Those centers that implement both private pay and state vouchers, as well as participate in the USDA food program typically have higher margins and six-figure cash flows. Centers over 100 students should have annual revenues between $700,000 and $1,000,000 or higher.
- Revenue should be minimum $10K per unit of licensed capacity; however, this may vary due to practical capacity that is lower than approved capacity (due to ratios of quality limit).
- Size is important. Most desirable size is 125+ capacity; 75–125 is acceptable; difficult to profit on less than 75.
- All operating ratios depend on each state's level of regulations. Heavy regulated states with low student-to-teacher ratios are significantly less profitable. There are no common, national benchmarks accurate across all states.
- Revenue should be minimum $10K per unit of licensed capacity however this may vary due to practical capacity that is lower than approved capacity (due to ratios of quality limit). Size is important. Most desirable size is 125+ capacity. 75–125 is acceptable. Difficult to profit on less than 75.

Expenses (% of Annual Sales)

Cost of Goods	10%
Occupancy Costs	10% to 20%
Payroll/Labor Costs	40% to 55%
Profit (pretax)	10% to 18%

Questions

- Ask the buyer if he loves education and is willing to help young learners.
- How many students are you licensed for? Do you accept state tuition vouchers? Do you participate in the USDA food program? What percentage of your revenues are private pay vs. subsidized tuition? Have you had any negative complaints filed against you, or any DHS violations? How would you as the owner increase revenues and cash flow? How old is your playground equipment? Do you provide meals for the students, and if so, how many meals or snacks? What type of curriculum are you using? How many full-time vs. part-time employees do you have? Are any of your teachers certified teachers? How many competitors are in your market—private centers, church-owned centers, state-owned centers, etc.? When was your last DHS inspection? What are your current tuition rates? When did you last raise these rates, and by how much?
- Occupancy records, look at competitors' occupancy as well. The future is more important than the past!
- Capacity, enrollment, rates, revenue, estimated profitability, facility. Does business owner or closely related 3rd party entity own the real estate? Detailed info on staff (hire dates & their credentials). Center's distinguishing characteristics. Describe local competition (reputation/rates/size/enrollment as % of capacity/advantages/disadvantages). Reason for sale?
- Are you on the food program? Subsidized care? Gold Seal?
- Does the provider have a contract with the children's parents? If yes, ask for the contract. Does the provider have a rate schedule? Is the same schedule used for all children or do some have a special rate? Determine which children have a different rate and the amount. If the provider does not have the rate schedule for the year in question, ask for the current rate schedule and then ask how it differed in the tax year under exam. Does the provider furnish year-end statements to the parents as to how much they paid in the tax year?
- Any state subsidies? Review price schedule. Listing of all licenses-NAEYC accredited? Any claims against center? Confirm enrollment counts. Discuss curriculum. Education/experience of staff.

Industry Trend

- I see child care businesses thriving over the next few years, especially as the economy continues to improve. The trend in this industry is toward centers that provide an excellent curriculum and educational activities for children, as well as a safe and monitored environment. Child care is becoming more and more of a necessary expenditure for families, as opposed to 20 years ago when it was considered a discretionary household expense.
- Parents love being able to access a live video feed of their students via a smart phone app being coordinated with closed-circuit video monitoring of the facility.
- Stable; however, there is volatility related to employment. Child care spending is usually the first expense cut when unemployed.

D

- "Child care is evolving, and most care providers and parents agree the changes are for the best. What are some of the latest trends in child care and what should parents be looking for when making an all-important child care decision?
  - ✓ Child Care Is Catering to Budget-Minded Families
  - ✓ Child Care is Now Early Education
  - ✓ Drop-In Child Care is More Common
  - ✓ Corporate Child Care is Raising Quality Bar
  - ✓ Technology is Changing Provider/Parent Connection
  - ✓ Most Child Care is Becoming Safer
  - ✓ More Child Care Options Exist
  - ✓ The Internet Can Help You Find Child Care
  - ✓ Communications Are More Frequent, More Useful
  - ✓ Child Care Caters to Time-Crunched, Working Parents
  - ✓ Vacation Destinations, Kid-Friendly Hotels Offering On-Site Care
  - ✓ After-School Programs and Care Provide Child Care Flexibility"
    Source: Robin McClure, April 19, 2016, https://www.verywell.com/top-trends-in-child-care-616937

- Average growth; declining profits with increased regulations; labor shortages of qualified teachers.

Expert Comments

This industry is very location sensitive.

If buying, find out the licensing capacity of the business. Also ask about recent equipment and playground upgrades, specifically along the lines of fire suppression systems; and if the facility possesses a kitchen, make sure the kitchen is compliant with fire code and DHS standards. Buyers should be aware of square footage of the facility as this comes into play with future revenues and expansion. If the facility is maxed out on its ratio of students per square foot, the buyer should look to outside services such as before- and after-school programs, as well as infant care, for potential avenues to increase sales. Be very careful to maintain confidentiality over the course of acquiring a center, as parents will pull children from the center if it gets out that the facility is selling. Selling a business creates a negative psychological impression on customers if they find out, whether the business is struggling or not.

If selling, make sure your financial records are in line and up to date. If the center accepts state tuition vouchers and participates in the USDA food program, make sure the documentation is in order for each of these revenue streams. Documentation is critically important in selling a center, especially if accepting state and federal monies. Make sure documentation is up to date and compliant! This is the most important thing sellers can do. If the real estate is owned, get an updated appraisal or broker's opinion of value prior to listing so the real estate value can be ascertained and verified. Do not tell employees or parents if considering selling as this will lead to employees leaving and children being pulled out of the center, reducing revenues and consequently the overall value of the business. Confidentiality is very, very important.

Child care has proven itself to be a relatively recession-proof industry. The demand for child care has increased as parents have gone back to work and now require supervision. The nature of the supervision itself has changed as parents are more aware of early childhood development and want centers that educate children, rather than simply babysit children. Thus a center's curriculum can play a big role in marketing the business. Privately owned facilities are becoming fewer and fewer as church-owned facilities are increasing, due to low overhead and an already established location and space. However, these businesses are very profitable and if properly run should carry a significant cash flow. Due to increased regulations and strict DHS requirements, ease of entry for start-up centers is extremely difficult. Any individual thinking of entering the industry should do so through the acquisition of an existing center.

Buy a business that the owner is retiring from and has run for a long time, or is moving out of state or area. Look at two areas: payroll should be between 40 and 50%, and rent/mortgage no more than 20%.

Run it like a business, not as an educator or on passion.

Replication more difficult in states with high regulatory compliance

Be careful to make sure that the seller isn't being taxed twice on any reimbursements from any governmental agencies.

Seller Financing

- Both lender financing and seller carry back
- Businesses in this industry can usually be financed by a third party, but in order to achieve maximum sales price desired some owner financing as well will be required. If the center owns the real estate, then conventional financing is available through a bank, as well as an SBA secured loan. In nearly every transaction, though, the seller should be prepared to finance at least a small portion of the deal. This helps the seller get the most amount of money for the business possible, while also keeping the most amount of money possible by reducing tax consequences and spreading out the taxable proceeds.
- A business without real estate should look to its equipment/playground to use as collateral for financing. Even in this situation, a lender will look heavily at revenues, cash flow, and buyer experience. Financing for businesses without real estate is usually via the SBA route.
- Most if not all sales are financed with an SBA program. If the seller helps with a note, the SBA loan will not allow the seller to get a payment for some time as it is on full standby.
- Depends on size—more seller financing with smaller centers.
- 5% to 10% seller financing; the rest of the financing is from SBA loans.

Resources

- National Association for the Education of Young Children: http://www.naeyc.org
- Association for Early Learning Leaders: http://www.earlylearningleaders.org
- National Association for Family Child Care: http://www.nafcc.org
- National Child Care Association: http://www.nccanet.org/
- Childcare Brokers: http://www.childcarebrokers.com
- IBISWorld, June 2017: http://ibisworld.com
- Child Care Exchange: https://www.childcareexchange.com/
- Child Care Aware—Arkansas: http://www.childcareaware.org/state/arkansas/

D

	Franchise

Deck the Walls

Approx. Total Investment		$112,500–$202,000
	NAICS 442299	Number of Businesses/Units 200

Rules of Thumb

➢ 35% of annual sales plus inventory

Resources

- Deck the Walls: http://www.dtwfraninfo.com

Delicatessens

SIC 5812-09	NAICS 445110	

Rules of Thumb

➢ 40% of annual sales plus inventory

➢ 2 x SDE plus inventory

➢ Retail: 40% of annual sales plus inventory

➢ Industrial: 50% of annual sales plus inventory

➢ Office Buildings: 50% of annual sales plus inventory

Pricing Tips

- It's important to recognize the distinction between sandwich shops and a real delicatessen. A real deli sells cold cuts plus many other traditional deli items; it usually does make and sell sandwiches, but it represents only a portion of their business. A sandwich shop is like a Subway or Quiznos.

Industry Trend

- "Retailers have seen huge increases in certain categories, spurred on by new products and increasing variety. Specialty cheese may be the best example. From a self-service case with under 50 varieties, specialty cheese has evolved into its own sub-department in many stores. High-volume and specialty retailers often have cheese as a separate department with its own buyers and merchandisers.

  "Younger consumers, particularly those located in larger cities, lead the market for natural meats. Because these younger people are key to the market, social media is particularly important in merchandising. 'Millennials are the biggest group of consumers driving food trends,' says Holt. 'This demographic also is driving the social media movement. They use Facebook, Twitter, Instagram and Snapchat to get advice, learn about what they want to buy, and are excited to share anything new they find through social media."

  Source: http://www.delibusiness.com/media/ebooks/16decjan.pdf

Resources

- International Dairy-Deli-Bakery Association: http://www.iddba.org
- Deli Business: http://www.delibusiness.com/

Delivery Services (Courier Services)

SIC 4212-05	NAICS 492210	Number of Businesses/Units 201,047

Rules of Thumb

➤ 70% of annual sales plus inventory (if any)

➤ 3 x SDE including Inventory

➤ 2 x EBITDA for businesses under $1 million

➤ 3 x EBITDA for businesses from $1 to $5 million

➤ 4 x EBITDA for businesses over $5 million

Pricing Tips

- FedEx has more pricing flexibility because its deliveries are handled by independent contractors while UPS employs unionized drivers.

Benchmark Data

Statistics (Courier and Local Delivery Services)

Number of Establishments	201,047
Average Profit Margin	9.8%
Revenue per Employee	$111,700
Average Number of Employees	4.3
Average Wages per Employee	$36,957

Products and Services Segmentation

Ground deliveries	56.8%
Air transit services	41.9%
Other services including messengers and local deliveries	1.3%

Major Market Segmentation

Business to consumers, including households	51.9%
Business to business	40.2%
All other	7.9%

Industry Costs

Profit	9.8%
Wages	33.3%
Purchases	9.4%
Depreciation	4.0%
Marketing	0.4%
Rent & Utilities	3.7%
Other	39.4%

Market Share

United Parcel Service Inc.	54.8%
FedEx Corporation	23.2%

- Of the online retailers profiled in the Top 500 Guide, 184 list UPS as their shipping carrier, 139 FedEx and 107 USPS, according to Top500Guide.com

D

Expenses (% of Annual Sales)

Cost of Goods	42%
Occupancy Costs	0%
Payroll/Labor Costs	30%
Profit (pretax)	25% to 28%

Industry Trend

- "In our latest research 'Adding Value to Parcel Delivery' we identified more than a dozen trends impacting parcel delivery service, an industry that is projected to grow 9 percent annually to more than $343 billion globally by 2020. As postal organizations around the world continue to face revenue challenges created by dramatically reduced mail volumes, focusing on competitive parcel delivery products, services and supply chains can help close the revenue gap."

  Source: https://www.accenture.com/us-en/insight-new-delivery-trends

- We predict that these small groupings are going to be purchased by larger investment groups that will dominate the industry as freight carriers.

Expert Comments

It is worthy to note that the Frontier study (Frontier Economics, London) did research on why businesses use and value express delivery for global shipments. Here are the value points for the global customer according to the study:

- ✓ Global Reach-ability to send items anywhere
- ✓ Reliability-knowing the items arrive on time
- ✓ Transparency-being able to track the items
- ✓ Speed-ability to reach destination quickly
- ✓ Security-knowing the items move in a secure supply chain

Seller Financing

- Cash purchase. Very difficult to finance.

Resources

- IBISWorld, August 2017: http://ibisworld.com
- Express Delivery & Logistics Association: http://www.expressassociation.org
- eTruckBiz: http://www.etruckbiz.com/

Del Taco	Franchise
Approx. Total Investment	$960,700–$1,866,500
Estimated Annual Sales/Unit	$1,370,000
NAICS 722513	Number of Businesses/Units 241

Rules of Thumb

➢ 70% of annual sales plus inventory

Resources

- Del Taco: http://www.deltacofranchise.com

Dental Laboratories

SIC 8072-01	NAICS 339116	

Rules of Thumb

➢ 45% of annual sales plus inventory

➢ 1 x SDE plus equipment and inventory

➢ 2 x SDE includes equipment & inventory

Benchmark Data

- Industry Asks FDA to Improve Regulation of Dental Restorations to Protect Patient Safety in $5.5 billion U.S. dental-restoration products industry. Most domestic dental laboratories are exempt from registering with the FDA, and most typically employ just 3.5 people.

Industry Trend

- "Over the next five years, the Dental Laboratories industry will benefit from growth in private health insurance, which will increase access to dental insurance and, as a result, bolster industry revenue. Furthermore, the number of adults aged 65 and older is anticipated to grow at an annualized rate of 3.3% over the five years to 2021, stimulating demand for industry products. As per capita disposable income grows during the five-year period, more individuals will be able to incur high out-of-pocket expenses for dental care, particularly for elective or cosmetic products such as veneers and other customized dentistry products. As a result, industry revenue is forecast to grow at an annualized rate of 2.4% to $5.8 billion over the five years to 2021. Profit is expected to remain steady, decreasing from an estimated 9.5% of industry revenue in 2016 to 9.4% in 2021."

Source: IBISWorld Industry Outlook

Resources

- National Association of Dental Laboratories: https://nadl.org/home-page.cfm
- IBISWorld, January 2017: http://ibisworld.com

Dental Practices

SIC 8021-01	NAICS 621210	Number of Businesses/Units 191,992

Rules of Thumb

➢ 60–70% of annual sales includes inventory

➢ 1.3–2.5 x SDE includes inventory

➢ 3–4 x EBIT

➢ 2–4 x EBITDA

➢ 50–70% of annual collections

Pricing Tips

- Earnings are the critical factor in any valuation. Be careful of Rules of Thumb valuations. Earnings can be all over the board. Some Rules of Thumb use earnings before doctors' salaries, others after. A thorough analysis is needed to get an accurate value.

- 50% to 70% of annual collections, depending on percentage of managed care versus private fee for service (cash) and type and condition of equipment
- Performing a valuation on a dental practice, or any business for that matter, involves looking at more than one variable. You have to look at the adjusted net income, the equipment market value and the risk attributes of a practice. A simple rule of thumb may be 65% of gross annual sales, but what if the practice has poor margins? Then, the rule of thumb goes out the window. The best valuation would be to use a net income approach, a book value method and a capitalization method. Taking a weighted average of these three approaches will provide an accurate value of a practice.

Benchmark Data

Statistics (Dentists)

Number of Establishments	191,992
Average Profit Margin	14.6%
Revenue per Employee	$127,900
Average Number of Employees	5.4
Average Wages per Employee	$49,406

Products and Services Segmentation

Restorative dental services	22.3%
Preventative services	16.3%
Dental consultations and diagnostic services	15.9%
Other	15.1%
Prosthodontics (fixed and removable)	9.4%
Orthodontics	9.3%
Surgical oral and maxillofacial services	7.0%
Nonsurgical endodontic services	4.7%

Industry Costs

Profit	14.6%
Wages	38.6%
Purchases	11.8%
Depreciation	3.0%
Marketing	1.6%
Rent & Utilities	6.3%
Other	24.1%

- $20,000 to $25,000 per employee per month in revenues. $25,000 per operatory per month in revenues. National average margin of 35%. National average overhead of 65%.

Expenses (% of Annual Sales)

Cost of Goods	07% to 14%
Occupancy Costs	04% to 09%
Payroll/Labor Costs	25% to 35%
Profit (pretax)	30% to 35%

Questions

- Payor mix, market share, patient demographic data
- What procedures do you do? What's your philosophy? Any specialty procedures? How many staff and how much are they paid? How many years left on the lease? How much is the lease? How much hygiene production is there? What opportunities are there for growth? Why are you selling?
- Type of practice? Hours worked? Amount of hygiene revenue? # of operatories? Annual production by procedure code? Payer mix? Insurance contracts? Operations data including management systems and reports in the practice? Age of practice and specific pieces of equipment (obtain tax depreciation schedule)? Demographics of practice? Call-back programs? Average annual billing per patient? Aged accounts receivable? Are billing practices compliant? Any staffing issues—personal or professional?
- What are the revenues comprised of? What 3rd party payer sources exist? Age and condition of equipment, how they market.
- Besides all the typical questions, how many active patients do they have; do they want to stay on or leave; and if they own the real estate (50%-60% do), do they want to rent or sell it.

Industry Trend

- More practices merging together. More practices coming on the market. Corporates and small groups picking up a higher percentage of the market place.
- "One major change in the dental industry in recent years has been, and will continue to be, the rise of the group practice. In the past, it was more common for dentists to open up a solo practice or maybe have one partner, but group practices are becoming increasingly common.

  "According to dentist and practice management consultant Dr. Marc B. Cooper, as interviewed by Dental Products Report, 86% of dentists still practice solo, but this figure is shrinking. Rising costs and the growing influence of PPOs and third parties are some reasons for this trend. Student loan debt — averaging $221,000 for graduating dentists — is another huge factor. Average educational indebtedness of graduating dental students has increased an average of 3.7% annually.

  "From this AEGIS Communications article, here are some statistics on this trend:

  - ✓ The percentage ratio of females to males enrolling in US dental schools is approaching 50%
  - ✓ The percentage of females currently practicing dentistry has risen to more than 20% of the total number of practicing dentists
  - ✓ 60% of practicing dentists under the age of 44 are women"

  Source: "What Are The Trends In Dentistry In 2017? How Will They Impact You?" by Tyson Downs, January 23, 2017, https://titanwebagency.com/blog/dental-industry-trends/

- Dependent on insurance coverage allocated to dental practices
- Improvements in technology, quality of materials, and education of consumers regarding services available and transparency in pricing will continue to accelerate.

Expert Comments

50% of doctors are over the age of 55. In metropolitan areas there tends to be an oversaturation of practices. The trend is for existing practices to buy practices that are for sale and merge them into their practices. Corporate and small group buyers are also becoming more prevalent in the market.

D

Improvements in technology, quality of materials, and education of consumers regarding services available and transparency in pricing will continue to accelerate.

Seller Financing

- Outside financing
- Banks are financing dentists fairly easily. The failure rate on dentists is approximately .025%.
- Bank financing and 3rd party financing is readily available. Up to 100% plus working capital over 5 to 7 years.

Resources

- Dental Economics: http://www.dentaleconomics.com
- American Dental Association: http://www.ada.org
- IBISWorld, March 2017: http://ibisworld.com
- Washington State Dental Association: http://WSDA.org
- Dentaltown: http://Dentaltown.com

Diagnostic Imaging Centers

	NAICS 621512	Number of Businesses/Units 16,481

Rules of Thumb

➤ 4 x–5.5 x SDE includes inventory

➤ 100% of annual sales includes inventory

➤ 4 x EBIT

➤ 5 x EBITDA

Benchmark Data

Statistics (Diagnostic Imaging Centers)

Number of Establishments	16,481
Average Profit Margin	14.0%
Revenue per Employee	$178,500
Average Number of Employees	6.3
Average Wages per Employee	$64,157

Products and Services Segmentation

Computed tomography (CT) scanning	27.5%
Magnetic resonance imaging scans	27.1%
All other diagnostic imaging	21.4%
Ultrasound imaging	10.8%
Radiographic imaging (Including x-rays)	10.0%
Other services	3.2%

Major Market Segmentation

Private insurance payments	40.3%
Medicare and Medicaid payments	19.5%
Other	12.9%
Health practitioner payments	11.1%
Hospital payments	10.3%
Out-of-pocket payments	5.9%

Industry Costs

Profit	14.0%
Wages	35.9%
Purchases	28.5%
Depreciation	4.8%
Marketing	1.0%
Rent & Utilities	5.7%
Other	10.1%

Expenses (% of Annual Sales)

Cost of Goods	10%
Occupancy Costs	05% to 10%
Payroll/Labor Costs	25%
Profit (pretax)	40%

Questions

- Payor mix, market share, patient demographic data

Industry Trend

- "Over the five years to 2022, revenue for the Diagnostic Imaging Centers industry is forecast to increase 1.8% per year on average to $19.9 billion, including growth of 1.2% in 2017. Despite potential market changes in the next five years, several factors will positively influence the volume of diagnostic imaging, including increased patient access to industry services. The aging US population and a rising number of tests that are readily available for cancer and infectious diseases due to technological advancements and improved cost efficiencies will also likely lead to volume growth. However, Medicare's and other third-party payers' increased control over laboratory service are expected to partly offset the positive effects of these growth factors."

Source: IBISWorld Industry Outlook

Seller Financing

- Outside financing

Resources

- IBISWorld, January 2017: http://ibisworld.com

Dialysis Centers		
	NAICS 621492	Number of Businesses/Units 10,096

Rules of Thumb

➢ 2.7 x SDE

➢ 78% of annual sales

➢ 5–10 x EBITDA

Pricing Tips

- Patient mix (types of payer sources) is key; geography is also important given differences in reimbursement in different areas and regulations.

D

Benchmark Data

Statistics (Dialysis Centers)

Number of Establishments	10,096
Average Profit Margin	14.1%
Revenue per Employee	$168,700
Average Number of Employees	13.0
Average Wages per Employee	$41,544

Products and Services Segmentation

Outpatient hemodialysis	73.0%
Peritoneal dialysis	12.9%
Home-based hemodialysis	8.0%
Hospital inpatient hemodialysis	4.1%
Other	2.0%

Major Market Segmentation

Medicare	50.0%
Private insurance	38.5%
Medicaid	5.3%
Patient (out-of-pocket)	0.6%
Other	4.7%

Industry Costs

Profit	14.1%
Wages	24.4%
Purchases	26.9%
Depreciation	2.7%
Marketing	0.5%
Rent & Utilities	4.7%
Other	26.7%

Market Share

Fresenius Medical Care AG & Co. KGaA	52.4%
DaVita HealthCare Partners Inc.	41.5%

Expenses (% of Annual Sales)

Cost of Goods	13%
Payroll/Labor Costs	06%
Profit (pretax)	05% to 15%

Questions

- Whether they are the medical director, and what relationships they have with patient referral sources; whether they would continue to work in the unit post transaction, etc.

Industry Trend

- "The two leading dialysis companies, German conglomerate Fresenius Medical Care and Colorado-based DaVita Healthcare Partners, control about 70% of the U.S. market. Together they operate about 3,900 locations nationwide— roughly the same number of Target, Best Buy, and Publix Super Market stores combined.

"Despite the patient acuity, dialysis is enormously profitable for both DaVita and Fresenius. DaVita reported adjusted net income of $828 million for 2015, up more than $100 million from 2014. Three-quarters of its cash flow stems from dialysis services. Fresenius fared even better, netting more than $1 billion in after-tax profit for 2015. For the first quarter of this year, its revenue was up 6%, net income up 9%. The pharmaceutical industry also benefits tremendously from dialysis. Aside from regularly receiving blood thinners, many patients also receive Epogen, a drug that stimulates blood cell production (kidneys perform this when functioning properly).

"It currently costs about $88,000 a year for a patient to undergo dialysis, according to the USRDS. That's about 60% more than what the average U.S. household earns in a year."

Source: "The Big Business of Dialysis Care," June 9, 2016,
http://catalyst.nejm.org/the-big-business-of-dialysis-care/

Resources

- IBISWorld, January 2017: http://ibisworld.com

Dick's Wings & Grill		Franchise
Approx. Total Investment		$100,000 per restaurant plus a net worth of $500,000
	NAICS 722513	Number of Businesses/Units 22

Rules of Thumb

➤ 35% of annual sales

Resources

- Dick's Wings and Grill: http://www.dickswingsandgrill.com

Diners		
	NAICS 722511	

Rules of Thumb

➤ 30–35% of annual sales plus inventory

Direct Mail Advertising		
SIC 7331-05	NAICS 541860	Number of Businesses/Units 2,503

Rules of Thumb

➤ 40–50% of annual revenues plus inventory

➤ 2–2.5 x SDE not including inventory

Pricing Tips

- Valpak used to be the gold standard for this industry at a multiple of 3. Considering new technology and the economy most have been selling at 2 X SDE or slightly less.

D

Benchmark Data

Statistics (Direct Mail Advertising)

Number of Establishments	2,503
Average Profit Margin	7.2%
Revenue per Employee	$242,700
Average Number of Employees	16.9
Average Wages per Employee	$51,443

Products and Services Segmentation

Full direct mail services	51.3%
Printing and fulfillment services	19.6%
Other services	13.7%
Lettershop services	12.4%
Mailing list support services	3.0%

Major Market Segmentation

Retail Stores	35.0%
Other	20.0%
Restaurants and travel companies	16.8%
Finance, banking and insurance institutions	16.1%
Business-to-business market	12.1%

Industry Costs

Profit	7.2%
Wages	21.4%
Purchases	32.9%
Depreciation	1.2%
Marketing	5.5%
Rent & Utilities	5.2%
Other	26.6%

Market Share

Valassis Communications Inc.	13.8%

Expenses (% of Annual Sales)

Cost of Goods	65%
Occupancy Costs	05%
Payroll/Labor Costs	05% to 10%
Profit (pretax)	20% to 25%

Questions
- How many recurring agreements are in place? How large is your biggest client?
- How many active clients? What is your average net profit?

Industry Trend
- "In 2015, we predicted personalization, increased mobile device adoption and multi-channel analysis as some of the biggest trends for 2016. These predictions turned out to be right in line with what we saw from the industry this past year. For 2017, we foresee some of the same trends continuing, while we

think others will take a more commanding place in the spotlight.
- ✓ Omnichannel Marketing—Many marketers understand the benefits of omnichannel marketing and unified campaigns across different media.
- ✓ Data for Targeted Marketing—Targeted messaging has been a big direct marketing trend over the last few years, and it continues to grow without showing signs of stopping.
- ✓ Direct Mail—Despite worries from marketers that direct mail is becoming outdated and undesirable, research is showing the opposite to be true."

Source: "Keep an Eye Out for These 3 Direct Marketing Trends in 2017," by Jim Leone, December 9, 2016, https://www.iwco.com/blog/2016/12/09/direct-marketing-trends-2017/

Expert Comments

On-line coupon technology has hurt this industry.

Marketability is high. Location and facilities are solid because this biz thrives in metropolitan areas and can be run out of your home.

Resources
- Direct Marketing Association: https://thedma.org/
- IBISWorld, February 2017: http://ibisworld.com
- Direct Marketing News: http://www.dmnews.com/

Direct Selling Businesses		
SIC 5963-98	NAICS 4543	Number of Businesses/Units 705,016

Rules of Thumb
➢ 4.5–5 x EBITDA

Pricing Tips
- It all depends on who is buying and who is selling. Buyer and seller motivation is key. If the seller is very successful and getting in the way of larger companies, that would tend to dramatically increase the price.

Benchmark Data

Statistics (Direct Selling Companies)

Number of Establishments	705,016
Average Profit Margin	7.0%
Revenue per Employee	$51,600
Average Number of Employees	1.1
Average Wages per Employee	$9,112

Products and Services Segmentation

Home and family care products	30.9%
Wellness and personal care products	30.8%
Other products and services	19.3%
Leisure and educational products	10.0%
Clothing and accessories	9.0%

D

Industry Costs

Profit	7.0%
Wages	17.7%
Purchases	64.8%
Depreciation	0.7%
Marketing	1.9%
Rent and Utilities	4.3%
Other	3.6%

- $150,000 annual sales per employee

Expenses (% of Annual Sales)

Cost of Goods	60%
Occupancy Costs	01% to 04%
Payroll/Labor Costs	01%
Profit (pretax)	07% to 10%

Questions

- You need to have detailed information on all the customers. See what trends have been the last 3 years. Who are the suppliers? Many times the key supplier is the buyer. About the employees, how long they have been there and their roles in the company. Need to see all financial information including tax returns for the last 3 years. What equipment is being included like trucks, forklifts and warehouse equipment? Are the bottles, racks, water coolers and coffee brewers in good shape? What is the age of the equipment? What about accounts receivable? Need A/R aging reports, totals for each customer.

Industry Trend

- Increasing consolidation

Seller Financing

- Both are common, many times it is a combination of the outside financing and seller financing.

Resources

- IBISWorld, February 2017: http://ibisworld.com

Disability Facilities		
	NAICS 623210	

Rules of Thumb

- ➢ 42% of annual sales includes inventory
- ➢ 2.6 x SDE includes inventory
- ➢ 6.3 x EBIT
- ➢ 3.8 x EBITDA

Benchmark Data

Statistics (Elderly & Disabled Services)

Number of Establishments	145,273
Average Profit Margin	4.5%
Revenue per Employee	$39,200
Average Number of Employees	9.6
Average Wages per Employee	$19,468

Products and Services Segmentation

In-home personal care services	30.8%
Senior community centers	16.4%
Other services	15.8%
Home-delivered meals and transportation	14.8%
Day care services for the physically disabled	12.4%
Day care services for the learning disabled	6.5%
Disability support groups	3.3%

Major Market Segmentation

People aged 65 years and older	40.0%
People with a physical disability	18.3%
People with a mental disability	10.4%
People with an employment disability	9.2%
People with a sensory disability	8.4%
People unable to leave the home	8.3%
People with a self-care disability	5.4%

Industry Costs

Profit	4.5%
Wages	49.3%
Purchases	13.7%
Depreciation	2.2%
Marketing	1.8%
Rent & Utilities	4.2%
Other	24.3%

Statistics (Residential Intellectual Disability Facilities)

Number of Establishments	63,515
Average Profit Margin	6.7%
Revenue per Employee	$44,600
Average Number of Employees	9.5
Average Wages per Employee	$23,137

Products and Services Segmentation

Facilities for patients with profound disabilities	41.6%
Facilities for patients with severe disabilities	21.7%
Facilities for patients with moderate disabilities	19.7%
Facilities for patients with mild disabilities	17.0%

Industry Costs

Profit	6.7%
Wages	51.8%
Purchases	10.3%
Depreciation	2.7%
Marketing	0.8%
Rent & Utilities	6.0%
Other	21.7%

Expenses (% of Annual Sales)

Cost of Goods	18%
Payroll/Labor Costs	08%
Profit (pretax)	04%

Questions
- Payor mix, market share, patient demographic data.

Industry Trend
- Revenue, profit, and demand projected to grow, industry expected to expand.

Seller Financing
- Outside financing

Resources
- The National Institute of Mental Health (NIMH): http://www.nimh.nih.gov
- American Health Care Association:
  https://www.ahcancal.org/Pages/Default.aspx
- IBISWorld, April 2017: http://ibisworld.com
- IBISWorld, November 2016: http://ibisworld.com

Distribution/Wholesale—Durable Goods

	NAICS 423	

Rules of Thumb

➤ 4 x EBITDA

➤ 4.5 x EBIT

➤ 2–2.5 x SDE plus inventory

Pricing Tips
- Inventory (durable or non-durable) is critical to the sale and must be current, well managed with appropriate controls and real time valuation processes in place.
- Worth approximately one-half of sales volume; watch out for large, stale inventory.
- Percentage of annual gross sales is a poor guide to follow. EBITDA drives ROI and ability to service debt.
- Add cost of replacing current ownership with professional management to SDE, and then multiply this number by 4 to 6 to get price. variance is for security of earnings, competition, assets, etc.

Benchmark Data

- Distribution costs are sensitive to energy prices. Direct competition from manufacturers is increasing which creates a challenge for many distributors and a need to find service and delivery differentiation for the clients.
- Cost of goods should be less than 74%, with 70% as ideal; operating expenses of less than 20%; sales/assets ratio of 3.0; W/C ratio of 13% to 15% of revenues; current ratio of 3.0 or greater; A/R turnover ratio of 12.0; inventory turns of 6.0 or greater; sales per employee greater than $250,000; sales per sq. ft. in excess of $300,000.

Expenses (% of Annual Sales)

Cost of Goods	70% to 80%
Occupancy Costs	03% to 08%
Payroll/Labor Costs	10% to 20%
Profit (pretax)	08% to 15%

Questions

- Does the business belong to any distributor buying groups/co-ops?

Expert Comments

There are significant competitive cost barriers to entry into this industry, where size does matter along with quantity and quality of product lines, adequate logistical distribution channels, good supplier pricing and terms, adequate facilities sizing and location. Solid, well-diversified customer base mitigates risk and wards off competitive challenges.

Seller Financing

- Banks like the industry and will generally provide SBA 7(a) credit to qualified buyer and where consistent cash flow is evident.

Resources

- National Association of Wholesaler-Distributors: http://www.naw.org

Distribution/Wholesale—Electrical Products	
NAICS 423610	Number of Businesses/Units 15,404

Rules of Thumb

> 35% of
> annual revenues plus inventory

Benchmark Data

Statistics (Electrical Equipment Wholesaling)

Number of Establishments	15,404
Average Profit Margin	4.4%
Revenue per Employee	$859,100
Average Number of Employees	13.9
Average Wages per Employee	$74,606

Products and Services Segmentation

Other electrical equipment.. 28.3%
Wiring.. 23.3%
Lighting fixtures and light bulbs 17.3%
Switchgear and switchboard apparatus... 9.6%
Relay and industrial controls... 8.7%
Motors and generators... 7.1%
Power and distribution transformers 5.7%

Major Market Segmentation

Construction... 44.5%
Industrial users 28.6%
Commercial, institutional and governmental...................................... 14.1%
Utility 12.8%

Industry Costs

Profit 4.4%
Wages.. 8.7%
Purchases.. 74.9%
Depreciation.. 0.5%
Marketing 0.3%
Rent & Utilities 2.0%
Other.. 9.2%

Resources

- IBISWorld, March 2017: http://ibisworld.com

Distribution/Wholesale—Grocery Products/Full Line		
SIC 5141-05	NAICS 424990	Number of Businesses/Units 5,454

Rules of Thumb

➢ 4 x EBIT

➢ 3–4 x SDE

➢ 4–4.5 x EBITDA

Pricing Tips

- Use 25%-30% of GPM [gross profit margin] times 4 to arrive at goodwill price including all F F & E. To this number, add the dollar amount of net working capital, if any, to be included in the sale.

Benchmark Data

Statistics (Grocery Wholesaling)

Number of Establishments... 5,454
Average Profit Margin 3.0%
Revenue per Employee $1,347,300
Average Number of Employees 26.5
Average Wages per Employee $57,025

Products and Services Segmentation

Other	23.5%
Fresh meat and meat products	20.0%
Canned food	17.7%
Frozen food	13.0%
Dairy products	10.0%
Specialty food	6.0%
Fresh fruits and vegetables	5.4%
Paper and plastic products	4.4%

Major Market Segmentation

Food service outlets	53.5%
Supermarkets and other grocery retailers	30.8%
Other wholesalers	11.9%
Other	3.8%

Industry Costs

Profit	3.0%
Wages	4.2%
Purchases	82.3%
Depreciation	0.4%
Marketing	0.5%
Rent & Utilities	1.9%
Other	7.7%

Market Share

SYSCO Corporation	24.7%
C&S Wholesale Grocers Inc.	17.0%
US Foods	12.1%
Performance Food Group	7.2%
Wakefern Food Corporation	5.0%

Expenses (% of Annual Sales)

Cost of Goods	80% to 83%
Occupancy Costs	05%
Payroll/Labor Costs	12%
Profit (pretax)	07% to 08%

Questions
- Stability of gross profit margins?

Resources
- IBISWorld, January 2017: http://ibisworld.com

Distribution/Wholesale—Industrial Supplies		
	NAICS 423840	Number of Businesses/Units 10,123

Rules of Thumb

➢ 50% of annual revenues plus inventory

➢ 4–5 x EBITDA

D

Pricing Tips

- Many distributorships for larger equipment do not order high dollar inventory until they receive a request from a customer to order that equipment. Therefore, inventory levels may not be extremely high as they try to not hold excess inventory. If the business you are evaluating is not operated this way and there is a large amount of inventory, you may need to consider that in your working capital calculations.

Benchmark Data

Statistics (Industrial Supplies Wholesaling)

Number of Establishments	10,123
Average Profit Margin	4.3%
Revenue per Employee	$784,100
Average Number of Employees	9.6
Average Wages per Employee	$70,361

Products and Services Segmentation

Abrasives, strapping and tape	30.8%
Industrial containers	19.0%
Other supplies	16.5%
Mechanical power transmission supplies	15.4%
Industrial valves and fittings	14.4%
Welding supplies	3.9%

Major Market Segmentation

Industrial users for production inputs	49.0%
Other wholesalers for resale	25.7%
Businesses for end use	10.3%
Other	7.0%
Retailers for resale	5.0%
Building contractors	3.0%

Industry Costs

Profit	4.3%
Wages	9.1%
Purchases	74.8%
Depreciation	0.7%
Marketing	0.4%
Rent & Utilities	1.0%
Other	9.7%

Questions

- Who are your distributor agreements with? What restrictions do you have regarding geography and other products? How many additional products can your current sales force add to their sales book?

Expert Comments

Companies that represent quality lines of products are desired. Contracts with customers to consistently provide their equipment or supplies or maintenance are a major plus.

Resources

- Industrial Supply Association: http://www.isapartners.org
- IBISWorld, April 2017: http://ibisworld.com

Distribution/Wholesale—In General

Rules of Thumb

➤ 3–3.2 x EBIT

➤ 3.5 x–4.5 x EBITDA

➤ 2.75 x–3.75 x SDE plus inventory

➤ 60–65% of annual sales includes inventory

Pricing Tips

- Scale, location and profitability are the key strategic indicators of value in the business. Inventory turns and accounts receivable are equally important especially if it is tied to the apartment industry. Does the company have capital reserves to handle the cyclical nature of the industry while maintaining high inventory and AR? Multiple locations and long-running customer relationships, along with contracts for preferred customer discounts, will increase the multiples for pricing. Large wholesalers like Home Depot and Lowe's service the apartment industry on a national level, but smaller companies in the southern states are more nimble and provide a higher quality of personal service.
- Typically, the larger the cash flow, the higher the multiple. Every deal is different.
- Revenue multiple only relevant with multi-year contracts and no concentration issues
- The cost of inventory can be a significant barrier to entry even if it is easy to replicate the distribution model.
- Distribution companies that are profitable with a strong history and diversified customer base can command high multiples.
- Assumes SDE in excess of $500K. Where less than $500K, lower multiples; where over $1M, multiples exceed 3 and escalate as SDE increases.
- Suppliers, how many, and will that continue for a new owner, under the same or better terms. Current contracts with customers and account concentration issues all of high importance in determining value.
- Debt service will have great impact on ultimate rule of thumb multiple considering "living wage" necessary by locality after debt is serviced.

Benchmark Data

- 8–10 times annual inventory turnover, gross margins 40%, AR collections less than 10% over 90 days, receiving to stock within 24 hours, 97% fill rate
- $200K per employee.
- Over $700,000 revenue per employee. Can be quite a bit more for efficient operators.
- The occupancy costs can vary considerably depending if the seller is the landlord or not.
- High margins for the most part

D

- Low rent can be easy to achieve for these types of 'warehouse' businesses.
- Cost of goods sold varies from 60%–70% depending on product.

Expenses (% of Annual Sales)

Cost of Goods	60% to 70%
Occupancy Costs	04% to 05%
Payroll/Labor Costs	20% to 25%
Profit (pretax)	10% to 15%

Questions

- Determine how many employee and customer relationships are tied to the owner(s). Will the owner stay on for a year or more to transition the customers and employees along with providing an in-depth knowledge of the business and industry? Structure and earnout with the owner? Is the industry cyclical and or seasonal? Who are the largest competitors?
- Customer concentration percentages, vendor concentration percentages, recent revenue and cash flow trends
- How much have margins shrunk in the past 5 to 10 years?
- In the middle market, the buyers are usually smarter than the seller, in that they have bought and sold many companies, whereas the seller is often selling for the first time.
- What other products or lines can they distribute, are there any restrictions given by current suppliers?
- Get financials for past 3 years and year-to-date. What has changed in your industry? Do you sell to distributors? If so, what are the margins? What is the source of your product and is there an agreement to assure continued supply?
- What is the current method of finding and keeping customers? How do they expect the current sales to grow? Does China or overseas production cause any future issues for the current products sold?
- How many clients do you have and how many are regularly serviced?

Industry Trend

- "Plenty of companies are angling to get in on the coming legalized pot bonanza. Some, however, are lobbying the state to carve off a piece just for them: cigarette wholesalers. The companies that track, deliver, and tax all the cigarettes sold in Massachusetts are seeking a similar monopoly on recreational marijuana when sales begin in 2018. They've asked state officials to require marijuana producers to sell all their pot products through them—just as most alcohol has to pass through a wholesaler on its way to bars and package stores."

  Source: "Tobacco wholesalers want similar monopoly with legalized pot," by Dan Adams, *Boston Sunday Globe*, June 11, 2107

- Smaller companies will emerge as the market continues to consolidate due to the high service levels and personal relationships at the end user's level. Larger supply companies with brand recognition and buying power will compete on a national level to gain market share with large REIT's and other national management companies.
- Strong market for the sale of distribution businesses. Online sales cutting into business at some distribution companies.
- Tightening margins
- High-tech distribution and value add services distributors will continue to grow and outperform competition. Those that have figured out a recurring revenue model (30 to 50% of revenue) are appraised at considerable higher multiples.

Expert Comments

They will need a high level of working capital and bank financing to purchase these types of businesses. Inventory turns will identify dead inventory and the percentage of AR over 90 days should be discounted. Understand the needs of the in user and the relationship with the sales force. The outside sales staff should sign new non-compete agreements as it is usually not enforceable with a stock sale. Incentive key employees to stay.

Look carefully and customer and vendor concentration. Look at whether the product being distributed is under attack by firms such as Amazon. Are the manufacturers showing signs of going direct and cutting out the distributor?

Currently, more buyers than sellers. Some distribution companies are being squeezed out by manufacturers selling direct.

Firm up contracts and solve any customer concentration issues.

Small distributorships attract a great deal of interest even though the barrier to entry is quite low.

Make sure you understand the technology and have good management and financial skills.

Sellers—Start preparing for your sale as much as five years in advance. Selling a business is very complex and you need to develop a good team of advisors. Five years in advance is not always possible but I recommend the seller hire an exit planner with experience in this industry to help with the complexities of the process. I also suggest you hire an experience investment banker. They have sold many businesses and understand they types of advisors required (Tax and Audit CPA, Transaction Attorney, Financial Advisor and more - all should have M&A experience, if you have an important advisor without the experience let them help you find one to augment their skills and experience). No matter how much the advisors cost they should easily pay for themselves many times over.

Buyers—Assuming you know the industry, please put a high-quality team of advisors together as mentioned above. You will need a forensic CPA (audit), a good tax CPA, transaction attorney and more.

Seller Financing
- Outside financing and long personal guarantees for previous owners. Middle Market M&A and Private Equity Companies provide the valuation and terms of the deals in this space.
- Typical deals involve SBA or conventional bank financing. Sale to private equity groups may involve no outside financing and small holdback or promissory note.
- Seller financing: 24 months at 5% for 10 to 15% of the deal.

Resources
- Modern Distribution Management: http://www.mdm.com/
- National Association of Wholesaler-Distributors: http://www.naw.org
- List of Trade Associations: http://www.ceostrategist.com/links-wholesale-distribution.html
- American Supply Association: http://www.asa.net/

D

Distribution/Wholesale—Janitorial

	NAICS 423850	Number of Businesses/Units 2,580

Rules of Thumb

➢ 30–40% of annual sales plus inventory

Benchmark Data

Statistics (Cleaning & Maintenance Supplies Distributors)

Number of Establishments	2,580
Average Profit Margin	3.6%
Revenue per Employee	$312,400
Average Number of Employees	11.8
Average Wages per Employee	$31,815

Products and Services Segmentation

Paper and plastics products	46.5%
Chemical supplies	23.6%
All janitorial supplies and accessories	22.3%
Power equipment	7.6%

Major Market Segmentation

Industrial and commercial buildings	28.3%
Healthcare Centers	15.1%
Janitorial service companies	14.0%
Others	12.8%
Schools, colleges and universities	12.5%
Retail, malls, department stores, grocery stores and other	10.8%
Government buildings	6.5%

Industry Costs

Profit	3.6%
Wages	10.3%
Purchases	70.1%
Depreciation	0.6%
Marketing	0.6%
Rent & Utilities	4.9%
Other	9.9%

Market Share

Essendant, Inc.	17.0%
SupplyWorks	10.7%

Resources

- IBISWorld, May 2017: http://ibisworld.com

Distribution/Wholesale—Medical Equipment & Supplies

	NAICS 42145	Number of Businesses/Units 13,455

Rules of Thumb

➢ 4 x EBITDA

➢ 4 x SDE

➢ 50% of annual revenues plus inventory

Pricing Tips

- It is important to look at the licensing issues to determine who can legally purchase the business. If it is restricted to a doctor or licensed professional then the buyer pool is smaller and the multiple needs to be reduced.
- Pricing on medical equipment tends to be a higher percentage of sales than medical supplies. While the percentage of annual sales price might be a bit higher than the multiple in the Rule of Thumb above, the price based on percentage of annual sales for medical supplies could be lower.

Benchmark Data

Statistics (Medical Supplies Wholesaling)

Number of Establishments	13,455
Average Profit Margin	6.8%
Revenue per Employee	$886,800
Average Number of Employees	16.6
Average Wages per Employee	$103,996

Products and Services Segmentation

Surgical, medical and hospital instruments and equipment	53.4%
Surgical, medical and hospital supplies	24.1%
Orthopedic and prosthetic appliances and supplies	10.4%
Dental equipment, instruments and supplies	6.5%
Other	4.2%
Pharmaceuticals, cosmetics and toiletries	1.4%

Major Market Segmentation

Hospitals	63.5%
Clinics	20.7%
Alternate care providers	11.1%
Dentists	4.7%

Industry Costs

Profit	6.8%
Wages	11.7%
Purchases	73.3%
Depreciation	0.8%
Marketing	0.7%
Rent & Utilities	0.7%
Other	6.0%

Market Share

Cardinal Health Inc.	7.1%
Owens & Minor Inc.	5.0%

Expenses (% of Annual Sales)

Cost of Goods 14%

Industry Trend

- Due to the aging of the population, medically related transactions will be in huge demand.

Expert Comments

Use an attorney familiar with the industry.

Seller Financing

- Fairly easy to get outside financing, but often a small earnout or seller carry component.

Resources

- IBISWorld, May 2017: http://ibisworld.com

Distribution/Wholesale—Paper		
	NAICS 425120	Number of Businesses/Units 1,496

Rules of Thumb

➢ 5 x EBITDA

➢ 3–4 x SDE plus inventory

➢ 4–5 x EBIT

Pricing Tips

- Use 25–30% of GPM [Gross Profit Margin] times 4 to arrive at goodwill price including all FF&E. To this number, add the dollar amount of net working capital to be included in the sale.

Benchmark Data

Statistics (Paper Wholesaling)

Number of Establishments 1,496
Average Profit Margin 2.3%
Revenue per Employee $2,306,700
Average Number of Employees 8.4
Average Wages per Employee $69,740

Products and Services Segmentation

Printing and writing paper 59.8%
Fine roll paper 21.0%
Paper and plastic products 8.8%
Other 7.6%
Newsprint 2.8%

Major Market Segmentation

Paper converters	30.0%
Other industries	29.6%
Book and magazine publishers	26.5%
Commercial printing	8.9%
Newspaper publishers	3.0%
Exports	2.0%

Industry Costs

Profit	2.3%
Wages	3.1%
Purchases	79.6%
Depreciation	0.2%
Marketing	0.5%
Rent & Utilities	1.1%
Other	13.2%

Market Share

Veritiv Corp.	26.3%

Expenses (% of Annual Sales)

Cost of Goods	70% to 75%
Occupancy Costs	04%
Payroll/Labor Costs	10%
Profit (pretax)	08% to 10%

Questions

- Stability of gross profit margins, number of inventory turns per year. Percentage of slow moving inventory and the need for adjustments thereof.

Industry Trend

- Stable

Resources

- IBISWorld, November 2016: http://ibisworld.com

Distribution/Wholesale—Tools	
NAICS 423171	Number of Businesses/Units 7,916

Rules of Thumb

➢ 55% of annual sales includes inventory

➢ 3.7 x SDE includes inventory

Pricing Tips

- Higher multiples for the higher net profit industries

D

Benchmark Data

Statistics (Tool and Hardware Wholesaling

Number of Establishments	7,916
Average Profit Margin	5.0%
Revenue per Employee	$668,900
Average Number of Employees	11.7
Average Wages per Employee	$62,578

Products and Services Segmentation

Bolts, nuts, rivets and other fasteners (excludes nails)	55.7%
Hand tools and power tools	29.7%
Miscellaneous hardware	8.0%
Plumbing and hydronic heating equipment	6.6%

Major Market Segmentation

Retailers	43.7%
Other wholesalers	19.8%
Manufacturing and mining industries	13.6%
Building contractors and heavy construction	12.0%
Businesses and others for end use	10.9%

Industry Costs

Profit	5.0%
Wages	9.4%
Purchases	57.0%
Depreciation	0.5%
Marketing	1.0%
Rent & Utilities	3.5%
Other	23.6%

Market Share

Stanley Black & Decker Inc.	8.3%
Ace Hardware Corp.	7.9%

- Very hands-on with the key customers. Must maintain knowledge of the products they need to service their clients.

Expenses (% of Annual Sales)

Cost of Goods	74%
Occupancy Costs	01%
Payroll/Labor Costs	08%
Profit (pretax)	15%

Questions
- Do you need a mechanical background or inclination to be successful?

Industry Trend
- Good

Expert Comments

Location is not typically important since there is not much drop-in traffic.

Resources

- IBISWorld, April 2017: http://ibisworld.com

Document Destruction		
	NAICS 561990	

Rules of Thumb

➤ 150% of annual sales includes inventory

➤ 4 x SDE includes inventory

➤ 6 x EBIT

➤ 6 x EBITDA

Pricing Tips

- Prices range from 1.25 to 2.0 times gross revenues
- Mobile shredding operations include price adjustments to compensate for the age of the fleet.

Benchmark Data

- Well-run businesses can generate $250K–$300K revenue per vehicle in fleet.
- EBITDA margins should exceed 30% for mobile operations and 35% for plant-based operations.

Expenses (% of Annual Sales)

Cost of Goods	40%
Occupancy Costs	05%
Payroll/Labor Costs	25%
Profit (pretax)	30%

Questions

- Age of fleet and the output of plant facilities are important. Industry standard equipment is a must.
- What % of the business is recurring versus one-time purge service revenues? Is the service provided on-site at the customer location via a mobile shredding truck or destroyed in a plant environment off-site?

Industry Trend

- "The maturity of the document destruction industry in the United States has resulted in a saturated market where any new entrants will find it tough going and existing companies will likely grow their businesses faster in the future through acquisitions and mergers, according to one industry veteran. 'I don't believe you're going to see a lot of new document destruction services entering the industry in North America,' says Bob Johnson, chief executive officer at the National Association for Information Destruction (NAID)."

Source: "Consolidation, Drop in Service Providers Predicted for Saturated Shred Industry," by P.J. Heller, http://www.securityshreddingnews.com/in-the-news/articles/2016-articles/230-consolidation-drop-in-service-providers-predicted-for-saturated-shred-industry

D

- Industry revenues should continue to grow. Consolidation has reduced the number of larger independently owned businesses.
- Revenue trends exceed 20% growth due to heightened awareness of confidentiality and identity theft concerns. Many state regulations require shredding of confidential information.

Expert Comments

In a world of daily data breaches, identity theft and privacy concerns, ensuring the protection of information is dire. Companies are looking for better protection in regard to the secure destruction of their private documents as confidentiality and security top businesses' list of importance.

High revenue growth rates have attracted new market competition.

This is a high-growth industry, with low technology requirements and relatively few barriers to entry.

Resources

- National Association for Information Destruction: http://www.naidonline.org/nitl/en
- Security Shredding and Storage News: http://www.securityshreddingnews.com
- Recycling Today: http://www.recyclingtoday.com/magazine/code/sdb/

Dog Kennels		
SIC 0752-05	NAICS 812910	

Rules of Thumb

➢ 4.5 x EBITDA

➢ 1 x annual sales plus inventory

➢ 2.7 x EBIT

➢ 2–3 x SDE plus inventory

Pricing Tips

- Annual Gross Multiplier not accurate reflection, comparable sales range from 0.2 to 1.2, would not advise using. SDE multiplier the most consistent method of establishing value and it varies from 2 to 3.3. Low end multiplier for more risky businesses; i.e., high owner dependency and large amount of revenue from grooming or training. Higher end multiplier for facilities with management, less owner dependency, well trending revenues, long term lease or property owned by seller.
- Careful consideration of multiplier of add backs, revenue trend, geographic location.
- American Boarding Kennel Association (ABKA) uses 1 to 1.5 times gross sales plus real estate. These transactions can be very real estate intensive and often business does not support debt service. That needs to be taken into consideration when pricing. Location and zoning influence pricing considerably.

Benchmark Data

- Overnight boarding annual occupancy rate should be above 50%.
- Labor is the largest expense, should be around 30% to 35% but can be as high as 50%.
- SDE above 30%, EBITDA minimum 25%
- Too varied. Payroll should be below 35% of gross revenue.
- Occupancy! A successful facility should have a year-round occupancy level of at least 50%. Per-run revenue can be measured; but, as many facilities also provide grooming and daycare services, not a reliable benchmark. Payroll below 40% of Gross Income. Overall, SDE should be close to, or above, 30% of Gross Income.

Expenses (% of Annual Sales)

Cost of Goods	03%
Occupancy Costs	10% to 17%
Payroll/Labor Costs	35% to 40%
Profit (pretax)	20% to 30%

Questions

- Describe your daily and weekly duties; what exactly do you do at the business? (Sellers are the biggest risk factors in a sale in this industry.)
- Do you have direct client contact and if yes, how much?
- History of staffing to learn of turnover
- Investigate owner involvement with customers. Verify licenses, zoning, allowed use. If seller grooms or trains, expect that income to be eliminated with a sale.

Industry Trend

- Consolidation from corporate buyers. The industry will continue to grow due to consumer's affection for their pets. Rover.com will take some of the market.
- Growth, more franchises, more 'resort' style facilities, more competition.

Expert Comments

Buyers: Learn about dogs and pack management as it's a risk mitigation tool. Volunteer at a facility to really experience what it means to work in the environment; this industry is quite romanticized and often different from what one expects. Understand the staffing structure and the needs of clients who are emotionally tied to their dogs. Sellers: Minimize your involvement. Don't directly generate income (grooming, training). Hire a GM and empower him.

There are limited barriers to entry except the cost of facilities. No professional licenses required, kennel license requirement varies by state, county and city (typically easy to obtain). Risk factors are mainly centered around the seller's involvement in business; this is a highly loyalty & trust based industry. High profit industry if properly managed, SDE typically 25% to 30% of gross revenue. Often seller owns the real estate, so Rent expense needs to be adjusted to FMV of rent (some owners don't charge rent at all so a recast needs to account for that negative adjustment). Industry trending very strongly upwards.

D

Seller Financing

- SBA financing as long as business cash flow qualifies. Corporate buyers pay cash.
- Combination of both. SBA loans are readily available if business cash flow is sufficient.

Resources

- National Association of Professional Pet Sitters: http://www.petsitters.org
- International Boarding and Pet Services Association: http://www.ibpsa.com
- Barkleigh Pet Boarding and Daycare Magazine: http://www.petboardinganddaycare.com

		Franchise
Dollar Discount Stores		
Approx. Total Investment		$99,000–$195,000
	NAICS 452990	Number of Businesses/Units 140

Rules of Thumb

➤ 20% of annual sales plus inventory

Benchmark Data

- For Benchmark Data see Dollar Stores

Resources

- Dollar Discount: http://dollardiscount.com

Dollar Stores		
	NAICS 452990	

Rules of Thumb

➤ 15–20% of annual sales plus inventory

➤ 2–2.5 x SDE plus inventory

➤ 2–2.5 x EBITDA

➤ 1.5–2 x EBIT

Pricing Tips

- With the increase in competition, margins must be looked into carefully.
- Sells easily, as mom-and-pops are moving in, and it's day hours only.
- Very competitive market. More diversification and the astute marketers are moving to the $1-$5 spread.
- There seems to be a downward pressure on profitability but the dollar stores are expanding into higher priced and higher margin items.

Benchmark Data

Statistics (Dollar and Variety Stores)

Number of Establishments 55,249
Average Profit Margin 4.7%
Revenue per Employee $170,100
Average Number of Employees 7.0
Average Wages per Employee $15,981

Products and Services Segmentation

Kitchenware and home furnishings 19.6%
Others 19.2%
Soaps, detergents, cleaning supplies and paper related products 18.7%
Groceries 16.7%
Drugs, health aids and beauty cosmetics 13.9%
Men's and womenswear, and other textile products 11.9%

Industry Costs

Profit 4.7%
Wages 9.3%
Purchases 64.2%
Depreciation 0.8%
Marketing 1.1%
Rent and Utilities 7.9%
Other 12.0%

Market Share

Dollar General Corporation 33.4%
Dollar Tree Stores Inc. 29.2%
Big Lots Inc. 7.5%

Expenses (% of Annual Sales)

Cost of Goods .... 70% to 75%
Occupancy Costs 10%
Payroll/Labor Costs .... 15% to 17%
Profit (pretax) .... 20% to 25%

Questions

- Tax returns and all invoices
- Paperwork, and sit and observe
- Margins and vendor contacts

Industry Trend

- "Dollar stores have grown sales fast. From 2010 through 2015, the top four chains grew their combined total annual sales from $28 billion to an estimated $42 billion, representing a compound annual growth rate (CAGR) of 8.5%."

   Source: "How The Dollar Store Boom May Shake Up Big Grocers," by Deborah Weinswig, May 9, 2016, https://www.forbes.com/sites/deborahweinswig/2016/05/09/how-the-dollar-store-boom-may-shake-up-big-grocers/#42e485eb60db

- Next to supercenters, dollar stores remain the fastest growing channel among food, drug, and mass retailing. No-frills stores, low prices, and a small, easy-to-shop and easy-to-access format gives shoppers a convenient option to big box discount retailers, like Wal-Mart. 'Dollar stores combine pricing power, efficient operations, and small stores to make the model work,' comments Skrovan.

Source: www.retailindustry.about.com/od/seg_dollar_stores/a/bl

Expert Comments

Not too difficult to replicate; needs a large amount of inventory; the larger the store, the better the variety and the sales.

Resources

- IBISWorld, December 2016: http://ibisworld.com
- Dollar$tores: http://www.buckstore.com

Domino's Pizza	Franchise
Approx. Total Investment	$119,950–$461,700
Estimated Annual Sales/Unit	$925,000
SIC 5812-22 NAICS 722513	Number of Businesses/Units 12,900

Resources

- Domino's Pizza: https://biz.dominos.com/

Donut Shops	
SIC 5461-05 NAICS 722515	Number of Businesses/Units 25,144

Rules of Thumb

➤ 45–50% of annual sales plus inventory (and can go much higher for a great store)

➤ 2–2.5 x SDE plus inventory

Pricing Tips

- Higher coffee sales (60 percent of sales) produce higher value. Very low coffee sales produce lower values.
- Length & cost of lease? Retail vs. wholesale business? Percentage of business that is coffee (the higher the percentage of coffee sales, the higher the price).

Benchmark Data

Statistics (Doughnut Stores)

Number of Establishments	25,144
Average Profit Margin	6.6%
Revenue per Employee	$62,600
Average Number of Employees	9.5
Average Wages per Employee	$15,957

Products and Services Segmentation

Donuts in bulk	25.0%
Coffee	20.0%
Other beverages	18.0%
Other items	18.0%
Yeast donuts	10.0%
Mini donuts and donut holes	5.0%
Other donuts	4.0%

Industry Costs

Profit	6.6%
Wages	25.5%
Purchases	38.8%
Depreciation	3.1%
Marketing	3.4%
Rent & Utilities	12.5%
Other	10.1%

Expenses (% of Annual Sales)

Cost of Goods	21% food
Occupancy Costs	10%
Payroll/Labor Costs	20% to 23%

Industry Trend

- "When the three most popular bakeries in the United States are donut shops, based on a Travel + Leisure magazine report citing Instagram data, it may be time to officially proclaim the donut as America's favorite sweet baked good, surpassing the once beloved cupcake.

  "U.S. retail sales of donuts at supermarkets and convenience stores reached $1.97 billion for the 52 weeks ended Nov. 27, 2016, which was up 3.4% from the previous 52 weeks, according to Information Resources, Inc., a Chicago-based market research firm. Over the past four years, supermarket sales of fresh donuts have risen by an average of 5.2% a year."

  Source: "Wild about donuts" by John Unrein, March 3, 2017,
  http://www.bakingbusiness.com/articles/news_home/Trends/2017/03/Wild_about_donuts.
  aspx?ID=%7BA68A0EEB-6174-462F-9264-BD9619C48CAF%7D&cck=1

Resources

- IBISWorld, March 2017: http://ibisworld.com

			Franchise
Dream Dinners			
Approx. Total Investment			$273,200–$418,000
	NAICS 445299		Number of Businesses/Units 87

Rules of Thumb

➤ 40% of annual sales plus inventory

Resources

- Dream Dinners: http://www.dreamdinners.com

D

Drive-in Restaurants

	NAICS 722513	

Rules of Thumb

➢ 40–45% of annual sales plus inventory

➢ 5–6 x monthly sales plus inventory

Drive-in Theaters

	NAICS 512132	Number of Businesses/Units 595

Rules of Thumb

➢ 2% of annual sales plus equipment and real estate

Benchmark Data

- "In 2015, there were 595 Drive-ins in the U.S., up from 366 in 2012."

Source: natoonline.org—an interesting website

Industry Trend

- "As of June 2016:
    - ✓ 324 theatre locations in the USA
    - ✓ 299 Locations are digital
    - ✓ 595 total screens"

Source: http://www.uditoa.org/media.html

- Drive-ins and small-town movie theaters have been challenged in the past few years since the movie industry has been phasing out film prints and implementing the use of digital protection. Adapting to digital, however, can cost theater owners $70,000-$80,000 per projector.

Resources

- National Association of Theatre Owners: http://www.natoonline.org/
- United Drive-in Theatre Owners Association: http://www.uditoa.org/

		Franchise
Dr. Vinyl		
Approx. Total Investment		$44,000–$69,500
	NAICS 325211	Number of Businesses/Units 170

Rules of Thumb

➢ 75% of annual sales plus inventory

Resources

- Dr. Vinyl: http://www.drvinyl.com

D

Dry Cleaners

SIC 7212-01	NAICS 812320	Number of Businesses/Units 36,199

Rules of Thumb

- 70–80% of sales plus inventory. Plants with on-site laundry equipment will get a higher multiple.
- 2.5–3 x SDE plus inventory
- 2–3 x EBIT
- 2.5–3 x EBITDA

Pricing Tips

- Smaller dry cleaners sell for 2.5x SDE; larger dry cleaners sell for 3x–3.5x SDE.
- I personally don't rely on gross revenue; that is a starting point. I form my opinion of value based on SDE, and I take a consideration for the dry cleaner machine. There is a big price difference if the dry cleaner plant has a perc. machine vs. hydrocarbon or wet machine, for example. Front assigned parking is critical for dry cleaners, the location etc.
- "There are several formulas to determine selling price. Most of them work on some version of a multiple of net profit over the last three years, giving more preference for recent years. This profitability factor translates to what the business is worth, and is used to assess the 15% to 30% rate of return a buyer wants to achieve. So, if a buyer wants to achieve a 15% rate of return, and the business churns out a $30,000 net profit per year, the buyer will not pay more than $200,000 for the business (because a $200,000 investment will return exactly a 15% return of $30,000, which is the current profitability)."

  Source: https://americandrycleaner.com/articles/right-way-sell-your-drycleaning-business-conclusion

- Business that has good equipment and has its own shirt machine and does mostly retail business and is not a discount store will always be in high demand.
- Dry cleaners grossing under $500,000 sell for about 1X gross sales, 2.5X cash flow. Dry cleaners grossing over $500,000 sell for about 3X cash flow. Dry cleaners with a cash flow over $500,000 can sell for 4X cash flow.
- Dry cleaning machine and shirt machine play a big key role in pricing. There will be a significant price difference between a dry cleaner plant with an extra large size and good brand hydro carbon machine and very good condition shirt machine vs. dry cleaner with perc machine and no or older type shirt machine. Perc dry cleaner machine will be obsolete in 2020, therefore it has no value; it's the same with a shirt machine, if the owner does it with old press machine, creative old way vs. newer shirt machine. A good brand 60-lb. hydro- carbon dry cleaning machine and shirt machine will run approximately $80,000 to $100,000 after delivery and installation, and configuring, plumbing and electrical. Other important equipment overlooked are all pressers and the boiler-are they installed correctly and are they up to the current code?
- Dry cleaner plant with high volume over-the-counter (retail vs. wholesale) will get more SDE multiple. Ample parking is very important with 1 or 2 assigned parking spaces in the front.
- Owner who is involved and works in the business will get lower SDE multiple vs. owner who only oversees the business and has all employees in place including front counter.

D

Benchmark Data

Statistics (Dry Cleaners)

Number of Establishments	36,199
Average Profit Margin	8.5%
Revenue per Employee	$62,300
Average Number of Employees	4.0
Average Wages per Employee	$21,394

Products and Services Segmentation

Retail dry cleaning and laundry services	63.6%
Commercial full-service laundry	15.9%
Commercial dry cleaning services	12.4%
Other	8.1%

Industry Costs

Profit	8.5%
Wages	34.0%
Purchases	16.0%
Depreciation	4.7%
Marketing	2.6%
Rent & Utilities	17.9%
Other	16.3%

- Profit on a dry cleaner should be between 35% and 40% depending on owner involvement.
- COGS above in expenses as a % of annual sales is for dry cleaner agencies; the plants will have way less COGS, but the labor cost will be higher.
- Dry cleaner agencies have higher COGS because the garment will be picked up and delivered by dry cleaner plants.
- Typical breakeven for a dry cleaning store is approximately $150,000 annual sales. Average is $250,000

Expenses (% of Annual Sales)

Cost of Goods	30%
Occupancy Costs	11% to 15%
Payroll/Labor Costs	25% to 28
Profit (pretax)	15% to 25%

Questions

- Always the first question I ask for plants is what type of dry cleaner machine do they have? Do they have a shirt machine, what type and the brand? Do you have computerized POS system to verify the sales? Ask the seller if he knows about any EPA problems. Are they a discount cleaner or a full-price cleaner? How many hours the seller or family member works in the cleaner. Who does the alterations? This is a very important question that is overlooked by the buyers.
- Do you have computerized cash registers so verification of the sales can be made?
- Make sure that the store doesn't have any EPA problems.
- How much does a seller actually work in the business?

- Buyer should ask for all the brands and sizes of all the equipment including laundry machines and determine if the capacity will be enough in case of growth. Number of slots on conveyor line, discount or full service, prices for garment, delivery retail or wholesale. If they do delivery is the van included in the price? Tailoring-if so, who does it? How to handle work in process/accounts receivable.
- Books and records, age of equipment and what solvent is being used.
- Who are the biggest competitors?
- The age of the boiler and the dry cleaning machine. Anything newer than 10 years is good.

Industry Trend

- Many more dry cleaners are being built, much more competition.
- Lot of dry cleaner plants with perc. machine will go out of business especially those with lower revenue because of environmental AQMD law; all perc. machines will be removed by end of 2020.
- This industry is very stable if the following is applied: customer relationship and quality of service is the key.
- Dry cleaners are consolidating. Individual owners are owning more than one location.
- Dry cleaners with perc. machines will be closing down unless they are in a great location and their volume is high. More and more bigger cleaners will be replacing the little cleaners, including discount cleaners. It is very difficult for discount cleaners to make a profit in a high-cost area like California.
- Sales will be up as more and more employees are trending to looking and feeling good about how they present themselves.
- I believe we are in the beginning of a growth phase. Consumer confidence, fabrics, clothing costs and economy are some of the reasons. It's easy to copy but hard to replicate a successful operation. Our industry is very detailed in nature. The removal of small stains, professional pressing, replacing missing or cracked buttons are all fairly easy tasks but you need someone on staff that will actually look for and complete. It is this consistency of quality and caring that will build your sales. Customer service is the primary reason people either stop coming or continue to become loyal customers.

Expert Comments

There are a lot of dry cleaners. Small ones are more easy to replicate, large cleaners in a good location are much more difficult to replicate.

Do a lot of research before buying a dry cleaner; the buyer should know all state and local environmental restrictions, and be ready to work hard.

Buyer: the age of the dry-cleaning unit, condition of the equipment, and don't overpay. Seller: have an expert/business valuator give you a price for the business, not your accountant or business broker who has no expertise of the industry.

Dry cleaners are fairly easy to replicate, however location is most important. The dry cleaning industry trend is very good, but there are more and more dry cleaners being built constantly.

Dry cleaners with plants are very costly, with all the environmental and state and city requirements. Landlords who rent to dry cleaners are very careful about contamination, especially the dry cleaners with perc. machines that have the history of causing contamination. All the perc. machines will be replaced with hydrocarbon, wet dry cleaner machines, etc.

Age of the equipment and the care of it is very important. The trend is for dry clean business owners to eliminate the use of perchlorethylene as the cleaning solvent. Buyers should take into consideration the cost of a new dry cleaning machine that will use the environmentally friendly solvents.

Seller Financing

- About 40% are seller financing, 40% bank financing, 20% all cash.
- Seller financing is very typical, usually 3 to 5 years depend on the loan amount, and the monthly payment. The seller has to be reasonable with the monthly payment when they structure the deal.
- Dry cleaners sell with SBA financing 30% of the time, seller financing 30% of the time, all cash or 401k rollovers 40% of the time. SBA loans are 10 yrs., seller financing 3 to 5 yrs.
- Seller financing is a must, usually 50 to 60% down and the rest will be carried by the seller for 4 to 5 years with 5% to 7% interest depending on the monthly payment.
- Bank financing is difficult to get for dry cleaners although not impossible. Seller financing is preferred although a lot of sellers do not want to provide any financing.
- In my experience, existing stores sell using some percentage of seller financing. New plants with expensive equipment are typically leased or bank financed.

Resources

- National Clothesline: http://www.natclo.com
- American Dry Cleaner: http://www.americandrycleaner.com
- National Cleaners Association: http://www.nca-i.com
- IBISWorld, January 2017: http://ibisworld.com
- Drycleaning and Laundry Institute International: http://www.dionline.org

Dry Cleaning Pickup Outlets/Stores		
SIC 7212-01	NAICS 812320	
Rules of Thumb		
➢ 30 x Weekly Sales		
➢ 25–50% of annual sales		

Dry Cleaning Routes		
SIC 7212-01	NAICS 812320	
Rules of Thumb		
➢ 15–40% of annual revenues		

	Franchise
Dry Clean USA	
Approx. Total Investment	$300,000–$750,000
SIC 7212-01 NAICS 812320	Number of Businesses/Units 45

Rules of Thumb

➢ 55% of annual sales plus inventory

Resources

- Dry Clean USA: http://www.drycleanusa.com

	Franchise
Dunkin' Donuts	
Approx. Total Investment	$109,700–$1,637,700
Estimated Annual Sales/Unit	$953,000
SIC 5812-06 NAICS 722515	Number of Businesses/Units 12,000

Rules of Thumb

➢ 4 x SDE plus inventory

➢ 5 x EBITDA

➢ 60–100% of annual sales plus inventory

➢ Prices typically run 5 times EBITDA on groups of 3 or larger. Rule of thumb, which is still very strong in the marketplace, is about 1.25 times annual sales in very high coffee sale areas of New England. It is closer to 1x the sales in the Mid-Atlantic where coffee sales are still very good, but not as high as in New England. Where coffee sales are much less, values run about .75 times annual sales. These numbers can be affected (up or down) by unusually low or high rents, and/or the requirement to undergo a major remodel in the near future.

Pricing Tips

- The higher values are ascribed to units with a greater percentage of coffee sales.
- "Dunkin' Donuts' minimum cash required is $750,000 with a net worth of at least $1,500,000. Minimum 5-store development required."

  Source: Dunkin' Donuts

- The value is decreased if the unit or units require substantial remodeling in less than 4–5 years.
- Sufficient length of leases and franchise agreements, percentage of businesses coming from coffee/beverages.

Benchmark Data

Expenses (% of Annual Sales)

Cost of Goods + supplies	23% to 24% +4%
Occupancy Costs	08% to 10%
Payroll/Labor Costs	22%
Profit (pretax)	15% to 20%

E

Questions

- When are remodels due? Lease details are critical, and length of time remaining on the franchise agreements. Does the seller have expansion rights in adjacent areas?
- What percent of sales is beverages?

Industry Trend

- "Dunkin' Donuts plans to double its locations in the United States over the next 20 years, the company announced Wednesday. The coffee and doughnut chain currently operates nearly 7,000 stores nationwide. Each new store adds an average of 20 to 25 new employees, both full and part time a Dunkin' spokeswoman said."

  Source: "Dunkin' Donuts to double U.S. locations" by Annalyn Censky, CNNMoney

Expert Comments

It is a well-known franchise, but there is stiff competition from Starbucks and McDonald's.

The marketability is not as high as one would expect for such a profitable and growing business. The reason is that the franchisor has very strict requirements to approve a buyer.

Seller Financing

- 7 years—usually are bank/SBA financed

Resources

- Dunkin Franchising: http://www.dunkinfranchising.com

Franchise

Eagle Transmission Shop

Approx. Total Investment			$194,000–$292,500
SIC 7537-01	NAICS 811113		Number of Businesses/Units 27

Rules of Thumb

➢ 40% of annual sales

➢ 2.5 x SDE

Benchmark Data

- Cost to get to breakeven is the same as AAMCO—approx. $200,000 (this is my targeted bottom sale price).
- Franchises with an owner overseeing a manager in the expenses are still selling for 2.5 to 3 X SDE. Franchised shops with SDE of at least $100,000 with high percentage retail are very marketable. Franchised shops that historically are not breaking even with a manager in the expenses are very hard to sell.
- If the location seems OK, the price seems to bottom out at about $125,000. Small independents are getting more and more difficult.

E

Resources
- Eagle Transmission: http://www.eagletransmission.com

E-Cigarette Stores/Vapor Stores		
	NAICS 453998	

Rules of Thumb
➢ 1.7 x SDE plus inventory

Pricing Tips
- The relative cost of the products is cheap, allowing a sizeable margin of profit.
- The industry is undergoing lots of change with the regulations that were just announced. Buyers are very nervous about how this will affect the business. Many vapor stores sell high volumes of liquids, and this could all be removed with the new regulations requiring all liquids to be pre-packaged.

Benchmark Data

Expenses (% of Annual Sales)
Cost of Goods	20%
Occupancy Costs	25%
Payroll/Labor Costs	15%
Profit (pretax)	40%

Questions
- Why are you selling?

Industry Trend
- The public's perception of vaping is changing for the better, and scientific studies are being conducted to determine the medical effects of vaping. This, coupled with state and federal legislation, will prove to be the deciding factors of the industry.
- There is lots of uncertainly with the newly announced regulations. The business models may have to change drastically and the profit margins may erode.

Expert Comments
Don't let the tidal effects of legislation and regulation wear you down. Many are certain that this industry will weather the storm and come out more lucrative than ever.

With the public's opinion of e-cigarettes and vaporizers finally looking up, the only real bottleneck within the industry is the legislative aspect. Lawmakers and governing bodies are still clamoring to come to accurate conclusions regarding the safety of vaping in general.

E-Commerce (Internet Sales)

SIC 5731-24	NAICS 454111	Number of Businesses/Units 175,125

Rules of Thumb

➢ 30% of annual sales includes inventory

➢ 2–4 x SDE includes inventory

➢ 3–6 x EBITDA

Pricing Tips

- Gross sales are not necessarily important to determine value because of tendency for very high gross margins. A business with little or no inventory is more valuable. Businesses with very high inventory are very difficult to value and sell; the business is the inventory.
- High inventory businesses will be harder to sell. Higher multiples with SDE over $100K are more easily sold. The ease of the operation will determine marketability. Many are too complicated for the average buyer.
- The more niche-related the product, the higher the multiple.
- Prices vary depending on age of business...at least three years is excellent...12 months is usually necessary.

Benchmark Data

Statistics (E-Commerce & Online Auctions)

Number of Establishments	175,125
Average Profit Margin	6.4%
Revenue per Employee	$832,300
Average Number of Employees	3.0
Average Wages per Employee	$41,733

Products and Services Segmentation

Other merchandise	26.5%
Clothing, footwear and accessories	17.7%
Computer, electronics and appliances	17.3%
Home and office	12.9%
Media	8.1%
Sporting goods, toys, hobby items and games	7.6%
Medication and health aids	7.3%
Food, beer and wine	2.6%

Industry Costs

Profit	6.4%
Wages	4.9%
Purchases	60.5%
Depreciation	0.7%
Marketing	3.7%
Rent & Utilities	3.8%
Other	20.0%

Market Share

Amazon.com Inc.	22.6%

- Always look at current market comps when pricing as conditions may be subject to change.
- On average, the gross margin is 20%. The expenses tend to be very low because many Internet businesses are relocatable and do not require an office or warehouse.
- Profits can be as high as 50–90%

Expenses (% of Annual Sales)

Cost of Goods	20% to 50%
Occupancy Costs	0% to 10%
Payroll/Labor Costs	0% to 50%
Profit (pretax)	50% to 60%

Questions

- Why are you selling?
- What is the learning curve for the business operations?
- Where do you generate customers from?
- What is the competition?
- Ask the sellers before you analyze numbers if all the revenues generated are from products that either do not require a license to be sold, or, if they do require a license or some kind of special permission, that it transfers or can be transferred to a new owner. Look at 3-year trends in annual sales. Why are you selling? Ask to see payment gateway record for the past 3 years to help verify financials, i.e., company PayPal Account or other merchant gateway. Is all of the income shown on the company Payment Gateway Record only from income generated from that particular company?
- Does the seller inventory the product? Who does the credit card processing and what are their fees? Who does the Web hosting and how much traffic can the website handle? How do they maintain their Internet rankings? What are they doing to increase their Web presence?

Industry Trend

- From "7 Predictions on What to Expect in 2017"
  - ✓ "Chat bots
  - ✓ Artificial Intelligence
  - ✓ Mobile. Mobile. Mobile
  - ✓ Mobile payment and loyalty apps
  - ✓ Personalization and customization
  - ✓ Increasing same-day delivery
  - ✓ Social selling"

  Source: "E-commerce Trends: 7 Predictions on What to Expect in 2017," by Kit Smith, December 7, 2016, https://www.brandwatch.com/blog/ecommerce-trends-2017/
- "In the fourth quarter, U.S. e-commerce sales grew 14.3% to $123.61 billion from $108.18 billion. The growth rate for Q4 is the smallest year-over-year increase since the fourth quarter of 2014, when online retail sales grew 13.9%. Still, online sales are growing much faster than store sales, which suggests that e-commerce remains a primary growth driver in the retail industry as a whole."

  Source: " U.S. E-Commerce Share of Total Retail Sales by Quarter," *Internet Retailer*, January 9, 2017
- Increasing positive trends

E

- "E-commerce sales are expected to grow to more than $400 billion in the next several years, with Forrester Research estimating $414.0 billion in sales in 2018 and eMarketer estimating $491.5 billion in 2018."

  Source: eMarketer, Forrester Research

- "As more B2B buyers choose to do much of their purchasing online, the number of sales reps in the United States will decline rapidly over the next several years. By 2020, the number will drop by 1 million, a decrease of 22% between 2012 and 2020. Sales reps that offer extra services to assist the purchasing of complex products for big companies will fare better."

  Source: Forrester Research Inc.

- Unlimited growth potential for the next 3–5 years.

Expert Comments

Do complete due diligence. Watch out for erroneous claims of proprietary product or systems.

E-Commerce niche businesses are extremely desirable if profitable and easy to operate. Little or no inventory on hand is best and increases the potential for sale and added value.

A unique product with aggressive marketing will usually succeed.

Internet companies can be replicated structurally, but very difficult to replicate from an SEO stand point.

Seller Financing

- Seller financing or all cash deals are the norm especially without hard assets.
- Recently it's buyer financing.
- 1–5 years

Resources

- E-Commerce Times: http://www.ecommercetimes.com/
- IBISWorld, April 2017: http://ibisworld.com
- Internet Retailer: https://www.digitalcommerce360.com/internet-retailer/

Electricians		
	NAICS 238210	Number of Businesses/Units 220,496

Rules of Thumb

➤ 2 x SDE plus inventory

Pricing Tips

- Strong order book is essential. Wide range of customers.

Benchmark Data

Statistics (Electricians)

Number of Establishments	220,496
Average Profit Margin	5.5%
Revenue per Employee	$177,100
Average Number of Employees	4.5
Average Wages per Employee	$58,458

Products and Services Segmentation

Electric power and systems installation and servicing 66.7%
Other services 9.5%
Telecommunications installation and servicing 9.2%
Electronic control system installation and servicing 7.5%
Fire and security system installation and servicing 7.1%

Major Market Segmentation

Commercial buildings 35.9%
Institutional, educational, and civic organization buildings 18.2%
Nonbuilding construction 14.4%
Industrial buildings 13.9%
Single-family homes 12.5%
Multifamily housing (e.g. apartment buildings) 5.1%

Industry Costs

Profit 4.8%
Wages 33.0%
Purchases 38.5%
Depreciation 0.7%
Rent & Utilities 0.2%
Marketing 3.3%
Other 18.8%

Expenses (% of Annual Sales)

Cost of Goods 50%
Occupancy Costs .... n/a
Payroll/Labor Costs 30%
Profit (pretax) 06%

Questions

- 1. Details of job costing, current and bids 2. List of staff, experience, and time with business 3. Usual financial and due diligence.

Industry Trend

- Directly dependent on construction industry but can work related areas if necessary to cover slack period.

Expert Comments

Underpricing of bids is a serious risk but may be used to increase order book in preparation for sale. Good demand for sound business. Location is relatively unimportant.

Resources

- IBISWorld, January 2017: http://ibisworld.com

E

Electric Motor Repair

SIC 7694	NAICS 811310	

Rules of Thumb

➢ 33% of annual sales plus inventory

➢ 3 x SDE plus inventory

➢ 5 x EBIT

➢ 4 x EBITDA

Pricing Tips

- Condition of equipment and customer concentration are significant factors.
- Industry is always a mix of repair of customer motors and resale of new motors and related products. Rule of thumb for pricing is one-third of annual repair sales plus 15% of annual product sales, plus inventory. Most successful buyers for smaller businesses in the industry have electric motor background. Condition of equipment and extent of machine shop tools is important.

Benchmark Data

- $150,000 sales per employee is an average for companies with approximately 2/3 repair, 1/3 new sales.

Expenses (% of Annual Sales)

Cost of Goods	25%
Occupancy Costs	10%
Payroll/Labor Costs	25%
Profit (pretax)	05%

Questions

- Technical strengths of shop employees? Concentration of customers? Where is future growth coming from?
- Buyer needs to establish the repeatability and retainability of current customers after change in ownership.

Industry Trend

- Repair lags general industry trends. Emphasis on power generation and distribution including wind energy.

Expert Comments

This is a mature industry. The repair market (higher margins) is stable to declining slightly as increased costs force higher horsepower standard motors to be replaced (lower margins) rather than repaired. Other technological factors and the shift to more offshore manufacturing have resulted in no net growth and eroding profits. Successful shops have either good niche customer markets and/or services or a long- term approach to partnering with customers to reduce customer's motor operating costs. Sales growth for individual companies usually comes from taking sales away from competitors.

Embroidery Services/Shops

| SIC 7389-42 | NAICS 314999 | |

Rules of Thumb

➤ 55–60% of annual sales plus inventory

Engineering Services

| | NAICS 54133 | Number of Businesses/Units 156,475 |

Rules of Thumb

➤ 40–45% of annual revenues; add value of fixtures & equipment; may require earnout

Benchmark Data

Statistics (Engineering Services)

Number of Establishments	156,475
Average Profit Margin	8.8%
Revenue per Employee	$214,700
Average Number of Employees	7.5
Average Wages per Employee	$84,149

Products and Services Segmentation

Industrial and manufacturing project	25.7%
Other projects and services	23.5%
Energy projects	11.8%
Transportation projects	11.6%
Commercial, public and institutional projects	9.8%
Project management services	8.4%
Municipal utility projects	6.0%
Telecom Projects	3.2%

Major Market Segmentation

Private businesses	43.4%
Government bodies	38.2%
Engineering firms	8.3%
Architectural firms	4.5%
Construction firms	4.1%
Individuals	0.9%
Nonprofit organizations	0.6%

Industry Costs

Profit	8.8%
Wages	39.5%
Purchases	12.5%
Depreciation	1.5%
Marketing	1.3%
Rent and Utilities	3.9%
Other	32.5%

E

Resources
- IBISWorld, August 2017: http://ibisworld.com

Environmental Testing		
	NAICS 541380	

Rules of Thumb
➤ 60% of annual sales plus inventory

➤ 2–2.5 x SDE plus inventory

Pricing Tips
- SDE must at least be equal to new debt service using a 1.5 ratio, owner's salary and any capex requirements, or it's priced too high.
- Be sure the accounting is on the accrual method so there is no confusion as to how values are arrived at.

Benchmark Data
- It can be a roll-up-your-sleeves kind of business.

Expenses (% of Annual Sales)
Cost of Goods	02%
Occupancy Costs	03%
Payroll/Labor Costs	30%
Profit (pretax)	16%

Questions
- Why did you get in the business and why are you getting out at this time?

Industry Trend
- "The environmental testing market is projected to reach a value of USD 11.82 Billion by 2021, at a CAGR of 6.9% from 2016 to 2021. The market is driven by factors such as increasing regulations regarding environment protection, and active participation of different government and regulatory bodies to monitor environmental conditions. The high growth potential in emerging markets and untapped regions provides new opportunities for market players."

  Source: http://www.marketsandmarkets.com/PressReleases/environmental-testing.asp
- Steady, but real estate activities have a big influence.

Expert Comments
Owner and his contacts are more the driving, networking force than the location or the facilities.

Resources
- Environmental Business International: http://www.ebionline.org

Environment Control (Commercial Cleaning Services)

Approx. Total Investment		$55,000 plus $150,000 net worth
	NAICS 561720	Number of Businesses/Units 50

Rules of Thumb

➤ 42% of annual sales plus inventory

Pricing Tips

Resources

- Environmental Control: http://www.environmentcontrol.com

Event Companies

SIC 7389-44	NAICS 812990	

Rules of Thumb

➤ 3 x EBITDA plus asset value

Pricing Tips

- Are there events on the books going forward? How many repeat clients?

Benchmark Data

Statistics (Trade Show and Conference Planning)

Number of Establishments	5,055
Average Profit Margin	9.0%
Revenue per Employee	$167,700
Average Number of Employees	17.0
Average Wages per Employee	$41,049

Products and Services Segmentation

Exhibit sales and design services	44.0%
Registration, analytics and show services	23.9%
Sponsorships, entertainment and advertising sales	21.0%
Shipping, logistics and other services	11.1%

Major Market Segmentation

Other	34.6%
Consumer goods, sporting goods, travel and other services	18.7%
Medical and healthcare	18.1%
Business services	10.6%
Producers of commodities, chemicals and materials manufacturers	9.1%
Communications and information technology	8.9%

E

Industry Costs

Profit	9.0%
Wages	24.5%
Purchases	32.0%
Depreciation	0.5%
Marketing	20.3%
Rent & Utilities	6.4%
Other	7.3%

Market Share

The Freeman Companies	13.3%
Viad Corp.	6.1%

Statistics (Party & Event Planners)

Number of Establishments	137,696
Average Profit Margin	9.2%
Revenue per Employee	$34,800
Average Number of Employees	1.0
Average Wages per Employee	$10,395

Products and Services Segmentation

Corporate social events	43.1%
Weddings	28.4%
Birthday parties	15.8%
Other	12.7%

Industry Costs

Profit	9.2%
Wages	29.5%
Purchases	24.9%
Depreciation	2.6%
Marketing	5.8%
Rent & Utilities	7.3%
Other	20.7%

Industry Trend

- "What event trends should you be keeping an eye on next year?
    - ✓ One of the big trends we're going to see a lot in 2017 is live streaming for events.
    - ✓ Social will be at the heart of marketing campaigns for both audience acquisition and content amplification.
    - ✓ The growing dominance of event production and experience production agencies.
    - ✓ This'll be the year of data playing a big role in determining the effectiveness of events.
    - ✓ Visitors with smart badges. Exhibitors with lead capture devices. Venues with wifi networks. Exhibition stands with smart cameras. Seminars capturing audience engagement.
    - ✓ Personalization is a trend that has impacted many industries – particularly eCommerce – and it's going to make an impact in the events industry in 2017."

Source: Excerpts from interviews with experts in the event planning industry in "The Event Trends That Will Shape Your 2017: Over 50 Expert Predictions," January 2, 2017, https://www.eventbrite.com/blog/event-trends-2017-ds00/

Seller Financing

- 2 ½ years

Resources

- IBISWorld, February 2017: http://ibisworld.com
- IBISWorld, September 2016: http://ibisworld.com

Fabric Stores

SIC 5949-02	NAICS 45113	Number of Businesses/Units 23,594

Rules of Thumb

> ➢ 3 x monthly sales plus inventory

Benchmark Data

Statistics (Fabric, Craft & Sewing Supplies Stores)

Number of Establishments	23,594
Average Profit Margin	4.7%
Revenue per Employee	$73,600
Average Number of Employees	2.6
Average Wages per Employee	$10,651

Products and Services Segmentation

Fabrics	60.3%
Sewing and craft supplies	37.0%
Fabrics and other	2.7%

Industry Costs

Profit	4.7%
Wages	14.5%
Purchases	44.4%
Depreciation	0.9%
Marketing	1.8%
Rent & Utilities	9.2%
Other	24.5%

Market Share

Michaels Stores Inc.	27.0%
Jo-Ann Stores Inc.	25.0%
Hobby Lobby Stores Inc.	14.0%

Industry Trend

- "The family-run Paron Fabrics has been in business for 76 years, but like two other fabric stores on the block of W. 39th Street, it will be closing due to rising rents and landlords who would rather have their tenants serving up craft beers than bolts of fabric. 'We're losing the heart of New York with all these mom-and-pop stores closing,' Amy Nurtig, a Paron Fabrics customer, told PIX11

F

News. 'There are going to be no garments in the garment district,' Paron's owner Mark Lynn said. 'I've had customers in here crying in total disbelief.'"

Source: "Fabric stores close as Garment District continue decades-long decline" by Magee Hickey, September 16, 2016, http://pix11.com/2016/09/16/fabric-stores-close-as-garment-district-continue-decades-long-decline/The Fabric Shop Network: http://www.fabshopnet.com

Resources
- IBISWorld, February 2017: http://ibisworld.com
- The Fabric Shop Network: http://www.fabshopnet.com

Family Clothing Stores

SIC 5651	NAICS 448140	Number of Businesses/Units 45,728

Rules of Thumb

➢ .75–1.5 x SDE plus inventory

➢ 2.4–2.8 x SDE includes inventory

➢ 40–45% of annual sales includes inventory

Pricing Tips
- Women's Apparel: try 23 percent of annual sales + inventory and/or 1.1 times SDE.

Benchmark Data

Statistics (Family Clothing Stores)

Number of Establishments	45,728
Average Profit Margin	4.7%
Revenue per Employee	$141,500
Average Number of Employees	16.5
Average Wages per Employee	$15,941

Products and Services Segmentation

Women's casual wear	24.2%
Children's wear	19.7%
Other women's wear	18.7%
Men's casual wear	17.3%
Women's formal wear	8.9%
Other men's wear	7.2%
Men's formal wear	4.0%

Major Market Segmentation

Generation X	35.5%
Baby boomers	24.5%
Generation Y	22.5%
Seniors aged 65 and over	10.0%
Children aged nine and under	7.0%
Commercial buyers	0.5%

Industry Costs

Profit	4.7%
Wages	11.3%
Purchases	59.9%
Depreciation	0.5%
Marketing	2.0%
Rent & Utilities	6.0%
Other	15.6%

Market Share

The TJX Companies Inc.	15.5%
Ross Stores Inc.	13.2%
Gap Inc.	9.7%

Expenses (% of Annual Sales)

Cost of Goods	46% to 52%
Occupancy Costs	06% to 10%
Payroll/Labor Costs	14% to 18%
Profit (pretax)	12% to 15%

Seller Financing

- 5 to 10 years

Resources

- IBISWorld, June 2017: http://ibisworld.com

Family Entertainment Centers		
	NAICS 713120	

Rules of Thumb

➢ 3 x EBITDA

		Franchise
Fantastic Sam's		
Approx. Total Investment		$136,100–$247,100
	NAICS 812112	Number of Businesses/Units 1,143

Rules of Thumb

➢ 35–40% of annual sales plus inventory

Resources

- Fantastic Sam's: http://www.fantasticsams.com

F

	Franchise
Fast-Fix Jewelry and Watch Repairs	
Approx. Total Investment	$170,000–$498,000
SIC 7631-01	NAICS 811490	Number of Businesses/Units 153

Rules of Thumb
> ➢ 80–85% of annual sales plus inventory

Resources
- Fast Fix: http://www.fastfix.com

Fast Food	
	NAICS 722513	

Rules of Thumb
> ➢ 35–45% of annual sales plus inventory

Industry Trend
- "Fast food had been thought to be largely recession proof, and indeed the industry did not suffer nearly as much as other discretionary spending sectors. In fact, there was some increase in consumer visits as people choose cheaper fast food options over fast casual or traditional restaurant choices. But overall, the recession hurt spending, and consumers overall purchased less with each trip. Fast food franchises fared reasonably well but still felt some pain."
  Source: https://www.franchisehelp.com/industry-reports/fast-food-industry-report/

Resources
- National Restaurant Association: http://www.restaurant.org
- Nation's Restaurant News: http://www.nrn.com

	Franchise
FastFrame	
Approx. Total Investment	$105,800–$150,300
SIC 7699-15	NAICS 442299	Number of Businesses/Units 128

Rules of Thumb
> ➢ 32% of annual sales

Resources
- Fast Frame: http://www.fastframe.com

FasTracKids

	Franchise
Approx. Total Investment	$48,717–$203,517
NAICS 624410	Number of Businesses/Units 270

Rules of Thumb

➢ 45% of annual sales plus inventory

Resources

- FasTracKids: http://www.fastrackids.com/

Fast Signs

		Franchise
Approx. Total Investment		$151,140–$293,525
SIC 3993-02	NAICS 541890	Number of Businesses/Units 621

Rules of Thumb

➢ 42–46% of annual sales plus inventory

Resources

- Fast Signs: http://www.fastsigns.com

Fertility Clinics

NAICS 621410	Number of Businesses/Units 499

Rules of Thumb

➢ 3 x EBIT

➢ 2.9x EBITDA

➢ 78% of annual revenues plus inventory

➢ 2.7 x SDE plus inventory

Benchmark Data

Statistics (Fertility Clinics)

Number of Establishments	499
Average Profit Margin	10.5%
Revenue per Employee	$108,100
Average Number of Employees	35.9
Average Wages per Employee	$43,545

Products and Services Segmentation

ART using fresh embryos	57.9%
ART using frozen embryos	19.3%
Intrauterine Insemination	18.6%
Other services	4.2%

Industry Costs

Profit	10.5%
Wages	40.3%
Purchases	18.2%
Depreciation	2.7%
Marketing	0.7%
Rent & Utilities	6.1%
Other	21.5%

Market Share

IntegraMed Inc.	14.3%

Expenses (% of Annual Sales)

Cost of Goods	10%
Payroll/Labor Costs	04%
Profit (pretax)	12%

Questions
- Payor mix, market share, patient demographic data.

Industry Trend
- Competition should remain low in many segments; family planning industry may struggle due to regulation.

Seller Financing
- Outside financing

Resources
- The National Women's Health Foundation: http://womenshealthfoundation.org
- The National Family Planning and Reproductive Health Association: http://www.nationalfamilyplanning.org
- IBISWorld, November 2016: http://ibisworld.com

Fire Suppression Systems Sales & Services		
	NAICS 238220	

Rules of Thumb
➢ 80% of annual sales plus inventory

➢ 2.2 x SDE plus inventory

Pricing Tips
- Business does not have to be profitable to obtain price, but must have good accounts, preferably with contracts in place.
- The value of the customers can depend on whether the owner is the primary contact or the employees.
- Most of these businesses are small and run by a family. There are larger companies that are actively seeking to roll up smaller companies. Their primary

interest is retaining the current customers and the pricing of the products and services. They are more focused on gross sales than SDE or EBITDA.

Benchmark Data

Expenses (% of Annual Sales)

Cost of Goods	20%
Occupancy Costs	05% to 06%
Payroll/Labor Costs	24%
Profit (pretax)	15%

Questions

- Revenue per customer? Are there contracts in place for service? Employees interact with customers, so questions about their capabilities are important. Ask questions about relationships with local fire marshals and fire departments which can be very important. You want them on your side because they are often the enforcement arm for fire safety compliance.

Industry Trend

- "The fire protection systems (FPS) market revenue market is expected to grow from $33.58 billion in 2013 to $79.18 billion in 2020 at a CAGR of 11.53%. The global fire protection systems market exhibits a lucrative growth potential for the next six years. The growth of the market is propelled by the government mandates and political support, increased fire protection expenditure from the enterprise segment, and technological innovations in equipment and networking. The lack of integrity in system interfaces and higher initial investments for the fire protection systems' installation are restraining the growth of fire protection systems globally.

  "Some of the major players in this market include Gentex Corporation (U.S.), Halma PLC (U.K.), Hochiki Corporation (Japan), Honeywell International Inc. (U.S.), Johnson Controls (U.S.), Robert Bosch GmbH (Germany), Siemens AG (Germany), Tyco (Switzerland), United Technologies Corporation (U.S.), VT MAK (U.S.)."

  Source: "Fire Protection Systems (FPS) Market worth $79.18 Billion by 2020,"
  http://www.marketsandmarkets.com/PressReleases/fire-protection-systems.asp

Resources

- National Fire Sprinkler Association: http://www.nfsa.org
- National Fire Protection Association: http://www.nfpa.org
- Fire Suppression Systems Association: http://www.fssa.net/

Fish & Seafood Markets

	NAICS 445220	Number of Businesses/Units 4,711

Rules of Thumb

- ➤ 20–25% of annual sales plus inventory

F

Benchmark Data

Statistics (Fish and Seafood Markets)

Number of Establishments..4,711
Average Profit Margin 4.3%
Revenue per Employee $189,700
Average Number of Employees 3.0
Average Wages per Employee $22,876

Products and Services Segmentation

Fresh fish for human consumption 45.6%
Frozen fish for human consumption 29.7%
Fish meal and fish oil 17.2%
Canned fish.. 4.0%
Animal food and other... 3.1%
Cured fish 0.4%

Major Market Segmentation

Consumers 69.7%
Restaurants 13.0%
Wholesalers and other... 10.2%
Retailers.. 7.1%

Industry Costs

Profit 4.3%
Wages... 12.0%
Purchases.. 68.8%
Depreciation... 1.7%
Marketing 0.7%
Rent & Utilities 4.8%
Other 7.7%

Industry Trend

- "Over the five years to 2022, consumers are likely to continue their dietary preference for seafood; however, slow growth will do little to improve demand for goods sold at fish and seafood markets. However, a steadily growing economy and improving per capita disposable income will help consumers purchase premium products at fish markets. The rising price of seafood may cause Americans to turn to more affordable retail channels, including grocery stores and warehouse clubs, to obtain their seafood products. Additionally, more consumers are expected to opt for alternative sources of protein, such as red meat and poultry, provided that various health and safety concerns surrounding these animal products are put at ease and the average retail price of red meat does not grow rapidly. Meanwhile, aquaculture will play an important role in stabilizing supplies of fish and seafood, moderately mitigating the volatility of seafood prices. Over the five years to 2022, IBISWorld forecasts industry revenue to grow at an annualized rate of 1.1% to $2.8 billion."

Source: IBISWorld Industry Outlook

Resources

- IBISWorld, January 2017: http://ibisworld.com

Fitness Centers

SIC 7991-01	NAICS 713940	Number of Businesses/Units 110,480

Rules of Thumb

➤ 70–100% of annual sales plus inventory

➤ 2–3.5 x SDE plus inventory

➤ 4–5 x EBIT

➤ 3–5 x EBITDA

Pricing Tips

- Competition is becoming more significant every day in this crowded space. Personal trainers and instructors (yoga, Pilates, etc.) are able to set up studios inexpensively and draw away training clients. Big-box gyms can open large facilities with low membership rates by cutting a deal to become an anchor for a new retail center and draw away memberships. The value of a studio is similar to an accounting (or other professional) practice; it's in the revenues that will stay after an ownership transition, as there are almost no other assets of value. This can be achieved by offering some funds at closing, and the remainder after the next year based on retained client revenues. The seller may need to be involved that year to assist with competition. Large facilities can open very successfully because of their newness and low cost. These may see a decline in cash flow after five years as the newness wears off and another, newer big box opens in the same area. It will be important to include CAPEX in determining real cash flow, especially if the facility is being sold within its five-year honeymoon period in the market. Also consider the likelihood of a new retail center bringing in a new competitor nearby. Midsized facilities that can offer a community feel are making a comeback in between these approaches; however, their success is often driven by the personality of the owner or manager, and they bear some of the problems of studios in transition.
- 12x the monthly preauthorized debits minus returns and taxes
- The median selling price for gyms, health clubs, Pilates studios, and dance studios tends to be around 2x SDE. Businesses with reasonable long-term leases in good locations and with recurring revenue can generally sell for up to 2.2x SDE.
- This is a capital-intensive business, so first break apart tangible and intangible assets. Sadly, the market value of used fitness equipment is generally low, so the primary value will be from cash flow; however, it will be easier to break this out first to better value large from smaller facilities. For intangible value average the cash flow quantity and quality. Use 2x SDE for intangible quantity and average that with 10x monthly contract revenues to reflect the quality (or dependability) of that cash flow. Finally, calculate the value of outstanding paid-in-full contracts and subtract that from the consideration.
- Pricing varies by size. Smaller fitness studios with little infrastructure may sell for 3X EBIT. Larger businesses, with multiple locations, upscale clientele and solid management team, will be much higher.
- If the business model is based on member's paying monthly through pre-authorized payments this business can be very stable. Most facilities have a good value in assets if the owner takes care in maintaining the equipment. The greatest challenge is often from rising occupancy cost so if an owner can purchase the building they occupy or secure a long term favourable rental

F

agreement, they can ensure their continued profitability. Many facilities have gone with great success to a model that includes multiple revenue streams (personal training, group fitness, nutritional consultation, juice bar, pro shop, etc.) to provide a better and more even cash flow.

- Drivers are quality of equipment and facilities. 5% of annual revenues needs to go into CAPEX annually so best driver of value is EBITDA minus CAPEX (Capital Expenditures). Facilities get a lot of wear and tear and they need to be updated regularly. Retention also drives multiple and value. Facilities with excellent retention (better than 80%) will garner higher multiples and valuations than those at 60% or less. 60% is usually average retention rate for a quality facility 50% or less for poorer run facilities. Be wary of value of smaller storefront facilities/franchises. Many are often upside down, meaning a multiple of EBITDA doesn't justify the original purchase price on the business.

Benchmark Data

Statistics (Gym, Health & Fitness Clubs)

Number of Establishments	110,480
Average Profit Margin	12.9%
Revenue per Employee	$38,900
Average Number of Employees	7.2
Average Wages per Employee	$14,499

Products and Services Segmentation

Membership fees	68.1%
Personal training services	12.1%
Other	6.7%
Meals and beverages	5.1%
Guest admission	3.1%
Merchandise sales	3.0%
Spa services	1.9%

Industry Costs

Profit	12.9%
Wages	37.1%
Purchases	7.2%
Depreciation	6.9%
Marketing	3.0%
Rent & Utilities	21.5%
Other	11.4%

Market Share

Fitness International LLC	6.3%

- "In 2016, health club membership grew by 3.6% from 2015, while the total number of users, including members and non-members, rose by 3.1%, according to IHRSA's recently released *2017 Health Club Consumer Report*."
  Source: "3 Ways Youth Are Shaping the Health Club Market" by Melissa Rodriguez, September 28, 2017, http://www.ihrsa.org/blog/category/research

- "The global health club industry continues to grow, with more than 200,000 clubs serving 162 million members and generating $83.1 billion in revenue in 2016, according to the *2017 IHRSA Global Report: The State of the Health Club Industry*."
  Source: "Worldwide Health Club Revenue Up in 2016, Passing $83 Billion," June 2, 2017, http://www.ihrsa.org/blog/category/research

- Value-added services, such as training, are becoming more necessary to maintain profitability, as competition squeezes revenues. Historically, fitness centers have seen about 15% of new members taking advantage of these. Centers that can attract higher conversion rates are very valuable.
- It is recommended to keep rent and payroll costs under 50% of revenue, as other costs including liability, workers comp insurance, and marketing can be quite high.
- Having the majority of the clients on preauthorized payment for membership fees is critical to the long-term success and salability of the club.
- Contract sales should be at least 75% of total revenues in a healthy sales environment.
- Good benchmark numbers to look at are the total number of active members (paying monthly) and the average amount each of those members pays. Member growth and attrition over a three-year period can be a good indicator as to future performance.
- Urban is $200 per square foot; suburban is $100 per square foot. Occupancy costs of 15% average; 20% OK but high; less than 10%, excellent. Location is key; need highly visible, easily accessible locations.

Expenses (% of Annual Sales)

Cost of Goods	05% to 15%
Occupancy Costs	20% to 30%
Payroll/Labor Costs	25% to 35%
Profit (pretax)	15% to 20%

Questions

- How do you close?
- The buyer should always ask about the previous membership promotions (two for one, decreasing rate) and cancellation policy to see if they will affect the membership in the future.
- What is the current member retention in months? How long is the occupancy lease, and do the terms change over its duration? Does the rent go up?
- Pricing model; staffing levels; how much recurring revenue; in terms of marketing, what works and what doesn't work; what new competitors have emerged in the area?
- Recurring revenue, opportunities for growth, lease transferability, value and state of equipment, potential deferred maintenance
- Do you use Mind Body Online for scheduling? How are instructors paid? Are the instructors on payroll (which they should be) vs. 1099s?

Industry Trend

- Continued growth through 2020
- The industry is looking for more ways to develop a community with its members without depending so much on the personality of an owner or manager. Franchise programs and technology are being developed toward this effort.
- Small location with higher service and higher cost
- Significant growth in the smaller boutique centers with a heavy focus on personal training

F

- Group fitness is the hottest trend in physical fitness. Any business that can capitalize on the intersection of community, data, and varying full-body workouts should do very well.

Expert Comments

It is a fantastic industry if you are a fitness enthusiast and plan on working 70+ hours minimum during the first 3 years; otherwise I would advise you not to consider.

Like many verticals, it is an industry going through transition, especially since the 2008 economic downturn.

Make sure you understand the sales and marketing necessary to overcome competition and that you are comfortable with it.

As the market becomes more fitness aware, the competition is taking many forms, not just other businesses. At-work and at-home programs are becoming more prevalent everywhere.

Purchase a business with a very strong preauthorized debit program. Monthly payments are the most secure way to ensure long-term success.

The biggest challenge these days for fitness centers is the cost of occupancy. Large facilities need many members to cover these costs. The industry seems to be trending towards smaller facilities that offer higher service (personal training, diet consulting, yoga, Pilates, etc.).

Perform due financial and operational diligence. Be prepared to put down personal guaranty on lease.

Competition for fitness-based business is especially fierce in Los Angeles, with many new concepts starting all the time; however, parking and zoning are limited, so it is a challenge for business owners to easily relocate and open new gyms. In general, the greater LA market is a thriving one for gyms, and ones that have established a critical mass of members (150+) with recurring revenue will command attention from multiple buyers.

Sellers should be able to articulate a reasonable growth strategy. Buyers should be able to understand the skills of each staff member, trainer and understand all aspects of revenue—how much is subscription, one time, etc.

The fitness/health club industry is a very competitive one as barriers to entry are low, member retention is always an issue, and business models and the focus of gyms tend to change every few years. The group fitness concept is quickly emerging at the expense of one-size-fits-all gyms like Bally and 24 Hour Fitness. In addition, members are more likely to be interested in paying on a class-by- class basis as opposed to annual subscriptions.

Fitness is enjoying a lot of popularity right now, which has brought in a great deal of competition. It is about sales production, and often people get into it thinking it is about fitness, Because of their failures, the equipment, while expensive, isn't worth that much although recurring revenues from contracts in place are worth a great deal.

In the CrossFit space specifically, competition is increasing to keep up with consumer demand, which has grown several fold over the past 5 years. Gyms can command a premium if they:

- ✓ have established themselves deeply in the local market and build strong brands

✓ have trainers that have built large and engaged followings

✓ have sent delegates to compete in the CrossFit games

✓ are in Tier 1 locations (but not crippled by rent)

This is a competitive industry with a lot of different segments; low-cost, low-service to high-touch, high-cost facilities. You need to understand where a facility fits in its competitive landscape.

The biggest risk to fitness center business is capitalization. It takes 12–18 months to get to breakeven. They get hurt if they don't adequately capitalize their companies. Once you get to breakeven, 70-90% of the next dollar flows to the bottom line, so depending on its profitability trend, bringing a little bit of growth can be very accretive.

Seller Financing

- Many lenders do not like this space. Often it's cash or seller financing, with many using retirement funds as well.

- These businesses typically sell with a combination of outside source financing as well as vendor financing. I most often see a 1/3, 1/3, 1/3 buying scheme where the purchaser has 1/3 of the money in cash, they borrow 1/3 from a bank, and the vendor provides the balance in the form of vendor financing.

- Both are equally common. Sellers should be prepared to carry 10%–20% of the purchase price.

- Conventional lenders see fitness centers like restaurants, assets that are not worth much if they have to be liquidated. It will require a solid history of cash flows to attract one to finance a deal. Because of this, seller financing is often used in creative ways.

Resources

- HealthClubs.com: http://www.healthclubs.com
- IDEA Fitness: http://www.ideafit.com
- International Health, Racquet & Sportsclub Association: http://www.ihrsa.org
- Club Industry: http://www.clubindustry.com
- IBISWorld, August 2017: http://ibisworld.com
- CrossFit: https://www.crossfit.com/
- British Columbia Recreation and Parks Association: http://www.bcrpa.bc.ca/

Flower Shops (Florists)		
SIC 5992-01	NAICS 453110	

Rules of Thumb

➤ 2 x EBITDA

➤ 30–35% of annual sales includes inventory

Pricing Tips

- Review the Profit and Loss Statement to determine if wire service revenues and expenses (FTD, Teleflora, etc.) are tracked on separate line items to ensure that the sales are not overstated and cost of goods is not understated.

F

- A premium should be given for stores with a significant number of commercial accounts (especially if there is a credit card on file for ease of billing) which helps protect revenues from big box stores that also sell flowers and plants.

Benchmark Data

Statistics (Florists)

Number of Establishments	31,087
Average Profit Margin	2.2%
Revenue per Employee	$66,600
Average Number of Employees	2.3
Average Wages per Employee	$15,816

Products and Services Segmentation

Arranged cut flowers	61.9%
Giftware and other	12.8%
Potted plants	12.7%
Unarranged cut flowers	12.6%

Industry Costs

Profit	2.2%
Wages	23.8%
Purchases	43.9%
Depreciation	1.9%
Marketing	2.3%
Rent & Utilities	10.2%
Other	15.7%

Statistics (Online Flower Shops)

Number of Establishments	243
Average Profit Margin	4.3%
Revenue per Employee	$1,277,300
Average Number of Employees	10.6
Average Wages per Employee	$75,155

Products and Services Segmentation

Potted plants	35.6%
Arranged cut flowers	22.4%
Unarranged cut flowers	17.8%
Giftware and others	15.1%
Floral network services	9.1%

Industry Costs

Profit	4.3%
Wages	5.8%
Purchases	46.9%
Depreciation	1.2%
Marketing	11.4%
Rent & Utilities	5.9%
Other	24.5%

Market Share

1-800-Flowers.com Inc.	30.2%
FTD Companies Inc.	24.8%

Expenses (% of Annual Sales)

Cost of Goods	33%
Occupancy Costs	10%
Payroll/Labor Costs	20%
Profit (pretax)	20%

Questions

- Percentage of local business versus wire service?

Industry Trend

- "Consumers will continue to purchase industry products from e-commerce sites and supermarkets rather than florists over the next five years. To maintain favorable profit margins, many florists will increasingly specialize in creative, individualized arrangements, allowing them to stand out from competitors and increase prices. As a result, profit is expected to increase slightly despite falling revenue. Demand from wedding services and funeral homes is anticipated to account for an increasing percentage of sales because these services are less sensitive to pricing and convenience concerns. Overall, industry revenue is expected to decline at an annualized rate of 0.3% over the five years to 2020, totaling $5.7 billion as external competition continues to drain revenue from industry operators."

    Source: http://clients1.ibisworld.com/reports/us/industry/industryoutlook.aspx?entid=1096

Expert Comments

Owning a flower shop continues to be a desirable lifestyle business for creative entrepreneurs who wish to provide an artistic and meaningful contribution to their community.

The floral industry has been deeply affected by the economy and online 'orders.' Grocery stores and discount warehouses have also taken market share from retail florists.

Seller Financing

- 2 to 5 years

Resources

- Florists' Review: http://www.floristsreview.com
- Wholesale Florist & Florist Supplier Association: http://www.wffsa.org
- Society of American Florists—for members only: http://www.safnow.org
- IBISWorld, May 2017: http://ibisworld.com
- IBISWorld, July 2017: http://ibisworld.com

Food Service Contractors

	NAICS 722310	Number of Businesses/Units 55,837

Rules of Thumb

➤ 3.5 x EBITDA

➤ 40–45% of annual sales plus inventory

➤ 2.5–3x SDE plus inventory

➤ 2.5–3.5x EBIT

Pricing Tips

- Location. Location. Location. A rule of thumb: one person will occupy a building for every 200 square feet of total building space. This number is very important to calculate a frequency rate depending on the building usage/mix (customer count and average ticket is key). Also, if there are multiple buildings in the center, assume that one person for every 450 square feet of buildings more than 25 yards away from primary building will frequent the shop.
- A better operator can create 25% to 40% more sales quickly. You can still sell potential in this industry.

Benchmark Data

Statistics (Food Service Contractors)

Number of Establishments	55,837
Average Profit Margin	8.3%
Revenue per Employee	$69,300
Average Number of Employees	11.9
Average Wages per Employee	$21,468

Products and Services Segmentation

Cafeteria dining services	31.7%
Retail outlets and concessions	24.7%
Food and nutrition services	14.0%
Catering and banquet	12.3%
Other	10.3%
On-site restaurants	7.0%

Major Market Segmentation

Business and industry	28.5%
Educational institutions	27.5%
Healthcare	23.3%
Sports and entertainment	12.6%
Other	6.0%
Airlines and airports	2.1%

Industry Costs

Profit	8.3%
Wages	30.8%
Purchases	41.5%
Depreciation	1.8%
Marketing	0.7%
Rent & Utilities	7.9%
Other	9.0%

Market Share

Compass Group PLC	23.2%
Aramark Corporation	17.1%
Sodexo	16.6%
Delaware North Companies Inc.	5.1%

Expenses (% of Annual Sales)

Cost of Goods	31% to 39%
Occupancy Costs	04% to 10%
Payroll/Labor Costs	16% to 25%
Profit (pretax)	12% to 20%

Questions

- 1) The lease is very important (get a copy and read it slowly). 2) Agreement with company is very important (get a copy and read it slowly). 3) What are the sales trends for the last 2 years? 4) What improvements or repairs are needed? 5) Count the people in the building. 6) Get information on employees. 7) Make a spreadsheet of the compatible operations. 8) Outside setting is a big value. If they don't have it, can you add outside set? 9) Do you like the food they sell? 10) What equipment will you need and is there room for it? 11) Make sure the common areas are kept up nicely. 12) How many hours does the owner work? 13) Call health department for inspection ASAP. 14) Can you increase the hours? 15) Equipment age is important. 16) When is the last time seller had a price increase?

Industry Trend

- "The Food Service Contractors industry will continue to benefit from increased consumer spending and higher corporate profit over the next five years. As unemployment rates remain steady and incomes rise, consumers will increasingly spend on luxuries such as dining out. Various private and public institutions and facilities will recognize the benefits of outsourcing food services to professionals that can deliver quality and consistent food options. Over the five years to 2022, industry revenue is projected to rise at an annualized rate of 1.8% to $49.8 billion."

Source: IBISWorld Industry Outlook

Expert Comments

The location is everything...so good location and it is easy to sell and hard to replicate.

More and more operators are getting as close to office and workforce personnel as possible with smaller units. This will create pressure on price and profit.

Seller Financing

- There is very little outside financing the sales, and lack of increased sales volume prohibits banks from participating in the financing. Will most likely be owner financing.
- 3 to 5 years is common with about 30% down.
- Finance no longer than the current lease term. 3 to 5 years is average.

F

Resources

- IBISWorld, February 2017: http://ibisworld.com

Food Service Equipment and Supplies		
	NAICS 423440	

Rules of Thumb

➢ 45% of annual sales plus inventory

➢ 2.5 x SDE plus inventory

➢ 4.5–5 x EBIT

➢ 5–6 x EBITDA

Pricing Tips

- 10 times EBITDA for dealerships
- All assets saleable? Obsolete equipment?

Benchmark Data

Expenses (% of Annual Sales)

Cost of Goods	30%
Occupancy Costs	05% to 07%
Payroll/Labor Costs	30%
Profit (pretax)	10%

Industry Trend

- ". . . the National Restaurant Association (NRA) projects the restaurant industry will grow to $799 billion in revenues in 2017, up 4.3 percent from 2016. In real terms, though, this translates into a growth rate of 1.7 percent, consistent with the past few years. 'The past several years, and even the first quarter of this year, have definitely been one of the slower growth environments,' says B. Hudson Riehle, senior vice president of research for the NRA. Looking ahead to 2018 and beyond, the restaurant industry should anticipate much of the same moderate growth rate. That's because, according to most industry observers, macroeconomic indicators, such as national employment levels and disposable personal income, can be expected to continue edging up but will not experience a period of rapid growth. 'It is sustained real growth for the industry, but it is definitely a sustained moderate growth environment,' Riehle says."

  Source: "FE&S' Forecast 201: Steady as the Foodservice Industry Grows" by Joseph M. Carbonara, September 1, 2017, http://www.fesmag.com/research/industry-forecast/15056-fe-s-forecast-2018-steady-as-the-foodservice-industry-grows

Resources

- Foodservice Equipment Reports: http://www.fermag.com
- Food Service Equipment & Supplies Magazine: http://www.fesmag.com

Food Stores—Specialty

	NAICS 44529	Number of Businesses/Units 54,523

Rules of Thumb

➤ Candy Stores—30 to 35% of annual sales plus inventory

➤ Bakeries—40 to 45% of annual sales plus inventory

➤ Dairy Stores—25% of annual sales plus inventory

➤ Other—35 to 40% of annual sales plus inventory

Pricing Tips

▪ This category also includes the following retail businesses: confectionery products, gourmet foods, organic and health foods, packaged nuts, spices and soft drinks.

Benchmark Data

Statistics (Specialty Food Stores)

Number of Establishments	54,523
Average Profit Margin	4.6%
Revenue Per Employee	$73,800
Average Number of Employees	2.4
Average Wages per Employee	$14,064

Products and Services Segmentation

Other	27.2
Candy, chocolate and snacks	26.8%
Bakery Products	24.4%
Refrigerated and frozen meats, seafood and eggs	9.5%
Coffee and tea	6.6%
Dairy products	5.5%

Industry Costs

Profit	4.6%
Wages	19.2%
Purchases	48.7%
Depreciation	2.1%
Marketing	1.5%
Rent & Utilities	10.4%
Other	13.5%

Statistics (Ethnic Supermarkets)

Number of Establishments	45,460
Average Profit Margin	2.5%
Revenue per Employee	$207,600
Average Number of Employees	4.0
Average Wages per Employee	$19,0212

Products and Services Segmentation

Other food items	38.9%
Meats	16.5%
Produce	14.0%
Non-food items	9.7%
Beverages (including alcohol)	9.3%
Dairy items	7.4%
Frozen foods	4.2%

Industry Costs

Profit	2.5%
Wages	9.2%
Purchases	71.0%
Depreciation	1.3%
Marketing	1.1%
Rent & Utilities	6.5%
Other	8.4%

Industry Trend

- "The Specialty Food Stores industry is expected to continue expanding steadily during the next five years as economic conditions improve and more Americans develop a taste for specialty, premium or all-natural foods. During this period, the industry is expected to benefit from heightened consumer confidence and a rise in per capita disposable income. Furthermore, the national unemployment rate is expected to remain low as more Americans return to work, which will enable consumers to increase their spending on discretionary products, such as specialty foods sold by this industry. Despite these favorable economic conditions, operators will continue to experience escalating competition from mainstream grocery stores, supermarkets and other retail channels during the next five years. Consequently, IBISWorld expects industry revenue to rise at an annualized rate of 2.4% to $10.7 billion over the five years to 2022. In 2018, revenue is forecast to increase 2.9% as health and wellness claims made by organic, unprocessed and all-natural food manufacturers and rising health consciousness drive up demand for specialty foods across all retail channels."

Source: IBISWorld Industry Outlook

Resources

- Specialty Food: http://www.specialtyfood.com
- IBISWorld, September 2017: http://ibisworld.com
- IBISWorld, January 2017: http://ibisworld.com

Food Trucks		
	NAICS 722330	Number of Businesses/Units 3,817

Rules of Thumb

➤ 25–30% of annual sales plus inventory

Pricing Tips

- A big difference between food trucks and catering trucks is that the food truck is many times named after a restaurant or recognizable chef. This is often difficult to transfer and most likely neither the restaurant nor chef will be willing to allow a stranger to operate under their name. In other words, a good portion of the value (and goodwill) is the name. If franchises such as Chili's or one of the steakhouse franchises get into the food truck business-that would be transferable with franchisor approval. Some food trucks do not use a well-known name, but rather specialize, such as the grilled cheese sandwich truck that did so well on a TV show. A food truck specializing in a particular food category would be transferable, again with permission.

Benchmark Data

Statistics (Food Trucks)

Number of Establishments	3,817
Average Profit Margin	7.9%
Revenue per Employee	$65,000
Average Number of Employees	3.6
Average Wages per Employee	$23,688

Products and Services Segmentation

American (burgers, sandwiches and hot dogs)	34.0%
Asian	18.3%
Desserts	13.8%
Central and South American	12.0%
Other	11.8%
Mixed Ethnicity	6.4%
Greek Mediterranean	3.7%

Industry Costs

Profit	7.9%
Wages	36.4%
Purchases	39.7%
Depreciation	2.1%
Marketing	1.7%
Rent & Utilities	7.5%
Other	4.7%

- Most Common Truck Specialties: Cheeseburgers, Mexican/Tacos, Desserts, American Classics, Sandwiches

Industry Trend

- "They're restaurants on wheels, churning out everything from pan-seared dumplings to juicy porchetta sandwiches for the city's hungry lunchtime crowds. But food trucks, which are proliferaing at a rapid pace around Boston, are more likely to be temporarily shut down for serious health violations than their brick-and-mortar counterparts, most commonly for violating a basic requirement for proper sanitation: running water."

  Source: "Food trucks more likely than restaurants to be temporarily shut for serious violations," by Megan Woolhouse and Matt Rocheleau, *Boston Sunday Globe*, June 11, 2017

- "From Urban Sugar Donuts in Portland, Maine, to Homegrown Smoker Vegan BBQ in Portland, Ore., there's a food truck for every taste in every state in the U.S., including Alaska's Quickie Burger and Hawaii's Giovanni's Shrimp Truck. The fast-growing industry (more than 4,000 food trucks roam the U.S., generating $1.2 billion in annual revenue) traces back to push cart vendors in 17th century New Amsterdam (New York City) and post-Civil War chuck wagons. Gourmet food trucks became a thing in 2008, when Kogi BBQ began selling $2 Korean barbecue tacos on L.A. streets. Now websites and apps like Food Truck Fiesta, Eat Street and Roaming Hunger help you find food trucks in your neighborhood in real time."

  Source: *Parade Magazine*, July 16, 2017

- "The current $650 million revenue estimate by food trucks, will be hitting about $2.7 billion in 2017! That is almost a four times increase. This hike has made it one of the best revenue generating segments in the overall food industry, currently producing $1.2 billion per year from 4,130 food trucks all over the United States. That's $290,556 on average per food truck. The average meal ordered at food trucks costs about $12.40, which is much less than a restaurant dine-in.

"Because of the food court areas located in almost all the shopping malls, the least revenue is generated by food trucks in nearby areas which consist of 12% of the total revenue. Coming after this, is the industrial and construction work sites where about 15% of the total sales take place. Other locations like event venues produce 18% of the total industry revenue. And the highest percentage of revenue is generated from random roadside locations and street corners which make up 55% of the total revenue. Random placements are the most profitable way of achieving more sales. These areas usually include residential or office-majority locations where there aren't many restaurants nearby, which make food trucks an attraction for that place."

Source: "The Growth of the Food Truck Industry," April 7, 2016,
http://www.foodtruckhq.com/growth-food-truck-industry/

- "The food truck business has grown 80% since 2009, and it's on the way to becoming a billion-dollar Industry by 2020."

Source: Matthew Twombly, NGM Staff Sources; Todd Schifeling, University of Michigan; Daphne Demetry, Northwestern University, Roaming Hunger; National Restaurant Association

Expert Comments

"Food trucks are difficult for a couple of reasons. A lot of laws are outdated when it comes to running a food truck. Permits can tend to be a big headache. You can't just pull up on a corner and start selling food—I wish it were that easy! You need permits and inspections for everything, and those all cost money."

Source: "Hybrid Vehicles" by Peter Lombardi in *PMQ Pizza Magazine*, March 2017

Resources

- Mobile Cuisine: http://mobile-cuisine.com
- IBISWorld, November 2016: http://ibisworld.com

Foot Solutions		Franchise
Approx. Total Investment		$85,000–$240,000
	NAICS 448210	Number of Businesses/Units 113

Rules of Thumb

➢ 60–65% of annual sales plus inventory

Resources

- Foot Solutions: http://www.footsolutions.com

Framing & Art Centre		Franchise
Approx. Total Investment		$118,200–$179,400
SIC 5999-27	NAICS 442299	Number of Businesses/Units 50

Rules of Thumb

➢ 60% of annual sales plus inventory

Benchmark Data
- For Benchmark Data see Picture Framing

Resources
- Framing Art Centre: http://www.framingartcentre.ca

Franchise Food Businesses		
	NAICS 722	

Rules of Thumb
➤ 4 x EBIT

➤ 3.5 x EBITDA

➤ 52–60% of annual sales plus inventory

➤ 2.5 x SDE plus Inventory

➤ Asset value + 1 year's SDE plus Inventory

Pricing Tips
- Franchise resales can skew these metrics higher depending on the quality of the franchise or the current 'hotness' of the franchise concept.
- Rule of thumb: will list for 60% of gross and sell for 60% of list. Add cost of franchise fee on top of selling price. Non-traditional sites ... very lease dependent!
- Establish seller-adjusted cash flow and multiply times 2.5 to 3.5
- Stability of income, down payment & quality of franchisor
- Check the franchise agreement. Who pays transfer and training fees? Does the franchisor have the first right to purchase the business? Will the transition require the facilities to be upgraded to franchisor's current standards? If yes, the upgrade cost can be substantial.

Benchmark Data

Expenses (% of Annual Sales)
Cost of Goods	30%
Occupancy Costs	07%
Payroll/Labor Costs	19%
Profit (pretax)	22%

Questions
- What would you do to improve sales? Would you do it again?

Seller Financing
- 5 to 7 years; however, SBA loans up to 10 years can be obtained.

Resources
- We Sell Restaurants Blog: http://blog.wesellrestaurants.com/

F

Franchise Resales

Pricing Tips

- "Omitting a step, or even performing a step late, could have disastrous effects on the resale transaction. For example, franchisors often require upgrades and enhancements at time of transfer (costing thousands of dollars). If detailed information is not provided to both seller and buyer prior to executing an agreement, buyers-typically the party responsible for upgrades-may decide to walk away from the transaction. To make matters worse, this often occurs right before the closing table. Surprises like that may not always kill the transaction, however corporate will receive stressful, time-consuming phone calls from frustrated buyers unaware of the upgrades required of them.

  "If the seller gets tied into a listing agreement with a local broker who does not educate the seller on proper pricing techniques, the franchisee will be tied into a one-year listing agreement to find their overpriced, or mispriced, business never sells. Therefore, their sales and profits decrease; royalties decrease; the business is worth less; or they are in jeopardy of going dark. It is critical that sellers are educated on the pricing of their business, and the steps involved to properly value their business prior to market."

Source: Jon Franz, *Franchise Times*,
http://digitaledition.qwinc.com/display_article.php?id=935202

Resources

- Franchise Times: http://www.franchisetimes.com

Franchises

Rules of Thumb

➤ We have listed franchises with a quick rule of thumb, or range, usually expressed as a percentage of sales. For many of them we have based it on quite a few actual sales; others may have been based on just a few; and in some cases just one where we felt it was appropriate. They can be a good starting point for pricing the business. Many of the franchises are well known while others are very new with just several units. By the time this goes to press, some of the franchises may have folded, sold or merged. We try to keep this as up-to-date as possible.

➤ Keep in mind that Rules of Thumb are just that. Every business is different and Rules of Thumb will never take the place of a business valuation or even an opinion of value, but, everything else being equal, they will give you a rough idea of what the business might sell for. A rule of thumb will tell you whether a seller is in the ballpark when he or she tells you what they think their business is worth or what they want to sell it for. For up-to-date information, go to the websites of the specific companies.

➤ Several other factors can greatly influence the selling price of a franchise. One is the question of the transfer fee levied by the franchisor and who pays it. This amount can be substantial, so find out the information on this prior to going to market. Another factor is the franchisor requiring a major change in outside appearance and a change in the interior of the unit—or both. This should also be investigated before attempting to sell it. The costs involved in either requirement can be substantial.

Name of Franchise	Selling Price as % of Sales
AAMCO Transmission	40%–42%
A&W Restaurants	45%
Ace Cash Express	1.25%
Ace Hardware Stores (1)	45%
Adam and Eve Stores	35%
Aero Colours	70%
All Tune & Lube	20%–25%
Allegra Painting	70%
AlphaGraphics	60%–65%
American Poolplayers Association (2)	1.4x SDE
Andy on Call	25%
Anytime Fitness	2.5x SDE
Atlanta Bread Company	25%–30%
Baskin Robins Ice Cream	46%–56%
Batteries Plus	30%–35%
Beef O'Brady's	25%
Beltone Hearing Aids	50%
Ben & Jerry's	35%–40%
Between Rounds Bagel Deli & Bakery (3)	
Big Apple Bagels	35%–40%
Big City Burrito	55%–60%
Big O Tires	35%
Blackjack Pizza	40%
Blimpie	45%–50%
Boba Loca	30%
Bruster's Ice Cream	45%–50%
Budget Blinds (4)	50%–55%
Burger King	35%
Carl's Jr.	40%
Cartridge World	30%–35%
Carvel Ice Cream/Restaurants	55%
Car X Auto Service	35%–40%
CertaPro Painters	45%
Cheeburger Cheeburger	35%–40%
Chick-Fil-A	60%–70%
Closet Factory	45%–50%
Closets by Design	45%
Cold Stone Creamery	30%
Cost Cutter's Family Hair Care	55%–60%
Coverall North America (5)	2–3x monthly sales
Culligan Dealerships	80%–120%
Curves for Women (6)	30%
Dairy Queen	45%
Deck the Walls	35%
Del Taco	70%
Dick's Wings and Grill	35%
Domino's Pizza	45%–50%
Dream Dinners	40%
Dr. Vinyl	75%
Dry Cleaners USA	55%
Dunkin' Donuts (7)	60%–100%
Eagle Transmission Shops (8)	40%
Environmental Control	42%
Fantastic Sam's (9)	35%–40%
Fast Fix (Jewelry)	80%–85%
Fast Frame	32%
FasTrac Kids	45%

F

Fast Signs 42%–46%
Foot Solutions 60%–65%
Framing & Art Centre 60%
Friendly Computers 30%
Friendly's Restaurant 40%
Gatti's Pizza 30%–35%
Geeks on Call 60%
General Nutrition Centers 40%
Godfather's Pizza 25%–30%
Goin' Postal 30%–35%
Goodyear Store (Business Opportunity) 35%
Grease Monkey International 58%
Great Clips .... 1–1.5x SDE
Great Harvest Bread Co. (10) ....
Great Steak 55%–60%
Grout Doctor 85%–90%
Harley Davidson Motorcycles (11) 85%–90%
Home Helpers 40%–45%
Home Team Inspection 35%
Honest-1 Auto Care 70%–75%
House Doctor 24%
Hungry Howie's Pizza & Subs 35%
Huntington Learning Center 60%
Iceberg Drive Inn 40%–45%
i9 .... 60%–70%
Jani-King 25%–30%
Jersey Mike's Subs 50%
Jiffy Lube 45%–50%
Jimmy John's 65%–70%
Johnny Rockets 70%–75%
Jon Smith Subs 20%
Juice It Up 20%–25%
Kentucky Fried Chicken (KFC) 30%–35%
Kumon Math & Reading Centers 80%–90%
Kwik Kopy (printing) 50%–60%
Lady of America 45%–50%
Laptop Xchange 80%–85%
Lenny's Subs 15%–20%
Liberty Tax Service 45%–50%
Li'l Dino Subs (12) 64%
Little Caesar's Pizza 55%
Logan Farms (honey-glazed hams) 30%
MAACO Auto Painting and Bodyworks 40%
MaggieMoo's Ice Cream (13) 25%
Maid Brigade 45%
Mama Fu's 30%
Marble Slab Creamery 45%
Martinizing 55%–60%
McGruff's Safe Kids ID System 52%
Meineke Car Care Center 30%–35%
Merry Maids 45%
Midas Muffler 30%–35%
Minuteman Press 65%
Miracle Ear Hearing Aids 60%
Molly Maid 40%
Money Mailer 40%–45%
Moto Photo 72%
Mountain Mike's Pizza 27%
Mr. Jim's Pizza 35%–40%

F

F

U-Save (auto rental) (20) 10%
Valpak Mailers... 40%–45%
Valvoline Instant Oil Change.. 50%
Wienerschnitzel 30%–35%
Wild Birds Unlimited... 30%–35%
Wine Kitz (Canada)... 55%
Wingstop Restaurants 30%–35%
Wireless Toyz... 45%–50%
Worldwide Express 50%–55%
Your Office USA... 60%
You've Got Maids.. 60%
Ziebart International (auto services) 42%
Zoo Health Club.. 20%

(1) Sales seem to indicate that smaller sales bring a higher multiple (50% +) than stores with sales over $1 million, which seem to bring lower multiples. Price is plus inventory which may be the cause of lower multiples for larger stores. (2) $1,000 to $1,800 per team in sales; selling price: $2,000 to $2,500 per team (3) 3–4 times earnings (4) 2 times annual EBIT, plus inventory & equipment (5) Master/Area developer—Sell for 3 to 5 times earnings plus some blue sky for size and potential of market (some cases). (6) Prices for Curves for Women seem to be all over the place. Some sales have been reported at 75+% of sales. One sale reported was 1.31 times sales for four units. (7) Dunkin Donuts shops now sell for 75–125% of annual sales, depending mainly on geography. It's about 125% in New England, 100% of sales in the Mid-Atlantic States, and lower in the South and Midwest. There really is not a Dunkin' Donuts market in the West, however they are now moving into the West Coast market. A sale in Colorado was reported that sold for 22% of sales. (8) Eagle is a Texas-based franchise www.eagletransmission.com. They are the strongest transmission franchise in the Dallas area with 21 locations and are a minor player in Houston and Austin. The attraction is the royalties at 4% in Dallas and 6% in Houston and Austin, and the training is "hands on" locally. (9) These stores sell for maximum 2 times SDE versus $120,000 to $150,000 + for new. 10 to 12 sales have been reported at 2 times SDE for absentee owner stores (most are) and 2 times SDE + manager's salary of owner operated. (10) 3.3–3.4 times SDE (11) Netted $2,100,000 and seller retained 20% of ownership (12) One sold for 80% of sales, but it was located in an office building with vending rights. (13) One MaggieMoo's Ice Cream & Treatery sale was reported at 92%, three years old, great location, growth at approximately 15% a year; but only 15% down payment (14) 1–4 times SDE plus hard assets. The number between 1–4 depends on several factors such as the owner operating a truck, etc. (15) The only sale reported of Papa John's was a 3-store chain which sold for $475,000 with $150,000 down and grossed $1,191,700. (16) Pizza factory has approximately140 units in the 10 western States. (17) Quiznos, which has struggled as a higher-priced alternative to Subway, has closed an estimated 1,000 of its U.S. shops (the company won't confirm the number) and has begun putting mini-stores in gas stations in a bid to boost sales— from www.msn.com April 2011 (18) One sale was reported at 70% of sales. (19) "As a former multi-unit Subway franchisee and a Development Agent, now a business broker for Subway stores, there are many different formulas I have seen. 30 to 40 weeks' sales, or 60 to 70% of sales is a popular one. Actual sales price depends on supply and demand and is closer to 70% of sales in So. CA." "On stores with gross sales of $300,000 to $500,000, multiple of 40% of annual sales. On stores with sales of $500,000+, multiple of 50% of annual sales. Franchisor would like 30% as a down payment on resales." (20) Price does not include cost of vehicles, and revenues do not include auto sales.

Pricing Tips

- Very much depends on SDE and the franchise itself. Can be as low as a 2 and as high as a 4 multiple.
- Typical rule is 1–4 times SDE and it may or may not include inventory, depending on the business. With so many different brands and industries represented within the franchise industry, it truly varies. It's difficult to give a single, broad-based rule.

- Middle Market can vary wildly depending on size of the system and industry.
- Presumes profitability on top of market-rate wages to the owner(s) for the time spent working in and on the business. I have observed about 90 business categories of franchised enterprises. It is hard to generalize about 'franchised enterprises' in general. Other considerations can be time left on the license and franchiser transfer fees. Still another consideration can be the history and SIZE (number of units regionally-nationally) reflecting the strength of the brand.
- "Pricing the franchise resale obviously depends on the franchise. Is the franchise value added or-as in some cases-value subtracted? Does franchising add value to the business or would the same business-independent of a franchise label-bring as high a price in the marketplace? When calculating a multiple of annual sales, is it before subtracting the royalty fees, or are they included in the annual sales? After all, 6 percent of just $500,000 in annual revenues is $30,000, but just $12,000 at 40 percent of annual sales. The $12,000 probably doesn't have much of an impact on pricing unless the sales are really astronomical.

"McDonald's has always been the franchise that everyone compares others to, but that has changed recently. However, it probably hasn't hurt the price of a McDonald's-it is still a very strong brand. One disadvantage of franchising is that, like Burger King, the company gets sold several times, and the direction of the new owners can play havoc with operational support, advertising and growth of the company. In most cases, franchisees have no control over this. The strength of a franchise is the success of the brand name and the reputation created in the marketplace. Many franchises have been able to create that brand-identity and awareness to add a lot of value to the price of one of the units. And, if you want to buy a very popular franchise in a particular geographical marketplace, you have to pay the going rate.

"Some prospective business buyers like the security and the support of a franchise. Still others want the independence of owning and controlling their own business. Buying an independent business provides just that. No answering to the franchisor, no royalties and no heavy advertising fees, no forced purchasing from certain suppliers-and no politics. Owning your own independent business also allows you to expand, change, add or delete products and/or services. Independent businesses can be very quick to adjust to changes. Franchises, especially large ones, are very cumbersome and slow to adapt to new trends and ideas.

"The choice is a personal one. Some very strong independent operators have chosen, after years of independence, to buy a franchise, while some franchisees felt stifled and changed to an independent business.

"As for pricing a franchise, we don't see much of a difference between an independent business and the franchised one, except for the very big players, where the franchise label probably adds a lot of value, maybe 10 to 20 percent, based on the same gross. On the other hand, the fledging franchise with just a few units has some real problems on the resale side. If it's fairly new, there are plenty of new units available, the name doesn't really mean anything yet, and the age-old question is asked—why is the business for sale? In cases like this, the percentage multiples might be reduced by the same figure as is added for the well-known brand name-most likely lower.

"Despite what the franchise industry would like us to believe, not all franchises are successful. What has always struck us as strange is the buyer who is very number- oriented and turns down a very good business due to some slight

F

anomaly in the financial statement from two years ago, but will be the same buyer who purchases a franchise (a new one) where he has seen no books and records and has no idea whether the location will work out or not."

Source: The Business Broker (Business Brokerage Press)

- "Key Considerations When Pricing a Franchise
    - ✓ Lease Terms—If the lease doesn't contain a provision for at least 10 years remaining, the price can be affected accordingly.
    - ✓ Franchise Rights—If there aren't at least 10 years left in the franchise agreement, a price adjustment downward should be made. This may not be applicable in those states where the franchisor may not terminate the agreement unless there is a default.
    - ✓ Territorial Rights—If the franchise agreement does not provide for territorial rights, this could be a minus. In other words, if the franchisor can open additional units in the immediate area, the value of the existing franchise could be diminished. However, if the franchisee has additional territorial rights then the value may be increased.
    - ✓ Business Mix—If the bulk of the sales is in low-profit items, value may be diminished; whereas if high profit items make up a substantial part of the business, value may be increased. Is there wholesale business? Do one or two customers make up a majority of the business? Business mix should be considered.
    - ✓ Remodel Requirements—Does the franchise agreement state that the business has to be remodeled periodically? How often and how much remodeling? The value of the business may be reduced by the cost of the remodeling, depending on when it has to be done.
    - ✓ Hours of Operation—Does the franchisor require specific hours and days open? Some franchisors, especially food related, donuts/convenience stores, may state that the business has to be open 24 hours a day, seven days a week. The shorter the hours, the better the price.
    - ✓ Location—Obviously, the better and more desirable the location, the better the price.
    - ✓ Cash Flow—The price of a small business may be based on its sales history rather than on reported profitability. Some businesses are just not operated efficiently from a cash management point of view. Certainly, strong cash flow benefits the price asked, but a poor cash flow coupled with strong historical sales does not necessarily detract from the price."

Excerpted from a presentation to the American Institute of Certified Public Accountants by Bernard Siegel, Siegel Business Services, Philadelphia, PA.

Benchmark Data

- Franchise metrics vary depending upon the category. Fast food tends to have higher margins but is more labor intensive with higher occupancy costs. Service franchises tend to produce less revenues with lower operational costs. In addition, a number of franchises are now home based which results in much lower expenses.
- This varies greatly depending on the business and the specific industry it's in within the franchise industry. I can't really generalize since so many various industries are included in franchising.
- I value most business based on multiple of SDE plus assets.

Questions

- Why are they selling? Have they been receiving the support of the franchise system that they are paying for with their royalties? What have been the pros and cons of the business model and the company?
- What do you wish you had done differently in the last six months, three years, five years? Where do you feel better controls over the business could be put in place?
- It's important to use the services of professionals Be sure to understand the terms of a new franchise agreement, study most recent sales trend. Review who franchise competes against. Ask if a remodel of the building and location is due. Meet the franchisor staff so as a buyer you will know who you'll be dealing with.
- Would you invest in this opportunity if you had it to do again?

Industry Trend

- Stable
- Service franchises, both B2B and B2C, are seeing continued growth. Other popular trends are the passive/semi-absentee owner models and multi-unit models.
- "1.The franchise categories, that led the industry in 2015, will continue to dominate franchising in 2016:
  - ✓ QSR—look for more specialty and ethnic based franchise concepts.
  - ✓ Personal Services—especially the home care and children services sectors will remain vibrant. The wellness and fitness sectors will remain strong.
  - ✓ Lodging—fueled by a stronger U.S. economy and lower oil prices, more people will travel and use lodging services in 2016.
  - ✓ Residential and Commercial Services—will continue to grow and will benefit from an aging population of home owners that seek home maintenance services, as well as a resurgence of the residential housing market.

2. Any increase in interest rates such as the recent ¼ point increase by the Federal Reserve will tighten credit for small businesses and franchising. Look for third party lenders that specialize in the franchise industry to grow in popularity

3. There will be continued acquisitions and mergers by private equity firms in 2016. The favorable returns and scalability that franchising offers will increase the amount of investment in franchise companies by financial firms.

4. The Joint Employer issue promulgated by recent NLRB decisions, especially the Browning-Ferris Industries ruling, will cause the most vulnerable franchisors to increase their oversight and increase control over their franchisees by tweaking their franchise contracts to avoid direct and immediate control over franchisee employment. Franchising will continue to seek relief from the further NLRB decisions regarding Joint Employer rulings through congressional action.

5. Politicians will remain divided and polarized over particular issues regardless of the 2016 election outcomes.

6. Item 19 disclosures will increase in use and detail, as Financial Performance Representations become a significant competitive issue.

7. The franchise industry will continue to experience positive growth.

8. Franchisors, especially in the QSR sector, will adapt to increases in minimum wages by increasing the use of technology."

Source: "Franchise Know How" by Ed Teixeira

F

- Franchise resales are increasingly popular while independent sales are tougher. There are pockets of the country (California for example) where a combination of the new minimum wage laws, occupancy costs and cost to build are rendering restaurants almost impossible to resell. The East Coast is not as affected.
- It is getting harder to start an unbranded business. It is easier to open multiple locations with a branded business. Franchising is being driven on a commercial and consumer level. Despite the economy, new franchisers are entering all markets-everywhere nationwide.
- Continued growth and interest as confidence in corporate jobs decreases.

Expert Comments

Research franchisor

Do your due diligence to be sure it's a fit for you—your skills, your goals, your interests, and your financial capabilities.

Industry stats show continued growth for the franchise industry over the next couple of years, on top of the growth it's seen in the past few years. Corporate America is changing and more and more skilled executives are looking to be business owners but they need a plan, a system, a structure. They don't want to reinvent the wheel and franchises offer them what they need (over-used phrase but I'll say it anyway: be in business for themselves but not by themselves).

Franchises are operated under the terms of a franchise agreement which requires a buyer to utilize a competent franchise attorney and accountant. In addition, certain franchisors require a location to be remodeled upon a sale. This could cost the buyer more capital than anticipated. Most importantly, be sure the terms of the new franchise agreement, which a buyer must execute, don't contain higher royalties which will distort the financial statements the buyer is relying on.

Call other franchisees in the system to validate. Speak with both those who are successful and those who might be struggling to get a realistic expectation.

Regarding the ease of replication-typically it's difficult because one must develop a concept, develop the business structure, develop the systems, and prove the model in multiple locations before expanding through franchising. It takes a lot in the beginning, but it offers great value down the road to investors looking for such proven models!

A franchisee must be committed to following the franchise system. Franchisees that sway from the franchise standards seem to struggle. The learning curve for a franchise is much, much quicker than a typical business with systems, controls and procedures normally in place. This makes is much simpler for the franchisee to expand the business in size and/or locations

Besides brand strength, the business system of the franchiser has a lot to do with success. Franchisees (new & re-sales) have to follow the business system.

Seller Financing

- For franchise resales, we almost always see banks lending at 10-year terms with 6% rates with 20% down. We are also getting identical terms for independent restaurants. Seller financing is more common for independent sales and there we see 30% or so held on a note payable in typically three years or less.
- Outside financing for the majority, but sellers seem to be carrying part of the deal lately.
- In the sale of an existing franchise, it is usually a combination of personal funds, outside financing and seller financing. In the sale of a new unit or location, there is no seller financing.
- Most franchises, especially existing profitable franchises, can be financed.

Resources

- FranNet: http://www.frannet.com
- FranchiseKnowHow: http://www.franchiseknowhow.com
- American Association of Franchisees & Dealers: http://www.aafd.org
- Franchise Times: http://www.franchisetimes.com
- International Franchise Association: http://www.franchise.org
- American Bar Association - Forum on Franchising: http://www.americanbar.org/groups/franchising.html
- Franchise Gator: http://www.franchisegator.com
- Franchise Grade: http://Franchisegrade.com
- Blue MauMau: http://www.bluemaumau.org

Freight Forwarding

SIC 4731-04	NAICS 488510	Number of Businesses/Units 89,882

Rules of Thumb

➤ 50% of annual sales

➤ 2.6 x SDE

Benchmark Data

Statistics (Freight Forwarding Brokerages & Agencies)

Number of Establishments	89,882
Average Profit Margin	4.5%
Revenue per Employee	$420,700
Average Number of Employees	4.0
Average Wages per Employee	$50,085

Products and Services Segmentation

Domestic freight transportation arrangement services	52.2%
International freight forwarding and customs brokerage services	35.5%
Non-vessel operating common carrier services	8.9%
Other	3.4%

Major Market Segmentation

Manufacturers	33.4%
Exporters	24.7%
Importers	23.0%
Wholesalers	18.9%

Industry Costs

Profit	4.5%
Wages	12.0%
Purchases	49.3%
Depreciation	0.6%
Marketing	0.8%
Rent & Utilities	3.5%
Other	29.3%

Questions

- Do you need a customs license?

Expert Comments

Just sold a niche market, owner plus one employee freight forwarder, for $1.1 million at these figures.

Resources

- IBISWorld, July 2017: http://ibisworld.com

	Franchise
Friendly Computers	
Approx. Total Investment	$56,980–$109,480
NAICS 811212	Number of Businesses/Units 260

Rules of Thumb

➢ 30% of annual sales plus inventory

Resources

- Friendly Computers: http://www.friendlycomputers.com

	Franchise
Friendly's	
Approx. Total Investment	$482,200–$1,959,600
Estimated Annual Sales/Unit	$1,150,000
NAICS 722511	Number of Businesses/Units 144

Rules of Thumb

➢ 40% of annual sales plus inventory

Resources
- Friendly's Restaurant: http://www.friendlys.com

Fruits and Vegetables (Wholesale)		
SIC 5148-01	NAICS 424480	Number of Businesses/Units 9,425

Rules of Thumb
➤ 25% of annual sales plus inventory

➤ .75 x EBIT

➤ .75 x EBITDA

➤ .50–1 x SDE plus inventory

Pricing Tips
- What is the average per basket or package profit the company normally charges/expects?
- How much commission/profit does wholesaler charge its customers per basket/box? It usually is about $2.50 to $3 per . . . anything less makes the wholesaler merely a shipping company.

Benchmark Data

Statistics (Fruit & Vegetable Wholesaling)
Number of Establishments	9,425
Average Profit Margin	3.6%
Revenue per Employee	$784,600
Average Number of Employees	12.5
Average Wages per Employee	$48,103

Products and Services Segmentation
Fruits	55.7%
Vegetables	39.7%
Other	4.6%

Major Market Segmentation
Other wholesalers	42.1%
Retailers	33.7%
Foodservice providers	15.2%
Others	9.0%

Industry Costs
Profit	3.6%
Wages	6.1%
Purchases	87.3%
Depreciation	0.6%
Marketing	0.2%
Rent & Utilities	0.5%
Other	1.7%

F

Expenses (% of Annual Sales)

Cost of Goods	40% to 50%
Occupancy Costs	10%
Payroll/Labor Costs	30%
Profit (pretax)	10% to 20%

Industry Trend

- If the hothouse effect is a reality for our environment and fuel prices continue an upward trend, the produce business will be adversely affected.
- Smaller wholesalers either going out. . . or taking on additional food lines.

Expert Comments

It is perhaps one of the least expensive businesses to start and operate, but just as easy to destroy without a strong paying customer base. One can grow this business through adding of multiple delivery trucks and yet not even have to rent warehouse space.

Seller Financing

- Both outside financing and seller financing, depending on what the corporate tax returns look like and the amount/age of equipment owned by the company.

Resources

- IBISWorld, September 2017: http://ibisworld.com

Fruit & Vegetable Markets (Produce)

	NAICS 445230	Number of Businesses/Units 12,805

Rules of Thumb

➤ 35–40% of annual sales

Benchmark Data

Statistics (Fruit and Vegetable Markets)

Number of Establishments	12,805
Average Profit Margin	4.2%
Revenue per Employee	$163,000
Average Number of Employees	2.3
Average Wages per Employee	$17,590

Products and Services Segmentation

Vegetables	54.4%
Fruit	32.8%
Meat, fish, seafood and poultry (including prepackaged meats)	4.9%
Dairy products and related foods (including milk, eggs and cheese)	3.9%
Frozen foods (including frozen packaged foods)	2.1%
Delicatessen items (including deli meats)	1.9%

Industry Costs

Profit	4.2%
Wages	10.8%
Purchases	67.8%
Depreciation	0.6%
Marketing	0.6%
Rent & Utilities	4.6%
Other	11.4%

Industry Trend

- "Revenue for the Fruit and Vegetable Markets industry is expected to continue to grow over the five years to 2022, albeit at a slower pace than it did during the previous five-year period. Sharp increases in the price of fruits and vegetables, the industry's top two revenue-producing product segments, will continue to bolster growth. Despite these price increases, per capita fruit and vegetable consumption is estimated to remain fairly steady, declining at an annualized rate of 0.2% over the five years to 2022. Despite slight declines in demand for fruit and vegetables, US consumers' preferences have been shifting away from red meats and toward white meats; per capita poultry consumption is expected to increase an annualized 0.4% over the five years to 2022, burgeoning industry growth. Moreover, governmental and school programs, which encourage individuals to eat more fresh fruits and vegetables, will continue to spur demand, despite rising prices. Such demand will help operators maintain profit margins by letting them pass on price increases to consumers. Rising per capita disposable income will also bolster revenue growth, as consumers will have more money to spend on locally grown and organic price-premium products. Consequently, over the five years to 2022, revenue is expected to rise at an annualized rate of 1.2% to $5.1 billion, with an expected increase of 1.3% in 2018 alone."

Source: IBISWorld Industry Outlook

Resources

- The Packer: http://www.thepacker.com
- IBISWorld, March 2017: http://ibisworld.com

Fuel Dealers (Wholesale)

	NAICS 424720	

Rules of Thumb

➤ 1.5 x SDE plus inventory

➤ 1.5 x EBITDA plus vehicle value (over 15 vehicles)

Pricing Tips

- Wholesalers/distributors are large-volume, low-margin operators; therefore the price is 1–2 times EBITDA.

Benchmark Data

- Typical wholesaler does $30 million in annual sales.

F

Industry Trend

- "While crude oil prices are expected to rise, industry revenue is anticipated to gradually decline. Over the five years to 2022, industry revenue is expected to decline an annualized 0.5% to reach $31.5 billion. As in previous years, severe weather patterns could also have a profound influence on industry demand. On a broader level, the continued retrofitting of residential and nonresidential buildings from heating oil to natural gas heating systems is anticipated to spur competition between the Fuel Dealers industry and Natural Gas Distribution industry (IBISWorld report 22121). However, industry performance over the next five years will continue to be influenced by the prices of crude oil and natural gas, as well as the severity of winters."

Source: IBISWorld Industry Outlook

Resources

- National Propane Gas Association: http://www.npga.org
- Butane Propane News: http://www.bpnews.com

Funeral Homes/Services

SIC 7261-02	NAICS 812210	Number of Businesses/Units 28,310

Rules of Thumb

➢ 200% of annual sales includes inventory and real estate

➢ 6 x EBIT includes real estate

➢ 1.5–3 x SDE

➢ 5 x EBITDA

➢ 5–6 x w/real estate, 4x w/o real estate SDE plus Inventory

➢ Under 75 funerals/year: 3–4.5 x EBITDA plus vehicle value (over15 vehicles)

➢ 75–100 funerals/year: 4–5 x EBITDA plus vehicle value (over 15 vehicles)

➢ 150+ funerals/year: 4.5–6 x EBITDA plus vehicle value (over 15 vehicles)

➢ 6–6.5 x (if real estate included) EBITDA plus vehicle value (over 15 vehicles)

Pricing Tips

- "Today, more than 60% of mortuary science students in the United States are women. Many of these women have discovered and are attracted to the skills and traits needed as a funeral director, including communication skills, compassion, a desire to comfort those coping with a death, as well as organizational and event-planning skills."

Source: "Trends in Funeral Service," http://www.nfda.org/news/trends-in-funeral-service

- The standard valuation method within the industry is to use a mutiple of EBITDA, typically between 4-6 times. This valuation method assumes everything is included, FF&E, vehicles, inventory and real estate. It is also common for funeral homes to purchase items at cost for families as a courtesy; these are referred to as cash advance items, and should be subtracted from the gross revenue to obtain a true picture of the gross revenue. Common cash advance items are obituaries, flowers, clergy honorariums, cemetery expense, crematory expense, organist/musician, death certificates, etc. Take the Gross Revenue, subtract all cash advance items to arrive at an adjusted Gross Revenue, and multiply the Adjusted Gross Revenue by 25% to arrive at a realistic estimated EBITDA number. That estimated EBITDA number would then have a multiple of between 4 and 6 applied to it to arrive at a realistic asking price range. The multiple depends on things such as condition of the real estate and vehicles, competition in the area, revenue trend, etc. When it comes to prepaid funerals/cremations there is no value placed on them; the funeral home does not own them, and the families can go somewhere else. However, a strong prepaid funeral backlog may result in a higher EBITDA multiple because a buyer may have more confidence in the continued success of the business. A low prepaid account may result in a lower multiple. A non-compete agreement is a must, as it is a relationship-based business. Common non-compete agreements in the industry are from 10–20 years, and they are for 10–20% of the total asking price (not in addition to it).

- Funeral homes that are larger in size and have more traditional funeral services are slightly more valuable than the standard Rules of Thumb.
- Valuations can be negatively affected by high cremations or eroding market share; valuations can be positively affected by strong real estate values, high growth areas, or increasing market share.

Benchmark Data

Statistics (Funeral Homes)

Number of Establishments	28,310
Average profit Margin	9.8%
Revenue per Employee	$132,200
Average Number of Employees	4.4
Average Wages per Employee	$28,785

Products and Services Segmentation

Funeral planning services	29.8%
Resale of merchandise	28.2%
Body preparation and internment	13.9%
Other	13.1%
Cremation	10.4%
Transportation	4.6%

Industry Costs

Profit	9.8%
Wages	22.0%
Purchases	24.0%
Depreciation	3.1%
Marketing	3.0%
Rent & Utilities	5.7%
Other	32.4%

Market Share

Service Corporation International	10.9%

- Adjusted EBITDA should be in the 25% area of gross revenue after subtracting out cash advance items.

F

- A typical single location funeral home can be run at an EBITDA in a range of 28–32%; any more than that, and they are likely not putting money back into the facility and equipment.
- Employment of funeral service workers is projected to grow 12 percent from 2012 to 2022.

Expenses (% of Annual Sales)

Cost of Goods	20%
Occupancy Costs	15% to 25%
Payroll/Labor Costs	28% to 30%
Profit (pretax)	25% to 35%

Questions

- What are their plans after the sale? Will they be staying In the area? Make sure to ask about the prepaid funeral accounts and the last time they were audited.
- Ask if the firm has ever been cited by the state regulators for anything, ask if they have ever been cited by the FTC. Ask to see copies of the facility license from the state and make sure it is current.
- Make sure your attorney has a clause in the purchase agreement that states you are only assuming the prepaid funeral liabilities specifically disclosed and that can be verified. Get advice from someone experienced in the business.

Industry Trend

- Lower gross revenues and declining profit as more and more families choose cremation over burial. There will be more consolidation and some outright closings as the drop in revenue/profits from cremation makes it unprofitable to own a small funeral home.

Expert Comments

Buyers: Do not go into this for the money. Make sure your attorney has a clause in the purchase agreement that states you are only assuming the prepaid funeral liabilities specifically disclosed and that can be verified.

Sellers: Valuations have changed since the consolidation by the public companies in the '80s and '90s. Be prepared to carry-back 10–20% of the asking price as a non-compete agreement.

With the aging of the baby boomers, there will be an increase in the number of deaths annually; the funeral homes that keep up with changing preferences will see continued success.

High cost of real estate and zoning laws make it difficult for new players to enter the local market. In addition, if an existing funeral home has a strong prepaid funeral marketing program they can lock up future business and protect their market. Profits are declining as cremation is increasing exponentially in many areas of the country.

The historical profit trend is declining with the rise in the number of families choosing cremation which is a lower priced service. Marketability is fair to good, as a fairly priced funeral home should sell. It is typically hard for a new funeral home to enter an established market, as it is a relationship based business, and it is expensive to build a new funeral home, so the ease of replication is hard to very hard.

1. 200 percent of annual sales includes inventory and real estate

The rule of thumb has been around for a long time, but it always used to be a range of '1.5 to 2 times annual sales including inventory and real estate,' plus the math of 2X is easier than 1.5X to do in your head).

There are two big issues with this method. First, it does not take into account cash advance items. These are items that the funeral home purchases for the family and puts on the contract, but there is no mark up. These items are easily identified in a contract analysis, or if the funeral home has accurate P&L's as they should be line items.

Things like obituaries, flowers, death certificates, opening/closing the grave, crematory fee, required permits, etc. These can add up to between $1,000 and $2,000 per service. Since there is no profit to the funeral home, there should be no mark-up/multiple assigned to these items when trying to value a funeral home. If anything, a slight discount should be applied, because many funeral homes give families 30 days to pay, so they are giving an interest fee loan to the families served.

As an example, most industry participants use a multiple of EBITDA to value a funeral home, if we compare the two, here is what we get. (assuming we already subtracted out cash advance items): revenue is $1,000,000 so 2 times sales would be a value of $2,000,000.

However, using EBITDA it would be $1,800,000 (A funeral home can be run at a 30% EBITDA, so in this case $300,000 and the average multiples used are 4 to 6, so 6 times $300,000= $1,800,000). While it is only 10% over-priced using this method, if cash advance items are not subtracted first, it can be 20–30% overpriced.

If we used the 1.5 times sales, we would be at $1,5000,000 and since EBITDA multiples are 4-6 most of the time, we use a multiple of 5, since it is in the middle of the range. A $300,000 EBITDA x 5= $1,500,000. We have a match!! This is the area that 90%+ of the deals actually get done.

2. 5 to 6 times SDE includes inventory and real estate, 4 times SDE without real estate

The issue with this rule of thumb as it is written is that it is also the same (or even higher) as the EBITDA method listed in the guide and since the SDE method adds back all the owners earnings and the EBITDA method allows for a reasonable owners salary, obviously one of the methods in the guide is wrong.

The one that is wrong here is the SDE as it overinflates the value of the funeral home, and since most general business brokers use the SDE method, it is causing a lot of funeral homes to be listed, but not being sold. If we stick with the fictional funeral home doing $1 million in revenue, it would not be out of the question for an owner or manager to have a salary of $90,000/year and use of a company car. So, if using SDE that $90,000 is added back in and say $10,000 for use of a car, we would be adding back in $100,000 which could increase the sale price by up to $600,000 or more above the EBITDA method.

If we stick to the fictional funeral home we have been using in the previous example, the EBITDA was $300,000 and at a multiple of 6 would value the funeral home at $1,800,000 a multiple of 4 would be $1,200,000. The SDE method would add back the $100,000 owner's compensation/benefits and give us a figure of $400,000. Based on that, to arrive at a similar valuation as the EBITDA method you are looking at an SDE multiple between 3 and 4.5 times. (3 x $400,000=$1,2000,000 and 4.5 x $400,000 = $1,800,000). This range would bring it in line with the EBITDA method, allow general business brokers to arrive at a realistic value and get deals done.

3. Under 75 funerals per year 3 to 4.5 times EBITDA; 75 to 150 funerals, 4 to 5 times EBITDA; and 150+ funerals, 4 to 6 times EBITDA

These numbers are pretty close, the lower multiples for the smaller businesses are because nobody really wants a firm under 100 services per year as there is typically not enough money to hire another licensed funeral director, so the buyer is really buying a job and may be better off to just stay working somewhere else and making about the same amount of money, getting some time off, and having no financial risk.

4. 6 to 6.5 times EBITDA if real estate is included. If real estate is not included, a long-term triple net lease is a must (8 to 10 percent of sales); purchase price would be 4 times EBITDA or approx. 1 times trailing 12 months' sales.

Obviously, this one is on the high end of the EBITDA range. Because this is the top of the range, the real estate, furniture, fixtures, equipment, vehicles better be in pristine condition, if not, the cost to update repair or replace these items should be subtracted from the valuation arrived at.

Also, while a long-term lease is a must, the difference between a gross lease and a triple net lease depends on if you are the buyer of seller, although the 8–10 of net sales is about the right percentage.

5. 6 times EBIT includes real estate

Seller Financing
- The standard is outside financing for 75-80% of the purchase price, with the seller carrying back the balance in the form of a non-compete agreement over several years. Since this is a relationship based business, the non-compete helps to protect the buyer and helps to insure the seller will assist in transitioning the relationships in the community to the new buyer.
- 10–15 years
- 15–20 percent of purchase price for 10 years

Resources
- International Cemetery, Cremation & Funeral Association: http://www.iccfa.com
- National Funeral Directors Association: http://www.nfda.org
- IBISWorld, August 2017: http://ibisworld.com

Furniture Refinishing		
SIC 7641-05	NAICS 811420	Number of Businesses/Units 23,567

Rules of Thumb
➢ 50% of annual sales plus inventory

Benchmark Data

Statistics (Furniture Repair & Reupholstery)

Number of Establishments... 23,567
Average Profit Margin 9.4%
Revenue per Employee $59,800
Average Number of Employees... 1.4
Average Wages per Employee $20,070

Products and Services Segmentation

Office and institutional furniture repair 55.8%
Upholstery repair of household furniture... 18.9%
Wooden household furniture repair... 13.3%
Other furniture repair services 12.0%

Major Market Segmentation

Households.. 51.7%
Businesses 44.3%
Government 4.0%

Industry Costs

Profit 9.4%
Wages... 33.7%
Purchases... 29.5%
Depreciation.. 1.6%
Marketing.. 1.5%
Rent & Utilities 7.5%
Other.. 16.8%

Industry Trend

- "The Furniture Repair and Reupholstery industry is expected to experience sluggish yet steady growth over the next five years. As economic conditions continue improving, particularly consumer disposable income, individuals will increasingly opt to purchase new furniture instead of repairing it, making long-term demand for the industry dismal at best. Less expensive furniture, especially from low-cost manufacturing countries, will continue to lure customers away from repair services. Overall, industry revenue is forecast to increase at an annualized rate of only 0.7% to total $2.0 billion over the five years to 2022."

Source: IBISWorld Industry Outlook

Resources

- IBISWorld, July 2017: http://ibisworld.com

Furniture Stores		
SIC 5712-16	NAICS 442110	Number of Businesses/Units 39,192

Rules of Thumb

➤ 60% of annual sales includes inventory

F

Pricing Tips

- Analyze gross profit margin & ratio of repeat clientele to new customers.

Benchmark Data

Statistics (Furniture Stores)

Number of Establishments	39,192
Average Profit Margin	4.9%
Revenue per Employee	$268,600
Average Number of Employees	5.7
Average Wages per Employee	$34,104

Products and Services Segmentation

Living room furniture	50.4%
Bedroom furniture	19.5%
Other furniture	16.3%
Dining room furniture	13.8%

Industry Costs

Profit	4.9%
Wages	12.8%
Purchases	53.8%
Depreciation	0.9%
Marketing	3.3%
Rent & Utilities	8.1%
Other	16.2%

Market Share

Inter IKEA Systems BV	9.7%
Ashley Furniture Industries Inc.	6.3%

Expenses (% of Annual Sales)

Cost of Goods	30%
Occupancy Costs	20%
Payroll/Labor Costs	15%
Profit (pretax)	35%

Questions

- What is the reason for selling? Will the purchaser assume ownership of the client base? Is there already a fully functional website?

Industry Trend

- "While the shift to online is perhaps not surprising, the pace of the shift is. In a furniture market that is growing at a rate of 2.9% annually, e-commerce sales are expected to double, from $15 billion in 2012 to $32 billion by 2018. E-commerce accounted for 21% of total furniture sales in 2014, and it is forecast to grow to 30% by 2018, according to research firm eMarketer. Recent trends support this forecast. For example, in 2014, sales at Overstock.com, Amazon and Wayfair, the three largest online retailers of furniture, grew by 14.8%, 19.5% and 44.0%, respectively."

Source: "Seismic Shift to Millenials Driving Dramatic Changes in U.S. Furniture Market," by Deborah Weinseig, February 15, 2016, https://www.forbes.com/sites/deborahweinswig/2016/02/15/seismic-shift-to-millennials-driving-dramatic-changes-in-us-furniture-market/#4010373d1cab

- "IBISWorld anticipates revenue for the Furniture Stores industry will increase over the next five years as per capita disposable income and homeownership rates rise. Rising demand for furniture will result in revenue growth, but falling consumer confidence and increased competition will greatly constrain revenue and margin expansion. As more consumers buy homes, operators will benefit because homeowners often purchase furniture to outfit the home initially. The residential market will continue to expand slightly for that reason. With more per capita disposable income, consumers will be more easily able to outfit new homes with industry products. However, consumer confidence declines will make consumers more hesitant to make big-ticket purchases in existing homes, constraining revenue growth. Consequently, over the five years to 2021, revenue is expected to rise at an annualized rate of 0.6% to $61.5 billion, slower than the previous five-year period."

Source: IBISWorld Industry Outlook

Resources
- Bedding Today: http://www.furnituretoday.com/
- IBISWorld, January 2017: http://ibisworld.com

Garage Door Sales & Service		
SIC 5211-02	NAICS 444190	Number of Businesses/Units 912

Rules of Thumb

> 25% of annual sales plus inventory

Benchmark Data

Statistics (Garage Door Installation)

Number of Establishments	912
Average Profit Margin	6.5%
Revenue per Employee	$339,400
Average Number of Employees	1.4
Average Wages per Employee	$123,265

Products and Services Segmentation

Maintenance and service work	62.2%
Automatic door installation	19.5%
Manual door installation, door openers and accessories	18.3%

Major Market Segmentation

Residential construction	57.0%
Retail merchants	33.3%
Utilities construction	9.7%

Industry Costs

Profit	6.5%
Wages	36.3%
Purchases	32.8%
Depreciation	1.2%
Marketing	1.1%
Rent & Utilities	3.79%
Other	18.2%

G

Resources
- IBISWorld, January 2017: http://ibisworld.com

Garden Centers/Nurseries		
SIC 5261-04	NAICS 444220	Number of Businesses/Units 20,566

Rules of Thumb
➢ 25% of sales

➢ 3–5 x SDE plus inventory

Pricing Tips
- Customer database indicating the amount of recurring revenue per customer

Benchmark Data

Statistics (Nursery and Garden Stores)
Number of Establishments	20,566
Average Profit Margin	4.0%
Revenue per Employee	$303,000
Average Number of Employees	6.5
Average Wages per Employee	$31,278

Products and Services Segmentation
Equipment	50.4%
Grain and animal feed	19.2%
Chemicals	17.2%
Plants	7.8%
Tools and other supplies	5.4%

Major Market Segmentation
Farmers	44.8%
Consumers aged 55 and older	22.6%
Consumers aged 35 to 54	17.4%
Corporate entities	8.5%
Consumers aged 34 and younger	6.7%

Industry Costs
Profit	4.0%
Wages	10.4%
Purchases	50.3%
Depreciation	1.4%
Marketing	1.6%
Rent & Utilities	4.5%
Other	27.8%

- "Greenhouse Grower's 2016 State Of The Industry Survey included separate questions for growers and for suppliers. Of our 358 respondents, 103 were suppliers, 111 were grower-retailers, 109 were wholesale growers, and 35 were young plant growers. Among growers, 57% indicated their operations were small (less than 100,000 square feet), 21% were medium-sized (100,000

G

to 399,999 square feet), and 22% said they were large growers (400,000 square feet or larger).

- "Annual Sales Volume:

Less than $100,000	31%
$100k to $249,999	13%
$250k t0 $999,999	13%
$1 million to $4.99 million	14%
$5 million to $9.99 million	11%
$10 million to $19.99 million	08%
$20 million to $29.99 million	04%
$30 million to $39.99 million	03%
$40 million to $49.99 million	01%
More than $50 million	02%"

Source: "Growers And Suppliers Move Forward With Cautious Optimism In 2016," by Laura Drotleff, January 18, 2016, http://www.greenhousegrower.com/business-management/growers-and-suppliers-move-forward-with-cautious-optimism-in-2016/

Expenses (% of Annual Sales)

Cost of Goods	48%
Occupancy Costs	05%
Payroll/Labor Costs	28%
Profit (pretax)	04%

Questions

- What am I not seeing in your numbers? Is unaccounted cash being removed from the business? How current and complete is your customer database?

Industry Trend

- "Over the next five years, the Nursery and Garden Stores industry is expected to continue its upward climb. Increased consumer spending and continued strength within the housing and construction markets are expected to bolster demand for industry goods. However, heightened external competition from big-box stores is expected to threaten industry operators. As big-box stores continue to offer lower prices, industry operators will need to strengthen their position within their local communities to compete. Due to the competitive environment, industry revenue is expected to rise less rapidly than in the previous period, increasing at an annualized rate of 0.4% to reach $41.1 billion by 2022."

Source: IBISWorld Industry Outlook

Expert Comments

This is a maturing industry but the right business location and a good marketing and management of finances makes all the difference. Affluent customer base is necessary to compete effectively with mass merchants. A service component of the business is helpful but increases risk.

Seller Financing

- 5 to 15 years

Resources

- Garden Center Magazine: http://www.gardencentermag.com/
- IBISWorld, July 2017: http://ibisworld.com
- Greenhouse Grower: http://www.greenhousegrower.com/

28th Edition

293

Gas Stations—Full- and/or Self-Serve

SIC 5541-01	NAICS 447190	

Rules of Thumb

➢ 10–15% of annual sales plus inventory

➢ 2.5–3 x SDE plus inventory

➢ 2.5–3.0 x EBIT

➢ 2.5–3.5 x EBITDA (business only)

Pricing Tips

- Buyers are looking for high volume gas stations; the norm is the higher the gasoline volume per month the more attractive the business becomes. That being said you also need to be aware of the margin on each gallon of gas sold. Find out if the tanks underground have been inspected in the last year and meet or exceed EPA and local standards. Ask if any leaks or hazardous waste has been found/detected on the premises in the last ten years. If the gas station has a convenience store associated the value is higher, if there is a car wash the value increases again.

- Age of tanks; does station have canopy (is it cantilever or mech. attached); is it clean (environment); location, location, location.

Benchmark Data

Statistics (Gas Stations)

Number of Establishments	14,707
Average Profit Margin	1.6%
Revenue per Employee	$764,300
Average Number of Employees	8.3
Average Wages per Employee	$22,423

Products and Services Segmentation

Diesel	49.2%
Gas	41.8%
Other	5.6%
Nonautomotive fuel	1.8%
Automotive services (repairs, car washes and general parts	1.6%

Major Market Segmentation

Consumers	68.8%
Businesses	26.1%
All other	5.1%

Industry Costs

Profit	1.6%
Wages	3.1%
Purchases	82.3%
Depreciation	0.7%
Marketing	1.5%
Rent & Utilities	2.6%
Other	8.2%

Market Share

Royal Dutch Shell PLC 8.9%

Expenses (% of Annual Sales)

Cost of Goods.. 75%
Occupancy Costs...05% to 10%
Payroll/Labor Costs ....08% to 10%
Profit (pretax)..03% to 05%

Questions

- 5 years' financial and gallonage history; phase I & II environmental reports
- Any new competition? Security & safety? Road construction? Introduction to vendors.

Industry Trend

- "The Gas Stations industry is expected to grow over the five years to 2021. Operators will experience more competition from retail sites in the Gas Stations with Convenience Stores industry (IBISWorld report 44711), while demand for gasoline will decline due to the growing popularity of fuel-efficient vehicles. However, a mild rebound in the world price of crude oil over the next five years is expected to enable industry operators to moderately raise prices for fuel. Higher per capita disposable income will mitigate these price increases somewhat, by allowing consumers to opt for the most convenient retail sites, despite higher prices, and by raising demand for diesel fuel and premium grades of gasoline. As a result, IBISWorld anticipates industry revenue to grow at an annualized rate of 1.9% to $97.4 billion during the five years to 2021."

Source: IBISWorld Industry Outlook

Expert Comments

Major oil companies are getting out of owning properties and managing labor. More and more newer immigrants are getting into locations as owners across the country. Oil companies primarily want to be in the fuel supply busness as their core profit driver.

It is getting very expensive to build a new ground-up facility. Average does cost close to $2 million, therefore it is not that easy to replicate. Not to mention the uphill battle with most urban zoning requirements which causes lengthy delays and adds to the soft costs.

Seller Financing

- 3 years, on average 8 percent interest per annum
- As much as 50 percent of sales price could be financed; 3 to 5 years typical.

Resources

- IBISWorld, November 2016: http://ibisworld.com

G

Gas Stations w/Convenience Stores/Minimarts

SIC 5541-01	NAICS 447110	Number of Businesses/Units 110,238

Rules of Thumb

➤ 80% of annual sales with real estate plus inventory

➤ 20–25% of annual sales plus inventory

➤ 3.5–4.5 x SDE plus inventory, when a full-service car wash is included (min. $250k SDE) 3–5 x EBIT

➤ 2.5–3.75 x EBITDA (business only)

Pricing Tips

- If sold with real estate, expect a 9–11 multiple of SDE.
- Business Asset: 1.25 X Cash Flow
- 1) What type of gas supply agreement is in place; rack deal gets a high price; dtw (dealer tank wagon) average price; commission agent low price. Buy a commission agent gas station only if there is at least a 10-year lease.
- 2) Gas volume and pool margin on gas.
- 3) Convenience store gross profit preferred 30% or higher.
- 4) Independent or brand name. Independent are valued at a higher price.
- 5) If it has a car wash it has a higher value.
- 6) Low rent, high value.
- 7) If diesel is also sold, higher value as pool margin on diesel is high.
- 8) The more the revenue stream, the higher the price.
- Location, years history of proven growth, modern facility, and attention to competition.
- The number and breadth of variables makes ROT pricing invalid, and largely misleading-we don't use it.
- 1) Valuation is 2–3 times net income for owner-operated gas stations and for absentee owned 3-4 times.
- 2) Potential buyers must consider rent, pool margin on gas, mechanics on salary or commission.
- 3) Age of the car wash equipment. Most car washes last 10 years.
- 4) Land owned by the oil company is a plus; if third party owns the land, check the underlying lease between the oil company and the landlord.
- 5) Check transfer fee and security deposit charged by the oil company.
- The most valid pricing comes from capitalizing adjusted cash flow, or SDE. If the gas station acquisition includes the real estate, this either needs to be broken out and priced in addition to the business, or digested in the capitalization calculation. Severely reduced transaction volume, little or no new construction, and poorly defined interest rate scale to define risk (& CAP rates) due to government intermediation make the standard approaches to pricing uncertain.
- Gasoline volume and gasoline margin are key indicators of value; beer/wine license receives a higher price; store size greater than 1000 sq. ft. gets a higher price; length of time and type of fuel contract; franchised vs. independent impacts price, but depends on area.

Benchmark Data

Statistics (Gas Stations with Convenience Stores)

Number of Establishments...110,238
Average Profit Margin 2.8%
Revenue per Employee $412,300
Average Number of Employees... 7.8
Average Wages per Employee 18,890

Products and Services Segmentation

Regular gasoline..58.9%
Groceries 12.8%
Mid-grade and premium gasoline 12.1%
Other.. 10.7%
Diesel... 5.5%

Industry Costs

Profit 2.8%
Wages...4.6%
Purchases... 88.6%
Depreciation... 1.1%
Marketing 0.1%
Rent & Utilities 2.2%
Other.. 0.6%

Market Share

Alimentation Couche-Tard Inc.. 6.7%

- It's often said that 80 percent of a convenience store's sales come from just 20 percent of its customers.
- CGS, operating expenses, and net profit as a percent of sales varies greatly as a function of fuel-to-store sales, and the price of fuel. Also, the revenue centers in the store, whether there is a QSR, a carwash, or mechanical service as part of the non-fuel sales mix provides too much variance to make simple comparisons meaningless.
- Average profit pretax is about 10%. Gas volume should be minimum 1.2 million gallons per year. $600,000 in convenience store sales with 30–40% gross profit. Car wash must do minimum $100–$150k per year
- Case by case, customer count to average sale $12.00+ per transaction.
- Gross profit % of in-store sales is an important metric, and many of the major players will use gasoline as a lost leader to get you in the store.
- Benchmarks for success depend upon revenue centers on the property and the sales mix among the centers, most easily illustrated by considering fuel and c-store. Fuel sales for a metro station might be 60–80% of sales with a profit margin of 2–4%, and the balance under-the-roof at 30% gross margin. (Fuel margins are expressed in pennies/gallon, called blended or pooled margin-easily converted into percent.) Rural stations tend to function more as a grocery store where fuel is the convenient item. These might do 80–90% under the roof and 10–20% or so in fuel. Store margins in rural settings can approach 40%, and fuel pooled margins $.30/gal. (vs., currently, $.12-.18/gal. in metro settings) Additional products and services also are a factor in this evaluation, e.g., carwash, alcohol sales, QSR (franchised or not), quick lube, etc.

G

- Gross Profit margins in C-Stores should not be less than 30%, for delis not less than 50%, car wash GP margins 90%. Gasoline pool margins should be a min. of $.15/gallon.

Expenses (% of Annual Sales)

Cost of Goods	65% to 80%
Occupancy Costs	06% to 16%
Payroll/Labor Costs	08% to 15%
Profit (pretax)	04% to 10%

Questions

- Get all the financials and documentation from Z reports to sales tax returns and purchase invoices to figure out real bottom-line profit.
- Buyer asks seller who the toughest competitor is and why.
- When do you know it's time to sell?
- How much financing can the seller do? What is your gas pool margin? Do you have a supply agreement with an oil company or are you independent? What is the gross profit on your convenience store sales? How old is the car wash equipment? If repair, how old is the equipment in the bays? Do you have emission/inspection? Do you have any fleet contracts for gas? Do you own the ATM or is it leased? What is your lotto commission? If buying real estate also: how old are the tanks, any road widening plans, how much insurance premiums does he pay. What is the workers comp insurance premium especially if there is a repair shop with the gas station? Who is the nearest competitor?
- Ask for 5 years' financial statements and tax returns; petroleum equipment detail; environmental assessments.
- 1) Potential buyers must consider rent, pool margin on gas, if mechanics are on salary or commission.
- 2) Age of the car wash equipment. Most car washes last 10 years.
- 3) Land owned by the oil company is a plus; if third party owns the land, check the underlying lease between the oil company and the landlord.
- 4) Check transfer fee and security deposit charged by the oil company.
- What would you do differently to enhance sales?

Industry Trend

- "US-based fuel retailer Sunoco has agreed to divest around 1,100 convenience stores for $3.3bn to 7-Eleven, a subsidiary of Japanese retail group Seven & I."
  Source: http://conveniencestoresgasstations.retail-business-review.com/news/sunoco-to-divest-1100-convenience-stores-to-7-eleven-for-33bn-070417-5781604 April 7, 2017
- " U.S. convenience stores experienced record in-store sales of $233.0 billion in 2016 and the third straight year of more than $10 billion in pretax profits, according to newly released NACS State of the Industry data:

U.S. store count	154,535
Inside sales	$233.0 billion
Fuel sales	$316.8 billion
Total sales	$549.9 billion
Pretax profit	$10.2 billion"

  Sources: Nielsen/TDLinx; NACS; U.S. Energy Information Administration
- "Convenience stores, which sell more than 80% of the fuel purchased in the country, reported a 9.2% decline in fuel sales. This was driven by another year

of low gas prices, which averaged $2.17 for the year compared with $2.44 in 2015."

Source: "2016 a Record Year for Inside Sales in Convenience Stores," April 4, 2017,
http://www.cspdailynews.com/industry-news-analysis/corporate-news/articles/
2016-record-year-inside-sales-convenience-stores

- More corporate locations, fewer independent owners.
- Continued reasonable growth for larger originations and the demise of smaller operations.
- Continuing trend to food service in the store. In AZ, not a great amount of alternative fuels emerging yet. We have started seeing more electronic charging stations showing up at non-gas station retail, e.g., fast food restaurants, larger shopping centers (malls).
- "Freedom to choose where to stop was cited by 59 percent of those stating they will travel by car this summer, also a 7-percent jump. Once consumers do stop, c-stores are certain to benefit. Three-quarters (76 percent) of vacationers on the road this summer plan to stop to use the bathroom; 69 percent expect to get gas; and 67 percent expect to get food or drinks, reported NACS. Those in the 18-to-34 age group are expected to visit c-stores the most."

Source: http://www.csnews.com/product-categories/fuels/more-summer-vacationers-will-take-road?cc=1

- High competition amongst major convenience retailers. Bigger and better stores, more varieties and add-ons.

Expert Comments

This is a seller's market so you can ask higher prices.

Gas stations are in high demand; corporate entities are buying the traditional private dealers all over the country.

Have your exit plan well in advance of your decision to sell and prepare your business plan conservatively for buying.

Consumer demand continues to improve year over year.

Be conservative on growth forecast and be ready to invest in upgrades, when needed, to the facility and promotion of the business.

To buyers: work in a station for a minimum 6 months before buying one. Make sure you have 2–3 months working capital after the purchase. To sellers: start preparing two years prior to selling so you have clean financials. Not having proper financials will lead to lower valuation. Prepare a good management/employee team so the station is on auto pilot.

Gas stations are a retail business with a very high barrier to entry. Same inventory keeps changing hands as opening a new location is tough due to zoning laws and regulations and it costs over $2 million to get a new one started. It's a recession-free business. You don't need a lot of employees, mostly one, unless you have a great hot food program.

Municipalities dictate barriers to entry. Licensing (privileged licenses) are provided to qualified applicants only.

This industry is dominated by large national and regional players with deep pockets.

Use a broker, and find a specialist for the market you're going into. Business standards of practice, jobber relationships, environmental regulations, etc., vary greatly among regions of the country and the various states.

The overall appetite for profitable businesses in this class is trending upward.

G

Seller Financing

- All cash first, then second financing typically at 30% down and institutional financing 70% of sale price, not including inventory.
- Outside financing is more typical. If seller financing is available, only a small portion of the sales price and for a short term that is secured with a personal guarantee.
- The most common financing is only for inventories for merchandise in the convenience store and fuel in the tanks. It normally will not exceed six months and will require some guarantee.
- If real estate is part of the seller's assets, outside financing. If it's the business only with a lease, you can still get SBA financing, but often times the seller will need to provide 'filler' or 'gap' financing.
- 70% of the purchase price plus inventory paid by the buyer at closing and 30% seller financing for 2–4 years at 6–7% interest rate.

Resources

- PA Petroleum Association: http://www.ppmcsa.org
- Retail Business Review: http://www.conveniencestoresgasstations.retail-business-review.com
- New York Association of Convenience Stores: http://www.nyacs.org
- American Petroleum Institute: http://www.api.org
- Fuel Oil News: http://fueloilnews.com
- Arizona Petroleum Marketers Association: http://www.apma4u.org
- Gasoline & Automotive Service Dealers of America: http://www.gasda.org
- Convenience Store News: http://www.csnews.com
- Convenience Store/Petroleum News: http://www.cspnet.com
- IBISWorld, February 2017: http://ibisworld.com
- Convenience Store Decisions: http://www.cstoredecisions.com/
- Association for Convenience and Fuel Retailing (NACS): http://www.nacsonline.com

Gatti's Pizza		Franchise
Approx. Total Investment		$511,975–$3,430,445
Estimated Annual Sales/Unit		$1,000,000.
SIC 5812-22	NAICS 722513	Number of Businesses/Units 77

Rules of Thumb

- ➢ 30–35% of annual sales plus inventory
- ➢ The company also offers a larger restaurant, GattiTown, for $2,900,000 to $3,200,000. The size of a Gatti's Pizza is 3,000 to 8,000 square feet; GattiTown is 18,000 to 25,000 square feet.

Resources

- Gatti's Pizza: http://www.gattispizza.com

		Franchise
Geeks on Call		
Approx. Total Investment		$53,350–$82,150
	NAICS 811212	Number of Businesses/Units 123

Rules of Thumb

➢ 60% of annual sales plus inventory

Resources

- Geeks on Call: http://www.geeksoncall.com

		Franchise
General Nutrition Centers		
Approx. Total Investment		$165,000–$200,000
SIC 5499-04	NAICS 446191	Number of Businesses/Units 935

Rules of Thumb

➢ 40% of annual sales plus inventory

Resources

- GNC: http://www.gnc.com

Gift Shops		
SIC 5947-12	NAICS 453220	

Rules of Thumb

➢ 30%–40% of annual sales plus inventory

➢ 2.5–3.5 x SDE includes inventory

➢ 3–4 x EBITDA

➢ Inventory @ cost + FF&E + 1 - 2x SDE

Pricing Tips

- Specialty stores; boutique with exclusive lines; location is important.
- If the store has a good location, has a customer tracking system and a good website that is providing at least 10% of annual sales, the values above will hold. Fortunately, most buyers believe that they could run and manage a retail gift business. It is a fun business; most folks don't go into a gift shop unhappy. It is a feel good business.

Benchmark Data

- For additional Benchmark Data see Card Shops
- Needs high traffic area location
- The open hours make for a long work day. Most successful stores are owner run to keep wages in balance. Also, most stores use part-time help to keep the hours at lower wages.

G

Expenses (% of Annual Sales)

Cost of Goods	48% to 55%
Occupancy Costs	06% to 12%
Payroll/Labor Costs	08% to 18%
Profit (pretax)	05% to 25%

Questions

- Why selling. Require the seller to attend at least one industry trade show with introductions to vendors and other sources of inventory.
- Look for a business that you would like to own and be proud to say that you owned it. The decision should be a blend of #1) what the seller has been doing for the last 3 years and #2) what ways do you see to improve and grow the business.

Industry Trend

- Location will remain important; however, building a loyalty client program and customer contact & relationships with customers will continue to be critical to success.
- More use of good websites to sell more to repeat customers that do not have to actually come back into the store. Also, build up customer list with reminders and specials.
- I don't have the statistics, but I believe there are fewer gift shops in business every year. The successfully operated gift stores appear to be in tourist locations and affluent communities. It is extremely difficult to secure unique gift products to sell, and many gift products are available at major retailers and discounters nationally at often discounted prices, making it virtually impossible for small stores to compete.

Expert Comments

The buyer needs to feel comfortable that they can manage and run the business; and they need to feel comfortable with the vendor/ trade-show sourcing of inventory.

Competition from Internet shopping/on-line shopping expansion.

Gifts make people smile. An owner needs to be able to have joyous empathy with their customers-especially those looking for that special gift for someone special to them. And, you need to have good taste for what your customers may want. Providing services such as gift baskets and shipping can add to the business, especially with developing corporate sales.

Seller Financing

- Seller financing, five years.
- 3 to 7 years

Resources

- Association for Creative Industries (AFCI): http://www.afci.global

Godfather's Pizza	Franchise

Approx. Total Investment$100,000–$300,00 depending on the business model

Estimated Annual Sales/Unit	$455,600

SIC 5812-22	NAICS 722513	Number of Businesses/Units 425

Rules of Thumb
➢ 25–30% of annual sales

Resources
▪ Godfather's Pizza: http://www.godfatherspizza.com

Goin' Postal	Franchise

Approx. Total Investment	$48,865–$139,500

SIC 7331-01	NAICS 561431	Number of Businesses/Units 350

Rules of Thumb
➢ 30–35% of annual sales plus inventory

Resources
▪ Goin Postal: http://www.goinpostal.com

Golf Courses		
SIC 7997-06	NAICS 713910	Number of Businesses/Units 11,490

Rules of Thumb
➢ Private: 2.5–5 x SDE plus inventory
➢ 4 x golf-related income, including greens fees, golf carts, driving range
➢ Public: net income—8–11 x SDE, typically 9–10 x SDE plus Inventory

Pricing Tips
▪ I'm not a fan of Rules of Thumb in this industry as the principles of alternatives and replacements are typically at play. Additionally, the northeastern U.S. is unique to the industry in terms of seasonality, premiums on land costs and housing, weather, and value added services such as food and beverage, banquet facilities, private vs. public, instruction, leagues, group outings vs. public daily play, etc. Economic factors resulting from the recession have had a huge impact on the industry as well, especially on private courses where we appraised three for banks planning auctions. Two of three sold for less at auction than what we appraised them for but were bought by past members who formed a consortium hoping to get a good deal (and did). New England also has more 9- hole courses than most other areas of the country which skews industry rules.

G

- Personal property + equipment (FF&E) usually accounts for 3 to 10 percent of the purchase price depending on the amount of equipment leased and type of operation (daily fee vs. private). From 4 to 7 percent of price is typical.
- Due to weather-related conditions, a 5-year average for cash flow should be used- capital reserves of 5 percent should always be accounted for.

Benchmark Data

Statistics (Golf Courses & Country Clubs)

Number of Establishments	11,490
Average Profit Margin	1.9%
Revenue per Employee	$76,500
Average Number of Employees	26.2
Average Wages per Employee	$30,881

Products and Services Segmentation

Food and beverages	33.7%
Memberships	33.1%
Green fees	17.6%
Equipment rentals and sales	11.5%
Other sales and services	4.1%

Industry Costs

Profit	1.9%
Wages	40.3%
Purchases	16.2%
Depreciation	9.2%
Marketing	1.5%
Rent & Utilities	6.6%
Other	24.3%

Expenses (% of Annual Sales)

Cost of Goods	20%
Occupancy Costs	15%
Payroll/Labor Costs	45%
Profit (pretax)	20%

Questions

- Question to ask seller: Is there adjoining acreage that could be used for golf community homes? This can greatly increase value of the golf course.

Industry Trend

- "Yes, far more courses are closing than opening, yet that's because the market is going through a natural correction caused by over-saturation during the boom years. The PGA Tour last year said that the percentage of millennials who play golf (28%) mirrors that of group's percentage of the total population, although they only play about half as frequently as previous generations. The PGA Tour has actively embraced digital to try to engage with millennials, including active social media content and the creation of a cool Internet-only network called SkratchTV."

Source: "Here's Why We Should Be Bullish About Golf in 2017," January 23, 2017, https://www.forbes.com/sites/erikmatuszewski/2017/01/23/heres-why-we-should-be-bullish-about-golf-in-2017/#31edb0f55660

- "Now there are finally signs of an upswing. Apollo Global Management is acquiring country-club operator ClubCorp Holdings Inc. in the industry's biggest takeover in years. New golf personalities are taking the place of Woods, and the sport is looking to attract younger players with Topgolf entertainment venues and other tactics. The push helped bring 2.5 million new participants to the game last year, the most in more than a decade.

  "More broadly, golf has seen a resurgence in so-called avid players, those who play at least 25 rounds on a regulation course per year. The number rose to 8.8 million last year, up 400,000 from 2015, according to the National Golf Foundation. Avid players are critical to the health of the sport because they account for 80 percent of industry spending."

  Source: "Golf's New Stars Help Boost a $70 Billion Industry After Tiger" by Taylor Cromwell, July 10, 2017,
  https://www.bloomberg.com/news/articles/2017-07-10/
  golf-s-new-stars-duffers-buoy-70-billion-industry-after-tiger

- "Here's a look at a few interesting trends in 2016 that caught our attention:
  - ✓ Shorter is better
  - ✓ Growing youth golf
  - ✓ Fighting Mother Nature's wrath
  - ✓ Investing in the game
  - ✓ A monumental year in flexible golf course routings
  - ✓ New courses
  - ✓ The Brexit bargain
  - ✓ Fun with technology"

  Source: "Looking Back: The 10 encouraging golf trends that caught our attention in 2016," by Jason Scott
  Deegan, December 13, 2016, http://www.golfadvisor.com/articles/2016-golf-trends-16189.htm

Expert Comments

Golf is a nearly $70B U.S. industry, impacting 2 million jobs w/ an annual wage income of $55.6B.

"Further, golf courses are a breeding ground for lawsuits. Golf and legal issues can be found in every square inch of a golf facility. From defective golf carts to improperly designed fairways; from wetlands to wrongful serving of alcohol to minors. Are all entitlements in place? Are all liquor licenses proper? Will the new buyer inherit some old tax problems?"

Source: http://www.hospitalitynet.org/news/4063485.html

Seller Financing

- 5 to 7 years
- 20 years

Resources

- National Golf Course Owners Association: http://www.ngcoa.org
- Golf Course Industry: http://www.golfcourseindustry.com
- IBISWorld, February 2017: http://ibisworld.com
- "Golf Property Analysis and Valuation: A Modern Approach" by Laurence A. Hirsh: http://www.appraisalinstitute.org/appraisal-institute-book-shares-methods-for-valuing-golf-courses/

G

Golf Driving Ranges & Family Fun Centers

SIC 7999-31	NAICS 713990	Number of Businesses/Units 57,317

Rules of Thumb

➢ Golf Driving Ranges—70% to 75% of annual sales including inventory

Benchmark Data

Statistics (Golf Driving Ranges & Family Fun Centers)

Number of Establishments	57,317
Average Profit Margin	13.9%
Revenue per Employee	$73,700
Average Number of Employees	3.1
Average Wages per Employee	$19,061

Products and Services Segmentation

Other	23.7%
Amusement and recreation services	33.2%
Coin-operated games and rides	8.8%
Amateur sports teams and club services	10.1%
Meals and beverages	7.9%
Fitness and recreational sport center services	7.6%
Registration for sports tournaments and matches	5.3%
Golf course and country club services and memberships	3.4%

Industry Costs

Profit	13.9%
Wages	25.9%
Purchases	22.0%
Depreciation	5.8%
Marketing	4.0%
Rent & Utilities	6.0%
Other	22.4%

Industry Trend

- "Over the five years to 2022, the Golf Driving Ranges and Family Fun Centers industry will continue to expand as industry operators specialize their product portfolios to attract particular demographics. Time spent on leisure and sports is expected to stagnate over the next five years, which will drive individuals to place an increasing premium on the value of free time. To generate continued growth in consumer attendance rates at golf driving ranges and family fun centers, industry operators must focus on the value of the experience they provide. Furthermore, while per capita disposable income is expected to rise, consumer confidence is forecast to decline. This is anticipated to reduce the portion of consumer spending allocated to entertainment purchases, which will intensify competition for the industry. Although consumer spending is still expected to increase, the rate of growth for discretionary purchases will likely be lower than the previous period.

  "Moreover, over the five years to 2022, industry revenue is forecast to grow at an annualized rate of 0.6% to $13.3 billion, driven partly by growth in the number of individuals aged 20 to 64, a demographic that accounts for a large share of industry revenue. This age range encompasses both young adults, adults with children and older individuals with increased discretionary income. Industry trends toward more diversified product portfolios and better concession options are anticipated to help improve revenue from this demographic range. Additionally, profit is expected to decline to 12.5% of industry revenue in 2022. The rapid gain in profitability during the previous period is expected to taper off, as high margins support increased industry entrance, thereby increasing competition. Increased competition, combined with the variety of services and activities provided by the industry, tends to cannibalize profitability as increased options for consumers pushes down prices."

Source: IBISWorld Industry Outlook

Resources
- IBISWorld, September 2017: http://ibisworld.com

Golf Shops		
	NAICS 451110	

Rules of Thumb
➢ 30% of annual sales plus inventory

Questions
- Is the seller willing to allow the buyer a 10% rejection on the inventory (or some other fixed amount)?

Industry Trend
- "Golf equipment makers are suffering. Nike Inc. pulled out of the market, while Adidas AG recently agreed to sell its equipment business. New online competitors, and the ability to trade gear on the internet, have depressed equipment prices. Nike and Adidas still make golf clothing, but most of it can be worn on or off a course. And the association with the sport allows the brands to charge premium prices, says Chen Grazutis of Bloomberg Intelligence."

Source: "Off for a Round of Golf? Didn't Think So" by Andrea Felsted and Elaine He, https://www.bloomberg.com/gadfly/articles/2017-05-25/off-for-a-round-of-golf-this-weekend-didn-t-think-so

Resources
- National Golf Foundation: http://www.ngf.org
- Professional Golfers Career College: http://www.golfcollege.edu/

Goodyear Tire Stores		
	NAICS 441320	

Rules of Thumb
➢ 35% of annual sales plus inventory

G

Gourmet Shops

SIC 5499-20	NAICS 445299	

Rules of Thumb

➢ 20% of annual sales plus inventory

Benchmark Data

- For Benchmark Data see Food Stores—Specialty

		Franchise
Grease Monkey		
Approx. Total Investment		$190,000–$335,000
	NAICS 811191	Number of Businesses/Units 230

Rules of Thumb

➢ 50% of annual sales plus inventory

Resources

- Grease Monkey: http://www.greasemonkeyfranchise.com

		Franchise
Great Clips		
Approx. Total Investment		$132,250–$253,100
	NAICS 812112	Number of Businesses/Units 4,100

Rules of Thumb

➢ 1–1.5 x SDE plus inventory

Resources

- Great Clips: http://www.greatclipsfranchise.com

		Franchise
Great Harvest Bread Company		
Approx. Total Investment		$93,022–$690,393
	NAICS 311811	Number of Businesses/Units 200

Rules of Thumb

➢ 3.2–3.4 x SDE plus inventory

Resources

- Great Harvest: http://www.greatharvest.com

Franchise

Great Steak

Approx. Total Investment	$146,600–$511,050
Estimated Annual Sales/Unit	$425,000

SIC 5812-19	NAICS 722513	Number of Businesses/Units 76

Rules of Thumb

➢ 50–55 % of annual sales plus inventory

Resources

- Kahala Management: http://www.kahalamgmt.com

Green Businesses

	NAICS 541620	

Rules of Thumb

➢ 120% of annual sales includes inventory

➢ 5.5 x SDE plus inventory

➢ 6.5 x EBIT

➢ 5 x EBITDA

Pricing Tips

- They do vary a lot based on the unique aspect of their environmental services. Emergency response companies will have higher margins and less predictable monthly revenues and cash-flows. Those that are doing more regular industrial/environmental services will be more valuable, i.e., 2 men and a truck for $3500 a day. These are typically worth 5 to 6X EBITDA.

Expenses (% of Annual Sales)

Cost of Goods	30%
Occupancy Costs	10%
Payroll/Labor Costs	36%
Profit (pretax)	10%

Benchmark Data

- Sales per employee: $200 to $300k; CAPEX is 4% to 5% of annual revenues and is a real expense.
- The specific infrastructure will vary materially based on the niche they are providing, i.e., oil recycling, wastewater treatment, remediation of other environmental wastes

Questions

- How much is project oriented versus recurring "milk-run" type services.

G

Industry Trend

- There is plenty of regulation in place that will continue to drive the need for good environmental services.
- "The Eco and Green Certification Providers industry will continue to grow over the next five years. Although a less budget-friendly federal government may constrain growth, companies across all sectors will strive to remain abreast of any regulatory changes. The increased emphasis on environmental sustainability will lead to industry revenue growth. As construction activity continues to increase, demand for sustainable green products will persist. Additionally, companies in high-polluting industries, such as those in the energy and manufacturing sectors, will come under increased pressure to present themselves as environmentally friendly. The combination of shifting consumer preferences and rising corporate pressure to appear green will continue to propel industry growth over the next five years. As a result of these conditions, over the next five years, IBISWorld forecasts revenue will grow at an annualized rate of 1.3% to $510.0 million."

Source: IBISWorld Industry Outlook

Expert Comments

The equipment to get into this industry is usually pretty expensive. Vac trucks are $300-$400k on average so you're not talking $40k pickup trucks. With that said, there iscompetition but most competitors play nice and if they do a good job, they can retain customers well.

Seller Financing

- 40% equity with balance in senior debt and mezzanine financing.

Resources

- IBISWorld, August 2017: http://ibisworld.com

Ground Transportation		
	NAICS 484110	

Rules of Thumb

➢ 50% of annual gross sales plus inventory

➢ 2–3 x SDE plus inventory

➢ 3 x EBITDA plus vehicle value (over 15 vehicles)

➢ 4 x EBITDA plus vehicle value (over 15 vehicles)

Pricing Tips

- You must look at ODCF before you use a multiple. It is important to know if the vehicles are owned, leased or financed. Depreciation will not be a total add-back because you must factor in the life of the vehicle so that only a portion of depreciation is added back. You must reduce Fair Market Value by outstanding debt.
- Maintenance records? Facility?

- Who controls the groups? The quality of the drivers and how long have they been with the company? Are the groups preformed or do they sell into them? Condition of equipment counts.

Benchmark Data

Statistics (Airport Shuttle Operators)

Number of Establishments	619
Average Profit Margin	8.5%
Revenue per Employee	$64,900
Average Number of Employees	20.8
Average Wages per Employee	$26,389

Products and Services Segmentation

Local shuttle services for leisure	67.0%
Local shuttle services for business	30.5%
Other	1.9%
Long-distance shuttle services	0.6%

Industry Costs

Profit	8.5%
Wages	40.5%
Purchases	13.1%
Depreciation	6.1%
Marketing	0.5%
Rent & Utilities	3.2%
Other	28.1%

Expenses (% of Annual Sales)

Cost of Goods	30% to 40%
Occupancy Costs	10%
Payroll/Labor Costs	30%
Profit (pretax)	20%

Questions

- What has been your biggest frustration?

Industry Trend

- "Global consumers are increasingly spending their disposable income on experiences rather than material goods. And consumers' desire for these life experiences is spurring a growth in luxury travel that is outpacing the rest of the travel industry, according a new report commissioned by global travel technology company, Amadeus.

  "The report, Shaping the Future of Luxury Travel, reveals the fresh challenges and opportunities that the luxury travel market will face over the next decade. Some key findings from the report include:

  ✓ We have entered a new age of luxury travel, where luxury is curated, real-time and experience-led

  ✓ North America and Western Europe account for 64% of global outbound luxury trips, despite only making up 18% of the world's population

  ✓ From 2011-2025, Asia Pacific's luxury travel market will see faster overall

G

growth than Europe's, but this growth will decelerate from 2015–2025

✓ India's luxury market of CAGR of 13% is higher than any of the other BRIC nations, and is the highest of the 25 countries explored in this report

✓ A human desire for more rewarding experiences provides an essential catalyst to evolve and improve travel industry quality and service standards

✓ A hierarchy of luxury travel needs is identified, ranging from 5-star quality and service standards to exclusive VIP privacy and security"

Source: "Luxury travel outpaces the rest of the travel industry, according to new Amadeus report," May 18, 2016

Expert Comments

It is a business with low barriers to entry. Now that the economy is improving, this is a discretionary expenditure that has started to increase.

Seller Financing

- Based on the price of the vehicle and the down payment, the term should be 5 to 7 years.

Resources

- Limousine, Charter, and Tour: http://www.lctmag.com
- IBISWorld, August 2016: http://ibisworld.com

Grout Doctor	Franchise
Approx. Total Investment	$14,405–$37,415
NAICS 811411	Number of Businesses/Units 70

Rules of Thumb

➢ 85–90% of annual sales plus inventory

Resources

- Grout Doctor: http://www.groutdoctor.com

Guard Services		
SIC 7381-02	NAICS 561612	

Rules of Thumb

➢ 30% of annual sales plus inventory

➢ 3 x SDE includes inventory

➢ 3 x EBITDA

Pricing Tips

- Non-union are worth more
- If guards are 1099's, business is worth less.

Benchmark Data

- For additional Benchmark Data see Security Services/Systems
- Cost is different for an armed guard, for an event security, or 24-hour security service.

Expenses (% of Annual Sales)

Cost of Goods	05%
Occupancy Costs	05% to 10%
Payroll/Labor Costs	70%
Profit (pretax)	15% to 20%

Questions

- Most guard companies have major clients; explain anything over 20%, could become an earnout event.
- Relationship to customers?

Industry Trend

- "The Security Service industry will benefit from a projected increase in corporate profit levels, which will lead to an increase in security budgets over the five years to 2022. In addition, the industry will continue to benefit from increased residential, commercial and public construction over the next five years, improving demand for industry operators to safeguard real estate and infrastructure development projects. Rising industrial activity and investments in new manufacturing facilities will also lead to an increase in demand for security services. The industrial production index, the Federal Reserve's measurement of output from mining, manufacturing, electric and gas sectors, is expected to increase at an annualized rate of 1.3% over the next five years. Private investment in manufacturing structures is also expected to increase at an annualized rate of 2.8% during this period. An increase in the total number of US factories will subsequently lead to rising demand for security services, as industry operators will be needed to protect manufacturing facilities, equipment and finished goods.

  "Due to these factors, industry revenue is expected rise in line with US economic growth. However, like the prior five years, consolidations, mergers and acquisitions will remain commonplace, as major international security service corporations continue their trend of acquiring smaller domestic companies. Although the Security Services industry will endure stiff competition from high-tech security systems, which employ alarm monitoring and closed-circuit television systems, the industry's major players will be able to incorporate these new technological tools into their current staffed security systems to provide enhanced and comprehensive services. As a result, industry revenue is expected to increase at an annualized rate of 1.4% to $36.2 billion over the five years to 2022."

  Source: IBISWorld Industry Outlook

Expert Comments

As crime increases, so does security.

It is easy to lose a client if you have to go to bid every year.

G

Resources

- IBISWorld, June 2017: http://ibisworld.com

Gun Shops and Supplies		
SIC 5941-29	NAICS 451110	Number of Businesses/Units 6,804

Rules of Thumb

➤ 30–35% of annual sales plus inventory

Benchmark Data

Statistics (Gun & Ammunition Stores)

Number of Establishments	6,804
Average Profit Margin	3.0%
Revenue per Employee	$106,600
Average Number of Employees	12.0

Products and Services Segmentation

Ammunition	25.0%
Pistols	23.2%
Rifles	20.8%
Other equipment, apparel and supplies	18.3%
Shotguns	6.3%
Revolvers	4.4%
Other firearms	2.0%

Industry Trend

Profit	3.0%
Wages	23.3%
Purchases	62.8%
Depreciation	0.8%
Marketing	2.1%
Rent & Utilities	6.2%
Other	1.8%

Industry Trend

- "The total economic impact of the firearms and ammunition industry in the United States increased from $19.1 billion in 2008 to $51.3 billion in 2016, a 168 percent increase, while the total number of full-time equivalent jobs rose from approximately 166,000 to more than 300,000, an 81 percent increase in that period, according to a report released today by the National Shooting Sports Foundation® (NSSF®), the industry's trade association. On a year over year basis, the industry's economic impact rose from $49.3 billion in 2015 to $51.3 billion in 2016, a nearly 15 percent increase."
  Source: "Firearms Industry Economic Impact Rises 168% since 2008," April 10, 2017, http://www.nssfblog.com/firearms-industry-economic-impact-rises-168-since-2008/

- "In spite of the fact that gun ownership is becoming increasingly restrictive due to government legislation in both the United States and Canada, opening and operating a retail business that buys, sells, and trades guns still has the potential to be profitable. In addition to gun sales you can also sell ammunition and hunting-related products as well as offer a gun repair service. Promote the business by establishing alliances with gun clubs and shooting ranges as well as firearm instructors, as these clubs and individuals can refer your business to others. Starting this type of business will require a substantial investment and you will also have to clear a few legal hurdles before you can open. A well-promoted and operated gun shop could return the owner a six-figure yearly income."

Source: "Gun Shop-Business At A Glance" www.entrepreneur.com

Resources
- National Shooting Sports Foundation: http://www.nssf.org
- IBISWorld, November 2016: http://ibisworld.com

Hardware Stores

SIC 5251-04	NAICS 444130	Number of Businesses/Units 20,094

Rules of Thumb
➤ 3.5 x SDE includes inventory

➤ 45–50% of annual sales plus inventory

➤ 3–3.5 x SDE plus inventory

Benchmark Data

Statistics (Hardware Stores)
Number of Establishments	20,094
Average Profit Margin	2.3%
Revenue per Employee	$160,300
Average Number of Employees	7.4
Average Wages per Employee	$25,712

Products and Services Segmentation
Hardware, tools, plumbing and electrical supplies	53.4%
Other	19.9%
Lumber and other building materials	10.9%
Lawn, garden and farm supplies	8.6%
Paint and sundries	7.2%

Major Market Segmentation
Do-it-yourself consumers	52.7%
Businesses	19.0%
Contractors	12.6%
Do-it-for-me consumers	8.7%
Other	7.0%

Industry Costs
Profit	2.3%
Wages	16.0%
Purchases	64.9%
Depreciation	1.1%
Marketing	1.6%
Rent & Utilities	3.8%
Other	10.3%

Market Share

True Value Company	22.5%
Ace Hardware Corp.	22.3%
Do It Best Corp.	18.6%

- Should turn their inventory 2.5 to 3 times per year. Fixtures and equipment should not exceed 16 percent of the average stock carried per year. These stores are sold for fixtures and equipment at depreciated value plus the inventory at wholesale cost.
- Markup runs from 35 to 40 percent.

Expenses (% of Annual Sales)

Cost of Goods	50% to 60%
Occupancy Costs	05% to 08%
Payroll/Labor Costs	12% to 15%
Profit (pretax)	01% to 03%

Questions

- How do you value your ending inventory on the books? Is there concealed inventory or understated inventory? How often do you do a physical inventory? Is your cash register point-of-sale system read barcodes? Are your inventory counts computerized?

Industry Trend

- "Over the five years to 2022, revenue for the Hardware Stores industry is forecast to increase at an annualized rate of 0.3% to $24.2 billion, including a 0.4% jump in 2018. Strong demand for hardware will persist as new home acquisitions and delayed purchases carry over from the recession. However, industry profitability will remain stagnant as continued competition from home improvement stores and online retailers will threaten industry operators.

  "Continued strength in the housing market and consumer spending will bolster demand for the industry's products over the next five years. Per capita disposable income is forecast to increase at an annualized rate of 2.9% over the five years to 2022. Rising incomes will encourage consumers to engage in more do-it-yourself (DIY) projects, along with larger-scale home renovations. Expected increases in housing starts and existing home sales will also benefit industry operators. When consumers purchase homes, they often renovate their new living spaces. As a result, demand for hardware will increase as the housing market flourishes, thereby boosting industry revenue over the next five years."

  Source: IBISWorld Industry Outlook

Expert Comments

Stores in good locations will still bring premium prices. Rural locations are often insulated from the effects of big boxes.

Reasonably profitable hardware stores sell very quickly.

Seller Financing

- A good, qualified buyer should bring at least 25% down to the table. In such cases a ten-year amortized note is fairly common.

Resources

- North American Retail Hardware Association: http://www.nrha.org
- HBS Dealer: http://www.hbsdealer.com/
- IBISWorld, July 2017: http://ibisworld.com

Harley-Davidson Motorcycle Dealerships

SIC 5571-06	NAICS 441228	

Rules of Thumb

➢ 1–4 x EBITDA

➢ 2.5–3 x SDE plus net assets plus inventory

Benchmark Data

- For Benchmark Data see Motorcycle Dealerships

Questions

- Why are you selling? What are the strengths and weaknesses of your business? Are there any add-backs? What is your reputation in the marketplace? What is the upside potential?

Resources

- Harley Davidson: http://www.harley-davidson.com

Health Food Stores

SIC 5499-01	NAICS 446191	Number of Businesses/Units 97,162

Rules of Thumb

➢ 40% of annual sales plus inventory

➢ 1–1.5 x SDE plus inventory

Benchmark Data

Statistics (Health Stores)

Number of Establishments	97,162
Average Profit Margin	6.0%
Revenue per Employee	$127,900
Average Number of Employees	2.0
Average Wages per Employee	$23,544

Products and Services Segmentation

Vitamin and mineral supplements	26.6%
Orthopedic equipment	24.5%
Sports nutrition products	12.6%
First-aid products	12.2%
Other	12.2%
Convalescent care products	11.9%

H

Industry Costs

Profit	6.0%
Wages	18.4%
Purchases	53.6%
Depreciation	1.3%
Marketing	3.2%
Rent & Utilities	6.0%
Other	11.5%

Market Share

General Nutrition Centers Inc.	7.1%
Vitamin Shoppe Inc.	5.0%

Industry Trend

- "Whole Foods Market sales increased $3.7 billion in the second quarter, driven by America's insatiable appetite for organic, healthy food. As consumers become more discerning about what they eat and more are willing to pay for better-quality foods or those for special diets, many small food makers are carving out toeholds in this fast-growing marketplace.

  "The trend is not surprising, considering that about $45 billion is spent on organic food every year in the United States. Today, organic products are available across America in more than 20,000 food stores and nearly 3 out of 4 grocery stores, according to TechSci Research. And it is projected to grow at a compounded annual rate of 16 percent through 2020."

  Source: "The organic food revolution that is minting millionaires," by Elaine Pofeldt, May 6, 2016, http://www.cnbc.com/2016/05/05/the-whole-foods-economy-sparks-organic-food-start-ups.html

Resources

- Specialty Food Association: http://www.specialtyfood.com
- IBISWorld, May 2017: http://ibisworld.com
- Organic Trader Association: https://www.ota.com/

Hearing Aid Clinics

SIC 5999-79	NAICS 446199	Number of Businesses/Units 4,387

Rules of Thumb

➢ 4 x EBITDA

➢ 40–45% of annual revenues plus inventory

Pricing Tips

- Larger practices with multiple offices and support infrastructure sell at higher multiples. The more trained audiologists and dispensers that a practice maintains, the more stability the practice will offer to purchasers.
- Transition agreements for long periods are common.

Benchmark Data

Statistics (Hearing Aid Clinics)

Number of Establishments	4,387
Average Profit Margin	12.1%
Revenue per Employee	$184,600
Average Number of Employees	2.7
Average Wages per Employee	$42,699

Products and Services Segmentation

Digital hearing aids 50.0%
Analog hearing aids 33.0%
Batteries and accessories... 14.8%
Other.. 2.2%

Major Market Segmentation

Consumers older than 65 .... 41.9%
Consumers aged 55 to 64 .... 25.6%
Consumers aged 45 to 54 .... 14.0%
Consumers aged 18 to 34 .... 7.0%
Consumers aged 35 to 44 .... 7.0%
Consumers younger than 18 .... 4.5%

Industry Costs

Profit 12.1%
Wages.. 23.2%
Purchases... 47.8%
Depreciation... 2.0%
Marketing 3.3%
Rent & Utilities 5.7%
Other.. 5.9%

Market Share

Starkey Hearing Technologies 19.2%
Amplifon USA... 10.0%
Sonova.. 6.9%
William Demant Holding AS 6.3%

Expenses (% of Annual Sales)

Cost of Goods.. 30% to 35%
Occupancy Costs.. 05% to 10%
Payroll/Labor Costs 20%
Profit (pretax) .... 18% to 20%

Questions

- Is this business free from liens/encumbrances with vendors that would prohibit the sale of the practice?
- Are any loyalty agreements or right of first refusals in place?

Industry Trend

- Continuing to increase as baby boomers enter market and stigma of wearing hearing aids decreases.
- "The market, driven by technological advancements in cochlear implants, bone-anchored hearing-aids and the introduction of wireless Bluetooth capability from Starkey, GN Resound and Cochlear America, is expected to touch almost $8 billion in annual sales by 2018."

Source: headsets.tmcnet.com

Expert Comments

Market for audiology and hearing aids is expanding as baby boomers enter the market. Franchises such as Miracle Ear (1,300 franchised units) and Beltone reduce obstacles to entry and increase ease of replication.

H

Seller Financing

- Manufacturers offer financing if customers commit to purchasing their products. Many acquisitions require an earn-out based on sales and/or profit.
- 3 years

Resources

- IBISWorld, January 2017: http://ibisworld.com

Heating Oil Dealers		
	NAICS 454310	

Rules of Thumb

➢ 25% of annual sales plus inventory

➢ 2.5 x SDE plus inventory

➢ 3–3.5 x EBIT

➢ 3–4 x EBITDA.

Pricing Tips

- Purchase price is typically based on FMV of assets plus retained gallonage.
- Gross profit per gallon is the main value driver—the higher the better.
- There is slow turnover in this industry, as most dealers are 2nd or 3rd generation in the business.
- Industry buyers used to price on the basis of gallons delivered, especially automatic gallons. They now price at 4 to 5.5 times EBITDA, based upon number of automatic vs. 'will call' customers, margins per gallon, location, competition from discounters, condition of equipment, etc.
- Low margin, high risk business since there is credit risk involved.

Benchmark Data

- As heating oil prices rise, savings from switching to gas heat grow. PSE&G's average customer would pay $1,122 for the year beginning last October, the company announced when it set its yearly rate last May. It would take 757 gallons of oil to produce the same amount of heat as gas.
- Gross profit per gallon is a key benchmark. The higher the better.
- Less desirable companies (discounters) are very difficult to sell.
- EBITDA is the most common benchmark. Another would be number of automatic gallons x margin per gallon x a multiple of 1 to 1.5 but in the end, industry buyers will look at EBITDA.

Expenses (% of Annual Sales)

Cost of Goods	60% to 70%
Occupancy Costs	02% to 05%
Payroll/Labor Costs	10% to 15%
Profit (pretax)	05% to 10%

Questions

- Are there any environmental concerns; compliance with government regulations?

- 5 years' financials and gallonage history; customer base breakdown by class of customer and type of delivery (automatic or will call); asset listing; phase I & II environmental reports.

Industry Trend

- Slow decline as customers switch to other fuels

Expert Comments

Consider the risk involved in getting into this industry as it is a mature industry on the decline.

Mature industry; customers are switching to other fuels; environmental concerns, industry image.

Seller Financing

- Outside financing for the assets; seller financing for retained gallonage/intangible value.
- We typically get cash at closing for fixed assets, and finance the intangibles over 2 to 5 years.

Resources

- Petroleum Marketers Association of America (PMAA): http://www.pmaa.org
- Empire State Energy Association: http://www.eseany.org/index.php
- PA Petroleum Association: http://www.ppmcsa.org
- New England Fuel Dealers: https://nefi.com/index.php
- American Petroleum Institute (API): http://www.api.org

Heavy Equipment Sales & Service		
	NAICS 811310	

Rules of Thumb

➤ 50% of SDE plus fixtures, equipment and inventory

Pricing Tips

- Value is based upon Fair Market Value of balance sheet including real estate. Low ROI based upon required 40% equity.

Benchmark Data

- Have to look at how numbers are assembled. Manufacturers can supply specific targets as well as how they see your client. Balance sheet composition has a great deal to do with profitability.

Questions

- What are issues with the local manufacturer representative?

Industry Trend

- Strong. Many of the manufacturers are worldwide companies and industry leaders.

H

Expert Comments

Buy quality name on the sign.

Suppliers want large, professionally managed dealerships. Move is towards multi-unit operations. Size does matter.

Seller Financing

- Minimal seller financing. Manufacturer may want up to 40% equity in the deal.

Hobby Shops		
SIC 5945-08	NAICS 451120	Number of Businesses/Units 21,512

Rules of Thumb

➢ 20% of annual sales plus inventory

➢ 1.5 x SDE plus inventory

Pricing Tips

- "Don't buy too much inventory. In the hobby business, October through January are the busiest sales months while many find February, March, August and September are slower. When approaching a heavy selling season, you need to increase inventory. When it ends, you need to move whatever seasonal or outdated inventory that did not sell out the door as quickly as you can."

Source: www.nrhsa.org

Benchmark Data

Statistics (Hobby & Toy Stores)

Number of Establishments	21,512
Average Profit Margin	6.8%
Revenue per Employee	$137,600
Average Number of Employees	6.7
Average Wages per Employee	$16,585

Products and Services Segmentation

Hobby, craft and art supplies	31.0%
Toys	27.9%
Other	24.7%
Games (including electronic and video games)	16.4%

Industry Costs

Profit	6.8%
Wages	11.9%
Purchases	57.8%
Depreciation	0.8%
Marketing	2.4%
Rent & Utilities	8.7%
Other	11.6%

Market Share

Michaels Stores, Inc. 21.2%
Toys 'R' Us Inc. 16.0%
Hobby Lobby Stores Inc. 10.9%

Industry Trend

- "IBISWorld expects Hobby and Toy Stores industry revenue to grow sluggishly over the five years to 2021. Improved economic conditions will boost consumer spending and confidence, encouraging consumers to spend more on toys and hobby goods. However, the industry will continue to face challenges from discount department stores and e-commerce channels, as these retailers continue to provide popular items at discounted prices. Despite mounting competition, the industry is expected to rise an annualized 1.5% during the next five years to reach $21.4 billion by 2021."

Source: IBISWorld Industry Outlook

Resources

- Model Retailer magazine: http://www.modelretailer.com
- IBISWorld, December 2016: http://ibisworld.com
- National Retail Hobby Stores Association: http://www.nrhsa.org
- Association for Creative Industries (AFCI): http://www.afci.global

Home-Based Businesses

Rules of Thumb

➤ The best way to price a home-based business is to first find out if the business is dependent on the owner. If so, it may be impossible to price, as it may have little or no value. However, if the business is transferrable it does have value. Prepare for an SDE figure and then create a multiple (see introduction for more information on SDE and a corresponding multiple) to arrive at an approximate price. If the business corresponds to a business listed in this *Guide*, see if the information there helps.

Pricing Tips

- "The primary objective that you need to accomplish when selling your home business is to come up with a fair price for it that you are willing to take and a reasonable buyer will be willing to pay. Setting a realistic price early on will allow you to negotiate more easily down the line.

  "Be ready to show your potential buyers all your assets, liabilities and cash flow. These will be your convincing reasons for an interested buyer to buy. All figures must be absolutely honest. Never fudge on your figures. Nothing will chase away an interested buyer faster than this. Count on them checking everything closely. If they see you are well prepared their interest will rise real fast."

  Source: http://www.streetdirectory.com/travel_guide/22035/home_businesses/
  when_and_how_to_sell_your_home_business.html

- "Run your business without getting too involved: When you are ready to sell your business, make sure that your business is able to operate without you. If a single-person business is totally dependent on its current owner for smooth operation, then the business will be a hard sell. Potential buyers will be unwilling to purchase such business because there's no value without the current owner. Buyers have to be assured that, new staff and technology alone can run the business. A fully functional home-based business, regardless of the owner will get a higher selling price.

"Offer to stay with the business for a certain period: One major problem with home-based service businesses is that the whole business revolves around the existing owner. The current owner can offer to stay with the business for a certain period. This offer will lower the risks and thus add value to the selling price. Current owners can stay and ensure a smooth transition."

Source: http://exitadviser.com/seller-status.aspx?id=sell-homebased-business

Industry Trend

- After 37 years of following small and home business launches, the National Mail Order Association (NMOA) predicts a new explosion in people starting a business because of layoffs and fears of salary reductions. 53 percent of small (businesses with one or more owners but no paid employees) businesses in the U.S. are home- based businesses.

Home Centers	
NAICS 444110	Number of Businesses/Units 9,148

Rules of Thumb

➤ 2 x SDE plus inventory

➤ 40–45% of annual sales includes inventory

Pricing Tips

- Tend to be asset value sales

Benchmark Data

Statistics (Home Improvement Stores)

Number of Establishments	9,148
Average Profit Margin	10.0%
Revenue per Employee	$241,400
Average Number of Employees	81.2
Average Wages per Employee	$27,906

Products and Services Segmentation

Lumber and other building and structural materials	38.6%
Household appliances, kitchen goods and housewares	27.3%
Hardware, tools and plumbing and electrical supplies	19.6%
Lawn, garden and farm equipment supplies	14.5%

Major Market Segmentation

Professionals (commercial projects)	48.3%
Professionals (do-it-for-me consumer projects)	32.2%
Do-it-yourself customers	19.5%

Industry Costs

Profit	10.0%
Wages	11.5%
Purchases	70.3%
Depreciation	1.0%
Marketing	1.2%
Rent & Utilities	2.5%
Other	3.5%

Market Share

The Home Depot Inc.	45.9%
Lowe's Companies Inc.	32.1%
Menard Inc.	5.6%

Expenses (% of Annual Sales)

Cost of Goods	65% to 70%
Occupancy Costs	05% to 06%
Payroll/Labor Costs	12% to 15%
Profit (pretax)	10% to 15%

Questions

- How do you compete with the competition? Is it through franchise-type buying power?
- Why are you selling? Are there any potential franchise or refurbishment costs that may be included in the sale?
- Does any one contractor represent more than 10% of your lumber business? This is a personality business. If the old owner goes, the customer might leave too.

Industry Trend

- Steady if you have the labor available to compete service-wise with the big box stores.

Expert Comments

The high capital costs for inventory and fixtures and the lack of good locations are significant barriers to entry.

Resources

- IBISWorld, May 2017: http://ibisworld.com

Home Health Care—Equipment and Supplies

SIC 8082-01	NAICS 532291	

Rules of Thumb

- ➢ 85% of annual sales plus inventory
- ➢ 4 x EBITDA excluding rental equipment depreciation
- ➢ 4 x EBIT
- ➢ 4 x SDE plus inventory

H

Pricing Tips

- Payer mix: rental vs. sales
- Depends on type of contracts (Medicare-Medicaid, private pay, nursing home, etc.) and length of contracts.
- The age of the equipment may make it subject to obsolescence. A careful inventory of equipment located in patients' homes must be made and evaluated by an expert.

Benchmark Data

- See additional Benchmark Data under Home Health Care Rental
- 20% + EBITDA margins. Need to show annual growth in sales and profits. Stable referral sources.

Expenses (% of Annual Sales)

Cost of Goods	35%
Occupancy Costs	05%
Payroll/Labor Costs	20%
Profit (pretax)	35%

Questions

- Any outstanding Medicare audits? Are they accredited?

Industry Trend

- Continued consolidation due to competitive bidding.
- Declining profits because of Medicare pricing pressures

Expert Comments

Substantial pressure on margins due to Medicare implementing cost controls and national competitive bidding.

Resources

- HME News: http://www.hmenews.com

Home Health Care/Home Nursing Agencies

	NAICS 621610	

Rules of Thumb

➢ 60–70% of annual sales plus inventory

➢ 2–4 x SDE plus inventory

➢ 4–6 x EBIT

➢ 3–5 x EBITDA

Pricing Tips

- Licensing requirements are state specific and reimbursements are a key to pricing and margins, also the medical vs. nonmedical services are a consideration. It is a highly fragmented industry and we are seeing consolidation in some states with favorable reimbursement rates, licensing

---

requirements and demographics. There are many small mom-and-pop home care companies because of low barriers to entry and many of them are franchises. The consolidation is happening with the larger companies and they are in high demand. People-/employee-intensive business and payroll costs are 55%–60%.

- Case-by-case basis. Factors to consider are service area senior demographics, experience and tenure of staff, owner role, referral sources, percent of recurring revenue, breakdown of revenue (private pay vs. insurance vs. Medicaid vs. nonmedical vs. skilled care).
- Current agency I am selling includes two franchise agreements valued at $115,000. Seller will pay franchise transfer fee of $50,000. That is $165,000 of value regardless of SDE. Seller will keep AR. These must be factored into pricing. A good agency generating over $1 million revenue will produce a return of 15–17%. Very important to plot at least 3-year growth track. This franchise has over 300 successful agencies that can provide great stats.
- The range of multiple for home care companies ranges from 2.5X to 3.5X. What allows for a higher valuation are several factors including: 1) Revenues over $1MM, 2) Growth in revenues and profit year over year, 3) Sustainability, i.e., number of referral sources, key personnel in place, role of the owner, demographics of the territory covered, 4) types of clients, etc. 5) if a franchise, the brand.
- Businesses that have $600K to $1M of SDE tend to sell for 4x SDE. The multiple gradually goes lower with less than $600 SDE. The multiples are the same for both franchises and non-franchises. However, it's easier to sell franchises because of the additional support, branding and marketing. Businesses with $2M+ in revenue are easier to sell.
- Businesses with $2M+ in revenue often turn down business because of a lack of caregivers. Recruiting and retaining caregivers is the industry's biggest challenge.

Benchmark Data

Statistics (Home Care Providers)

Number of Establishments	417,966
Average Profit Margin	7.4%
Revenue per Employee	$49,800
Average Number of Employees	4.4
Average Wages per Employee	$24,715

Products and Services Segmentation

Traditional home healthcare and home nursing care	56.5%
Home hospice	23.2%
Home therapy services	8.6%
Homemaker and personal services	6.4%
Other	5.3%

Major Market Segmentation

Medicare	38.9%
Medicaid	36.7%
Private insurance	10.6%
Out-of-pocket	9.8%
Other	4.0%

Industry Costs

Profit 7.4%
Wages.. 49.6%
Purchases 6.5%
Depreciation.. 1.0%
Marketing 1.5%
Rent & Utilities 4.4%
Other.. 29.6%

Statistics (In-Home Senior Care Franchises)

Number of Establishments... 9,758
Average Profit Margin 13.1%
Revenue per Employee $24,800
Average Number of Employees.. 40.2
Average Wages per Employee $15,771

Products and Services Segmentation

Traditional home healthcare and home nursing care........................... 57.3%
Home hospice (end of life) care services... 22.6%
Home therapy services 9.1%
Homemaker and personal services 6.1%
Other.. 4.9%

Major Market Segmentation

Out-of-pocket 40.1%
Medicare 22.7%
Medicaid 18.4%
Private insurance 13.5%
Other sources 4.0%
Other government (e.g., Veterans Affairs, Indian Affairs, etc.)............... 1.3%

Industry Costs

Profit 13.1%
Wages.. 62.9%
Purchases.. 8.0%
Depreciation.. 1.6%
Marketing 3.8%
Rent & Utilities 4.4%
Other.. 6.2%

Market Share

Home Instead Inc.. 9.1%
Interim HealthCare Inc... 7.4%
Comfort Keepers... 5.1%
Living Assistance Services Inc.. 5.0%
Right at Home Inc. 4.9%
Griswold Special Care 3.8%

- Billable hours > 1,000 per week
- Gross Profit over 40% indicates an agency with pricing power.
- Net profits closer to 20% margin
- Price should generate a 50%+ gross profit margin on direct labor costs.

- When comparing terminations and ceased operations, home care franchises were only 4.9% compared to 6% for the franchise industry.

Expenses (% of Annual Sales)

Cost of Goods	05% to 09%
Occupancy Costs	05% to 10%
Payroll/Labor Costs	50% to 60%
Profit (pretax)	20% to 27%

Questions

- Payor mix, market share, patient demographic data
- Key questions: percent of skilled care, percent of nonskilled care, percent Medicaid payor, percent Medicare payor, percent private payor
- What are the reimbursement rates for each payor? What is the regulatory environment for that state, census historical data?
- What is your experience modification for workers' comp? What are your billable hours per week? What is your net margin?
- Past caregiving incidents? Owner's roles and responsibilities? Number of clients driving 10%, 50% of revenue? 3-year monthly trend of revenue?

Industry Trend

- Heavy competition, strong growth, reimbursement cuts continue to pressure profitability, consolidation expected to continue.
- Consolidation between larger companies over $4 million in sales and smaller companies under $1.5–$2 million are struggling with state regulations and low reimbursement rates in Medicaid specifically.
- Strong growth in demand
- Agencies that offer medical and non-medical care will continue to grow as baby boomers age and the cost of healthcare rises.
- Demand continues to grow as the senior population increases. Many seniors prefer to age in place as long as they can.
- "Home Health Care Industry Focus—In 1994, approximately one in eight Americans was age 65 and older. But by 2030, one in five Americans will be a senior citizen. From 2010 to 2030, the number of baby boomers age 65 to 84 will grow by an estimated 80 percent while the population age 85 and older will grow by 48 percent. In addition, between 1994 and 2020, the nation's population of 85 years and older is projected to double to 7 million, and then increase to between 19 and 27 million by 2050. So it's easy to see why those in the home health care industry see another boom on the horizon-one of ever-increasing demand for services."

Source: ww.missouribusiness.net/iag/focus

Expert Comments

Industry is growing. Barriers to entry relatively low. Takes two years to get strong traction for start-ups.

Sellers should have a sales force in place. The owner will participate in the sales process but must not be the face of the business. Most agencies have excellent financial records and sellers should make sure they are up to date at all times. For buyers you must understand the sales process and be willing to follow the franchise business model. There are many opportunities in specialized areas and buyers should be prepared to look for these opportunities.

There are several national franchises operating in this space. Each has its benefits. Starting an agency is a relatively high-risk process because it takes a long time to reach profitability. Many startups are under-capitalized. All of the agencies I have worked with show great growth and this industry will continue to grow with the aging of baby boomers. Marketability is OK, but it takes a special buyer to operate these agencies and financing the purchase for a relatively new agency is extremely difficult.

The home-care industry has exploded with the aging population. Today, with 10,000 Americans turning 65 every day, the demand for senior care is ever increasing. The U.S. senior population currently sits at approximately 50 million and by 2030, it is expected to swell to 81 million (Source: U.S. Census Bureau). An estimated 70 percent of people over 65 will require home-care services at some point in their lives.

Sellers—Work with a broker who really understands the industry and has a proven track record. Buyers—Both franchises and non-franchises are valued with similar multiples, so buying a franchise gives you much more bang for the buck (support, marketing, branding....)

Seller Financing
- Outside financing
- Outside financing with small seller financing bridging any gaps
- SBA financing very common. Buyer 25% down, or 15% down and seller 10% carry, 75% loan.
- A mature agency can probably be purchased with SBA financing. The agencies I have sold are relatively new (under 5 years) and the licensing process and historical numbers make SBA nearly impossible.
- SBA financing is the norm (75%) for 10 years. 10% seller financing with a 3 year hold back period (8 years in total),

Resources
- IBISWorld, August 2017: http://ibisworld.com
- California Association for Health Services at Home: http://cahsah.org/
- American Board of Home Care: http://www.americanboardofhomecare.org/
- National Association for Home Care and Hospice: http://www.nahc.org
- IBISWorld, October 2016: http://ibisworld.com

Home Health Care Rental		
SIC 5999-20	NAICS 532291	Number of Businesses/Units 7,826

Rules of Thumb
➢ 4 x EBITDA

Pricing Tips
- Payor mix (Medicare, Medicaid, commercial, etc.). How many "capped" patients?

Benchmark Data

Statistics (Home Medical Equipment Rentals)

Number of Establishments	7,826
Average Profit Margin	6.4%
Revenue per Employee	$133,100
Average Number of Employees	5.4
Average Wages per Employee	$41,828

Products and Services Segmentation

Oxygen and respiratory therapy equipment	65.0%
Mobility aid equipment	23.3%
Diabetic therapy equipment	5.9%
Other medical equipment	5.8%

Major Market Segmentation

Medicare insured individuals	42.8%
Other insured individuals	28.2%
State and local governments	14.6%
Out-of-pocket individuals	14.4%

Industry Costs

Profit	6.4%
Wages	31.2%
Purchases	11.7%
Depreciation	27.8%
Marketing	1.2%
Rent & Utilities	6.2%
Other	15.5%

Market Share

Lincare Holdings Inc.	8.6%

Expenses (% of Annual Sales)

Cost of Goods	10%
Occupancy Costs	04%
Payroll/Labor Costs	20%
Profit (pretax)	18%

Industry Trend

- "Medicare's competitive bidding program is likely to remain in effect over the next five years. In fact, the White House has suggested expanding the program to regulate Medicaid reimbursements for home medical equipment purchases and rentals. As a result, the industry will continue to face adverse pricing conditions that constrain revenue and limit profitability. Still, after the completion of Round 2 of the program in 2016, IBISWorld expects revenue to recover slowly but steadily, as prices stop falling and operators adjust to the new system. Overall, revenue is expected to grow an annualized 0.6% through 2021 to $5.8 billion."

Source: IBISWorld Industry Outlook

- Continued pricing pressures and uncertainty of Medicare reimbursement rates. Implementation of competitive bidding will further erode profit margins.

Expert Comments

Industry demand is growing but margins continue to decline as CMS (Center for Medicare & Medicaid Services) reduces reimbursement to providers.

Resources

- IBISWorld, July 2016: http://ibisworld.com

		Franchise
Home Helpers		
Approx. Total Investment		$70,850–$117,600
	NAICS 621610	Number of Businesses/Units 635

Rules of Thumb

➤ 40–45% of annual sales plus inventory

Resources

- Home Helpers: http://www.homehelpershomecare.com

Home Inspection		
	NAICS 541350	Number of Businesses/Units 24,581

Rules of Thumb

➤ 45% of annual sales includes inventory

Benchmark Data

Statistics (Building Inspectors)

Number of Establishments	24,581
Average Profit Margin	24.9%
Revenue per Employee	$90,200
Average Number of Employees	1.6
Average Wages per Employee	$31,229

Products and Services Segmentation

Home inspection services	29.8%
Specific element inspection services	23.8%
Other	21.6%
Commercial building inspection services	19.3%
New home construction inspection services	5.5%

Major Market Segmentation

Commercial and other markets	32.5%
Home buyers and sellers	30.1%
The government	22.6%
Contractors	14.8%

Industry Costs

Profit	24.9%
Wages	34.6%
Purchases	11.2%
Depreciation	1.3%
Marketing	2.6%
Rent & Utilities	3.8%
Other	21.6%

Resources
- Home Inspector Magazine, published by the Organization of Real Estate Professionals: http://www.workingre.com/home-inspector-magazine-news/
- National Association of Home Inspectors—a good site: http://www.nahi.org
- IBISWorld, September 2017: http://ibisworld.com
- International Society of Home Inspectors: http://www.ishionline.org/

		Franchise
Home Team Inspection Service		
Approx. Total Investment		$37,400–$70,600
SIC 7389-96	NAICS 541350	Number of Businesses/Units 160

Rules of Thumb
➢ 35% of annual sales plus inventory

Benchmark Data
- For Benchmark Data see Home Inspection

Resources
- Home Team: http://www.hometeam.com

		Franchise
Honest-1 Auto Care		
Approx. Total Investment		$169,975–$457,975
	NAICS 811111	Number of Businesses/Units 43

Rules of Thumb
➢ 60–65% of annual sales plus inventory

Resources
- Honest-1 Auto Care: http://www.honest-1.com

Hospital Laundry—Supply		
	NAICS 812331	

Rules of Thumb
➢ 50% of annual sales plus inventory

H

Pricing Tips

- An industry expert states that for laundry with hospital contracts a rule of thumb is 50 percent of gross annual sales. This is because that market is a very competitive one.

Benchmark Data

- For additional Benchmark Data see Uniform Rental
- "The size in value of the laundry market, including: healthcare, hospitality, and federal government is $10.5 billion annually, as follows:

Total Laundry Market Size and Value by Segment

Segment	Percent
Healthcare	45.9%
Hospitality	52.8%
Federal Government	1.3%
Total	100.0%

"As indicated, the size of the federal government market is small compared to the total laundry market. The statistics related to this market are as follows: healthcare-hospitals: 4,915, 823,560 beds; healthcare-nursing homes: 17,000, 1.6 million beds; hospitality-hotels: 53,500 rooms; and federal government: 1,231 locations."

Source: "Competition in the Laundry Industry," www.sourceamericalaundry.mindtouch.us/

Resources

- Textile Rental Services Association (TRSA): http://www.trsa.org

---

Hospitals—Medical and Surgical

	NAICS 622110	

Rules of Thumb

➢ 78% of annual sales plus inventory

➢ 2.7 x SDE plus inventory

➢ 3 x EBIT

➢ 2.9 x EBITDA

Pricing Tips

- Tremendous variation in types of hospitals today. Substantial due diligence is required to determine appropriate EBITDA multiples for a particular hospital at a particular point in time.

Benchmark Data

- The American Hospital Association provides an annual survey with basic statistics. Levin Associates tracks publicly announced transactions. The Healthcare Financial Management Association provides industry statistics and surveys.

Expenses (% of Annual Sales)

Cost of Goods	08%
Payroll/Labor Costs	03%
Profit (pretax)	06%

Questions

- Payor mix, market share, patient demographic data.

Industry Trend

- Tremendous changes in technology and the business model. More services will continue to move out of the inpatient setting. Value-based payment will continue to push focus to the full continuum of care. More personalized medicine will rely on genomics.
- Revenue is expected to grow, demand expected to grow, consolidation expected to continue, profit expected to decrease.

Expert Comments

Due diligence is essential!

Tremendous variation in types of hospitals today. Some are profitable and growing, some are bankrupt and closing. Some have excellent state-of-the-art facilities, while others are closing due to failure to meet required standards.

Seller Financing

- Outside financing

Resources

- American Hospital Association: http://www.aha.org
- Levin Associates: http://www.levinassociates.com

Hospitals—Psychiatric and Substance Abuse		
	NAICS 622210	

Rules of Thumb

➤ 3 x EBIT

➤ 2.9 x EBITDA

➤ 78% of annual sales plus inventory

➤ 2.7 x SDE plus inventory

Benchmark Data

Expenses (% of Annual Sales)

Cost of Goods	09%
Payroll/Labor Costs	03%
Profit (pretax)	06%

Questions

- Payor mix, market share, patient demographic data

Industry Trend

- Demand expected to grow, revenue projected to grow, consolidation expected to continue, costs projected to increase.

Seller Financing

- Outside financing

Resources

- National Association of Psychiatric Health Systems: http://www.naphs.org

Hospitals—Specialty

Rules of Thumb

➢ 51% of annual sales plus inventory

➢ 1.8 x SDE plus inventory

➢ 3 x EBIT

➢ 2.9 x EBITDA

Benchmark Data

Expenses (% of Annual Sales)

Cost of Goods	08%
Payroll/Labor Costs	03%
Profit (pretax)	06%

Questions

- Payor mix, market share, patient demographic data

Industry Trend

- Further consolidation; revenue projected to increase; profit projected to grow; demand expected to increase.

Seller Financing

- Outside financing

Resources

- American Hospital Association: http://www.aha.org

Hotels & Motels

SIC 7011-01	NAICS 721110	Number of Businesses/Units 93,869

Rules of Thumb

➢ 250–300% of annual sales plus inventory

➢ 8–11 x EBITDA

➢ 2.0–3.5 x annual room revenues—average 2.5

➢ Outside corridors—2.0–2.5 x annual room revenues

➢ Inside corridors—2.5–3.0 x annual room revenues

➢ Seldom seen—3.5 x annual room revenues

➢ $20,000 per room

➤ 10%–12% of cap rate

➤ 7–8 x SDE

Pricing Tips

- This sector is a hybrid between business and real estate. Valuations vary with multiple factors, including real estate value, brand, market trends, etc.
- Normalize repairs and maintenance to 4% of annual revenues, typically same for CapEx. Buildings built with concrete, aluminum or vinyl window, and concrete or stucco exterior, will typically have less maintenance/CapEx costs in the first 25–40 years. Consider current state of building and equipment; if there is any abnormal deferred maintenance or capital expenditure, adjust price accordingly. Consider going in CAP rate and all in CAP rate. Flag is important to lenders. Interior hallways and elevators are important. Normalize income based on future revenue expectations, adding back any "non-operating" expenses. CAP rate should be 8%–11% to arrive at final value. Look for quarterly industry publications for sales history, price per door, CAP rates.
- Independents 1.5–2 x room revenue; budget franchise 2–3 x room revenue; higher end franchise 4–5 x room revenue; larger full-service propitious 10 cap rate.
- "Now take the asking price and subtract what you will pay in the equity down payment. Consider if your offer will include a request that the seller finance some improvements. You might be able to negotiate this up to an amount equal to your down payment as the money will be going directly back into the hotel."

  Source: http://www.hotelonline.com/Trends/Payne/Articles/SoYouWanttoBuyaHotel.html

- Lease arrangements, age of equipment, management in place, length of existence.
- Large capital investment on front end makes the property susceptible to new, better-located competition. Need ongoing reserve for replacement of FF&E.
- Location and franchise make a great difference. Also, we must consider extended-stay motels.
- Check contracted room business and QA score if franchised.

Benchmark Data

Statistics (Hotels and Motels)

Number of Establishments	93,869
Average Profit Margin	16.6%
Revenue per Employee	$110,300
Average Number of Employees	18.0
Average Wages per Employee	$26,784

Products and Services Segmentation

Guest room rentals from properties with between 75 - 299 rooms	42.7%
Guest room rentals from properties with under 75 rooms	19.7%
Meals, nonalcoholic drinks and other items for consumption	9.8%
Guest room rentals from properties with over 500 rooms	8.3%
Conference room and venue space rentals for events	6.7%
Guest room rentals from properties with between 300-500 rooms	6.7%
Alcoholic beverages served for immediate consumption	3.1%
Other services	3.0%

Major Market Segmentation

Domestic leisure travelers	50.0%
International leisure travelers	19.5%
Business travelers	18.2%
Meeting, events and incentive travelers	12.3%

Industry Costs

Profit	16.6%
Wages	24.3%
Purchases	26.9%
Depreciation	9.5%
Marketing	2.0%
Rent & Utilities	8.2%
Other	12.5%

Market Share

Marriott International Inc.	19.7%
Hilton Worldwide Holdings Inc.	13.5%
InterContinental Hotels Group PLC	6.9%

Statistics (Boutique Hotels)

Number of Establishments	2,174
Average Profit Margin	16.2%
Revenue per Employee	$116,800
Average Number of Employees	30.0
Average Wages per Employee	$30,823

Products and Services Segmentation

Lodging	69.0%
Food and beverages	24.5%
Spa and wellness services	6.5%

Major Market Segmentation

Domestic leisure travelers	50.0%
Business travelers	30.5%
International leisure travelers	19.5%

Industry Costs

Profit	16.2%
Wages	26.3%
Purchases	27.9%
Depreciation	9.7%
Marketing	2.3%
Rent & Utilities	8.2%
Other	9.4%

Market Share

Marriott International Inc.	20.4%
InterContinental Hotels Group PLC	14.4%
Two Roads Hospitality	7.2%

- A select service property in a proper location with a good brand should be able to generate 27% NOI
- Price per unit varies upon condition, location, brand and type of hotel

Penn State Index of U.S. Hotel Values

Value	Annual Per Room	% Change
Overall 2017	$130,459	1.2%
Luxury 2017	$397,560	-2.1%
Upper Upscale 2017	$210,324	0.4%
Upscale 2017	$153,252	0.5%
Upper Midscale 2017	$113,906	-0.6%
Midscale 2017	$73,892	1.7%
Economy 2017	$39,983	2.0%

Source: "Penn State Index of U.S. Hotel Values, The Pennsylvania State University

Expenses (% of Annual Sales)

Cost of Goods	01% to 10%
Occupancy Costs	50% to 60%
Payroll/Labor Costs	20% to 30%
Profit (pretax)	10% to 25%

Questions

- STR report, CAPEX reports, 3 years' financials
- PIP requirements? STAR reports?
- ADR, occupancy, RevPar, punch list, recent inspection reports
- Are there capital expense items that need attention? How much contracted room business do they have? How much room business do they have on the books and for how long a period of time? What was their last QA score if it is a franchise hotel? Do they know of any new highways being constructed in the future that may divert traffic to or away from the hotel? Any new competition coming up in the area?

Industry Trend

- "In the U.S., hosts renting out two or more entire-home units generated nearly $2 billion in revenue in 2016. In the 13 markets highlighted, revenue reached $700 million. 81% of Airbnb's U.S. revenue—$4.6 billion—comes from whole-unit rentals (those rentals where the owner is not present during the time of the rental)."

Source: "New Study Shatters Airbnb Homesharing Myth," March 9, 2017, https://ahla.com/press-release/new-study-shatters-airbnb-homesharing-myth

- Currently on an upward trend; will level out in the next year or so.
- "MMGY Global predicts a record number of vacations and new highs in vacation spending among American travelers in the next 12 months. The market's intention to vacation during the next 12 months represents a 10-year high that surpasses the pre-recession record.
  - ✓ 28 percent of travelers indicated an intention to take more vacations, while only 14 percent reported that they plan to take fewer resulting in a 14-point net positive variance.
  - ✓ Vacation spending has fully recovered from the Great Recession and spending intentions have soared well above to the pre-recessionary levels in recent quarters.

✓ In 2016, travelers reported having spent an average of $5,048 on vacations in the previous 12 months—an impressive 30 percent increase from 2010, and a 12 percent increase from an already-strong 2015.

✓ Travelers are planning to spend an average of $5,182 in the next 12 months—an astonishing 23 percent increase in only four years, and a nine percent increase in the past year."

Source: "Leisure travel and vacation spending will achieve record levels in the next 12 months," http://www.hotelnewsresource.com/article89709.html

- "In less than a decade Airbnb, the San Francisco-based home-sharing platform worth an estimated $25.5 billion, has become one of the biggest disruptors in the travel space. And the industry for whom Airbnb has been the most disruptive—hospitality—is keeping a very close watch on the company's every move. Every day, there seems to be a new headline suggesting the hospitality industry's demise at the hands of short-term rental sites like Airbnb."

Source: "What Americans Really Think About Airbnb and Home-Sharing," by Deanna Ting, May 20, 2016, https://skift.com/2016/05/20/what-americans-really-think-about-airbnb-and-home-sharing/

Expert Comments

Depending on location, some markets have become overbuilt, such as Alberta.

Look and compare several properties.

High cost of entry

One must be aware of trends but be careful it is not a fad. Location is a key ingredient, items like parking, traffic lights, visibility. Highly competitive for some, so locating near target audience is crucial.

Seller Financing

- Outside financing with a small portion of owner financing 10-15%, sometimes decreed for 2 years, 20- to 30-year amortization from most lenders
- Mostly outside financing, but many times deals are made with extremely creative and sophisticated financing models

Resources

- American Hotel & Lodging Association: http://www.ahla.com
- Hotel Business: http://www.hotelbusiness.com
- Lodging Magazine: http://www.lodgingmagazine.com
- Hotel Management: http://www.hotelmanagement.net
- IBISWorld, April 2017: http://ibisworld.com
- IBISWorld, June 2017: http://ibisworld.com

House Doctors	Franchise
Approx. Total Investment	$89,300–$124,450

	NAICS 236118	Number of Businesses/Units 54

Rules of Thumb

➢ 24% of annual sales plus inventory

Resources
- House Doctors: http://www.housedoctors.com

Hungry Howie's Pizza & Subs	Franchise
Approx. Total Investment	$253,075–$453,850
Estimated Annual Sales/Unit	$690,000

	NAICS 722513	Number of Businesses/Units 550

Rules of Thumb
➤ 35% of annual sales plus inventory

Benchmark Data
- For Benchmark Data see Pizza Shops & Sandwich Shops

Resources
- Hungry Howie's: http://www.hungryhowies.com

Huntington Learning Center	Franchise
Approx. Total Investment	$99,000–$204,000

	NAICS 611691	Number of Businesses/Units 237

Rules of Thumb
➤ 60% of annual sales

Resources
- Huntington Learning Center: http://www.huntingtonfranchise.com

HVAC—Heating, Ventilating & Air Conditioning		
	NAICS 238220	Number of Businesses/Units 110,337

Rules of Thumb
➤ 25–40% of annual sales plus inventory
➤ 2–3.5 x SDE plus inventory
➤ 3–4.5 x EBIT
➤ 2.75–3.5 x EBITDA

Pricing Tips
- Residential service and replacement is preferred over new construction.
- Heavy new construction lowers value by at least 25% to nearly half, depending on economy and integrity of database.
- Number of ongoing residential preventative maintenance agreements is key to

driving value.

- Service sales per service truck rankings:
  - ✓ Low = $150,000-$200,000
  - ✓ Mid =$201-000-$275,000
  - ✓ High = $276,000-$350,000
- "If you're looking to exit your business or acquire another company, there are two ideas to think of in terms of the value of that business. The reality value of the business would be 3 to 6 times its EBITDA, but the opportunity value, as Cassel points out, can be much higher. 'Most financial people will tell you that profit is king, but I'll tell you the phone number is king,' said [Lon] Cassel. 'No matter how you value your business, you'll have to find a buyer for it. Make sure you find someone who really knows the opportunity value of a residential service call, so both buyer and seller receive a fair return on their investment of time and money,' instructed Cassel.

  "Cassel also emphasized the importance of planning for your exit. 'The fact is that everyone is going to exit their business someday, and, depending on how you exit, it could be with a lot of money or very little money. Some may value your company on profits and some may value it on service calls or both. Just make sure it is a fair value,' he concluded."

  Source: http://www.achrnews.com/articles/90302-what-8217-s-your-hvac-plumbing-business-worth

Benchmark Data

Statistics (Heating and Air-Conditioning Contractors)

Number of Establishments	110,337
Average Profit Margin	4.0%
Revenue per Employee	$187,100
Average Number of Employees	4.4
Average Wages per Employee	$50,174

Products and Services Segmentation

New construction HVAC installations	51.7%
HVAC maintenance and repairs	31.8%
Existing structure HVAC installations (i.e. replacements)	10.6%
Refrigeration system installations, maintenance and repairs	5.9%

Major Market Segmentation

Single-family homes	25.6%
Manufacturing and industrial buildings	12.7%
Other	12.5%
Office buildings	11.6%
Retail and storage spaces	11.6%
Healthcare and public safety buildings	10.4%
Educational buildings	9.2%
Apartment buildings, dormitories and barracks	6.4%

Industry Costs

Profit	4.0%
Wages	26.7%
Purchases	44.2%
Depreciation	0.8%
Marketing	0.7%
Rent & Utilities	1.8%

Other...21.8%
- Ongoing preventative maintenance agreements are key to driving value.
- Residential service and replacements are key, rather than new construction.
- Need strong operations manager, service manager
- Must have 3 to 5 field techs to every 1 inside support to be successful.
- 10% pretax is expected; 20% pretax will increase value.
- Sales per employee, including administrative:
  - ✓ High = $250,000
  - ✓ Medium = $225,000
  - ✓ Low = $175,000
- Sales per Service Truck:
  - ✓ High = $350,000*
  - ✓ Medium = $300,000
  - ✓ Low = $250,000
- *Accessory sales are a must for higher service sales per truck. (i.e., Surge Protectors, Compressor Savers, UV Lights, Filtration, etc.)
- Sales per Field Technician Employee:
  - ✓ Optimal = $350,000
  - ✓ Average = $250,000
  - ✓ Poor < $175,000
- Field Techs to Inside Support Ratio:
  - ✓ Optimal = 5/1
  - ✓ Average = 3/1
  - ✓ Poor = 2/1

Expenses (% of Annual Sales)

Cost of Goods	35% to 65%
Occupancy Costs	02% to 03%
Payroll/Labor Costs	10% to 25%
Profit (pretax)	05% to 15%

Questions
- List of key employees
- Age of fleet; age of inventory
- Relationship with vendors
- How long with specific brand of equipment?
- Proof of ongoing preventative maintenance agreements
- Review list of active customers over previous three years, to see if service trends are solid.
- Ask for no less than five years of tax returns or financials. Ask for proof of PMA's. Ask for employee descriptions and longevity. Ask for list of recurring customers.

Industry Trend
- Very strong demand for quality businesses.
- The strong are slowly overtaking the weak.
- Relatively recession-proof industry.
- Continued consolidation, especially if/when the economy slows again.
- Consolidation will occur over next ten years, due to added cost of retaining qualified employees.
- Wider spread between haves and have nots. Larger and stronger are

consuming the mid-size and weaker. Home energy services are on the rise, but spotty acceptance per state. Home energy services have high barriers to entry, due to high certification and equipment costs.

Expert Comments

Document all processes and procedures; keep a clean database of customers; build your list of ongoing preventative maintenance agreements.

The trades are becoming high demand as younger talent becomes scarce, due to overall push for college education among high school grads. There are not enough young people joining the trades industries, so pricing is increasing, as manpower becomes less and less available.

Look for high number of service agreements.

Seller Financing

- Combination of owner financing and outside financing
- It seems best to keep the owner involved for 3–9 months, if possible.

Resources

- HVACNews.com: http://www.hvacnews.com
- Air Conditioning Refrigeration News: http://www.achrnews.com
- Kentucky Association of Master Contractors: http://www.kyamc.com
- The Indoor Environment and Energy Efficiency Association: https://www.eventbrite.com/o/acca-the-indoor-environment-amp-energy-efficiency-association-10598752539
- Air Conditioning Contractors of America: http://www.acca.org/home
- Heating Air-conditioning & Refrigeration Distributors International: http://hardinet.org/
- International Ground Source Heat Pump Association: https://igshpa.org/
- IBISWorld, January 2017: http://ibisworld.com

			Franchise
i9 Sports°			
Approx. Total Investment			$44,900–$69,900
	NAICS 713990	Number of Businesses/Units 125	

Rules of Thumb

➢ 65–70% of annual sales plus inventory

Resources

- i9 Sports: http://www.i9sportsfranchise.com

		Franchise
Iceberg Drive Inn		
Approx. Total Investment		$132,500–$556,000
	NAICS 722513	Number of Businesses/Units 16

Rules of Thumb

➤ 40–45% of annual sales plus inventory

Resources

- Iceberg Drive Inn: http://www.icebergdriveinn.com

Ice Cream Trucks		
	NAICS 722330	

Rules of Thumb

➤ 1 x SDE plus fair market value of the truck(s) plus inventory

Benchmark Data

- For Benchmark Data see Catering Trucks
- "... While the profits don't quite cover tuitions, Toll (Taylor) says it's a huge help in paying for books and other expenses. She says the truck (ice cream) can rake in up to $1,000 on a good day."

  Source: "Paying for College with an Ice Cream Truck" by Gabrielle Karol, June 5, 2013,
  www.smallbusiness.foxbusiness.com/entrepreneurs

Industry Trend

- "Good Humor's trucks will soon be hitting the road again after a decades-long hiatus, but the iconic ice cream brand's fleet will be announcing its presence with tweets instead of clanging bells. Customers looking for an ice cream fix will be able to summon the classic Good Humor trucks by tweeting @GoodHumor. And, in another modern twist, the throwback trucks will be blasting pop music and rock songs instead of ringing their iconic chime bells."

  Source: "Good Humor's iconic ice cream trucks are making a big comeback" by Tom Huddleston, Jr.,
  http://fortune.com/2015/06/23/good-humors-ice-cream-trucks/

Resources

- AllScream.com: http://www.allscream.com/icecreamstories.php
- International Dairy Foods Association: http://www.idfa.org
- International Association of Ice Cream Distributors and Vendors (IAICDV): http://www.iaicdv.org

Ice Cream/Yogurt Shops		
SIC 5812-03	NAICS 722515	

Rules of Thumb

➤ 60% of annual sales plus inventory

➤ 2.2 x SDE plus inventory (franchised only)

> ➤ 3 x EBIT
>
> ➤ 3 x EBITDA
>
> ➤ 15–20 x weekly sales (independent only)

Pricing Tips

- Condition of premises, age of equipment, and location of shopping center critical to resale value.
- 2.5 x SDE applies to franchised ice cream stores with minimum 8+ year lease remaining with transfer fee included in the price. If less than 8-year lease or if seller requires buyer pay transfer fee, appropriate modifications need to be made. Non-franchised ice cream businesses sell at 15–20 x weekly sales assuming condition and lease (8+) years are acceptable.

Benchmark Data

- For more Benchmark Information see Restaurants -- Limited Service

Statistics (Frozen Yogurt Stores)

Number of Establishments	3,109
Average Profit Margin	13.2%
Revenue per Employee	$101,100
Average Number of Employees	6.9
Average Wages per Employee	$18,125

Products and Services Segmentation

Self-serve yogurt	68.3%
Full-service yogurt	18.7%
Toppings and other products	13.0%

Industry Costs

Profits	13.2%
Wages	18.1%
Purchases	37.0%
Depreciation	5.3%
Marketing	3.1%
Rent & Utilities	11.6%
Other	11.7%

Market Share

Menchie's	15.9%
Yogurtland	11.1%
Sweet Frog	9.9%
TCBY	9.1%
Orange Leaf Frozen Yogurt	7.5%
Pinkberry	5.8%
Red Mango	5.6%

Expenses (% of Annual Sales)

Cost of Goods	28%
Occupancy Costs	10%
Payroll/Labor Costs	22%
Profit (pretax)	05%

Questions
- Equipment servicing questions, employee history, historical sales
- Owner operated or absentee? Any wholesale accounts.

Industry Trend
- It's not just frozen yogurt that's pulling away ice cream lovers-consumers are also enjoying gelato, Italian ice, custard, smoothies and other frosty concoctions.
- Dramatically increasing product costs will strain profitability, increase in number of franchised concepts will cause competition unseen in the marketplace in its history.

Expert Comments
Location-driven business with increasing competition in the marketplace. Co-branding is an ideal situation for this concept to offset the seasonality and utilize the facility to a greater degree.

Franchised operations protect many of the negatives, but increasing availability of premium desserts and ice cream limit expansion possibilities.

Resources
- International Dairy Foods Association: http://www.idfa.org
- IBISWorld, January 2017: http://ibisworld.com

Information and Document Management Service Industries		
	NAICS 541513	

Rules of Thumb
➤ 4–6 x normalized EBITDA

Industry Trend
- "Over the five years to 2022, the Document Management Services industry is expected to post steady growth, with industry revenue forecast to rise at an annualized rate of 2.6% to $6.5 billion. Industry growth will be supported by rising business formation and greater demand from healthcare institutions transitioning to electronic health records (EHRs). Although digital records use will increase among all businesses over the next five years, demand for paper-based systems will remain strong.
  "Over the next five years, the industry is projected to continue expanding slowly, with the number of industry operators growing at an annualized rate of 1.4% to 1,556 companies. Meanwhile, the number of employees is forecast to rise an annualized 2.3% to 65,235 workers during the same period.
  "The Document Management Services industry is expected to benefit from a projected upswing in the business cycle over the next five years. During the period, the number of businesses in the United States is projected to increase an annualized 0.8%. Low unemployment will continue to drive consumer spending, leading to a more favorable business environment. Increased business formation will expand the industry's target market. Additionally, the industry will experience sustained demand due to stricter records management

required by various federal regulations, as well as records requirements for potential litigation.

"Government clients are a key source of demand for document management services. Although increasing use of cloud-based systems is expected to continue among government clients, tape storage is likely to be a cost-effective system for long-term storage because it is significantly less expensive than cloud-based storage. Moreover, given that state and local governments are expected to continue facing budget cuts due to lower tax receipts recorded during the recession, there will likely be continued emphasis on cost-cutting strategies during the interim, likely resulting in continued demand for tape storage. This move will be further supported by continued technological improvements in tape storage. Recent technological improvements include expanded cartridge capacity of up to five terabytes, as well as improved shelf life, increasing tape lifespans to three decades."

Source: IBISWorld Industry Outlook

Resources
- IBISWorld, June 2017: http://ibisworld.com

Information Technology Companies		
	NAICS 541512	

Rules of Thumb
➤ 100–150% of annual sales
➤ 2.5–4 x SDE
➤ 3–4 x EBIT
➤ 3–6 x EBITDA

Pricing Tips
- Must understand vendor contracts, customer contracts, assignability, and how important employees are to the company having certain certifications.
- The range of value varies widely by size of company and deal structure. Smaller companies (under $1 million in revenue) tend to see SDE multiples around 2.5 times SDE. Larger companies with more than $1 million EBITDA tend to see multiples of 4 times EBITDA, and are more likely to use EBITDA as the earnings metric. Companies in the middle of the foregoing range tend to be valued around 3 to 3.5 times SDE or EBITDA. Revenue is not a significant factor, except that most buyers will place a ceiling at 1 times revenue. Companies with recurring revenue and predictable earnings will be valued higher, such as IT Managed Service Providers, SaaS, DaaS, and hosted services with annual contracts and recurring income. Staff, technical capabilities, and sales team strength tend to be value drivers as well.
- Might increase multiple if selling company has secured government contracts, especially if in secured agency.
- Consider any off-balance sheet value, i.e., IP, Gov't contracts, valued customer relationships, unique vendor relationships.
- Is there an SLA (Software License Agreement) for each type/copy of software being used? Are the SLA's assignable? Has the vendor given written

permission to assign them and under what conditions? Has the company been reported to the Software Consortium as a company using unlicensed software? Is the technology based on open standards and/or proprietary? Is there a complete inventory list of all software and hardware being used in the business? What 3rd parties are hosting applications and providing IT Services?

Benchmark Data

- "CompTIA projects global IT industry growth of 4.1 percent in 2017. If this growth materializes, it will push the $3.4 trillion global IT industry past the $3.5 trillion mark by year's end."

Source: "IT Industry Outlook 2017"

Expenses (% of Annual Sales)

Cost of Goods	05%
Occupancy Costs	05% to 10%
Payroll/Labor Costs	75%
Profit (pretax)	15% to 20%

Questions

- Describe your streams of revenue and your contract lengths. Are your key salespeople operating with a non-compete agreement? Who has the primary contacts with your top 10 customers?
- Do you have contracts with your client companies? How many users are under contract? Is this hardware, software, etc.? How do your technical representatives work in your company? Where are they located? Do they have individual specialties? How are they paid? Who sells to the customers? Who takes care of client concerns? What do you use to back-up data? Where do you co-locate storage and back-up? Do you own all or part of a data center?
- Stability of staff, will owner(s) stay on for a reasonable period
- Must have references and be able to demo product(s)

Industry Trend

- "A notable milestone was recently attained. For the first time ever, the five most valuable companies in the world were all technology companies. While stock market valuations should be taken with a grain of salt, it did mean technology supplanted the behemoths of the energy, finance, healthcare, and manufacturing sectors."

Source: "IT Industry Outlook 2017," January 2017,
https://www.comptia.org/resources/it-industry-trends-analysis-2017

- Significant growth overall for hardware, software, services, and storage
- Managed Service Providers, SaaS, DaaS, and other fully hosted services and cloud-based services will continue to gain momentum. Old-line technology companies (break-fix, staffing, hardware support, etc.) will decline in popularity and valuation.

Expert Comments

The world is becoming more computer and software dependent. Companies that address hardware, software, managed services, and data center storage are all poised to be in an industry that will experience vast growth into the future. Technology can get old very quickly, so companies must stay relevant.

Overall the industry enjoys above average characteristics, but not necessarily the home-run characteristics of previous time periods. Overall the industry is trending up, but is more favorable to companies with modern methods of business. Older companies that continue to do business the way they did 5 years ago tend to suffer and see reduce valuation.

Seller Financing
- While seller financing and earnout can be common, the industry tends to be a good fit for SBA 7(a) financing. This allows buyers to pay lower valuations in exchange for sellers receiving all cash at closing. When there is upside to be achieved or downside to mitigate, then revenue-based earnouts can be more effective here than other industries because fixed and variable expenses can often be more predictable.
- 3 years

Injection Molding		
	NAICS 333249	

Rules of Thumb

➢ 4.5–6 x EBITDA

Industry Trend
- "Over the five years to 2021, the Contract Injection Molding Manufacturing industry will experience slower growth as the economy continues more assuredly on the path of stable growth. Key downstream sectors are all poised to perform strongly, sustaining demand for long-term industry supply contracts and strengthening relationships that integrate production along the supply chain. Industry revenue is estimated to increase at an average annual rate of 1.7% to reach $8.4 billion in 2021, beginning with a 2.9% increase over 2017."

Source: IBISWorld Industry Outlook

Inns		
SIC 7011-02	NAICS 721110	

Rules of Thumb

➢ 8 x SDE including inventory

Pricing Tips
- "Firstly, you should always know what your occupancy levels are, as well as ADR (Average Daily Rate) per room. Knowing these numbers will help you to stay focused on your budget, sales and marketing plans each year."

Source: http://www.innconcierge.com/innkeeping-solutions/when-is-the-right-time-to-sell-your-inn/
- The smaller the inn and lower the business income, the more the real value factor weighs heavy in the formula. The larger the inn and the higher the business income, the less weight this factor affects total value. Many of the larger inns have been selling in the 8 to 10 capitalization rate of net income, less any needed repairs, and up to a 20% discount if seller financing is not involved.

Benchmark Data

- For additional benchmark information, see Bed and Breakfasts.
- In the middle part of U.S., B&Bs are selling for $80K–$100K/guestroom on average. The popular East & West Coast locations could be up to twice that amount. The larger the inn, the less value/guestroom. Values and expenses vary greatly due to the non-standardized structure of the buildings and locale.
- Operating expenses 40 to 50 percent

Expenses (% of Annual Sales)

Cost of Goods (food, cleaning supplies, & linens)	15%
Occupancy Costs	07% to 10%
Payroll/Labor Costs (not including owner)	10%
Profit (pretax)	10%

Questions

- Ask the broker/seller how their B&B will work for you with the buyer's down payment.

Industry Trend

- B&Bs primarily cater to affluent, baby boomer and millennial travelers. That market appears to be growing. This is also the market that the next generation of innkeepers is coming from.

Seller Financing

- On inns that are < $700K, conventional commercial financing is available. Over $700K, the seller and the SBA is usually involved. Typically, it's buyer 10%, seller 25% and lender 65%.
- Most large inns are seller financed, typically with 20 percent down and terms @ 9 percent, 30-year amortization with a 7-year balloon.
- 5 to 10 years

Resources

- bb-4-sale: http://www.bb-4-sale.com
- Michigan Lake to Lake Bed and Breakfast Association: http://www.laketolake.com
- Professional Association of Innkeepers International: http://www.paii.com/

Insurance Agencies/Brokerages		
SIC 6411-12	NAICS 524210	Number of Businesses/Units 429,311

Rules of Thumb

- ➤ 150–200% of annual sales includes inventory
- ➤ 150–200% of commission revenue
- ➤ 4–6 x SDE plus inventory
- ➤ 5–7 x EBITDA
- ➤ 5–7 x EBIT

I

Pricing Tips

- Agencies sell for 1–2X revenue depending on carrier selection, profitability with carriers, etc. Larger agencies, $1mm+, typically sell for 3–6X EBITDA; however, that's based on at least 15–20 different factors.
- Prices can be dependent on the buyers. A buyer who can purchase the book without taking over agency expenses can be willing to pay more than two times annual commissions.
- Pricing at the start of 2017 remains well above the norm, and it is mostly unchanged from the start of 2016.
- Pricing for small agencies is typically based on a multiple of commissions, typically 2.0 or higher for stable books of business with good loss ratios. One reason for pricing as a multiple of revenue is that the profitability of the book of business in the hands of the buyer is much more relevant than in the hands of its current owner. Quite often the buyer will be able to combine the purchased book of business with the buyer's existing production and achieve improved overall profitability as a result.

  Larger agencies sell for a multiple of sustainable cash flow in the hands of the buyer, starting at multiples of at least 7.0, and rising as high as 12 or more for well-run, large agencies. There is a very strong seller's market for agencies of this type.
- Must look at more than just size of agency in order to come up with appropriate price.
- Must consider type of agency, location, retention, expenses, reason for selling the agency, etc. All of these must be considered and factored into the price of the agency.
- Non-standard auto is approximately one times annual commissions. Standard agencies are currently selling for 2-2.25 annual commissions with increases for large agencies (more than $250,000 in annual commissions), desirable commercial policies and/or high-end homes.
- The multiple increases the larger the insurance agency. Agencies with less than $1M in commissions have multiple ranging from 1.25 to 1.75 annual commissions. Once commissions reach over $1M they start selling for 2X until they get to $3M and any agency over that can sometimes go as high as 3X annual commissions.
- There are really no Rules of Thumb. Each agency is so different; they each have their own valuations depending on many variables involved. Perhaps the average agency sells for 2x total revenues (without subtracting expenses), but 95% of agencies probably fall in the range of 1x to 3x revenues, depending on the quality of business, location and a number of other factors.
- Although competition is high, there are significant barriers to entry. Personal expertise is essential, as is good sales ability. Gaining contracts from insurance companies (carriers) is essential, and difficult for someone starting an agency from scratch to do.
- Length of time in business, reputation, possible cross-selling opportunities in the future, etc.

Benchmark Data

Statistics (Insurance Brokers and Agencies)

Number of Establishments	429,311
Average Profit Margin	14.2%
Revenue per Employee	$158,400
Average Number of Employees	2.3
Average Wages per Employee	$52,848

Products and Services Segmentation

Commercial P&C insurance	30.1%
Personal P&C insurance	27.6%
Health and medical insurance	14.4%
Other	12.2%
Life and accident insurance	9.4%
Annuities	5.0%
Insurance administration and risk consulting	1.3%

Major Market Segmentation

Businesses	65.6%
Individuals aged 45 to 54	7.1%
Individuals aged 35 to 44	6.7%
Individuals aged 65 and older	6.1%
Individuals aged 34 and younger	5.2%
Individuals aged 55 to 64	5.0%
Government	4.3%

Industry Costs

Profit	14.2%
Wages	33.4%
Purchases	0.9%
Depreciation	1.3%
Marketing	0.7%
Rent & Utilities	0.8%
Other	48.7%

Market Share

Aon Corporation	2.1%
Marsh & McLennan Companies Inc.	2.0%
Willis Towers Watson PLC	1.7%
Arthur J. Gallagher & Co.	1.6%

- 30–40% margins. Revenue multiple for "fold-In," which can be moved to buyer without assuming liabilities from seller.
- The best agencies can put 40% or more of revenues on the bottom line. These agencies are particularly sought after and command very high multiples of adjusted cash flow when they are sold.

Expenses (% of Annual Sales)

Cost of Goods	15%
Occupancy Costs	05% to 12%
Payroll/Labor Costs	30% to 50%
Profit (pretax)	15% to 30%

Questions

- Loss ratios, income growth, carrier contract percentages
- Is there any reason to expect carrier appointments not to transfer?
- Why is the agency for sale? Do your producers and other employees have employment contracts with some form of confidentiality and non-piracy provisions?
- What is your retention? How are your loss ratios? In your opinion, how likely is it that a new owner will be appointed by the carriers?
- Can I see your CSRP report? This is the agency report card.
- Are you willing to remain with the business for 2 to 4 years?
- What insurance companies do you represent and what premium and loss ratio have you had with each for last 3 yrs.? Employees and date of hire? Persistency? Top 10 clients and commission revenue from each? Copies of all producer agreements? Cash or accrual basis tax payer? Itemized list of commission receivables and premium payables?
- What is the product mix? (personal lines, commercial lines, benefits, and general description of any specialization). S vs. C corp status. Have tax issues been assessed? Will an asset sale generate tax issues for the seller? Are the employees subject to enforceable non-piracy agreements?
- Are you willing to do an earnout?
- Do your producers have vesting rights to their books of business?
- Size of book? Mix of book by product line? Expense ratio for agency? Loss ratio for P&C book? New business growth? Licenses held? Carrier appointments held? Written premium by carrier?

Industry Trend

- Same as today: high demand for sellers, aging ownership base.
- "Insurance agents and brokers are experiencing a major shift in what their customers and clients have come to expect. By 2017, 'digital natives' will dominate the workplace, which has huge implications for agents and brokers looking to engage with customers and grow their businesses. As the millennial generation matures and enters into its peak buying power, digital and more-automated ways of doing business will become a fundamental part of day-to-day workflows. As a result, insurance agents not only feel pressured to digitize their workflow, but also must streamline business processes to make the cost of doing business more efficient and in-line with these regulations.

  "While 63% of insurance businesses report that they are ready to move towards more digital practices, only 23% of these businesses are actually ready, reports a joint Forrester and Accenture study. To accelerate this process and ensure successful transition to digital workflows, there are three key areas we can expect insurers to embrace as they seek to create more automated, user-friendly processes."

  Source: "3 Technology Trends for the Insurance Industry in 2017" by Triinu Murumäe, November 7, 2016, https://www.insly.com/en/blog/3-technology-trends-for-the-insurance-industry-in-2017/

- "There are three major trends impacting the entire insurance journey. These trends will require brokers to re-think the existing operating model, in order to remain competitive in the future.

  ✓ Heightened demands from a new generation of customers

  ✓ Entrance of new 'digital' players

  ✓ New products and pricing"

  Source: "What's Next for the Insurance Brokerage Industry?", October 31, 2016, https://medium.com/zensur-ance/whats-next-for-the-insurance-brokerage-industry-89f203e9cd57

- Consistent sales as agency owners move into retirement.
- Most industry experts do not expect the current historically strong seller's market to be sustained long term, but there is currently no sign of pricing reverting to more typical levels.
- The insurance industry will continue to experience consolidation.
- As long as the stock market stays up, and the economy stays strong, these agencies will remain highly sought-after acquisition targets. If the economy turns down, the seller's market may end, but they are likely to weather the storm better than the average small closely held business.
- Managing the agency in a way that exploits these trends will lead the firm to success. With hard markets, there is a lot of work quoting for not a lot of reward in increased premiums and thus, commissions. In order to keep revenues up, agencies will still need to sell more—either cross-sell or sell additional coverages to new customers. Value added services should be offered and a fee charged, to increase revenue.
- Standard agencies' revenue will improve as business revenue increases. Small standard agencies will be relegated to small business. Consolidation will continue with regional brokers acquiring strong local standard agencies.

Expert Comments

Be prepared: get P&L, commission statements, management team, etc.

Verify commissions. Clean records help a seller get a better price and avoid a deal collapsing. The best documents for due diligence for buyers are commission statements.

The buyer's perceived probability of account retention, post sale, is critical. Sellers should be willing to help with account retention post sale.

Buyers should make sure the seller's employees are not likely to leave and compete with the new owner of the agency. If they do, account retention can suffer significantly.

Although competition between agencies is high, there are significant barriers to entry. Personal expertise is essential, as is good sales ability. Gaining contracts from insurance companies (carriers) is essential, and difficult for someone starting an agency from scratch to do.

Because an agency's client base tends to stay with an agency in good times and in bad, the typical agency can be sold based on the expectation of the buyer that those clients will be retained.

Seller Financing

- Sales are generally cash or third-party financing. Sellers may be asked to hold a small note as a matter of trust.
- Cash is king. Outside financing is readily available.
- Mostly both with the bank requiring the seller to have some 'skin in the game' of at least 10%.
- There are about six or so specialty lenders who target this industry, and it's desirable to lenders.
- Seller financing is very common when one independent agency buys another. If a national buyer is involved, the up-front cash is often a large portion of the sale, with the balance in an earnout. The earnouts can be very hard to achieve in full.

I

Resources

- American Association of Insurance Management Consultants: http://www.aaimco.com
- Agency Equity: http://www.AgencyEquity.com
- Insurance Journal: http://www.insurancejournal.com/magazines
- The Council of Insurance Agents and Brokers: http://www.ciab.com
- Professional Insurance Agents: http://www.pia.org
- Independent Insurance Agents and Brokers of America: http://www.independentagent.com
- Insurance Information Institute—lots of information and data: http://www.iii.org
- IBISWorld, February 2017: http://ibisworld.com
- American Agents Alliance Insurance Association: https://agentsalliance.com/

Insurance Companies (in general)		
	NAICS 524210	

Rules of Thumb

➢ 1–2 x capital and surplus

Pricing Tips

- "A couple of key metrics can be used to value insurance companies, and these metrics happen to be common to financial firms in general. These are price to book (P/B) and return on equity (ROE). P/B is a primary valuation measure that relates the insurance firm's stock price to its book value, either on a total firm value or a per-share amount. Book value, which is simply shareholders' equity, is a proxy for a firm's value should it cease to exist and be completely liquidated. Price to tangible book value strips out goodwill and other intangible assets to give the investor a more accurate gauge on the net assets left over should the company close shop. A quick rule of thumb for insurance firms (and again, for financial stocks in general) is that they are worth buying at a P/B level of 1 and are on the pricey side at a P/B level of 2 or higher. For an insurance firm, book value is a solid measure of most of its balance sheet, which consists of bonds, stocks and other securities that can be relied on for their value given an active market for them."

  Source: http://www.investopedia.com/articles/investing/082813/how-value-insurance-company.asp

Industry Trend

- "Top 10 Insurtech Trends for 2017:

  Trend 1. Massive cost savers in claims, operations and customer acquisition

  Trend 2. A new face on digital transformation: engagement innovation

  Trend 3. Next-level data analytics capabilities and AI, to really unlock the potential of IoT

  Trend 4. Addressing the privacy concerns

  Trend 5. Contextual pull platforms

  Trend 6. The marketplace model will find its way to insurance

  Trend 7. Open architecture

  Trend 8. Blockchain will come out of the experimentation stage

  Trend 9. Use of algorithms for front-liner empowerment

Trend 10. Symbiotic relationship with insurtechs"
Source: "Top 10 Insurtech Trends for 2017" by Reggy De Feniks and Roger Peverelli January 3, 2017, http://insurancethoughtleadership.com/top-10-insurtech-trends-for-2017/

Resources
- Digital Insurance: https://www.dig-in.com

Insurance Companies—Life	
NAICS 524210	Number of Businesses/Units 9,451

Rules of Thumb
➤ 1–2.5 x capital and surplus

Benchmark Data

Statistics (Life Insurance & Annuities)
Number of Establishments ... 9,451
Average Profit Margin ... 12.6%
Revenue per Employee ... $2,697,200
Average Number of Employees ... 37.8
Average Wages per Employee ... $103,955

Products and Services Segmentation
Variable deferred annuities ... 28.7%
Other ... 18.2%
Fixed rate deferred annuities ... 18.0%
Individual whole life premiums ... 11.3%
Group life premiums ... 6.7%
Individual term life premiums ... 6.7%
Individual universal life premiums ... 6.1%
Immediate annuities ... 4.3%

Major Market Segmentation
Individuals aged 35 to 44 ... 25.3%
Individuals aged 45 to 54 ... 24.3%
Individuals aged 34 and younger ... 21.6%
Individuals aged 55 to 64 ... 14.5%
Individuals aged 65 and older ... 14.3%

Industry Costs
Profit ... 12.6%
Wages ... 3.8%
Purchases ... 49.8%
Depreciation ... 1.3%
Marketing ... 0.6%
Rent & Utilities ... 0.7%
Other ... 31.2%

Resources
- IBISWorld, March 2017: http://ibisworld.com

I

Insurance Companies—Property & Casualty

	NAICS 524126	Number of Businesses/Units 16,764

Rules of Thumb

➤ ½–3 x capital and surplus

Pricing Tips

- With a strong demand and low inventory available for P&C agencies, the values have risen sharply. Buyers are most interested in the renewal commissions that are associated with the agency. Standard line P&C agencies sell around 2.5 times commissions. Non-standard line agencies tend to sell at lower multiples, 2.0. Other factors that positively influence the valuation: strong retention rates (85%+), low loss ratios, direct bill and quality of carrier appointments. Allstate agencies tend to sell at slightly higher multiples because of the generally strong retention rates. P&C agencies that contain a strong home owners' insurance book of business also make them more valuable. Many large buyers in the market looking to acquire books of business.
- Pricing in P&C insurance is based on commissions. Typically, 1.5-2.0 (or a little higher if over $1M in commission). Key factors will be loss ratios.

Benchmark Data

Statistics (Property, Casualty and Direct Insurance)

Number of Establishments	16,764
Average Profit Margin	9.7%
Revenue per Employee	$977,100
Average Number of Employees	39.0
Average Wages per Employee	$90,351

Products and Services Segmentation

Private passenger auto	37.1%
Other	15.8%
Homeowners multiple peril	15.4%
Other liability	8.8%
Workers compensation	8.7%
Commercial multiple peril	6.7%
Commercial auto	5.3%
Fire	2.2%

Major Market Segmentation

Other commercial market	41.1%
Private vehicle market	37.1%
Other private market	14.1%
Commercial vehicle market	5.3%
Other insurance carriers	2.4%

Industry Costs

Profit	9.7%
Wages	9.3%
Purchases	0.9%
Depreciation	0.8%
Marketing	0.6%
Rent & Utilities	0.7%
Other	78.0%

27th Edition

27th Edition

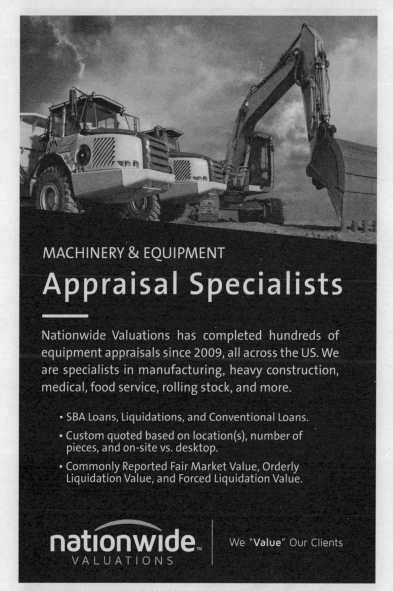

Market Share

State Farm Mutual Automobile Insurance Company	11.6%
Berkshire Hathaway Inc.	6.5%
Liberty Mutual Insurance Group	5.5%
Allstate Insurance Company	5.4%
The Travelers Companies Inc.	3.8%

- Insurance industry has very low COGS expenses. You can estimate one service agent for every $1 million in premiums.

Questions

- 1. 12-month renewal of commissions
  2. Retention rate
  3. List of carriers and volume of business
  4. Are there any large accounts that make up more than 10% of the book?
  5. Does agency accept cash payments? Direct bill or agency bill?
- What is their stockholders' equity? What management do they have? What is their marketing ability?

Industry Trend

- As larger companies acquire smaller agencies, I see consolidation in the market. Buyers are using the internet more frequently for their insurance needs, hence the brick and mortar agency is becoming less and less relevant. Still there are many years before they become extinct.

Expert Comments

If you're selling in this industry, work with a person/company that is experienced in this industry. Buyers should contact brokers and get on as many contact lists as possible. It's a very difficult market for buyers, as there is very low inventory and lots of qualified buyers.

Almost impossible to start a new agency from scratch. Most of the larger insurance companies (carriers) will not appoint with new start- ups. Current trend is that larger agencies are acquiring the small 'mom and pop' agencies and merging the business with their current business to reduce overhead. Another factor that is having a positive influence in the insurance industry is the availability of funds. Lenders like Oak Street, PPC and Crestmark are specialty lenders that have helped drive the market.

When selling a book of business, expect to have to carry tail insurance for 2-3 years after the deal is done. This is E+O insurance to protect the buyer from things that happened when the seller had the book of business. Also, many buyers will want to have earnouts to reduce their risk.

Seller Financing

- I see most deals have some seller financing (10%) involved. There are many specialty banks that lend to this industry. Also, cash buyers are prevalent as they are experienced buyers who currently own other agencies, hence they have the available capital to acquire.
- Personal lines books tend to get a higher multiple than commercial lines. Commercial lines usually have to rebid every year and this increases the risk.

I

Resources
- IBISWorld, June 2017: http://ibisworld.com
- FAIA: http://www.FAIA.com

Internet-Related Businesses

Rules of Thumb
➤ 80% of annual gross sales

Pricing Tips
- "The market is growing, not only in terms of deals closed but demand from buyers. We are seeing around 10 buyers for every seller as a ratio. If you look at the total deals closed trends you can see that total deals closed went from $53 million to $112 million in 4 years. That is over a 100% increase. Our predictions, for 2016, is we will see another growth year again. As of writing this post we have 5 businesses listed and another 5 in the pipeline."
  Source: http://www.digitalexits.com/whats-your-online-business-worth/
- It depends on if there is any profit. If there is, about 2 times SDE.
- "An important consideration during your search is the pricing of a potential web investment. According to Justin Gilchrist, a Manchester, England-based industry consultant and founder of FlipFilter.com, a website sales analysis tool, website buyers are typically paying between 12 and 24 months' revenue. You can usually expect to pay between $100,000 and $200,000 for an online business that is generating $100,000 in annual revenue."
  Source: http://www.entrepreneur.com/article/22342
- Drop ship companies are worth more than one which requires inventory. Internet companies can sell for between 20% of sales and 50% of sales depending on how hands-on the business is, if there is inventory or not, and what the growth potential is.

Benchmark Data
- Average gross margin is 20% of sales. Sales per square foot is difficult, as some drop-ship Internet companies operate out of a very small commercial space or even a home office.

Questions
- A buyer should ask to verify sales by using the credit card merchant account, as all online transactions are paid by credit card. Also, a buyer should ask if there is any product-specific knowledge needed to sell the product.

Industry Trend
- There is a strong growth pattern as more and more people are using the Internet.

Expert Comments
When buying an Internet company, be sure to include enough training to understand the website and to maintain the SEO and ranking. Many buyers assume that websites are a cash cow, then they fail to maintain the website and the business begins to decline.

A good Internet company with excellent SEO is hard to duplicate, as achieving high rankings and organic traffic in search engines can take years to develop.

Seller Financing

- Very short—2 to 4 years
- These businesses generally close with little or no bank financing. Most times, it is an all- cash deal or 75% cash with 35% seller financing.
- Currently the Internet Merger & Acquisitions space is an either all cash business or with a little seller financing thrown into the mix! Traditional banks are not at the point yet where they can evaluate how to protect their asset (the domain and its content). Unless you have free and clear real estate to put up as collateral, you're not getting a bank loan on an Internet company.

Investigative Services		
	NAICS 561611	

Rules of Thumb
➢ 70–75% of annual sales

Industry Trend

- "The Private Detective Services industry is expected to continue performing strongly over the five years to 2021, as demand for industry products is expected to remain robust. Additionally, sustained profitability and revenue growth are anticipated to encourage new participants to enter the industry. IBISWorld also expects wages to grow in the five years to 2021, which will also contribute to an expanding industry. In the five years to 2021, IBISWorld expects industry revenue to grow at an annualized rate of 1.4% to total an estimated $6.0 billion."

Source: IBISWorld Industry Outlook

Resources
- IBISWorld, January 2017: http://ibisworld.com

Investment Advice/Financial Planning		
	NAICS 523930	Number of Businesses/Units 115,168

Rules of Thumb
➢ 1.5 x SDE

➢ 1 x annual sales

Pricing Tips

- Contract persistency is critical to the continuation of fees. The demographics of the clientele base should be carefully analyzed. The range of valuation multiples is very wide and varies by the type of revenue stream and how it's paid. The numbers above are considered to be averages. Regulation violations by the owner can severely reduce the sales price.

Benchmark Data

Statistics (Financial Planning and Advice)

Number of Establishments	115,168
Average Profit Margin	25.5%
Revenue per Employee	$263,500
Average Number of Employees	1.9
Average Wages per Employee	$82,880

Products and Services Segmentation

Personal financial planning and advice	33.3%
Personal investment management	29.7%
Business and government financial planning and management	20.8%
Other Services	16.2%

Major Market Segmentation

Individuals and households	42.9%
Businesses	27.7%
Other clients	15.8%
Governments	13.6%

Industry Costs

Profit	25.5%
Wages	31.9%
Purchases	4.8%
Depreciation	1.2%
Marketing	1.7%
Rent & Utilities	2.8%
Other	32.1%

Market Share

Morgan Stanley Wealth Management	17.4%
Wells Fargo & Company	13.7%
Bank of America Corporation	13.1%
Ameriprise Financial Inc.	5.5%

Industry Trend

- "Over the five years to 2022, increased market valuations for various types of assets and securities are expected to push revenue growth for the Financial Planning and Advice industry upwards at an annualized rate of 5.1% to $71.7 billion. As the economy continues to grow, the number of wealthy households and institutions needing financial management services will also increase, raising the value of assets under management (AUM) for firms. The majority of this growth is expected to go to existing firms, rather than the limited number of new operators breaking into the industry. In 2018, total industry revenue is estimated to rise 4.3%. Rising interest rates, geopolitical tension and inflation over the next year are anticipated to encourage consumers to consult professional services for managing their finances and protecting their assets."

Source: IBISWorld Industry Outlook

Expert Comments

Industry consolidation and company marketing efficiencies are promoting the move away from commissioned sales force.

Resources
- IBISWorld, February 2017: http://ibisworld.com

Jani-King	Franchise
Approx. Total Investment	$8,170–$74,000

	NAICS 561720	Number of Businesses/Units 11,000

Rules of Thumb
➢ 25–30% of annual sales plus inventory

Resources
- Jani-King: http://www.janiking.com

Janitorial Services		
SIC 7439-02	NAICS 561720	Number of Businesses/Units 920,627

Rules of Thumb
➢ 1 x one month's billings; plus fixtures, equipment and inventory

➢ 4 x monthly billings; includes fixtures, equipment and inventory

➢ 45–53% of annual sales plus inventory

➢ 1.5–1.8 x SDE plus inventory

➢ 4 x EBITDA

Pricing Tips
- The janitorial service field has always been a good seller especially in highly populated areas. Commercial cleaning companies tend to demand a higher price especially if their SDE is above $300K. A good sales force and low customer concentration is vital. All staff should be W-2 compliant and W.C. should be in place, with a good record. Residential cleaning/maid service businesses are highly dependent on the number of clients under a professional fee agreement, and typically those with 50 or more clients (100–200 cleans per month) sell before smaller companies. Franchise cleaning companies are much harder to sell as there simply isn't enough profit to go around and the franchisor usually owns the client. The owner should be an operator and not a cleaner! Granted a small owner/cleaner business is salable to those in need of a job or to an acquisition minded buyer set on growth.
- "Basically, estimating value starts with adding up net annual sales and subtracting operating expenses to arrive at your annual operating profit. This number is then used to calculate how much the business is worth based on its future profit potential and by using a multiplier to arrive at an estimated value.

J

The multiplier is based on the risk in the cleaning industry in general as well as in your business in particular, such as the number of long-term cleaning contracts."

Source: http://smallbusiness.chron.com/sell-janitorial-business-73876.html

- 1.5 to 1.75 times SDE including a working inventory for commercial janitorial service companies. 1.25 to 1.60 times SDE including a working inventory for maid service/residential businesses. Commercial companies with Gross Sales in excess of $3 million–$20 million could fetch a 3–6 time multiple of SDE. Companies with long terms (3-5+ years) client contracts have more weight. Fully staffed with supervision in place has more weight. Government contracts offer nice security for buyers but are difficult to transfer. Minority owned businesses carry less weight if client contracts are based on such ownership. W-2 Employees carry more weight than 1099's. Quality of books and records are important.

Benchmark Data

Statistics (Janitorial Services)

Number of Establishments	920,627
Average Profit Margin	6.6%
Revenue per Employee	$29,800
Average Number of Employees	2.1
Average Wages per Employee	$15,002

Products and Services Segmentation

Standard commercial cleaning	57.1%
Other	22.0%
Residential cleaning	10.9%
Damage restoration cleaning	4.7%
Floor care services	3.0%
Exterior window cleaning	2.3%

Major Market Segmentation

Offices	32.8%
Educational facilities	22.1%
Retail complexes	12.1%
Residences	10.9%
Government	10.8%
Industrial plants	6.0%
Healthcare facilities	5.3%

Industry Costs

Profit	6.6%
Wages	50.0%
Purchases	19.1%
Depreciation	0.4%
Marketing	1.2%
Rent & Utilities	3.5%
Other	19.2%

Market Share

ABM Industries Inc.	5.4%

Expenses (% of Annual Sales)

Cost of Goods	01% to 03%
Occupancy Costs	07%
Payroll/Labor Costs	45%
Profit (pretax)	40%

Industry Trend

- "The Janitorial Services industry will grow over the five years to 2022 due to the continued expansion and growth of the US economy. Consequently, operators will benefit from the increase in nonresidential construction activity. Moreover, other US industries are expected to outsource cleaning activities to janitorial and cleaning service specialists. In particular, the education, health and medical industries, which outsource the majority of their cleaning requirements, will provide sustained growth for the industry. An aging US population and greater demand for healthcare services will bolster demand for cleaning services for medical and surgical hospitals, urgent care clinics, diagnostic labs and research facilities. As a result of these improving conditions, industry revenue is forecast to increase at an annualized rate of 1.1% to reach $58.9 billion in 2022.

"Over the next five years, high occupancy rates for offices and other commercial and industrial properties will yield growth prospects for operators. Residential and nonresidential construction activity will also accelerate, resulting in new cleaning contracts and more robust revenue growth. Demand for domestic cleaning services is also expected to rise, as the unemployment level drops and household disposable income continues to grow. Disposable income levels affect the industry because the main consumers of residential cleaning services are upper income bracket households. The percentage of households with annual incomes exceeding $100,000 is expected to increase from 26.5% in 2017 to 27.9% by 2022, which will result in greater demand for residential cleaning services."

Source: IBISWorld Industry Outlook

Expert Comments

Location and facilities are usually not important, as customers don't typically visit the premises. It's getting harder and harder to find a well-run commercial cleaning business for sale as many of the larger companies have bought up the small ones. Although the costs of supplies have gone up, in most cases the added expenses are handed down to the client. However, competition for new customers in the residential market is proving to be difficult when it comes to raising prices. As in most business, it's all about the demographics of your client base.

Seller Financing

- SBA and private equity group financing is certainly an option. Most small units are sold with at least 80–90% cash down.

Resources

- Building Service Contractors Association International: http://www.bscai.org
- C M Cleaning & Maintenance Management—informative site based on the magazine: http://www.cmmonline.com
- International Sanitary Supply Association: http://www.issa.com
- IBISWorld, June 2017: http://ibisworld.com

Franchise

Jersey Mike's Subs

Approx. Total Investment	$203,191–$680,827
Estimated Annual Sales/Unit	$738,000

SIC 5812-19	NAICS 722513	Number of Businesses/Units 1,020

Rules of Thumb
➢ 50% of annual sales plus inventory

Benchmark Data
- For Benchmark Data see Sandwich Shops

Resources
- Jersey Mike's Subs: http://www.jerseymikes.com

Jewelry Stores

SIC 5944-09	NAICS 448310	Number of Businesses/Units 71,275

Rules of Thumb
➢ 4–6 x EBIT if inventory included

Pricing Tips
- What return on assets would be expected if current owner left city?
- A destination upscale jeweler has a much better 'chance' of being sold as a going business.
- Highly capital intensive-inventory on hand most critical in pricing

Benchmark Data

Statistics (Jewelry Stores)

Number of Establishments	71,275
Average Profit Margin	4.7%
Revenue per Employee	$203,000
Average Number of Employees	2.4
Average Wages per Employee	$26,015

Products and Services Segmentation

Diamond Jewelry	44.1%
Other merchandise	21.6%
Watches	15.7%
Gold jewelry	10.0%
Pearl and other gemstone jewelry	8.6%

Industry Costs

Profit	4.7%
Wages	12.9%
Purchases	53.7%
Depreciation	1.0%
Marketing	2.8%
Rent & Utilities	9.3%
Other	15.6%

Market Share

Signet Jewelers Ltd.	15.2%

Expenses (% of Annual Sales)

Cost of Goods	55% to 58%
Occupancy Costs	n/a
Payroll/Labor Costs	22%
Profit (pretax)	06%

Industry Trend

- "Analysis suggests that consumer behavior has shifted due to the proliferation of competitive online marketplaces, such as Amazon, Facebook Marketplace, and eBay. Additionally, fashion trends have steered buyers away from high-end jewelry and watches toward more affordable designer diffusion lines and mid-market items. As an example, the Jewelers Board of Trade has cited increases in jewelry store closings in 2016 at 66 percent above 2015 levels. This shrinking of the jewelry industry displays the dramatic change in the desire for, and value of, jewelry, a core retail product for pawnbrokers."

Source: "Pawnbrokers Report Decrease in Retail Sales as Online Competition Grows and Buying Trends Shift," https://www.pawnshopstoday.com/trends/

Seller Financing

- Not seller financed, inventory too portable, high risk
- 3 years

Resources

- Instoremagazine: http://www.instoremag.com
- National Jeweler: http://www.nationaljeweler.com
- Jewelers of America (JA): http://www.jewelers.org
- IBISWorld, May 2017: http://ibisworld.com

	Franchise
Jiffy Lube International	
Approx. Total Investment	$220,000–$450,000
NAICS 811191	Number of Businesses/Units 1,915

Rules of Thumb

➢ 45–50% of annual sales plus inventory

J

Resources
- Jiffy Lube: http://www.jiffylube.com

	Franchise
Jimmy John's Gourmet Sandwiches	
Approx. Total Investment	$325,500–$555,000
Estimated Annual Sales/Unit	$1,365,000
SIC 5812-19 NAICS 722513	

Rules of Thumb
➢ 65–70% of annual sales plus inventory

Benchmark Data
- For Benchmark Data see Sandwich Shops

Job Shops/Contract Manufacturing		
	NAICS 332710	

Rules of Thumb
➢ 1.5–2 x SDE plus inventory

➢ 3–5 x EBIT

➢ 4–5 x EBITDA

Pricing Tips
- Customer concentration is an issue for most job shops and contract manufacturers. A customer over 30% or two customers over 50% is a major problem.
- 4 x EBITDA is just a rule of thumb. A range of 3 x to 8 x is realistic depending a range of factors (history, custom concentration, future prospects, etc.).
- Best rule of thumb in this industry to use as a barometer is FMV of FFE&M plus 1 X EBITDA.

Benchmark Data
- For additional Benchmark Data see Machine Shops
- Revenues per man-hour can be all over the place because newer, numerical controlled machines are much more productive. The higher the revenues per man-hour the better the business.
- Determine unused capacity. Buyers will want to determine potential without major capital investment.

Expenses (% of Annual Sales)

Cost of Goods	40% to 50%
Occupancy Costs	03% to 05%
Payroll/Labor Costs	25% to 28%
Profit (pretax)	12%

Questions

- Find out the seller's motivation. Could be issues related to hiring skilled machinists or constant battles with customers paying on time.
- Backlog, WIP, age, qualifications & tenure of staff, condition of equipment (look at line items for R&M closely to avoid machinery held together with band aids), need for CAPEX near and mid-term, etc.?
- Will the business be sustainable when owner leaves? Any known environmental issues?

Expert Comments

While some people consider ease of replication is easy they are wrong, wrong, wrong. The business might be easy to start but very difficult to get big-name customers until the company has established a track record.

Competition is high and the key to gross profit margins is using technology to be low-cost manufacturer.

Recent influx of orders from OEM's has contributed to better backlog. Receivable aging improving and more shops able to get 33%–50% deposits. Not as much used equipment in the field as prior years. Competitive edge goes to automated shops with palletized tool changing machining centers, wire EDM, etc.

Seller Financing

- Most deals to have some seller financing, usually 3 to 5 years at an interest rate between CD rates and bank loan rates. Our current experiences are interest rates in the 3% to 4% range.

Resources

- Design2Part Buyers Guide: http://www.D2PBuyersGuide.com

John Deere Dealerships

Pricing Tips

- Rules of Thumb are totally inappropriate. If DOT then dealership has future but if not DOT, the days are numbered and must be acquired by an adjoining dealership. Market share is huge to JD and rebates reducing to those not DOT or not achieving market share objectives. Need 40% equity so forget about high leverage deals. Be careful and look at aging of inventory and losses hidden in leases and conditional sales contracts-dealers are exposed.
- DOT is the term used for their Dealer of Tomorrow standards. The goal is to deal with $50 million plus dealers only. They no longer want 'Joe' who is a good salesman to be a dealer. They want organizations with sufficient size that they can afford to employ a full management team-general manager, controller/VP-Finance, sales manager, parts manager, and aftermarket manager. At $50 million, you can afford most of these people and at $100 million, you can afford better people and real economies of scale set in.

K

Johnny Rockets

Approx. Total Investment		$553,500–$1,098,500
Estimated Annual Sales/Unit		$1,150,000
	NAICS 722513	Number of Businesses/Units 205

Rules of Thumb

➢ 70–75% of annual sales plus inventory

Resources

- Johnny Rocket's: http://www.johnnyrockets.com

Franchise

Jon Smith Subs

	NAICS 722513	Number of Businesses/Units 8

Rules of Thumb

➢ 20% of annual sales plus inventory

Franchise

Juice It Up

Approx. Total Investment		$249,550–343,726
	NAICS 722515	Number of Businesses/Units 86

Rules of Thumb

➢ 20–25% of annual sales plus inventory

Resources

- Juice It Up: http://www.juiceitup.com

Franchise

KFC (Kentucky Fried Chicken)

Approx. Total Investment		$1,300,000–$2,500,000
Estimated Annual Sales/Unit		$1,062,000
	NAICS 722513	Businesses/Units 4,199

Rules of Thumb

➢ 30–35% of annual sales plus inventory

Franchise

Kumon Math & Reading Centers

Approx. Total Investment		$69,428–$140,626
	NAICS 611691	Number of Businesses/Units 25,811

Rules of Thumb
➢ 80–90% of annual sales plus inventory

Industry Trend
- "For the 15th consecutive year, Kumon, the world's largest after-school education company, has been ranked as the number one tutoring franchise in *Entrepreneur*'s annual Franchise 500 Issue. The ranking is considered to be the best and most comprehensive ranking based on objective, quantifiable measures of franchise success."

Source: January 13, 2016,
https://www.kumonfranchise.com/us-en/assets/pressrelease/release2016-0113.html

Resources
- Kumon: https://www.kumon.com/math-program

Franchise

Kwik Kopy Business Center

Approx. Total Investment		$219,578–$248,626
	NAICS 323111	Number of Businesses/Units 18

Rules of Thumb
➢ 50–60% of annual sales plus inventory

Franchise

Lady of America

Approx. Total Investment		$9,250
	NAICS 713940	Number of Businesses/Units 500

Rules of Thumb
➢ 45–50% of annual sales plus inventory

Resources
- Lady of America: http://www.loafitnessforwomen.com

L

Landscaping Services

SIC 0782-04	NAICS 561730	Number of Businesses/Units 528,250

Rules of Thumb

> ➤ 1.5 x SDE; plus fixtures and equipment (except vehicles) & inventory

> ➤ 45–50% of annual revenues plus inventory

> ➤ 2–4 x EBITDA (may be higher for larger firms)

Pricing Tips

- Multiples of EBITDA range from 2 to 6 depending on size, profitability and industry segment.
- "Landscape contractors need substantial capital investments for equipment. Startup costs of $100,000 are needed to compete in this industry. 'It's a difficult field unless you're a really large company' said Crabtree, who has been in the industry for over 15 years. Profit margins are typically 5%."

Source: www.urbanforest.org

Benchmark Data

Statistics (Landscaping Services)

Number of Establishments	528,250
Average Profit Margin	7.2%
Revenue per Employee	$80,000
Average Number of Employees	2.0
Average Wages per Employee	$25,947

Products and Services Segmentation

Maintenance and general services—commercial	51.0%
Maintenance and general service—residential	31.0%
Design-build-installation services	13.8%
Arborist services and other services	4.2%

Major Market Segmentation

Commercial markets	46.2%
Residential markets	43.9%
Government and institutional markets	7.5%
Non-profit organizations and other	2.4%

Industry Costs

Profit	7.2%
Wages	32.3%
Purchases	29.6%
Depreciation	1.8%
Marketing	2.6%
Rent & Utilities	3.8%
Other	22.7%

Expenses (% of Annual Sales)

Cost of Goods	50%
Occupancy Costs	05%
Payroll/Labor Costs	30%
Profit (pretax)	10% to 15%

Questions

- Does the company have contracts with its clients? Are all employees legal? How many customers are built on relationships with the seller, and what will happen to them if he or she sells?

Industry Trend

- "Landscape Trends for 2017:
  - ✓ Going green with all types of greenery
  - ✓ Bringing 'hygge' outdoors
  - ✓ Creating tech-savvy exterior kitchens
  - ✓ Mixing up materials
  - ✓ Prioritizing pollinators
  - ✓ Growing 'smart' lawns
  - ✓ Taking landscapes to new heights and unusual places"
    Source: "Landscape Trends for 2017" by Sally Benson, March 15, 2017,
    http://www.amerinursery.com/landscape/2017-landscape-industry-trends/
- "7 Green Industry Trends for 2017:
  - ✓ Maintenance, such as lawn mowing, weed control and fertilization, is your moneymaker, but design and build is catching up.
  - ✓ Water management, such as irrigation and landscape drainage, is becoming more and more important.
  - ✓ Millennial employees will continue to shape your business in the year ahead.
  - ✓ Overtime rules changed as of December 1.
  - ✓ Healthcare costs continue to impact most small-business owners.
  - ✓ Technology and its impact on your green industry business aren't going anywhere.
  - ✓ A generational shift in attitudes about lawn maintenance appears to be underway, with the younger demographic appearing more willing to pay someone else to care for their lawn."
    Source: "7 Green Industry Trends for 2017" posted on December 20, 2016 by Spring-Green,
    https://www.spring-green.com/franchise-opportunity/blog-7-green-industry-trends-2017/

Expert Comments

Competition is fierce and ease of replication is as easy as owning a lawnmower and weed whacker. Much better once the company reaches several million in sales.

Set yourself apart from the competition. Get long-term contracts. Focus on maintenance.

Seller Financing

- Generally difficult to finance because of lack of assets.

Resources

- Association of Professional Landscape Designers: http://www.apld.org
- National Association of Landscape Professionals: http://www.landscapeprofessionals.org
- Turf Magazine: http://www.turfmagazine.com

L

- Landscape Management: http://www.landscapemanagement.net
- Lawn and Landscape: http://www.lawnandlandscape.com
- IBISWorld, March 2017: http://ibisworld.com
- American Nurseryman: http://www.americannursery.com

Land Surveying Services

SIC 8713-01	NAICS 541370	Number of Businesses/Units 17,970

Rules of Thumb

➢ 40–80% of annual fee revenues; plus fixtures, equipment and inventory; may require earnout

Benchmark Data

Statistics (Surveying and Mapping Services)

Number of Establishments	17,970
Average Profit Margin	8.4%
Revenue per Employee	$132,800
Average Number of Employees	3.4
Average Wages per Employee	$51,827

Products and Services Segmentation

Cadastral, property line and boundary surveying	23.9%
Geospatial processing services	16.0%
Topographical and planimetric surveying and mapping	17.8%
Other services	16.5%
Construction surveying	16.5%
Engineering services	4.4%
Subdivision layout and design services	3.6%
Geophysical processing services	1.3%

Major Market Segmentation

Other	41.0%
Governmental bodies (federal, state and local)	22.0%
Construction companies	13.6%
Energy, utility and mining companies	15.6%
Professional technical companies	12.0%
Households	11.4%

Industry Costs

Profit	8.4%
Wages	39.2%
Purchases	7.7%
Depreciation	2.7%
Marketing	1.2%
Rent & Utilities	5.0%
Other	35.8%

Industry Trend

- "Over the five years to 2022, IBISWorld forecasts that revenue for the Surveying and Mapping Services industry will increase at an annualized rate of 1.5% to $8.3 billion, including growth of 1.2% in 2022. This growth will largely be driven by continued, but steadier growth across key downstream construction markets. Additionally, external competition is projected to intensify over the five years to 2022, as engineering operators and construction contractors increasingly offer value-added services, such as in-house surveying. While this factor will dampen industry growth over the next five years, the negative effect of increased competition will be partly offset by the public-sector agencies' increasing tendency to outsource surveying, mapping and data information services to industry operators."

Source: IBISWorld Industry Outlook

Resources
- Professional Surveyor magazine: http://www.profsurv.com
- The National Society of Professional Surveyors: http://www.nsps.us.com/
- IBISWorld, October 2017: http://ibisworld.com

Laptop Xchange		Franchise
Approx. Total Investment		$183,750–$267,800
	NAICS 443142	Number of Businesses/Units 20

Rules of Thumb
➢ 80–85% of annual sales plus inventory

Law Firms		
SIC 8111-03	NAICS 541110	Number of Businesses/Units 468,957

Rules of Thumb
➢ 4 x SDE includes inventory

➢ 3.5 x EBIT

➢ 3.5 x EBITDA

➢ 90–100% of annual fee revenue; estate work approaches 100%; may require earnout

Pricing Tips
- "Many considerations go into a valuation. Even if you have a standardized multiple-which does not exist-the end results won't be the same. The multiples I use by way of a shortcut valuation are .5 to 3 times the average annual gross revenue. That gives me a starting point. Then many factors come into play, like the geography and history of the practice, the longevity of the earnings cycle, and whether the practice is ascending or descending in gross revenue. The final number will be based on the experience of the evaluator."

Source: http://www.lawpracticetoday.org/article/selling-your-practice/

- Valuing law practices vary widely depending on practice area, geographic location, systems and other key value drives. Transition plan is a key factor in the value of the practice.

L

Benchmark Data

Statistics (Law Firms)

Number of Establishments	468,957
Average Profit Margin	21.2%
Revenue per Employee	$222,000
Average Number of employees	3.0
Average Wages per Employee	$80,142

Products and Services Segmentation

Commercial law services	44.2%
Other services	25.5%
Criminal law, civil negligence and personal injury	16.8%
Real estate law	8.1%
Labor and employment	5.4%

Major Market Segmentation

Business and corporate clients	70.8%
Households	23.9%
Government and not-for-profit clients	5.3%

Industry Costs

Profit	21.2%
Wages	36.2%
Purchases	1.5%
Depreciation	0.8%
Marketing	2.3%
Rent & Utilities	6.3%
Other	31.7%

Expenses (% of Annual Sales)

Profit (pretax)	30%

Questions

- Transition timeline. Claims history. Repeat clients. Systems. Key personnel. Key clients and ability to transition.
- What is their backlog? Customer concentration?

Industry Trend

- The Top 8 Digital Marketing Trends for Law Firms
    - ✓ "The focus will shift to social media conversion.
    - ✓ Law firms of all sizes will place a high importance on SEO (Search Engine Optimization).
    - ✓ Microsites will become the preferred thought leadership platforms for practice and industry groups.
    - ✓ Mobile will completely dominate desktop.
    - ✓ Intelligent content will replace content marketing as the new current trend.
    - ✓ Firms will focus on measuring ROI and actionable insight from their digital efforts.
    - ✓ Multichannel marketing will become the key to a firm's marketing strategy.
    - ✓ True marketing automation will emerge."

Source: "The Top 8 Digital Marketing Trends for Law Firms in 2016," by Guy Alvarez, January 19, 2016, https://good2bsocial.com/the-top-8-digital-marketing-trends-for-law-firms-in-2016/

- More consolidation and price competition for smaller practices. Attorneys looking to expand geographically, implement systems and software and become advisors as compared to transactions. As well, attorneys typically will work longer into retirement than other professionals and so many of the retirement age attorneys have delayed or have not planned for exit along with similar aged business owners.

Expert Comments

Practices vary greatly depending on practice area, attorney and overall firm setup. Some fields would be on higher end of scale and some on lower.

It is difficult to replicate, as the good businesses have reputations built over many years.

Seller Financing

- A mix, but mostly seller financing with small to medium practices. Max 50% down on practices with remaining being earnout or financed by seller.

Resources

- IBISWorld, July 2017: http://ibisworld.com

Lawn Maintenance & Service		
SIC 0782-06	NAICS 561730	

Rules of Thumb

➢ 50–60% of annual sales plus inventory

➢ 2–2.75 x SDE plus inventory

➢ 1.7–3 x EBIT

➢ 2–4 x EBITDA

Pricing Tips

- Multiples vary based on several factors, with the most important being the percentage of recurring revenues. Lawn care (fertilization & weed control companies) and landscape maintenance companies receive higher multiples than construction-oriented businesses. Larger companies (lawn care companies with revenues in excess of $1 million and maintenance companies with revenues in excess of $2.5 million) tend to get higher multiples. Companies with EBITDA margins in line with industry benchmarks will usually get a higher multiple.
- The age and condition of the fleet of vehicles and equipment used in the business may negatively impact the valuation if a buyer would expect to need a high level of capital expenditures.
- Companies with a larger working capital requirement (more money tied up in accounts receivable) may receive a lower valuation.
- Pre-billing or post-billing of clients—pre-bill is more valuable.

Benchmark Data

- For additional Benchmark Data see Landscaping Services
- Many companies in this industry classify labor costs as a part of direct costs in calculating gross profit. Benchmark profit percentages: maintenance

L

companies 10–15%, lawn care (fertilization and weed control companies) 15–30%, construction (design-build companies) 10–20%.

- Enhancements can/should be around 20% of the gross service revenue annually. 2-man residential crew should max generate $150k annually.

Expenses (% of Annual Sales)

Cost of Goods	20% to 45%
Occupancy Costs	02% to 05%
Payroll/Labor Costs	35% to 45%
Profit (pretax)	10% to 15%

Questions

- The most important question is why are you selling. Multiples are relatively low and so the payoff from a sale is often limited compared to the cash flow experienced owners can generate. As a result, it is very important to understand why an owner is selling and is it a good reason.
- What is your monthly service revenue? What types of properties do you do? (residential or commercial) What type of grass (blue, zosia, augustine, bahaia)? How many people in your crews? How many stops a day are they doing? Does your price per property include trimming, trees and shrubs (which drive labor)?
- Do they pre-bill or post-bill service? Is service billed monthly with cuts of 42 per year? What is the mix of service by commercial and residential? Density of the routes drives fuel and therefore labor and fuel consumption.

Industry Trend

- The industry weathered the Great Recession better than many observers expected. Business is recovering nicely and is expected to continue to expand as the construction sector strengthens. A robust merger and acquisition market has developed and is expected to continue in the near future led by high profile private equity transactions involving the industry's largest participants.

Expert Comments

Recognize the importance of both residential and commercial to cash flows due to terms.

Landscape maintenance companies are marketable since the industry has been impacted less compared to other businesses in the current economy. Their margins have been reduced, but businesses still need to maintain their properties.

Generally difficult to finance because of lack of assets

Seller Financing

- Smaller companies are usually sold with substantial seller financing, but transactions involving $2–$3 million purchase prices are often financed with SBA loans.
- Seller financing...guarantees are not the norm despite the rumors otherwise

Resources

- AmericanHort: http://www.americanhort.org
- National Association of Landscape Professionals: http://www.landscapeprofessionals.org
- Landscape Management magazine: http://www.landscapemanagement.net

- Turf Magazine: http://www.turfmagazine.com
- Lawn & Landscape: http://www.lawnandlandscape.com

Lenny's Subs

Franchise

Approx. Total Investment		$216,500–$369,000
SIC 5812-06	NAICS 722513	Number of Businesses/Units 150

Rules of Thumb

➤ 15–20% of annual sales plus inventory

Resources
- Lenny's Subs: http://www.lennys.com

Liberty Tax Service

Franchise

Approx. Total Investment		$58,700–$71,900
	NAICS 541213	Number of Businesses/Units 4,300

Rules of Thumb

➤ 45–50% of annual sales plus inventory

Resources
- Liberty Tax Service: http://www.libertytaxfranchise.com

Li'l Dino Subs

Franchise

Approx. Total Investment		$47,400–$240,800
	NAICS 722513	Number of Businesses/Units 15

Rules of Thumb

➤ 60% of annual sales plus inventory

Benchmark Data
- For Benchmark Data see Sandwich Shops

Limousine Services

SIC 4119-03	NAICS 485320	

Rules of Thumb

➤ 4 x EBITDA—companies with corporate accounts under contract plus vehicles

➤ 3 x EBITDA plus vehicles

➤ 50–55% of annual revenues plus vehicles

➤ 2–2.5 x SDE plus vehicles

L

Pricing Tips

- You need to look at Owner's Discretionary Cash Flow (also known as Seller's Discretionary Earnings). You also need to know whether the limousines are owned outright, financed or leased. Depreciation expense becomes an important consideration because the owned vehicles wear down rapidly and must be replaced to keep the business looking up-to-date.
- The figure needs to be adjusted for the fair market value of the vehicles less the outstanding debt.
- Note: Depreciation is usually considered an "add-back" and is therefore part of the Seller's Discretionary Earnings/EBIT/EBITDA. However, in this type of business it should not be added back as it is a necessary business expense. Vehicles are the mainstay of the business and replacement is ongoing business.

Benchmark Data

- "What percentages of your total gross revenues are devoted to the following business expenses?

Expenses	Small Operators (1–10 vehicles)	Medium Operators (11–50 vehicles)	Large Operators (51+ vehicles)
Payments	17%	14%	18%
Labor/Wages/Benefits	23%	31%	38%
Facilities Mortgage or Rent	7%	8%	7%
Technology/Systems	5%	5%	5%
Vehicle Insurance	15%	13%	9%
Vehicle Maintenance	11%	9%	9%
Fuel	16%	13%	10%
Marketing/Advertising/PR	6%	7%	6%

Source: "2015–2016 LCT Fact Book Industry Survey"

Expenses (% of Annual Sales)

Cost of Goods (auto purchases)	30% to 35%
Occupancy Costs	05% to 10%
Payroll/Labor Costs	25% to 35%
Profit (pretax)	10% to 20%

Questions

- You will want to see the repair and maintenance records for all the vehicles. You will want to know if there have been any accidents. You will want to know if there is outstanding litigation or workmen's compensation issues. What background checks and drug tests are performed on new hires?
- Look at the maintenance logs; have a mechanic check all vehicles.

Industry Trend

- "Increased demand from corporate travelers, tourists and private households is expected to result in the continued expansion of the Taxi and Limousine Services industry over the next five years. The industry mainly provides discretionary services that can be substituted when economic times are unfavorable. Therefore, taxis and limousines rely heavily on consumer and business spending, both of which are expected to improve gradually over the next five years. As a result of these positive trends, industry revenue is projected to increase at an annualized rate of 1.2% to $20.0 billion over the five years to 2021, including growth of 1.3% in 2017. However, growth during this period will be somewhat limited by external competition from Uber and other transportation network companies; the extent to which municipal and state governments can regulate these disruptors will greatly impact industry revenue moving forward.

"The luxury sedan and limousine segments of the industry are expected to lead growth over the next five years as businesses increase spending. Corporate profit is projected to increase an annualized 1.6% over the five years to 2021, reaching an all-time high of about $2.2 trillion. Moving forward, greater corporate profit means business travelers will increasingly opt for more convenient and personalized luxury town car services."

Source: IBISWorld Industry Outlook

- ". . . estimates that iPads save the company up to 8% on annual fuel costs and up to 25% savings in paper costs. It also reduces chauffeur phone calls to operations by 20%. Moreover, there are many benefits that can't be tied to hard dollars, but operators know from feedback and observation that iPads are spurring better customer service, customer relations, and most importantly, customer satisfaction."

Source: "Touch & Go: Tablet Access Speeds Up Operations," www.lctmag.com/technology/article/107388

Expert Comments

"Valuation Rules of Thumb: Limousine business owners commonly seek out a quick 'rule of thumb' to understand the value of their own business. Unfortunately, Rules of Thumb rarely apply to this industry. Relying on Rules of Thumb can be very misleading and very destructive if major financial decisions are based upon them. Depending on the size, profitability, location, and buyer of your business, a variety of valuation methods may be used to calculate the 'fair market value' for your business. Most likely, a combination of valuation methods will be applied and weighted accordingly to calculate the fair market value of your limousine business. When using an earnings valuation method, Seller's Discretionary Earnings (SDE) and Earnings Before Interest Taxes Depreciation & Amortization (EBITDA) are the most common formulas applied."

Source: http://www.limobusinessforsale.com/selling-limousine-business-101-part-1/

Seller Financing

- Seller should expect 50% down and offer 10-year amortization with a 3-year balloon at 6% interest.

Resources

- National Limousine Association—a lot of excellent information, with a study for members only: http://www.limo.org
- Limousine, Charter, and Tour: http://www.lctmag.com

Liquefied Petroleum Gas (Propane)		
SIC 5984-01	NAICS 454312	

Rules of Thumb

➢ 130% of annual sales plus inventory

➢ 4 x EBIT

➢ 6 x EBITDA (Good double-check is 2.5 to 3.5 gross profit)

➢ 3–4 x SDE plus inventory

L

Pricing Tips
- EBITDA multiples can range from 4. to over 7 times, depending on volume, gross profit, tank control/ownership, potential blending opportunities and other factors.

Benchmark Data
- Tank ownership 70% or above; gross profit margins vary greatly by market but companies with a minimum of $ 0.70/ Gal GP is appealing to most acquirers.
- COGs and GP margins vary greatly from company to company, area by area; as such there is no real average. GP can vary from $.35 cents per gallon sold to well over $2.00 per gallon, depending on many factors. Net Income and EBITDA amounts and percentages can also vary greatly.
- Can vary considerably by company, depending on customer mix between residential, commercial, farm & industrial type customer.

Expenses (% of Annual Sales)

Cost of Goods	40% to 50%
Occupancy Costs	02% to 05%
Payroll/Labor Costs	15% to 25%
Profit (pretax)	15%

Questions
- 5 years' financials and gallonage history; gross profit per gallon by segment of business; complete list of assets including tank inventory, bulk plants, trucks, etc.; real estate appraisal.
- Customer concentration, competition, age of fleet, tenure/age of employees, reason for exit
- Company ownership of customer tanks & cylinders is an important consideration. Where the company owns most of the customer field equipment, and there are good gross profits, a much better value can be obtained.

Industry Trend
- "And even with the downturn in crude oil prices since 2014, U.S. natural gas production has continued to increase. Forecasts call for output to rise above 30 trillion cubic feet (TCF) in 2020 and reach 40 TCF in 2035. At the same time, Marcellus gas production has proven to be extremely resilient and has not been significantly affected by the downturn in crude oil prices. Production has now grown to more than 18 million standard cubic feet per day (mmscfd)."
  Source: "Shale Revolution Changes Everything in Northeast," https://bpnews.com/index.php/publications/magazine/current-issue/1264-shale-revolution-changes-everything-in-northeast
- "ICF projects consumer propane sales to grow by about 800 million gallons (9 percent) between 2014 and 2025. Most of the growth will come from the propane engine fuel market, although lower propane prices associated with the growth in domestic propane supply and lower oil prices will also make propane more competitive in traditional propane markets, including residential and commercial space heating, and forklift markets."
  Source:http://www.afdc.energy.gov/uploads/publication/2016_propane_market_outlook.pdf

Expert Comments
The last 2 years of warm winters have impacted volume and earnings.

Capital intensive business; supply displacements during peak winter season; high level of training and technical expertise required to install and maintain equipment in the field; CDL requirements for drivers and technicians.

"If the objective is to sell in three to five years, important factors to consider include:

- ✓ Increase profitability. Retail propane companies are typically valued, bought and sold based on applying a multiple to the EBITDA (earnings before interest, income tax, depreciation and amortization).
- ✓ Focus on developing good records (financial, operational, employee, safety, etc.).
- ✓ Book all revenues for a minimum of three years.
- ✓ Stop selling tanks to customers. Buyers like high company tank ownership for multiple reasons. It increases the ability to keep the customers, and it shelters income for the buyer as they can restart the depreciation schedule on acquired assets. If a customer leases a tank, make sure you have a signed lease (by the customer) on file for each tank in the field. (Goes back to record keeping).
- ✓ Increase other income where available, such as charging tank rent to the customers who lease a tank (which also helps confirm who owns the tank).
- ✓ Work on improving the trends of the company.
- ✓ If you are considering selling within the next 12 months, get your records in order. It may be too late to make changes to profitability, but have good records available for due diligence. Buyers won't pay you for what they can't see."

Source: http://www.lpgasmagazine.com/in-the-know-factors-to-consider-when-selling-a-propane-businesses/

Large amount of capital needed for infrastructure & equipment, as well as for trucks and tanks; seasonal sales volume affects working capital requirements, depending on time of year.

Hire a professional intermediary who has extensive experience in the propane industry as offers for these types of businesses vary widely.

Seller Financing
- 100% all cash transactions typically (except for Invent & A/Recs which are paid within 90–180 days typically); non-compete allocations vary somewhat and these payments are sometimes tied to a payout period of 3–5 years
- Typically uses outside financing
- Typically cash at closing for fixed assets; intangibles are sometimes financed over five years.

Resources
- National Propane Gas Association: http://www.npga.org
- Propane Canada: http://www.northernstar.ab.ca
- Propane Education & Research Council: http://www.propanecouncil.org
- LP Gas Magazine: http://www.lpgasmagazine.com
- Butane-Propane News (BPN): http://www.bpnews.com

Liquor Stores/Package Stores (Beer, Wine & Liquor Stores)

SIC 5921-02	NAICS 445310	Number of Businesses/Units 46,493

Rules of Thumb

➢ 35–45% of annual sales plus inventory

➢ 2–4 x SDE plus inventory

➢ 2.5–3.5 x EBITDA

➢ 3–3.5 x EBIT

Pricing Tips

- Although 40% of revenue is the current rule of thumb, the following must be taken into consideration: gross profit, occupancy expense, location, category sales and payroll expense. (Keep in mind that every state has its own liquor laws and regulations.).
- Stores with sales above $1M are more desirable.
- Lottery Commission good indicator of area. Long hours and delivery reduce purchase price. Competition in area and parking are big concerns.
- Gross profit should be 24–39%, occupancy expense no more than 7.5%, and payroll expense 7% of revenue.
- Stores doing less than $1MM are trading at a lower multiple.
- Old inventory or lack of long, reasonable lease creates an un-marketable store.
- The percentage to gross is between 40–50% depending on factors such as rent, payroll, gross profit. SDE will fluctuate as well between 2.5–3.25%.

Benchmark Data

Statistics (Beer, Wine & Liquor Stores)

Number of Establishments	46,493
Average Profit Margin	3.0%
Revenue per Employee	$308,500
Average Number of Employees	3.8
Average Wages per Employee	$22,396

Products and Services Segmentation

Liquor	42.1%
Wine	32.4%
Beer	25.1%
Other	0.4%

Industry Costs

Profit	3.0%
Wages	7.3%
Purchases	74.9%
Depreciation	0.7%
Marketing	0.7%
Rent & Utilities	4.6%
Other	8.8%

- A store with payroll at 7% of revenue, occupancy expense between 3–7%, and gross profit of 25% is very marketable.

- Stores with revenue under $1M trade at lower SDE multiples and are essentially valued on the demand and need of the full retail liquor license. Stores with higher margins and higher sales of wine trade at higher multiples.
- Profit margin of 30% or higher typical to stores with high volume wine sales are very desirable and will trade at a higher multiple.
- Gross margins on retail sales should be at least 25%.

Expenses (% of Annual Sales)

Cost of Goods	65% to 80%
Occupancy Costs	05% to 15%
Payroll/Labor Costs	05% to 12%
Profit (pretax)	08% to 15%

Questions

- Reason for selling, lease term, gross profit, payroll expense, any additional income and category breakdown, i.e., beer, wine, liquor.
- What tier pricing is current ownership purchasing under? What are the category breakdowns of beer vs. wine vs liquor?
- Hours owner works? Delivery? Lottery? Employees' length of employment? Equipment maintenance records, compressors, HVAC etc.
- Cash flow, gross profits, occupancy expense, payroll expense and category percentage mix.
- Profit margin, category breakdown. How does the seller buy from the wholesalers?
- Review the sales and expenses over a two- or three-year period. See what trends are, up or down. Is theft a problem? Most sellers are either burned out or not making money.
- Seller: true margins, sales trends and mix; buyer: any experience in industry, reason for purchasing.
- Closest competition, term of lease, payroll cost, how computer system controls inventory and ordering. Do they work on margins or markup? How do store margins compare to any stores within 2–3 miles? How did they arrive at selling price? How would they grow the business, and how long will they provide training and distance for a covenant not to compete?
- Is there an option on the property or is it owned by the seller? What competition is nearby? Are there any other licenses available in the town? Do you owe any back taxes or fees that would hold up the transfer of the liquor license?
- What are your sales tax numbers and are you current?
- Security/surveillance system in place? Theft/shrinkage.

Industry Trend

- Liquor stores in Maryland are highly sought after by buyers from NJ, NY, DE and GA.
- In the Massachusetts marketplace there is a roll-up taking place. Multiple store owners are acquiring other locations in order to get to the maximum amount of licenses allowed in the state of Massachusetts (7). It is a strong seller's marketplace and we are seeing stores trade at multiples higher than previous years; inventory for strong performing stores is low (stores over $1M++). License values in capped towns are also at record high levels.
- The smaller volume stores closing and selling the liquor licenses. Larger stores thriving with bigger Gross Sales.

L

Expert Comments

Pay strict attention to the tax returns. Verify sales by looking at the monthly revenue reported to the comptroller's office.

The demand in Maryland is high for larger volume stores, $2M and above in annual revenue.

You need to be aggressive if in acquisition mode. There is no sitting on the sidelines; you are either a seller or buyer; there is no middle ground.

High grossing stores in proven locations are very hard to replicate, however the license expansion in the Massachusetts marketplace has allowed big box retailers and grocery stores to obtain more licenses and become strong competitors.

Be prepared to spend long hours in the store. Computerizing the business, if possible, will make running a successful operation much much easier.

"Liquor store owners have a reputation in the business world for skimming cash and keeping poor books (a very easy habit for some owners to fall into when dealing with a cash-heavy business). Although credit/debit cards are being increasingly used, this affects the potential buyer because it may be impossible to determine the business's real profits. The seller may also factor unreported income into his asking price, and employees may be following the owner's lead and skimming cash as well. It may be necessary to reconstruct the financials, but the buyer must insist that the seller provide ample documentation to support the asking price. However, if the buyer is adept at keeping books, then better financials may be all the business needs to thrive more successfully than with the previous owner."

Source: http://www.georgeandco.com/5-things-know-buying-liquor-store/

Ease of replication is restricted to local licensing rules.

Do your due diligence on competition and what big box stores could be coming into your geographic area that could impact business.

Good liquor businesses are in high demand, far more buyers than sellers.

Work with the seller to verify sales. Pay attention to details; do not try to reinvent the wheel.

Seller Financing

- Recently SBA financing has become available. This is typical for lack of hard assets as collateral. Seller financing with typically no less than 50% down.
- It is typical for short-term inventory financing and or seller note of 10% of sale price.
- Seller financing required. Usually 1/3 to 1/2 half down payment plus the inventory at cost.

Resources

- IBISWorld, August 2017: http://ibisworld.com
- Massachusetts Package Stores Association: http://masspack.org/

Little Caesars Pizza

	Franchise
Approx. Total Investment	$314,000–$1,335,500
Estimated Annual Sales/Unit	$856,300
NAICS 722513	

Rules of Thumb

➤ 55% of annual sales plus inventory

Resources

- Little Caesars: http://www.littlecaesars.com

Lock & Key Shops

SIC 7699-62	NAICS 561622	Number of Businesses/Units 21,921

Rules of Thumb

➤ 40–45% of annual sales plus inventory

Benchmark Data

Statistics (Locksmiths)

Number of Establishments	21,921
Average Profit Margin	4.7%
Revenue per Employee	$59,900
Average Number of Employees	1.5
Average Wages per Employee	$18,886

Products and Services Segmentation

Nonresidential security system installation and repair	51.4%
Residential security system installation and repair	23.4%
Key cutting and duplication services	8.6%
Resale of locks and security merchandise	8.3%
Other services	4.4%
Residential and nonresidential system services with monitoring	3.9%

Major Market Segmentation

Businesses	55.5%
Households	28.4%
Government entities	9.6%
Not-for-profit organizations	6.5%

Industry Costs

Profit	4.7%
Wages	31.5%
Purchases	33.5%
Depreciation	1.1%
Marketing	3.2%
Rent & Utilities	4.9%
Other	21.1%

Resources
- Associated Locksmiths of America: http://www.aloa.org
- Institutional Locksmiths' Association: http://www.ilanational.org
- IBISWorld, November 2016: http://ibisworld.com

		Franchise
Logan Farms Honey Glazed Hams		
Approx. Total Investment		$338,475–$418,125
	NAICS 445210	Number of Businesses/Units 11

Rules of Thumb
➤ 30% of annual sales plus inventory

Resources
- Logan Farms: http://www.loganfarms.com

Lumberyards		
SIC 5211-42	NAICS 444190	Number of Businesses/Units 48,014

Rules of Thumb
➤ 40% of annual sales includes inventory

➤ 4 x EBIT

➤ 4–6 x SDE includes inventory

➤ 4–6 x EBITDA

Pricing Tips
- These comments would apply to lumberyards dealing with contractors, sometimes called ProYards, not home centers (DIY business) . . . if profits (EBT) are 5%–10% of sales, the business would likely sell for 1.5 times book value; less profitable lumberyards sell for book value, or in an asset sale. In an asset sale, if profits are above 5% EBT, use lesser of cost or market on the inventory and FMV on equipment and real estate used in the business, plus one year's EBT for goodwill/non-compete.
- The major buyers were offering to pay for the best yards 5.5 x EBITDA

Benchmark Data

Statistics (Lumber & Building Material Stores)
Number of Establishments	48,014
Average Profit Margin	4.0%
Revenue per Employee	$310,400
Average Number of Employees	6.2
Average Wages per Employee	$44,893

Products and Services Segmentation

Lumber and other structural building materials.. 56.0%
Hardware, tools, plumbing and electrical supplies.. 23.2%
Doors and windows 10.4%
Flooring and roofing materials 8.6%
Other... 1.8%

Major Market Segmentation

Professional Contractors 60.0%
Other... 20.0%
Do-it-for-me customers 10.0%
Do-it-yourself customers... 10.0%

Industry Costs

Profit 4.0%
Wages... 14.6%
Purchases... 60.4%
Depreciation... 0.9%
Marketing 1.6%
Rent & Utilities 4.3%
Other... 14.2%

Market Share

Builders FirstSource 7.3%

Expenses (% of Annual Sales)

Cost of Goods... 75%
Occupancy Costs... 03% to 05%
Payroll/Labor Costs 20%
Profit (pretax)... 02% to 05%

Questions
- Why selling? Have audited 5 years' financials?
- Look carefully at profit, and if future earnings are possible.

Expert Comments

Lumberyards are very difficult to duplicate. High dollar investment keeps most competition out of a market. It also requires a minimum of 2 acres to runs a $5 million lumberyard. Cost of land these days makes it impossible to start a new store.

Seller Financing
- Very few sell on owner financing; the sales are generally to existing lumber dealers.

Resources
- National Lumber & Building Material Dealers Association: http://www.dealer.org
- IBISWorld, December 2016: http://ibisworld.com

M

MAACO Auto Painting and Bodyworks

Approx. Total Investment	$250,000–$350,000

	NAICS 811121	Number of Businesses/Units 457

Rules of Thumb

➢ 40% of annual sales plus inventory

Resources

- MAACO Auto Painting and Bodyworks: http://www.maacofranchise.com

Machine Shops

SIC 3599-03	NAICS 332710	Number of Businesses/Units 18,884

Rules of Thumb

➢ 50–65% of annual revenues includes inventory

➢ 3–5 x SDE plus inventory

➢ 4.5–7 x EBIT

➢ 3–5 x EBITDA

Pricing Tips

- The more the company has in the way of tier-one clients, contracts for critical components, and a history of reliable deliveries and quality, the higher the multiple.
- Valuation in this industry is tied to a multitude of factors: size of the shop, facilities list and type/condition of machinery, client concentration, industries served, age of machinists, backlog, WIP, etc. Multiples of gross sales are meaningless in this industry.
- "There are many factors that go into developing the EBITDA multiple, and here are just a few:
  - ✓ Position in a market. A company's position in a market, whether it is local, national, or international, also has a bearing on its value. A market leader is likely to have a higher value, yet a company's rate of growth or decline in a market will also be a factor. For example, a relatively small market share can be viewed positively if the company has shown sustained growth, while a large market share might be viewed negatively if the share has been steadily eroding.
  - ✓ Products and services. Products and services offered can also impact value. New products and services may provide greater sales potential in the future, while mature products, although likely a major reason for past sales, may be at the end of their life cycle and unable to offer much in the way of sales growth. A company with an obvious lack of any new products and services could be viewed as lacking innovation and take a hit on its valuation. As with customers, the right mix of products and services is important. If a majority of sales comes from one or two products or services, there is more risk than if a wide variety of products contributes equally.

✓ Assets. A company with a great deal of new, updated equipment may have a higher value, especially if the equipment has demonstrated productivity or quality improvements. Buildings, land, solar panels, and other energy-efficient and cost-saving systems can also increase a company's value.

✓ Technology. How a company develops or utilizes technology can go a long way in increasing value.

✓ Management team. An experienced, skilled management team also can increase a company's value. Of course, any positives associated with the management team can only last as long as the management team stays intact."

Source: http://www.mmsonline.com/columns/what-is-the-value-of-your-business

■ Client concentration remains an issue. Deduct 1 x for any concentration over 50%. Proprietary processes and expertise in working exotic metals/materials, add 1–2 X. ISO and other certifications along with lean processes, add 1 X. Five axis CAPEX adds 1–2 X. Important to examine the excess earnings approach when valuing a machine shop. Retrofit Bridgeports and other more labor-intensive equipment, deduct 1–2 X. In general, the larger the shop the higher the valuation multiples.

Benchmark Data

Statistics (Machine Shops)

Number of Establishments	18,884
Average Profit Margin	5.8%
Revenue per Employee	$160,900
Average Number of Employees	13.6
Average Wages per Employee	$50,527

Products and Services Segmentation

Milling	46.7%
Turning	25.9%
Other	11.3%
Grinding	9.1%
EDM and ECM	7.0%

Major Market Segmentation

Fabricated metal product markets	36.4%
Automotive, transportation and off-highway vehicle markets	13.8%
Industrial machinery and equipment markets (including components)	21.6%
Airline markets	9.3%
Medical markets	4.0%
Electronics and telecommunications markets	6.0%
Other markets	8.9%

Industry Costs

Profit	5.8%
Wages	31.4%
Purchases	34.1%
Depreciation	3.8%
Marketing	0.2%
Rent & Utilities	3.9%
Other	20.8%

M

- Sales should be at least $185K per employee per annum. If over $200K, the business is first class. If less than $150K, the business is not efficient.
- Smaller shops do not always put direct labor (machinists) or plant occupancy in COGS. Inventory is often stated for tax purposes. PE likes GP to be 70% or better. Capacity should be 70% or better. Backlog of orders tells a lot about the health (or lack thereof) of the shop.
- Watch for inconsistencies in reporting of COGS, i.e., is all occupancy under the line? Is only production labor in COGS? Is inventory accurately represented? Total inventory value of raw material, WIP and finished goods should be 10–15%. Average growth last 5 years has been 5–6%; watch for inconsistencies.
- Geographic location is important to buyers since machinery is expensive to move.
- Many shops like to get X dollars per hour per machine and then work towards 70%–80% capacity per machine or better.
- There are no major players in this industry.

Expenses (% of Annual Sales)

Cost of Goods	50% to 60%
Occupancy Costs	03% to 08%
Payroll/Labor Costs	30% to 35%
Profit (pretax)	05% to 15%

Questions

- 1) Concentration can be an issue in this business—sometimes 60% or more can be with one customer. Buyer needs to be assured that the relationship with customers is intact and will follow with a new owner. 2) Does the business rely on the owner or the company? 3) Are there sufficient skilled and knowledgeable supervisors/managers to help with the transition? 4) How much working capital is needed during seasonable slumps or plant closures during vacations?
- Backlog, client concentration, CAPEX, aging of receivables, organized labor, profit margins per category of equipment.
- Any equipment need to be replaced, account concentration issues are very important to be informed of.
- Personal salary & benefits, any unutilized or underutilized assets

Industry Trend

- "U.S. machine tool exports valued $175.58 million in March, up 6.2 percent from February's total of $165.29 million. Exports for year-to-date 2017 totaled $340.87, an increase of 7.1 percent when compared to the same period for 2016. Monthly machine tool imports valued $410.25 million in March, up 36.5 percent from February's total of $300.65 million. Imports for year-to-date 2017 totaled $710.91 million, a decrease of 6.1 percent when compared to the same period for 2016."

Source: May 10, 2017,

- http://www.amtonline.org/GatherIndustryIntelligence/IndustryTrends/
- This business is on a consistent growth track for the foreseeable future.
- The trend has been upwards and other experts in the industry expect continued growth.
- Offshore competition in certain areas remains a threat.
- Industry indications are growth through 2020.

Expert Comments

Sellers need to have an expert broker on their side to manage the sale process to obtain the best possible price and terms. Buyers need to ensure they are totally comfortable with any long-term contracts in place (or promised) and to ensure that gross margin integrity applies to all SKUs.

It usually takes a company a minimum of ten to an average of fifteen years or more to reach "critical mass" in this business. That is: consistent margins of 45% or more; minimum EBITDA of $1 million with minimum gross annual revenues of $5 million. There are 20 years of orders for airplanes, both passenger and defense, and in most cases, the large companies either prefer or have to buy American.

Like many industries, machine shops were affected by the recession but are rebounding with the automotive, medical and aerospace industries. CAPEX can be very expensive with pallet loading & auto tool changing 4+ axis machinery making barrier to entry higher than many industries. PE has a renewed interest in this industry especially those with excess capacity or a proprietary product(s). Shops producing 70%+ of capacity are considered healthy.

Barrier to entry becoming higher as cost of high-tech equipment increases and good programmers are less abundant. OEM's are experiencing slightly better growth and accordingly machine shop's backlogs are increasing. Gross income per employee should be in the $200K per range. Does the shop do a lot of prototyping/short runs or is it more of a mid- to long-run shop? Cost savings realized from longer runs.

Get involved with an industry association. Meet other owners. Stay abreast of new technology. Have equipment checked out as part of due diligence. Find out about quality issues with major customers. Focus on the retention of employees after the transaction is completed.

Seller Financing

- Small amount of seller financing—maybe 15% to 20%; buyer needs to have at least 50% in cash.
- Rarely do we see much seller financing, however earnouts are common due to client concentration.
- Generally, it is a blend of seller financing and outside financing unless the business is asset heavy.

Resources

- The Association for Manufacturing Technology: http://www.amtonline.org
- Fabricators and Manufacturers Association, International: http://www.fmanet.org
- Precision Machine Products Association: http://www.PMPA.org
- IBISWorld, October 2017: http://ibisworld.com

Franchise	
MaggieMoo's Ice Cream and Treatery	°
Approx. Total Investment	$25,000–$250,000
Estimated Annual Sales/Unit	$200,000
SIC 2024-98	NAICS 722515	Number of Businesses/Units 159

Rules of Thumb
➢ 25% of annual sales plus inventory

Resources
- MaggieMoo's Ice Cream and Treatery: http://www.maggiemoos.com

Franchise	
Maid Brigade	
Approx. Total Investment	$85,000–$115,000
	NAICS 561720	Number of Businesses/Units 420

Rules of Thumb
➢ 45% of annual sales

Resources
- Maid Brigade: http://www.maidbrigadefranchise.com

Maid Services		
	NAICS 561720	

Rules of Thumb
➢ 1.5 x SDE plus inventory

➢ 35–40% of annual sales plus inventory

Benchmark Data
- For Benchmark Data see Janitorial Services

Industry Trend
- "According to a study by the investment bank Scott-Macon, the cleaning and janitorial industry is expected to grow faster between 2014 and 2020, at 4.3%, than it did in previous years (2.7% growth per year between 2010 and 2013). As a result, the market sector is expected to be worth nearly $60 billion in 2016, and to surpass that amount by 2017.

  "One of the reasons the cleaning services industry can undergo such growth is because of the low barrier of entry to start a successful cleaning company. In fact, the 4 largest companies in the industry account for less than 10% of the available market, with much of the rest taken up by smaller, often independent companies."

  Source: http://www.slideshare.net/PSJanitorial/cleaning-industry-trends-for-2016

Resources
- AW Cleaning Services: http://awcleaning.com

Mail and Parcel Centers (Business Centers)		
SIC 7389	NAICS 561431	Number of Businesses/Units 25,611

Rules of Thumb

➢ 2–2.75 x EBIT

➢ 45–50% of annual sales includes inventory, less direct cost of goods sold (pass-throughs, e.g., stamps, money

➢ 2–3 x SDE for national franchises includes inventory

➢ 2–3 x EBITDA

Pricing Tips
- Generally, the value is a function of cash flow to owner SDE.
- Independents & Non-UPS Store franchises:
  - ✓ SDE <$50K, value is generally FFE (at FMV excluding buildout) + Inventory at cost + AR
  - ✓ SDE $50K–$100K, 1.5–2.5 x SDE
  - ✓ SDE $100K–$200K, 2.5–3.5 x SDE
  - ✓ SDE >$200K (rarely), 3–4 x SDE

  UPS Store franchises sell at 20% to 30% premium to above depending on costs for CURE (Compliance Upgrade Review Estimate); buyer pays transfer fees.
- Easy to own and operate along with endless add-on services (i.e., bookkeeping, legal documents, printing, fingerprinting, passport photos, etc.) make this a very appealing business for first-time business buyers.
- Those netting up to $40,000 sell at a 1 multiple. Those netting $50,000 to $60,000 sell for a 1.5 multiple of provable net income. From $70,000 to $85,000 of provable net, the multiple is usually 2. Those netting $90,000 and up, the multiple is usually 2.25 to 2.5.

Benchmark Data

Statistics (Business Service Centers)

Number of Establishments	25,611
Average Profit Margin	6.0%
Revenue per Employee	$108,800
Average Number of Employees	3.2
Average Wages per Employee	$31,527

Products and Services Segmentation

Copying and reproduction services	53.4%
Postal and shipping services and mailbox rentals	21.7%
Printing Services	11.6%
Other	11.0%
Packaging and labeling services	2.3%

M

Major Market Segmentation

Small Businesses	57.2%
Individuals and households	29.2%
Financial institutions	7.6%
Government	3.5%
Healthcare service sectors	2.5%

Industry Costs

Profit	6.0%
Wages	28.9%
Purchases	39.1%
Depreciation	2.2%
Marketing	0.7%
Rent & Utilities	3.3%
Other	19.8%

Market Share

United Parcel Service Inc.	23.0%
FedEx Corporation	14.5%
FedEx Corporation	13.0%

- Mailbox rental income should cover store rent.
- Must have an average 50% mark up on shipping (USPS, Fed Ex, UPS, etc.)
- There are a lot of startup stores or lower performing stores whose annual sales are under $200K. Be careful if it goes below $150K in annual sales, as fixed costs will eat up your profit.
- Location is important, do not need a lot of SF. Keep the rent low.
- Mailbox rentals should cover all operating expenses.
- Most stores must be doing at least $150,000 in annual sales before they start showing any real profit. Advertising is very important; stores should not skimp on advertising. The client base is primarily within a radius of a few miles.

Expenses (% of Annual Sales)

Cost of Goods	45% to 50%
Occupancy Costs	10% to 15%
Payroll/Labor Costs	15% to 20%
Profit (pretax)	10% to 20%

Questions

- What are the revenue splits by product lines?
- What is price of a pack of 20 first class stamps? Do they have any leased equipment? What is their POS system? (PostalMate is industry leader)
- How much prepaid mailbox rents have been collected; buyer should get this amount as cash back at the closing.
- Is the notary income being reported? If not, look at notary's journal to get idea of volume. Any accounts receivable (business accounts)? Any trade for mail box rental? Do you want to slap customers who complain about you selling stamps for a penny or two more than the post office?
- Do they charge for packing labor? How much? If not, this is a pure profit area to explore! It does depend on their markup otherwise.

Industry Trend
- Electronic at-home preprinting of postage and UPS/FedEx will continue to put downward margin pressure on the industry. Successful operators will add higher margin services to compensate.
- Further diversification into add-on products and services

Expert Comments

Look for mailbox rentals > Rent (including NNN)

Industry profitability is trending down as more consumers are opting to print their UPS or FedEx labels at home and drop off at these stores. Drop-off revenue is typically $0.35–$1.25 per piece and does not cover the labor cost for customer counter service and handling. More profitable stores will add printing, especially wide format (e.g., banners) and other higher margin services.

Buyer—plan on adding on products and services. Seller—get "Broker Price Opinions" from a few brokers and offer seller financing to get the highest sale price.

This is a proven successful business model; however, it's a mature industry that is always threatened with new technologies.

Seller Financing
- CFO > $75k + good, matching tax returns = easy SBA 7a deal with 20% down
- If tax returns have lot of seller addbacks, then seller financing 75% of the time:
- price < $150,000: 50% down, 50% SF for 5 years at Prime + 3%
- price > $150,000: 1/3 down, 2/3 SF for 5 years at Prime + 3%
- Outside financing is more typical due to sellers' hesitancy to finance the sale.

Resources
- Association of Mail and Business Centers (AMBC): https://ambc1.wildapricot.org/
- IBISWorld, April 2017: http://ibisworld.com
- Retail Shipping Associates (RSA): http://www.rscentral.org/

Mail Order		
SIC 5961-02	NAICS 454110	Number of Businesses/Units 58,082

Rules of Thumb
- 6 x EBIT
- 5 x EBITDA
- 80% of annual sales includes inventory

Pricing Tips
- Valuation of firm typically based on house account quality (house database of customers) and EBITDA sustainability and growth

M

Benchmark Data

Statistics (Mail Order)

Number of Establishments	58,082
Average Profit Margin	5.9%
Revenue per Employee	$652,400
Average Number of Employees	3.9
Average Wages per Employee	$51,218

Products and Services

Health and beauty products	62.2%
Other	15.4%
Computer hardware, software and office supplies	7.3%
Home furnishings	6.9%
Clothing, jewelry and accessories	5.8%
Sporting goods, toys, games and hobby items	2.4%

Industry Costs

Profit	5.9%
Wages	7.9%
Purchases	58.5%
Depreciation	0.7%
Marketing	3.7%
Rent & Utilities	3.7%
Other	19.6%

Market Share

Express Scripts Holding Company	31.4%

Expenses (% of Annual Sales)

Cost of Goods	60% to 67%
Occupancy Costs	01%
Payroll/Labor Costs	01%
Profit (pretax)	09% to 10%

Questions
- What experience do you have in the catalog or direct marketing industry?

Industry Trend
- "The Mail Order Industry is expected to continue its slow growth over the five years to 2022, as online shopping continues to steal customers and women's labor participation continues to decline. Revenue is expected to increase at an annualized rate of 1.3% over the five-year period to total $156.6 billion in 2022. Industry performance over the next five years is projected to be stronger than during the previous five-year period, as both discretionary spending and corporate profit are expected to accelerate, which will contribute to industry-related revenue growth. However, industry profit is expected to slightly decrease as wages pick up and the US dollar's growing strength slows.

  "As revenue growth is begins to accelerate, the number of industry enterprises will also begin to rise. Over the five years to 2022, the number of enterprises is expected to increase at an annualized rate of 1.0% to total 60,060 in 2022.

Industry employment will also increase, rising at an annualized rate of 0.9% over the period to total 237,479 employees. However, as the majority of new enterprises will be nonemployers, employment growth will come from already established companies, contributing to the continual increase in market share concentration.

"A main revenue stream for the industry is sales through TV home-shopping networks. However, changing consumer preferences away from traditional TV to online streaming services like Netflix and Hulu could jeopardize sales from this stream. Over the five years to 2022, the number of cable TV subscriptions, which distributes home shopping programs such as QVC and HSN, is estimated to decline at an annualized rate of 0.9%. As the number of cable TV subscriptions decreases, home-shopping networks' customer base also decreases."

Source: IBISWorld Industry Outlook

Expert Comments

Straightforward estimate of risk-reward. Margins declining, but from high past levels. Ease of replication reduces going concern values. Consolidation occurring.

Resources
- National Mail Order Association—an excellent site, loaded with information: http://www.nmoa.org
- IBISWorld, May 2017: http://ibisworld.com

Mama Fu's Asian House		Franchise
Approx. Total Investment		$407,000–$663,000
SIC 5812-08	NAICS 722513	Number of Businesses/Units 9

Rules of Thumb
➢ 30% of annual sales plus inventory

Resources
- Mama Fu's Asian House: http://www.mamafus.com

Management Consulting		
	NAICS 541611	Number of Businesses/Units 745,863

Rules of Thumb
➢ 2.5 x SDE

Pricing Tips
- "So What's My Firm Worth? That may be the question that popped into your head, so let's deal with it first. There are many factors involved in a valuation, however, in simple terms your firm is worth a multiple of the last 12 months profits.

  "Of course, there are substantial variations in the numbers. For example, the average EBIT multiple may be 10, but the range goes from 4 to 40, and there are many other factors to consider for the particular circumstances of your firm. Also, as I'll go on to explain, the real value of your firm is in your ability to reliably predict your profits into the future."

Source: http://managementconsultingnews.com/article-paul-collins-1/

- "A firm with a track record of erratic revenues and profits sends a concerning message to buyers and investors, so if you can show sustained revenue and profit growth and high margins, you have an attractive proposition. Before you take your firm to market, you want to be able to demonstrate consistent growth over the last 3 years. Sales and profit growth is a reflection, or an output, of your performance in the other 7 levers."

Source: http://managementconsultingnews.com/article-paul-collins-2/

- "There are four key performance indicators that would be taken into account in a valuation:
  - ✓ Pipeline-A premium value would be placed on a firm with 75% of its pipeline as business booked over the next three months and 50% booked over the next six months
  - ✓ Sales Growth-15% consistent year-on-year growth would be viewed as strong, but 25% would win a premium valuation
  - ✓ Repeat Business-A firm with 80% repeat business would be seen as strong, and 90% would win a premium value
  - ✓ Client Relationships-Valuation would increase where long-term client relationships are prominent, and a discount would be applied if too many eggs are in one basket in terms of client concentration.

"The best time to sell is when the following three areas are in line and on the increase:
  - ✓ A peak in market activity (such as now)
  - ✓ A peak in your own profits
  - ✓ A peak in your market sector.

"If these three things coincide and you go to market at a time when you have an excellent sales track record and clients are singing your praises, then you stand a very good chance of getting the maximum value for your firm."

Source: http://managementconsultingnews.com/article-paul-collins-3/

Benchmark Data

Statistics (Management Consulting)

Number of Establishments	745,863
Average Profit Margin	11.5%
Revenue per Employee	$145,900
Average Number of Employees	2.1
Average Wages per Employee	$61,370

Products and Services Segmentation

Corporate strategy	38.9%
Marketing and sales	19.4%
Organizational design	13.4%
Process and operations management	8.8%
Financial advisory	8.0%
Human resources advisory	6.9%
IT strategy	4.6%

Major Market Segmentation

Financial services companies	22.7%
Government organizations	19.2%
Consumer products companies	15.8%
Manufacturing companies	10.5%
Technology and media companies	9.3%
Life science and healthcare companies	7.7%
Energy and utilities companies	7.4%
Individuals and non-profit organizations	7.4%

Industry Costs

Profit	11.5%
Wages	41.7%
Purchases	11.7%
Depreciation	1.0%
Marketing	1.7%
Rent & Utilities	3.5%
Other	28.9%

Market Share

Accenture PLC	3.4%
Deloitte Touche Tohmatsu	2.9%
McKinsey & Company	1.5%

Resources

- IBISWorld, March 2017: http://ibisworld.com

Manufacturing—Aluminum Extruded Products		
	NAICS 331318	

Rules of Thumb

➢ 50% of annual sales plus inventory

➢ 6 x SDE plus inventory

➢ 5 x EBIT

➢ 4 x EBITDA

Pricing Tips

- Nature of contract with metal supplier; this is a low added value business.

Benchmark Data

- At least a ratio of added value/salaries cost (total) of 2.0.

Expenses (% of Annual Sales)

Cost of Goods	70%
Occupancy Costs	05%
Payroll/Labor Costs	35%
Profit (pretax)	08%

M

Questions
- Customer base, nature of metal contracts

Industry Trend
- Growing

Manufacturing—Chemical		
SIC 2899-05	NAICS 32599	Number of Businesses/Units 1,807

Rules of Thumb
> .5–2 x annual sales includes inventory

> 4–9 x EBITDA

Pricing Tips
- "As the owner of a chemical manufacturing firm, you may want to begin evaluating your options and take advantage of this rare opportunity known as a Seller's Market by planning ahead for your future and the future of your business. Every business owner should know the value of their business, even if they are not ready to sell, and we can tell you. To give you an idea of what formulas are used during the valuation process, we have provided some multiples below. Please keep in mind that many factors go into valuing a business and only a professional broker can tell you the true value."

  Source: http://www.vikingmergers.com/blog/2015/how-to-sell-a-chemical-plant-for-the-best-price
- Industry is very diverse (some businesses are state-of-the-art/cutting edge, some are very mature, and everything in between), therefore pricing depends on a variety of factors.

Benchmark Data

Statistics (Chemical Product Manufacturing)
Number of Establishments	1,807
Average Profit Margin	7.3%
Revenue per Employee	$694,200
Average Number of Employees	33.0
Average Wages per Employee	$63,688

Products and Services Segmentation
Other	36.0%
Custom-compounding of resins	28.4%
Photographic films, papers and plates	15.9%
Water-treating compounds	9.6%
Automotive chemicals	5.2%
Evaporated salt	2.8%
Gelatin	2.1%

Major Market Segmentation
Manufacturing sector	25.9%
Automobile industry	19.6%
Households	18.1%
Construction sector	15.6%
Other	3.9%

Industry Costs

Profit 7.3%
Wages 9.2%
Purchases 52.4%
Depreciation 1.6%
Marketing 0.1%
Rent & Utilities 2.1%
Other 27.3%

Expenses (% of Annual Sales)

Cost of Goods 25%
Occupancy Costs .... n/a
Payroll/Labor Costs .... n/a
Profit (pretax) 10%

Questions

- Normal due diligence type issues plus environmental/regulatory issues which are somewhat unique to the industry, and impact of overseas competition.

Industry Trend

- "North American chemical companies face workforce turnover issues, which if not resolved, could mean more unplanned operations disruptions, more hiring and training costs and more efforts to maintain safety - reports a new survey by Accenture (NYSE: ACN) and the American Chemistry Council (ACC). The survey was released today at the Council's annual business meeting.

  "Chemical companies face a shortage of experienced workers and must replace a substantial number of retiring baby boomers in the coming years. More than 20 percent of the chemicals workforce is approaching retirement in the next three to five years, said 40 percent of respondents.

  "If the aging workforce issue is not resolved in the next three to five years, 86 percent said the chemical industry's profitability will suffer significantly. This includes 49 percent of chemical companies that agree and 37 percent that strongly agree with this point of view at a time when industry expansion is expected to continue in North America."

  Source: "Turnover of Millennials and Other Workers Challenge North American Chemical Companies as Retirement Surge Looms, New Survey by Accenture and American Chemistry Reports," by Guy Cantwell, Matt Corser, Patrick Hurston, June 7, 2016, https://www.americanchemistry.com/Media/PressReleasesTranscripts/ACC-news-releases/Turnover-of-Millennials.html

- "The Society of Chemical Manufacturers and Affiliates (SOCMA) on Friday celebrated President Obama's signing into law the American Manufacturing Competitiveness Act of 2016 (H.R. 4923), bipartisan legislation that would create a Miscellaneous Tariff Bill (MTB) process to eliminate tariffs on inputs and other products that aren't produced or available in the United States.

  "'This landmark victory finally ends years of unnecessary tax increases on U.S. specialty chemical manufacturers, many of whom are already paying higher prices for raw materials not domestically produced,' said William E. Allmond, SOCMA Vice President of Government and Public Relations."

  Source: "President's Signing of New MTB Law Huge Victory for Specialty Chemical Manufacturers," May 23, 2016, http://www.socma.com/article/id/2095/presidents-signing-of-new-mtb-law-huge-victory-for-specialty-chemical-manufacturers

Expert Comments

Chemical industry in U.S. on upward trend because of natural gas availability in the U.S., making for lower raw material costs in many cases

Seller Financing

- 5 years

Resources

- Independent Chemical Information Service (ICIS): http://www.icis.com
- American Chemistry Council: http://www.americanchemistry.com
- IHS Chemical Week: http://www.chemweek.com
- Chemical & Engineering News: http://cen.acs.org
- The Society of Chemical Manufacturers and Affiliates (SOCMA): http://www.socma.com
- IBISWorld, June 2017: http://ibisworld.com

Manufacturing—Custom Architectural Woodwork and Millwork		
	NAICS 337212	

Rules of Thumb

➤ 3 x SDE includes inventory

Pricing Tips

- Growth and customer list affects multiple dramatically.
- Benchmarks

Expenses (% of Annual Sales)

Cost of Goods	50%
Occupancy Costs	10%
Payroll/Labor Costs	30%
Profit (pretax)	10%

Industry Trend

- China will affect every aspect of this industry. Must have niche to prosper.
- Most owners are getting older, and the industry will consolidate.

Expert Comments

China is becoming a big factor.

Manufacturing—Electrical		
	NAICS 33531	Number of Businesses/Units 2,126

Rules of Thumb

➤ 5 x EBITDA

Pricing Tips

- Client relationships and strength of long-term contracts is a major factor. Patents and proprietary processes must be evaluated. Work force productivity factor, minimum of $250K per man-year is essential.

Benchmark Data

Statistics (Electrical Equipment Manufacturing)

Number of Establishments	2,126
Average Profit Margin	5.9%
Revenue per Employee	$348,100
Average Number of Employees	53.3
Average Wages per Employee	$60,560

Products and Services Segmentation

Switches	31.4%
Motors and generators	27.3%
Transformers	27.3%
Relays and industrial controls	14.0%

Major Market Segmentation

Wholesalers	33.0%
Exports	32.4%
Retailers	11.8%
Utilities	11.7%
Downstream manufacturers	11.1%

Industry Costs

Profit	5.9%
Wages	17.5%
Purchases	50.7%
Depreciation	1.3%
Marketing	0.5%
Rent & Utilities	0.8%
Other	23.3%

Market Share

Eaton Corporation plc	10.2%
General Electric Company	7.5%
Schneider Electric SA	7.1%

Expenses (% of Annual Sales)

Cost of Goods	64%
Occupancy Costs	04%
Payroll/Labor Costs	07% to 08%
Profit (pretax)	12%

Seller Financing

- 5 years

Resources

- IBISWorld, February 2017: http://ibisworld.com

M

Manufacturing—Electrical Connectors

	NAICS 334510	

Rules of Thumb

➢ 3 x EBITDA

Pricing Tips

- Transferring the customers and good accounting of inventory are very important.
- Contract manufacturing companies sell for 3X SDE or under. Companies with proprietary products are 4–7 X SDE depending on growth.

Benchmark Data

- No customer bigger than 30%

Expenses (% of Annual Sales)

Cost of Goods	40% to 45%
Occupancy Costs	10%
Payroll/Labor Costs	30%
Profit (pretax)	10%

Questions

- How much engineering work do you do?

Industry Trend

- Major consolidation

Expert Comments

The industry is very cyclical.

Manufacturing—Food

	NAICS 311	

Rules of Thumb

➢ 4–7 x EBITDA

Pricing Tips

- Pricing Tips include brand, years in business, strong customer base and length of relationship with customers, vendor certifications (i.e., certified organic, 100% natural, etc.)

Benchmark Data

- Branded vs. private label, any notable long-term customers?
- Wide range, depending on product category, sales channel, branded vs. private label, etc.
- Food manufacturing gross margins (after material costs and direct labor) should be at least 40%, and preferably at least 50%.

M

Expenses (% of Annual Sales)

Cost of Goods	30% to 40%
Occupancy Costs	05%
Payroll/Labor Costs	10% to 15%
Profit (pretax)	05% to 10%

Questions

- Revenue, COGS, liabilities, owner involvement? Sales channel? Who are your customers? How long have you been supplying to these customers? Do you have contracts with clients? Any client that accounts for more than 10% of your sales? What is the production capacity? Type of equipment?

Industry Trend

- "According to the 2016 annual U.S. Food & Beverage Industry Study, released Tuesday by WeiserMazars LLP, a leading accounting, tax and advisory services firm, most food and beverage companies anticipate a significant increase in sales this year.

  "Survey participants—which were drawn from over 200 companies across the food and beverage industry—are confident sales will increase 14% compared to 2015 and project net profits will rise by 10%. Respondents attributed this growth prediction to secular industry trends currently favoring both private label and healthy/nutritious foods."

  Source: "WeiserMazars' Annual US Food And Beverage Industry Study Shows Companies Anticipate Substantial Sales Increase In 2016," June 14, 2016

Expert Comments

Food manufacturing businesses have high marketability

Seller Financing

- Depends on the size of the deal. Average seller financing is 2-10 years

Resources

- Food Engineering: http://www.foodengineeringmag.com/
- Food Manufacturing: http://www.foodmanufacturing.com

Manufacturing—Furniture/Household

SIC 2599-01	NAICS 33712	Number of Businesses/Units 9,605

Rules of Thumb

➤ 4–7 x EBITDA

Pricing Tips

- Size, growth, condition of plant, how profitable it is, place in the market, and management can play a part.

Benchmark Data

Statistics (Household Furniture Manufacturing)

Number of Establishments	9,605
Average Profit Margin	3.7%
Revenue per Employee	$194,900
Average Number of Employees	13.3
Average Wages per Employee	$37,942

Products and Services Segmentation

Upholstered household furniture	50.4%
Institutional furniture	19.8%
Nonupholstered wood household furniture	15.5%
Metal household furniture	10.3%
Other	4.0%

Major Market Segmentation

Furniture and home goods stores	32.2%
Independent wholesalers	24.0%
End users	13.3%
Exports	9.6%
Manufacturer-affiliated retailers	9.1%
Warehouse stores	5.3%
Department stores	3.5%
Other retailers	3.0%

Industry Costs

Profit	3.7%
Wages	19.6%
Purchases	54.2%
Depreciation	0.8%
Marketing	0.6%
Rent & Utilities	2.3%
Other	18.8%

Market Share

Ashley Furniture Industries Inc.	7.4%

- CURRENT U.S. OFFICE FURNITURE MARKET FORECAST

Year	Production	% Change	Consumption	% Change
2016	$10.3 billion	+1.0%	$13.4 billion	+3.9%
2017	$10.8 billion	+4.8%	$14.4 billion	+7.2%

Source: February 29, 2016, http://www.bifma.org/page/HistoricalData

Resources

- Business & Institutional Furniture Manufacturers Association: http://www.bifma.org
- IBISWorld, January 2017: http://ibisworld.com

Manufacturing—General

SIC 3999-03

Rules of Thumb

➤ 40–60% of annual sales includes inventory

➤ 2.5–3.5 x SDE (depending on size & quality) includes inventory

➤ 3–4 x SDE; must manufacture product; not be a job shop

➤ 3–5 x EBITDA

➤ 4–5 x EBIT

Pricing Tips

▪ A general CNC component manufacturer may trade at 5–6 X SDE, depending on their industry certifications and a host of other factors. However a medical instrument manufacturer can trade as high as 29 x. Manufacturing is one of those sectors that can't be put into a box; they are vastly different.

▪ Each business is different based on several factors such as the size, ownership, management team, assets, inventory, etc. Larger businesses typically use EBITDA while smaller businesses typically use SDE. Use more than one method to check.

▪ 4–8 x depending upon barriers to entry and low customer concentration.

▪ While it may prove worthwhile to target a 3.0 multiple, it's best to set the seller's expectations below 2.5.

▪ The equipment included is a key factor in the valuation and sale of the business.

▪ In terms of valuation, timing is less important than the EBITDA levels, growth prospects and quality of the underlying business. Companies that have patented products and proprietary methods will see a higher multiple. The transferability of the customer base will have a significant influence regarding price.

▪ Important to understand finished product, parts, inventory and work in progress and exactly how much of each will or will-not be included in the purchase price.

▪ Niche or proprietary products, processes, etc. require a premium. Repetitive long-term contracts generate a premium. ISO 2000 procedures in place deserve a premium. Discount for client concentration, labor unions and 'me too' products or services. Watch out for warranty exposure, product liability exposure, excessive WIP and old or obsolete inventory.

Benchmark Data

▪ Customer or supplier concentration is a major issue.

▪ Revenue per employee over $200,000 is good.

▪ The goal is to see $300K–$350K per shop employee.

▪ Successful manufacturers get significant amount of productivity from employees due to skills, training and efficiencies in automation. $150 K per employee in sales.

▪ Employee/labor costs are on the rise along with insurance costs. Understanding where efficiencies can be put into play can be helpful for a buyer. Cost of goods sold also important to understand if current pricing for materials, etc. will continue and for how long.

M

- 3–4 x adjusted-verifiable net.
- $1k sales per square foot, but it depends on what you are selling, power transmission products vs. electronics.

Expenses (% of Annual Sales)

Cost of Goods	40% to 60%
Occupancy Costs	03% to 10%
Payroll/Labor Costs	10% to 20%
Profit (pretax)	05% to 10%

Questions

- Does the company have a process/product that is exclusive or does it compete on price, quality, or service? Is there an opportunity to add new products or services? Does the manufacturing equipment utilize the latest technology? Are systems in place to manage the manufacturing process? What does the owner do every day? Is there a good management team in place?
- Sector concentration, customer concentration, remaining working years of key employees, what capacity the plant is running at, machine tool maintenance schedule.
- CapX requirements.
- Is vendor concentration an issue and who are the alternate suppliers? Is customer concentration an issue and how does the buyer maintain that business? If the company has multiple products, what is the gross margin per product? How much working capital will I need? Is there any equipment that will need major maintenance or replacement in the near future?
- Three- to five-year historical financials, asset list and values, inventory value and categorize by current, slow moving or obsolete, customer list and percentages of revenue, management team, contracts, agreements, royalties as a starting point.
- Product-line diversification by industry focus, i.e., not just products in the oil industry.
- Can the training transition period last longer with a phase-out period and compensation for the seller during transition?
- How much working capital is required? Who are your competitors? Do you have an up-to-date business plan? Who owns the working relationships with the customers? Are there any vendor concentration issues? Do you have many offshore competitors? What is your role in the business?
- Work in progress—how much and how it will be calculated. Inventory in both finished and unfinished product and how much included in the sale. Materials—how they can be accurately counted.
- What is the quality of your management team? Are your books and records audited by a national or large regional firm? Are you a planner and can you show me your strategic plan vs. execution, etc.?
- Customer concentration. By whom are technical and sales relationships owned? Environmental? Quality control standards? ISO compliance? Risk of obsolescence? Competitive products/threats?
- Raw materials—how much, will the current pricing continue? Long-term lease can be important; find out the status and if it is assignable or if a new one at the same or better rate is possible. Check the details carefully of all customer contracts.
- Do they have patents on their products?
- Is your product certified and if so what kind of certification?

Industry Trend

- "Current uncertainties in global manufacturing:
    - ✓ Escalating U.S. political and policy uncertainties,
    - ✓ Risks in China's financial system, and
    - ✓ Brexit's early impacts on the Eurozone.

    "Between 2017–2020, we expect annual U.S. GDP growth to be an average 2.2% and U.S. manufacturing growth to average 1.6% across the three-year period. However, today's global uncertainties and turmoil can quickly present head- or tail-winds to future U.S. growth. In addition to our quarterly scenario for U.S. manufacturing growth, this report also explores the boundaries of plausible factory sector growth through 2020."

    Source: "Stronger World Propelling U.S. Manufacturing" by Cliff Waldman, https://mapifoundation.org/economic/2017/6/1/stronger-world-propelling-us-manufacturing?external-link=yes

- Manufacturing is one of the most sought-after sectors for acquisition. Individual buyers are leaving executive positions at Fortune 500 companies for business ownership.

- According to the National Association of Manufacturers 2017 First Quarter Manufacturers' Outlook Survey, optimism has reached a 20-year high, with 93.3% of large and small manufacturers positive in their outlook of the economy. The expected growth rate for sales over the next 12 months is 4.9%.

- There will be additional investments in automation required to be successful due to labor shortages, and to reduce overall costs. Organization must continue to differentiate and provide value-added services.

- With assertive sales and marketing approaches, we should continue to see growth and even modest roll-ups among small manufacturers.

- Challenging, because U.S. manufacturing is under intense pressure from foreign competition, currency exchange and the U.S. government as well as governments in the Northeast are anti-business and anti-manufacturing.

- Growth including onshoring and manufacturing moving from China to U.S. and Mexico.

Expert Comments

The most important component for sellers in preparing the business for sale is to ensure the business is not dependent on them and have systems in place for everything.

You need to "know what you don't know" and engage the right consultants during due diligence. The buyer should consider having the equipment appraised.

The National Association of Manufacturers (NAM) released a new study in January, 2017 that "Manufacturers face 297,696 restrictions on their operations from federal regulations." Eighty-seven percent of the manufacturers surveyed say that if compliance costs were reduced permanently and significantly, they would invest the savings on hiring, increased salaries and wages, more R&D or capital replacement.

Understand all the potential options regarding how to sell or buy the business: financing, structure, management team, competitors, market trends and projections, equipment condition, customer and customer mix, etc.

Manufacturing is difficult to replicate or start due to the capital required and the availability of a good work force.

Capital expenditure is high in this industry but technology is not a barrier.

Focus on strong inside sales development.

Location has no bearing on the business other than overall distance to ship to customers. International customers are difficult to have continuity with because the strength of the U.S. dollar negatively impacts sales internationally, especially Canada.

Making strategic investments is essential for growth. Manufacturing technology is evolving faster than ever before and owners must lead with an eye toward that reality, and not merely the current bottom line.

The U.S. manufacturers have a structural cost disadvantage given the high corporate tax rates.

Seller Financing
- Outside financing with 10% seller's note
- Some seller financing is usually required for a business in this industry that sells for less than a few million dollars. The terms vary a lot from deal to deal.
- Depends on the size of the business and current ownership of the business. It can be owner financing or a variety of outside financing. The terms are dependent on the structure of the sale/who and how it is being sold.
- We typically see a blend of down payment (25%), outside financing (60%), and a blend of a seller note and earnout (15%).

Resources
- The Manufacturing Institute: http://www.themanufacturinginstitute.org
- The Manufacturers Alliance for Productivity and Innovation: http://www.mapi.net
- The National Association of Manufacturers: http://www.nam.org
- First Coast Manufacturers Association: http://www.fcmaweb.com
- The Association of Equipment Manufacturers: http://www.aem.org
- Manufacturers Association of Florida: http://www.mafmfg.com
- Fabricators & Manufacturers Association, International: http://www.fmanet.org
- National Tooling & Manufacturing Association: http://www.NTMA.org
- Association for Manufacturing Excellence: http://AME.org

Manufacturing—General Purpose Machinery		
	NAICS 3339	

Rules of Thumb
➤ 4.5 x EBITDA

Manufacturing—Guided Missile and Space Vehicle		
	NAICS 336414	Number of Businesses/Units 128

Rules of Thumb
➤ 100+ % of annual sales

> ➢ 3–4 x SDE plus inventory
> ➢ 6–10 x EBIT
> ➢ 5–8 x EBITDA

Pricing Tips

- Pricing is heavily impacted by third-party lending criteria and formal appraisals/ evaluations. Buyers and sellers are sensitive to industry standards and trends, and a certain segment is sensitive to environmental issues and political correctness.
- Usually need to sell as a stock sale due to the qualifications and licenses held by the seller.
- Value increases with the company's ability to meet high quality controls and production deadlines as specified by military and military contractors. Extremely high barriers to entry in this industry keep values high.

Benchmark Data

Statistics (Space Vehicle & Missile Manufacturing)

Number of Establishments	128
Average Profit Margin	10.3%
Revenue per Employee	$368,900
Average Number of Employees	546.4
Average Wages per Employee	$127,145

Products and Services Segmentation

Missile systems	42.6%
Space systems	35.4%
Propulsion systems	12.3%
Other missile and space vehicle parts	9.7%

Major Market Segmentation

US military	55.2%
Domestic civilian market	34.6%
Exports	10.2%

Industry Costs

Profit	10.3%
Wages	34.7%
Purchases	36.7%
Depreciation	2.1%
Marketing	0.1%
Rent & Utilities	1.9%
Other	14.2%

Market Share

Raytheon Company	29.7%
Lockheed Martin Corporation	28.6%
The Boeing Company	10.7%
Orbital ATK Inc.	8.2%
Aerojet Rocketdyne Holdings	7.3%

Expenses (% of Annual Sales)

Cost of Goods	31% to 35%
Occupancy Costs	15%
Payroll/Labor Costs	50%
Profit (pretax)	20% to 21%

Questions

- How are you going to pay for this business? If I carry back a note, what security are you going to provide and how many months of cash will you have at closing?
- Are the key employees willing to stay on post sale? Are qualifications and certifications up to current standards and valid?

Industry Trend

- "The industry's future performance will remain dependent on the defense market. While US defense spending is expected to remain constrained, it is anticipated to stabilize. The Pentagon will continue to invest in missile defense systems, a new generation of stealthy and partially autonomous cruise missiles (i.e. LARSM) and new missiles for next-generation platforms such as the F-35. Continued defense investment, combined with growth in export sales, will lead industry revenue to increase at a projected annualized rate of 1.1% to $27.6 billion over the five years to 2020."

Source: "Industry Trends: Space Vehicle and Missile Manufacturing," February 22, 2016, http://www.sme.org/MEMagazine/Article.aspx?id=8589938163

Expert Comments

Visual appeal of facility as well as the level of technology in equipment is very important.

Seller Financing

- A mixture of 10% to 20% seller financing, a typical 20% and up buyer cash down payment, and 3rd party financing.
- Five years at a premium over bank rates.

Resources

- IBISWorld, May 2017: http://ibisworld.com

Manufacturing—Machinery		
	NAICS 333	

Rules of Thumb

➢ 100% of annual sales includes inventory

➢ 4 x EBIT

➢ 3 x EBITDA

Pricing Tips

- Average of last 3 years' EBITDA plus stockholders' comp, multiplied by 2 to 4 depending on profit history and market share.
- Valuation method for work in process. Inventory turnover. Nature and situation

of officer's account with business. Indebtedness. How easy for the firm to get bonded on basis of financial credibility.

- A manufacturer of industry-specific machinery generally employs 50 to 500 people. A high price is 1 times sales figure (valid if market dominant worldwide). A good price is equal to total assets. A frequently observed price is twice net assets (Stockholders' Equity) or 5 times EBITDA for a firm in good standing. Multiple of net earning is meaningless since most owners minimize net earnings through various perks.

Benchmark Data

- Take sales figure minus costs of raw materials and components, which is added value. Divide added value by total salaries cost including management. If result is consistently above 2.0, it is a well-managed business. Watch out: In figures in expenses below, we consider total salaries costs, not labor costs (meaningless).
- Added value/salaries cost >2. Added value/sales figure >50%. Sales per employee >$250,000. Identified competitors are few, and far away.
- Sales per employee: $120,000 to $250,000; varies a lot as function of manufacturing integration. Our experience (300 clients during last 10 years) is that 80% of the world machinery industry is mismanaged because of lack of market focus and deficient customer service. The remaining can be highly profitable, and utilize market downturns to acquire competitors (most of our own business).

Expenses (% of Annual Sales)

Cost of Goods	60%
Occupancy Costs	05%
Payroll/Labor Costs	25%
Profit (pretax)	10%

Questions

- How many customers? Since when? How many customers amount to 50% of sales? How far away do they sell?
- Loans and advances to/from officers in balance sheet. Do they own their real estate (facility)? If so, is it undervalued in assets (historic value)?

Industry Trend

- It is moving to fast-growing economies where the biggest markets are China, India, other NICs.
- Favorable

Expert Comments

The machinery business is highly dependent on global market share (high), skills, reputation with customers based on customer service and availability of spare parts. Management predicament is how to control a high global market share when you are a business with between 50 and 500 employees.

Any sales require customized engineering, manufacturing and assembly, plus installation and startup which are always cursed with delays.

M

Manufacturing—Marine Products

	NAICS 336612	

Rules of Thumb

➤ 85% of annual gross sales plus inventory

➤ 2.1 x SDE

➤ 3.2 x EBIT

➤ 3.9 x EBITDA

Pricing Tips

- EBITDA must be adjusted to show owner's discretionary cash flow. The multiple that is used varies by industry segments, geographical location, and specific business and must be determined in a subjective manner by one knowledgeable of current market conditions.

Benchmark Data

- Sales per employee with a strong management team in place: $120,000 to $180,000 depending on WIP production. A mix of customers is key with no one customer >20%.

Expenses (% of Annual Sales)

Cost of Goods	32%
Occupancy Costs	06%
Payroll/Labor Costs	25%
Profit (pretax)	21%

Questions

- Customer concentration and percentage of revenue from the top 10 customers
- Equipment needs to be up to date-updating equipment in this industry can be a large expense.
- Are the contracts with manufacturers transferable to the new owner?
- Who is the competition?
- How is the business protected from offshore competition?
- Consider the WIP situation as these types of products can have significant amounts invested in work in progress.
- Insurance considerations-is the business properly insured? Consider the value and margin of the backlog and make sure it is accounted for regarding insurance needs.
- What are the capital expenditures required to maintain and grow the business?

Expert Comments

Niche products are key to success and to reducing competition.

Only the strong survived during the recession, which was particularly difficult for the marine industry from 2008 thru 2012. The weaker competitors fell away so the last couple of years have experienced a sharp increase in business for the survivors.

Location is also key. In order to control shipping costs, it is important to be located in active boating areas. Marine related manufacturing is typically a complex business with extensive processes creating attractive barriers to entry.

Manufacturing has been enhanced by technological systems which have greatly improved over the last 25 years. CADCAM systems and computerized equipment have greatly improved productivity in the industry.

Seller Financing
- Depending on the records, banks are doing SBA deals recently. If not, 60% to 70% down with 30% to 40% seller financing is common.

Resources
- National Marine Manufacturers Association: http://www.nmma.org
- Marine Industries Association of South Florida: http://www.miasf.org

Manufacturing—Metal Fabrication

SIC 1791-04	NAICS 238390	

Rules of Thumb
➤ 70%–80% of annual gross sales plus inventory

➤ 5–6 x EBIT

➤ 4–6 x EBITDA

➤ 3.5–4.5 x SDE plus inventory

Pricing Tips
- Likely will need an equipment appraisal to satisfy lender, so locating an appraiser early on can save some time with financing.
- Products, type of metal fab and recurring revenue have material impact on value.
- Equipment is a real expense so valuation will be dinged or improved based on how frequently seller updates equipment. Useful life of CNC equipment is typically 5–7 years depending on how hard it's used. CAPEX is a real expense of the business which keeps EBITDA multiples down. If they have any proprietary products, it improves value. Most contract manufacturers don't have proprietary products though.
- Having spoken to over a hundred owners, I can attest that each is very unique. Confirm they don't have customer concentration and identify gross margins for their work. 40–50% gross margins are healthy.
- Aerospace and defense fabrication typically garners better margins and multiples. It is common to have customer concentration in this space where one customer makes up 20–50% of sales. This brings value about a turn of EBITDA. Size matters too...$2M in EBITDA and below is limited to 5 X and below; $2M–$5M is 5.5–6 and more than $10M of EBITDA 5.5–7 X. 7 X is very rich, and that business will need a lot of other things going for it like heavy services (subassembly, kitting, supplier management, painting and e-coating, etc.)

M

Benchmark Data

- For additional Benchmark Data see Manufacturing—Metal Stamping
- 5% of gross revenue goes into CAPEX each year. It is a real expense of the business. Gross margins from 30% to 55% are found depending on market and type of metal fabrication. Less than 30% GM is too commodity based and will trade for lower multiple (4 or less) 40–50% gross margin will trade 5 X or above.
- 50 employees should generate $10M in revenues. You want to make sure you can pass commodity price increases along to customers.

Expenses (% of Annual Sales)

Cost of Goods	30% to 40%
Occupancy Costs	20%
Payroll/Labor Costs	20% to 30%
Profit (pretax)	15% to 20%

Questions

- What has been the maintenance schedule for the equipment, and what equipment is new in the last few years?
- What are gross margins? What are quality systems? How many new clients do you get a year? What percent of revenues have gone into CAPEX the last three years? Is your scrap revenue on your income statement?
- Check on your ability to sell metal fabricated parts. Getting new sales is important. Often owners are very good at building and challenged at selling. This is competitive and it's hard to get someone to change suppliers if they are doing a good job. Therefore, you're looking for new part numbers from OEMs. Buyers should ask about their quality programs, operating team, safety record and sales/customer retention history.
- Do you have any payment or performance bonds in place? Retainage? What is your backlog? Growing?

Industry Trend

- This industry's profit is now on the increase.
- More reshoring is going on in U.S. The trend for more metal parts fabrication domestically is growing.

Expert Comments

Look over the age of the equipment and how well it has been maintained, as this equipment can be very expensive. Often if the seller has been thinking of selling, they haven't been updating as needed.

There is significant variety in this industry. It's best not to rely on a rule of thumb, but focus on the specific attributes of the unique metal fabricator.

The customers of these businesses regularly get competitive pricing from the market. It's not uncommon that you'll have a customer and lose a customer and get them back. The point is there is not a lot of pricing power for the owner.

Pure welding and fabrication businesses that need less equipment are easier to sell than those that require more annual CAPEX spend.

Seller Financing

- Outside/bank financing is common. Also, often tied to an earnout depending on customer mix.
- Outside financing unless there is customer concentration.
- 90% outside financing, usually 5%–10% seller financing. They're usually asset heavy so financing is readily available.
- 3 to 5 years

Resources

- The Society for Mining, Metallurgy and Exploration: http://www.smenet.org
- Precision Metalforming Association: http://www.pma.org
- Fabricators & Manufacturers Association International (FMA): http://www.fmanet.org
- American Welding Society: http://www.aws.org

Manufacturing—Metal Stamping		
	NAICS 332119	Number of Businesses/Units 2,402

Rules of Thumb

➤ 5 x SDE plus inventory

➤ 3 x EBIT

➤ 4 x EBITDA

Pricing Tips

- Length of time in business. Customer base and spread of customer base by percentage.

Benchmark Data

Statistics (Metal Stamping & Forging)

Number of Establishments	2,402
Average Profit Margin	6.6%
Revenue per Employee	$337,300
Average Number of Employees	43.6
Average Wages per Employee	$58,380

Products and Services Segmentation

Non-automotive stamping	34.0%
Ferrous forging	26.0%
Custom rollforming	22.7%
Nonferrous forging	8.7%
Powder metallurgy	6.1%
Other	3.7%

Major Market Segmentation

Aerospace	38.6%
Off-highway and agriculture markets	18.1%
Other	12.8%
Exports	11.7%
Ordnance markets	9.5%
Industrial manufacturing	9.3%

Industry Costs

Profit	6.6%
Wages	17.3%
Purchases	52.7%
Depreciation	2.9%
Marketing	0.1%
Rent & Utilities	3.3%
Other	17.1%

Expenses (% of Annual Sales)

Cost of Goods	50%
Occupancy Costs	15%
Payroll/Labor Costs	15%
Profit (pretax)	20%

Questions

- How long in business? Cost of goods sold? Lease and rent? How long have employees been there? Diversification of customer base?

Industry Trend

- Lots of this work is going to China.

Expert Comments

Depending upon products being developed

Resources

- IBISWorld, March 2017: http://ibisworld.com

Manufacturing—Metal Valve and Pipe Fitting

	NAICS 332919	

Rules of Thumb

➢ 7 x EBIT

➢ 100% of annual sales

Benchmark Data

- Four inventory turns, 50 percent gross margin

Expenses (% of Annual Sales)

Cost of Goods	50%
Occupancy Costs	30%
Payroll/Labor Costs	20%
Profit (pretax)	15%

Expert Comments

High capital investment

Manufacturing—Miscellaneous Electrical and Components

| | NAICS 335999 | |

Rules of Thumb

➢ 8 x SDE

Pricing Tips

- Customer concentration and special skills required by owner drive the price model.

Expenses (% of Annual Sales)

Cost of Goods	50%
Occupancy Costs	15%
Payroll/Labor Costs	25%
Profit (pretax)	10%

Manufacturing—Office Products

| | NAICS 339940 | Number of Businesses/Units 444 |

Rules of Thumb

➢ 1 x sales plus inventory

➢ 5–8 x EBIT

Pricing Tips

- Key to higher valuation is the company's customer base. Does it include either:
  - (a) One or more office superstores? (Staples, OfficeMax/Office Depot)
  - (b) One or more national wholesalers? (United Stationers, etc.)
  - (c) One or more contract stationers?

Benchmark Data

Statistics (Art & Office Supply Manufacturing in the U.S.)

Number of Establishments	444
Average Profit Margin	13.1%
Revenue per employee	$325,300
Average Number of Employees	20.5
Average Wages per Employee	$42,532

Products and Services Segmentation

Pencils and art goods	43.0%
Pens and mechanical pencils	22.0%
Carbon paper and linked ribbon	21.3%
Marking devices	13.7%

Major Market Segmentation

Wholesalers	31.0%
Other industries	25.4%
Retailers	24.0%
Exports	19.6%

Industry Costs

Profit	13.1%
Wages	13.2%
Purchases	52.4%
Depreciation	2.2%
Marketing	3.8%
Rent & Utilities	0.9%
Other	14.4%

Market Share

Newell Brands Inc.	19.4%
Crayola LLC	15.4%
ACCO Brands Corp.	11.4%

Seller Financing
- Not very often. If it is a good company, it is a cash deal.
- 3 years

Resources
- IBISWorld, May 2017: http://ibisworld.com

Manufacturing—Ornamental & Architectural Metal		
SIC 3446-04	NAICS 332321	

Rules of Thumb
➢ 3–7 x EBITDA depending on the company, industry and buyer.

Questions
- Do you have to pay union or David-Bacon linked wages for government work?

Manufacturing—Personal Health Products		
	NAICS 325412	

Rules of Thumb
➢ 5 x SDE plus inventory

➢ 6 x EBIT

➢ 5.5 x EBITDA

Pricing Tips
- 30% of GPM [gross profit margin] x 5 should roughly equal a fair valuation.

Benchmark Data
- $200,000 sales per employee

Expenses (% of Annual Sales)

Cost of Goods	40%
Occupancy Costs	05%
Payroll/Labor Costs	12%
Profit (pretax)	10% to 12%

Questions
- Market share and stability of GPM [gross profit margin]

Manufacturing—Pharmaceutical Preparation & Medicine	
NAICS 325412	Number of Businesses/Units 4,939

Rules of Thumb
➤ 75% of annual sales
➤ 5 x SDE
➤ 6 x EBITDA
➤ 4–5 x EBIT

Pricing Tips
- Biotech, smaller pharma and R&D based companies are valued using a discounted cash flow of expected earnings less R&D expense and capital expenditures.
- Depends on the market size and developmental maturity of products in the pipeline
- Because of products manufactured, it is important that the products are not on the FDA hit list.
- Much of what the company is valued at will depend on how many products they manufacture, the concentration of clients to the gross revenues, the cost margin for each product, the number of short runs versus the number of long runs, and the opportunity for expansion through existing clients.

Benchmark Data

Statistics (Brand Name Pharmaceutical Manufacturing)
Number of Establishments	3,477
Average Profit Margin	22.5%
Revenue per Employee	$909,100
Average Number of Employees	60.1
Average Wages per Employee	$85,863

Products and Services Segmentation
Other	43.8%
Oncological products	10.8%
Antidiabetes products	9.4%
Mental health products	9.2%
Respiratory agents	7.9%
Pain products	7.2%
Autoimmune	6.9%
Antihypertensives	4.8%

Major Market Segmentation
Exports	24.7%
Chain stores	23.2%
Mail service providers	17.3%
Clinics	10.0%
Independent retailers	8.5%
Nonfederal hospitals	5.9%
Food stores	5.3%
Other	5.1%

M

Industry Costs

Profit	22.5%
Wages	9.5%
Purchases	31.3%
Depreciation	2.2%
Marketing	0.6%
Rent & Utilities	9.9%
Other	24.0%

Market Share

Amgen	10.9%
Johnson & Johnson	10.4%
Merck and Co., Inc.	9.6%
AbbVie Inc.	9.5%
Pfizer Inc.	8.8%
Sanofi	6.6%

Statistics (Generic Pharmaceutical Manufacturing)

Number of Establishments	1,462
Average Profit Margin	9.5%
Revenue per Employee	$846,700
Average Number of Employees	56.7
Average Wages per Employee	$84,141

Products and Services Segmentation

Nervous system disorders and antihypertensives	20.5%
Other	19.7%
Mental health and lipid regulators	18.5%
Pain and antibacterials	16.9%
Antidiabetics and respiratory	8.9%
Antiulcerants and thyroid	7.0%
Dermatologicals and hormonal contraceptives	4.7%
ADHD and anticoagulants	3.8%

Major Market Segmentation

Third-party payers	53.1%
Medicare	25.7%
Medicaid	13.3%
Out-of-pocket	7.9%

Industry Costs

Profit	9.5%
Wages	9.8%
Purchases	37.8%
Depreciation	2.4%
Marketing	2.4%
Rent & Utilities	3.2%
Other	34.9%

Market Share

Mylan Inc.	8.7%
Teva Pharmaceutical Industries Ltd.	7.0%
Sandoz Ltd.	5.8%

- Biotech and R&D companies do not follow the same matrix as many other companies because they are typically pre-revenue companies. Nonetheless, they carry intellectual and enterprise value which can be significant, even the smaller companies, to the right buyer. Finding the right buyers/bidders is the key to realizing the full value of the selling company.
- Development stage: number of drugs in pipeline, and the stage of development

Expenses (% of Annual Sales)

Cost of Goods .... 30% to 35%
Occupancy Costs .... 15% to 20%
Payroll/Labor Costs .... 30% to 32%
Profit (pretax) .... 20% to 30%

Industry Trend

- More and more U.S. companies are being sold outside the U.S. and this is expected to continue with the standardization of product approval requirements. This is driving values up, especially for many of the smaller companies. Yet it also is becoming more important to research competitors before selling a business in this industry because they are not just found in the U.S. Management should be able to tell you what the competitive landscape looks like, and any knowledgeable buyer will want to know in pre-due diligence.

Expert Comments

Seek outside advice for estimates of value. A thorough investigation of competing products is worth the effort. Consider taking an upfront retainer to cover some hard costs. Often when a company wants to sell it's because they are running out of cash. Therefore, it's critical to consider the company's burn rate alongside the length of the listing agreement.

Value in this industry predicated on intellectual property, which means replication is or should be difficult. The industry has been riding a three-year upswing where values and multiples have gone up substantially dovetailing several significant successes. Profit trends are historically lower as many companies are purchased by larger companies prior to the launch of their products. Marketability can be good but is hampered by a limited pool of buyers. This is a very high-risk industry but also highly rewarding, which can bring in competitors vying for the same treatment space.

Seller Financing

- Senior debt can be very hard to get as there is often very little in the way of hard assets and profitability
- 5 years

Resources

- FiercePharma: http://www.fiercepharma.com
- IBISWorld, April 2017: http://ibisworld.com

Manufacturing—Plastic and Rubber Machinery		
	NAICS 333249	

Rules of Thumb

➢ 9 x EBITDA

M

Pricing Tips

- Look at customer concentration; determine age and condition of equipment; look at industry diversification.

Expenses (% of Annual Sales)

Cost of Goods	50%
Occupancy Costs	08%
Payroll/Labor Costs	12%
Profit (pretax)	15%

Manufacturing—Plastic Products

SIC 3089-10	NAICS 3261	Number of Businesses/Units 6,575

Rules of Thumb

➢ 3.5 x SDE

➢ EBITDA is 4X to 7X; depending upon size, product mix (less for automotive or appliance, more for medical, and size of products produced (more for companies with larger products, less for smaller products).

➢ EBIT is 5X to 8X, depending upon same considerations as EBITDA.

➢ Both totals assume customer amounts of Working Capital (inventory+A/R+other; current minus A/P+accruals) transfer with the business.

Pricing Tips

- Multiples of EBITDA vary significantly based upon the seller's revenues, sales/employee, age/size of its equipment, and what industries are served. Companies supplying the automotive and appliance industries have lower multiples than those serving other industries. Companies supplying the medical industry have the highest multiples (especially if they have a clean-room operation). Furthermore, if the company has value-added services this results in a higher valuation. Generally speaking, the EBITDA multiple range for the industry is 4.5 x to 5.5 x for companies with less than $2 million of EBITDA, 5.0 x to 7.0 x for companies with $2 to $5 million of EBITDA and 6.0 x to 8.0 x for companies with more than $5 million of EBITDA. Companies serving the medical industry will have higher multiple ranges. Companies focused purely on automotive and/or appliances will have lower ranges.

- Good company should have net profits in the 15%-20% range. Multiples in the range of 5 to 7 times EBITDA are possible for good companies. Niche businesses can be very attractive. A model with some manufacturing in the U.S. and some in China also works well.

- Pricing depends on whether molding company has proprietary products or is a custom molder. Any proprietary products enhance the value. Concentration of customers is critical. High concentration = high risk. Machines vary significantly in capacity and are very expensive. They should be well-maintained and no more than 15 years old, depending on hours of usage. Capacity utilization is a critical question. With aging baby boomers, technical staffing is becoming an issue due to lack of apprenticeships. Mold makers are dying out. Few millennials are interested in becoming mold makers or molders. If a company relies on an aging in-house mold maker, be cautious. ISO certification is becoming more important, not only as a process control, but also as a marketing tool. ISO certified companies command a premium. Labor and insurance costs are rising, as is off-shore competition, and therefore robotic systems for removing and packaging parts add efficiency and command a premium. Molding is price competitive. Secondary operations, such as sonic welding, stamping, painting and assembly, are often the most, or only, profitable operations. It's important to look at the markets being served by the molder and whether the customers face production cycles or seasonal variations. Buyers should be knowledgeable in plastics operations. Otherwise, it's a very big learning curve.

Benchmark Data

Statistics (Plastic Products Miscellaneous Manufacturing)

Number of Establishments	6,575
Average Profit Margin	6.3%
Revenue per Employee	$266,700
Average Number of Employees	57.9
Average Wages per Employee	$47,557

Products and Services Segmentation

Consumer, institutional and commercial fabricated plastic products	23.1%
Fabricated plastic products for transportation applications	22.1%
Plastic packaging	18.2%
Fabricated plastic products for building applications	12.1%
Other plastic products	11.4%
Reinforced and fiberglass plastic products	5.5%
Plastic plumbing fixtures	3.9%
Fabricated plastic products for electrical/electronic applications	3.7%

Major Market Segmentation

Hardware and home improvement wholesalers	45.6%
Automotive manufacturers	26.7%
Other	14.3%
Plumbing fixture wholesalers	4.8%
Electrical and electronic manufacturers	4.5%
Furniture and furnishing wholesalers	4.1%

Industry Costs

Profit	6.3%
Wages	17.7%
Purchases	46.8%
Depreciation	2.5%
Marketing	0.3%
Rent & Utilities	3.3%
Other	23.1%

Expenses (% of Annual Sales)

Cost of Goods	60% to 74%
Occupancy Costs	05% to 10%
Payroll/Labor Costs	08% to 20%
Profit (pretax)	07% to 12%

M

Questions

- Most plastics companies are terrible at marketing. Ask the owner how they sell/market their products. Also ask what makes them different from their competitors.
- Customer concentration. Size, in tons, of equipment. How do they sell their products?

Industry Trend

- "Advances in resin materials, improved automation, and factory connectivity all point to a bright future for plastics manufacturing. The industry in the United States will also be challenged by foreign competition with cheaper labor and fewer regulations, but we have the technology and the innovative spirit to continue to find competitive solutions that will advance the use of plastics for years to come.

"Below we have outlined five key trends that we think will have significant impacts not only on the plastics industry but the world of manufacturing.

  ✓ Lightweighting—not just for cars anymore
  ✓ Automation and Customization—beyond the axis
  ✓ Three R's—reclaimable, recyclable, and renewable
  ✓ Near-Shoring
  ✓ The Connected Factory"

Source: "Top Trends for Plastics Manufacturing in 2016 and Beyond," January 11, 2016, https://info.rodongroup.com/top-trends-for-plastics-manufacturing-in-2016-and-beyond

Expert Comments

A lot of consolidation in the U.S. With competition from China, it is becoming easy to lose business.

Location matters. When shipping plastic products, most shipments 'dimension out' before they weigh out, which means most manufacturers are located within 500 miles of their customers. Many larger manufacturers build/buy factories near their larger customers. Also, 10 to 15 years ago, this industry suffered heavily from off-shoring manufacturing to Asia. However, most of the new work is staying in the USA, leading to a resurgence in the industry. Plus, the Great Recession wiped out many, many companies leaving those in operation today in a much better position than pre-2008.

It is a competitive industry but there is high demand for a well-run company. Proprietary niches are attractive. General commodity products get very little attention or value.

Seller Financing

- Typically, these businesses are financed with outside financing, especially senior debt. They are asset-laden businesses and customarily easy to finance.

Resources

- Injection Molding ReSource: http://www.injection-molding-resource.org
- Injection Molding Resource: http://www.injection-molding-resource.org
- Plastics Engineering Magazine: http://www.plasticsengineering.org
- Plastics News: http://www.plasticsnews.com

- Society of the Plastics Industry: http://www.plasticsindustry.org
- Society of Plastics Engineers: http://www.4spe.org
- Plastics Technology Magazine: http://www.ptonline.com
- IBISWorld, May 2017: http://ibisworld.com
- Manufacturers Association for Plastics Processors: http://www.mappinc.com

Manufacturing—Powder Metallurgy Processing		
	NAICS 332117	

Rules of Thumb

➢ 5 x EBIT

➢ 4.5 x EBITDA

➢ 60–70% of annual gross sales includes inventory

Pricing Tips

- Price could vary widely depending on growth prospects.
- If EBIT is 12% of sales, the multiple at 60% is 5X. Most of these businesses now are not bringing double digits down to the EBIT line, but they still have a lot of assets, most of which would be hard to sell.
- Industry is under significant stress due to the concentration in the auto industry. Companies with less exposure are performing better and will be more marketable than businesses with auto exposure over 50%.
- Gross margins consistency and diversification of the customer base add value to PM business.

Benchmark Data

- Sales per employee will vary based on the material mix. A good benchmark is $150,000 for a typical mix of iron powders.

Expenses (% of Annual Sales)

Cost of Goods	65%
Occupancy Costs	05%
Payroll/Labor Costs	20%
Profit (pretax)	10%

Questions

- Customer and industry diversification is very important as is the strength of engineering and manufacturing leadership.
- Percent breakdown of customer types by market segment. How large are the top 10 customers? What percent of sales do the top 10 account for? How large is the engineering and tooling staff? What experience does the technical staff have? How long have they been with the company?
- Customer trends; industry concentration; changes in key technical, management personnel and direct production supervisors.

Industry Trend

- Technical advances will support overall industry growth. There is a potential impact from "additive manufacturing" somewhere in the future. This alternative process method may become a companion processing method to complement the long-established powder compacting services.

M

Expert Comments

Pay for value, deliver value. This is not an industry to try to find a bargain or one to try to sell at inflated prices. Buyers have good information and understand the alternative available to any specific investment opportunity.

This is a capital-intensive industry that is strongly influenced by technical expertise.

Basic changes in the industry and individual company concentration will control the rate of recovery.

The industry is 70% automotive based which has had a significant effect on companies with a high percent of sales in this market segment. Non-automotive PM manufacturers are experiencing much better results.

Profit margins have been squeezed in recent years due to movement offshore and increased volatility in raw material costs. In addition, the cost of capital equipment has increased faster than industry sales growth.

The current trend to move manufacturing to China and India is affecting the key customer groups of many PM companies.

Seller Financing

- Little seller financing is involved in many transactions. Corporate acquirers are less active than in the past, but this may reverse with continued industry changes.

Resources

- Metal Powder Industries Federation: https://www.mpif.org/

Manufacturing—Prefabricated Wood Buildings		
	NAICS 321992	Number of Businesses/Units 885

Rules of Thumb

> 100% of annual sales includes inventory

Pricing Tips

- Modular plants sell at a premium. Log home companies sell at a discount.
- Dealer network is important, or if selling direct, quality of sales staff.

Benchmark Data

Statistics (Prefabricated Home Manufacturing)

Number of Establishments	885
Average Profit Margin	2.8%
Revenue per Employee	$201,200
Average Number of Employees	46.2
Average Wages per Employee	42,070

Products and Services Segmentation

Manufactured mobile homes	55.3%
Prefabricated wood buildings	33.6%
Nonresidential mobile buildings	11.1%

Industry Costs

Profit	2.8%
Wages	20.8%
Purchases	61.3%
Depreciation	1.3%
Marketing	0.3%
Rent & Utilities	1.4%
Other	12.1%

Market Share

Berkshire Hathaway Inc.	41.4%
Champion Enterprises Inc.	8.1%
Cavco Industries Inc.	7.1%

Gross profit over 35%

Expenses (% of Annual Sales)

Cost of Goods	50%
Occupancy Costs	03% to 05%
Payroll/Labor Costs	15%
Profit (pretax)	05%

Questions

- Warranty policy and expense. How much warranty exposure is there? Does company have a favorable reputation for taking care of warranties?
- What is your backlog? How many leads have you received over each of the last 5 years? How do you sell your product -through a dealer network or direct or both? What patented processed do you have? Do you have challenges meeting energy or structural/building codes? What info do you have for your sales performance by region for the last 5 years? How many competitors do you have and where are they located? Do you sell internationally? Brand name, length of time in business and type of building system are extremely important.

Industry Trend

- "The Prefabricated Home Manufacturing industry is expected to continue expanding over the five years to 2022 against the backdrop of rising home prices, greater access to credit and an increase in the homeownership rate. However, the industry is expected to struggle as consumers continue their longtime substitution away from prefabricated homes. In total, IBISWorld projects industry revenue to grow an annualized 1.0% to $8.5 billion over the five years to 2022, including a 1.7% expansion in 2018."

Source: IBISWorld Industry Outlook

Expert Comments

Difficult to develop designs and engineering and establish a reputation, so it is not easy to start business from scratch.

Resources

- IBISWorld, April 2017: http://ibisworld.com
- Manufactured Housing Institute: http://www.manufacturedhousing.org/

M

Manufacturing—Products from Purchased Steel

	NAICS 3312	

Rules of Thumb

➤ 3–5 x SDE includes inventory

Benchmark Data

- Payroll costs, equipment maintenance and age of equipment

Expenses (% of Annual Sales)

Cost of Goods	15%
Occupancy Costs	20%
Payroll/Labor Costs	35%
Profit (pretax)	20%

Questions

- How many customers does he have and what is the percentage of his business?

Industry Trend

- If you have a niche business, you will do well. If you are a job shop, chances are you will struggle.

Expert Comments

Product line is the main importance along with the ability to deliver.

Manufacturing—Proprietary Products

Rules of Thumb

➤ 75% of annual sales includes inventory

➤ 4 x SDE plus Inventory

➤ 5 x EBITDA

Pricing Tips

- Manufacturing typically uses a multiplier in the range of 3–6, with various quality issues moving the actual value up or down.

Expenses (% of Annual Sales)

Cost of Goods	40%
Occupancy Costs	15%
Payroll/Labor Costs	30%
Profit (pretax)	20%

Benchmark Data

- Revenue per employee is in the $100,000 to $200,000 range.

Questions

- How well are your procedures documented? What additional capital expense is needed? What has limited the growth of the company?

Industry Trend

- Above average growth compared to the services industry.

Expert Comments

Always use bank financing, since it provides another set of eyes on the business and the valuation.

Normally there is a regional coverage aspect to the value of the business, and the ability for the company to grow.

Seller Financing

- Outside financing and the addition of seller financing
- Buyer cash plus seller's note = 25 percent and 75 percent bank financing.
- Banks like to see seller financing as a level of confidence that the business can prosper with a new owner.

Resources

- Society of Manufacturing Engineers: http://www.SME.org
- The Association for Manufacturing Technology (AMT): http://www.amtonline.org

Manufacturing—Scientific Instruments

Rules of Thumb

➤ 3–6 x EBITDA

Pricing Tips

- Where are the products in the life cycle? What new products are about to be introduced? Do they have strong patents? What is the competitive situation?

Expenses (% of Annual Sales)

Cost of Goods	50%
Occupancy Costs	15%
Payroll/Labor Costs	25% to 30%
Profit (pretax)	10%

Manufacturing—Showcase, Partition, Shelving, and Lockers

	NAICS 337215	

Rules of Thumb

➤ 2–3 x SDE plus inventory

Pricing Tips

- Customer concentration and any special skills required to operate can make for a big difference in pricing.

M

Expenses (% of Annual Sales)

Cost of Goods	35%
Occupancy Costs	15%
Payroll/Labor Costs	40%
Profit (pretax)	10%

Expert Comments

Economy changes the profitability very quickly here.

Manufacturing—Signs

SIC 7389-38	NAICS 339950	Number of Businesses/Units 31,244

Rules of Thumb

➢ 45–50% of annual sales plus inventory

➢ 2–2.5 x SDE plus inventory

Benchmark Data

Statistics (Billboard and Sign Manufacturing)

Number of Establishments	31,244
Average Profit Margin	5.1%
Revenue per Employee	$149,400
Average Number of Employees	3.2
Average Wages per Employee	$37,729

Products and Services Segmentation

Traditional billboards and signs	44.2%
Digital billboards and signs	40.2%
Other	15.6%

Major Market Segmentation

Accommodation and food services	40.1%
Other retailers	17.5%
Car dealers and gas stations	13.7%
Government	9.2%
Professional services	7.3%
Outdoor advertisers	7.2%
Other	5.0%

Industry Costs

Profit	5.1%
Wages	25.3%
Purchases	44.0%
Depreciation	1.8%
Marketing	0.8%
Rent & Utilities	3.5%
Other	19.5%

M

Industry Trend

- "The Billboard and Sign Manufacturing industry is expected to continue expanding over the five years to 2022. Corporate profit is anticipated to rise, ultimately leading businesses to increase their advertising budgets and branding efforts over this period. During the five-year period, IBISWorld expects that total advertising expenditure will increase at an annualized rate of 2.0%. Furthermore, traditional mass-market print media is anticipated to continue declining, strengthening the appeal of billboards as one of the few remaining viable options for advertisers seeking to reach a broad audience.

  "Revenue from digital billboards, high-definition video displays and LED displays is forecast to be the driving force behind industry-wide growth. Advertisers will continue to demand digital products that can convey multiple advertising messages and effectively target specific demographics. Accordingly, companies in this industry will move to offer more digital billboards and smaller digital signage and displays. Digital signage is expected to grow to exceed more than 50.0% of the billboard segment over the next five years. Traditional signage, however, such as advertising displays and billboards, will remain an important product segment."

Source: IBISWorld Industry Outlook

Resources

- International Sign Association (ISA): http://www.signs.org
- IBISWorld, May 2017: http://ibisworld.com

Manufacturing—Small

Rules of Thumb

➤ 4–5 x SDE plus inventory

Pricing Tips

- For manufacturing companies with sales of $1 million to $5 million, a crude rule of thumb is 3 to 4 times SDE, assuming the company is reasonably well established and viable. As company size goes up, the multiple will go up.
- Factors to look for: sales/profitability trends; SDE (and trends); industry trends; years in operation; fixed asset value, seller financing. Risk factors: technology, competition, industry trends.

Manufacturing—Specialty Vehicle

Rules of Thumb

➤ 4 x SDE includes inventory

Pricing Tips

- Evaluate inventory closely as there is a tendency to accumulate difficult-to-use inventory.
- Look for amount of booked business. Lead times from getting the order to shipping the finished vehicle can run 12 months or more.
- Evaluate financials closely. Many in this industry do not know what their true costs are.

M

Benchmark Data
- Difficult to estimate sales per employee, but should probably be $175,000–$200,000 per hourly production employee.

Expenses (% of Annual Sales)

Cost of Goods	55%
Occupancy Costs	05%
Payroll/Labor Costs	25%
Profit (pretax)	10%

Questions
- Who has design experience in the company? Who has the manufacturing experience in the company? How do you accurately cost jobs?
- What portion of the business is municipal, corporate, & private? Who are the key employees with industry experience? What is your marketing/sales plan? What is your backlog of business?

Industry Trend
- Much of the business is tied to Homeland Security. If there are attacks on our soil, demand will increase. Otherwise budget cutbacks will dampen demand.
- The market for mobile command centers, bomb trucks, SWAT trucks, etc. will continue to be strong as long as the U.S. has to fight terrorists. Many corporations are developing mobile marketing vehicles which will also help drive demand.

Expert Comments

It is difficult to acquire the expertise to build these vehicles. Many can build them; few can build them well.

Homeland Security issues make this a growth industry. It is fairly easy to replicate the physical facility, but the real market advantage comes from experience in designing, building and using these vehicles.

Resources
- Specialty Vehicle Services: http://www.vehiclesuccess.com

Manufacturing—Sporting Goods & Outdoor Products	
NAICS 339920	

Rules of Thumb
➢ 4–7 x EBITDA

Pricing Tips
- Brand and customer concentration are extremely important factors in valuing a manufacturer of outdoor and/or sporting products. These consumer products include hunting equipment, ammunition, fishing equipment, camping gear, sporting goods, outdoor apparel, etc. Patents are also an important value driver by increasing barriers to entry and making these consumer products harder to imitate. Customer diversity and relationships with key distributors are important. Brand awareness and time in the market place also add value.

Many manufacturers outsource to contract manufacturers overseas to control costs and create a variable cost model. It's important to understand the sustainability of these supplier relationships.

Industry Trend

- "Over the next five years, the Athletic and Sporting Goods Manufacturing industry is expected to increasingly team up with retailers to directly supply sporting goods to the retail sector. This trend, coupled with greater integration along all aspects of the supply chain, is anticipated to prop up industry revenue, albeit at a slow pace. Demand from downstream markets, including sporting goods stores, will increase as more individuals adopt active, health-conscious lifestyles. As obesity remains highly prevalent, more businesses will implement incentives to enhance employee health and productivity.

  "In the five years to 2022, industry revenue is forecast to grow at an annualized rate of 0.6% to $8.5 billion. Moreover, this figure includes an expected 0.6% jump in revenue in 2018 alone. Profit is also expected to hold mostly steady, from 6.2% of revenue in 2017 to 6.0% in 2022. As sporting goods manufacturers consolidate, they will address changing customer preferences more quickly and gain the resources necessary to invest in specialized manufacturing processes. For example, many manufacturers will increasingly appeal to customers on the basis of customization, such as high-quality sporting goods that are individually tailored to a customer's measurements and skill level."

  Source: IBISWorld Industry Outlook

Resources

- IBISWorld, February 2017: http://ibisworld.com

Manufacturing—Stainless Steel Food Service Fabrication		
	NAICS 333319	

Rules of Thumb

➢ 3–6 x EBITDA depending on the company, industry and buyer.

Questions

- Are you a custom fabricator also? Do you install? Do you sell other food-service equipment? Do you sell to the cruise lines?

Manufacturing—Tactical Military Equipment

Rules of Thumb

➢ 5 x SDE

Pricing Tips

- There is significant roll-up activity by major firearms manufacturers seeking to diversify their wholesale and retail product offerings into streams with higher margins than firearms. Accessories, apparel, and collectables are popular acquisition targets. Government contracts (GSA) should be priced separately as contingent payments when orders are received. Intellectual property plays a large role in valuations above 5 x owner benefit. Manufacturing dies are also priced in addition to multiple, but should be amortized to reflect useful life from a tool and product demand perspective. Sellers should have sophisticated inventory management and manufacturing processes in place. Gross profits should be extremely high.

Expenses (% of Annual Sales)

Cost of Goods	20%
Occupancy Costs	15%
Payroll/Labor Costs	20%
Profit (pretax)	20%

Benchmark Data
- These metrics vary widely based upon the size of the target company.

Questions
- What does the company's intellectual property portfolio look like? Who competes with your products on a product by product basis, and what are your differentiators?

Industry Trend
- Increased sales and acquisitions by large strategic buyers

Expert Comments

Focus on growth potential and margins. The multiples will be higher than anticipated.

There are many competitors in most product categories. Designs must be original, functional, and cost effective.

Seller Financing
- Outside financing with a component of seller financing, especially when government contracts are in place

Manufacturing—Turbine and Turbine Generator Set Units		
	NAICS 333611	

Rules of Thumb
➢ 8–10 x EBITDA

Pricing Tips
- Use cap rate, similar to pricing commercial real estate.

Benchmark Data
- Revenue per kilowatt hour, capacity factor, PPA rate

Industry Trend
- "The world market for turbines and related products (turbine-based engines, generators, and generator sets) is forecast to rise 6.4 percent annually to $162 billion in 2016. Wind turbines will remain the largest and fastest growing

segment (albeit at a more moderate rate), while demand for gas combustion turbines will accelerate."

Source: http://www.freedoniagroup.com/World-Turbines.html

- Significant growth as the industry consolidates and becomes institutionalized.

Expert Comments

This industry is, for a number of reasons, going to grow dramatically over the next decade. The economic model is very similar to that of commercial real estate-high upfront capital costs followed by extremely consistent cash flows, with upside appreciation potential. Smart money will get in early and ride the wave.

Manufacturing—Valves		
	NAICS 332911	Number of Businesses/Units 1,318

Rules of Thumb

➢ 5 x EBITDA

Pricing Tips

- Special consideration given for special products, market share, industry recognition.

Benchmark Data

Statistics (Valve Manufacturing)

Number of Establishments	1,318
Average Profit Margin	7.6%
Revenue per Employee	$359,600
Average Number of Employees	72.4
Average Wages per Employee	$60,824

Products and Services Segmentation

Other	24.2%
Other industrial valves	17.2%
Hose, parts and accessories	14.0%
Hydraulic and pneumatic valves	12.3%
Plumbing fixture valves, fittings and trim	11.8%
Gate, globe and check valves	9.7%
Ball valves	5.9%
Valves for water works	4.9%

Major Market Segmentation

Exports	31.7%
Construction	20.6%
Oil and gas	15.6%
Heavy manufacturing and mining	14.6%
Utilities	8.7%
Aerospace	6.2%
Utilities	5.3%
General manufacturing	2.6%

M

Industry Costs

Profit	7.6%
Wages	17.0%
Purchases	42.9%
Depreciation	2.2%
Marketing	0.2%
Rent & Utilities	1.4%
Other	28.7%

Market Share

Parker Hannifin	6.5%
Emerson Electric Co.	5.6%

Expenses (% of Annual Sales)

Cost of Goods	60%
Occupancy Costs	20%
Payroll/Labor Costs	20%
Profit (pretax)	15%

Industry Trend

- "The industry is expected to perform well over the next five years as demand for valves and other flow control devices rebounds in line with domestic manufacturing activity and investment in infrastructure. Although volatility in oil prices is likely to have lingering effects on industry performance in the beginning of this five-year period, stronger performance within the domestic energy sector and chemical processing industries will continue to increase demand. IBISWorld expects industry revenue to increase as demand from petroleum production and refining, which fell significantly from late 2014 to 2016, rebounds. Overall, industry revenue is forecast to grow at an annualized rate of 0.8% to $35.0 billion over the five years to 2022."

Source: IBISWorld Industry Outlook

Expert Comments

A lot of competition with commodity type valves; the more specialized, the less competition.

Seller Financing

- 5 years

Resources

- Valve Magazine: http://www.valvemagazine.com/
- IBISWorld, July 2017: http://ibisworld.com

Manufacturing—Wood Kitchen Cabinets and Countertops		
	NAICS 337110	

Rules of Thumb

➢ 2–2.5 x SDE plus inventory

Pricing Tips

- Such companies are considered light manufacturing operations, and since demand for manufacturing is at a premium, pricing may command higher multiples. Considerations must be put on how dependent on the amount of customization and specialty product the companies produce. Franchised operations are easier to assess if the owner is part of the production or part of marketing and sales. Franchised resale operations could be truly turnkey. If franchise resale, the territory scope could have a bearing on the multiples as its demographic plays a role in the profitability and scalability of the opportunity.
- Some wood cabinet manufacturers have state-of-the-art equipment that increases the efficiency of the business. Analyzing and adding the value of the equipment is a component of the above.

Benchmark Data

- The ability to buy supplies (melamine, hardware, etc.) at a volume increases your profitability, as volume buy drives costs down.

Expenses (% of Annual Sales)

Cost of Goods	25%
Occupancy Costs	10%
Payroll/Labor Costs	35%

Questions

- How easy or difficult has it been to hire the production labor? What's your turnover rate in this area? Do you do the sales, are you in the production area or are you in the delivery area? How many vendors do you have to source the materials?

Industry Trend

- A steady trend for demand is expected. The millennial age group does have a tendency to rent versus buy homes. Most of the closet/cabinet/organizing industry lends to homeowners, but the ongoing home improvement of the baby boomer, coupled by high growth regions, will provide the steady growth. Not significant but steady.

Expert Comments

Pricing the business accordingly will help sell the business quickly. A seller asking or waiting for a premium price might be coached to be prepared to get to closing. If the transaction is franchise resale, obtain and find out the resale process from the franchisor early in the process.

Barriers to entry could be difficult unless someone has previous experience and a good handle on sales and marketing. Once established it could be 'auto pilot' as long as an ongoing marketing campaign is established. This industry sector is attractive to previous corporate executives and managers who have a penchant for light manufacturing operations.

Seller Financing

- A high percentage will be eligible for SBA financing so most owners/sellers are able to walk away with a good amount of cash at closing. Seller financing 10% at a minimum.

M

Resources

- National Association of Productivity & Organizing Professionals (NAPO): http://www.NAPO.net

Manufacturing—Wood Office Furniture		
SIC 2499-02	NAICS 337211	

Rules of Thumb

➤ 2.5–3 x SDE includes inventory

➤ 2.5–3 x EBITDA

➤ 35% of annual sales includes inventory

Pricing Tips

- Contracts are rare in the industry but client relationships are important. We would look at the percentage of sales to the largest clients. The value of the business increases with more dispersed clients rather than a few large clients.
- Very cyclical business

Benchmark Data

Expenses (% of Annual Sales)

Cost of Goods	40%
Occupancy Costs	15% to 20%
Payroll/Labor Costs	20% to 30%
Profit (pretax)	15% to 25%

- COGS below 30%

Questions

- Look to see the client distribution of work. You'd like to see how many clients they have and the percentage distribution of work.
- How much design work and fashion trends?

Industry Trend

- Generally, it has been trending up for the past 5 years.
- More consolidation and offshore competition

Expert Comments

This is clearly a niche industry which requires creative employees. Once established, the base of creative employees takes a long time to duplicate, therefore the low competition.

Really depends where you are on the food chain; these vary from high- to low-margin businesses.

Very dependent on economic cycles and affected by China

Seller Financing

- Seller financing for the business and outside financing for the real estate.

Resources
- Business and Institutional Furniture Manufacturers Association: http://www.bifma.org

	Franchise
Marble Slab Creamery	
Approx. Total Investment	$100,000–$550,000
Estimated Annual Sales/Unit	$225,000
SIC 2024-98 NAICS 722515	Number of Businesses/Units 340

Rules of Thumb
➢ 45% of annual sales plus inventory

Resources
- Marble Slab Creamery: http://www.marbleslab.com

Marinas	
SIC 4493-06 NAICS 713930	Number of Businesses/Units 11,669

Rules of Thumb
➢ 10 x EBIT

➢ 10–12 x SDE plus inventory

➢ 11–12 x EBITDA

Pricing Tips
- This is a very complicated business. Estimating the selling price has many factors such as: dock leases, leases with resorts, years of operation, strength of mid-level management, survey of the vessels, competition, market, etc. Bottom line, it would be foolish to use a multiplier without a great deal of study.
- Be very careful using multipliers as the price of waterfront land greatly distorts the valuation of a marina. The best rule of thumb is to ensure that slip rental and boat storage income will suffice to cover debt service, allowing the buyer to make a living off the other services offered by the marina.
- Waterfront property makes the earnings multiple much higher than most businesses. That and the fact that marinas are very difficult to start from scratch anymore.

Benchmark Data

Statistics (Marinas)
Number of Establishments	11,669
Average Profit Margin	15.7%
Revenue per Employee	$134,900
Average Number of Employees	3.0
Average Wages per Employee	$31,872

M

Products and Services Segmentation

Pleasure craft dockage services	27.3%
Fuel and merchandise sales	20.2%
Other	16.2%
Repairs and maintenance services	15.6%
Pleasure craft launching, storage, and utilities services	13.3%
Food and beverage sales	7.4%

Industry Costs

Profit	15.7%
Wages	23.7%
Purchases	32.0%
Depreciation	8.1%
Marketing	1.1%
Rent & Utilities	7.8%
Other	11.6%

- A marina is usually a combination of many businesses, each with its own benchmarks. You have a storage business, a service business, a gas station, boat sales, brokerage sales and sometimes a restaurant, all with different Rules of Thumb.
- Slip rental income and storage fees should cover 100% of debt service. Owner compensation and other benefits would come from sales and service charges and appreciation of real estate value(s).

Expenses (% of Annual Sales)

Cost of Goods	60% to 65%
Occupancy Costs	05% to 12%
Payroll/Labor Costs	20%
Profit (pretax)	05% to 10%

Questions

- Be ready for a lot of hard work. Ask about environmental history. Be careful of new boat sales as the floor plans/interest thereon will eat you up. Competition results in razor thin margins. Stick to brokerage if possible.
- Why are you selling? Are you environmentally clean? What would you do differently if you were starting again?

Industry Trend

- "Gradual revenue growth is expected for the Marinas industry over the five years to 2021, with industry revenue projected to rise at an annualized rate of 0.3% to $4.8 billion. This forecast includes a 0.2% increase in 2017 alone. Transporting and launching a boat oneself can be an arduous task and take considerable daylight time away from the activity itself. In 2016, time spent on leisure and sports by consumers is estimated to slightly decrease, placing more value on the limited time consumers have for recreational activities and the need for time-saving strategies. The increasing number of boats being built will also secure revenue for the future, as demand for storage services will increase."

Source: IBISWorld Industry Outlook

- With innovative design and consumer preferences for outboard power, many manufacturers are seeing the fishing boat replace the fiberglass inboard/outboard as the de facto family runabout.

Expert Comments

It is a tourist related industry. If the location requires costly travel and the economy is soft, the sales will be down.

Location and facilities are critical but vary greatly.

Seller Financing

- It is extremely difficult to obtain bank financing, since the assets can literally float away.
- Large down payments and seller's financing is the rule.
- Seller financing used as banks are loath to take any risks at all. They don't want foreclosure auctions which will only bring in a fraction of their loan.

Resources

- National Marine Manufacturers Association: http://www.nmma.org
- American Boat Builders and Repairers Association: http://www.abbra.org
- Association of Marina Industries: http://www.marinaassociation.org
- Boat Owners Association of the U.S.: http://www.boatus.com
- IBISWorld, January 2017: http://ibisworld.com

Marine/Yacht Services (Boat/Repair)	
NAICS 811490	Number of Businesses/Units 118,210

Rules of Thumb

➤ 100% of annual sales includes inventory

➤ 2.3 x SDE includes inventory

Pricing Tips

- Determine value of furniture, fixtures & equipment; any warranty work involved?

Benchmark Data

Statistics (Boat Dealership and Repair)

Number of Establishments	118,210
Average Profit Margin	5.6%
Revenue per Employee	$125,900
Average Number of Employees	1.3
Average Wages per Employee	$17,518

Products and Services Segmentation

New boats	56.7%
Parts and repair services	29.4%
Used boats	13.9%

M

Industry Costs

Profit	5.6%
Wages	13.8%
Purchases	63.6%
Depreciation	0.9%
Marketing	1.3%
Rent & Utilities	3.6%
Other	11.2%

Market Share

MarineMax Inc.	6.6%

Expenses (% of Annual Sales)

Cost of Goods	30%
Occupancy Costs	07%
Payroll/Labor Costs	15%
Profit (pretax)	40%

Questions
- Customer base, length of time in industry, employee turnover, specific services performed

Industry Trend
- Growth

Expert Comments

The mega-yacht (80-foot to 180-foot boats) is a major growth industry, especially in south Florida.

Resources
- IBISWorld, March 2017: http://ibisworld.com

	Franchise
Martinizing Dry Cleaning	
Approx. Total Investment	$305,000–$593,700

	NAICS 812320	Number of Businesses/Units 422

Rules of Thumb
➢ 55–60% of annual sales plus inventory

Benchmark Data
- "He said a franchisee could open a store for anywhere from $293,500 to $476,000, including the franchise fee and purchase of in-house dry cleaning equipment. A typical investment for a franchisee to open a store would be $390,000.
  "Four percent of the sales from a franchised store's gross sales go back to the company."

Source: "Martinizing Cleans Up" by Jeff McKinney, www.greenearthcleaning.com

Resources

- Martinizing Dry Cleaning: http://www.martinizingfranchise.com

	Franchise
McGruff's Safe Kids ID System	
Approx. Total Investment	$7,995–$9,995
	Number of Businesses/Units 26

Rules of Thumb

➢ 52% of annual sales plus inventory

Resources

- McGruff'sSafe Kids ID Systems: https://www.mcgruffstuff.com/

Meat Markets		
SIC 5421-07	NAICS 44521	Number of Businesses/Units 9,404

Rules of Thumb

➢ 40% of annual sales plus inventory

➢ 2.5 x SDE includes inventory

➢ 5 x monthly sales plus inventory

Benchmark Data

Statistics (Meat Markets)

Number of Establishments	9,315
Average Profit Margin	3.0%
Revenue per Employee	$176,400
Average Number of Employees	4.7
Average Wages per Employee	$21,921

Products and Services Segmentation

Broilers	42.3%
Beef	25.3%
Pork	23.5%
Turkey	7.7%
Other red meat and fish	0.6%
Other chicken	0.6%

Industry Costs

Profit	3.0%
Wages	12.4%
Purchases	68.0%
Depreciation	1.6%
Marketing	1.7%
Rent & Utilities	5.0%
Other	8.3%

M

Market Share

Omaha Steaks International Inc. 6.9%

Expenses (% of Annual Sales)

Cost of Goods	50%
Occupancy Costs	10%
Payroll/Labor Costs	15%
Profit (pretax)	15%

Industry Trend

- "Clean and ethical labels alongside intelligent packaging and the demand for organic produce are some of the key trends likely to dominate the food industry this year." (The information in the rest of this article is copyrighted, but it can be read be online at this website.)

  Source: "Food trend predictions for 2017" by Oscar Rousseau, January 3, 2017, http://www.globalmeatnews.com/Analysis/Food-trend-predictions-for-2017

- "According to a report from the USDA, 87 percent of households buy food from large grocery stores or supermarkets, forcing local butcher shops to change how they do business. Most grocery stores have butchers, but not all are meat cutters, which are what the butchers at Stoney Point Farm Market are called. Meat cutters are similar to butchers but have more finesse in breaking down meat into different cuts and tailoring those per individual customer requests. Some organizations predict the services offered by butcher shops will make a comeback this year. The National Restaurant Association forecasts that the No.1 trend in 2017 will be new cuts of meat and the No.1 concept trend will be hyper-local sourcing."

  Source: http://www.eveningsun.com/story/news/2017/04/26/family-butcher-shops-unique-hanover-area/99492530/

Resources

- National Cattlemen's Beef Association: http://www.beef.org
- IBISWorld, September 2017: http://ibisworld.com
- North American Meat Institute: http://www.meatinstitute.org

Medical and Diagnostic Laboratories

	NAICS 621511	Number of Businesses/Units 37,270

Rules of Thumb

- ➢ 4–5 x EBIT
- ➢ 4–5 x EBITDA
- ➢ 100–125% of annual gross sales
- ➢ 4–6 x SDE plus inventory

Pricing Tips

- Good diversity of accounts, good 3rd party payer contracts a must
- Multiple of SDE increases with profit levels.

Benchmark Data

Statistics (Diagnostic & Medical Laboratories)

Number of Establishments	37,270
Average Profit Margin	13.7%
Revenue per Employee	$182,100
Average Number of Employees	8.0
Average Wages per Employee	$61,847

Products and Services Segmentation

General pathology services	36.8%
Clinical pathology services	18.6%
Other	17.5%
X-ray/radiography imaging services	10.3%
Magnetic resonance imaging (MRI) services	10.0%
Anatomic pathology services	6.8%

Major Market Segmentation

Private insurance payments	41.6%
Medicare and Medicaid payments	20.3%
Health practitioners' payments	11.0%
Hospital payments	10.0%
Other	6.6%
Patient out-of-pocket	5.9%
Outpatient care facility payments	3.0%
Other healthcare providers payments	1.6%

Industry Costs

Profit	13.7%
Wages	33.9%
Purchases	10.0%
Depreciation	2.7%
Marketing	0.9%
Rent & Utilities	5.3%
Other	33.5%

Market Share

Quest Diagnostics Inc.	14.3%
Laboratory Corporation of America Holdings	13.3%

Expenses (% of Annual Sales)

Cost of Goods	13% to 20%
Occupancy Costs	03%
Payroll/Labor Costs	44% to 45%
Profit (pretax)	30% to 35%

Questions
- Payer mix, market share, patient demographic data

Industry Trend
- ". . .the aging US population will bolster demand for laboratory testing due

to this demographic's high prevalence of chronic illnesses, which will require frequent monitoring and testing by healthcare providers. As more insured individuals use industry services, such as magnetic resonance imaging and CT scans and biopsies for irregular screening results, revenue is expected to grow, increasing at an annualized rate of 2.7% to $60.7 billion in the five years to 2022. Profit is expected to remain steady at 13.7% or industry revenue over the next five years."

Source: IBISWorld Industry Outlook

- Heavy competition, steady growth for next 5 years, heavy regulation, low capital intensity.

Expert Comments

It would take over four years to replicate a new diagnostic clinic and that long to obtain a good strong client base.

Difficult to acquire accounts since physician groups don't like to make changes. 3rd party payer contracts are difficult to obtain.

This is a marketing business. Location, ease of service, and networking with doctors and attorneys is a must.

Seller Financing
- Outside financing

Resources
- Clinical Laboratory and Pathology News and Trends: http://www.darkdaily.com
- American Society for Clinical Laboratory Science: http://www.ascls.org
- IBISWorld, June 2017: http://ibisworld.com

Medical Billing		
	NAICS 541219	Number of Businesses/Units 2,409

Rules of Thumb

➤ 2.5–3 x SDE

➤ 3–4 x EBIT

➤ 85–90% of annual sales plus inventory

➤ 3–3.5 x EBITDA

Pricing Tips
- Determine how much of the revenue is recurring revenue and how active the owner is in the business. Locate any client concentration issues.
- Specialties of clients are a very important factor.
- The value of medical billing companies is heavily dependent upon the billing rates they charge their clients and the length of the contract. Billing rates are typically in the 5% to 8% range for larger accounts, but can be as high as 15% and as low as 2%.

Benchmark Data

Statistics (Medical Claims Processing Services)

Number of Establishments	2,409
Average Profit Margin	27.0%
Revenue per Employee	$489,800
Average Number of Employees	3.0
Average Wages per Employee	$86,479

Products and Services Segmentation

Claims processing	49.1%
Policy and claims examinations	21.1%
Claims investigations	19.4%
Back-office, administrative support and consulting	10.4%

Major Market Segmentation

Healthcare providers	66.1%
Private insurers	21.7%
Government insurers	12.2%

Industry Costs

Profit	27.0%
Wages	17.7%
Purchases	4.0%
Depreciation	1.0%
Marketing	1.0%
Rent & Utilities	1.1%
Other	48.2%

Market Share

HMS Holdings	14.5%

- No client representing more than 10% of revenue.
- Payroll typically runs 40–55% of revenue.
- Sales per FT employee are typically around $100,000.

Expenses (% of Annual Sales)

Occupancy Costs	05%
Payroll/Labor Costs	45% to 50%
Profit (pretax)	25%

Questions

- What do your client contracts look like? How long have you been in business? Can the business be easily scaled or the overhead reduced?
- A good question for a buyer to ask a seller would be if there are any client concentration issues.

Industry Trend

- "It is expected that healthcare industries will add 15.6 million jobs by the end of 2022. There have been a lot of issues regarding the billing process that include changes in maintaining healthcare records and the changes in Medicaid and Medicare policies. The operational costs are increasing in the medical industry almost every day. Complicated and rigid coding rules, the constant debate on fee structure, various attempts to reward for results and the heated negotiations are among the few constant struggles that go on in the medical billing world.

M

"2017 is considered to bring a transition in the healthcare sector, especially for the medical coders. A lot of advancements in the medical billing and coding sector will make the job more interesting and challenging.

"Let us have a look at the most important medical billing trends that will affect the healthcare industry in 2017.

- ✓ The Transition from ICD-9 to ICD-10
- ✓ Implementation of CPT codes
- ✓ Electronic Health Records Management

"The EHR trends to look out for in 2017 are as follows:

1. Patient access will increase
2. Cloud technology for Electronic Health Records will improve
3. Implementation of a nationalized electronic patient database
4. Adopting HER software will become mandatory for every healthcare provider."

Source: "Medical Billing Trends In 2017—What Can You Expect?" by Rajeev Singh, March 30, 2017, https://www.linkedin.com/pulse/medical-billing-trends-2017-what-can-you-expect-rajeev-singh

- Health care is a trillion-dollar industry that is always in need. Medical billing operations will continue to increase as more doctors outsource their billing and transfer their records into digital form.

Expert Comments

I would advise a buyer to act quickly due to the few number of business opportunities on the market. I would advise sellers to delegate their role and responsibilities in the business to their employees to make it a smoother transition for a buyer.

There are a large amount of buyers looking to buy medical billing businesses, and shifts in billing trends have made it easier and more cost effective for doctors to outsource their billing needs.

Due to new rules and regulations relating to Obamacare, the medical billing industry has recently seen significant growth.

Buyers should educate themselves on upcoming changes within the industry and find out the specific area of medicine that each client practices, example: surgeons, clinics, dialysis centers, etc.

This is a highly competitive industry that has a strong financial outlook with the changes in the health care field and complicated coding and billing procedures.

Seller Financing

- I typically see sellers carry notes for 24 months at 6% interest.
- Seller financing is very common. However, the buyers for Chiropractically Yours were able to secure SBA financing. I believe future medical billing transactions will include outside financing due to the increase of SBA loans we are currently experiencing.

Resources

- IBISWorld, December 2016: http://ibisworld.com
- Healthcare Business Management Association: http://www.hbma.org

Medical Practices (Physicians)

SIC 8011-01	NAICS 621111	

Rules of Thumb

➢ 35–45% of annual gross sales includes inventory

➢ 1–3 x SDE includes inventory

➢ 1.5–2.5 x EBITDA

➢ 2.5–3.5 x EBIT

Pricing Tips

- For medical practices, the average sales price is about 30% of annual gross income for smaller 1- to 5-doctor practices, though, the range can vary a great deal depending on practice characteristics and medical specialty. Understanding the industry compensation, income, expense norms for a particular specialty is key.
- Must sell at Fair Market Value (FMV) to comply with anti-kickback statute and Stark Laws. Physician compensation must be at Fair Market Value.
- Obamacare disrupted the market and supports large multispecialty entities, further eroding value. The Trump and Republican election is causing further erosion.
- Value of a practice will vary depending on the type of practice. For example, a primary- care practice will sell for roughly 30% of annual gross collections, where a veterinary practice will sell for roughly 75% of annual gross collections.
- Price Rules of Thumb vary greatly (I mean a lot) based on practice type. Most primary care practices will sell in the 30%-35% range as percentage of gross. But can vary from zero % to 50% for small 1-4 doctor practices. Averages for specialty practices tend to be lower, perhaps in the 20%-25% range. Physical therapy and psychology/psychiatric higher in the 40%-45% range. These prices can vary greatly depending on number factors. Carefully examine discretionary earnings compared to industry compensation exceptions for that particular specialty. Compensation expectations vary dramatically for different types of doctors. $200K might be good for one type of doctor, whereas in other specialties new grads might commonly make $350K. Look at patient load and hours worked compared to industry norms for that specialty.
- Most medical practices are created and run to create high income for labor, not profit or EBITDA. There is an excess of jobs available driving up salaries and driving down profits, so driving down value. The Goodwill Registry on sale-data is helpful in some cases, but the often-quoted running-average 10-year median goodwill-value as a percentage of gross is irrelevant; as the average of many specialties reflects the midpoint of 10 years' steady decline. You need to acquire the full database and evaluate the underlying data to be useful; and look in particular at the price:SDE data. The effect of the Medicare cuts which began in 2005 can distort the Registry summary statistics and need to be adjusted; and you need to remove results from court-valuations, divorces and other non-transactional data. The value of medical practices is generally at an all-time low. Decisions regarding what, where, when and how to practice are influenced by numerous factors, including: personal preferences, market forces, state and federal policies and programs, and institutions that constitute the health care system and medical education infrastructure. Increasing retirement, plus the trend toward shorter working hours, increases the supply

of practices for sale, and decreases the available FTE workforce available as buyers. The increasing rate of boomer retirement and decreasing count of new physicians contribute to a reduction of value of practices for sale. A significant shortfall of physicians could develop over the next 15 or more years in the absence of increased output from U.S. medical schools, increased recruitment of foreign-trained physicians, or both. The American College of Physicians is concerned that the practice environment for those in medical practice has become so encumbered with regulation and practice hassles, at a time when reimbursement for care provided by physicians is declining, that physicians are finding it increasingly difficult to provide for their patients. Of particular concern when determining value of a medical practice is ensuring not only that the purchase price is Fair Market Value, but also that the valuation method does not take into account the volume or value of referrals that the selling physician has made or may make to the purchaser, such that the purchase price could be challenged as a kickback or inducement. The OIG has provided guidance on the question of how to value a physician practice or other healthcare provider. The ailing economy is leading many Americans to skip doctor visits, skimp on their medicine, and put off tests. Employment by hospitals is paying more, and insurance-reimbursement and gross income is often dropping, so the results of the Income Approach of valuation identifying dividends [(SDE minus market rate compensation of one working owner) x 2 (i.e., 50% Cap rate)] is becoming more important for more specialties. Percentage of annual gross sales or SDE multiplier as valuation Rules of Thumb are obsolete, if ever valid. Growth Rates are available through the Congressional Budget Office reports; rarely above 2% historically. Medical practice is riskier-and demands higher Cap rates-than other professional practices like accounting, law, architecture and engineering which are not subject to clinical malpractice risks, or subject to Medicare or insurance company changing reimbursement limitations or denials. Many practices can't even sell at the value of the liquidated assets, since jobs pay more without asset purchase. The impact of specialty and location is profound, as is the FTE work schedule and leverage of employed licensed providers. Medicare is continually reducing reimbursement, which impacts other insurances which often base their payment on a percent of Medicare (i.e., 80-120% of Medicare), so dependence on insurance reimbursement is an important consideration in value. In addition, specific diagnosis and procedure (ICD/CPT) billing-code reimbursement changes-like what has happened in dermatology, ophthalmology, allergy, cardiology, and other specialties-have further reduced reimbursement and profits during the past decade. Cash and cosmetic practices are usually worth more since there is a higher profit for less work, and often provide a better lifestyle, but even those can be difficult to sell. Many specialties are having trouble attracting new doctors no matter the income, so guaranteed wages are increasing, sales are becoming more difficult, and values are dropping. Make sure to read the 'white papers' on supply and demand available on many specialty professional association websites. The best overhead statistics are usually available at http://www. NSCHBC.org. The best market rate compensation stats are usually available at http://www.MGMA.com.

- The rule of thumb in any of the medical fields (i.e., accepting Medicare) is 1.5 x dividends as defined by IRS RR59-60. (You can call it 1.5 x EBITDA, but that is slightly incorrect for non-capital, asset-heavy businesses.) Includes normal inventory but not excess inventory. %-of-gross hasn't applied to medicine in decades since the doctor shortage began.

- From SDE, I will subtract the estimate of the cost of employing one person at the same level of licensure, with the same work schedule, and with the same experience and sophistication as the current owner, at a market rate of compensation. This provides a perspective as if the owner was instead employed, and the balance was a return on investment to ownership. Another way to look at this is the result is the income available to the owner if the owner couldn't work and had to hire an equivalent replacement licensed professional to see the patients. This remainder income is equivalent to what the IRS defines as Dividends in RR59-60. Dividends will be the income stream analyzed in the Income Approach.
- The billing process in a medical practice is very complex, both in generating the charges using appropriate diagnosis and treatment codes, and in recording the payment and adjustments for uncollectable amounts. Accounts Receivable represent past gross charges for services rendered and as yet uncollected or adjusted-off. These receivables must be discounted to reflect both insurance company reimbursement disallowances, plus the decreasing value over time due to difficulty in collections of past due accounts. In other words, the historic collection ratio of the practice does not yet include the standing wave of uncollectable accounts at practice end, or at a particular point in time, as in a valuation at a particular date.

Benchmark Data

Statistics (Primary Care Doctors)

Number of Establishments	203,139
Average Profit Margin	14.4%
Revenue per Employee	$210,000
Average Number of Employees	6.5
Average Wages per Employee	$79,030

Products and Services Segmentation

Diagnosis of general symptoms	32.0%
Diagnosis, screening and preventative care	26.0%
Other	17.0%
Diagnosis of symptoms related to the musculoskeletal systems	12.0%
Disease treatment	7.0%
Diagnosis of symptoms related to the respiratory system	6.0%

Industry Costs

Profit	14.4%
Wages	37.8%
Purchases	13.6%
Depreciation	1.3%
Marketing	0.8%
Rent & Utilities	4.1%
Other	28.0%

Statistics (Specialist Doctors)

Number of Establishments	259,192
Average Profit Margin	12.2%
Revenue per Employee	$175,300
Average Number of Employees	5.8
Average Wages per Employee	$91,604

Products and Services Segmentation

Other	52.5%
Psychiatry	10.2%
Anesthesiology	8.9%
Obstetrics and gynecology	8.9%
Emergency medicine	7.5%
Radiology and diagnostic medicine	6.2%
General surgery	5.8%

Industry Costs

Profit	12.2%
Wages	52.3%
Purchases	13.6%
Depreciation	1.3%
Marketing	0.8%
Rent & Utilities	4.1%
Other	15.7%

- Be sure to use income/compensation levels for correct medical specialty.
- For solo practice the SDE should be higher than 50% of gross collections. Midlevel's production should be 3 times their income. Each full time equivalent provider should see at least 80-85 patients per week; 100–120 patients per week is better.
- Typically, a multi-doctor practice is considered less risky for an investor and is usually potentially more profitable.
- Per bed, per full-time employee (FTE); per physician; per square foot; per machine; per member per month (PMPM).
- Practice benchmarks vary with specialty. Look up statistics/benchmarks for the practice type in question. A psychiatry practice may be a solo operation in 200SF with no support staff and almost no assets. A cosmetic plastic surgeon may have $500K in equipment and an in-house accredited surgical suite with a lot of staff. An oncology or allergy practice may have a great deal of value in drug inventory, whereas a pediatric practice may have no drug inventory. So for some practice types (e.g., psychiatry) the cost of goods sold is very small. Others have significant COGS. For most practice types expect a support staff ratio of 3–5 per full-time doctor.
- Profit for physician practices should be above 50%

Expenses (% of Annual Sales)

Cost of Goods	n/a
Occupancy Costs	05% to 10%
Payroll/Labor Costs	20% to 30%
Profit (pretax)	25% to 35%

Questions

- Payer mix. hours of work, number of patient encounters per week, support staff ratio, ancillary services performed. What special training, education and services will buyer need to duplicate? Are there aged accounts receivable?
- Ask specific questions regarding details of 5 years of tax returns, financial statements, production reports including payer mix, accounts receivable and billing, procedure mix, etc. Also, discuss detailed tax depreciation schedule and details regarding specific assets.
- How many hours a doctor works is directly connected to gross revenue

collections. They should ask how many hours a week they work.

- Type of practice; hours worked per week; number of patient encounters per week; ancillary services % of revenue; types of procedures performed; drug inventory levels; in-house lab and equipment capabilities; industry trends for that particular specialty; number of providers; hospital/competition.
- An important fact is the type of medical practice, general or specialty! Number of Medicare and Medicaid patients? Billing process and whether in-house or farmed out.
- Accounts receivable in collections amount should be under 25%. Insurance accepted and type of billing to insurance companies. Employee retention and turnover.
- What are the ACO plans in this community? Is your ICD/CPT coding federally compliant? Are your provider employment and compensation plans and PECOS registrations state and federally compliant?
- Hours worked. Use of mid-level providers/physician extenders payer mix reimbursement trends up/down ancillary profit centers.
- Sustainability of projected revenue stream, based on probability of patients remaining with practice, level of reimbursement yield, regulatory restrictions on ASTC, etc.

Industry Trend
- The Affordable Care act keeps changing. Young doctors graduate with a lot of debt and so their preference is to work in a stable hospital environment with consistent hours, rather than take on the risk of owning and operating a private medical practice.
- Will still be in high demand. Baby boomers getting older/sicker. Highly regulated industry. Will continue to be highly regulated. I don't see the will in Congress/President (either political party) to significantly change regulatory environment.
- More doctors looking to add ancillary services as a way to increase revenue and compensate for burdensome cost of regulatory requirements.
- Payer mix, procedure mix, appropriate use of mid-level providers, and appropriate use of technology all have a tremendous influence on value. Medical practices that effectively manage these components of their practices will be more valuable and less risky.
- Consolidation into very large organizations in most specialties.
- Medical will continue to be in demand by buyers.
- Under PPACA (Obamacare) hospitals are the main buyers, and can charge double what the acquired physicians could.
- Increased merger & acquisition (M&A) activity, and steady growth in revenue.
- The market trend is lower profits for the next few years.
- A lot of turmoil due to regulatory changes. More practices trending to self-pay practices. Many doctors moving away from Medicaid and Medicare due to regulatory burden and low reimbursement. Still a very large part of the economy. Healthcare will still be strong in years to come. Likely to see more boutique practices and more capitation practices.
- Demand for services and costs to provide services increasing while reimbursements decreasing.
- Increasing competition; industry will tend to consolidate.
- PPACA is driving physicians into employment, reducing available buyers.

M

Expert Comments

The sale of a medical practice is unique and takes much longer to close than any other type of business or practice purchase.

Compare the subject practice against industry key performance indicators.

Competition is relatively low as demand for medical services is increasing. Profit trends are relatively stable. There is lots of downward pressure from government and insurance payers, but doctors are still finding ways to maintain income. Check the CMS Physician Fee Schedule to get an idea of if a particular specialty's reimbursements are going up or down this/next year.

Most doctors' offices are in decent facilities. Marketability is mixed. A good practice with good profits will sell. Large practice (EBITDA $1M+) are very desirable. A small practice where the doc is taking home a low income may not be sellable.

Hospitals will usually pay 10%–20%–30% of what another owner practitioner might pay. Hospitals won't pay for goodwill due to concern about Stark laws.

Normal income & expense ratios can vary greatly depending on practice specialty type.

Due diligence is essential. Review at least 5 years of tax returns, financial statements, production reports including payer mix, accounts receivable and billing, procedure mix, etc. Also, obtain an equipment appraisal if significant equipment is involved.

Regulatory pressures and changes in the marketplace, including demographics of physicians and patients, are driving decline in valuation in medical practices.

Owner will usually make more money by working just one more year.

Healthcare experience is essential for your advisors, including valuation professionals, accountants, attorneys, and others.

There is more variance than ever in healthcare providers and the way that they run their businesses. Some have excellent, state-of-the-art facilities and are extremely efficient. Others have poor facilities and outdated technology and business models. The regulatory environment is extremely challenging and ever changing.

The market is mostly doctors selling to other doctors. Very few non-doctors buyers/sellers outside of hospitals/large groups, though in some states and practice types non-physician ownership is allowed and you will find investor buyers.

Number of specialists per 100K population varies. Obamacare and healthcare reform is causing turmoil in industry. Industry is constantly evolving in response to government laws/regulations. Above-average practices can usually sell okay. Underperforming practices may have virtually no value and be unable to sell.

Managed care, political pressure on lowing reimbursements, regulatory pressures, uncertainties all are playing a part in valuation declines in the healthcare industry.

Physicians are very smart but often choose their advisors poorly. Selecting a team of trustworthy advisors (legal, accounting, transactional) is key to success.

Seller Financing
- It's possible for a buyer of a medical practice who is a licensed physician to borrow up to 90% of the practice purchase price, maybe even more.
- Financing is available through specialty bank departments. Sellers are also willing to finance. 5 to 10 years.
- Mostly outside financing, but seller financing is not uncommon in this industry. Many times a portion of the financed amount will be seller carry in order to make the deal happen.
- Seller financing is common, but outside financing is also available. Many hospitals are also purchasing medical practices.
- 100% financing is readily available through specialty bank departments.
- Lenders look very favorably towards funding these deals. Many have special terms available for financing professional practices.

Resources
- Physicians Practice: http://www.physicianspractice.com
- Medscape: http://www.medscape.com
- National Society of Certified Healthcare Business Consultants: http://www.nschbc.org
- Medical Economics: http://www.memag.com
- American Academy of Family Physicians: http://www.aafp.org
- American Medical Association: http://www.ama-assn.org/ama
- Medical Group Management Association: http://www.mgma.com
- IBISWorld, March 2017: http://ibisworld.com
- The BVR/AHLA Guide to Healthcare Valuation: https://www.bvresources.com/products/the-bvr-ahla-guide-to-healthcare-industry-finance-and-valuation-fourth-edition
- American Health Lawyers Association (AHLA): https://www.healthlawyers.org/Pages/home.aspx
- American Hospital Association (AHA): http://www.aha.org/
- Healthcare Financial Management Association (HFMA): https://www.hfma.org/
- IBISWorld, May 2017: http://ibisworld.com
- American Medical Group Association: https://www.amga.org/

Medical Spas		
	NAICS 812199	Number of Businesses/Units 23,175

Rules of Thumb
➢ 50% of annual gross sales plus inventory

➢ 2.5 x SDE includes inventory

➢ 3.5 x EBIT

➢ 5 x EBITDA

M

Pricing Tips

- Price varies according to the equipment as the industry is creating new treatments and new technologies every year. People are more aware of the newest treatments and the owners have to invest regularly in new equipment if they want to be able to keep the clientele.
- More and more competitors are entering in this market because it's very profitable. Investors partner with doctors to create different types of spas, and business owners need to invest more money in marketing and social media to maintain their clientele. Clients are ready to invest a lot of money for their beauty, but they are becoming more demanding and look for the newest trends.
- "The most simple rule of thumb—with any legitimacy, limited as it is—is using a grossly simplified Income Approach, the primary approach per IRS Revenue Ruling 59-60. This approach looks at the return on investment (i.e., dividends) to the buyer after market-rate compensation of one working owner."

Source: http://www.medicalpracticeappraisal.com/medspa-appraisal-valuation.html

Benchmark Data

Statistics (Health and Wellness Spas)

Number of Establishments	23,175
Average Profit Margin	10.6%
Revenue per Employee	$44,368
Average Number of Employees	16.6
Average Wages per Employee	$22,543

Products and Services Segmentation

Massage and bodywork treatments	35.6%
Skin-care treatments	24.1%
Hair and nail treatments	20.2%
Retail	10.8%
Other	9.3%

Major Market Segmentation

Adult women	52.7%
Seniors	18.9%
Adult men	18.1%
Teenagers and children	10.3%

Industry Costs

Profit	10.6%
Wages	50.7%
Purchases	15.7%
Depreciation	3.6%
Marketing	3.2%
Rent & Utilities	13.8%
Other	2.4%

Market Share

Massage Envy	9.0%

Expenses (% of Annual Sales)

Cost of Goods	05% to 10%
Occupancy Costs	08% to 10%
Payroll/Labor Costs	30% to 35%
Profit (pretax)	25% to 30%

Questions

- How did they get the clientele over the years, what the seller is intending to do after the sale, for how long the employees have been working in the business, their experience, and how do they get paid-on commission or fixed salary. How is the equipment: year, model, the maintenance? Is it all paid off? What are the nearest competitors in the area? Do a market search and go to the city hall or local business association to see if there are other projects for new spas that will open in the near future.
- Revenue/service mix. Liability for prepaids. Equipment leases. Reason for selling.

Industry Trend

- The spas are intended to be more specialized in certain treatments for certain parts of the body or the face as so many new treatments and trends are appearing on the market. The spas would need more space and more equipment and qualified employees to be able to propose such a variety of treatments.
- The trend is also to open larger spas with cafeteria, movement studio, retail accessories, beauty product store, and valet parking, to keep the clientele longer at the spa and to make them spend more money. So now the spa is becoming a leisure destination in itself!

Expert Comments

Verify if the team is highly trained and experienced and how to secure the employees and clientele after the sale.

Ease of replication is easy for new spas that don't have too much income, but very difficult to get the reputation and clientele built over the years; the number of good rated reviews on the Internet.

Seller Financing

- We see in 80% of the cases seller financing—30% to 50%.
- 3 to 5 years

Resources

- Spa Industry Association: http://www.dayspaassociation.com
- IBISWorld, August 2016: http://ibisworld.com

Medical Transcription		
	NAICS 561410	

Rules of Thumb

➢ 75–80% of annual sales

➢ 3–3.5 x SDE

➢ 4.5–5 x EBITDA

M

Pricing Tips

- MTSO's are almost always sold as a percentage of revenue with not too much attention paid to net profit but a great deal to gross profit. Most of the buyers are rolling up revenue and are therefore most concerned about the quality of the revenue and the cost of production (COGS.) MTSOs with revenue under $1.5M can generally expect to get about 75–80% of revenue as a purchase price, while those doing revenue of $1.5M plus can expect to see 80–100% of revenue.
- The lower the risk profile of the customer base the greater the percentage of revenue one can expect. Customer concentration and risk of losing the customer to EHR are central to evaluating this risk profile. If the work is post EHR, that is the MTSO is working within the healthcare provider's EHR, then the buyer is going to perceive the revenue to be less at risk of loss to EHR.
- Earnouts are virtually always a part of any MTSO transaction. Typically, the buyer will come in with 50–60% cash and the seller will carry the balance on an 18- to 36-month earnout tied to ongoing revenue. A greater risk profile will equate to a larger earnout, a lower profile to less earnout.
- Offshore, onshore or hybrid production models: The easiest MTSO to sell is where all the customers are U.S. based but most are OK with some or much of the production work being done offshore. If offshore production is allowed, many more buyers, especially from India, will come to the table with offers. Ideally the business has customers paying onshore rates but the buyers believe they can move much of the production off shore while keeping the customer pricing closer to onshore rates.

Benchmark Data

Statistics (Document Preparation Services)

Number of Establishments	87,171
Average Profit Margin	7.2%
Revenue per Employee	$37,000
Average Number of Employees	1.5
Average Wages per Employee	$16,628

Products and Services Segmentation

Document preparation services	55.8%
Typing services	38.1%
Printing services	3.7%
Other services	2.4%

Major Market Segmentation

Healthcare providers	55.9%
Small service-related business	19.8%
Individuals and households	10.1%
Other	9.0%
Federal, state and local government	5.2%

Industry Costs

Profit	7.2%
Wages	44.6%
Purchases	16.8%
Depreciation	2.8%
Marketing	1.8%
Rent & Utilities	4.6%
Other	22.2%

Market Share

Nuance Communications Inc. 9.3%

- Gross profit and EBITDA are very much tied to how much of the production is done offshore and or how much of the production is being processed via a speech engine. Use of technology and offshore labor will have a huge impact on how profitable the business is.
- For work being produced through onshore labor, line rates should be 12–15 cents per line (CPL) with labor costs at 7–9 CPL and platform cost at about 1.5 CPL. Offshore production line rates are about 6 CPL, mostly in India followed by the Philippines. When production is done offshore, frequently the customer can get a line rate of 10–12 CPL. In hospitals speech recognition technologies are used to produce 70–80% of the work. In this case the customer may pay 10–12 CPL while cost of production (i.e., the editor plus the technology) might be more like 4 CPL for the editor/labor and 2–3 CPL for the speech engine.
- Well-run MTSOs with only onshore operations can see gross profit margins in the 30–40% range; those with offshore operations can increase these margins by 10 points to the 40–50% range.

Expenses (% of Annual Sales)

Cost of Goods .... 50% to 70%
Profit (pretax) .... 15% to 20%

Questions

- Please describe each customer that accounts for more than 15% of your revenue. Have you or do you anticipate losing any business to EMR or to other competitors? Is your production being done onshore or offshore? Are you open to selling to someone with an offshore workforce? What platform, if any, are you using? Are your customer contracts assignable?

Industry Trend

- "Six Medical Transcription Predictions:
  - ✓ Age of technological breakthroughs
  - ✓ Outsourcing is expected to increase
  - ✓ Emerging markets will pave the way
  - ✓ Enhanced use of security mechanisms
  - ✓ Voice recognition technologies will be in demand
  - ✓ Fresh guidelines"
    Source: https://www.flatworldsolutions.com/healthcare/articles/medical-transcription-trends.php
- Consolidation of smaller MTSOs by the large players, such as Nuance and lots of mid-sized regional/national players. More revenues will be lost to EHR and speech recognition technologies but the declines in revenue are tapering off from the big declines of the past few years of government incentivized EHR adoption.

Expert Comments

The Medical Transcription industry has witnessed declines in revenue and profitability due to low-cost offshore labor, improvements in speech recognition technology and the government mandated adoption of Electronic Health Records.

M

Seller Financing
- Occasionally for the smaller MTSO, the buyer will purchase with an SBA loan and the seller will hold a note for 15% of the transaction rather than the typical earnout structure.
- Transactions typically involve 50-60% cash down with the seller doing a 24- to 36-month earnout for the balance.

Resources
- The Association for Healthcare Documentation Integrity: http://www.ahdionline.org
- American Health Information Management Association: http://www.ahima.org
- IBISWorld, May 2017: http://ibisworld.com

Meineke Car Care Centers	Franchise
Approx. Total Investment	$255,000–$320,000
Estimated Annual Sales/Unit	$700,000

	NAICS 811112	Number of Businesses/Units 972

Rules of Thumb
> 30–35% of annual sales plus inventory

Mental Health and Substance Abuse Centers	
NAICS 621420	Number of Businesses/Units 14,827

Rules of Thumb
> 78% of annual sales plus inventory

> 2.7 x SDE plus Inventory

> 11.3 x EBIT

> 1.7 x EBITDA

Benchmark Data

Expenses (% of Annual Sales)
Cost of Goods	12%
Payroll/Labor Costs	05%
Profit (pretax)	08%

Statistics (Mental Health & Substance Abuse Centers)
Number of Establishments	14,827
Average Profit Margin	8.0%
Revenue per Employee	$73,300
Average Number of Employees	15.7
Average Wages per Employee	$33,317

Products and Services Segmentation

Residential care for mental health 40.7%
Residential care for combined drug and alcohol abuse 32.3%
Residential care for drug abuse 13.8%
Residential care for alcohol abuse 8.9%
Home healthcare 2.5%
Other services 1.8%

Major Market Segmentation

Medicaid 32.9%
Other state and local entities 22.8%
Medicare 13.9%
Out-of-pocket payers 12.9%
Individuals with private insurance 8.4%
Other private payers 5.4%
Other federal entities 3.7%

Industry Costs

Profit 8.0%
Wages 45.4%
Purchases 12.2%
Depreciation 2.7%
Marketing 0.4%
Rent & Utilities 8.2%
Other 23.1%

Market Share

Universal Health Services Inc. 29.4%

Questions
- Payor mix, market share, patient demographic data

Industry Trend
- Revenue projected to grow, demand projected to grow, profit expected to grow, consolidation.

Seller Financing
- Outside financing

Resources
- National Institute of Mental Health: http://www.nimh.nih.gov
- National Association of Psychiatric Health Systems (NAPHS): http://www.naphs.org
- IBISWorld, March 2017: http://ibisworld.com

M

Mental Health Physicians

	NAICS 621112	

Rules of Thumb

➢ 43% of annual sales plus inventory

➢ 1.1 x SDE plus inventory

➢ 3 x EBIT

➢ 1.7 x EBITDA

Benchmark Data

Expenses (% of Annual Sales)

Cost of Goods	07%
Payroll/Labor Costs	05%
Profit (pretax)	10%

Questions
- Payor mix, market share, patient demographic data

Industry Trend
- Consolidation has caused stagnation; however, growth is expected as efficiency improves.

Seller Financing
- Outside financing

Resources
- American Academy of Family Physicians (AAFP): http://www.aafp.org
- American Medical Association (AMA): http://www.ama-assn.org

Mental Health Practitioners (Except Physicians)

Rules of Thumb

➢ 23% of annual sales plus inventory

➢ 5.5 x SDE plus inventory

➢ 2.7 x EBIT

➢ 2.8 x EBITDA

Benchmark Data

Expenses (% of Annual Sales)

Cost of Goods	07%
Payroll/Labor Costs	01%
Profit (pretax)	10%

Questions
- Payor mix, market share, patient demographic data

Industry Trend
- Increased consolidation, steady growth in revenue

Seller Financing
- Outside financing

Resources
- American Academy of Family Physicians (AAFP): http://www.aafp.org
- American Medical Association (AMA): http://www.ama-assn.org

		Franchise
Merry Maids		
Approx. Total Investment		$60,450–$185,850
	NAICS 561720	Number of Businesses/Units 1,433

Rules of Thumb
➢ 45% of annual sales plus inventory

Resources
- Merry Maids: http://www.merrymaids.com

		Franchise
Midas International		
Approx. Total Investment		$184,13–$433,0970
Estimated Annual Sales/Unit		$1 million+
	NAICS 811112	Number of Businesses/Units 2,098

Rules of Thumb
➢ 30–35% of annual sales plus inventory

Resources
- Midas International: http://www.midasfranchise.com

Middle Market Businesses (In General)

Rules of Thumb
➢ 2–5 x SDE plus inventory

➢ 3–5 x EBIT

➢ 3–5 x EBITDA

Pricing Tips
- Only accept audited financials. Always retain qualified legal and accounting professionals early on in the process to uncover any 'hidden' issues that you may not discover on your own. Determine whether the industry sector of the

M

business you are considering is trending up or down and what the long-term direction of the specific business's product line(s), within that industry, is projected to be. Determine what your exit strategy would be if you were to obtain control of the business.

Benchmark Data

Expenses (% of Annual Sales)

Cost of Goods .... 20% to 30%
Occupancy Costs 10%
Payroll/Labor Costs .... 25% to 30%
Profit (pretax) .... 30% to 40%

Questions

- What are their companies' goals for the future and how have they prepared to make that a reality? Have they prepared a contingency plan in the event of unforeseen developments and what are their contingencies?

Expert Comments

Middle market businesses have very sophisticated competitors and are quite risky. Therefore, they are historically more profitable than smaller, main street operations. Because of the high cost of entry, there is a limited market for many of these businesses. Additionally, these companies tend to often be quite specific in their product line and hold a large market share in their respective geographic location.

Mining—Metals		
	NAICS 212	

Pricing Tips

- 1. Does the property have an NI 43-101?
  2. What is the amount of proven, recoverable reserves?
  3. What is the value of the metal per ounce in the current market?
  4. Can the buyer get a 100% ROI in three years?
  5. Placer mines are more difficult to sell than hard-rock, lode, open-pit mines.
  6. Are the claims patented or unpatented? Are they on private land or BLM?

Benchmark Data

- Mining costs can run $400 to $600 an ounce for gold, and can vary for other minerals.

Questions

- 1. Will the owner joint-venture?
  2. Is the mine accessible year-round?
  3. Property status (e.g., patented, prospecting stage, pre-exploration, exploration, prefeasibility, feasibility, mining)?
  4. If not currently producing, how much time and money would it take to get into production?
  5. Executive summary? Business plan?

6. How much mineral has been removed from the mine?
7. What is the main mineral?
8. What other minerals are there and how much?
9. Is there a mill?
10. Accessibility to paved roads and railways?
11. Infrastructure, electricity, water?
12. Permitting status?
13. Acreage?
14. Grade % (grams/ton, or ounces/ton)
15. Brief history—when did the mine open?

Industry Trend

- We see precious and nonprecious metals increasing in price, which will be a benefit to the mining industry.

Expert Comments

Be extremely careful. Ask a lot of questions. Get a geologist's opinion.

Every mine is different. No two mines are alike. Every mine must be evaluated on its own merits.

Seller Financing

- Seller financing, anywhere from 10% to 50% down

Resources

- ICMJ Mining and Prospecting Journal: http://www.icmj.com/

Mining—Sand and Gravel

SIC 5032-11	NAICS 212321	Number of Businesses/Units 2,223

Rules of Thumb

➢ 100% of annual sales plus inventory
➢ 5 x EBITDA

Benchmark Data

Statistics (Sand and Gravel Mining)

Number of Establishments	2,223
Average Profit Margin	8.7%
Revenue per Employee	$512,200
Average Number of Employees	14.2
Average Wages per Employee	$63,930

Products and Services Segmentation

Construction sand and gravel	60.2%
Industrial sand and gravel	29.0%
Kaolin, common clay and other products	10.8%

Industry Costs

Profit	8.7%
Wages	12.6%
Purchases	16.2%
Depreciation	6.9%
Marketing	0.1%
Rent & Utilities	11.2%
Other	44.3%

Market Share

CRH PLC	7.1%
HeidelbergCement AG	10.5%

- At least 150,000 tons/year is the minimum usually necessary for a profitable site.

Industry Trend

- "The outlook of the Sand and Gravel Mining industry will remain heavily dependent on demand from downstream markets, particularly infrastructure construction and oil and gas applications. Over the five years to 2022, industry revenue is expected to rise at an annualized rate of 2.7% to $17.8 billion, including an anticipated 3.2% bump in 2018. Despite the end of federal stimulus programs, a stronger economy will spur greater demand in downstream construction markets, including residential, nonresidential and infrastructure. Demand for clay and refractory materials is projected to continue to deteriorate from several downstream manufacturing industries, but this decline will be offset by stronger demand from the housing market and buoyant demand from the highway and bridge construction market. As growth in housing starts accelerates over the period, public sector investment in the highway construction market is expected to improve. In addition, nonresidential construction is projected to increase, further contributing to industry growth."

Source: IBISWorld Industry Outlook

Resources

- IBISWorld, July 2017: http://ibisworld.com

	Franchise
Minuteman Press	
Approx. Total Investment	$100,000–$150,000
NAICS 323111	Number of Businesses/Units 956

Rules of Thumb

➢ 60–65% of annual sales plus inventory

Resources

- Minuteman Press: http://www.minutemanpress.com

Mobile Home Parks		
SIC 6515-01	NAICS 531190	

Rules of Thumb

➢ 3–8 x monthly income

Pricing Tips

- "As (Frank) Rolfe explains it, there are five issues an investor needs to watch out for when considering buying and owning mobile home parks—the infrastructure associated with the lots including utility access, local laws regarding maximum density per acre, the historical net income of the park, the age of the homes and the location. 'The best parks are the ones in real expensive areas,' Rolfe says. 'You will stay packed and will have a waiting list. You want to be the cheap alternative in an expensive world.'"

  Source: "Mobile Home Parks Are a Viable Investment," by Joel Cone, July 20, 2016, http://money.usnews.com/money/blogs/the-smarter-mutual-fund-investor/articles/2016-07-20/mobile-home-parks-are-a-viable-investment

- "Before you decide to sell your manufactured home community/mobile home park there are several ways to increase the value of your investment and in doing so increase the value of the park and make it more saleable.

  ✓ Submeter water, sewer and trash: By installing water meters at each mobile home and billing the residents back for water and sewer and trash, you are in effect increasing your bottom line.

  ✓ Enforce rules and leases: By enforcing reasonable rules and regulations, your mobile home community will be regarded as a safe and comfortable environment. Get rid of problem tenants.

  ✓ Buy manufactured homes for resale or rental. Buying used homes and placing them in your manufactured home community for resale or rental is another way to drastically increase the value of your community.

  ✓ Increase the curb appeal: Encourage residents to clean up their yards and property. Hold cleanup days on a monthly basis. Have new and attractive signs installed at the entrances."

  Source: http://www.ebay.com/gds/Increasing-the-Value-of-your-Mobile-Home-Park-/10000000003154759/g.html

- Note: Mobile-home parks are generally real-estate-intensive—a real estate license is probably necessary to handle the sale.

Industry Trend

- "Still, (Frank) Rolfe estimates that of the roughly 50,000 mobile home parks in the country only about 10,000 are professionally owned, leaving the remainder of the market up for grabs by small investors looking to either diversify their portfolio or change direction with a whole new investment strategy.

  "Why mobile home parks? Mobile home parks provide a viable form of affordable housing—especially for the nation's low-wage earners and people living at or below the national poverty level. According to the U.S. Census Bureau's 2016 Poverty Guidelines, a family of four that earns $24,300 or less is living in poverty. Last time it was measured (2014), the Census reported the nation's official poverty rate was 14.8 percent, or 46.7 million people.

  "A report released in May by the Social Security Administration notes that 38 percent of all wage earners in the U.S. make less than $20,000 a year. This April, the Census Bureau reported that the national median asking price for

M

vacant rental units was $870. Rolfe estimates that roughly 8 percent of the U.S. population or 20 million Americans presently live in mobile homes. At the state level South Carolina has the most with 16 percent of its population living in mobile homes, he notes."

Source: "Mobile Home Parks Are a Viable Investment," by Joel Cone, July 20, 2016, http://money.usnews.com/money/blogs/the-smarter-mutual-fund-investor/articles/2016-07-20/mobile-home-parks-are-a-viable-investment

Expert Comments

"'We don't want to be in the home business. We want to be in the land business,' says Frank Rolfe, owner of the Mobile Home University based in Cedaredge, Colorado. Rolfe, along with his partner Dave Reynolds, boasts being the sixth-largest owner of parks in the country, with 170 parks totaling more than 15,000 lots in 22 states. 'We want the park tenants to own their own homes.'"

Source: "Mobile Home Parks Are a Viable Investment," by Joel Cone, July 20, 2016, http://money.usnews.com/money/blogs/the-smarter-mutual-fund-investor/articles/2016-07-20/mobile-home-parks-are-a-viable-investment

Modeling Agencies

SIC 7363-01	NAICS 711410	Number of Businesses/Units 7,840

Rules of Thumb

➢ 20% of annual sales

Pricing Tips

- Smaller agencies may be one-person businesses, and the goodwill may be difficult to transfer. Earnouts may be necessary.

Benchmark Data

Statistics (Model Agencies)

Number of Establishments	7,840
Average Profit Margin	10.5%
Revenue per Employee	$103,900
Average Number of Employees	1.8
Average Wages per Employee	$45,450

Products and Services Segmentation

Commissions from advertising agencies	32.0%
Commissions from creative clients	21.2%
Performance or project related contract	18.9%
Commissions from other commercial clients	17.1%
Other	7.1%
Product Licenses	3.7%

Major Market Segmentation

Advertising agencies	45.5%
Creative clients	30.2%
Other commercial clients	24.3%

Business Reference Guide **2018**

Industry Costs

Profit	10.5%
Wages	43.7%
Purchases	17.8%
Depreciation	0.8%
Marketing	2.9%
Rent & Utilities	4.6%
Other	19.7%

Market Share

IMG Models	5.2%
Wilhelmina International Inc.	5.2%

Resources
- IBISWorld, September 2017: http://ibisworld.com

	Franchise
Molly Maid	
Approx. Total Investment	$89,200–$137,200
NAICS 561720	Number of Businesses/Units 620

Rules of Thumb
➤ 35–40% of annual sales plus inventory

Resources
- Molly Maid: http://www.mollymaid.com

	Franchise
Money Mailer	
Approx. Total Investment	$50,000–$75,000
NAICS 541870	Number of Businesses/Units 190

Rules of Thumb
➤ 40–45% of sales plus inventory

Resources
- Money Mailer: http://www.moneymailer.com

Montessori Schools	
NAICS 611110	

Rules of Thumb
➤ 35% of annual gross sales plus inventory

➤ 1.5–2 x SDE

➤ 3–4 x EBITDA

M

Pricing Tips

- The demographics profile—is it changing? Are the tuition rates within market too low such that when increased will significantly affect enrollment and profits? Verify financials through due diligence by a knowledgeable CPA. Is the owner the director, or simply the administrator overseeing operations? Are maintenance expenses being performed by the owner that would have to be assumed by the buyer? Is the enrollment going to change because of the personal goodwill of the owner and/or a director or key teacher who might leave? Why is the owner selling? Have there been any incidents or outstanding events that have not been disclosed. Verify continuation of enrollment due to possible aging of children in the area served. Is there a new school moving in or under construction nearby? Certifications of the teachers and their salaries. Teacher to student ratio. Are there foreseeable expenses in bringing the facility into code? What is the ethnic background of the owner/director and parents/ students as compared to the buyer? Historic enrollment, actual enrollment, and maximum enrollment.

Benchmark Data

Expenses (% of Annual Sales)

Cost of Goods	n/a
Occupancy Costs	30% to 45%
Payroll/Labor Costs	25% to 35%
Profit (pretax)	20% to 35%

Questions

- Ethnic ratio of students and the owner/director. Qualification and tenure of teachers.
- Are any of the teachers interns that will have to be replaced or higher paid later on?

Industry Trend

- Growing in areas where there are children in the pre-K through third grade. Trends down if they are above this level and there are good public schools. There is a very strong demand for special education for handicapped children.

Expert Comments

Focus on why the facility is for sale and what the owner plans to do after sale.

Most successful if enrollment is over 200 students, has a solid curriculum with stable teachers in a high-income area.

Seller Financing

- We have sold large facilities with enrollment of more than 200 students for 3 X EBITDA. Smaller are more difficult and sell for about 2 X.

Resources

- The International Montessori Index: http://www.montessori.edu
- Montessori Foundation: http://www.montessori.org
- American Montessori Society: https://amshq.org/

Franchise

MotoPhoto

	NAICS 81292	Number of Businesses/Units 16

Rules of Thumb

➤ 60% of annual sales plus inventory

Resources

- MotoPhoto: http://www.motophoto.com

Motorcycle Dealerships

SIC 5571-06	NAICS 441228	Number of Businesses/Units 20,610

Rules of Thumb

➤ 12–14% of annual sales plus inventory

➤ 2–3 x SDE plus inventory

➤ 3–4 x EBITDA

Pricing Tips

- It can be sold for a little higher multiple of SDE because of the hobby aspect.
- 2 x to 5 x SDE; includes parts, garments, & accessories inventory (PG&A); can include used vehicles, but not new vehicles. High multiples for Harley dealerships, and lower multiples for Japanese or other brands.

Benchmark Data

Statistics (Motorcycle Dealership and Repair)

Number of Establishments	20,610
Average Profit Margin	3.0%
Revenue per Employee	$344,200
Average Number of Employees	4.1
Average Wages per Employee	$35,163

Products and Services Segmentation

New motorcycles	46.9%
Motorized sports vehicles	21.0%
Used motorcycles	19.3%
Other	7.5%
Independent repairers	5.3%

Major Market Segmentation

Male consumers	69.5%
Businesses	15.4%
Female consumers	14.0%
Government	1.1%

M

Industry Costs

Profit	3.0%
Wages	10.3%
Purchases	74.3%
Depreciation	0.6%
Marketing	1.2%
Rent & Utilities	1.8%
Other	8.8%

Expenses (% of Annual Sales)

Cost of Goods	77% to 85%
Occupancy Costs	01%
Payroll/Labor Costs	05%
Profit (pretax)	02% to 03%

Questions

- PG&A inventory and new vehicle value requirements for a new buyer can be the most difficult and complex aspect to understand. A good deal of time should be spent understanding what inventory is there and how much is really needed. Inventory should turn on an average of 4 times to 6 times per year in a healthy dealership. Slower turns suggest the business is carrying too much inventory or is very seasonal.

Industry Trend

- "Motorcycle and all-terrain vehicle maker Polaris Industries Inc. plans to launch an electric bike under its marque Indian brand in the next four or five years, a senior executive said. Polaris and larger rival Harley-Davidson Inc are increasingly targeting price-conscious millennials as demand skids for big bikes in the United States, where the core customer group of baby boomers is aging."

  Source: "Polaris to launch new electric bike in 4-5 years -exec"
  by Ankit Ajmera, February 28, 2017, by Ankit Ajmera,
  http://www.cnbc.com/2017/02/28/reuters-america-polaris-to-launch-new-electric-bike-in-4-5-years-exec.html
- Stable

Expert Comments

Several years ago, motorcycle dealerships were easy to sell. Some regions of the country have experienced a downward trend in sales. The southeastern U.S. is still very strong. Currently, smaller dealerships can be very difficult to sell.

The original equipment manufacturers (Honda, Harley-Davidson, Yamaha, Suzuki, Kawasaki, etc.) control the number of dealers permitted in a marketplace. An existing dealership can block the establishment of a competing dealership of the same brand within a geographical proximity to the existing dealership.

Seller Financing

- Seller financing, all cash.

Resources

- PowerSports Business: http://powersportsbusiness.com/
- IBISWorld, July 2017: http://ibisworld.com

M

Mountain Mike's Pizza	Franchise
Approx. Total Investment	$197,000–$598,000
Estimated Annual Sales/Unit	$525,000

SIC 5812-22	NAICS 722513	Number of Businesses/Units 160

Rules of Thumb
➢ 30% of annual sales plus inventory

Resources
- Mountain Mike's Pizza: http://www.mountainmikes.com

Movie Theaters		
SIC 7832-01	NAICS 512131	Number of Businesses/Units 4,788

Rules of Thumb
➢ 4 x SDE

➢ 6 x annual adjusted earnings, 1000-plus seating

➢ 4–6% of annual sales; add fixtures & equipment

Pricing Tips
- Concession sales usually make up 24 percent of movie-theater sales. It has been said that, without concession sales, the movie theater business would not be viable.

Benchmark Data

Statistics (Movie Theaters)
Number of Establishments	4,788
Average Profit Margin	7.4%
Revenue per Employee	$115,900
Average Number of Employees	30.4
Average Wages per Employee	$13,312

Products and Services Segmentation
Admissions	66.8%
Food and beverage sales	29.9%
Other	3.3%

Industry Costs
Profit	7.4%
Wages	11.5%
Purchases	25.4%
Depreciation	5.9%
Marketing	3.9%
Rent & Utilities	5.2%
Other	40.7%

M

Market Share

Regal Entertainment Group	20.1%
AMC Entertainment Inc.	19.4%
Cinemark Holdings Inc.	14.5%

Industry Trend

- "Domestic box office receipts broke a new record at $11.37 billion in the U.S. and Canada. That is a 2.1% increase from 2015 and the eighth straight year revenues have exceeded $10 billion. There were nine titles that grossed over $300 million in 2016, while there were only six in 2015. But in an equally encouraging sign that runs counter to earlier trends, films that grossed between $50 and $100 million accounted for $250 million more in 2016 than in the prior year.

  "In 2001, domestic box office totaled $8.11 billion. Last year, domestic ticket sales brought in $11.37 billion. In the last fifteen years, domestic movie theaters and their distribution partners have seen box office revenue increase by 40%."

  Source: Remarks made by John Fithian, President and CEO,
  National Association of Theater Owners, at the CinemaCon, March 28, 2017,
  http://www.natoonline.org/wp-content/uploads/2017/03/Fithian-CinemaCon-Speech-2017.pdf

Resources

- Motion Picture Association of America: http://mpaa.org
- National Association of Theatre Owners: http://www.natoonline.org
- Business of Show Business: The Valuation of Movie Theaters," published by the Appraisal Institute: http://www.appraisalinstitute.org
- IBISWorld, February 2017: http://ibisworld.com

Moving and Storage		
SIC 4214-01	NAICS 484210	Number of Businesses/Units 16,070

Rules of Thumb

➢ 50% of annual sales

Benchmark Data

Statistics (Moving Services)

Number of Establishments	16,070
Average Profit Margin	9.4%
Revenue per Employee	$166,500
Average Number of employees	6.7
Average Wages per Employee	$35,915

Products and Services Segmentation

Residential moving	60.8%
Commercial moving	16.4%
Other	12.1%
Warehousing services	10.7%

M

Major Market Segmentation

Consumers	66.5%
Corporate customers	21.7%
Government	11.8%

Industry Costs

Profit	9.4%
Wages	21.7%
Purchases	32.7%
Depreciation	2.3%
Marketing	2.7%
Rent & Utilities	8.2%
Other	23.0%

Market Share

UniGroup Inc.	10.0%
Sirva Inc.	7.4%

Resources
- American Moving and Storage Association—an informative site: http://www.promover.org
- IBISWorld, September 2017: http://ibisworld.com

Mr. Jim's Pizza		Franchise
Approx. Total Investment		$75,000–$150,000
Estimated Annual Sales/Unit		$440,000
SIC 5812-22	NAICS 722513	Number of Businesses/Units 75

Rules of Thumb
➢ 35% of annual sales plus inventory

Resources
- Mr. Jim's Pizza: http://www.mrjimspizza.net

Mr. Payroll		Franchise
Approx. Total Investment		$68,800–$328,000
Estimated Annual Sales/Unit		$100,000–$325,000
	NAICS 522390	Number of Businesses/Units 45

Rules of Thumb
➢ 130% of annual sales

Resources
- Mr. Payroll: http://www.mrpayroll.com

M

Franchise

Mr. Rooter Plumbing

Approx. Total Investment		$76,775–$180,195
SIC 1711-05	NAICS 238220	Number of Businesses/Units 241

Rules of Thumb
➤ 1–4 x SDE

Franchise

Murphy's Deli

Approx. Total Investment		Net Worth of $200,000
	NAICS 722513	Number of Businesses/Units 80

Rules of Thumb
➤ 50% of annual sales plus inventory

Resources
- Murphy's Deli: http://www.murphysdeli.com

Franchise

Music Go Round

Approx. Total Investment		$261,500–$334,800
SIC 5736-08	NAICS 451140	Number of Businesses/Units 35

Rules of Thumb
➤ 40% of annual sales plus inventory

Resources
Music Go Round: http://www.musicgoround.com

Music Stores (Record Stores, Musical Instruments)

SIC 5736	NAICS 451140	Number of Businesses/Units 14, 397

Rules of Thumb
➤ 25% of annual sales

Pricing Tips
- Inventory of tapes, CD's, DVD's at FMV (used) is in addition to the above.
- Usually in a store of this kind inventory turns about twice a year. The store should be located in an area where rent will not exceed 4 percent of the gross sales. National average shows a gross profit of approximately 54 percent before expenses of wages, repairs, maintenance, advertising, bad debts, utilities, insurance, taxes, etc. National average net profit is approximately 10 to 18 percent.

Benchmark Data

Statistics (Musical Instrument and Supplies Store)

Number of Establishments	10,740
Average Profit Margin	4.6%
Revenue per Employee	$135,200
Average Number of Employees	3.3
Average Wages per Employee	$21,912

Products and Services Segmentation

Violins, drums, guitars, and other instruments	49.5%
Sheet muSIC 19.7%	
Pianos and organs	16.1%
Audio equipment, components, parts and accessories	12.4%
Other goods (includes tapes, CDs and audiobooks)	2.3%

Major Market Segmentation

Hobbyists	52.1%
Professional	30.3%
Students	10.6%
Education	4.9%
Other	2.1%

Industry Costs

Profit	4.6%
Wages	16.2%
Purchases	50.5%
Depreciation	0.9%
Marketing	1.8%
Rent & Utilities	7.4%
Other	18.6%

Market Share

Guitar Center Inc.	39.4%

Statistics (Record Stores)

Number of Establishments	3,657
Average Profit Margin	1.2%
Revenue per Employee	$95,900
Average Number of Employees	4.4
Average Wages per Employee	$14,338

Products and Services Segmentation

Compact discs, records, tapes & audio books	39.7%
Digital Video Discs (DVDs) and video tapes	33.6%
Other	16.6%
Toys, hobby goods & games	10.1%

Industry Costs

Profit	1.2%
Wages	15.1%
Purchases	63.1%
Depreciation	1.2%
Utilities	2.0%
Rent	7.7%
Other	9.7%

M

Market Share

Trans World Entertainment Corporation	19.4%

Expenses (% of Annual Sales)

Cost of Goods	35%
Occupancy Costs	15%
Payroll/Labor Costs	25% to 30%
Profit (pretax)	20% to 25%

Industry Trend

- "U.S. will continue to account for a leading share of the global musical instruments market. The prominence of keyboard stringed instruments will continue over the forecast period, creating consistent growth opportunity for keyboard manufacturers. The increasing number of music reality shows, live music bands, and concerts is projected to pose a positive impact on the increase in the demand for modern, high-tech, expensive instruments."
  Source: "Musical Instruments Market: Global Industry Analysis and Opportunity Assessment 2016-2026," http://www.futuremarketinsights.com/reports/musical-instruments-market

Expert Comments

Independent brick and mortar locations are a dying breed.

Resources

- IBISWorld, January 2017: http://ibisworld.com
- International Music Products Association: http://music.us/namm/
- National Association of Music Merchants Inc: http://www.namm.org

	Franchise
My Favorite Muffin	○
Approx. Total Investment	$254,300–$379,628
NAICS 722513	Number of Businesses/Units 70

Rules of Thumb

➤ 30–35% of annual sales

Resources

- My Favorite Muffin: http://www.myfavoritemuffin.com

Mystery Shopping Companies		
	NAICS 561990	

Rules of Thumb

➤ 50 percent of annual sales—the larger the company, the higher the percentage of annual sales over 50%

Pricing Tips

- Large mystery service companies can sell for considerably more than 50 percent of sales.

Benchmark Data

- "How much can someone realistically expect to earn as a mystery shopper? Compensation for mystery shopping significantly varies depending on a number of factors, including the type of industry, the level of difficulty required to complete the assignment and the detail required by the mystery shoppers. Compensation for the typical shop ranges from $5 to $20. Some complex assignments, such as video mystery shop, can pay $75 or more.

  "It is hard to find out more specifics on which companies get mystery shopped and how much shoppers are paid because shoppers are not allowed to divulge specific information, such as the name of the company they've shopped or how much they make per assignment. The shoppers are required to sign confidentiality agreements at the request of the mystery shopping providers and their customers."

  Source: www.mysteryshop.org

Industry Trend

- General Mystery Shopping Industry Information:
  - ✓ Mystery shopping is estimated to be more than a $1.5 billion industry
  - ✓ Current estimates indicate there are 1.5 million mystery shoppers
  - ✓ The scope of mystery shopping spans many industries and geographies
  - ✓ MSPA Americas and the industry combat scams that attempt to legitimize themselves by claiming affiliation with the industry and/or industry participants

  Source: http://www.mspa-na.org/news

Resources

- Mystery Shopping Providers Association (MSPA): http://www.mspa-na.org/

Nail Salons		
SIC 7231-02	NAICS 812113	

Rules of Thumb

➢ 25% of annual sales plus inventory

Pricing Tips

- "So, what records do you need to be able to provide? Kopsa provides the following list to get you started:
  - ✓ the last three years of tax returns
  - ✓ the last three years of the salon's accounting software records (such as QuickBooks or Sage 50)
  - ✓ the last three years of sales tax reports (to verify your retail sales)
  - ✓ the last three years to present day of your salon appointment records
  - ✓ a list of all employees, including how long they've been with the salon
  - ✓ the salon handbook (the new owner will likely need to carry over benefits, such as the number of vacation days, for employees who choose to stay with the salon)
  - ✓ the lease (which must be assignable to the new buyer)
  - ✓ the depreciation schedule"

  Source: http://www.nailsmag.com/article/109714/sell-your-salon-with-savvy

N

Benchmark Data

- For additional Benchmark Data see Beauty Salons

Industry Costs (Hair and Nail Salons in the U.S.)

Profit	8.2%
Wages	44.6%
Purchases	13.9%
Depreciation	1.7%
Marketing	1.8%
Rent & Utilities	15.5%
Other	14.3%

- "Nail Tech Demographics

Ethnicity	Percentage
Vietnamese	56%
Caucasian	36%
Other	08%

Gender	Percentage
Male	03%
Female	97%

How many nail technicians work at this location (including yourself)?

Number of Technicians	Percentage
I am the only technician	52%
2 nail techs	18%
3 nail techs	09%
4 nail techs	08%
5 nail techs	03%
6 nail techs	02%
7+ nail techs	07%

Who are your clients?

	Percentage
Girls under 12	01%
Girls 12–15	01%
Girls 16–20	04%
Women 21–25	11%
Women 26–35	19%
Women 36–45	28%
Women 46+	33%
Men	03%

On average what is your total weekly income?

	Average
Service Income	$630
Tip Income	$115
Incentives or earnings from retail sales	$82

Which best describes your current employment situation?

Salon owner keeping what I make from services I personally do	28%
Booth renter paying rent to the salon and keeping all service fees	24%
Booth renter paying a percentage of services as rent	03%

Employee receiving just a percentage of services, no salary 09%
Employee paid by the number of clients I serve 02%
Salon owner paying myself a salary 17%
Employee receiving salary plus a percentage of service fees 03%
Student or apprentice 02%
Employee receiving a salary 04%
Other arrangement 08%

What license(s) do you have?

Nail technician/manicurist 82%
Cosmetologist/hairstylist 20%
Esthetician 09%
I am not licensed 04%
Nails & Cosmetology 20%
Nail Tech & Esthetician 13%

- "$8.53 billion was spent on nail services in 2016. 9% of nail techs currently
  work at more than one salon. There are 393,581 active nail licenses in the U.S.
  63% of respondents had another career before they started doing nails."

  Source: "Nails Magazine," 2016–2017 Big Book statistics

Resources

- Nails Magazine—interesting and useful site, has an interesting survey of the
  nail salon business: http://www.nailsmag.com

  Source: IBISWorld, October 2017

		Franchise
Nathan's Famous		
Approx. Total Investment		$50,000–$1,000,000
	NAICS 722513	Number of Businesses/Units 300

Rules of Thumb

➢ 85–90% of annual sales plus inventory

Benchmark Data

- Units range from 120 sq. ft. to 3,000 sq. ft.

Resources

- Nathan's Famous: http://www.nathansfamous.com

		Franchise
Natural Chicken Grill		
	NAICS 722513	Number of Businesses/Units 14

Rules of Thumb

➢ 25–30% of annual sales plus inventory

N

		Franchise
Nature's Way Café		
Approx. Total Investment		$129,500–$253,900
	NAICS 722513	Number of Businesses/Units 8

Rules of Thumb

➢ 45% of annual sales plus inventory

Resources
- Nature's Way Cafe: http://www.natureswaycafe.com

Newspaper Routes		
	NAICS 454390	

Rules of Thumb

➢ 90–100% of annual sales plus inventory

Newsstands		
SIC 5994-01	NAICS 451212	

Rules of Thumb

➢ 25% of annual sales plus inventory

Nursing Homes/Skilled Nursing Facilities		
SIC 8051-01	NAICS 623110	Number of Businesses/Units 31,326

Rules of Thumb

➢ 45% of annual sales plus inventory

➢ 2.5 x SDE plus inventory

➢ 3 x EBIT

➢ 4 x EBITDA

Pricing Tips
- The long-term care industry values properties vastly differently than most other businesses. Value is determined not by a simple multiple of SDE or EBITDA but actually determining Net Operating Income (NOI) that starts with EBITDA and subtracts things like a reserve, a 5% management fee based on gross revenue, etc. and then applying a Capitalization Rate (CAP rate) to that number. For Skilled Nursing Facilities (SNFs) this is running about 9.9% (you take NOI and divide by this percentage). Assisted Living Facilities (ALFs) are running very strong around 7.7%, and Independent Living (IL) around 8.5%. For a well-run home, you can apply these CAP rates to the NOI with confidence. For poorly performing homes where EBITDA is depressed, sometimes falsely, you can normalize the revenue to a 95% census (this is

how HUD 232 analysis does it), make the same adjustements and still apply NOI. Now your challenge is to find the buyer for this type of under-performing company!

- Do not allow a general appraiser or even a commercial appraiser to conduct the appraisal. It must be done by a nursing-home or long-term care appraisal specialist.

Benchmark Data

Statistics (Nursing Care Facilities)

Number of Establishments	31,326
Average Profit Margin	14.0%
Revenue per Employee	$74,200
Average Number of Employees	56.8
Average Wages per Employee	$31,029

Products and Services Segmentation

For-profit skilled nursing facilities	43.6%
For-profit nursing homes	33.0%
Nonprofit skilled nursing facilities	10.3%
Nonprofit nursing homes	7.8%
Government nursing homes and skilled nursing facilities	4.7%
Hospice centers	0.6%

Industry Costs

Profit	14.0%
Wages	42.0%
Purchases	7.2%
Depreciation	2.3%
Marketing	0.3%
Rent & Utilities	7.1%
Other	27.1%

- Common pricing guideline is to use per-bed pricing. SNFs are generally $60,000 to $90,000; ALFs can range all over the board from $100,000 to $200,000 depending on the condition, size and ammentiies. CAP rates with SNFs are 9.9%, ALFs 7.7% on NOI.

Expenses (% of Annual Sales)

Cost of Goods	15%
Occupancy Costs	10%
Payroll/Labor Costs	40% to 50%
Profit (pretax)	15% to 20%

Questions

- Let me see your last 3 surveys. Surveys are conducted on life safety and health issues at the homes and detail any violations and corrective measures the home took to resolve the problem. If it's a SNF, what's their CMS rating? This ranges from 1 star to 5 star. 1- star homes will have challenges getting referrals in from hospitals, as many won't refer patients to nursing homes with such a low rating.

N

Industry Trend

- "The belief is that nursing homes are a place for old people. Today, that's not an accurate picture of what it really is.
    - ✓ Rehabilitation is a big part of what nursing homes do today. In some states, one-fourth or more of the residents in one come to one after hospitalization for an acute problem like stroke or hip fracture.
    - ✓ Because of short-term care, residents leave making wait lists shorter or non-existent. But check with you local nursing homes, in some states long wait lists do exist. As noted in the research study above, certified bed occupancy rates are going down. The rate of nursing home real estate development increases due to the surge of older boomers.
    - ✓ There's an increase of nursing home facilities in preparation for the aging baby boomers. Improved care: Today, nursing homes provide services and medical procedures offered in hospitals. Physical therapy, occupational therapy and speech therapy are now provided by nursing homes.
    - ✓ Nursing homes no longer just offer nursing care for the elderly. Due to post-acute care needs, nursing homes add hospital-like services to assist patients post-surgery. More variety: Skilled nursing facilities now offer upscale communities and provide care exclusively to residents.
    - ✓ Nursing homes have changed from the older institutional setting to contemporary, comfortable, and home-like. Some even offer arts and cultural events for residents and sports and games and crafts. Individualized care: More nursing homes focus on resident-centered care.
    - ✓ Individualized care is a goal of the new nursing home facility. Today, facilities advocate for culture change in long-term care. Residents get involved in their care plan and even operations of the home. Radical changes incorporate all-purpose workers who cook, clean, and help with daily activities."

    Source: "Trends in Nursing Homes," https://www.skillednursingfacilities.org/resources/nursing-home-trends/

- "A one-time giant among skilled nursing facility (SNF) operators has decided to entirely exit that business. After years of pruning its SNF portfolio, Kindred Healthcare (NYSE: KND) will be getting out for good, the Louisville-based company announced Monday. The move is meant to achieve stronger cash flow and higher margins while reducing the capital needs for the company. Kindred currently operates 91 skilled nursing facilities.

    "Owners of skilled nursing facilities, including large public real estate investment trusts (REITs), have been seeking to limit their exposure to the skilled nursing asset class. Last week, several transactions were announced in which REITs offloaded or spun off these properties."

    Source: "Kindred to Cease Owning, Operating Skilled Nursing Facilities," by Tim Mullaney, November 7, 2016, http://seniorhousingnews.com/2016/11/07/kindred-to-cease-operating-skilled-nursing-facilities/

- Strong activity for homes over 100 beds. Small facilities under 50 beds not sought after by larger buyers but are perfect for the individual buyer looking to enter marketplace.
- Further consolidation, revenue projected to increase, profit projected to grow, demand expected to increase

Expert Comments

Don't think you're going to slap a paragraph on a website and sell these businesses. You need detailed offering memorandums that go over the plethora of information these buyers are looking for whether that's census information, resident mix (private, Medicare, Medicaid), payrolls by department, food costs, CAP-EX history, etc.

Most states have moratoriums on new licenses making existing facilities pretty valuable. In most situations, you can't build a new home unless you buy an existing home or purchase a vacant license and the state approves you to move that license wherever it is you want to build. Long-term care has been very marketable for quite some time now even though CMS (Medicare/Medicaid) continues to put pressure on rates and regulations. The very good SNF homes have some level of private pay and a good Medicare mix. How the MDS and MMQ nurses are managing the nursing staff and grading residents is absolutely critical to maximizing rates and making a home profitable. ALFs (assisted living) are becoming more and more elegant with more and more ammenities, so the very good ones go for big numbers. You'll see per bed pricing at $150,000 to $200,000 per bed. Compare that to an SNF (skilled nursing facility) where per bed pricing is generally $60,000 to $90,000.

It really helps both sides if they have representation to assist them. Sellers absolutely should want and need a skilled broker assisting them. An honest review of the facility and suggested changes/improvements can be critical to the overall value. Buyers likewise would want assistance as to what to look for and to guide them through the lending process and due diligence.

Seller Financing
- If the selling price is under $10 million then SBA is a good source. HUD is the sourcing of choice for SNFs and ALFs but the process is long and it can take a year to complete the financing. Buyers love HUD, though, because they are non-recourse loans (no personal guarantees) and have the longest amortizations (typically 35 years) and lowest interest rates. Smaller, older homes oftentimes don't qualify for HUD financing, and this is when SBA is a good fit. Fixed interest rates and they'll break-out loans into a 7(a) a 504 on the real estate and a 3rd loan, another 7(a) for a working capital loan.
- Outside financing

Resources
- American Health Care Association: http://www.ahca.org
- IBISWorld, August 2017: http://ibisworld.com
- The National Investment Center for Seniors Housing & Care (NIC): http://www.nic.org/
- McKnight's Long-Term Care News: http://www.mcknights.com/
- LeadingAge: http://www.leadingage.org

Office Staffing and Temporary Agencies		
SIC 7363-03	NAICS 61320	Number of Businesses/Units 37,418

Rules of Thumb
➤ 3 x SDE plus inventory

➤ 6–12 x EBITDA

➤ 1–2 x annual sales plus inventory

➤ 2–5 x EBIT (smaller deals under $25 million)

➤ 5–7.5 x EBIT (larger deals over $25 million)

➤ 6–9 x EBIT (Information Technology)

O

Pricing Tips

- Client attrition and A/R information very important in valuing a staffing business.
- "One of the most common misconceptions I hear from staffing company owners is that the valuation of their business is directly tied to their annual revenue. While larger companies do tend to receive higher valuation multiples, staffing companies continue to be valued almost exclusively on a multiple of trailing 12-month (TTM) earnings before interest, taxes, depreciation and amortization (EBITDA), so growing the EBITDA of your business, not just its revenue, is the key to maximizing valuation.

  "The misconception that the purchase price paid by buyers in staffing industry transactions is based on revenue rather than EBITDA is largely based upon the fact that for most publicly announced transactions, earnings information is simply not available. So in the absence of earnings information, observers may attempt to link the seller's annual revenue to the purchase price if the revenue of the business is disclosed. Further complicating transaction analysis, in the situations where EBITDA is publicly stated, information concerning any non-recurring expense adjustments are usually not disclosed, so the implied transaction multiple may be overstated and often misleading.

  "Many buyers will also conduct a 'quality of earnings' assessment as a part of their transaction due diligence. Not only will this review include a confirmation of the annual or TTM EBITDA of the selling company, but factors such as the validity of the expense adjustments and the sustainability of the earnings will also be considered.

  "The majority of companies in the staffing industry sell for between four to seven times their TTM EBITDA on a cash free, debt free basis, with the working capital of the seller (the receivables and payables) going to the buyer. In the rare cases where the seller keeps the working capital, then the purchase price is reduced by a comparable amount. Some fast-growing professional staffing companies may even sell for above seven times TTM EBITDA, while less differentiated and/or smaller commercial staffing businesses may trade for less than four times TTM EBITDA. Because this valuation range is so large and based upon a variety of factors, speaking with multiple potential acquirers is critical to achieving the best possible valuation.

  "While staffing industry buyers may acquire for a variety of reasons, including access to new customers, expand the geography of their business, add a new service offering or bring additional management talent into their organization, they will almost always use EBITDA as their basis for valuation. Therefore, owners contemplating a future transaction should always be focused on the earnings line of their income statement, not revenue, in order to maximize the value of their staffing business in a sale."

  Source: "EBITDA, Not Revenue, Drives Staffing Company Valuations," by John Niehaus, July 11, 2016, www.thestaffingstream.com/2016/07/11/ebitda-not-revenue-drives-staffing-company-valuations/?utm_source=feedburner&utm_medium=feed&utm_campaign=Feed%3A+TheStaffingStream+%28The+Staffing+Stream%29

- "Staffing companies that use the cash basis—only counting income or expenses when the money changes hands—for their accounting method will be at a significant disadvantage when approaching a transaction. Investment bankers, transaction attorneys and accountants agree that financial statements prepared using generally accepted accounting principles (GAAP) present a clearer and more easily understood snapshot of a company's financial health. GAAP uses an accrual basis which recognizes revenue when the services occur, regardless of when the money is received or paid. Because GAAP is consistently used by most companies, it is a powerful tool for ensuring a fair business valuation."

  Source: http://wblcpa.com/maximize-your-staffing-business-value-now-eight-key-accounting-tax-and-finance-tips-to-prepare-your-staffing-business-for-sale/

Benchmark Data

Statistics (Office Staffing & Temp Agencies)

Number of Establishments 37,418
Average Profit Margin 4.1%
Revenue per Employee $48,600
Average Number of Employees 90.4
Average Wages per Employee $31,485

Products and Services Segmentation

Industrial staffing 22.6%
Office, clerical and administrative staffing 17.5%
Professional and managerial staffing 16.9%
Information technology staffing 16.8%
Healthcare staffing 9.8%
Engineering and scientific staffing 9.0%
Other 7.4%

Major Market Segmentation

Professional, retail and other service-oriented sectors 44.2%
Technical sectors 25.8%
Industrial 22.6%
Other 7.4%

Industry Costs

Profit 4.1%
Wages 64.2%
Purchases 4.5%
Depreciation 0.2%
Marketing 3.0%
Rent & Utilities 2.0%
Other 22.0%

Expenses (% of Annual Sales)

Cost of Goods 10%
Occupancy Costs 10%
Payroll/Labor Costs .... 50% to 60%
Profit (pretax) .... 08% to 10%

Questions

- Typical questions for any service business, customer concentration, staff non-competes, contracts with clients, ability to speak to next level of management when the time is right, historical growth, gross margins, etc.
- Background. Financial strength. Industry experience.
- Length of service by account. Gross Profit by account. Bad debt experience.
- Who in the organization has the relationships with the clients? What is the gross margin? Which clients have vendor management systems in place? How frequently do they put these out to bid? What is the turnover of the recruiting and sales staff?
- Need to understand working capital requirements. Will sellers include some accounts receivable in seller price? Review client hiring patterns for past three years and match against their payment history.

O

Industry Trend

- "U.S. staffing companies employed an average of 3.07 million temporary and contract workers per week in the first quarter of 2017. Staffing employment growth eased (-0.5%) compared with the same period in 2016, according to data released today by the American Staffing Association. Average weekly staffing employment has exceeded three million for 12 consecutive quarters. Temporary and contract staffing sales totaled $32.05 billion in the first quarter of 2017, 3.6% higher compared with the same period in 2016.

  "'Temporary and contract employment is an indicator of where the economy is today,' said Richard Wahlquist, ASA president and chief executive officer. 'The good news at this stage of the economic cycle is that while staffing employment growth was constrained in the first quarter by talent shortages across a wide range of occupations, the demand for temporary and contract employees is steady and is expected to remain so.'"

  Source: "Staffing Employment Easing Continues in First Quarter," June 5, 2017,
https://americanstaffing.net/posts/2017/06/05/staffing-employment-eases-first-quarter/

- Continued strong demand for staffing as industry consolidators seek acquisitions for branding and economic scale.

Expert Comments

High demand for temporary personnel due to economic uncertainly (use temps instead of adding to overheads).

Continuation of Obamacare should be positive for staffing.

Seller—prepare well in advance and work with a business intermediary to recommend steps to improve the potential marketability. Buyer—spend time at conferences such as the American Staffing Association's Staffing World, or meetings of Staffing Industry Analysts to learn about the field and to meet people in the business before considering starting to evaluate potential acquisitions.

Hire top recruiters, carefully interview temps, watch outstanding accounts receivable with credit weak customers.

Gross profit and accounts receivable performance influence the multiple selection as does strength of locations (near bus lines). Factoring is common in this industry and net factoring expenses can impact profitability. Customer concentration issues require analysis with balanced weighting across several segments supporting higher valuations.

Workers' comp., risk management, and mod factors affect light industrial staffing\PEO firms substantially.

Seller Financing

- For the more substantial transactions ($10million in sales and up) normally these are financed internally or with lines of credit for larger buyers. Smaller sellers, especially those with lower margins that are less desirable may be willing to consider seller financing.
- 50% or more owner financing common on transactions with less than $2 million in consideration. Owner financing declines to 20% level as transaction values climb over $5 million.
- Outside financing is very common. Owner financing can be expected if there are client concentration issues.
- This industry has an above average requirement for seller financing. Not uncommon for sellers to provide up to 50-70% financing.

Resources

- American Staffing Association: http://www.americanstaffing.net
- Staffing Industry Analysts: http://www.staffingindustry.com
- IBISWorld, May 2017: http://ibisworld.com
- National Association of Personnel Services: http://www.naps360.org

Office Supplies and Stationery Stores		
SIC 5943-01	NAICS 453210	Number of Businesses/Units 10,153

Rules of Thumb

➢ 25% of annual sales plus inventory

➢ 1.5 x SDE plus inventory

Pricing Tips

- Check inventory levels and FF&E carefully. Owners of these types of businesses tend to hide cash flow in excessive inventory and FF&E.

Benchmark Data

Statistics (Office Supply Stores)

Number of Establishments	10,153
Average Profit Margin	2.1%
Revenue per Employee	$178,000
Average Number of Employees	6.8
Average Wages per Employee	$22,091

Products and Services Segmentation

Office supplies and equipment	44.6%
Office machines	28.5%
Technology	13.0%
Services	8.2%
Office furniture	5.7%

Major Market Segmentation

Small businesses	27.8%
Households for education purposes	22.5%
Large businesses	16.8%
Households for general purposes	15.3%
Other	8.5%
Households for satellite work	7.2%
Federal, state and local government	1.9%

Industry Costs

Profit	2.1%
Wages	12.4%
Purchases	62.8%
Depreciation	0.8%
Marketing	1.0%
Rent & Utilities	3.2%
Other	17.7%

O

Market Share

Office Depot Inc.	41.3%
Staples Inc.	39.7%

Resources
- IBISWorld, May 2017: http://ibisworld.com

Oil and Gas Related Businesses

Rules of Thumb

➢ 2–4 x EBITDA

➢ 65% of annual sales includes inventory

➢ 5 x EBIT

➢ 4 x SDE plus Inventory

Pricing Tips

- Service industries in Oil & Gas many times have an inordinate amount of business with just a few customers, or sometimes only a few customers make up a large percentage of revenues. Who those customers are and how long they have been customers will determine how much, if any, discounts will apply. If there are disposal wells included, many times there will be no discounting.
- Very few sales are based on a percent of sales, most are a multiplier of EBITDA. When EBIDTA is above $2.0 million, it is not unusual to see a sale in the 6 x; above $4.0 million, depending on customer concentration and other issues similar to any other industries, they could value in the 6–8 x. Drilling companies may be priced more on the value of their equipment as opposed to EBITDA.
- Industry rule of thumb for:

  Roustabout (SIC 1389)
    - ✓ 2 x SDE plus FFE & inventory
    - ✓ 3–4 x SDE
    - ✓ 75–90% of sales (100%+ when talking over $10 million+ in sales)

  Drilling (water well) (SIC 1781) [O&G companies need water wells and core samples]
    - ✓ 2 x SDE plus FFE & inventory
    - ✓ 3 x SDE
    - ✓ 3.5 x EBITDA
    - ✓ 150% of sales

  Excavation/Construction (NAICS 213112) [specifically for O&G industry with MSAs (other excavations site preps {SIC 1794} are vulnerable to the housing/ real estate market and deem lower pricing)]
    - ✓ 1.5 x SDE plus FFE & inventory
    - ✓ 3–4 x SDE
    - ✓ 80–90% of sales
- Adjust for age/condition of equipment.
- The typical discount for all cash versus terms applies.
- The oil and gas industry is a very broad cross section of industry segments and

varies widely in size. Value parameters will vary widely and are probably most associated with individual market segments such as manufacturing or services.

- The typical measure of earnings used is EBITDA. The multiple will range between 3.2 X and 4 X for transactions up to $20 million. The variance is based upon qualitative factors such as customer concentrations, equipment age and condition, middle management depth and experience, safety records, and nature of services being performed. Equipment rental companies will be higher in the range while companies providing products or services with material intensive cost of sales will be somewhat lower, again depending upon qualitative factors.
- A key factor is the number of Master Service Agreements (MSA's) a company has in place. These are master agreements with an oil company. They do not guarantee any certain volume of work, but rather indicate the manner in which work will be performed, liabilities and hold harmless, rate sheets, insurance coverage required, etc.

Benchmark Data

- This industry doesn't have benchmarks such as sales per square foot or by employee. It is more geared toward the amount of equipment it possesses, such as the number of Frac tanks to rent, or the number of trucks for hauling wastewater, etc.
- All costs are dependent on the particular nature of the business. Is it service, manufacturing, repair, drilling, waste water hauling and disposal? All are unique in their own way.
- **Roustabout (SIC 1389)**
  - ✓ Payroll 40–45%
  - ✓ Profit 25%

  Drilling (water well) (SIC 1781) [O&G companies need water wells and core samples]
  - ✓ Payroll 15%
  - ✓ Profit 50%

  Excavation/Construction (NAICS 213112)
  - ✓ Payroll 15%
  - ✓ Profit 20–25%
- The cost of goods sold percentages vary widely. Companies providing materials in addition to their service or value-added features tend to have much lower gross profit per dollar of revenues.

Questions

- Customer concentration, who is key person in company, and who has customer connections. Otherwise, same questions as any customer.
- Why is he selling? How can I grow the business? What specific relationships does the seller have with customers, suppliers, etc.?
- Equipment should be the number one question-age/condition. Ask for service maintenance logs. Find out the turnover rate. How often is the equipment replaced with better and newer equipment? Get a third-party equipment appraisal.

Industry Trend

- The next few years should be up even if oil prices don't increase.
- Improving economics, with oversupply causing substantial price and economic risks. Strong economy should be a positive factor.

O

- Generally up, but with ups and downs. Rapid increases are unlikely, but rapid falls are possible as the world supply seeks equilibrium.
- Because of the low price of oil, all businesses in this space are affected in a negative manner. However, we know oil will come back. It usually takes about one to two years for a rebound to come into play for these businesses, so the future looks very bright. No one knows if oil will get back to $100 per barrel but the good news is it doesn't have to for these businesses to flourish. We should see an upward trend beginning in 2017 and in 2018 we should see that trend continue.
- Difficult profitability issues will likely remain over the short term. The long-term trend has been positive, but there are substantial periods of high volatility.

Expert Comments

Make certain you keep your service personnel; they are usually the ones with customer connections.

Location, outside of the region you are in, is insignificant. Marketability has little to do with success. Because of the investment of equipment, it is very difficult to replicate.

Research the opportunity carefully. Be prepared for large cycles driven by new technologies and geopolitics.

Boom–bust cycle. Long term is a growing profitable business segment, but capital costs are high.

It is no different than any other industry. Find the right buyer! To do that, the seller must take the time to clearly understand what kind of transaction he is most interested in. Will there be enough money after taxes and expenses for me and my family to live in style for the rest of my life? What will I do after I sell? For a buyer, ask himself, can I see myself working in this business? Does it fit my skill set? Exactly why is the seller wanting out? Are there key people in the business and will they remain after the sale? If I decide this business isn't for me, can I successfully sell it? And the most important of all: what is my exit plan?

All businesses geared to the O & G industry are potentially high profit with a high degree of risk due to the relationship of the price of a barrel of oil. However, many service and repair companies not only survive the downturns but also flourish. Because of the high cost of entry due to the equipment required, it is a difficult industry for new businesses.

Industry trends are heavily influenced by commodity based pricing of the underlying oil and gas products. The industry may be subject to boom-bust cycles.

Seller Financing

- Like many industries, 60% to 70% cash at closing with some carry by owner and possibly some reinvestment by seller.
- Buyer capital. In smaller deals, private equity backing and owner financing. Bank financing can be difficult from banks inexperienced in the industry and for purchase of goodwill.
- In today's market, buyers, including private equity, look to the owners for some financing and or investment back into the business, usually in the 25% range

of owner carry or investment. Many owners are willing to do this due to the tremendous upside in the industry.
- Normally a combination of owner and institutional financing
- Most have significant third-party financing, with some seller financing, frequently in the form of an earnout or clawback. The factors affecting that are usually the customer diversity or customer concentration.

Resources
- Petroleum Marketers Association of America (PMAA): http://www.pmaa.org
- American Association of Professional Landmen: http://www.landman.org
- Shale Play Water Management: http://www.shaleplaywatermanagement.com
- American Petroleum Institute: http://www.api.org
- Society of Petroleum Engineers: http://www.spe.org
- Pipe Line Contractors Association: http://www.plca.org
- Hart Energy: http://www.hartenergy.com
- The Oil & Gas Journal: http://www.ogj.com
- The American Association of Petroleum Geologists: http://www.aapg.org/

		Franchise
Once Upon A Child		
Approx. Total Investment		$254,500–$392,200
SIC 5932-05	NAICS 453310	Number of Businesses/Units 348

Rules of Thumb
➤ 25% of annual sales plus inventory

➤ 30% of annual sales includes inventory

Optical Stores		
	NAICS 446130	Number of Businesses/Units 14,969

Rules of Thumb
➤ 2 x SDE includes inventory (Sales do not include regular exam fees)

➤ 50–60% of annual sales includes inventory (sales do not include regular exam fees)

Pricing Tips
- Adjust price up or down depending on how updated the equipment is.
- How many days do they perform exams? For whom?

Benchmark Data

Statistics (Eye Glasses & Contact Lens Stores)
Number of Establishments	14,969
Average Profit Margin	7.7%
Revenue per Employee	$147,900
Average Number of Employees	5.5
Average Wages per Employee	$31,096

O

Products and Services Segmentation

Prescription eyeglasses	66.1%
Nonprescription eyewear	14.6%
Contact lenses	11.0%
Other optical goods	4.9%
Eye examinations	3.4%

Industry Costs

Profit	7.7%
Wages	21.0%
Purchases	43.1%
Depreciation	1.4%
Marketing	2.7%
Rent & Utilities	9.2%
Other	14.9%

Market Share

Luxottica Group S.p.A.	38.6%
National Vision Inc.	10.5%
Highmark Inc.	7.8%

- Should give exams at least one full day a week. The more days they offer exams, the better.

Expenses (% of Annual Sales)

Cost of Goods	35% to 45%
Occupancy Costs	15% to 20%
Payroll/Labor Costs	10% to 15%
Profit (pretax)	25% to 30%

Questions

- Contact lens sales? Do they keep the profits from opticians?
- Probability of staff retention. Number of active patient records.
- Days they have exams. If only one or two, could be tough to generate sales.
- What kind of equipment? Leased? Referral sources? Insurances accepted?

Industry Trend

- "Over the next five years, eye glasses and contact lens store revenue growth is expected to be driven by the aging US population's rising demand for prescription lenses. As the number of visits to the optometrist rises due to the growing incidence of eye diseases and vision impairment associated with diabetes and heavy computer use, demand for eyewear is expected to increase. While corrective eye surgery will constrain demand for prescription eyewear from many demographics, the industry will still benefit from age-related vision impairment, such as presbyopia, which cannot be amended with corrective eye surgery.
- "Over the five years to 2022, industry revenue is forecast to grow at an annualized rate of 2.6% to $13.5 billion due to growing demand for corrective eyewear from more individuals who have chronic diseases. Rising industry revenue is expected to place upward pressure on industry profit margins. However, profit gains are anticipated to be relatively minor, as strengthening

leverage among eyewear manufacturers will increase their ability to negotiate higher product prices, adding to this downstream retail industry's purchase costs. As a result, industry profit is expected to account for 8.1% of revenue in 2022, up slightly from an estimated 7.7% in 2017."

Source: IBISWorld Industry Outlook

Expert Comments

Very limited buyer pool; must have OD degree and state license.

National chains seem to be weaker. Mom and pops seem to be hanging in there, so they may be keeping optometrists busy.

Resources

- Eyecare Business: http://www.eyecarebusiness.com
- IBISWorld, September 2017: http://ibisworld.com

Optometry Practices

SIC 5999-04	NAICS 621320	Number of Businesses/Units 35,587

Rules of Thumb

➤ 60–70% of annual revenues includes inventory

➤ 2–2.5 x EBIT

➤ 2.5–3.5 x EBITDA

➤ 3–5 x SDE includes inventory

Pricing Tips

- 1.0 x SDE PLUS tangible assets
- The price should be discounted for a practice that doesn't have up-to-date equipment.
- Metro area and larger practices (more than $1 million in revenues) command higher multiples.
- Location, brand name optical and sufficiently stocked inventory are all very important in this industry. They will significantly affect time on the market.
- Practices with EHR systems in place sell for a higher multiple.
- Optometry professional fees are generally 40% of total sales if the office includes dispensary, 60% sales from eyewear and contacts. Cost of goods averages about 25%. Premises expense about 8%–12%.
- Pricing based on percentage of sales and cash flow are more applicable at sales exceeding $500,000.

Benchmark Data

Statistics (Optometrists)

Number of Establishments	35,587
Average Profit Margin	12.5%
Revenue per Employee	$113,200
Average Number of Employees	4.0
Average Wages per Employee	$38,915

O

Products and Services Segmentation

Eye exams	38.6%
Contact lenses	32.4%
Prescription eyewear	29.0%

Major Market Segmentation

Patients' out-of-pocket payments	42.4%
Private insurers	36.4%
Government payers	13.7%
Other patient care revenue	7.5%

Industry Costs

Profit	12.5%
Wages	34.3%
Purchases	8.9%
Depreciation	2.2%
Marketing	0.4%
Rent & Utilities	3.4%
Other	38.3%

- $300 gross revenue per exam; 60% recall within a three-year period; 30% new patient visits each year.
- Collections per FTE = $200,000. Collection per OD = $685,000.
- The 33% profit reflects SDE (income before a production wage for the owner/doctor).
- After all expenses, including a reasonable production wage for the owner, the net profit will average 10% to 15%.
- Ideally each doctor should generate over $700,000 annual gross revenue.
- New patient ratio should be at least 25%.
- 43 annual complete exams per 100 active patients. Eyewear sales as 43% of gross revenue. $550,000 annual revenue per full-time OD.
- 25% profit is SDE before paying doctor wages. Net profit to owner after all doctor wages is around 10%. Must be optometrist or ophthalmologist to own a practice. Many states and opticians cannot hire a doctor to do exams.

Expenses (% of Annual Sales)

Cost of Goods	25% to 35%
Occupancy Costs	05% to 15%
Payroll/Labor Costs	10% to 20%
Profit (pretax)	20% to 30%

Questions

- What are the growth opportunities for your practice, and why haven't you already taken advantage of them?
- Do you plan to continue practicing optometry in any way after the sale, and what are the details?
- Have any current or recent optometrist employees signed a noncompete agreement?
- Is there any current or pending litigation against the practice?
- What is the true cash flow for the practice? How up-to-date are the equipment and technologies? What are the demographics of the patients and what percent of patients is new each year?

- Insurance makeup (payors), review patient records.
- Carefully check out the risks associated with the seller continuing to practice in an area or in a manner that would siphon past patients to him/her. The details of the noncompete agreement are very important.

Industry Trend

- "The latest numbers from the Vision Council's VisionWatch survey, released today, reflect that the overall vision care market grew 0.7 percent, or nearly $282 million, in the 12 months ending March 2017, compared to the same period the prior year. Results from VisionWatch, the largest continuous survey of consumer purchasing attitudes toward eyewear and eyecare, indicated that the total vision care industry has generated $40.36 billion in revenue for the 12 months ending March 2017.

  "Looking at the vision care industry market over the past year, from March 2016 to March 2017, the report indicates that eyeglasses accounted for the largest share of the vision correction market at 55.6 percent, representing $22.43 billion in revenue—a decline of 0.3 percent over the past year."
  Source: "VisionWatch Survey Shows Nearly $300 Million Growth for $40.4B Vision Care Industry," June 21, 2017, http://www.visionmonday.com/latest-news/article/visionwatch-survey-shows-nearly-300-million-growth-for-404b-vision-care-industry/

- "In a move designed to bring not just eyewear but prescriptions to the masses via the Internet, online eyeglass purveyor Warby Parker has announced a mobile refraction service that allows customers to get a prescription renewal/update from their phone."
  Source: Warby Parker Unveils Mobile Rx Service" by Susan Tarrant, May 23, 2017, http://www.eyecarebusiness.com/news/2017/warby-parker-unveils-mobile-refraction-service

- "Luxexcel, a Belgium-based tech company that developed a technology to 3D-print ophthalmic lenses, has received up to $10 million in equity financing from a group of financial and strategic investors."
  Source: "3D-Printing Lens Co. Gets $10M Investment," May 3, 2017, http://www.eyecarebusiness.com/news/2017/3d-printing-lens-co-gets-$10m-investment

- Decline in single-doctor practices, increase in group practices
- Increasing reliance on social media
- Continued growth in coordinated care
- The burgeoning elderly population will create an increasing demand for medical optometry.
- Private practices are becoming more difficult to sell due a general shortage of willing and able buyers. This trend is much more pronounced in rural practices and will have a negative impact on selling prices.
- Older optometrists are looking to get out as the complexity of insurance, billing and medical records increases. Many would prefer to sell rather than try to implement an EHR.
- "The number of Americans with visual impairment or blindness will climb to more than eight million by the year 2050—approximately twice the current number—and an additional 16.4 million Americans are expected to have vision impairment due to uncorrected refractive error, based on a National Institutes of Health analysis of six large studies."
  Source: Visual Loss, Blindness to Double by 2050, by Bill Kekevian, June 15, 2016, https://www.reviewofoptometry.com/article/visual-loss-blindness-to-double-by-2050

- Competition continues to increase, consolidation has slowed the growth of business entities.
- More use of the Internet (online appointments, etc.) and social media. (marketing, patient relations, etc.). Movement towards multiple OD practices with larger patient bases. Expanding role of OD's in healthcare. OD alliances

28th Edition

O

will be on the increase to keep independent OD's competitive.

- The scope of optometry practice will continue to broaden as the supply of ophthalmologists fails to expand at the necessary pace.

Expert Comments

Be patient; it can take a year to find a buyer. Like all businesses, sell when it's doing well, not as it declines toward retirement.

For someone selling, start preparing at least three to five years in advance. For both buyers and sellers, get competent professional assistance.

Make sure the practice stands out in some way. It should either be known for its cutting- edge eye care treatment or for its unique assortment of frames and lenses.

Sellers—keep clean financial records with very little in the way of personal expenses. The valuation is heavily based on your practice's financial performance in the past two years. To get the most value for your practice, your tax returns should show a minimum of $140,000 in salary and net profit for a single practitioner. Larger ($750,000) and multi-office locations are in demand.

A buyer should examine the practice momentum. Is the practice declining, stable, or growing-and what is the perceived reason?

Competition would be lower if not for increased pressure from the growth of chains and the impact of the Internet on retailing (eyewear sales).

While entry is rather easy (provided you are a doctor), it's customer service oriented and that takes years to build goodwill if you are starting from scratch. Other pressures include changes in healthcare reimbursements and retail online and store eyewear and contact lens sales.

Seller Financing

- Outside financing. Specialty divisions of most large lenders handle these businesses. Ten-year fixed is most common.
- Typically, outside financing with little or no personal collateral required
- Loan terms can be up to ten years.
- Interest rates on par with other business purchase rates
- Banks typically love to lend to buyers in this industry, often with no money down, so, bank financing is very prevalent.
- It's almost all outside financing. Zero down is very common and financing is available for debt restructuring, relocation, remodeling, expansion and acquisition-good credit is the key.

Resources

- Optometric Management: http://www.optometricmanagement.com
- Optometry Times: http://optometrytimes.modernmedicine.com
- Review of Optometry: http://www.revoptom.com
- OptiBoard: http://www.optiboard.com
- Vision Monday: http://www.visionmonday.com
- American Academy of Optometry: http://www.aaopt.org
- American Optometric Association: http://www.aoa.org
- IBISWorld, September 2017: http://ibisworld.com

Orange Julius	Franchise
Approx. Total Investment	$345,000–$375,000
NAICS 722515	Number of Businesses/Units 465

Rules of Thumb
➤ 32% of annual sales plus inventory

Resources
• Orange Julius: http://www.orangejulius.com

Original Italian Pie	Franchise
Approx. Total Investment	$328,000–$617,500
NAICS 722513	Number of Businesses/Units 14

Rules of Thumb
➤ 35–40% of annual sales plus inventory

Resources
• Original Italian Pie: http://www.italianpie.com

OXXO Care Cleaners		Franchise
Approx. Total Investment		$475,500–667,000
SIC 7212-01	NAICS 812320	Number of Businesses/Units 40

Rules of Thumb
➤ 60% of annual sales plus inventory

Resources
• OXXO Care Cleaners: http://www.oxxousa.com

Packaging (Industrial)	
NAICS 561910	Number of Businesses/Units 11,193

Rules of Thumb
➤ 5–6 x EBIT
➤ 60–70% of annual sales plus inventory

P

Benchmark Data

Statistics (Packaging & Labeling Services)

Number of Establishments	11,193
Average Profit Margin	7.4%
Revenue per Employee	$165,200
Average Number of Employees	5.2
Average Wages per Employee	$37,564

Products and Services Segmentation

Packaging	47.2%
Other	20.7%
Assembly and fulfillment	17.9%
Repacking	8.6%
Labeling	5.6%

Major Market Segmentation

Personal care and cosmetics	40.0%
Pharmaceuticals and medical	27.1%
Other	23.0%
Electronics	6.2%
Apparel and textiles	3.7%

Industry Costs

Profit	7.4%
Wages	23.0%
Purchases	55.1%
Depreciation	2.3%
Marketing	0.7%
Rent & Utilities	3.2%
Other	8.3%

Expenses (% of Annual Sales)

Cost of Goods	60% to 65%
Payroll/Labor Costs	08% to 10%
Profit (pretax)	10% to 15%

Questions
- How stable is your customer base—what is your customer retention record? What percentage of total sales do your top 10 accounts represent? Is there really any real free cash flow in the business?

Industry Trend
- "Over the five years to 2022, macroeconomic growth and stability will continue to be the primary drivers of the Packaging and Labeling Services industry's growth. In particular, employment and consumer spending are projected to boost demand for industry services. Growth in household disposable incomes will likely lead to greater consumer spending on items that require packaging, spurring greater demand for industry services. Moreover, demand for niche, specialist and pharmaceutical packaging and labeling is expected to exhibit robust growth. Pharmaceutical packaging and labeling services will be in especially high demand as the baby boomer population ages and require more

pharmaceutical products. However, demand from food manufacturers is not expected to grow rapidly, and the Consumer Confidence Index is forecast to decline. As a result, IBISWorld expects industry revenue to only grow at an annualized rate of 2.6% to $10.5 billion over the five years to 2022."

Source: IBISWorld Industry Outlook

Resources
- IBISWorld, July 2017: http://ibisworld.com

Paint & Decorating (Wallpaper) Retailers		
SIC 5231-07	NAICS 444120	Number of Businesses/Units 9,135

Rules of Thumb
➢ 20% of annual sales plus inventory

Pricing Tips
- They should have a nationally known brand name plus 2 competitive paint lines. A wide variety of wallpaper from lesser priced to higher priced lines should be offered. National averages tell us these stores make from 16 to 17 percent plus reasonable wages for the owner/operators. The average markup is 40 percent. These stores are sold for fixtures, equipment plus inventory at cost.

Benchmark Data

Statistics (Paint Stores)

Number of Establishments	9,135
Average Profit Margin	12.6%
Revenue per Employee	$311,200
Average Number of Employees	4.1
Average Wages per Employee	$35,610

Products and Services Segmentation

Interior paint	44.0%
Stains, varnishes and other coatings	20.5%
Exterior paint	17.3%
Painting equipment and supplies	16.1%
Wallpaper and other flexible wall coverings	2.1%

Major Market Segmentation

Professional contractors	53.5%
Household consumers	29.3%
Other	17.2%

Industry Costs

Profit	12.6%
Wages	11.5%
Purchases	59.3%
Depreciation	0.8%
Marketing	1.8%
Rent & Utilities	6.1%
Other	7.9%

P

Market Share

The Sherwin-Williams Company	63.9%
PPG Industries Inc.	10.3%

Industry Trend

- "With an anticipated acquisition of Valspar in the air, The Sherwin-Williams Company posted consolidated net sales of $2.76 billion in the first quarter, up 7.3% from the same quarter last year. Net income increased to $239,152,000, up from $164,876,000. Net sales in the Paint Stores Group increased 12.1% to $1.81 billion in the quarter due primarily to higher architectural paint sales volume across all end market segments, selling price increases. There are more than 4,100 company-operated stores and facilities selling Sherwin-Williams products. The company said it opened 10 net new store locations in the Paint Store Group during the quarter."

  Source: "Sherwin-Williams reports record sales," April 20, 2017, http://www.hbsdealer.com/article/sherwin-williams-reports-record-sales

- "The global market for paints and coatings is expected to reach $155 billion by 2020, which would represent a compound annual growth rate of 4%, according to BCC Research. Asia is expected to post significant gains, especially China and India.

  "The US paint and wallpaper store industry includes about 7,000 establishments (single-location companies and units of multi-location companies) with combined annual revenue of about $10 billion."

  Source: http://www.firstresearch.com/Industry-Research/Paint-and-Wallpaper-Stores.html

Resources

- Paint and Decorating Retailers Association (PDRA): http://www.pdra.org
- IBISWorld, February 2017: http://ibisworld.com

		Franchise
Pak Mail		
Approx. Total Investment		$151,500–$224,450
	NAICS 561431	Number of Businesses/Units 220

Rules of Thumb

➢ 50% of annual sales plus inventory

Resources

- Pak Mail: http://www.pakmail.com

		Franchise
Panera Bread		
Approx. Total Investment		net worth of $7.5 million
Estimated Annual Sales/Unit		$2,585,000
	NAICS 722513	Number of Businesses/Units 1,926

Rules of Thumb

➢ 35– 40% of sales plus inventory

Industry Trend

- "Digital sales at Panera Bread Company-those made via mobile, web, or kiosk-have surpassed $1 Billion on an annualized basis and could double in 2019. Since the inception of its Panera 2.0 program in 2014, the company has emerged as an industry-leading restaurant e-tailer. Panera's end-to-end digital pathways, including Rapid Pickup, Fast Lane Kioskks, Catering and Delivery, enable a better guest experience for people to eat the way they want.

  "As of the end of Q1 2017, system-wide digital sales were 26 percent of total company sales-the highest rate in the restaurant industry outside of the pizza segment. Approximately 1.2 milliion digital orders are placed per week, as Panera continues to seamlessly integrate new services with the digital experience. Panera Delivery, which can only be ordered digitally and is supported by cutting-edge order tracking technology, is the latest way Panera is enhancing the guest experience."

  Source: https://www.panerabread.com/panerabread/documents/press/
  2017/panera-tech%20-leadership-release.pdf

Resources

- Panera Bread: http://www.panerabread.com

	Franchise
Papa John's Pizza	
Approx. Total Investment	$250,000–$300,000
Estimated Annual Sales/Unit	$885,500

SIC 5812-22	NAICS 722513	Number of Businesses/Units 2,666

Rules of Thumb

➢ 38–40% of annual sales

Benchmark Data

- For Benchmark Data, see Pizza Shops

Resources

- Papa John's Pizza: http://wwwpapajohns.com

	Franchise
Papa Murphy's Take 'N' Bake Pizza	
Approx. Total Investment	$216,430–$381,220
Estimated Annual Sales/Unit	$575,000

	NAICS 722513	Number of Businesses/Units 1,537

Rules of Thumb

➢ 35–40% of annual sales plus inventory

Benchmark Data

- See Pizza Shops

P

Resources

- Papa Murphy's Take 'N' Bake Pizza: http://www.papamurphys.com

		Franchise
Parcel Plus		
Approx. Total Investment		$206,720–$245,795
	NAICS 561431	Number of Businesses/Units 59

Rules of Thumb

➢ 25% of annual sales plus inventory

Resources

- Parcel Plus: http://www.parcelplus.com

Parking Lots and Garages		
	NAICS 812930	Number of Businesses/Units 20,683

Benchmark Data

Statistics (Parking Lots and Garages)

Number of Establishments	20,683
Average Profit Margin	18.1%
Revenue per Employee	$63,900
Average Number of Employees	7.6
Average Wages per Employee	$20,717

Products and Services Segmentation

Off-street parking - hourly or daily	38.3%
Off-street parking in buildings - weekly or monthly	24.3%
Valet parking	12.7%
Off-street parking on lots - weekly or monthly	9.1%
Management fees for the operation of parking facilities	9.0%
Other	6.6%

Major Market Segmentation

Privately operated central business district	40.5%
College and university	14.2%
Off-premise airport	12.3%
On-premise airport	12.2%
Hotel	10.3%
Hospital	5.5%
Municipal central business district	5.0%

Industry Costs

Profit	18.1%
Wages	32.1%
Purchases	8.4%
Depreciation	1.0%
Marketing	1.0%
Rent & Utilities	28.2%
Other	11.2%

Market Share

SP Plus Corporation	15.3%
Vinci	9.4%
ABM Industries Inc.	6.5%

Industry Trend

- "However, while data suggests positive events on the horizon for the parking industry, there are a number of risk factors, such as increased taxes and increased government regulation."

  Source: http://weareparking.org/?page=Parking_Demand.

- "In the five years to 2021, IBISWorld expects revenue for the Parking Lots and Garages industry to increase at an annualized rate of 1.0% to $11.3 billion. Employment, domestic trips and vehicle registrations will rise during this period, increasing the need for parking services at airports, entertainment venues and central business districts."

  Source: http://clients1.ibisworld.com/reports/us/industry/industryoutlook.aspx?entid=1739

Resources

- International Parking Institute: http://www.parking.org
- National Parking Association: http://weareparking.org
- IBISWorld, December 2016: http://ibisworld.com

Parking Lot Sweeping

SIC 1611-04	NAICS 561790	

Rules of Thumb

➢ 60–65% of annual sales includes inventory

➢ 2–2.5 x SDE includes inventory

➢ 5–5.5 x EBIT

➢ 5–6 x EBITDA

Benchmark Data

- $125K/employee or $150–$200K/driver

Expenses (% of Annual Sales)

Cost of Goods	20%
Occupancy Costs	05%
Payroll/Labor Costs	15%
Profit (pretax)	10% to 12%

Questions

- Must establish the quality of the accounts, condition of equipment, review contracts, examine labor force, etc. Is the owner tied to any special interests, people or other connections responsible for a significant portion of his company's business? If so how will this affect these accounts/sites? Future growth in a local area or region? Competition?

P

Industry Trend

- "Over the next five years, parking lot cleaning services are expected to continue making up the majority of industry services. As demand for public street cleaning falls, this service will make up a larger portion of industry revenue. Demand for parking lot cleaning is relatively stable, as parking lots need to be cleaned to maintain safety and quality, so demand is not likely to fluctuate. Over the next five years, aggregate private investment is projected to rise at an annualized rate of 3.9%, illustrating strong performance from private businesses. As a result, demand from businesses for parking lot cleaning will likely grow during the coming period."

Source: IBISWorld Industry Outlook

Expert Comments

This industry has been unable to support national or regional consolidation. Mostly local, statewide, or small regional players.

Resources

- IBISWorld, July 2017: http://ibisworld.com
- C & L Services: http://www.sweeping.com
- North American Power Sweeping Association (NAPSA): http://www.powersweeping.org
- World Sweeper: http://www.worldsweeper.com

Pawn Shops		
SIC 5932-29	NAICS 522298	Number of Businesses/Units 11,138

Rules of Thumb

➢ 3 x SDE includes inventory

➢ 3.5 x EBITDA

➢ 3–5 x EBIT

➢ 40–70% of annual sales plus inventory. Since money is loaned using items of value belonging to the customer and said items serve as collateral for the loan, inventory against money loaned has to be taken into account.

Pricing Tips

- Pricing pawnshops usually is far from the norm of a multiple of SDE, EBIT or EBITA. Typically the values that drive a pawnshop are the "money on the street" (value of the daily loans) and the inventory, with great interest in the mix of all the items that have been taken and used as collateral and the type of inventory, i.e., if a certain shop has 80% jewelry and 20% guns, tools, and electronics the inventory will be worth more than cost since gold and silver are extremely valuable. If the mix is 20% jewelry and 80% tools and electronics then it possibly could be worth less than cost due to depreciation. Not all shops handle guns but if they are a large percentage or even half of the inventory then it is a pretty safe bet it should be valued no less than cost. Today's buyers are typically corporate buyers and rely heavily on good records and computer systems. They will shy away from shops that are not computerized and the seller is telling them (wink, wink) the shop makes more than it shows.

Keep a close eye on the scrap gold sales and whether or not they are being recorded in the income for the shop. It is very common for those sales to not be recorded and will generally be $15,000–$25,000 per month for a shop doing $2 million in gross sales. This will drastically change the SDE for you.

Benchmark Data

Statistics (Pawn Shops)

Number of Establishments	11,138
Average Profit Margin	10.1%
Revenue per Employee	$227,800
Average Number of Employees	2.4
Average Wages per Employee	$30,769

Products and Services Segmentation

Merchandise sales	54.5%
Secured loans for personal collateral	42.4%
Other sales	3.1%

Industry Costs

Profit	10.1%
Wages	13.5%
Purchases	40.5%
Depreciation	0.9%
Marketing	1.8%
Rent & Utilities	6.5%
Other	26.7%

Market Share

EZCorp Inc.	10.4%
Cash America International Inc.	8.5%

- "The average pawn customer:
  - ✓ Age: 36
  - ✓ Household Income: $29,000
  - ✓ 80% are employed
  - ✓ 82% have high school diploma or GED
  - ✓ 33% are homeowners
  - ✓ All ethnicities
  - ✓ National Average Loan Amount: $150"

Source: http://pawnshopstoday.com/the-customer/

- According to the National Pawnbrokers Association, 80 percent of all customers do end up reclaiming their items.

Expenses (% of Annual Sales)

Cost of Goods	62%
Occupancy Costs	04%
Payroll/Labor Costs	09%
Profit (pretax)	18%

P

Questions

- What type of software do you use to track pawn receivables and inventory? How do you value pawned items? What is the quality of your pawn receivable? How do you measure and track bad inventory? What are the state laws regarding pawn shops, gun sales, and interest rates on loans?

Industry Trend

- "The National Pawnbrokers Association (NPA) announced today the results of the NPA 2016 Trend Survey. The survey, which was conducted in early 2017, focuses on industry trends as reported by pawnbroker members of the NPA for the 2016 calendar year. One notable survey result indicated that 47 percent of pawnbrokers cited a decrease in retail sales. 'Pawnbrokers' core business is making collateral loans. However, we depend on retail sales to liquidate defaulted collateral,' notes NPA president, Larry Nuckols. He continued, '2016 proved to be a competitive year in retail, as many brick and mortar jewelry and consumer electronics businesses have been negatively affected by the growth in online sales.'

  "'Americans continue to turn to pawn stores for non-recourse, collateral-based loans,' said Nuckols. 'While the pawn industry has grown more conservatively in recent years, increased public awareness, a positive image, and consumer-friendly stores attract new customers to pawn stores every day, and pawnbrokers have an optimistic outlook that all business will continue to increase in 2017.'"

  Source: Pawnbrokers Report Decrease in Retail Sales as Online Competition Grows and Buying Trends Shift," https://www.pawnshopstoday.com/trends/

- Trend is more competition and a steady customer base.

Expert Comments

Risk is actually very low if you make educated loans on a daily basis. There are many factors that weigh in on this and typically education in this field comes from learning the hard way, but several large chains have been very successful in training personnel quickly to run shops successfully.

Seller Financing

- 2–3 years max

Resources

- Pawn Shops Today: http://www.pawnshopstoday.com
- National Pawnbrokers Association: http://www.nationalpawnbrokers.org
- IBISWorld, September 2017: http://ibisworld.com

Payday Loans		
	NAICS 522291	Number of Businesses/Units 16,545

Rules of Thumb

➢ 70% of annual sales

Benchmark Data

Statistics (Check Cashing & Payday Loan Services)

Number of Establishments	16,545
Average Profit Margin	13.3%
Revenue per Employee	$136,300
Average Number of Employees	4.9
Average Wages per Employee	$39,849

Products and Services Segmentation

Payday loans for recurring expenses	46.0%
Check cashing	33.3%
Payday loans for unexpected emergencies/expenses	10.7%
Payday loans for other reasons	10.0%

Industry Costs

Profit	13.3%
Wages	28.9%
Purchases	33.9%
Depreciation	1.6%
Marketing	2.3%
Rent & Utilities	2.1%
Other	17.9%

Market Share

AARC LLC	5.5%

- "Miscellaneous statistics:
  - ✓ 97 percent of borrowers agree that their payday lender clearly explained the terms of the loan to them, including nearly nine in 10 (88 percent) who strongly agree.
  - ✓ 68 percent prefer a payday loan over incurring a late fee of approximately $30 (4 percent) or an overdraft fee of $35 from their bank (3 percent) when faced with a short-term financial crisis and unable to pay a bill.
  - ✓ Fewer than one in 10 (8 percent) said that a payday loan was their only option and they had no other resources available.
  - ✓ 95 percent say payday loans can provide a safety net during unexpected financial difficulties.
  - ✓ 94 percent say they were able to repay their loan in the amount of time they had expected to.
  - ✓ 89 percent say they feel more in control of their financial situation because of this option when they need it.
  - ✓ 68 percent say they would be in worse financial condition than they are now without the option of taking out a payday loan."
    Source: "New Harris Poll: 9 in 10 Payday Loan Borrowers Felt Product Met Their Expectations," http://cfsaa.com/our-resources/communications/recent-news/article-detail/newsid/77.aspx

Industry Trend

- "Sweeping new rules proposed Thursday by the Consumer Financial Protection Bureau (CFPB) could upend the payday loan industry, which consumer advocates say often traps cash-strapped workers into a vicious cycle of borrowing. If enacted, the rules generally will require lenders to verify that borrowers can afford the loans and cap the number of times people can take out successive loans. The rules also would go beyond payday loans to target other costly short-term loans, including some high-interest installment loans and car title loans.

"The CFPB says that because of the way the loans work now, borrowers who use them can often be overwhelmed by fees and trapped into a cycle of debt that forces them to skip important bills or make other difficult financial choices. For instance, theagency found that about 80 percent of payday loans are rolled over into a repeat loan, causing fees to pile up for borrowers. Roughly 45 percent of payday customers take out at least four loans in a row.

"And each loan comes with steep fees. The CFPB found that payday borrowers pay a median $15 in fees for every $100 they borrow, amounting to an annual percentage rate of 391 percent on a median loan of $350. The rates on installment loans and auto title loans can be similarly high."

Source: by Steve Helber, https://www.washingtonpost.com/news/get-there/wp/2016/06/02/what-consumers-need-to-know-about-the-rules-proposed-for-payday-loans/

- "The Check Cashing and Payday Loan Services industry is forecast to continue declining over the five years to 2021, albeit at a greater rate than the current period. The unemployment rate is anticipated to rise gradually during the five-year period at an annualized rate of 0.8%. Moreover, the percentage of services conducted online is anticipated to remain elevated in the years ahead, representing rising competition from online vendors. As regulation also increases, industry revenue is expected to continue to suffer under mounting government oversight.

"External competition is anticipated to increase substantially during the five-year period, predominately from companies that solely distribute check cashing and payday loan services online. Consequently, over the five years to 2021, industry revenue is anticipated to decrease at an annualized rate of 1.5% to reach $10.7 billion, including a 3.4% decrease in 2017."

Source: IBISWorld Industry Outlook

Resources
- IBISWorld, January 2017: http://ibisworld.com
- Community Financial Services Association of America: http://www.cfsaa.com

Pest Control		
SIC 7342-01	NAICS 561710	Number of Businesses/Units 27,308

Rules of Thumb

➢ 80–90% of annual sales plus inventory

➢ 2–3 x SDE plus inventory

➢ 3–4 x EBIT

➢ 3–4 x EBITDA

Pricing Tips
- 1. You really need to look at the individual selling the business or the management of the corporation, analyze them and check their background to see if they were sucessful previously.

2. Hire an expert who knows what the P & L should be if you do not know for sure yourself.

3. Is equipment shipshape or abused and dirty? How does the office appear? Are all of the records kept on the new and updated computer or on cards?

- Price should equal 4 to 5 times real profit where provable.
- Pest control companies tend to be less based on a multiple of cash flow than other industries. The multiple is taken into account along with whether the customers are under contract, the longivity of the customer base, as well as whether they are serviced monthly, bi-monthly or quarterly and the cost per service.

Benchmark Data

Statistics (Pest Control)

Number of Establishments	27,308
Average Profit Margin	10.3%
Revenue per Employee	$110,700
Average Number of Employees	4.6
Average Wages per Employee	$39,959

Products and Services Segmentation

Insect control, including bed bugs, cockroaches and ants	53.6%
Termite control	18.0%
Other services, including bird-proofing	16.1%
Rodent extermination and control	12.3%

Major Market Segmentation

Residential homes	68.0%
Commercial establishments	28.4%
Government institutions and not-for-profit organizations	3.6%

Industry Costs

Profit	10.3%
Wages	36.1%
Purchases	16.5%
Depreciation	1.2%
Marketing	4.9%
Rent & Utilities	4.7%
Other	26.3%

Market Share

The ServiceMaster Company	12.0%
Rollins Inc.	11.3%
Rentokil Initial	5.5%

Expenses (% of Annual Sales)

Cost of Goods	05% to 15%
Occupancy Costs	03% to 05%
Payroll/Labor Costs	25% to 30%
Profit (pretax)	25% to 35%

P

Questions

- Why are you selling and will you be available after the sale to assist with customers if necessary?
- Any recent significant changes in your business such as the loss of a major account? What portion of your business is your largest customer?
- Why are you getting out of the business? What is your employee turnover rate? Have you paid all of your federal and state taxes and can you prove it?
- Breakdown of services: commercial versus residential; general pest versus wood destroying.

Industry Trend

- More efficiency in production and more natural products
- Mergers and acquisitions, big fish eating little fish.
- In this industry there are always more buyers than sellers. I believe this should continue in the future.

Expert Comments

A lot of demand. Marketing plays a big role as well as market spread. There are many categories to choose from.

Takes 3 years to be a certified operator.

Most states require licensing which makes it more difficult to get into the industry. It eliminates those wanting to get into the industry without proper training.

Owner needs a pest control license; 4 categories-be sure you know the one you are working in. Possibly hire a certified operator. Use consultants as often as possible. Get a good marketing manager because things are changing as fast as technology.

Seller Financing

- Mostly owner financing unless the buyer has other assets. Banks typically will not loan money on a list of accounts.
- Some owner financing and not more than 70% in cash up front.
- Since this is not an inventory or equipment intensive business, the majority of buyers rely on seller financing or pay cash for the business. Lender financing is frequently based on the profits of the business.
- Depends on the size of the business. Normally 3 to 5 years. A larger company would be eligible for an SBA loan or other lender financing and could be financed for up to 10 years.

Resources

- Al Woodward, pest control brokerage specialist: http://www.servicebusinessconsulting.com
- PestWeb: http://www.pestweb.com
- Pest Management Professional—an excellent site with lots of informative articles: http://www.mypmp.net
- National Pest Management Association: http://www.pestworld.org
- IBISWorld, March 2017: http://ibisworld.com
- Arizona Pest Professional Organization: http://www.azppo.org

Pet Grooming

SIC 0752-04	NAICS 812910	Number of Businesses/Units 117,882

Rules of Thumb

➤ 1.5 x SDE plus inventory

➤ 40–45% of annual sales plus inventory

Pricing Tips

- Gross Income is not a reliable Rule of Thumb at all. SDE most accurate revenue stream against which multiplier is to be used, as most of these businesses are owner operated. Deduct any income owner/seller directly generates (grooming, training) as that revenue will most likely disappear with a sale. Owner involvement and client dependency on the owner needs to be carefully examined as the owner is a high-risk factor in this loyalty based, customer service industry. If owner also owns property, a Fair Market Value of Rent needs to be adjusted in the recast. Some owners pay no rent, some pay too little or too high.

Benchmark Data

Statistics (Pet Grooming and Boarding)

Number of Establishments	117,882
Average Profit Margin	11.7%
Revenue per Employee	$39,100
Average Number of Employees	1.8
Average Wages per Employee	$14,785

Products and Services Segmentation

Pet boarding	39.8%
Pet grooming	29.6%
Other	15.4%
Pet sitting and dog walking	7.7%
Pet training	7.5%

Industry Costs

Profit	11.7%
Wages	37.7%
Purchases	12.2%
Depreciation	4.1%
Marketing	2.5%
Rent & Utilities	11.6%
Other	20.2%

- Annual occupancy for boarding should be around 50% to 55%. Labor between 35% to 45%, excluding owners. SDE in the 25% range.

Expenses (% of Annual Sales)

Payroll/Labor Costs	35%

28th Edition

P

Industry Trend

- "For 2017, it's estimated that $69.36 billion will be spent on our pets in the U.S. Estimated Breakdown:

Food	$29.69 billion
Supplies/OTC Medicine	$14.93 billion
Vet Care	$16.62 billion
Live animal purchases	$2.01 billion
Other Services	$6.11 billion"

Source: http://americanpetproducts.org/press_industrytrends.asp

- "According to industry trends and projections, the pet business will continue to boom unabated in the future. While the forecast is healthy across the board, certain segments in the pet industry are seeing a significant amount of growth.

  "Natural products, in general, are gaining wide-spread popularity. This is because people have become more conscious about improving and sustaining the health of the planet. Consumers are also increasingly leery of the potential toxicity of synthetic chemicals and other harmful materials. In addition to a desire to decrease their pets' carbon paw prints, pet parents are opting to purchase natural products in an effort to maintain and/or improve the health and well-being of their beloved companion animals.

  "Specialty Pet Services Propel Pet Business Growth—The American Pet Products Association (APPA) predicted that spending in this arena would increase from $510 billion for 2013 to $620 billion in 2016. The demand for high-end pet grooming services is expected to continue to be particularly brisk.

  "Other pet services that are increasing in popularity are
  - ✓ Dog training
  - ✓ Upscale and holistic spa services such as 'paw-tinctures,' reiki and pet massage
  - ✓ Pet behavioral consulting
  - ✓ Pet portrait photography
  - ✓ Pet sitting
  - ✓ "More hot pet industry trends:
  - ✓ Mobile pet grooming
  - ✓ Pet-friendly travel
  - ✓ Pet health insurance"

Source: 5 Hot Trends in the Pet Industry" by Alissa Wolf, April 23, 2017,
https://www.thebalance.com/hot-industry-trends-in-pet-businesses-2660622

Expert Comments

Low barriers to entry of competition, except due to zoning requirements. High growth, high profit industry that attracts a lot of dog lovers. Competition includes pet sitters, friends & family. Industry expected to grow 3% to 5% annually for the next 5 years.

Boarding revenue is more protected from economic fluctuations than daycare, which relies heavily on discretionary income.

Seller Financing

- SBA financing for solid businesses, owner financing for others.

P

Resources

- American Pet Products Association: http://www.americanpetproducts.org
- National Dog Groomers Association of America: http://www.nationaldoggroomers.com
- PetGroomer—an amazing site, well worth visiting if you have any interest at all in the subject: http://www.petgroomer.com
- IBISWorld, January 2017: http://ibisworld.com

		Franchise
Petland		
Approx. Total Investment		$400,000–$850,000
	NAICS 453910	Number of Businesses/Units 142

Rules of Thumb

➢ 50% of annual sales plus inventory

Resources

- Petland: http://www.petland.com

Pet Stores		
SIC 5999-30	NAICS 453910	Number of Businesses/Units 17,945

Rules of Thumb

➢ 2 x SDE plus inventory

➢ 25–30% of annual sales plus inventory

Pricing Tips

- Be sure to check inventory turnover rate to make sure inventory is saleable.
- Dealing with reputable breeders increases value.

Benchmark Data

Statistics (Pet Stores)

Number of Establishments	17,945
Average Profit Margin	4.2%
Revenue per Employee	$154,600
Average Number of Employees	6.9
Average Wages per Employee	$20,323

Products and Services Segmentation

Pet food	45.7%
Pet supplies	40.6%
Pet services	9.0%
Live animals	4.7%

P

Industry Costs

Profit	4.2%
Wages	13.2%
Purchases	54.3%
Depreciation	0.8%
Marketing	1.9%
Rent & Utilities	10.2%
Other	15.4%

Market Share

PetSmart Inc.	38.0%
PETCO Animal Supplies Inc.	24.5%

- Number of U.S. Households that Own a Pet (millions)

Bird	7.9
Cat	47.1
Dog	60.2
Horse	2.6
Freshwater Fish	12.5
Saltwater Fish	2.5
Reptile	4.7
Small Animal	6.7

Source: http://www.americanpetproducts.org/press_industrytrends.asp

Expenses (% of Annual Sales)

Cost of Goods	50% to 60%
Occupancy Costs	04% to 05%
Payroll/Labor Costs	08% to 10%
Profit (pretax)	20% to 25%

Questions
- Where do you get your puppies from and what is their guarantee?
- Do they have a publicly accepted way of selling pets?

Industry Trend
- "The Pet Stores industry will continue fetching a growing share of the consumer dollar over the next five years as pet owners opt to spoil pets. In addition to rising pet ownership, improving economic conditions will boost consumer spending and encourage customers to purchase price-premium pet products and services. As a result, industry revenue is projected to increase at an annualized rate of 1.3% to $19.6 billion over the five years to 2022. Despite this growth, the Pet Stores industry will continue combating strong competition from grocery stores, mass merchandisers and a growing number of online-only retailers."

Source: IBISWorld Industry Outlook

Expert Comments

This takes into consideration that the store would be privately owned and not a big box store. Many of these privately owned businesses have been able to successfully compete on price against the big box stores. Stores in small towns tend to do well.

Location is a key factor in pricing, as many people travel to pick out the 'right' dog. Location to major intersections is a definite plus. Although it is fairly easy to duplicate a pet or pet supply store, knowing the mechanics of the industry can be tricky. Risk is primarily associated with dealing with reputable breeders that stand by their product; diseases such as parvo and kennel cough can cost quite a bit.

Resources

- Pet Industry Joint Advisory Council: http://www.pijac.org
- American Pet Products Association: http://www.americanpetproducts.org
- World Pet Association: http://www.worldpetassociation.org
- IBISWorld, March 2017: http://ibisworld.com

Pharmacies and Drugstores

SIC 5912-05	NAICS 446110	Number of Businesses/Units 55,086

Rules of Thumb

➤ 70 x average daily sales (range 60 to 80 times) plus inventory

➤ 25% of annual sales (range 20% to 30%) plus inventory

➤ 6.5 x EBIT (range 5 to 8 times) plus inventory

➤ 18–42% of annual sales—depending on profits and includes inventory

➤ 3 x SDE

➤ 5 x EBITDA

Pricing Tips

- Average total prescriptions filled daily, percent new, percent refills, and total prescriptions average price for year; percent prescription third-party insurance and Medicaid, and percent cash sales, percent charge sales. Inventory value in date and salable. Inventory turns per year; total cost of goods sold + inventory on hand (8 times); age analysis of all accounts receivable including welfare, Workers' Comp; hours open per day, per week, per month, number of days per year open; lease.

Benchmark Data

Statistics (Pharmacies and Drug Stores)

Number of Establishments	55,086
Average Profit Margin	4.9%
Revenue per Employee	$415,700
Average Number of Employees	13.8
Average Wages per Employee	$37,310

Products and Services Segmentation

Branded prescription drugs	51.5%
Generic drugs	20.1%
Other	11.2%
Nonprescription medicines	5.1%
Personal health supplies	4.8%
Groceries and food items	4.0%
Cosmetics	1.8%
Vitamins, minerals and dietary supplements	1.5%

P

Industry Costs

Profit	4.9%
Wages	9.5%
Purchases	68.4%
Depreciation	0.4%
Marketing	0.6%
Rent & Utilities	5.1%
Other	11.1%

Market Share

Walgreen Co.	28.6%
CVS Health Corporation	21.7%
Rite Aid Corporation	11.6%

Expenses (% of Annual Sales)

Cost of Goods	70% to 75%
Occupancy Costs	02% to 05%
Payroll/Labor Costs	09%
Profit (pretax)	03% to 07%

Questions

- Financials, average price per prescription, average amount of reimbursement of third-party payments, demographics, physicians in vicinity
- Number of years on lease? Do you own the building?

Industry Trend

- "Pharmacies and drug stores will prove to be indispensable over the next five years, as the industry will be an integral component in providing preventive care. As the number of insured individuals is expected to rise over the period due to healthcare reform, many individuals will have lower out-of-pocket costs for prescriptions. This trend, coupled with rising per capita disposable income, will enable more individuals to be compliant with their prescription dosages and refills, thus benefiting the industry.

  "Over the five years to 2022, industry revenue is forecast to rise at an annualized rate of 5.7% to $393.1 billion due to the projected shortage of primary care physicians, according to the US Department of Health and Human Services. This trend will enable more pharmacies and drug stores to provide preventive care services. Profit is expected to rise from 4.9% of industry revenue in 2017 to 5.9% in 2022, which can be attributed to the industry dispensing more high-margin drugs, including biologic drugs."

  Source: IBISWorld Industry Outlook

- Health care reform will encourage growth. Demographics (65+ population is increasing in U.S.) favorable for industry growth.
- "Most independent community pharmacists consistently encounter misleading and confusing fees imposed by prescription drug middlemen that negatively impact both pharmacies and patients and distort medication costs and reimbursement rates, according to a recent survey of 640 pharmacists conducted by the National Community Pharmacists Association (NCPA).

  "Sometimes weeks or months after medication is dispensed to a patient and a pharmacy is reimbursed, community pharmacies are assessed DIR fees that can turn a modest profit into a financial loss."

  Source: "Pharmacists Survey: Prescription Drug Costs Skewed by Fees on Pharmacies, Patients by NCPA," June 28, 2016, http://www.ncpanet.org/newsroom/news-releases/2016/06/28/pharmacists-survey-prescription-drug-costs-skewed-by-fees-on-pharmacies-patients

- "The Pharmacy Forecast 2016-2020 from the American Society of Health-System Pharmacists (ASHP) Foundation analyzed pharmacy trends and described strategies for health-system pharmacists to keep pace with the evolving scope of their practice. Here are 4 pharmaceutical market trends to watch in the year ahead:
  - ✓ Generic Drug Pricing
  - ✓ Enforced Product Tracing
  - ✓ Specialty Drug Spending
  - ✓ Limited Drug Distribution Channels"

Source: "4 Pharma Market Trends to Watch in 2016," by Allison Gilchrist, January 25, 2016, http://www.pharmacytimes.com/news/4-pharma-market-trends-to-watch-in-2016

Seller Financing

- Seller financing and outside financing are both involved. Most of the time startup pharmacies' inventory is financed by wholesaler for initial few months.
- Mostly all cash sales. Owner finance 3 to 7 years with interest at prime +/- 1% or 2 %
- 10 years

Resources

- National Community Pharmacists Association: http://www.ncpanet.org
- IBISWorld, January 2017: http://ibisworld.com
- www.salary.com: http://www.salary.com/
- American Pharmacists Association: http://www.pharmacist.com/
- American Society of Health-System Pharmacists: https://www.ashp.org/

Photographers & Photographic Studios

	NAICS 541921	Number of Businesses/Units 202,504

Rules of Thumb

- ➢ 45–50% of SDE; add fixtures, equipment & inventory
- ➢ 2.5–3 x monthly sales; add inventory

Pricing Tips

- They are usually sold for the new cost of fixtures and equipment, plus inventory, plus 30 percent of one year's net profit. National average states the gross profit usually runs about 62 percent, leaving a net profit of about 24 percent after expenses.

Benchmark Data

Statistics (Photography)

Number of Establishments	202,504
Average Profit Margin	11.7%
Revenue per Employee	$43,000
Average Number of Employees	1.2
Average Wages per Employee	$13,219

Products and Services Segmentation

Personal and group portrait photography 32.3%
Commercial and technical photography 30.0%
School portrait photography.. 14.4%
Weddings, holidays and other special occasions photography 14.0%
Other.. 9.3%

Industry Costs

Profit 11.7%
Wages.. 30.6%
Purchases.. 18.2%
Depreciation.. 3.5%
Marketing 2.1%
Rent & Utilities 6.6%
Other.. 27.3%

Market Share

Lifetouch Inc. 15.6%

Industry Trend

- "9 trends that will change photography in 2017:
  - ✓ Several linked trends: compact cameras c'est la mort
  - ✓ Desktop printers as an endangered species
  - ✓ Smartphone photography creates more photographers
  - ✓ Selfies. How is that still a thing?
  - ✓ More connectivity
  - ✓ Fashion camera bags
  - ✓ Vertical video?
  - ✓ Better cameras, not bigger cameras
  - ✓ The slow death of the trade show"

  Source: "9 Trends That Will Change Photography in 2017" by Joe Farace, January 6, 2017,
  https://www.shutterbug.com/content/geared-9-trends-will-change-photography-
  next-year-imaging-will-go-back-future-and-future-and

- "Despite a constantly evolving technological landscape that has dramatically altered consumer preferences for photographic services, the Photography industry is expected to grow moderately over the five years to 2022. This growth will come as consumers continue to gain spending power and players offer a broader range of products and services beyond conventional photography. Increased spending on advertising is also expected to propel growth in commercial photography services. Thus, IBISWorld anticipates total industry revenue to expand an annualized 1.8% to $11.1 billion over the five-year period."

  Source: IBISWorld Industry Outlook

Resources

- Imaging Alliance: https://www.theimagingalliance.com/
- IBISWorld, July 2017: http://ibisworld.com

Physical Therapy

	NAICS 621340	Number of Businesses/Units 117,849

Rules of Thumb

➤ 60–75% of annual sales
➤ 1.8–2.5 x SDE
➤ 1.5–2 x EBIT
➤ 1.5–3 x EBITDA

Pricing Tips

- Obamacare disrupted the market and supports large multispecialty entities, further eroding value. The Trump and Republican election is causing further erosion.
- Physical therapy record charts are not a true asset of the physical therapy practice since they can't be put on the balance sheet as an asset using the Asset Approach valuation methodology. Physical therapy record valuation is only used to specifically allocate intangibles, assuming they exist at the time of the valuation. The PT has the physical chart but usually cannot legally sell or dispose of it without the patient's consent (per state statutes), only transfer custodianship. The PT is basically a custodian of the physical therapy record rather than an owner of an asset with independent value. When paper charts are involved, I have come to the opinion that the value of the chart is zero because of the attendant custodianship liability costs. With EMR, a digital record may need to be converted from one digital platform to another either by custodianship transfer or technology succession, in which case a printout and re-entry may be required, probably exceeding in labor costs any physical value to the original digital chart.

  The billing process in a physical therapy practice is very complex, both in generating the charges using appropriate diagnosis and treatment codes, and in recording the payment and adjustments for uncollectable amounts. Accounts Receivable represent past gross charges for services rendered and as yet uncollected or adjusted-off. These receivables must be discounted to reflect both insurance company reimbursement disallowances, plus the decreasing value over time due to difficulty in collections of past due accounts. In other words, the historic collection ratio of the practice does not yet include the standing wave of uncollectable accounts at practice end, or at a particular point in time, as in a valuation at a particular date.

- Don't try to use boilerplate broker contracts to sell physical therapy practices, as it is easy to violate state or federal regulations; have all the paperwork and terms done by a medical practice transaction specialist attorney.
- The value of PT and medical practices dependent on insurance reimbursement is generally at an all-time low. Decisions regarding what, where, when and how to practice are influenced by numerous factors, including: personal preferences, market forces, state and federal policies and programs, and institutions that constitute the health care system and medical education infrastructure. Increasing retirement, plus the trend toward shorter working hours, increases the supply of practices for sale, and decreases the available FTE workforce available as buyers.

P

The increasing rate of boomer retirement and decreasing count of new physicians contributes to a reduction of value of practices for sale. A significant shortfall of physicians could develop over the next 15 or more years in the absence of increased output from U.S. medical schools, increased recruitment of foreign-trained physicians, or both. The American College of Physicians is concerned that the practice environment for those in medical practice has become so encumbered with regulation and practice hassles, at a time when reimbursement for care provided by physicians is declining, that physicians are finding it increasingly difficult to provide for their patients.

Of particular concern when determining value of a medical practice is ensuring not only that the purchase price is Fair Market Value, but also that the valuation method does not take into account the volume or value of referrals that the selling physician has made or may make to the purchaser, such that the purchase price could be challenged as a kickback or inducement. The OIG has provided guidance on the question of how to value a physician practice or other healthcare provider. The ailing economy is leading many Americans to skip doctor visits, skimp on their medicine, and put off tests. Employment by hospitals is paying more, and insurance-reimbursement and gross income is often dropping, so the results of the Income Approach of valuation identifying 'dividends' [(SDE minus market rate compensation of one working owner) x 1.5 (ie 65% Cap rate)] is becoming more important for more specialties. Percentage of annual gross sales or SDE multiplier as valuation Rules of Thumb are obsolete, if ever valid. Growth Rates are available through the Congressional Budget Office reports; rarely above 2% historically.

Medical practice is riskier-and demands higher Cap rates-than other professional practices like accounting, law, architecture and engineering which are not subject to clinical malpractice risks, or subject to Medicare or insurance company changing reimbursement limitations or denials. Many practices can't even sell at the value of the liquidated assets, since jobs pay more without asset purchase. The impact of specialty and location is profound, as is the FTE work-schedule and leverage of employed licensed providers. Medicare is continually reducing reimbursement, which impacts other insurances which often base their payment on a percent of Medicare (i.e., 80–120% of Medicare), so dependence on insurance reimbursement is an important consideration in value. In addition; specific diagnosis and procedure (ICD/CPT) billing-code reimbursement changes-like what has happened in dermatology, ophthalmology, allergy, cardiology, and other specialties-have further reduced reimbursement and profits during the past decade. The Goodwill Registry on sale data is helpful in some cases, but the often-quoted running average 10-year median goodwill value as a percentage of gross is irrelevant; as the average of many specialties reflects the midpoint of 10 years' steady decline. You need to acquire the full database and evaluate the underlying data to be useful; and look in particular at the Price:SDE data. The effect of the Medicare cuts which began in 2005 can distort the Registry summary statistics and need to be adjusted; and you need to remove results from court valuations, divorces and other non-transactional data.

- Most appraisers favor the Income Approach in valuing small, privately held professional services businesses, as it best reflects the impact of profit or dividends rather than just gross collections. It is the income above what the buyer could earn in employment that creates value in medical practices.

Benchmark Data

Statistics (Physical Therapists)

Number of Establishments	120,814
Average Profit Margin	12.9%
Revenue per Employee	$71,000
Average Number of Employees	4.0
Average Wages per Employee	$39,196

Products and Services Segmentation

Diseases of the musculoskeletal system and connective tissue	59.3%
Other	17.6%
Symptoms, signs and ill-defined conditions	8.2%
Injury and poisoning	7.3%
Diseases of the nervous system and sense organs	4.4%
Mental disorders	3.2%

Industry Costs

Profit	12.9%
Wages	54.7%
Purchases	8.7%
Depreciation	1.0%
Marketing	1.3%
Rent & Utilities	6.8%
Other	14.6%

- Employs at least 2–3 PTs and 2–3 PT aides.
- At least a 2-week waiting list for new patient visits. No PPACA ACOs locally.
- The best benchmark is revenue per employee. Revenue per full-time PT and patient visits by month are also helpful.
- Need to have 3–4 patients per hour for high utilization. Each physical therapist should account for approximately $250,000 of billing.

Expenses (% of Annual Sales)

Cost of Goods	27%
Occupancy Costs	06% to 10%
Payroll/Labor Costs	15% to 25%
Profit (pretax)	12% to 25%

Questions

- Compliance with state and federal regulations.
- How long have they been practicing physical therapy? Have they managed people before? Why are they looking for a practice? What location is important to them and why?
- Patient visits per hour, per day, per week are critical. Trends in the revenue. Orthopedic referral sources and relationships. Hospital contacts. Length of lease and terms.

Industry Trend

- "While the PT industry experienced modest growth from 2010 to 2015, it has entered a new era of growth and is expected to increase by 3.6% annually to become a $34.6 billion sector by 2020. U.S. Physical Therapy (the only public pure play ORF provider) anticipates the outsourced rehab market could grow at +5% over the same period. Growth within the ORF and IRF sectors are largely being fueled by the aging US population, healthcare reforms and the recognized benefits of rehabilitation services."

Source: CapStone LLC

- "The physical therapy and rehabilitation care industry market is large and growing. Merger and acquisition activity continues to be on the radar for many of our nation's largest rehab therapy providers with six of the ten largest players now owned by private equity firms. There are several reasons for this industry phenomenon, which has driven multiples to a 20-year high and has attracted both financial and strategic buyers from all walks of life.

  "We are seeing one to five clinics drive one to three multiple of EBITDA while larger groups of 20 or more exceed ten times EBITDA. These are general observations and may vary for a variety of reasons."

Source: https://www.webpt.com/blog/post/mastering-metrics-exit

- According to the US Department of Labor, Employment of physical therapists is expected to increase for all occupations. The impact of proposed Federal legislation imposing limits on reimbursement for therapy services may adversely affect the short-term job outlook for physical therapists. However, over the long run, the demand for physical therapists should continue to rise as growth in the number of individuals with disabilities or limited function spurs demand for therapy services. Job opportunities should be particularly good in acute hospital, rehabilitation, and orthopedic settings, because the elderly receive the most treatment in these settings. The growing elderly population is particularly vulnerable to chronic and debilitating conditions that require therapeutic services. Also, the baby-boom generation is entering the prime age for heart attacks and strokes, increasing the demand for cardiac and physical rehabilitation. Further, young people will need physical therapy as technological advances save the lives of a larger proportion of newborns with severe birth defects. Future medical developments also should permit a higher percentage of trauma victims to survive, creating additional demand for rehabilitative care. A growing number of employers are using physical therapists to evaluate worksites, develop exercise programs, and teach safe work habits to employees in the hope of reducing injuries in the workplace.

- PT reimbursement is legislated to also decrease like physicians, but the PT shortage will keep salaries stable, so costs will be going up while reimbursement is going down, decreasing profits.

- Under PPACA, many hospitals and other entities are forming vertically integrated systems, taking control of physician referrers to PTs, and likely following with integration of PT practices, keeping services in-house and reducing referrals to independent PTs.

- Integration into ACOs

- Declining reimbursements will force owners to increase patient time with aides and assistants, and reduce time with highly paid physical therapists.

- Rollups and combination due to insurance issues. However, with the aging of the population and more joint replacements, there will be a demand for services.

Expert Comments

Working one more year will commonly net more income than a sale.

You have to be a licensed PT or physician in most states to be an owner. There is currently a national shortage of physical therapists. There are over 2,700 PT jobs posted on the American Physical Therapist Association website, up from 2,300 just last year. A PT shortage reduces the availability of prospective purchasers of practices and drives up wages, reducing future profits-above-wages (i.e., 'dividends') for owners.

A PT can learn how to start and run a practice in a day's consult with an expert. As a field of medicine, it is subject to most of the same hassle factors, like insurance and laws. Obamacare is causing ACOs to take over PT and control referrals. On the other hand, larger chains of PT practices are selling for a premium to private equity groups at up to 4–5 x EBITDA, but I think it can't last due to PPACA laws and ACOs.

Owners of practices need to have a managing physical therapist. Many PTs are now incurring very high education expenses and the debt load on many of them may prevent them from owning practices in the future.

The reductions in insurance reimbursements have affected buyer's interest level in owning a practice.

Investment should include a gym and treatment area.

Seller Financing
- Bank financing is available.
- 100% bank financing
- 75% SBA guaranteed financing is generally available.
- Seller financing is low especially if referral sources is widely diversified. 10-20% of a deal is seller financing with the remaining amount in the form of an SBA loan.
- Financing is available through SBA guaranteed loans for those with good financial statements. Otherwise, they are seller financed. Banks generally approve of financing doctor practices although this has not been extended to physical therapists (unlike dentists and other medical and doctor practices).

Resources
- Physical Therapy Practice Valuation: http://medicalpracticeappraisal.com
- American Physical Therapy Association: http://www.apta.org
- IBISWorld, April 2017: http://ibisworld.com
- National Society of Certified Healthcare Business Consultants: http://www.NSCHBC.org
- MGMA: http://www.MGMA.com

Picture Framing		
SIC 5999-27	NAICS 442299	Number of Businesses/Units 9,973

Rules of Thumb
➤ 45% of annual sales plus inventory

P

Pricing Tips

- Not a lot of activity to report in the framing industry. While there have been some transactions, most involve private sales where numbers aren't reported. I have valued a few businesses in the past year and found the same formulae apply as in the past. Values were less, but that is as a result of lower sales, inventories and other assets.
- Perhaps most critical is the impact of a change in ownership. If the shop is small, that is the owner is the face of the business, rarely is the business worth any more than 10% of sales.

Benchmark Data

Statistics (Picture Framing Stores)

Number of Establishments	9,973
Average Profit Margin	5.5%
Revenue per Employee	$118,200
Average Number of Employees	2.3
Average Wages per Employee	$24,393

Products and Services Segmentation

Custom framing	67.5%
Ready-made frames	15.6%
Photo frames	9.4%
Other	7.5%

Industry Costs

Profit	5.5%
Wages	20.7%
Purchases	53.3%
Depreciation	0.7%
Marketing	2.7%
Rent & Utilities	4.6%
Other	12.5%

Market Share

Aaron Brothers Inc.	17.8%

Expenses (% of Annual Sales)

Cost of Goods	25%
Occupancy Costs	10%
Payroll/Labor Costs	12%
Profit (pretax)	14%

Questions

- In addition to the usual financial questions, you should conduct a market evaluation to determine the viability of the present pricing structure.

Industry Trend

- "As with much of the service-based retail sector, the Picture Framing Stores industry experienced a period of heightened volatility over the past five years.

While the period challenged framers, it also highlighted the importance of operational efficiencies and the adoption of sound business practices. The industry benefits from a primary market that exhibits some degree of resistance to recessionary periods. While affluent households earning more than $76,000 are more likely to remain consistent customers to their local framers in periods of economic uncertainty, the lower-tiered income earners turn to discount chains and ready-made frames available at big-box retailers functioning outside this industry. To compete over the next five years, independent frame shops will have to improve operational efficiencies through the adoption of technology and aggressive marketing. Growing plastic prices will likely weigh on profit, though it is still forecast to continue improving in line with overall economic expansion. IBISWorld expects industry revenue will increase at an annualized rate of 1.5% to $2.9 billion over the five years to 2022."

Source: IBISWorld Industry Outlook

Expert Comments

Location and co-tenancy is extremely important to value as long as lease is secure.

Resources
- Professional Picture Framers Association: http://www.ppfa.com
- IBISWorld, March 2017: http://ibisworld.com

		Franchise
Pillar to Post—Home Inspection		
Approx. Total Investment		$31,550–$36,550
	NAICS 541350	Number of Businesses/Units 455

Rules of Thumb

➢ 25–30% of annual sales plus inventory

Resources
- Pillar to Post: http://www.pillartopost.com

		Franchise
Pizza Factory		
Approx. Total Investment		$150,000–$400,000
Estimated Annual Sales/Unit		$375,000
	NAICS 722513	Number of Businesses/Units 110

Rules of Thumb

➢ 30%–35% of annual sales plus inventory

Resources
- Pizza Factory: pizzafactory.com

P

Pizza Inn

Approx. Total Investment		$80,000—$764,000
Estimated Annual Sales/Unit		$450,000
	NAICS 722513	Number of Businesses/Units 181

Rules of Thumb

➤ 45% of annual sales plus inventory

Resources

- Pizza Inn: http://www.pizzainn.com

Pizza Shops

SIC 5812-22	NAICS 722513	Number of Businesses/Units 92,780

Rules of Thumb

➤ 35% of annual sales plus inventory for independent shops

➤ 38% of annual sales plus inventory for franchised or chain pizza shops

➤ 1.5 x EBITDA

➤ 4 x monthly sales plus inventory

➤ 1.5–2 x SDE; plus fixtures, equipment and inventory

➤ 1.5–1.6 x EBIT

Pricing Tips

- "As a baseline, Edelstein says a restaurant valuation is typically anywhere from two to three times the adjusted cash flow, a number that rarely matches the cash flow number listed on the restaurant's P&L since so many operators place various expenses on the business--cars, cell phones, life insurance, and the like--to maximize deductions."
  Source: http://www.pizzatoday.com/departments/back-office/valuation-whats-pizzeria-worth/

- Good books can help raise all of the pricing Rules of Thumb. If there is substantial 'goodwill' being included in the sell price, positive online reviews will play an important part of the marketing of the pizza shop for sale.

- "Pizza Franchise Rules of Thumb and Annual Sales-Quick Check
  Blackjack's Pizza ....40% of annual sales
  Domino's Pizza ....50% of annual sales–$800,000
  Gatti's Pizza...30% of annual sales–$1,000,000
  Godfather's Pizza ....25% of annual sales–$380,000
  Hungry Howie's Pizza..35% of annual sales–$550,000
  Little Caesar's Pizza ....50% of annual sales–$830,000
  Mountain Mike's Pizza ....30% of annual sales–$525,000
  Mr. Jim's Pizza..35% of annual sales–$440,000
  Papa Murphy's Take 'N' Bake ....35% of annual sales–$550,000
  Pizza Factory ....30% of annual sales–$375.000
  Pizza Inn ....45% of annual sales–$450,000"
  September 2016

- Note: Several of the businesses had a percentage multiple of, for example, 35% to 40%. The lower figure was the one used in tabulating an average. This produced an average rule of thumb of 38% of annual sales = the ballpark price. The above represent an average rule of thumb for franchised pizza restaurants. As you can see, independent pizza shops have an average rule of thumb of 35%. This slight difference may be due to more information being available for franchised units than for independents.

Benchmark Data

Statistics (Pizza Restaurants)

Number of Establishments	92,780
Average Profit Margin	5.8%
Revenue per Employee	$45,000
Average Number of Employees	10.9
Average Wages per Employee	$11,237

Products and Services Segmentation

Takeout and delivery	53.0%
Sit-down service	33.0%
Catering	14.0%

Industry Costs

Profit	5.8%
Wages	24.9%
Purchases	37.2%
Depreciation	2.8%
Marketing	2.6%
Rent & Utilities	12.7%
Other	14.0%

Market Share

Pizza Hut Inc.	13.0%
Domino's Inc.	11.5%
Little Caesar's	8.8%
Papa John's International Inc.	6.6%

- Sales per employee should exceed $40,000. Food costs can vary depending on what you are doing with the dough; scratch dough can bring the food cost to 30%, where buying a fully sheeted pie could bring food cost to 34%.
- Imperative to watch food costs for this business. Cannot be run absentee. Theft by employees sometimes a problem. Trend was seven days per week, seems to be changing in some areas to six. Expect 11 a.m. to 11 p.m. hours. Delivery is a must.

Expenses (% of Annual Sales)

Cost of Goods	30% to 32%
Occupancy Costs	07% to 10%
Payroll/Labor Costs	25% to 30%
Profit (pretax)	08% to 12%

P

Questions

- What is the reason for selling? Will you open another pizza shop and where? How long have you been in business and what were your sales trends?
- Why is the business for sale? Net Income? Unreported Income? Employees off the books? Number of employees? Amount of hours he or she personally works?

Industry Trend

- "Forty-one percent of consumers polled say they now eat pizza once a week, a big jump from 26% just two years ago. And a Harris Poll found pizza is Americans' No. 1 favorite comfort food, earning twice as many votes as any other dish.

  "A total of 5,377 new pizzerias opened their doors in the past year, while 6,006 closed down. But if you dig a little deeper, you find that independent pizza shops held their own compared to the chains in terms of opens and closes. Independents opened 3,614 stores and closed 3,656 stores, for a net loss of only 42 units. Chains, meanwhile, opened 1,763 stores and closed 2,410, for a net loss of 647. The total impact on the industry was a net loss of only 689 stores—less than 1%.

  "But the chains, while closing more stores, still outsold the independents. Independents now comprise 55% of America's pizza restaurants while brining in only 42.5% of the sales. With a total of 42,455 units operating as of September 30, 2016, independents logged sales of $18,879,367,505 this year, while the chains raked in $25,552,998,951 with only 34,268 units, according to CHD Expert. Independents averaged $444,691 in sales per unit, compared to $745,681 per unit for the chains.

  "A Morgan Stanley study found delivery is a $30 billion industry, but it has the potential to be worth more like $210 billion—the total amount currently spent on off-premise dining. Of the $30 billion figure, $11 billion in delivery orders are placed online, and nearly two-thirds of those online orders are for pizza."

  Source: "2017 Pizza Power Report"

- "Technology is killing off independent pizzerias in the United States at the rate of roughly 2,549 locations per year (in 2015 alone). The pizza category is being reshaped by both big new tech deployed by chains and fresh threats from sophisticated emerging brands that are taking slices of the pie from tens of thousands of ill-equipped and low-tech independent pizzerias.

  "With an Average Unit Volume (AUV) of $657,000 (on par with the segment average), Domino's now sees over 50 percent of its sales generated by online platforms (though, in some regions like the U.K., that number is higher, with 75 percent of the company's 2015 pizza orders made through digital channels). Take away these sales, and you're left with an AUV of $328,500.

  "If that number looks familiar, it absolutely should-it's only $56,000 less than the AUV of your typical independent pizza restaurant. The evidence is pretty plain that, in the case of the plummeting mom-and-pop pizza profits, the failure to get with the program and get online, once categorized by consultants and onlookers as a 'highly recommended' strategy, is now requisite, not just to compete but to stay in business."

  Source: "How Tech is Killing Off Independent Pizzerias," by Aaron D. Allen, LinkedIn.com, March 3, 2016

- A lot of the same as far as total numbers of establishments. Turnover of pizza shops is high because of competition. People are always interested in buying for the relatively low entry costs.

Expert Comments

Location is important, as most shopping centers have an existing pizza shop. It is important to get in on the ground floor.

High profile locations are not as important if there is emphasis being put on delivery service. If that is the case, more rooftops in the area of the shop becomes the important factor.

You must make the process as simple as possible if you are going to expand to multiple locations.

Seller Financing

- Seller financing with 35-50% down with the balance being paid back in 3-5 years.
- Five to seven years

Resources

- National Restaurant News: http://www.nrn.com
- Pizza Magazine Quarterly: http://www.pmq.com
- Franchise Times: http://www.franchisetimes.com
- IBISWorld, January 2017: http://ibisworld.com
- Pizzabusiness.com: http://www.pizzabusiness.com

		Franchise
Planet Beach		
Approx. Total Investment		$177,000–$351,000
	NAICS 812199	Number of Businesses/Units 205

Rules of Thumb

➤ 35–40% of annual sales

Resources

- Planet Beach: http://www.planetbeach.com

		Franchise
Play It Again Sports		
	NAICS 453310	Number of Businesses/Units 283

Rules of Thumb

➤ 40–45% of annual sales plus paid-for inventory

Resources

- Play It Again Sports: http://www.playitagainsports.com

P

Podiatrists

SIC 8043-01	NAICS 621391	Number of Businesses/Units 12,314

Rules of Thumb

➤ 1.5 x EBITDA

➤ 40–50% of annual sales plus inventory

➤ 3–4 x SDE plus inventory

Pricing Tips

- Obamacare disrupted the market and supports large multispecialty entities, further eroding value. The Trump and Republican election is causing further erosion.

- The value of podiatry practices is generally at an all-time low. Decisions regarding what, where, when and how to practice are influenced by numerous factors, including: personal preferences, market forces, state and federal policies and programs, and institutions that constitute the health care system and podiatry education infrastructure. Increasing retirement, plus the trend toward shorter working hours, increases the supply of practices for sale, and decreases the available FTE workforce available as buyers. The increasing rate of boomer retirement and decreasing count of new physicians contributes to a reduction of value of practices for sale. A significant shortfall of physicians is expected over the next 15 or more years in the absence of increased output from U.S. podiatry schools, increased recruitment of foreign-trained physicians, or both; both of which are being further limited instead of expanded. The American College of Physicians is concerned that the practice environment for those in medical practice has become so encumbered with regulation and practice hassles, at a time when reimbursement for care provided by physicians is declining, that physicians are finding it increasingly difficult to provide for their patients.

  Of particular concern when determining value of a podiatry practice is ensuring not only that the purchase price is Fair Market Value, but also that the valuation method does not take into account the volume or value of referrals that the selling physician has made or may make to the purchaser, such that the purchase price could be challenged as a kickback or inducement. The OIG has provided guidance on the question of how to value a physician practice or other healthcare provider. The ailing economy is leading many Americans to skip doctor visits, skimp on their medicine, and put off tests. Employment by hospitals is paying more, and insurance-reimbursement and gross income is often dropping, so the results of the Income Approach of valuation identifying dividends [(SDE minus market rate compensation of one working owner) x 1.5 (i.e., 65% Cap rate)] is becoming more important for more specialties. Percentage of annual gross sales or SDE multiplier as valuation Rules of Thumb are obsolete, if ever valid. Growth Rates are available through the Congressional Budget Office reports; rarely above 2% historically. Podiatry practice is riskier—and demands higher Cap rates—than other professional practices like accounting, law, architecture and engineering which are not subject to clinical malpractice risks, or subject to Medicare or insurance company changing reimbursement limitations or denials. Many practices can't even sell at the value of the liquidated assets, since jobs pay more without asset purchase. The impact of specialty and location is profound, as is the

FTE work-schedule and leverage of employed licensed providers. Medicare is continually reducing reimbursement, which impacts other insurances which often base their payment on a percent of Medicare (i.e., 80–120% of Medicare), so dependence on insurance reimbursement is an important consideration in value. In addition, specific diagnosis and procedure (ICD/CPT) billing-code reimbursement changes have further reduced reimbursement and profits during the past decade.

Make sure to read the white papers on supply and demand available on many specialty professional association websites. The best overhead statistics are usually available at http://www.NSCHBC.org. The best market rate compensation stats are usually available at http://www.MGMA.com. The Goodwill Registry on sale data is helpful in some cases, but the often-quoted running average 10-year median goodwill value as a percentage of gross is irrelevant, as the average of many specialties reflects the midpoint of 10 years' steady decline. You need to acquire the full database and evaluate the underlying data to be useful; and look in particular at the price:SDE data. The effect of the Medicare cuts which began in 2005 can distort the Registry summary statistics and need to be adjusted; and you need to remove results from court valuations, divorces and other non-transactional data.

Podiatry record charts are not a true asset of the podiatry practice since they can't be put on the balance sheet as an asset using the Asset Approach valuation methodology. Podiatry record valuation is only used to specifically allocate intangibles, assuming they exist at the time of the valuation. The physician has the physical chart but usually cannot legally sell or dispose of it without the patient's consent (per state statutes), only transfer custodianship. So the physician is basically a custodian of the podiatry record rather than an owner of an asset with independent value. When paper charts are involved, I have come to the opinion that the value of the chart is zero because of the attendant custodianship liability costs. With EMR, a digital record may need to be converted from one digital platform to another either by custodianship transfer or technology succession, in which case a printout and re-entry may be required, probably exceeding in labor costs any physical value to the original digital chart.

The billing process in a podiatry practice is very complex, both in generating the charges using appropriate diagnosis and treatment codes, and in recording the payment and adjustments for uncollectable amounts. Accounts Receivable represent past gross charges for services rendered and as yet uncollected or adjusted-off. These receivables must be discounted to reflect both insurance company reimbursement disallowances, plus the decreasing value over time due to difficulty in collections of past due accounts. In other words, the historic collection ratio of the practice does not yet include the standing wave of uncollectable accounts at practice end, or at a particular point in time, as in a valuation at a particular date.

- Don't try to use boilerplate broker contracts to sell podiatry practices, as it is easy to violate state or federal regulations—have all the paperwork and terms done by a medical practice transaction specialist attorney.
- Most podiatric practices are small. Most of the practices have only one or two doctors. The average partnership has two doctors and the typical podiatric medical group has three podiatrists, according to an APMA study. The median podiatrist has about $750,000 in annual collections, with a $180,000–$200,000 income, including benefits. Prescription foot orthoses are a foundation of

P

non-surgical treatments utilized by podiatrists. The vast majority of orthotics dispensed by podiatrists are custom functional orthoses. The custom orthotic industry is headed into a crisis based upon a number of issues: ethics and accountability, verification of outcomes, coding and reimbursement, increased operational costs, and reduced profitability. As insurance companies look to reduce their services or payments, they have looked to orthotics as a way to cut costs, according to an article in *Podiatry Today.*

Benchmark Data

Statistics (Podiatrists)

Number of Establishments	12,314
Average Profit Margin	14.7%
Revenue per Employee	$123,200
Average Number of Employees	3.5
Average Wages per Employee	$44,437

Products and Services Segmentation

Musculoskeletal system and connective tissue diseases	37.4%
Skin and subcutaneous tissue diseases	20.3%
Other	14.6%
Infectious and parasitic diseases	7.7%
Endocrine, nutritional and metabolic diseases	7.1%
Merchandise Sales	5.2%
Circulatory system diseases	5.1%
Nervous system and sense organ diseases	2.6%

Industry Costs

Profit	14.7%
Wages	36.1%
Purchases	9.1%
Depreciation	1.3%
Marketing	1.5%
Rent & Utilities	7.4%
Other	29.9%

- The value of podiatry practices is generally at an all-time low.
- At least a 2-week waiting list for patient appointments
- Most podiatrists see approximately 100 visits per 40-hour workweek
- Variables include whether mid-levels like nurse practitioners or PA's are employed; orthotic sales or referral; surgical components.

Expenses (% of Annual Sales)

Cost of Goods	05% to 06%
Occupancy Costs	06% to 07%
Payroll/Labor Costs	16% to 23%
Profit (pretax)	35% to 40%

Questions

- State and federal compliance
- Do you have nursing home contracts? Do you have Medicaid patients?

538 Business Reference Guide 2018

Industry Trend

- "The Bureau of Labor Statistics reports that podiatry is poised to grow by 14 percent from 2014 to 2024, resulting in 1,400 new jobs. Since the U.S. population is both increasing and aging, the BLS predicts that more people will have foot- and ankle-related ailments. The diabetes epidemic is also driving the job growth, since diabetics often suffer from foot problems. "Quick Stats
  - ✓ $119,340 Median Salary
  - ✓ 1.7% Unemployment Rate
  - ✓ 1400 Number of Jobs"

  Source: https://money.usnews.com/careers/best-jobs/podiatrist

- An American Podiatric Medical Association (APMA)-commissioned study of the podiatric workforce confirmed what many in the profession have suspected for years: the number of podiatrists practicing and graduating over the next 10 years will be insufficient to meet a projected surge in demand for foot-care services. The number of graduating podiatrists needs to triple in order to meet the health needs of a population that is increasingly older, heavier, and diabetic. There is the possibility that an ongoing shortage also could force referring physicians to seek out other medical professionals to care for their patients. Many current podiatrists also will be nearing retirement age over the next decade. Only about 6.5 percent of podiatric physicians are younger than age 30, while about 56 percent are age 45 or older. Expansion of podiatry is facing strong opposition from various state physician orthopedic medical associations.

- Congress passed Health System Reform Legislation (H.R. 3590). We now have a federal law applicable to ERISA plans that makes it against the law for insurance companies to discriminate against Doctors of Podiatry and other providers relative to their participation and coverage in health plans. The legislation establishes a National Health Care Workforce Commission to review needs in the healthcare workforce, and specifically includes podiatrists by defining them as part of the healthcare workforce, and includes them in the definition of health professionals. A number of states quickly filed lawsuits seeking to block it, the outcome of which will not be known for some time. The future of podiatric economics is still unclear.

Expert Comments

Working one more year will often provide more net income than selling. Buying at the right price is an excellent investment because values are so low.

Easy for a podiatrist to learn how to do a startup in a day. Podiatry is a field of medicine accepting all the same insurances and Medicare, and subject to the same laws.

Serious shortages expected, plenty of jobs available, reduces need to buy business.

Seller Financing

- 80–100% bank financing is readily available.
- SBA will finance 75%.

P

Resources

- American Academy of Podiatric Practice Management: http://www.aappm.org
- American Podiatric Medical Association: http://www.apma.org
- Podiatry Today: http://www.podiatrytoday.com
- IBISWorld, April 2017: http://ibisworld.com
- National Society of Certified Healthcare Business Consultants: http://www.NSCHBC.org
- Medical Group Management Association: http://www.MGMA.com

Pool Service (Swimming)		
SIC 7389-09	NAICS 561790	Number of Businesses/Units 52,956

Rules of Thumb

➤ 2 x SDE

➤ 10 to 12 times the monthly service gross income; swimming pool routes throughout the country sell for this multiple.

➤ Note: The monthly service gross income is just that. It does not include income from maintenance or repair. This is already considered in the multiple, because most pool service technicians agree that whatever your monthly service billing is, half of that again will translate into maintenance/repair income.

Pricing Tips

- Most pool service routes sell for 1 year's gross service billing, not including repairs.
- Pricing is typically 10–12 times monthly service income. This usually does not include repairs or other services, but does include inventory.
- These figures will vary based upon a solo business owner and one that has employees. A great estimate of profit without employees will be 80%; if employees are a factor, you should anticipate 40% profit margins. Both of these issues will affect pricing of a business for sale, and will also affect sale price.
- "As stated, there are two main sources of income, monthly service billing and maintenance/repair income. Throughout the United States the purchase price of a pool service route is based on a multiple times the Monthly Service Billing Only income. The multiple will vary from state to state and even within some states. However, it is an industry standard to use a multiple times the Monthly Service Billing Only income. In other words, the maintenance/repair income should not be included to arrive at a fair purchase price. Any other method of appraising the value of a pool route would be contrary to the industry standards. The maintenance and repair income is already considered in the multiple, because most pool service technicians agree that whatever your monthly service billing is, half of that again will translate into maintenance/repair income.

"We have been selling businesses for over 28 years. Pool routes are our specialty. We can tell that the most important step in purchasing a pool route is in verifying the monthly service billing. Financial statements, profit and loss statements, and balance sheets are usually not available, mainly because it is not necessary to keep an expensive bookkeeping system for one person operating out of their home. Therefore, there are not usually records available to satisfy a bank or financial institution to borrow the money to buy the route. Individual tax returns usually will not help either, because if you were buying 50 accounts of a route of 100, the tax returns would not be broken down that way. Also, if he is a pool builder or does a lot of business in major pool repairs or pool remodeling, again the tax returns would reflect all this income. What if he had 100 accounts and sold 50 accounts? His tax return would show an income for 100 accounts and you would have no way of knowing this.

"Pool routes are sold for cash and no terms are generally available. Therefore, you should have the funds available at the time of purchase, unless you are arranging for an equity loan, line of credit or other means to enable you to purchase a pool route.

Source: Contributed by Frank Passantino, Pool Route Brokers, Inc. Frank is a veteran business broker and the information provided has been taken from his Web site--www.poolroutebrokers. He is one of the country's leading pool route brokers. His firm is in California and the phone number is 800-772-6002

Benchmark Data

Statistics (Swimming Pool Cleaning Services)

Number of Establishments... 52,956
Average Profit Margin... 9.0%
Revenue per Employee... $47,900
Average Number of Employees... 1.4
Average Wages per Employee... $15,599

Products and Services Segmentation

General cleaning services... 43.9%
Equipment cleaning and maintenance... 26.4%
Chemical adjustments... 16.4%
Other... 13.3%

Industry Costs

Profit... 9.0%
Wages... 32.5%
Purchases... 26.9%
Depreciation... 1.2%
Utilities... 1.6%
Rent... 5.5%
Other... 23.3%

- Customer service is the backbone of a successful business.
- On a well-designed route, each employee should generate $100k of gross sales based simply upon service; this figure should increase if repairs are included.
- "How many pools can I service in a day? A good question, but difficult to answer. The average pool service technician will service approximately 16 full-service pools a day, while some can service 25 to 30 in a day. It depends on the individual and what type of pools he or she is servicing. The average pool service technician will service two pools an hour including driving time. If the accounts are chemical only, he can do many more. If the accounts are commercial, he or she will do less.

P

"The average pool service technician, if running his route correctly, should be netting between $75,000.00 and $80,000.00 per year. If you have a monthly gross service billing income of $4,000.00 per month, that equates to $48,000.00 per year generated from weekly 'service only.' Your expenses should be approximately 2 months of your service income or in this example $8,000.00. This will cover your three major expenses, gas, insurance and chemical replacement. Therefore, your service income totaling $48,000.00 for the year, less estimated expense of $8,000.00, should produce a net profit of $40,000.00, assuming you are operating in a diligent manner. In addition to this profit, you will have a second income on the same accounts for maintenance (filter cleaning, algae, conditioner treatments and other preventive maintenance) charges that you will bill your account extra, plus repairs (motors, pumps, heaters, etc.). This second income should be fifty percent of your service net. If your net income from service is $40,000.00 then your net from maintenance and repairs should be $20,000.00. This is assuming that you are providing full service to your accounts."

Source: Contributed by Frank Passantino, Pool Route Brokers, Inc.

Expenses (% of Annual Sales)

Cost of Goods	20%
Payroll/Labor Costs	40%
Profit (pretax)	40%

Questions
- Payment history of accounts
- How long have you had the pools? Any previous problems with payments from customers. Where did your pools come from (did you buy route, build it, etc.?)

Industry Trend
- Growing industry
- I think profits should continue to increase with the new construction of more pools.
- "On the franchising side, most of the attention has been given to the service-tech side of the industry. There's an important reason for that: It costs less. Return on investment is the major concern when starting a franchise, so prospects like the relatively low start-up costs of a service business. 'The ones that tend to grow fastest are the ones that have the lowest level of investment,' Siebert (Mark, CEO of iFranchise Group) says. 'So the service industry would probably be the one that would ultimately get the most franchisees.'

"When Baron (Kevin, President of Probity Pools) wanted to expand his company, he chose the franchise model because he figured it best suited the kind of work done by service companies. To just grow a company organically removes the company owner farther and farther from the work itself as the organizational chart expands, he says, while franchising allows the owners to stay near those maintaining the pools.

"While some professionals are quick to point out examples where these types of models did not work in the pool industry, others say the time for franchising and outside investment has come, and examples will only become more prevalent. But Porter (Paul, CEO of Premier Pools Management Corp.) doesn't see the transition going smoothly. 'It will happen … kicking and screaming because we have a lot of people who are very resistant to change in our industry,' he says. But Baron expects it will be long-term. 'I think when the dust settles in 10 years, every city's probably going to have a half dozen or so major pool-maintenance brands,' he says."

Source: http://www.poolspanews.com/business/coming-together_o.aspx?dfpzone=general

- This industry should expand.
- Competition getting stronger and more government enforcement of licensing

Expert Comments

Sellers: Disclose all material facts. Buyer's: Disclose any health issues that could affect your responsibilities.

Sellers: Document all of your accounts and work so you can verify income. Minimize expenses where possible. Take great care of your customers so they trust you. Buyers: Buy a route that is closely run with minimal driving. You lose money any time you are sitting in the truck. Make sure you are making enough money per pool to justify the price.

As a seller: Provide the necessary training and support to the buyer and keep good books to verify income. As a buyer: Provide your best customer service skills to keep your customers, learn the trade and attend trade shows and training classes.

A business that has a strong long-term customer base should anticipate receiving a higher multiple of sales than one with a short-term history. If someone is willing to wait for the right buyer, expecting a 12-month multiple is realistic; however, if someone is looking for a quick sale on a well-designed route, 10 times monthly income is realistic.

Seller Financing

- Typically they are all-cash deals, but if any financing is involved it is typically very short-term owner financing.
- All cash, or 3rd party financing

Resources

- Independent Pool and Spa Service Association: http://www.ipssa.com
- Pool Pro: http://www.poolpro.com
- Florida Swimming Pool Association: http://www.floridapoolpro.com
- Pool and Spa News: http://www.poolspanews.com
- Association of Pool and Spa Professionals: http://www.apsp.org
- National Swimming Pool Foundation: http://www.nspf.org
- IBISWorld, September 2016: http://ibisworld.com
- AQUA Magazine: http://www.aquamagazine.com
- Pool Route Brokers (PRB): poolroutebrokers.com

Portable Toilet Companies		
SIC 7359-22	NAICS 562991	Number of Businesses/Units 8,741

Rules of Thumb

➢ 85–90% of annual revenues

➢ $1,000 per unit

P

Benchmark Data

Statistics (Portable Toilet Rental & Septic Tank Cleaning)

Number of Establishments.. 8,741
Average Profit Margin 13.0%
Revenue per Employee $132,800
Average Number of Employees.. 4.6
Average Wages per Employee $44,201

Products and Services Segmentation

Portable toilet rental.. 26.8%
Other services.. 25.9%
Septic tank maintenance services 25.0%
Drain and sewer services 22.3%

Major Market Segmentation

Businesses 44.6%
State and local governments 37.7%
Individuals... 13.8%
Federal government.. 2.3%
Nonprofits 1.6%

Industry Costs

Profit 13.0%
Wages... 33.3%
Purchases... 13.9%
Depreciation... 5.6%
Marketing 1.5%
Rent & Utilities 6.3%
Other... 26.4%

- "The portable sanitation industry has developed into a $4 billion-a-year business. There are an estimated 3 million portable restrooms in use, serviced by a fleet of over 10,000 trucks. The industry includes more than 3,600 businesses and 39,000 employees worldwide."

    Source: Portable Sanitation Association International

Industry Trend

- "Demand for the Portable Toilet Rental and Septic Tank Cleaning industry is expected to continue growing over the five years to 2022. Construction activity is expected to increase over the next five years, underpinned by gains in the broader economy. Since construction contractors are the largest market for portable toilet rental, a boom in construction markets is anticipated to translate into demand for industry services. With the rise in construction activity, demand for waste-holding and drain-cleaning services is also expected to rise. Consequently, industry revenue is forecast to grow at an annualized rate of 0.9% during the period, totaling $5.6 billion."

    Source: IBISWorld Industry Outlook

Resources

- Portable Sanitation Association International: http://www.psai.org
- IBISWorld, July 2017: http://ibisworld.com

Power/Pressure Washing

| | NAICS 561790 | |

Rules of Thumb

➤ 50% of annual revenues

| | | Franchise |

Precision Tune Auto Care

| Approx. Total Investment | | $123,000–$208,075 |
| | NAICS 811118 | Number of Businesses/Units 384 |

Rules of Thumb

➤ 35–40% of annual sales plus inventory

Resources

- Precision Tune Auto Care: http://www.precisiontune.com

Printing/Flexographic

| | NAICS 323111 | |

Rules of Thumb

➤ 3 x EBIT

➤ 2–5 x EBITDA

➤ Note: It is a different area—they print labels on Web presses using plates that are made of curved rubber. Web presses use rolls of material rather than sheets. Think newspaper printing. However, apparently the pricing multiples are similar.

Pricing Tips

- Depending on size, EBITDA ranges from 2 to 4 unless special circumstances are present like exceptional profit or none.
- Multiples range from 2 to 5 depending on size and sector.

Benchmark Data

- Look for stable customer base with no heavy concentration with one or two clients.

Expenses (% of Annual Sales)

Cost of Goods	43%
Occupancy Costs	05%
Payroll/Labor Costs	43%
Profit (pretax)	05% to 09%

P

Questions

- Does the owner handle major customers personally and can they be transitioned to a new owner? Do they have contracts? What sets this company apart from others? Do you have non-compete agreements with your salesmen?

Industry Trend

- "According to Hitesh Bhatia, a lead paints, coatings, and pigments research analyst from Technavio, 'The corrugated cardboard application held the highest market share, accounting for 32% of the global flexographic printing inks in 2016. Corrugated cardboard finds use as a packing material for many brands and industries. The growth in e-commerce is expected to drive the demand for corrugated cardboard, thereby fostering the global flexographic printing inks.'
  "'Flexible packaging is used in a variety of applications such as goods, consumer products, medical products, and others. In 2016, the flexible packaging market held the second-largest share in the packaging segment, representing more than 19% of the total packaging market,' says Hitesh."

  Source: http://www.businesswire.com/news/home/20170823005493/en/
  Flexographic-Printing-Inks-Market---Trends-Growth

Expert Comments

There is generally lots of competition but less than those of commercial printers. Profits have stabilized in recent years. Marketability is generally high. Replication is relatively easy, but can you get the business and can you keep going until you make a profit? This is a good sector of the printing industry.

Resources

- Greeneville Plate Services: http://www.greenevilleplateservices.com

Printing—Label		
	NAICS 323111	

Benchmark Data

Expenses (% of Annual Sales)

Cost of Goods	45%
Occupancy Costs	04%
Payroll/Labor Costs	18%
Profit (pretax)	20%

Questions

- How do you plan to finance the deal? What are the strategic advantages?

Industry Trend

- Growth markets—up 4–5% annually

Seller Financing

- Outside and private financed

Resources

- Tag and Label Manufacturers Institute: http://tlmi.com

Printing/Silk Screen		
SIC 7336-09	NAICS 23113	

Rules of Thumb

➤ 40–45% of annual sales plus inventory

➤ 2.5–3 x SDE includes inventory

➤ 3.5–4 x EBITDA

➤ 3.5–4 x EBIT

Pricing Tips

- SDE 2.5–3.0 range. Sales growth, market potential, age/quality of equipment, staffing, lease will determine which end of range to use.
- Value affected by equipment, customer base, skilled labor, location and sales growth.
- Value of any long-term contracts that are in place. Are contracts assignable?
- National/corporate accounts vs. small local accounts increases value.

Benchmark Data

Expenses (% of Annual Sales)

Cost of Goods	60%
Occupancy Costs	05%
Payroll/Labor Costs	20% to 25%
Profit (pretax)	05% to 10%

Questions

- Sales and profit trend over past 3 years, and especially over most recent 12-month period.
- Monthly revenue over past 3 years to gauge seasonality of business and to analyze competitive environment.
- Provide concentration of customers. Any range, one-time orders in sales figures? Maintenance schedule for all equipment?

Industry Trend

- "Digital technology, specifically inkjet printing, was forecast by many to be the death knell of screen printing when the first systems were first showcased at the SGIA Expo in the early 1990s. While inkjet has taken much of the large-format graphics market and DTG printers are extending their reach into textiles, inkjet has not forced screen printing into obsolescence. In fact, the two disciplines seem to complement each other, giving screen printers more choices and variety of services to sell."

  Source: "Stencilmaking in the Age of CTS," by Dave Dennings, May 3, 2016, http://www.screenweb.com/content/stencilmaking-age-cts#.V42Dn6KhmQ8

- Consolidation as weaker competitors are either sold or shut the doors.
- Increased competition and pressure on margins
- Growth due to U.S. society continuing to be more visually oriented

P

Expert Comments

Can be high capital investment to start up.

Anyone can open a small screen printing shop or store. Most companies do screen printed and embroidered products. They also sell small signs, graphics, etc. This industry can be capital intensive. High-speed equipment is necessary to produce larger volume and some companies add a second and third shift.

Resources

- ScreenWeb: http://www.screenweb.com/

Print Shops/Commercial Printers		
SIC 2752-02	NAICS 323111	

Rules of Thumb

➤ 3.5 x recast EBITDA if sales $5 to $25 million

➤ 4 x EBIT

➤ 50–55% of annual sales plus inventory

➤ 2–3 x SDE includes inventory

➤ 2.5–3 x recast EBITDA if sales under $2 million

➤ 2.5–3.5 x recast EBITDA if sales $2 to $5 million

Pricing Tips

- "As with other small businesses, commercial printers can be valued using a number of income and asset-based business valuation methods. For owner-operator managed printers, the Multiple of Discretionary Earnings method is a frequent choice. This well-known method lets you determine the value of your business based on its earnings and a set of financial and operational performance factors. For a well-established commercial printing business, the Capitalized Excess Earnings method is a good choice. You can calculate the value of your business and its goodwill-an important part of what makes a successful business worth more."
Source: https://www.valuadder.com/blog/2008/11/19/valuing-printing-businesses/ (dated, but still of interest)

- Smart sellers are well positioned and organized relative to qualitative and quantitative monitoring systems. Buyers buy on potential of the seller's enterprise.

- There are two primary ways of valuing printing companies. Fair value of assets plus a half multiple of EBITDA for goodwill and customer lists. The other is 2–4 times EBITDA depending on size, profitability, equipment, sector, etc.

Benchmark Data

- For additional Benchmark Data see Print Shops (General)

Expenses (% of Annual Sales)

Cost of Goods	40% to 50%
Occupancy Costs	03% to 10%
Payroll/Labor Costs	35% to 45%
Profit (pretax)	05% to 15%

Questions

- Do you have skilled and experienced people in place?
- Real estate options; IP advantages; lean or sustainability programs; owner financing options; proforma forecasts; management skill set; supplier discounts
- Why are you leaving and are there any contracts still honored?
- Commercial account base? Outside salespeople? What role(s) does owner fill? Product mix? Specialty vs. commodity.
- Look for any niche they serve; client concentration is a risk; client contracts are rare and would be a premium multiple.
- Is production equipment leased or owned?
- How up-to-date is their equipment? Do they have a niche? Do they do digital printing? What is their salesperson(s) situation? Do they have noncompete agreements with salespeople?
- How tied to the customers is the owner, why do customers use this printer over others, does any customer account for more than 10% of revenue.
- How has the business been trending over the past five years?

Industry Trend

- Consolidation—vast exit of baby boomers
- Because (1) new production equipment is becoming increasingly available and appropriate for the largest customers of printing companies; (2) traditional printing work is continuing to be replaced by digital media-for email and the Web; and (3) much of the printing equipment [digital & analog] remains in operation, long after they might be considered obsolete, there is an imbalance of supply (of services) and demand, so downward pressure on prices will continue for the foreseeable future.
- Positive outlook—big players expanding with M&A strategies.

Expert Comments

Because of the various types and sizes of printing companies (large- vs. small-format equipment, digital vs. analog, screen vs. digital signage, etc.) the speed of technological changes makes the above factors inconsistent throughout this industry. More than any other industry I've seen through my 12 years in M&A, there is no greater challenge than selling a printing company.

Market share, customer base, equipment capabilities, niche markets

Person-to-person relationships are still very important.

The current regional market shows excess capacity and possibly short-term declines in sales. There is brisk competition, but capitalization costs are high to replicate these businesses. Consolidations are needed.

Printing is a mature industry that is growing at barely the growth in population.

Price competition from on-line providers. Short-run color work is being done on in-house printers and copiers. Pleasing quality has become acceptable for the small-business owner.

P

Seller Financing
- New owner and outside financing
- More typical to be outside financing

Resources
- Idealliance + Epicomm: http://my.idealliance.org/
- Specialty Graphic Imaging Association: http://www.sgia.org
- Tag and Label Manufacturers Institute: http://www.tlmi.com
- American Printer: http://www.americanprinter.com
- Printing Impressions: http://www.piworld.com
- Printing Industries of America: http://www.printing.org
- "Valuing Printing Businesses, Handbook of Business Valuation," West & Jones, 2nd Edition: http://www.wiley.com

Print Shops (General)		
SIC 2752-02	NAICS 323111	Number of Businesses/Units 47,088

Rules of Thumb
- 30–45% of annual sales plus inventory
- 2–3.5 x SDE plus inventory
- 3.5–4 x EBITDA

Pricing Tips
- Look to current certified appraisers; know RMA ratios, trade association benchmarks; identify correct NAICS code.
- Pricing is based on EBITDA-multiples are determined by the buyers-buyers are strategic and financial.
- EBIT, EBITDA, 3-5 years of financial statements, outsourced industry specific appraisal, best to have audited statements every 5 yrs.
- Market share in region, quality of accounts, no more than 20% of annual revenues per key account. Profit margin vs. industry benchmarks
- Owner benefit add-backs, IP protection, key account loyalty, key employees and non-compete agreements.

Benchmark Data

Statistics (Printing)

Number of Establishments	47,088
Average Profit Margin	5.7%
Revenue per Employee	$195,000
Average Number of Employees	8.2
Average Wages per Employee	$46,546

Products and Services Segmentation

Commercial lithographic printing	41.7%
Other printing	15.4%
Digital printing	13.2%
Commercial flexographic printing	10.5%
Commercial screen printing	9.4%
Book printing	5.6%
Commercial gravure printing	4.2%

Major Market Segmentation

Manufacturers	24.9%
Advertisers	16.3%
Publishing	18.6%
Other	25.4%
Financial and legal firms	8.4%
Exports	6.4%

Industry Costs

Profit	5.7%
Wages	24.0%
Purchases	45.7%
Depreciation	3.4%
Marketing	0.4%
Rent & Utilities	3.8%
Other	17.0%

Market Share

RR Donnelley & Sons Co.	4.0%
Quad/Graphics Inc.	4.1%
Deluxe Corporation	1.4%

- Per employee—$250,000

Expenses (% of Annual Sales)

Cost of Goods	40% to 50%
Occupancy Costs	04% to 05%
Payroll/Labor Costs	20% to 25%
Profit (pretax)	20%

Questions

- 1. Current valuation—transparency
- 2. Future plans
- 3. Leadership team
- 4. Culture—integration experience
- 5. Terms
- 6. Post-transaction—transition plans
- Competitive advantages? Retained talent pool for transitions? Last year of 3rd party valuation of business? Reasons for selling? Best identified and suited buyers of your business?
- What is the business plan? Vision of business? Key employees secured by noncompete? IP status? What do the next 3 years look like in contacts, sales revenues?
- Systems, controls, leadership team, competitive advantages, ideal clients.
- Who are your largest customers and what percentage of the total do they account for?
- Are these relationships personal and can they be transitioned to a new owner? What has been done to grow the business?
- What is customer mix? What is age and type of equipment?

P

Industry Trend

- "Over the next five years, the printing industry will continue to struggle as digital media replaces traditional paper products. As a result, industry revenue is forecast to decline at an annualized rate of 2.4% to $67.8 billion in 2022. Profit margins are also expected to stagnate because low demand has left excess capacity in the industry and has led to significant price-based competition. The industry remains firmly embedded in its decline phase, as falling demand for print is a structural trend that is expected to continue regardless of improvements in the overall US economy. For example, IBISWorld expects that print advertising expenditure will fall at an annualized rate of 5.1% over the next five years, even as overall US ad spending is projected to grow an annualized 2.0% during the five-year period.

  "Most notably, rapid growth in digital media will adversely affect the circulation and advertising volumes of print periodicals. Moreover, book publishers will increasingly seek shorter print runs due to ongoing advancements in digital technology, further contributing to industry declines. Electronic books that can be read on devices such as Amazon's Kindle or Apple's iPad will continue to grow in popularity as a result of further innovation and expected low prices, which will make them more accessible to consumers. These trends, coupled with the continually rising cost of paper, will make printed material less attractive to downstream markets and fuel steady revenue declines for the industry."

  Source: IBISWorld Industry Outlook
- Growth—M&A strategies in labels and packaging converting
- Growth for print leaders; packaging, wide-format and labeling all growing. Baby boomers exiting; less family succession plans. Consolidation continues.
- Higher capability and lower cost for in-house equipment to handle short-run requirements.

Expert Comments

Partner where required

Be strategic. Invest in people, culture, and technologies. Keep your promises.

Focus on your niche; stay the course; be strategic and buy right; don't overpay on the short term.

Talent pool, key sales relationships, special capabilities, owner financing

Key accounts, brand awareness, strong sales force, experience of leadership, documented business plans and vision, funding and vendor relationships, diversity of markets, product mix.

Seller Financing

- Outside financing is the standard; sellers want out. Cash is king.

Resources

- Idealliance + Epicomm: http://my.idealliance.org/
- IBISWorld, June 2017: http://ibisworld.com
- Specialty Graphic Imaging Association: https://www.sgia.org/

- Tag and Label Manufacturers Institute: http://tlmi.com/
- International Sign Association: http://www.signs.org/
- Printing Association of Florida: http://flprint.org/
- Printing Industries of America: https://www.printing.org/
- Label & Narrow Web: http://www.labelandnarrowweb.com/
- Printers Broker and Buyers Association: http://www.pbba.org
- Independent Carton Group: http://www.independentcartongroup.com/

Print Shops/Quick Print

SIC 2752-02	NAICS 323111	Number of Businesses/Units 8,683

Rules of Thumb

➤ 4 x EBIT

➤ 3–4 x EBITDA

➤ 45–55% of annual sales plus inventory

➤ 2.5–3.5 x SDE plus inventory

➤ 2–5 x SDE plus inventory—SDE (Owner's compensation) treats depreciation as an expense and thus it is not included in SDE.

Pricing Tips

- Fair market salary adjustment required prior to calculating SDE or excess earnings.
- Quick printer valuations have been on the decline.
- The terms of the leases on the digital equipment will affect the operating income and price.
- Competitive equipment is very important, including lease terms and click charges.
- Review replacement cost of assets; percentage of business with top ten clients; receivable turn.

Benchmark Data

Statistics (Quick Printing)

Number of Establishments	8,683
Average Profit Margin	4.8%
Revenue per Employee	$156,900
Average Number of Employees	2.9
Average Wages per Employee	$29,995

Products and Services Segmentation

Printing	63.9%
Other services	14.8%
Bindery and finishing services	8.2%
Prepress services	7.1%
Mailing services	6.0%

P

Major Market Segmentation

In-store customers	47.0%
Small businesses	23.5%
Non-employing businesses	18.5%
Online customers	11.0%

Industry Costs

Profit	4.8%
Wages	19.3%
Purchases	41.0%
Depreciation	3.9%
Marketing	0.9%
Rent & Utilities	6.2%
Other	23.9%

Market Share

FedEx Corporation	13.9%

Expenses (% of Annual Sales)

Cost of Goods	30% to 40%
Occupancy Costs	05% to 10%
Payroll/Labor Costs	25% to 30%
Profit (pretax)	10% to 20%

Questions

- Percent of sales represented by top 3–5 customers?
- Describe competition, percentage of sales by category (products and customers).
- What percentage of customers makes up 80% of the business?
- Type of equipment, lease terms, click charges. What related services do they offer? How do they get and maintain sales?
- Sales per employee, how old is the equipment-and number of impressions. How long have the employees been with the business? How up-to date is the pre-press department?

Industry Trend

- "The Quick Printing industry's decline is expected to slow somewhat over the next five years, with revenue expected to decrease at an annualized rate of 0.6% to total $3.9 billion by 2022. This is a continuation of the industry's long-term decline, primarily a result of a continued decline in print advertising expenditure and the increasing propensity for smaller businesses to complete industry services in-house as computer peripheral equipment becomes more sophisticated and continues to decrease in price."

  Source: IBISWorld Industry Outlook
- Very good for someone who is technically literate regarding computers and networks and has specific skills found in the printing industry.

Expert Comments

Printing customers today do not necessarily buy on price, but they are buying small quantities and cutting back . . . this favors smaller printers.

Industry is equipment intensive and requires a high degree of marketing skills to succeed.

These are marketable companies suitable for corporate dropouts or general business people.

Resources

- Idealliance + Epicomm: http://my.idealliance.org/
- IBISWorld, September 2017: http://ibisworld.com
- PrintingNews.com: http://magazine-directory.com/Quick-Printing.htm

Process Serving

	NAICS 541199	

Rules of Thumb

> 35–40% of annual sales includes inventory

Benchmark Data

Statistics (Conveyancing Services)

Number of Establishments	37,729
Average Profit Margin	12.0%
Revenue per Employee	$146,200
Average Number of Employees	2.9
Average Wages per Employee	$46,229

Products and Services Segmentation

Conveyancing and title abstract services	43.6%
Settlement and closing services	24.1%
Title search and other document filing services	12.7%
Other legal services	12.1%
Process services	5.3%
Patent copyright and other intellectual property document services	2.2%

Major Market Segmentation

Businesses	61.4%
Individuals	35.8%
Government and nonprofit organizations	2.8%

Industry Costs

Profit	12.0%
Wages	31.8%
Purchases	6.3%
Depreciation	1.0%
Marketing	2.3%
Rent & Utilities	8.6%
Other	38.0%

Market Share

Fidelity National Financial, Inc.	11.2%
First American Financial Corporation	9.2%
Stewart Information Services Corporation	6.2%

P

Industry Trend

- "The trends show that as technology grows more pervasive into everyday life, it also has made its way into the civil process service industry. The bulk of the new rules implemented in 2016 are focused on modernizing processes, making them more efficient and compatible with today's technology. This should continue throughout 2016 and in the years to come.

  "Just as the U.S. Post Office was revolutionized by the advent of email, we may see electronic service options increase for those who seek out civil process service. But, just as the US Post Office continues to be a communications staple in the U.S., so shall the traditional means of hand-delivered service.

  "Be on the lookout for bills in the U.S. Congress that aim to streamline processes (e.g., decreasing time limits to get things done), as well as requiring and/or creating more options for civil process service. Hopefully, these changes will make processes easier-not more difficult -for process servers."

  Source: https://www.serve-now.com/articles/2175/2016-new-rules-in-process-serving

Resources

- IBISWorld, January 2017: http://ibisworld.com

Property Management Companies		
SIC 6531-08	NAICS 531311	Number of Businesses/Units 271,253

Rules of Thumb

➤ 100% annual revenues

➤ 2.5–5 x SDE based on a cash sale

➤ 3.5–6 x SDE with sales involving notes and/or contingencies

➤ 3–6 x EBIT

➤ 3–5 x EBITDA

➤ 6 to 7 months' revenues for firms selling under $500K

➤ 10 to 12 months' revenues for firms above $500K

Pricing Tips

- Rule of thumb of 50% of gross revenue should not include rent collected for tenants, as some property managers do not collect rent but pass that directly to the owner.
- When pricing for property management, particularly short-term rental homes, we take into consideration the number of properties managed by the business owner and the amount they charge as a management fee. Also whether or not the properties are good rentable homes which generate a decent nightly rental income.
- These businesses have a tendency to sell between 2 and 2.6 times the owner benefit. In some cases, individual contracts are sold, i.c., a seller may have 50 management contracts and sell off say 20, in which case they are sold on a contract basis according to the quality of the contract.
- There are critical elements to valuation of these businesses that do not show in the financials. Booking sources for tenants, mortgage position of the property

owners. In addition, the escrow monies must be measured and transferred at closing.

- Occupancy is critical as is markup on services. Discovery of proximity of properties to attractions.
- Key item is the longevity of accounts (i.e., any property managed for more than 3 years is good). Also, the transition period should have the owner (seller) remain visible for 2 to 3 months.

Benchmark Data

Statistics (Property Management)

Number of Establishments	271,253
Average Profit Margin	23.2%
Revenue per Employee	$97,700
Average Number of Employees	3.0
Average Wages per Employee	$46,384

Products and Services Segmentation

Residential property management	55.4%
Non-residential property management	24.7%
Other	14.2%
Real estate brokerage	2.8%
Land management	1.9%
Construction	1.0%

Major Market Segmentation

Residential properties	67.5%
Other nonresidential properties	16.3%
Commercial	5.7%
Industrial buildings	5.8%
Office buildings	4.7%

Industry Costs

Profit	23.2%
Wages	47.3%
Purchases	7.5%
Depreciation	3.4%
Marketing	1.0%
Rent & Utilities	6.9%
Other	10.7%

- This business can be grown very well by the owners if they are willing to put effort into the business. I have seen this kind of business grow from 20 contracts at time of purchase to almost 100 within 4 to 5 years. This kind of business sells very fast.
- It is difficult to give an average for occupancy, labor and cost of goods sold, due to the fact these businesses are so diverse and you have to determine according to the business being sold. Some businesses have a higher owner involvement, i.e., the owner may do some of the maintenance work, lawn and pool care as well as the administration; whereas in other businesses the owner simply handles the administration, including placing rentals into the properties, which creates a much higher income for the business.

- This type of business allows an owner to do a variety of work within the business, which makes it attractive to a buyer. It is not too difficult to expand this type of business providing the owner is an organized person. Over the last 10 years or so I have seen contracts per house for short-term rental homes sell from $5,000 to $8,000 per unit, subject to the type of property and age.

Expenses (% of Annual Sales)

Cost of Goods	20% to 35%
Occupancy Costs	05% to 10%
Payroll/Labor Costs	40% to 50%
Profit (pretax)	15% to 25%

Questions

- Longevity of each client is important; once over 2 years, the retention rate increases dramatically.
- Age of equipment, as replacement values could be high.
- Employee retention is important; find out how long each employee has been with the company.
- Determine how much of the labor is performed in-house versus outsourced.
- Ask what special licenses are required to perform the work, such as Real Estate or Community Association Manager (CAM) licenses.
- Ask the seller if there are any lawsuits or outstanding complaints.
- Are any of your owners in debt to you (seller) and if so how much and for how long have they owed that money.
- Escrow account/operating account terms and transfer
- Homeowner mortgage? How do you generate occupancy? What is the occupancy rate?
- What exactly do you do in the business? Do you hold escrow for the owners? Do you pay their bills without holding escrow? Can you show a contract for each of the owners you manage properties for?
- Insure that deposits and owner operating account funds transfer at closing.
- Why are you selling? Have there been any lawsuits or complaints?

Industry Trend

- Vacation properties are quickly becoming a key retirement and income source for the middle class. Because renting out such properties has become easier and cheaper, the owners are providing this service, but providing the ground services will continue to be in high demand. Property management companies are learning how to service short-term rentals. Outsourcing of services (by the property manager) has been increasing as more subcontractors can provide adequate services for reduced costs. Some trades now require certifications (such as arborists and pesticide and chemical applicators); it is becoming harder for the property management company to obtain because they don't perform enough of the type of work. In addition, more building owners prefer not to manage the services on their own buildings because they can't find an adequate pool of employees. Software systems to control scheduling within the organization and also connecting to subcontractors are becoming a standard tool.

Expert Comments

Best advice for sellers is to obtain long-term contracts that automatically renew and allow assignment to a new owner. Advice to the buyer is to look at the mix of clientele both in type of business and percentage of work. It is best if the property manager has a diverse client base to avoid an industry recession.

Because most clients are under automatically renewing contracts, the risk involved in new business owners continuing to service these clients is very strong. Most employees in this industry really enjoy their job and tend to stay. It is very hard to create a new business in this space, as many clients are very satisfied to stay with their existing property management company.

Make sure you carry out your due diligence, check the books and records, do not just believe what someone tells you, get the facts.

This is a very popular business in Central Florida. It lends itself to people from all walks of life, as there are numerous income streams and you can earn from rentals, management fees, lawn care, pool care, cleaning, maintenance. I find that it is very popular with people who are willing to work in a business doing any of the manual work; those who only wish to do administrative work can employ sub-contractors to carry out the cleaning, maintenance etc.

Seller Financing

- The seller is generally open to financing a high portion of the price if their confidence level is high that the clients will retain.
- I have been successful in obtaining SBA Loans for this kind of business.
- I have been able to achieve all manner of financing. Many people have paid cash. I have also had success in SBA lending for a good solid business. Not much seller financing, the reason being, this is a very personal type of business and the sellers understand this. If a buyer does not have a good attitude, it could prevent the business expanding, and this is a fear for sellers, so they do not like to carry a large note.
- Seller financing is less common for property management companies larger than $500,000 gross income, but for smaller companies it would be 3 to 5 years.
- 30% owner financing

Resources

- Institute of Real Estate Management: http://www.irem.org
- Property Management Association: http://www.pma-dc.org
- IBISWorld, August 2017: http://ibisworld.com
- Florida Vacation Rental Managers Association: https://fvrma.wildapricot.org/
- National Property Management Association: http://www.npma.org
- Building Owners and Managers Association International: http://www.boma.org
- Onsite Property Management Association: http://theopma.org
- Vacation Rental Management Association: http://www.vrma.com

P

Publishers—Books

SIC 2731-01	NAICS 511130	Number of Businesses/Units 4,338

Rules of Thumb

➢ 70% of annual sales plus inventory

➢ 4–6 x EBIT

➢ 4–6 x EBITDA

Pricing Tips

- Professional publishing is valued higher than educational publishing, and both are valued higher than consumer publishing. Proprietary and niche-specific publishing is most attractive.

Benchmark Data

Statistics (Book Publishing)

Number of Establishments	4,338
Average Profit Margin	7.5%
Revenue per Employee	$432,500
Average Number of Employees	14.4
Average Wages per Employee	$81,352

Products and Services Segmentation

Textbooks	31.6%
Professional, technical and scholarly books	27.5%
Adult trade books	24.0%
Other books and services	10.3%
Children's books	6.6%

Industry Costs

Profit	7.5%
Wages	18.8%
Purchases	44.5%
Depreciation	1.4%
Marketing	5.0%
Rent & Utilities	3.6%
Other	19.2%

Market Share

Bertelsmann SE & Co. KGaA	7.5%
Pearson PLC	9.9%

Industry Trend

- "Publishers' book sales for trade (consumer) books from Jan. to Dec. 2016 were flat -0.2% at $7.1 billion. While Religious Presses and Children's & Young Adult Books (Children's/YA) saw growth in 2016, the Adult Books category (which comprises more than 65% of all revenue for trade books) saw a 2.3% decline.

  "Overall publisher revenue for 2016 was $14.3 billion, down 6.6% from 2015. These numbers include sales for all tracked categories (Trade—fiction/non-fiction/religious, PreK–12 Instructional Materials, Higher Education Course

Materials, Professional Publishing, and University Presses).

"Some of the 2016 trends include:

- ✓ Reading preferences continue to shift. Print books saw growth, and for the second consecutive year publisher revenues from eBook sales declined and downloaded audio grew.
- ✓ Trade publishers fared better than educational or scholarly publishers, who saw declining revenue.
- ✓ Children's/YA titles and Religious Presses fared better than Adult Books, the opposite of 2015, when Adult Books did well and Children's/YA and Religious Presses declined.

"For the first time in years, publisher revenue for all print formats saw growth: hardback books grew 2.2%, children's board books grew 7.7% and paperback/mass market grew 4.1% compared to 2015 revenues. The news for digital books was mixed, as downloaded audio continued its double-digit growth from 2015, up 25.8% for 2016 vs 2015 and eBooks continued their decline, down 15.6%.

"Trade Formats:

- ✓ Within the Adult Books category, which saw revenue decline in 2016 vs. 2015, revenue for downloaded audio was up 24.9%; paperback revenue was up 5.3% for the year; eBook revenue was down 13.9%; and hardback revenue was down 3.7% for the year.
- ✓ Within Children's & Young Adult Books, hardback revenue was up 10.7%; paperback revenue was up 0.9%; board book revenue was up 7.7%; and eBook revenue declined 32.6%.

"Educational Materials:

- ✓ Revenues for PreK-12 instructional materials declined 9.0% to $2.8 billion for 2016, compared to $3.1 billion in 2015.
- ✓ Revenues for Higher Education course materials declined 13.4% to $3.6 billion for 2016, compared to $4.1 billion in 2015.

"Professional and Scholarly Publishing: Revenues for Professional Publishing, which includes business, medical, law, scientific and technical books and journals, were down significantly, by 20.8% at $628.8 million for 2016. University Press revenues were down 2.5% compared to 2015."

Source: "AAP StatShot: Book Publisher Trade Sales Flat for 2016," June 15, 2017,
http://newsroom.publishers.org/aap-statshot-book-publisher-trade-sales-flat-for-2016/

Resources

- Association of American Publishers: http://www.publishers.org
- American Booksellers Association: http://www.bookweb.org
- Independent Book Publishers Association: http://www.ibpa-online.org
- IBISWorld, May 2017: http://ibisworld.com

Publishers—In General

	NAICS 511130	

Rules of Thumb

- ➢ 75–100% of annual sales includes inventory
- ➢ 3–6 x SDE includes inventory
- ➢ 4–6 x EBIT
- ➢ 4–7 x EBITDA

P

Pricing Tips

- The issue with publishing is the diversity of publishing companies. Today, involvement in digital publishing such as website, e-magazine, or e-newsletter is critical. Higher valuations are obtained for digital properties. Also, valuations are clearly higher to strategic buyers versus nonstrategic or individuals. Margins for a strategic buyer can be very high, particularly for larger properties. This makes it very difficult for an individual to purchase a publishing or information property.

- The size of the business is critical to valuation-larger higher multiples.. Also, publishing is a diverse business. The niche of a publishing company is critical. Also, the competitive situation. A business to business magazine which is #1 in its niche is worth far more than the #4 publication as an example. I try to sell a publishing property to synergistic publishers. They will pay far more for the publication due to cost savings and the advantages of integration into a current portfolio.

- Pricing varies significantly by segment or niche, from a high of 1.5 times revenue and 8 to 10 times EBITDA for scientific technical publishing to 3 times EBITDA for trade book publishing.

- Publishing is a diverse business. Electronic publications have higher multiples. Specialties such as scientific and technical publications have higher multiples. Books would have the lowest multiple. Magazines would be somewhere in the middle, with good trade magazines worth more than consumer magazines. City and local magazines are worth the least of the magazines with competition intense. Most print publications will have an electronic or digital component, and if they do not, the value is negatively impacted. The publications of sufficient size and strategic interest to the major publishers such as Elsevier, Wiley or Wolters Kluwer are worth considerably more.

Benchmark Data

- Sales per employee, gross profit margin, ad rates versus the competition's. For magazines, the rank of the magazine in its niche is critical; ad dollars flow to the leading magazines.

- For magazines we use profit per page, cost per page, and various other metrics of profitability and productivity.

Expenses (% of Annual Sales)

Cost of Goods	20% to 25%
Occupancy Costs	05% to 08%
Payroll/Labor Costs	10% to 25%
Profit (pretax)	15% to 20%

Questions

- Competition, where does it rank among competitors, years in business, other opportunities for growth such as adding digital or adding salespeople, opening other offices. The reputation of a publication is critical.

- Buyer has many questions to ask. For example, is there a database of customers and how up to date is it? This may be the number 1 question.

- For magazines, what is the definition of your market segment and what is your rank in the segment? Number 1 can be worth considerably more than number 2 for a business-to-business magazine. Where do you print, who

P

are your suppliers? Questions about subscribership are critical for consumer magazines. Newsstand distribution is difficult for consumer magazines-how do you do it? Is the magazine paid or free, and so on.

Industry Trend

- More and more digital and Internet properties. There are paid properties and free content. Free poses problems for profitability. The number of visitors to websites and that of page views are critical markers for buyers.
- The trend is clearly to digital and electronic products. Also, the valuable properties have a very highly defined niche and a leadership position in that niche.

Expert Comments

There has been consolidation across the publishing industry. Competition is intense. Distribution is difficult for the smaller players.

Get a valuation. Price the business properly. Work with a broker who specializes in publishing. It is a unique and difficult business.

Print publishing is on a downward trend. More publishers of value will have a digital component or a secondary marketing component such as trade shows. Print is not dead; there is a market for print publications, however, the publishers should be moving towards digital delivery if not already there.

Publishing is a risky, competitive but profitable business for those who are successful. There are some declining segments which you should be aware of, such as general book publishing.

Seller Financing

- Smaller businesses are seller financing; as they range large, there may be opportunity for outside financing. In any case, these businesses are an air ball for banks; unless there is real estate, there is no collateral. It is all goodwill, and banks are not enthusiastic generally.
- Both. Large businesses are outside financing generally.

Resources

- Booklist: http://www.booklistonline.com
- Publishers Weekly: http://www.publishersweekly.com
- The Association of American Publishers: http://www.publishers.org
- Editor and Publisher: http://www.editorandpublisher.com
- International Association of Scientific, Technical & Medical Publishers: http://www.stm-assoc.org
- The Association of Magazine Media (MPA): http://www.magazine.org
- Independent Book Publishers Association: http://www.ibpa-online.org/
- Association of Educational Publishers: http://publishers.org/our-markets/prek-12-learning
- Software & Information Industry Association: http://www.siia.net/
- Book Industry Study Group: http://bisg.org/

P

Publishers—Internet (and Broadcasting)

	NAICS 519130	

Rules of Thumb

➤ 100% of annual revenue includes inventory

➤ 6 x SDE includes inventory

➤ 6 x EBIT

➤ 5 x EBITDA

Pricing Tips

- Size matters. Multiples for larger companies >$5 million will be in the 10X range. Same goes for companies with a subscription base that represents recurring revenues.
- Faster growing companies will provide higher multiples. Higher multiples will also be paid for companies that can document recurring revenue streams, such as subscriptions or annual advertiser contracts. Publishers who provide original content or who own assets such as proprietary databases also can expect greater buyer interest.

Benchmark Data

Expenses (% of Annual Sales)

Cost of Goods	10%
Occupancy Costs	05% to 10%
Payroll/Labor Costs	65%
Profit (pretax)	20%

Questions

- I would ask about stability of earnings, renewal rates, staff turnover, number of advertising contracts, and if there is any revenue/customer concentration.
- 1. How much of your revenue base is recurring? 2. What is your renewal rate? 3. How much do you spend on customer acquisition?

Industry Trend

- Businesses will continue to grow as 'old' media ad dollars continue to migrate to Web-based 'new' media.
- There will be significant consolidation as smaller operations are rolled into larger ones.

Expert Comments

Ease of replication; it really depends on the content provided. The best businesses have proprietary content and/or a market niche in which they operate.

Online publishing is a popular business. The barriers to entry are low and the financial reward can be great. The key is developing something original that keeps users coming back to a site. Competition is growing, a factor that will make good sites more valuable while leading to the demise of weaker ones.

The Web is the world's largest printing press. Everyone wants to be a publisher and competition for eyeballs, ad dollars, subscribers and market share is intense. Barriers to entry are low. On the flip side, publisher and broadcaster audiences tend to be loyal. If they like your site they will stay with you. This leads to lots of repeat business and higher profit margins.

Publishers—Magazines/Periodicals

SIC 2721-02	NAICS 511120	Number of Businesses/Units 21,253

Rules of Thumb

➤ 7 x SDE includes inventory

➤ 2–5 x EBIT

➤ 2–5 x EBITDA

Pricing Tips

- Publications generally sell for a multiple of EBITDA and have very little inventory. Depending on size, industry, if it is a consumer publication or business to business, profitability, etc., smaller ones will sell in the 2 to 5 times range, while the large companies will sell for as much as 12 times EBITDA.

- Circulation questions are key, including various details of subscriptions and newsstand: how many advertisers, number of new advertisers, share of market in the specific specialty area such as log-home or fishing magazines, number of pages and revenue dollars.

- Prices have been hurt due to low advertising and magazines not embracing an Internet strategy.

Benchmark Data

Statistics (Magazine & Periodical Publishing)

Number of Establishments	21,253
Average Profit Margin	7.4%
Revenue per Employee	$237,400
Average Number of Employees	5.5
Average Wages per Employee	$76,278

Products and Services Segmentation

Entertainment magazines	32.5%
Academic and professional	23.1%
General interest magazines	16.3%
Political, social and business	12.2%
Home and living magazines	9.4%
Other periodicals	6.5%

Industry Costs

Profit	7.4%
Wages	32.2%
Purchases	34.3%
Depreciation	1.9%
Marketing	2.6%
Rent & Utilities	4.3%
Other	17.3%

P

Market Share

Advance Publications Inc.	12.6%
Hearst Corporation Inc.	9.6%
Time Inc.	6.4%

Expenses (% of Annual Sales)

Cost of Goods	50%
Occupancy Costs	05%
Payroll/Labor Costs	35%
Profit (pretax)	10%

Questions

- What are advertisers telling you? Look at circulation trends and costs.
- What have you done to grow the company and how would you grow it in the future?

Industry Trend

- "The volume of magazines mailed annually has dropped for 15 years in a row, according to data released yesterday by the U.S. Postal Service. During those 15 years, 'Outside-County' Periodicals Class volume-by far the best proxy for total magazine volume-has dropped 44%. That means 4 billion fewer copies were mailed in 2015 than in 2000. (Outside-county periodicals are almost exclusively magazines and represent the vast majority of U.S. magazine distribution.) During that time, entire categories have disappeared or shrunk to the point of insignificance. For the past three years, the Outside-County declines have been 6%, then 5%, and then 4% in Fiscal Year 2015."

  Source: "A Magazine Resurgence? The Numbers Say No," July 13, 2016, http://deadtreeeedition.blogspot.com/2016/07/a-magazine-resurgence-numbers-say-no.html

- "The Association of Magazine Media released The Magazine Media 360° Brand Audience Report for March and the Social Media Report for first quarter 2016 today, showing that magazine media brands continue to deliver meaningful growth across platforms, engaging consumers in all formats, including social media."

  Source: "Magazine Media Continues to Grow Audiences," April 28, 2016, http://www.magazine.org/industry-news/press-releases/mpa-press-releases/mpa/magazine-media-continues-grow-audiences

Expert Comments

Publishing, especially trade publishing, is declining rapidly. People are looking to the Internet for trade information because it can be delivered daily and weekly and be received long before a magazine can even be produced.

Resources

- The Association of Magazine Media (MPA): http://www.magazine.org
- IBISWorld, September 2017: http://ibiworld.com
- Editor & Publisher: http://www.editorandpublisher.com

Publishers—Monthly Community Magazines

	NAICS 511120	

Rules of Thumb

> ➤ 3 x SDE includes inventory
>
> ➤ 3.5 x EBITDA
>
> ➤ 65–85% of annual sales includes inventory
>
> ➤ 3.5 x cap rate

Pricing Tips

- The page count of the magazine and the size of the distribution is a key to attaining the higher number and the greater multiple suggested above. Most publications in this segment will be focused on an area or group within a geographical area, i.e., Lake Norman Woman, Carolina Living, or Iredell County Life, and will require that targeted readers identify themselves with the title implication and market. The attraction to a segment of the market creates a loyalty that should translate into long-time advertisers. Make sure the renewal rate is over 75% to confirm this loyalty is real and present.
- If gross revenues exceed $500,000 then 1 X sales is common. That usually equates to 3 X SDE. A monthly that has the owner doing all of the sales is worth less than one with a good sales staff. Publications under $500,000 will sell closer to 2 X SDE or 50% to 75% of sales.

Benchmark Data

- The average cost is about $700 a page to print and distribute. The average sales commission should not exceed 25% of the sale. Most vanity magazines will operate out of a home or key-man office space with the occasional use of conference rooms for sales meetings. In any case, occupancy cost should not exceed 5% of sales.
- Look for sales per salesperson of around $20,000 a month. That should pay a commission of $4,000 which is the minimum you need to keep good salespeople.

Expenses (% of Annual Sales)

Cost of Goods	25%
Occupancy Costs	05%
Payroll/Labor Costs	25% to 30%
Profit (pretax)	20% to 30%

Questions

- What are the top five advertisers? How long have they been with you? Could you grow the circulation? How long have you been with your current printer? Describe your layout process.
- How long have you been publishing and what are your historical trends? How many salespeople and how long have they worked for you? Who do you consider your competition?

Industry Trend

- The boutique magazine industry trend is positive as a larger number of people see this industry as attractive because it affords them the opportunity for a specific lifestyle in a targeted community setting without a significant liability and risk

P

Expert Comments

The advertising industry as a whole is very competitive, which will show in the last 3 years' sales, but there is a strong opportunity for a great salesperson to make good money. Hiring great salespeople is very hard and a new owner should not count on a salesperson making a material difference in sales. This is the owner's primary responsibility.

Monthlies are easy to start up and competition is great. Look for the thickest book (largest number of pages). Advertising should be around 70% of total pages. The thinner books will have the hardest time staying alive. Advertisers tend to stick with the publication they are in, so it's hard to be the new kid on the block.

Publishers—Newsletters		
	NAICS 511120	

Rules of Thumb

➤ 1 x annual sales

Pricing Tips

- High renewal rate (70 percent plus) increases value

Publishers—Newspapers—Dailies		
SIC 2711-98	NAICS 511110	Number of Businesses/Units 7,226

Rules of Thumb

➤ 50% of annual sales includes inventory (only very large will get higher)

➤ 4 x EBITDA

➤ 4 x EBIT

➤ 5 x SDE includes inventory

Pricing Tips

- "EBITDA valuation multiples for mid and small market papers range from 3 x to 6 x. Publishing company values are currently in the 3 x to 6 x trailing EBITDA range with most transactions at 4 x to 5 x. Prices over 5 x tend to be strategic acquisitions. Buyers typically look at the most recent performance, and the multiples indicated here are based on stable or improving performance. Companies with declining revenues and EBITDA tend to be valued at the lower end of the multiple scale."

  Source: www.cribb.com—An excellent site, full of valuable information on the publishing business, especially newspapers.

- In today's market, most valuation methods for newspapers are out the window.
- Key factors include: size of market, years in business. Is the newspaper geographically desirable by contiguous publishers or buyers looking to roll-up smaller publications into larger groups and take advantage of economies of scale? How active and dominant is the publication in its market and how dominant are its online activities?

Benchmark Data

Statistics (Newspaper Publishing)

Number of Establishments	7,226
Average Profit Margin	5.5%
Revenue per Employee	$133,600
Average Number of Employees	23.6
Average Wages per Employee	$42,941

Products and Services Segmentation

Print Advertising	38.2%
Subscription and newsstand sales	32.0%
Digital Advertising	15.6%
Other	5.6%
Third-party printing services	6.0%
Third-party distribution services	2.6%

Industry Costs

Profit	5.5%
Wages	32.0%
Purchases	28.8%
Depreciation	3.3%
Marketing	2.2%
Rent & Utilities	3.8%
Other	24.4%

Market Share

Gannett Co. Inc.	12.4%
News Corp.	10.2%
Tronc Inc.	6.3%
The New York Times Company	6.8%

- Benchmarks vary greatly by type of publication. For instance, sellers of daily paid circulation newspapers may find that valuations based on subscriber base may be most advantageous. Publishers of free distribution publications are often tied to multiple of discretionary cash flow.
- Generally multiple of EBITDA. Another is $50 to $400 per paid subscriber.
- Sales per subscriber, number of subscribers, revenue per household reached (if free distribution publication).

Expenses (% of Annual Sales)

Cost of Goods	50% to 55%
Occupancy Costs	05%
Payroll/Labor Costs	30%
Profit (pretax)	15%

Questions

- How effectively are you competing with online media? How are your renewal rates compared to your competitors'?
- How he would increase the circulation and advertising revenue and why he has not been successful if that is the case. Is the circulation audited?

P

Expert Comments

While the industry is certainly on a decline, there are still many strategic consolidation opportunities.

Competition generally comes from other media such as TV and cable rather than other newspapers. As newspapers face new challenges, the risk will increase. Profits have historically been very high, reaching 30% EBITDA. Marketability is still strong but will probably decrease. Industry trend is down as circulation and advertising decline. You can replicate but you must sustain the losses for some time.

Subscriber acquisition and gaining solid market position takes many, many years for paid circulation newspapers, therefore time is the greatest barrier to entry.

Seller Financing

- 5 years

Resources

- Editor & Publisher: http://www.editorandpublisher.com
- National Newspaper Association: http://www.nnaweb.org
- Cribb, Greene and Associates—a newspaper appraisal and brokerage firm: http://www.cribb.com
- IBISWorld, June 2017: http://ibisworld.com
- News Media Alliance: https://www.newsmediaalliance.org/

Publishers—Newspapers (In General)		
SIC 2711-98	NAICS 511110	

Rules of Thumb

➤ 25% of annual sales includes inventory

➤ 3 x SDE plus inventory

➤ 3–5 x EBIT

➤ 3–5 x EBITDA

Pricing Tips

- Depends on size and segment; for example, it would be very hard to sell a daily newspaper in today's environment.
- Price can vary greatly depending on the size and frequency of publication, i.e., weekly, daily publication; if the company has its own printing plant; the value of printing equipment; and approximately 50% of gross revenue for recurring outside print work.
- A stable weekly will sell for 5 to 7 times EBITDA. A strong weekly in a growth area can sell for as much as 9 to 11 times EBITDA. Variation in price is based upon age of property, market potential, competition, stability, growth history, community acceptance, reputation and market penetration. If printing equipment is owned, add value of equipment. If income is generated from outside printing, the profits for the printing portion of the business need to be separated and valued at 3 to 5 times EBITDA.

Benchmark Data

- For additional Benchmark Data see Publishers—Newspapers—Dailies
- At one time $200 per daily newspaper subscriber, but not anymore. It is a matter of profitability. Some smaller newspapers in rural areas have a better chance because there are not as many advertising options.
- The ratio of advertising space to editorial space has a lot to do with profitability. Ideally one should have two-thirds advertising, one-third profit.

Expenses (% of Annual Sales)

Cost of Goods	35% to 45%
Occupancy Costs	05% to 10%
Payroll/Labor Costs	25% to 35%
Profit (pretax)	15% to 25%

Questions

- What is your online market position and share of market in each market that you serve?
- What are the reasons why you feel your media will continue to be relevant in the years to come?
- How would you increase the circulation and advertising? Why haven't you been successful in doing so?
- Revenue by category, cash flow, paid circulation and free circulation, average advertising percentage, competition, owner's duties, who sells the ads, number of ad contracts in place and dollar value?
- What contracts do you have; how are you handling the changes in the newspaper environment? Is it an all-cash sale or is the owner willing to carry some of the sale price?
- Subscription base, number of subscribers, subscriber retention, revenue trends, strength of online initiatives, years established
- Why they are selling; what their daily involvement is; what investment has been made to adapt to new technologies; how they reach the individual reader and advertiser.

Industry Trend

- "Last year, the estimated total U.S. daily newspaper circulation reached 35 million Americans for weekday delivery and 38 million for Sunday. It is an audience that not only believes in the importance of journalism, but also understands that print is a pretty good technology. In 2016, 56 percent of American subscribers still only read print newspapers. The 'death of print' has been greatly exaggerated. In fact, circulation revenue has been steady over the past few years, rising from $10.4 billion in 2012 to $10.9 billion in 2015 and 2016."

  Source: "The sky is not falling and print is still here" by David Chavern, August 23, 2017, https://www.newsmediaalliance.org/august-ceo-print-alive/

- "Perhaps the biggest shift in the newspaper world is the revenue driven from circulation is now greater than revenue from advertising. But one area that everyone is worried about is adblocking!
  - ✓ 47% of internet users use some form of adblocking (Reuters Institute—June 2015)
  - ✓ 55% in the 18–24-year-old demo
  - ✓ 16% of all US traffic adblocked at start of 2015—20% now (Adobe)
  - ✓ Global loss of ad revenue to adblocking—$21.8 billion (Adobe)
  - ✓ AdBlock Plus averaging 2.3M global downloads a week for 2 years

P

✓ Higher income users more likely to adblock (their time is more important to them)

✓ Adblocking effecting your analytics tags

✓ CBS Interactive—5%–40% of pageviews adblocked across 20 properties "So what does this all mean? Newspapers are hungry for new revenue streams. While this should not come as a surprise, one area that newspapers are successfully recouping losses is online recruitment advertising. As the job advertisement becomes more similar to a hybrid of native advertising and an SEM result, job ads are the prime content for a newspapers audience. Whether in New York, Philadelphia, Eastern Tennessee, or numerous places across America, newspapers are using their local influence to help employers and job candidates find each other."

Source: "State of the Newspaper Publishing Industry," by Yoav Guttman, May 25, 2016,
http://blog.realmatch.com/publishers/state-of-the-newspaper-publishing-industry/

Expert Comments

The growth of online advertising has significantly reduced profitability and gross revenues of newspapers.

Amount of competition from all media in the market is important because there is a limited amount of advertising dollars to go around. Historic performance and competition will be large factors in determining the amount of risk. Location is of minor importance because the customer rarely goes to the business. Most publications with reasonable profits are marketable as there are sufficient buyers in the market for local community operations. While the trend in large metro dailies is declining revenue and profits, smaller community publications continue to do well. It is easy to start a new publication, but a lot more difficult to build a reader and advertising base.

Seller Financing

- About 50% of sales are financed. Larger papers generally sell for cash. Smaller papers will sell for as little as 30% down with terms averaging seven years.
- Seller financing is typical with terms of five years or longer.

Resources

- Cribb, Greene and Associates: http://www.cribb.com
- Editor and Publisher Magazine: http://www.editorandpublisher.com
- News Media Alliance: https://www.newsmediaalliance.org/

Publishers—Newspapers—Weeklies/Community Papers		
	NAICS 511110	

Rules of Thumb

➢ 100% of annual sales

➢ 3 x SDE

➢ 3 x EBIT

➢ 3 x EBITDA

➢ 1 x annual income for mid-sized weekly newspaper

➢ Some smaller weekly papers will have lower multiples in the 3–5 EBITDA area.

➢ Community monthlies will sell for 3 x SDE if they produce at least $150,000 in SDE. Otherwise, multiple comes down to the 2 x SDE area.

Benchmark Data

- Advertising to editorial should run 2/3rd to 1/3rd for maximum profitability.
- Look for businesses where the owner does very little selling. You have to make a negative adjustment to SDE to account for sales commissions to replace an overactive seller.

Expenses (% of Annual Sales)

Cost of Goods	25%
Occupancy Costs	05%
Payroll/Labor Costs	25%
Profit (pretax)	20%

Questions

- How many salespeople do you have?

Industry Trend

- Up. Local merchants are looking for a cost-effective way to reach their local customers. Major dailies are too expensive and provide too much reach for the local markets.
- Community papers are following the rise in the housing market. New communities are receptive to local papers that educate them as to local restaurants, salons, etc. This trend will continue.

Expert Comments

Barriers to entry are low. This is a selling business. Getting good salespeople is very difficult. The buyers of this type of business should expect to spend half of their time selling.

Resources

- National Newspaper Publishers Association (NNPA): http://www.nnpa.org
- Cribb, Greene & Associates—a newspaper appraisal and brokerage firm: http://www.cribb.com
- Association of Free Community Papers: http://www.afcp.org

Publishers—Software		
	NAICS 511210	Number of Businesses/Units 10,026

Benchmark Data

Statistics (Software Publishing)

Number of Establishments	10,026
Average Profit Margin	37.4%
Revenue per Employee	$450,000
Average Number of Employees	49.7
Average Wages per Employee	$159,298

Products and Services Segmentation

Application software publishing	38.2%
System software publishing	31.4%
All others	18.3%
Re-sale of computer hardware and software	4.8%
Information technology technical consulting services	4.5%
Custom application design and development	2.8%

Major Market Segmentation

Businesses	76.8%
Household consumers and individual users	14.8%
Government	8.4%

Industry Costs

Profit	37.4%
Wages	35.2%
Purchases	5.0%
Depreciation	2.1%
Marketing	4.0%
Rent & Utilities	1.2%
Other	15.1%

Market Share

Microsoft Corporation	20.3%
Oracle Corp.	5.3%
International Business Machines Corp.	8.8%

Industry Trend

- Increasingly competitive

Expert Comments

Market momentum of software products can change quickly, both up and down. With specialized niche firms, buyers can be international companies. This is a trans-national market.

Resources

- IBISWorld, October 2017: http://ibisworld.com

	Franchise
Pump It Up	
Approx. Total Investment	$366,250–$790,000
NAICS 713990	Number of Businesses/Units 130

Rules of Thumb

➢ 30% of annual sales plus inventory

Resources

- Pump It Up: http://www.pumpitupparty.com

		Franchise
Purrfect Auto		
	NAICS 811118	Number of Businesses/Units 100

Rules of Thumb

➢ 45% of annual sales plus inventory

Resources

- Purrfect Auto: http://www.purrfectautoservice.com/franchise-information/

		Franchise
Quaker Steak & Lube		
Approx. Total Investment		$1.2 million–$4.4 million
Estimated Annual Sales/Unit		$3.07 million
	NAICS 722513	Number of Businesses/Units 44

Rules of Thumb

➢ 45% of annual sales

Resources

- Quaker Steak & Lube: http://www.thelube.com

		Franchise
Quiznos Classic Subs		
Approx. Total Investment		$182,912–$231,246
Estimated Annual Sales/Unit		$325,000
SIC 5812-19	NAICS 722513	Number of Businesses/Units 540

Rules of Thumb

➢ 20–25% of annual sales plus inventory

Benchmark Data

- For Benchmark Data see Sandwich Shops

Resources

- Quiznos Classic Subs: http://www.quiznos.com

Radio Communications, Equipment and Systems		
	NAICS 443142	

Rules of Thumb

➢ 2–4 x SDE plus inventory

Pricing Tips

- It is important to consider the revenue per customer and industry figures. A well-diversified company can weather downturns in business cycles that this industry may be subject to.

Benchmark Data

- GP of 40%, payroll 20%, advertising 4%

Expenses (% of Annual Sales)

Cost of Goods	60%
Occupancy Costs	07%
Payroll/Labor Costs	20%
Profit (pretax)	10% to 12%

Questions

- Product line diversification? Service and installation capabilities? Employee tenure?

Industry Trend

- FCC rule changes mandate replacement of older 2-way radio equipment being used.

Expert Comments

Not location dependent, but a well-trained staff and diversified product lines are important.

Radio Stations		
SIC 4832-01	NAICS 515112	Number of Businesses/Units 6,885

Rules of Thumb

- ➢ 15 x cash flow in large markets
- ➢ 8–10 x EBITDA
- ➢ 10–12 x cash flow in medium markets
- ➢ 1.5–6 x annual sales

Pricing Tips

- "Some Advice for Sellers
- You are not going to get 22 times cash flow on a small market station. Yes, I know that some stations in the past and one in particular in Texas were reported as having sold for 22 times cash flow. This is only going to happen in probably the top 50 markets. Most banks will only (if you can get them to look at the deal) do 4-5 times cash flow. That means the buyer will have to put in the balance in cash unless you carry the paper yourself (and be in 2nd position behind the bank). The only way you are going to get a big premium is if your FM station has the potential to upgrade into a much larger market. . .There are lots of people wanting to get into the radio station ownership
- business but pricing has got to be realistic in relation to market size."

Source: http://radiobroker.com/

Benchmark Data

Statistics (Radio Broadcasting)

Number of Establishments	6,885
Average Profit Margin	19.8%
Revenue per Employee	$216,800
Average Number of Employees	13.8
Average Wages per Employee	$59,796

Products and Services Segmentation

Other	10.2%
Country	15.1%
News, Talk and Sports	17.8%
Rock and Alternative	13.1%
Urban	8.6%
Top 40	11.8%
Adult Contemporary	23.4%

Industry Costs

Profit	19.8%
Wages	27.8%
Purchases	18.0%
Depreciation	4.8%
Marketing	3.3%
Rent & Utilities	3.7%
Other	22.6%

Market Share

Sirius XM Radio Inc.	26.4%
iHeartMedia Inc.	16.9%
Cumulus Media Inc.	5.6%

Questions

- "Can your signal be upgraded or moved to cover a larger market? How are you spending your revenue? How much do you do in trade? Can any barter be converted to cash? Do you really need to buy that new gadget, just because you have a few extra bucks this month? Spend the money to find out what can be done to expand or move that signal to more ears. Are you being a partner in your advertisers' business? The more you expand your advertisers' businesses, the more you expand yours and are therefore able to ask for more dollars on the selling market."

Source: www.buysellradio.com

Industry Trend

- "Of all media, radio will undergo the most dramatic change in the coming decade, and these changes will radically transform the industry. Below are some of the most important of those changes, based in insights by various media forecasters and analysts and media buyers, and the Media Life radio advisory panel.
- 1) The collapse of Big Radio.
  2) A renaissance of local radio.

3)   Radio will go entirely digital.

4)   The merging of radio, TV and news under single operators.

5)   A revolution in radio content.

6)   A transformation of the industry around this broader definition of radio as encompassing all things audio.

7)   An opportunity for radio to grab a larger share of consumers' time and attention."

Source: "The future of radio: Seven important trends," December 27, 2016,
http://medialifemagazine.com/future-radio-seven-important-trends/

- "Radio is the leading reach platform:
    - ✓ 93% of us listen to AM/FM radio over the airwaves, which is higher than TV viewership (85%), PC use (50%), smartphone use (74%), and tablet use (29%);
    - ✓ 265 million Americans 6+ listen to the radio each week;
    - ✓ 66 million millennials use radio each week;
    - ✓ Audio consumers are listening for more than 12 hours each week; and
    - ✓ The majority of radio usage comes from employed listeners; nearly three-quarters of Generation X listeners work full-time."

Source: "Radio Facts and Figures,"
http://www.newsgeneration.com/broadcast-resources/radio-facts-and-figures/

Seller Financing

- Rarely is there seller financing except for smallest of deals.

Resources

- David Garland, Media Brokerage, also, a brokerage site, but well worth a visit: http://www.radiobroker.com
- IBISWorld, July 2017: http://ibisworld.com

Real Estate Agencies		
SIC 6531-18	NAICS 531210	Number of Businesses/Units 894,342

Rules of Thumb

➢ 2 x SDE; may require earnout

➢ 33% of annual sales (real estate offices) includes inventory

Pricing Tips

- Price will depend on agent splits.
- Time in the market and number of listings

Benchmark Data

Statistics (Real Estate Agency Franchises)

Number of Establishments	19,031
Average Profit Margin	13.7%
Revenue per Employee	$454,600
Average Number of Employees	2.9
Average Wages per Employee	$42,823

Products and Services Segmentation

Residential real estate agency franchises 68.5%
Commercial real estate agency franchises 31.5%

Major Market Segmentation

Sellers 45.0%
Lessors 30.0%
Buyers 25.0%

Industry Costs

Profit 13.7%
Wages 9.5%
Purchases 15.2%
Depreciation 0.7%
Marketing 5.4%
Rent and Utilities 7.1%
Other 48.4%

Statistics (Real Estate Sales and Brokerage)

Number of Establishments 875,311
Average Profit Margin 20.4%
Revenue per Employee $146,700
Average Number of Employees 1.3
Average Wages per Employee $45,325

Products and Services Segmentation

Residential sales 67.0%
Commercial rentals 11.3%
Transaction, advisory and other services 8.8%
Commercial sales 8.3%
Residential rentals 4.6%

Major Market Segmentation

Married or partnered residential homeowners and renters 54.2%
Single residential homeowners and renters 17.6%
Office and professional space 12.1%
Retail space 9.8%
Warehousing and other commercial space 4.0%
Manufacturing space 2.3%

Industry Costs

Profit 20.4%
Wages 31.1%
Purchases 7.4%
Depreciation 1.8%
Marketing 5.5%
Rent & Utilities 3.5%
Other 30.3%

Expenses (% of Annual Sales)

Cost of Goods .... 65% (commission
Occupancy Costs .... 05% to 10%
Payroll/Labor Costs 10%
Profit (pretax) 15%

R

Questions

- Are you in production? What contract do you have for advertising and services? Where do you get your leads? Have you recently lost top-producing agents?
- Do you produce? What are your splits? Do you have noncompetes?
- Will the owner be available?

Industry Trend

- "These 5 Trends Will Shape the Housing Market in 2017:
  - ✓ Rising Rates
  - ✓ More Credit
  - ✓ More New Homes
  - ✓ The Continued Rise of Medium-sized Cities
  - ✓ Foreign Buyers Aren't Going Away"
  - Source: Chris Matthews, December 29, 2016, http://fortune.com/2016/12/29/real-estate-trends-2017-2/

Expert Comments

There is a wide variety of real estate firm types, from residential to commercial and from tenant-rep leasing to agency leasing for landlords. However, barriers to entry remain low and access to capital is increasing through both community banks and private lenders.

Seller Financing

- Banks are generally friendly to borrowers with collateral. So on the investment or development side, inexpensive capital is often easy to come by. However, the increase in private lending has been a boon to quick-moving developers who don't mind a higher, short-term rate.

Resources

- IBISWorld, June 2017: http://ibisworld.com
- IBISWorld, July 2017: http://ibisworld.com

Records Management		
	NAICS 541611	

Rules of Thumb

➢ 8 x SDE

➢ 200% of annual sales

Benchmark Data

- Internal account growth of 5% to 7%. Sixty percent storage revenues with 40% service revenues.

Expenses (% of Annual Sales)

Cost of Goods	0%
Occupancy Costs	25%
Payroll/Labor Costs	35%
Profit (pretax)	30%

Industry Trend

- Continued industry growth with emphasis on document-destruction services

Recruiting Agencies

SIC 7361-03	NAICS 56131	Number of Businesses/Units 28,097

Rules of Thumb

➤ 50% of annual revenues; may require earnout

➤ 1–1.5 x SDE; add fixtures equipment & inventory; may require earnout

Benchmark Data

Statistics (Employment and Recruiting Agencies)

Number of Establishments	28,097
Average Profit Margin	4.9%
Revenue per Employee	$92,900
Average Number of Employees	10.9
Average Wages per Employee	$38,458

Products and Services Segmentation

Permanent placement services	50.2%
Executive search services	34.0%
Temporary staffing services	7.9%
Independent contractor placement services	6.0%
Other	1.9%

Major Market Segmentation

Executive and managerial	34.0%
Industrial	33.9%
Administrative and clerical	12.2%
Technical	11.1%
Healthcare	8.8%

Industry Costs

Profit	4.9%
Wages	40.9%
Purchases	16.6%
Depreciation	0.2%
Marketing	1.6%
Rent & Utilities	3.2%
Other	32.6%

Market Share

LinkedIn Corp.	6.7%
Randstad Holding NV	6.6%

Industry Trend

- The online recruitment business is challenging. There are many new and free and very inexpensive competitors.

R

- "When LinkedIn and online job applications first began to gain traction, they were seen as supplements to the traditional paper résumé and in-person interview. Today, the world of recruiting has gone nearly 100-percent digital. "'From the résumé to the search to the interview, we're moving toward a digital hiring model,' said Bob Myhal, director of digital marketing at CBC Advertising and former CEO of NextHire. 'Résumés will be displaced by constantly evolving representations of individual experiences, skills and aptitudes that exist purely in the digital realm. Innovative tools that use social media, big data and other technologies to give tremendous insight into individual job seekers will [be] the primary screening method.
- "Jon Bischke, CEO of Entelo, noted that digital profiles can provide far more insight into a candidate than a traditional résumé can, and many recruiters have realized that."

  Source: "Hiring in the Digital Age: What's Next for Recruiting?" by Nicole Fallon Taylor, January 11, 2016, http://www.businessnewsdaily.com/6975-future-of-recruiting.html

Seller Financing
- Typically uses outside financing

Resources
- IBISWorld, April 2017: http://ibisworld.com

Recycling		
	NAICS 562920	Number of Businesses/Units 1,582

Rules of Thumb
➢ 3–5 x SDE includes inventory

➢ 3–6 x EBIT

➢ 3–6 x EBITDA

Pricing Tips
- Value is based on land and improvements, inventory (aged), earnings, and goodwill.
- Once the EBITDA exceeds $1,000,000 most buyers will assume that normal levels of inventory, A/R, and FFE will be included in the transaction as working capital. The key is to understand how the buyer is structuring their offer and how they are accounting for these values.

Benchmark Data

Statistics (Recycling Facilities)

Number of Establishments	1,582
Average Profit Margin	4.5%
Revenue per Employee	$252,900
Average Number of Employees	14.2
Average Wages per Employee	$40,669

Products and Services Segmentation

Recyclable material recovery and processing 47.3%
Sale of recycled materials 39.3%
Other 8.2%
Recyclables collection services 5.2%

Major Market Segmentation

Private businesses, including recycling commodity wholesalers a 75.5%
Municipal governments 22.8%
State governments, nonprofit organizations and individuals 1.7%

Industry Costs

Profit 4.5%
Wages 16.0%
Purchases 44.4%
Depreciation 6.0%
Marketing 0.5%
Rent & Utilities 3.4%
Other 25.2%

Market Share

Waste Management Inc. 20.0%
Republic Services Inc. 8.0%

Expenses (% of Annual Sales)

Cost of Goods 50%
Occupancy Costs 10%
Payroll/Labor Costs 12%
Profit (pretax) 08%

Questions

- What kind of contracts do you have with your paper suppliers? Are you contracted to sell your paper to certain mills or brokers? Who is your competition within 100 miles?

Industry Trend

- "A study by Rob Taylor with the State Recycling Program in the North Carolina Department of Environmental Quality estimated that the average market value of a ton of mixed recyclable material arriving at a recovery facility in the state dropped from just over $180 in early 2011 to less than $80 at the end of 2015. That value has since rebounded a bit, Taylor found, to a little over $100, but it still leaves the industry struggling to extract profit from the millions of tons of recyclable material Americans throw away every year.

  "There are a host of reasons for the decline in the recycling market, ranging from global trade policy to the decline in newspaper readership, said David Biderman, executive director and CEO of the Solid Waste Association of North America. Much of reclaimed American waste is shipped overseas, but China erected new limits on imported waste in 2013. In other nations, 'there has been a decrease in demand for that material as growth rate in foreign countries has leveled off,' Biderman said. Low oil prices have made it cheaper to produce new plastic bottles, so manufacturers don't have as much need for reclaimed plastic. In addition, packaging producers have figured out how to make bottles and cans thinner, so they don't need as much raw material.

"And as the circulation for print newspapers has plummeted, the recycling industry has lost both a massive customer for reclaimed paper fiber and a huge source of incoming recyclable material. Across the recycling industry, 'what was once a valuable commodity five years ago is less valuable now,' Biderman said. The change is perhaps most dramatic for glass. In most American cities, the glass bottle you toss in the recycling cart is essentially worthless, and if it breaks, the shards may make the paper in a mixed cart worthless as well.

"But it is not all bad news in the industry, Napa's Miller said. The growth of online shopping has generated an explosion of cardboard packaging coming into the recycling stream. 'There is more corrugated cardboard in the system than ever before,' he said, which is a valuable and readily recyclable product— as long as it is not contaminated in a recycling bin by a dirty diaper or broken bottle."

Source: "Recycling is in trouble — and it might be your fault" by Paul Singer, April 28, 2017, https://www.usatoday.com/story/news/politics/2017/04/20/weak-marketsmake consumers-wishful-recycling-big-problem/100654976/

- "Six waste and recycling trends to watch in 2017
  - ✓ Commodity prices likely to make a comeback
  - ✓ Recyclers to move away from weight-based goals
  - ✓ Flexible packaging to continue growing (and presenting challenges)
  - ✓ Shifts in politics to create more division
  - ✓ Increased infrastructure spending to present competitive opportunities
  - ✓ Technology to transform operations — whether or not the industry is ready"

Source: http://www.wastedive.com/news/6-waste-and-recycling-trends-to-watch-in-2017/433337/

Resources
- IBISWorld, April 2017: http://ibisworld.com

Red Robin Gourmet Burgers		Franchise
Approx. Total Investment		$1,800,000–$3,000,000
Estimated Annual Sales/Unit		$2,842,000
	NAICS 722513	Number of Businesses/Units 500

Rules of Thumb

➢ 30–35% of annual sales

Resources
- Red Robin Gourmet Burgers: http://www.redrobin.com

Registered Investment Advisors		
	NAICS 523930	Number of Businesses/Units 118,485

Rules of Thumb

➢ 150% of annual sales

➢ 3–5 x SDE plus net assets plus inventory

Pricing Tips

- The structure of your deal will depend on the willingness of the seller to hold an earnout vs. a note and cash down payment at closing.

Benchmark Data

Statistics (Financial Planning and Advice)

Number of Establishments 118,485
Average Profit Margin 25.5%
Revenue per Employee $263,500
Average Number of Employees 1.9
Average Wages per Employee $82,880

Products and Services Segmentation

Personal financial planning and advice 33.3%
Personal investment management 29.7%
Business and government financial planning and management 20.8%
Other services 16.2%

Major Market Segmentation

Individuals and households 42.9%
Businesses 27.7%
Other clients 15.8%
Governments 13.6%

Industry Costs

Profit 25.5%
Wages 31.9%
Purchases 4.8%
Depreciation 1.2%
Marketing 1.7%
Rent & Utilities 2.8%
Other 32.1%

Market Share

Morgan Stanley Wealth Management 17.4%
Wells Fargo & Company 13.7%
Bank of America Corporation 13.1%
Ameriprise Financial Inc. 5.5%
Average account per client

Expenses (% of Annual Sales)

Cost of Goods .... 05% to 10%
Occupancy Costs .... 05% to 15%
Payroll/Labor Costs .... 10% to 20%
Profit (pretax) .... 20% to 45%

Questions

- Gross commissions? Net? Broker-dealer? Overhead? Fee-based or commission-based? Average fees? Average client investment, net worth?

R

Industry Trend

- "Consolidation in the registered investment adviser space has become fast and furious, with no slowdown in sight, according to the latest research from Echelon Partners. The 138 transactions last year set a new record for RIA M&A activity, representing a 10% increase over the 2015 record of 125 deals and a 16% compound annual growth rate since 2009, which saw just 48 deals completed. 'The many macro trends impacting the RIA industry is setting up for a perfect storm of M&A for the wealth management industry,' said Daniel Seivert, Echelon's CEO.

  "The report also includes data on breakaway broker activity — brokers leaving major broker-dealers to go independent — showing more than 400 teams leaving last year for the second consecutive year. More than 15% of all breakaways have become RIAs, reflecting a new high. Last year 66 breakaway teams joined RIAs, representing an increase from 64 in 2015, 57 in 2014, and 30 in 2013. Last year marked the third time in the past five years that the average deal size exceeded $1 billion in assets under management.

  "RIAs were the acquirer in 42% of the transactions, which is down from 47% in 2013. The trend is reflective of the growing impact of strategic acquirers and consolidators, Mr. Seivert said. 'There are 300,000 advice-providing professionals, and 30,000 RIAs at 10,000 firms,' Mr. Seivert said. 'We're reporting roughly 1% deal activity, and we think the actual number is between 3% and 5%, which means three to five times the number being reported.'"

  Source: "RIAs merging at a record clip, more breakaways become RIAs" by Jess Benjamin, January 18, 2017, http://www.investmentnews.com/article/20170117/FREE/170119936/ rias-merging-at-a-record-clip-more-breakaways-become-rias

Expert Comments

There will be continued major consolidation in the industry.

Resources

- IBISWorld, February 2017: http://ibisworld.com

Remediation Services		
	NAICS 562910	Number of Businesses/Units 4,457

Rules of Thumb

➢ 40% of annual sales includes inventory

➢ 4–5 x EBITDA

➢ 2–3 x SDE includes inventory

Pricing Tips

- "Worldwide, the remediation and cleanup services industry generates about $60 billion in revenue, according to BCC Research. Due to access to advanced technology, developed countries account for most of the world's remediation services. The largest markets are the US, Western Europe, and Japan.

  "The US remediation and environmental cleanup services industry includes about 4,000 establishments (single-location companies and units of multi-location companies) with combined annual revenue of about $14 billion."

  Source: www.firstresearch.com/Industry-Research/Remediation-and-Environmental-Cleanup-Services.html

- Union vs non-union work force. Private vs. public projects.
- Contract and client direct relationships will be worth more than those performed as a subcontractor for a general contractor. Size makes a big difference in price-larger businesses with $1 million + EBITDA sell for higher multiples.
- Value of future jobs under contract is a major factor in value and salability.

Benchmark Data

Statistics (Remediation & Environmental Cleanup Services)

Number of Establishments	4,457
Average Profit Margin	6.4%
Revenue per Employee	$198,800
Average Number of Employees	16.4
Average Wages per Employee	$60,399

Products and Services Segmentation

Site remediation services	49.9%
Building remediation services	26.0%
Environmental emergency response services	12.7%
Other services	11.4%

Major Market Segmentation

Businesses	53.3%
Federal government	29.1%
State and local government	10.4%
Other	7.2%

Industry Costs

Profit	6.4%
Wages	29.4%
Purchases	26.0%
Depreciation	2.4%
Marketing	1.4%
Rent & Utilities	5.5%
Other	28.9%

Market Share

CH2M Hill Companies Ltd.	8.3%
CB&I	6.7%

Expenses (% of Annual Sales)

Cost of Goods	70%
Occupancy Costs	04%
Payroll/Labor Costs	07%
Profit (pretax)	03% to 05%

Questions
- Have there been any DEP violations? Worker's comp claims?
- Check for hidden liabilities. Union vs. non-union is important difference.

R

Reputation is also important-how many jobs have they abandoned or not completed on time?

Industry Trend

- Project opportunities are a function of the overall commercial construction industry. Business will pick up when commercial renovation work picks up.

Expert Comments

Industry has become increasingly competitive as more players are chasing fewer projects.

Competition varies based on union vs. non-union, and public vs. private market. Revenue varies with commercial real estate renovation and development.

Resources

- IBISWorld, September 2017: http://ibisworld.com

		Franchise
Renaissance Executive Forums		
Approx. Total Investment		$61,500–$150,000
	NAICS 611430	Number of Businesses/Units 54

Rules of Thumb

➤ 70% of annual sales includes inventory

Resources

- Renaissance Executive Forums: http://www.executiveforums.com

Rental Centers		
SIC 7359-59	NAICS 532310	Number of Businesses/Units 21,558

Rules of Thumb

➤ 5 x SDE (party and tent rental)

➤ 95–100% of annual sales includes inventory

➤ 3 x SDE includes inventory

➤ 4 x EBITDA

➤ Depending on type of business (general, tool, construction, industrial, party) values will range from 3.0 to 5.5 EBITDA, $1.00 to $2.00 per annual revenues.

Pricing Tips

- Age of equipment, depreciation expense. If equipment is old and depreciation expense getting lower each year, then examine equipment carefully. Equipment may be old and worn out requiring replacement with new.
- Percentage of rent to sales; capitalization versus expense policy for equipment

purchases; age of rental fleet (inventory for rent); rental inventory is a fixed asset, not a current asset such as inventory for sale.

- Return on Investment (ROI—annual rental revenues divided by original cost of equipment varies from $0.70:$1.00 to $2.00:$1.00, 1:1 depending on whether equipment is construction, general tool, or party. Values primarily based on multiple of EBITDA, net revenues, value of assets plus goodwill factor, customer base, organizational structure/employees and staff, physical plant facilities, including location and expansion area availability.

Benchmark Data

Statistics (Tool and Equipment Rental)

Number of Establishments	9,364
Average Profit Margin	18.7%
Revenue per Employee	$144,100
Average Number of Employees	2.7
Average Wages per Employee	$37,103

Products and Services Segmentation

Contractor equipment	47.2%
Home tools and DIY equipment rental	26.4%
Rental of other goods	12.9%
Consumer goods rental	8.8%
Delivery, repair and other services	4.7%

Major Market Segmentation

Independent builders and contractors	24.0%
Private households	22.2%
Construction companies	21.1%
Industrial companies	18.1%
Other	7.6%
Government	7.0%

Industry Costs

Profit	18.7%
Wages	25.8%
Purchases	25.5%
Depreciation	6.0%
Marketing	1.5%
Rent & Utilities	7.7%
Other	14.8%

Market Share

United Rentals Inc.	56.3%
Sunbelt Rentals	15.9%
Hertz Global Holdings Inc.	6.9%

Statistics (Party Supply Rental)

Number of Establishments	12,194
Average Profit Margin	11.0%
Revenue per Employee	$103,200
Average Number of Employees	4.1
Average Wages per Employee	$33,218

R

Products and Services Segmentation

Wedding rentals	34.8%
Corporate event rentals	31.3%
Other event rentals	18.7%
Birthday rentals	15.2%

Industry Costs

Profit	11.0%
Wages	32.2%
Purchases	20.2%
Depreciation	9.5%
Marketing	2.0%
Rent & Utilities	9.7%
Other	15.4%

Expenses (% of Annual Sales)

Cost of Goods	<10%
Occupancy Costs	<10%
Payroll/Labor Costs	<30%
Profit (pretax)	05% to 15%

Questions

- Get a depreciation schedule and verify equipment age and condition. Do a thorough due diligence. If a stock sale, find out about lawsuits and environmental issues.
- How does business account for equipment maintenance-expense or capitalize?

Industry Trend

- "The new five-year forecast for equipment rental industry revenues released by the American Rental Association (ARA) continues to call for steady gains, and expectations for growth are greater than in the February forecast. ARA now projects U.S. equipment rental revenue to reach $49.4 billion in 2017, up 4.5 percent over last year. The May 3 forecast calls for U.S. rental revenue to grow 4.7 percent in 2018, 5.1 percent in 2019, 4.6 percent in 2020 and 4.4 percent in 2021, to reach $59.4 billion combined for the three segments of the industry, including construction/industrial, general tool/light construction and party/special event."

Source: http://www.ararental.org/Portals/0/Documents/Press%20Releases/
Rental%20revenue%20forecast%20strengthens_2.27.17.pdf

Expert Comments

Business location is very important relative to competition and accessibility for customers.

Seller Financing

- Limited to 20 percent of the sales price
- 7-year amortization

Resources

- Rental Management: http://www.rentalmanagementmag.com
- American Rental Association: http://www.ararental.org
- IBISWorld, March 2017: http://ibisworld.com
- IBISWorld, January 2017: http://ibisworld.com

Rent-To-Own Stores

SIC 7359-30	NAICS 532310	

Rules of Thumb

➤ 55% of annual sales includes inventory

Pricing Tips

- Eight (8) times monthly gross receipts (tops), includes lock, stock (inventory) and barrel. All underlying debts would be paid off by seller at this price. I think the multiple is now less because the industry has sustained a shakeout.

Benchmark Data

Statistics (Consumer Electronics & Appliances Rental)

Number of Establishments	8,587
Average Profit Margin	10.8%
Revenue per Employee	$376,500
Average Number of Employees	2.6
Average Wages per Employee	$49,832

Products and Services Segmentation

Electronics	45.3%
Appliances	39.1%
Computers	14.5%
Other	1.1%

Industry Costs

Profit	10.8%
Wages	13.2%
Purchases	24.1%
Depreciation	11.3%
Marketing	1.9%
Rent & Utilities	7.3%
Other	31.4%

Market Share

Rent-A-Center Inc.	21.5%
Aaron's Inc.	19.7%

Industry Trend

- "There were 7,100 rent-to-own stores in 2014, 6,900 in 2015 and 6,700 in 2016. Brick-and-mortar stores suffered a small decline, $100 million, between 2014 to 2016. During that same period, e-commerce revenue shot up $800

R

million—and that only factors in e-commerce data generated from publicly traded companies.

"According to annual reports from the three e-commerce companies, the number of stores increased by 17,000 in the past three years, which reflects an $800 million increase in revenue. But while the number of rent-to-own e-commerce stores is exploding, the revenue for those concerns is not matching proportionally. Not even close.

"Another interesting revelation in the new survey is the customer count. Ignoring e-commerce and focusing only on U.S. brick-and-mortar stores for a moment, the customer count for 2016 was 3.4 million, which matches 2007 and 2008 numbers, but that's 700,000 fewer customers than in 2011, which came to 4.1 million. Calculating a total customer count and store count for e-commerce is difficult. Progressive is the only company to offer such data, reporting more than 500,000 customers per year. That would increase the total 2016 customer count—brick-and-mortar plus e-commerce—to around 4 million, and that doesn't factor in RAC Acceptance, Flex Shopper or the many other e-commerce companies."

Source: "The Shape of Rent-to-Own by the Numbers" by Valerie Villarreal, August 7, 2017, https://www.rtohq.org/2017/08/shape-rent-numbers/

Resources
- Association of Progressive Rental Organizations (APRO)—a very good site: http://www.rtohq.org
- IBISWorld, July 2017: http://ibisworld.com
- Rent-to-Own Industry Statistics, www.rtoonline.com.: http://www.rtoonline.com

Repossession Services

	NAICS 561491	

Rules of Thumb
- 4 x SDE
- 85–95% of annual sales includes inventory
- 2.5–3.5 x EBITDA

Pricing Tips
- Some industry consolidation is happening by various large conglomerates.
- Be careful of the depreciation associated with trucks. Towing is also a supplement of this industry.

Benchmark Data
- A successful company tracks on average how much fuel is consumed per recovery and also makes an allocation for insurance cost.
- The average repo fee is $300.00 +.

Expenses (% of Annual Sales)

Cost of Goods	10% to 15%
Occupancy Costs	10% to 15%
Payroll/Labor Costs	35% to 45%
Profit (pretax)	35% to 45%

Industry Trend
- The business will grow as the economy continues to improve.

Expert Comments

There are barriers to entry in certain states which require licensing. The insurance costs are very high.

Resale Shops		
	NAICS 453310	

Rules of Thumb

➢ 40–45% of annual sales plus paid-for inventory

Benchmark Data
- For additional Benchmark Data see Used Goods
- "According to America's Research Group, a consumer research firm, about 16–18% of Americans will shop at a thrift store during a given year. For consignment/resale shops, it's about 12–15%. To keep these figures in perspective, consider that during the same time frame, 11.4% of Americans shop in factory outlet malls, 19.6% in apparel stores and 21.3% in major department stores.

  "Resale is a multi-billion dollar a year industry. First Research estimates the resale industry in the U.S. to have annual revenues of approximately $16 billion including revenue from antique stores, which are 13% of their statistics."
  Source: "Industry Statistics & Trends," NARTS, The Association of Resale Professionals

Industry Trend
- "Apparel resale, offline and online, is an $18B industry; expected market size in 2021 is $33B. The resale market by segment consists of: clothing, shoes, accessories—49%; other—16%; books—14%; media—11%; electronics—10%. Millennials (30%) and grandmas (32%) are the most likely age groups to shop secondhand; Gen X 25%; Baby Boomers 26%. High-income shoppers are 35% more likely to try secondhand than low-income shoppers."
  Source: https://cf-assets-tup.thredup.com/resale_report/2017/thredUP_resaleReport2017.pdf

- "Currently, an average of 15 percent of Americans shop at resalt stores in a given year, compared with 11 percent of shoppers at outlet malls, less than 20 percent in apparel stores and just over 21 percent at major department stores. The industry has experienced an average growth of seven percent a year for the past two years, and, according to IBISWorld, is expected to increase at an annualized rate of nearly three percent until the year 2021.

  "Fifty of the largest U.S. companies account for about 30 percent of sales. Despite market competition, the resale industry remains lucrative for its ability to offer both consumers and storeowners a variety of benefits over traditional retailers. These include:
  - ✓ Being eco-friendly
  - ✓ Customizing their look
  - ✓ Saving consumers and owners money
  - ✓ Letting consumers earn money"
  Source: "What does the $17 billion resale industry look like?" February 28, 2017, http://www.winmarkfran-
chises.com/blog/2017/february/what-does-the-17-billion-resale-industry-look-li/

R

- "A majority of women 18–24 say they consider the resale value of an item before they purchase something new. I've seen the financial statements of a number of secondhand clothes stores and they're never very appealing. It's a challenging business for a number of reasons. Store rents are quite high. The quality of products depends on what people give to the store. Garments get overpriced and underpriced all the time since it's up to store personnel to judge their value.

"Now the business is changing. The combination of millennial customers' attitudes and the boom of online shopping are creating a threat to some retail models that isn't going away. There's a report out this morning from thredUP, a fashion resale website, that highlights what's happening in the market.

"Where is this growth coming from? Primarily from the online resale sector. The traditional thrift store market is growing by 8% per year but the online resale market is growing more than four times faster at 35% per year. That's 17 times faster than the broader apparel market overall.

"Why is this happening now? The women who have the highest likelihood of shopping for secondhand clothes are women over 65 and women 18-24. Both groups are motivated by the savings but the younger consumers are almost 2.5 times more likely to be motivated by environmental consciousness when shopping for secondhand clothes. More than half of those women have shopped secondhand in the last 12 months or say they will in the next 12 months. A majority of women 18-24 say they consider the resale value of an item before they purchase something new. The training that retailers have given consumers to shop only when the price is reduced has also helped power the growth in secondhand—94% of women say they rarely buy clothing that's not reduced in price."

Source: "Fashion Retailers Have to Adapt to Deal with Secondhand Clothes Sold Online" by Richard Kestenbaum, https://www.forbes.com/sites/richardkestenbaum/2017/04/11/fashion-retailers-have-to-adapt-to-deal-with-secondhand-clothes-sold-online/#11abe2ac1a7f

Restaurants—An Introduction

Restaurants-QUICK CHECK-2017

Bagels	30% to 35% of annual sales (not as much interest today)
Bars	50% of annual sales (very much in demand)
Bar & Grill (50% liquor)	40% of annual sales (very popular)
Barbecue	30% of annual sales (limited pool of buyers)
Bistros	30% of annual sales (typically chef owned)
Brew Pubs	40% of annual sales (a lot of interest in craft beers)
Billiard Parlors	45% of annual sales (limited pool of buyers)
Cajun	30% of annual sales (not big in New England)
Catering Businesses	30% of annual sales (seller may have to stay for an earnout)
Caribbean	30% of annual sales
Chicken	30% of annual sales
Chinese	30% of annual sales (of reported sales)
Coffee Houses	30% to 40% of annual sales
Continental	30% of annual sales (heavy/rich menus, not in vogue today)
Delis	30% to 40% of annual sales (higher value if only 5/6 days)
Diners	30% to 35% of annual sales (competing with coffee shops)
Fine Dining	30% of annual sales (goodwill lost when chef/owner leaves)
Full-Service/no liquor	30% of annual sales
Full-Service/with liquor	30% to 35% of annual sales
Gourmet Shops	20% of annual sales (+ cost of inventory which can be expensive)
Hamburgers	30% to 40% of annual sales (very popular today)
Ice Cream	30% to 40% of annual sales (higher price in warmer climate)
Irish	40% of annual sales (if higher liquor sales)

Italian .... 30% to 35% of annual sales (popular because of low food costs)
Mexican .... 30% of annual sales (popular concept today)
Night Clubs .... 20% of annual sales 2 x EBITDA (high risk rate lowers value)
Pancake Houses .... 30% of annual sales
Pizza (if delivery) .... 30% of annual sales
Pizza (if no delivery) .... 40% of annual sales
Sandwiches .... 40% of annual sales (not expensive to open)
Seafood ....30% of annual sales (very high food costs)
Sports Bars ....40% to 45% of annual sales (beverage sales over 40%)
Steakhouses .... 30% of annual sales (higher food costs)

Source: Business Brokerage Press and the Boston Restaurant Group, 2017

VALUING A RESTAURANT

- FAIR MARKET VALUE

"The asking price is what the seller wants. The selling price is what the seller receives. Fair Market Value is the highest price the buyer is willing to pay and the lowest price the seller is willing to accept."

There is no formula for valuing a restaurant. Each business needs to be considered on an individual basis. There are, however, certain benchmarks and valuation approaches and methods that enable an experienced appraiser to determine the most probable price for which the business could be sold on the open market.

- INCOME STATEMENT ANALYSIS

The restaurant's operating expenses will be consolidated into four categories to more accurately reflect industry format and to allow for more meaningful comparisons with the industry averages:

SALES	$	%	COMMENTS
Cost of Goods			
Payroll/Benefits			
Other Expenses			
Occupancy Costs			
Income			

- CASH FLOW ANALYSIS

When valuing a company, it is customary to analyze the financial statements and make adjustments, where necessary, to better indicate the true earnings capacity of the business:

ADJUSTMENTS
1.
2.
3. etc.
Total Adjustments

R

- VALUATION ANALYSIS

The following approaches and methods should be considered in the valuation of any restaurant:

Approaches/Methods	Sales/Cash Flow		Multiple	Indicated Value
Multiple of Sale		X		
Multiple of Cash Flow		X		
Sales to Investment Ratio		%		
Appraisal Databases		X		
Industry Rules of Thumb		X		

Source: Charles Perkins, Boston Restaurant Group, Inc.

Pricing Tips

- "In the valuation of a restaurant business, a multiple of from 1 to 3 times adjusted cash flow is considered as being most reflective of a buyer's investment criteria and takes into consideration some of the risk factors that are inherent in the industry: changing consumer tastes, the economy, unemployment, competition, etc.
". . .depending upon the condition of the facility, the terms of the lease, the cost of the renovation and the concept, the business will sell in a range of from 25% to 40% of sales."

Source: Charles Perkins, Boston Restaurant Group, Inc.

- "The restaurant industry is expected to add 1.6 million jobs over the next decade, with employment reaching 16.3 million by 2027. More than 9 in 10 restaurants have fewer than 50 employees. More than 7 in 10 restaurants are single-unit operations. Sales per full-time equivalent employee at eating and drinking places in 2016 were $79,400."

Source: National Restaurant Association's 2017 Restaurant Industry Pocket Factbook

Benchmark Data

- "Summary of Industry standards
Prime Cost
  - ✓ Full-service—65% or less of total sales
  - ✓ Table-service—60% or less of total sales

Food Cost
  - ✓ Generally—28% to 32% of total food sales

Alcoholic Beverage Costs
  - ✓ Liquor—18% to 20% of liquor sales
  - ✓ Bar consumables—4% to 5% of liquor sales
  - ✓ Bottled beer—24% to 28% of bottled beer sales
  - ✓ Draft beer—15% to 18% of draft beer sales
  - ✓ Wine—35% to 45% of wine sales

Nonalcoholic Beverage Costs
  - ✓ Soft drinks (post-mix) 10% to 15% of soft drink sales
  - ✓ Regular coffee—15% to 20% of regular coffee sales
  - ✓ Specialty coffee—12% to 18% of specialty coffee sales

✓ Iced tea—5% to 10% of iced tea sales

Paper Cost

   ✓ Full-service—1% to 2% of total sales

   ✓ Limited-service—3% to 4% of total sales

Payroll Cost

   ✓ Full-service—30% to 35% of total sales

   ✓ Limited-service—25% to 30% of total sales

Management Salaries

   ✓ 10% or less of total sales

Hourly Employee Gross Payroll

   ✓ Full-service—18% to 20% of total sales

   ✓ Limited-service—15% to 18% of total sales

Employee Benefits

   ✓ 5% to 6% of total sales

   ✓ 20% to 23% of gross payroll

Sales per Square Foot

   ✓ Losing Money: Full-service—$150 or less; Limited-service—$200 or less

   ✓ Break-even: Full-service—$150 to $250; Limited-service—$200 to $300

   ✓ Moderate Profit: Full-service—$250 to $350; Limited-service—$300 to $400

   ✓ High Profit: Full-service—More than $350; Limited-service—More than $400

Rent and Occupancy

   ✓ Rent—6% or less of total sales

   ✓ Occupancy—10% or less of total sales"

Source: Information provided by Jim Laube, founder of www.RestaurantOwner.com

- "Profitability Standards

Full-service

   ✓ Under $150/square foot = little chance of generating a profit

   ✓ At $150 to $250/square foot = breakeven up to 5% of sales

   ✓ At $250 to $325/square foot = 5% to 10% of sales

Limited-service

   ✓ Under $200/square foot = little chance of averting an operating loss

   ✓ At $200 to $300/square foot = break even up to 5% of sales

   ✓ At $300 to $400/square foot = 5% to 10% of sales (before income taxes)"

Source: www.bakertilly.com

- "Facts at a Glance 2017

   ✓ $799 billion: Restaurant industry sales.

   ✓ 1 million+: Restaurant locations in the United States.

   ✓ 14.7 million: Restaurant industry employees.

   ✓ 1.6 million: New restaurant jobs created by the year 2027.

   ✓ 10%: Restaurant workforce as part of the overall U.S. workforce.

   ✓ Nine in 10: Restaurant managers who started at entry level.

   ✓ Eight in 10: Restaurant owners who started their industry careers in entry-level positions.

   ✓ Nine in 10: Restaurants with fewer than 50 employees.

   ✓ Seven in 10: Restaurants that are single-unit operations."

Source: www.restaurant.org/News-Research/Research/Facts-at-a-Glance

R

- "Top challenges facing restaurant owners:
  Finding and keeping quality employees.. 48%
  Minimum wage increases or pressures 27%
  Health care costs 10%
  Changing consumer menu expectations 06%
  Securing prime real estate 04%
  Other .... 04%"

Source: NRN 2016 Operator Survey

Industry Trend

- "Mapping the Technology Landscape:
  - ✓ 81 percent of restaurants use a POS or electronic register system.
  - ✓ 68 percent of restaurants offer Wi-Fi for guests.
  - ✓ 37 percent of restaurants offer online ordering.
  - ✓ 32 percent of restaurants accept mobile payment.
  - ✓ 53 percent of restaurant operators say they would implement predictive ordering technology if it were available to them today.
  - ✓ 37 percent of restaurant operators believe the most important area of technology development in the next five years is customer ordering.
  - ✓ 32 percent restaurant operators consider their operations to be lagging when it comes to technology use; 12 percent consider their operations to be leading-edge"

Source: http://www.restaurant.org/News-Research/Research/Mapping-the-Technology-Landscape

- "Top 10 Concept Trends
  1. Hyper-local sourcing (e.g., restaurant gardens, onsite beer brewing, house-made items)
  2. Chef-driven fast-casual concepts
  3. Natural ingredients/clean menus
  4. Environmental sustainability
  5. Locally sourced produce
  6. Locally sourced meat and seafood
  7. Food waste reduction
  8. Meal kits (e.g., pre-measured/prepped raw ingredients for home preparation)
  9. Simplicity/back to basics
  10. Nutrition"

Source: "Chefs Predict 'What's Hot' for Menu Trends in 2017,
National Restaurant Association Surveys American Culinary Federation Chefs, December 8, 2016,
http://www.restaurant.org/Pressroom/Press-Releases/What-s-Hot-2017

- "2017 Industry Sales Projection

Commercial Restaurant Services	$736.3
Eating Places	$551.7
Bars and Taverns	$19.8
Managed Services	$53.6
Lodging Places	$36.1
Retail, Vending, Recreation, Mobile	$75.2
Noncommercial Restaurant Services	**$59.7**
Military Restaurant Services	$2.7"

Source: National Restaurant Association's 2017 Restaurant Industry Pocket Factbook

R

- "Foodservice research firm Technomic has identified five consumer trends that will drive consumer behavior in 2017. A confluence of healthy intentions, technology, community, and economic status will define how restaurants operate and meet consumer expectations this year.
  - ✓ Serving economically polarized consumers
  - ✓ Creating a sense of community
  - ✓ Modern comfort food and experiences
  - ✓ Food as more than just 'fuel'
  - ✓ Drone and droid delivery"

Source: "Top Five Consumer Trends of 2017,"
http://www.nightclub.com/operations/technomic-s-5-key-consumer-trends-2017

- "U.S. restaurant industry traffic will remain stalled in 2017 in much the same manner it did in 2016, reports The NPD Group, a leading global information company. The new year will bring little to no traffic growth for the total U.S. foodservice market. Quick service restaurants (QSRs), however, will increase visits by an estimated 1 percent, faring better than the flat growth achieved in 2016. The modest gain for QSRs will offset the anticipated 2 percent decline for full service restaurants, resulting in no-growth traffic for the industry overall, according to NPD Group's daily tracking of U.S. consumers' use restaurants and other foodservice outlets.

"Trends for 2017 include:
  - ✓ The future is now
  - ✓ Personal choice reigns
  - ✓ Home sweet home
  - ✓ Technology
  - ✓ Delivery
  - ✓ Restaurant loyalty programs"

Source: "Total U.S. Restaurant Industry Visit Growth Will Remain Stalled in 2017," January 3, 2017,
http://www.nightclub.com/the-scene/news/news/total-u-s-restaurant-industry-visit-growth-will-remain-stalled-2017-12421

Resources

- Baker Tilly: http://www.bakertilly.com
- Jim Laube, founder of www.RestaurantOwner.com: http://www.RestaurantOwner.com
- National Restaurant Association: http://www.restaurant.org/
- NRN 2016 Operator Survey: http://www.nrn.com/

Restaurants—Asian

| | NAICS 722511 | |

Rules of Thumb

➢ 30–32% of annual sales plus inventory

Benchmark Data

Statistics (Sushi Restaurants)

Number of Establishments	3,450
Average Profit Margin	7.2%
Revenue per Employee	$77,300
Average Number of Employees	8.9
Average Wages per Employee	$27,044

Products and Services Segmentation

Full-service dining sushi sales 62.0%
Beverage sales 26.0%
Take-out sushi sales 12.0%

Industry Costs

Profit 7.2%
Wages 35.0%
Purchases 24.8%
Depreciation 2.4%
Marketing 4.6%
Rent/Utilities 5.5%
Other 20.5%

Industry Trend

- Asian in general is one of the fastest growing categories in the U.S., though it's very fragmented.

Resources

- IBISWorld, June 2016: http://ibisworld.com

Restaurants—Full Service		
SIC 5812-08	NAICS 722511	

Rules of Thumb

➤ 20–35% of annual sales includes inventory

➤ 1–3 x SDE includes inventory

➤ 2.5–3.5 x EBIT

Pricing Tips

- 39 percent of reported sales +/-
- Three times cash flow, after owner salary
- Good books and records will help increase the price.
- SDE range, 2.0–2.5. Can be lower than 2 x if net is not at least $50K and can be max 3 x for the exceptional business with stable and high cash flow.
- EBITDA range of 3–4 x = ROI of 33 to 25 percent. Strong national franchise brands and multiple locations can go for higher, but not the independents.
- Pricing is function of sales volume, profitability, concept, duration, need for renovation, lease, liquor license, grandfathered C.O. issues, build-out, owned vs. lease assets,
- scalability....
- For nonfranchise:
  - ✓ if CFO is $50–$100K, price is 1.5–2.5 x
  - ✓ if CFO is $100–$250K, price is 2.5–3.5 x
  - ✓ if CFO is $250–$500K, price is 3–4 x
  - ✓ if CFO is $500K–$1M, price is 3.5–4.5 x
- Ranges for the sale of restaurants—and we always refer to Toms West's Business Reference Guide—vary between 1.8 and 2.5 net, depending on the

year. Everything depends on the type of business it is, whether full-service, franchise, fast casual; condition of books and records; location; rent; etc.

- Including real estate, the sale price should go up to 1 x gross sales, but then you have to calculate debt service and make sure there is still a reasonable owner's salary available.
- Pay close attention to food and payroll costs. Food cost should be between 28 and 32 percent for a well-managed restaurant. If cost controls are in place, the multiple leans toward the high end. Quality of product is important along with online reviews.
- Placing a simple multiple on earnings isn't where the art is. The art resides in developing an objective way to derive the multiplier to use on the earnings. I like to break down a restaurant business into four categories, scoring each category from 1 to 6, with 6 being great and 1 being awful.
  The four categories are (1) strength of revenue—is it growing, flat, or declining; (2) strength of cost management—are the cost percentages in line with industry or not; (3) lease, rent, location condition—is the lease fair and transferable; how strong is the location; how is the rent compared to market as well as revenues; (4) condition and building and FF&E—what is the condition of the facility, the parking lot, the equipment? Then I apply that average to a chart I use to determine what multiple to use.
  The following factors will affect the multiple of SDE: franchise or independent; location of restaurant; parking; rent has to be in line; number of seats; any patio seating; equipment condition; any entertainment license; ABC liquor—what type; any governmental agency code or permit violations; if restaurant has a grease trap and what kind.
  Usually the taxes and/or P&Ls don't show the true owner benefit. Reconstructing the financial data can be troublesome. I focus on the cost of goods to determine a likely gross sales figure. Other factors are the lease rate, and equipment and facility condition.
- I perform mostly franchise resales so my numbers will be on the higher end. Independent restaurant concepts will adjust by a factor of 0.5 to each number above, i.e., x SDE 2.5; x EBIT 3.0; x EBITDA 3.5. All numbers quoted are for single-store opportunities, not multistore.
- National franchise restaurants sell for higher prices than mom-and-pop units. Food costs and payroll costs are the two most important factors, followed closely by lease; rent should not exceed 6 percent of sales for most restaurants, 8 percent for some national franchised units.
- 13 times the weekly gross sales
- Occupancy costs/rent as percentage of volume; COGS; food to liquor volume; wages and salaries (owner vs. management)
- Price will be adjusted based on the condition of the equipment and build-out.
- All major costs should be compared to industry indexes. Percentage and ratios should be reduced, as financials exceed those standards.
- Each deal is a stand-alone situation. Many factors determine value. Use above only as a guideline. Use more technical value appraisals to get a true value:
  1. Number of years in business plays a vital part in the value of a business. A minimum of three years is essential to see what the sales pattern is for the concept.
  2. The rent is a very important factor and should not exceed 8 to 10 percent of gross sales.

R

3. A very important factor in the valuation is how verifiable the numbers are. Gross sales must be backed up with a combination of credit card deposits along with cash deposits.

4. Have the seller finance part of the purchase as that will keep him involved in the success of the restaurant.

5. Restaurant experience is a requirement of the buyer. The failure rate for inexperienced operators is too high to take that risk.

6. Keep the operation as simple as possible. The more complicated the concept, the higher the rate of failure.

7. A good business plan is essential to keep everything on track.

8. Consistency is a key element to success.

9. Location, location, location

- EBIT and EBITDA are too shallow of an estimation for restaurant valuation. For recasting, I work with the seller, using a weighted average of the last three years of income and SDE based on tax returns and income statements: 50 percent of the most current year, 33.5 percent of the previous year, and 16.5 percent of the year before that.

- In some instances, I'll annualize the current year, and if it does not deviate much from the previous years' trends, I'll use it in the valuation calculations.

- Discount for restaurants with rent close to, or over, 10 percent of gross sales. Discount if prime costs are more than 33 percent of gross sales.

- Profitable restaurants are being sold between 2 to 3 times SDE. However, distressed or closed restaurants sell as an Asset Sale and sometimes are a great buy. Even some landlords are asking for key money for a closed or second-generation restaurant. Removing an unprofitable seller from the lease liability may be a good deal for the seller... even if the seller does not make money.

- Location and the value of the lease (is it undermarket? Length of time left on the lease)

- The value of a license to sell alcohol varies from town to town. It is critical to find out what the market value of a license is in a subject's particular town or city. For example an all-alcohol license in Boston can cost $375,000–$400,000 in today's marketplace.

- Another pricing tip is to make sure the rent is competitive within the market place. If the rent is high on a dollar-per-square-foot basis or the annual escalations are unsustainable it will have an adverse impact on the selling price of the business.

- Unlike in other industries, many buyers in this sphere care more about top line revenues and significant fixed costs like rents than they do cash flow. This is the case because most experienced operators know the expense ratios a given operation should be able to achieve.

- Generally there are four different valuation methods used to place a value to a restaurant or bar.

  A. PERCENTAGE OF REVENUE: One method is the percentage of revenue method. To derive a value, one merely selects a percentage, say 30%, and multiplies it by the revenue or sales of the business not including sales taxes. For example, if the business had revenues of $1,000,000 and the percentage factor of 30% was used, then the business value is $300,000. This method is used when the financials are not readily available or are not accurate.

  To determine the percentage to use, one takes into account five factors. (1)

the strength of the revenue, (2) the condition of the facility, (3) the lease and location (4) the strength of the management and cost management of the business and finally (5) the type of restaurant business. I generally look at each item and assign a number between 1 and 4, 4 being it's awesome and 1 being it's awful. The closer the average is to 4, the closer the percentage factor is to 40%-45%. The closer to 1, then the percentage will be closer to 20%. This method, in my opinion, has some serious flaws and leads to bad valuations. I don't suggest using it.

B. SELLER'S DISCRETIONARY INCOME (SDI): This method takes some education and skills to accurately apply the concepts, but it is the standard the banks use to give loans to buyers. Simply put, SDI attempts to identify all the seller's perks including salary, payroll taxes, personal auto expenses, medical insurance and any other personal items included in the profit and loss statement that's truly not a business expense. To arrive at a value, one uses the SDI and multiples it by a market multiple. Every region and country has differing multiples and only a well-trained and educated broker can help you determine what you should use. For example, the average multiple across the U.S. is about 2.2 times. That means one takes the SDI and multiples it by 2.2 to determine the value. However, every region has differing multiples. In New Jersey for example, the multiple tends to be significantly higher than say Delaware. Why? I think it is in the variability of the earnings. The higher the variability, the lower the certainty; therefore the lower the multiple. I use the same logic to determine the multiple as I do in the example of Percentage of Revenue method described above, and adjust for regions. A 4 will receive a multiple in the 2.8–3.0 range, while a 1 will receive a 1–1.5 range.

C. CAPITALIZATION OF INCOME: This technique is widely used to value income producing assets such as commercial real estate. The premise is based on what the market expected return on investment is at the time the transaction takes place. The SDI must be calculated first as described above. Then that income is divided by the capitalization rate (Cap rate) to derive the value. For example, if the business' SDI is $100,000 and the determined Cap Rate is 30%, then the math is $100,000/.3 or $333,333.

To determine the cap rate is the challenge and a simple drop of a few percentage points can make a huge difference in price. For example, in the above example, if the Cap Rate were 35% the value would be $285,000. There are several considerations to think about when trying to determine the proper Cap Rate. First, the higher the risk of the investment, the higher the percentage used. In other words, when the income is risky, the expected return the market demands is higher. Restaurants are very risky. So I like to start out at the 35-40% range and go from there. Then again I apply the method described above and assign a number to the business. The closer the number is to 4, the closer my cap rate will be to 25-30%. The closer the number is to 1 the closer my cap rate will be to 50%.

D. REPLACEMENT COST METHOD: Finally, the replacement cost method assumes a buyer pays the seller a large premium over the income value and annual gross revenue techniques in order to benefit from the existing investment in the restaurant facility, the lease and the location of the restaurant. In other words, a buyer will pay for the right to avoid spending hundreds of thousands and even possibly a million+ dollars to avoid all the city regulations, delays and headaches of building a new restaurant. How much a buyer pays depends on the buyer's need. Some buyers will pay more for

R

the same space because they may see the value in a lease or location while others may see that they have too much improvements to make to convert to their existing concept.

- Rent and lease terms are an important part of the equation. Lease costs need to stay under 9% annually. Longevity can boost value. Sales numbers need to be verified against bank deposits along with credit card statements. Cash that can not be verified will not justify an add back for valuation purposes. A lot of times small Mom & Pop type restaurants have family members working there. If that is the case a negative add-back needs to be done to show cost of replacing that person or persons. Seller financing will help increase the value of the restaurant.

- Equipment age and maintenance important. Lease with market rent and good terms very important.

- Most restaurants with liquor sell for 70% multiple. Without liquor the ratio drops to 35-40% of sales. Light menu a big plus. Home cooking hard to duplicate for a buyer.

- Does the owner just manage the business or is he the chef or cook? Business is more valuable if owner just manages the business.

- Ease of operation—five-day operation worth more than a seven-day. Always look at food to bar sales as to what percent.

- Lease should be no more than six to eight percent of sales. Food cost and payroll costs are the key items to control after lease costs.

- Much depends on the size of the revenues and earnings; the multiples increase above $500k in sales. Gross profit should be 70% or better.

- We never use gross sales to determine a price. Only a multiple of SDE is used. For businesses that rent their space, the average is 2 X SDE with 1.7–1.8 X selling faster than 2 X. For businesses that own their real estate, the formula becomes 1.4 X SDE plus real estate—either appraised value or agreed.

- The main factor that drives pricing from a sales perspective is if the restaurant has liquor or is just food. From an EBITDA or SDE provable figures drive the multiple as well as the condition of the equipment and decor in addition to the lease terms. The type of food served also will be a factor; the more ethnic, the more difficult to sell.

- Pricing based on cash flow can range from 2.0 to approx. 2.5 depending on several factors: lease terms, condition of FF&E, stability and years established, hours of operation, complexity of operations. Location is always a factor but is generally already reflected in the financials. Unprofitable restaurants are marketable based on location, infrastructure in place, ABC Licensing, quality of FF&E, and lease terms.

- Including real estate, the price can be up to gross sales and up to 35–40% in leased space, but debt service should always be calculated to see if it makes sense for a buyer. This is going down as restaurants have become less desirable in recent years. The higher end restaurants are the toughest to sell, as the down payment needed is greater.

- Proper use of the SDE formula is the most accurate way of valuing an independent restaurant with sales under $3 million per year.

- The multiples increase as revenue and earnings increase due to economies of scale. Cost of goods should be at or below 30%. Must look for cash that is unaccounted for and non-operating assets and expenses.

- Twice the probable yearly seller's profit

- 100% of gross sales if the real estate is included and 30% if in leased space.

- Rent ratio over 10% lowers the SDE, EBIT, EBITDA and the percent of annual sales. The percent of annual sales is reduced point for point on every point rent ratio above 10%.

- Percentage of annual gross needs to be supported by SDE, so higher prices get higher percentage of sales and lower percentages may have no SDE and may be just the sale of the tangible and intangible assets. Lots of other factors to consider including comps for like businesses.
- Compare COG to industry standards. Rent factor vs. sales. Extraneous cost to generate sales, e.g., music, price deals, advertising, hours of operation.
- Restaurants with small profits are worth more as an asset sale than based on sales or net cash flow. The cost of opening a new restaurant makes over 50% of the restaurants for sale only worth what the buyer feels he would have to spend to open a new one. The cost of permits and fees has driven the cost of new restaurants through the roof, and buyers should always consider taking over an existing one even if not profitable.

Benchmark Data

Statistics (Chain Restaurants)

Number of Establishments	32,924
Average Profit Margin	4.9%
Revenue per Employee	$59,900
Average Number of Employees	58.0
Average Wages per Employee	$19,356

Products and Services Segmentation

American food	56.6%
Breakfast foods	17.0%
Italian-American food	9.3%
Seafood	5.8%
Other food	5.7%
Specialty burgers	3.8%
Asian cuisine	1.8%

Industry Costs

Profit	4.9%
Wages	32.3%
Purchases	32.1%
Depreciation	2.2%
Marketing	2.2%
Rent & Utilities	12.9%
Other	13.4%

Market Share

DineEquity Inc.	7.3%
Darden Restaurants Inc.	6.7%

Statistics (Single Location Full-Service Restaurants)

Number of Establishments	267,141
Average Profit Margin	4.9%
Revenue per Employee	$52,600
Average Number of Employees	13.6
Average Wages per Employee	$18,231

R

Products and Services Segmentation

Asian restaurants	25.5%
American restaurants	20.2%
European restaurants	14.5%
Other	13.7%
Mexican restaurants	12.9%
Pizza restaurants	6.4%
Seafood restaurants	4.0%
Steakhouses	2.8%

Industry Costs

Profit	4.9%
Wages	34.7%
Purchases	38.9%
Depreciation	2.2%
Marketing	2.2%
Rent & Utilities	11.9%
Other	5.2%

Statistics (Premium Steak Restaurants)

Number of Establishments	2,536
Average Profit Margin	6.6%
Revenue per Employee	$72,200
Average Number of Employees	45.8
Average Wages per Employee	$21,050

Products and Services Segmentation

Classic steak restaurants	35.0%
Steak and seafood restaurants	32.6%
Other premium steak restaurants	22.0%
Premium Brazilian steak restaurants	10.4%

Industry Costs

Profit	6.6%
Wages	29.2%
Purchases	36.1%
Depreciation	2.2%
Marketing	2.7%
Rent & Utilities	8.3%
Other	14.9%

Market Share

Ruth's Hospitality Group, Inc.	9.1%
Darden Restaurants Inc.	5.5%

- Sales per square foot: full service $500; fast food $700
- Ratio of sales to the investment (what it costs to open for the build-out and equipment): sales 2.5 times to investment 1.0
- Most important factor in the restaurant business is the lease expense. Parking is very important.
- Food costs, 28 to 40 percent depending on concept; rent including NNN, 6 to10 percent; direct labor (excluding owner), 15 to 30 percent depending on

concept; Seller's Discretionary Income, 10 percent

- Benchmarks fluctuate per segment, such as $52,600 for chain restaurants to $100,700 per employee for a premium steakhouse. Per-square-foot and rent numbers were always 10 percent as an occupancy with a big turn in reducing that number dramatically, prior to executing a lease. Food cost percentage can fluctuate from the high twenties to the high thirties depending on menu.
- Food costs should be around 30 percent; liquor, 15 to 20 percent.
- The restaurant should try to achieve 6 percent rent, meaning if the rent is $5,000 a month, the revenues need to be $83,000 a month to earn a fair profit.
- Owner has to control the food cost and make sure the employees don't waste a lot of food.
- Food costs can only be stated as a single number but vary by cuisine and service. For example, BBQ restaurants or other high-protein concepts can be much higher in food costs, while taco shops will be much lower.
- Food costs vary depending on the type of restaurant. Dinner house will be closer to 35 to 40 percent; most fast food units run between 28 and 33 percent. Sometimes paper goods are counted separately; they often run about 3 percent of sales. Most restaurants will not make it if the lease costs are over 6 percent of sales.
- Have over 200 comparable transactions and can correlate based on volume, SDE, EBIT, EBITDA, and other complied data.
- Very hard to keep the food cost down; price of goods going up but tough to raise profits.
- The most important key performance indicators are rent (10 percent), food cost (33 percent), and labor cost (27 percent).
- Sales per square foot: $425.00
- The more alcohol in the sales mix, the greater the profitability should be; requires inventory controls.
- Too often the RE has gotten too valuable for the sales level, thus the occupancy cost to the next buyer could go higher than industry averages, thus the seller is going to have to carry back more of the deal to make it work.

Expenses (% of Annual Sales)

Cost of Goods	25% to 35%
Occupancy Costs	06% to 12%
Payroll/Labor Costs	25% to 35%
Profit (pretax)	08% to 20%

Questions

- How long have you been in business? When it was established? Did you start it? How much is gross revenue? How much is your food cost? Any secret recipe? Any key employees and, if chef, will stay after the sell? Equipment conditions? Any code violations? Grease trap—what kind and the location?
- Financial books and records: tax returns, POS records; use a third-party broker or consultant to analyze for hidden costs.
- What can I do to build business?
- What are the strengths and weaknesses of the business?
- Will any seller financing be provided?
- Ask about landlord and facility issues; any deferred maintenance or repairs

needed? Understand responsibilities of landlord and tenant based on the lease. Ask about key employees; health department open items; ABC restrictions; future opportunities; local competitive environment; reason for sale, of course. Understand owner's labor and also whether family members are working, on/off payroll. Are employees all paid on payroll 100 percent?

- Why are you selling? Will you offer support after closing? Will staff stay? Will you sign a noncompete and, of course, are books and records verifiable? Due diligence of books and record and inspection of equipment and landlord negotiations must be to the full satisfaction of buyer.
- Is there any new competition coming to the area? Which employees would you suggest I keep?
- Are there any sources of income that do not show on the books? If so, can it be proven?
- What do you do with the cash? Why are you selling? Who works at the restaurant? Need tax returns and financial statements. What's the biggest challenge you've had in this business? How long have the key employees been around?
- I like to ask buyers if they have any experience and how much cash they have to invest.
- The basics: Why are you selling? What would you change? Where is the opportunity you haven't capitalized on? What is the single most successful marketing technique you've used?
- How many hours a week have they worked in the restaurant? How difficult is it to find qualified restaurant employees, i.e., employees with restaurant experience?
- Why are you selling the business? How many years left on the lease? Fixed costs? Variable costs?
- How long have employees worked there? What is the food cost? Length and terms of the lease. Does the owner manage the business or perform a specific task, such as cooking?
- What would you do to improve the business if you were to stay here for the next 10 years? Sellers should be prepared to answer that question in today's market.
- How much is it making? Reason for selling, seasonal trends, food cost, employees' tenure, social media items, list of vendors. Do any family members work in the restaurant? Are you willing to give me all your recipes? Will you sign a noncompete? Are all licenses transferable? Are there any unresolved health department issues? Is the liquor license transferable? Is the lease transferable? Is anything leased?
- If you could have done anything differently, what would it have been? What do you wish you knew when you opened? What is your relationship with your neighbors? What is the smartest thing you did as a restaurant operator?
- 1. Tell me about your typical bad day. 2. How much money do you set aside for your worst month? 3. Why are none of the employees here interested in buying this business? 4. What is your highest cost menu item and why do you keep it on the menu? 5. Who is your toughest competition? 6. How many customers are on your mailing list? 7. How do you determine who your vendors should be? 8. How do you determine where to spend marketing dollars?
- Do your financials reflect cash and credit card sales? Is the business free and clear of any liens or encumbrances? Have you had employee relations issues?

- Make sure to understand the labor picture in detail, including how people are being paid. Ask about any discounting programs that have been used (Groupon for example). These can distort both sales and expenses and have liabilities that must be considered. Gift cards and Inventory can also be sticky issues with a sale. Knowing the reason for selling and whether it makes sense is a good idea for any business. Ask if recipes and menus are documented and included.
- How much time a week has the seller spent in the business-the buyer will need to know what adjustments need to be made for management if the seller has been very hands on and the buyer does not plan to be hands on.
- Why are you selling? Why did you pick this type of food and why this location? Is your equipment-including hoods, grease traps, septic system-in sound working condition and in compliance with all city/county codes and regulations? Can the new owner get a certificate of occupancy and or a liquor permit for this type of business in this exact location?
- How many employees; do you perform maintenance on equipment.
- Verify funds or credit, secure loan with buyers outside interest.
- How many hours owner works, if it's more than 40 to 45; I do adjust for employees.
- Staff loyal? Menu same for how long? Personal receipt? Age of kitchen equipment? Delivery?
- Learn about the landlord. Understand the cost of goods. Know whether there are promos and discounts being used to generate revenue and what may be outstanding. Know who the key employees are in the kitchen and whether any are being paid outside of normal channels. Look into past health department reports and ABC conditions.
- 1.) Is the seller in good standing with the state Department of Revenue (DOR) and Department of Unemployment Assistance (DUA)? Failure to comply can result in delay of transfer and delay in transfer of liquor license. 2.) How old/ how many tons are the heating/cooling units. I advise purchasers to inspect these, as this can be a large unforeseen cost.
- How many hours have you been working? Are all sales recorded? Are there any employees being paid in cash? Do you know of any new competition coming to the area?
- How old is the air conditioning unit(s)? Inspect the A/C thoroughly. This is commonly overlooked by inexperienced buyers and can be a large unforeseen expense. Read your lease thoroughly and hire an attorney to review/negotiate it. Make sure to look at the gross sales to rent ratio.
- Why did you buy or start this business and what do you think of it now?
- How many hours the owner works, food and beverage costs and payroll costs. How long is the lease-is there percentage rent, what are the escalations in the lease?
- Reason for selling, history of the business, what makes it special compared to competitors, any lawsuits pending, three years' P&Ls and tax returns, list of FF&E, personnel info (duties, tenure, pay, hrs. worked weekly, any benefits), hours worked by owner, competitors' names and estimated market shares, areas for growth of the business, catering done, monthly sales for past 3 years, published newspaper or magazine articles, names of professional advisers, zoning-license or EPA issues, inventory value, business hours, etc.
- How much are liabilities?

R

- What does the future look like for the location? Zoning, competition, lease rate, etc.
- Percentage of cash vs. credit. Is there reliance on a key chef?
- Which equipment is leased and which is paid, and the condition of the equipment. Is there a grease trap? What kind and what size? Any key employee, especially the cook, and whether he or she wants to stay.
- Will the owner offer financing, training, non-compete (for how many miles); is the lease assignable; is all equipment approved by the NSF (many states do not allow domestic appliances in a commercial location); are trade name, Website, recipes and training manuals included in the deal?
- It is useful to know if the owner has experimented with different hours (breakfast, lunch, dinner, weekend brunch, late night entertainment). Of course the reason for sale is good to know. Any expected modifications from health dept. or franchisor? Any liquor license violations or restrictions?
- Ask about cash payroll. Many sellers pay all or part of their payroll in cash. Check if the POS computer is connected to the corporate headquarters or franchise. How long the seller has owned the business might be a good indication that after they bought it they decided that they made a mistake and want out.
- Work histories of staff? Staffing resources? What vendors should I not deal with and why? Suggestions for growth or expansion?
- Do they have good and current tax returns; are the federal, state and payroll taxes current; and does the family have non-essential employees on the payroll? Are sales taxes and gratuities being included in the sales? Some accountants will permit the operator to do that, then remove them as an expense.
- What is your strongest area in your business? What part of your business needs the most improvement?

Industry Trend

- "'The only part of casual dining that's growing right now is the off-premise side,' said Bonnie Riggs, foodservice industry analyst for NPI. 61% of all 2016 restaurant visits were for to-go orders; $15.16 was the average on-premise check, and $12.11 was the average carryout order."

  Source: "Casual dining finds a ray of light: Takeout" by Jonathan Maze, National Restaurant News, May 29, 2017

- Due to labor costs, in our area at least (CA), the trend is moving toward quick and limited service versus full service.
- Continued growth, especially in North Texas (Dallas–Fort Worth) market
- The trend will always be strong within a core business market or with high-income demographics. Daytime traffic will drive more fast-casual and the higher-priced restaurants, whereas lunch will be slower in the suburbs missing an office market. I believe we are on an upward trend.
- This industry has gotten tougher and likely will continue with minimum wage increases, etc.
- Should see an increase in franchises due to the baby boomer cycle.
- Landlords are squeezing tenants; minimum wages are squeezing them too. Price increases will happen but be rolled out slowly.
- Since a lot of restaurants closed or have been purchased or the concept replaced in the last decade, if the owner is a restaurateur, the trend will be up

for them; however, the rise in employee wages will reduce their profit if they can't raise the prices.

- This industry is good; there is a good amount of sellers who want to sell and buyers who want to buy.
- Continued sluggish growth for the industry (+3 percent or less) with pressure on costs, but smart operators and concepts are making plenty of money.
- I am concerned with the number of fast casual restaurants in the marketplace, and I see some thinning of the herd occurring as competition continues to heat up.
- As the economy improves, i.e., discretionary earnings improve, restaurants tend to do better.
- Many more owner-operators and national companies will take over this field. Absentee owners will fade out.
- Very competitive, particularly in fast casual, with overall sales volumes in decline.
- Business should hold steady.
- Food costs will rise slightly if we see an improving economy. Beef and seafood will rise regardless because of the payroll costs at the manufacturing level and the rising cost of raw material.
- Occupancy cost will also see a sharp rise because of the demand by chain owner-operators for triple-A sites. Smart business owners are looking at secondary sites and doing something unique instead of trying to do it better. If you have good food and service and a unique atmosphere or product, they will find you!
- I see diminishing profits in the next five years due to governmental payroll increases and increasing food costs.
- I see the trend continuing the same as it has been. Trend is to more quick-service restaurants as it is easier to run because of the lower employee count. The industry is improving; however, it is very highly competitive.
- In fine dining, there is a movement away from haute cuisine toward a nutrition-based menu. Healthful food enjoys an elevated status.
- Lots of new restaurants are appearing with a different kind of concept. QSR, quick service restaurants, are becoming more popular since there is no waiter service, and there is no tip, which is 15% to 20% in some restaurants.
- Good, particularly in more affluent areas like SF Bay area. The more money people make, they are less inclined to eat at home. This is true for people under 50 working in our Silicon Valley.
- Farm-to-table demands from consumers are high, but tourists, travelers and budget-conscious consumers like the convenience and familiarity of chain restaurants, so both will be contenders. Greatest challenge will be employee costs and retention. The large focus should be on millennials who eat out often and are a growing population.
- Though a high-risk opportunity, restaurant business will continue to be a desirable form of investment.
- Due to increased costs, labor in particular, I think the true mom & pops may continue to thrive if they don't require paid staff for key positions. The large multi-unit chains and franchisees may continue to grow but will operate on very thin margins. I am concerned about those who own 2-5 restaurants, especially in the full-service category. These may find it challenging, as minimum wage in our area is increasing to $15 per hour and waitstaff are paid minimum wage

R

with no offset for tips. This also creates disparity between what the servers earn as compared to kitchen staff. I think there will always be an active market for restaurants though, because people will continue to eat out.

- Increased move to automation, lower human labor, smarter equipment including iPad style ordering at the table. This can help improve business efficiency and standard daily costs.
- Strong growth, higher rent and stiff competition for prime real estate.
- Authentic restaurant in right location will do great, since people are looking for original and unique types of restaurants. People are tired of seeing the same franchise restaurant and will want something different. Of course the taste and the service is very critical, therefore, hiring a great chef is a must.
- High-end steakhouses will continue to feel the pressure as more restaurants enter the market and the restaurant industry continues to become more promotionally driven.
- Expect things to remain very competitive-tough to compete against national chains, but it can be done if management is exceptional.
- Restaurants and bars will continue to be a sought-after type of business. Turnovers will remain high. As rent will continue to rise, restaurant owners will be more creative in finding less popular locations and turn to social media for marketing and to promote their locations.
- The demand for restaurants in general seems stable and strong, but it may become more difficult for the independently owned single operators to maintain market share when dealing with costs and regulatory environment including minimum wage increases. California is more burdensome than many other states in this regard and some franchises and chain restaurants have avoided expansion to the area. People are more health conscious and particular with their food in general and there is an opportunity to cater to this market if the restaurant can provide a good value for the product. Bars and clubs including microbreweries and craft cocktail houses are doing well.

Expert Comments

Restaurant revenues in Florida are climbing and expect to increase 6.2 percent this year. Availability of gas and a strong economy will boost the industry this year.

Good opportunity for someone who is organized, is willing to work hard, and who likes responsibility

Seller: Keep good books and records. Buyer: Look for a business with good books and records.

Experienced food players may not look at the numbers but will look at the conditions, equipment (hood and grease trap, walk-in cooler-freezer), Internet reviews, violations, location.

While someone is buying a restaurant, someone else is selling a restaurant. Find out the real reason and confirm it. Determine if it still makes sense to purchase or if simply buying someone else's problem.

Buyers—look for something reasonably priced that has some possibility for growth and improvement. If less experienced, keep it smaller or simple, or buy one with very solid and consistent cash flow and sales.

Sellers—be able to document the add-backs. The revenue is fairly easy to verify these days due to the POS and merchant services (credit/debit), although catering is often not documented and should be accounted for. Don't slack off on marketing and general maintenance during the sale process.

Profit margins are thin in some market areas due to high labor costs and rents. It is relatively expensive to duplicate on a new build-out basis, so there is a barrier to entry, but it is fairly easy for competitors to replicate a good concept. On the positive, dining out in general continues to grow in terms of customer base, and existing restaurants can be sold for asset value in most cases, whether profitable or not.

Seller:

1) Maintain good books/records, especially two years before sale.

2) Report all income, especially two years before sale.

Buyer:

1) Do not buy if you don't have food service experience.

2) Must have adequate working capital.

3) Hold back 10 percent of purchase price for 30 to 90 days to ensure all bills are paid.

4) Is the concept scalable?

Have a strong cushion and do extensive due diligence before buying.

The market in Georgia currently is incredible. We have an explosion of growth whereas other parts of the country do not. We are selling many restaurants, and when the economy was down a few years ago, we sold less with demand to leave vacant space higher.

Buying: Plan to work it and it will pay off well. Selling: You need to be flexible with price and terms/financing.

Make sure you understand the commitment and be prepared to monitor all operations closely.

Location matters.

Be thorough in the analysis. There are a lot of thieves and liars in this business.

The buyer should have a lot of restaurant experience; otherwise the chance of failing will be very high. The buyer has to be ready to work very hard and long hours, and the seller has to be understandable and help the buyer during transfer of ownership; the seller has to provide high quality training after closing of escrow, and introduce good customers to new owner.

Very difficult and time consuming to start up a full serve restaurant with all the city or county and health department requirements.

Restaurants are facing increasing pressure from saturation of concepts, especially fast casual.

Buy on verified past performance. Good books and records are not a myth in this industry. They are real.

R

The fast-casual segment in particular, after years of growth, is seeing signs of oversaturation, and for that reason, we are seeing many more units hit the market and more competition for operators. There is also a limited amount of vacant restaurant space on the market.

A buyer should get some hands-on training in order to be successful. A seller should not carry financing for a sale to someone without restaurant experience. Be very careful with any claims of nonreported cash.

Location is critical. Fast food units require high visibility and easy access; generally require a drive-thru. Dinner houses are more of a destination place; high visibility is not as critical.

Make sure you can prove all of your numbers so the transition is much easier for all sides and there are no surprises.

Buyer should watch to see if the employees are good quality. Seller should expect to have to do some seller financing.

Look closely at the numbers; they say a lot. Learn how to interpret them or hire someone that can.

All these factors are important but the amount of competition. I always look at the industry trends against the individual business performance, usually an indication of a poor operator or location. Then start looking deeper.

Take your time with investigation. Often, it's wise to hire an expert to review the numbers.

Verify all the numbers and make sure you are comfortable running the type of concept you are buying.

The large chains are hurting the small independent restaurants. They build expensive beautiful stores, offer the employees benefits, and have large advertising budgets; and the general public eats there because they are familiar with the names.

Sellers: Your CPA's valuation of the business is almost always three to four times higher than what the restaurant will sell for in the open market. Assets are worth the revenue they generate. Do not expect to recoup opening costs in the sale of a restaurant; either stay in business long enough to depreciate the costs, or sell it for its worth. Buyers: Buying an existing business and changing the concept is much less expensive than building out a restaurant from a vanilla shell.

Labor costs, occupancy costs, and food costs are high and rising in California. It is rare that a business operates with prime costs below 30 percent of annual sales. The farm-to-table and organic trends have become the norm in northern California, and the market demand has increased greatly.

Buying a restaurant may take a couple of months, so it is very important to prepare the buyer or the seller for this event. It is not an easy task.

The buyer should have experience and reserves before even thinking of owning a restaurant. It is a real job that requires long hours and lots of energy. The most important items on the list are the lease and the landlord's approval. If the buyer does not have extensive restaurant experience, a sandwich/sub shop or a smoothie or juice bar will be recommended. A long lease with options is highly desirable. The ideal lease will be a percentage over the gross (8% to 12%).

Experienced restaurant owners are looking for 2nd generation restaurants either closed or in distress. The value, even if it is closed, is immense. Most likely there is a hood and grease trap fire suppression system, and all the impact fees have been paid. It may take up to a year or more to open a restaurant from zero. Buying a second generation one will save you time and money.

Restaurants are a very risky business, and lots of competition is always present. 70% to 80% of restaurants close the doors within 5 years or less.

Buy when you have plenty of money to carry you for 6 months. Sell when you're making money! Never wait until you must sell!

SDE is and should be a key factor in any analysis of this business.

BUYING: Use a seasoned consultant and broker in the restaurant industry who knows how to interpret the seller's financials and look for hidden problems. SELLING: Again, use a seasoned consultant and business broker who can properly vet your potential buyers for a match that will succeed. Closing a sale is not enough-you want to see a buyer candidate who has the skills and resources to continue to be successful in this very challenging business.

For a small- to moderate-sized operation, ease of replication is very high. Location is often key.

With all of the TV shows and glamorization around restaurants, we see more people diving in from other backgrounds.

Restaurants have high turnover rates.

If the person has a family, it is important to have their support due to the long hours involved. I try to give sellers advice on how to categorize their expenses and make sure they can validate any addbacks. Buyers don't accept the creative adjustments to cost of goods these days. Sales must be documented, including catering which is often outside of the POS system. Sellers should continue with maintenance of both the front of the house and kitchen. Make sure to always ask for another option on the lease whenever exercising an option to extend. It is not a good idea to be on a month-to-month basis when trying to sell.

In my market area, consumers continue to dine out so the customer base is strong, but expenses continue to increase so the margins are thin. There is a trend toward more limited service versus full-service, due to the cost of labor.

Restaurants have become a bit of a commodity. The plus side of this is there is a large and fluid market. The negative is that barriers to entry are low and competition high.

Be smart and keep the owner involved if you are the buyer and the seller finances the sale.

The industry is experiencing shrinking profitability and shrinking disposable income per household. All making the risk greater for start up restaurants. Startups are needed to find the best locations and fair rent. Today, because the leasing market is recovering, the search for the ideal location and rent is becoming increasingly difficult but more important. 'Better to buy a printing press already printing money rather than building a new one and hoping it works.' This is my philosophy when speaking with a client who wants to open a new restaurant business.

The restaurant/food service industry can be volatile and needs hard work. If a restaurant has systems and procedures in place, it can be very valuable and worth a lot.

Food industry is highly competitive and easily duplicated in some cases. Real estate has become more critical in recent years.

The industry can change quickly depending on many factors. Consumer spending is the key economic factor to consider---when the economy slumps, restaurants have a tougher time. Facilities need periodic remodeling and upgrades in order to remain competitive. The minimum wage battle is of great concern to restaurants.

Buyer should consider the minimum wage increase for the next 5 years and factor that into the labor expenses. Sales should be in the financial statement; today's buyers are very careful, and don't want to pay for just guessing. If the seller wants top dollar, then the seller has to show the top books. Gone are those days of buying a restaurant with observation only, with no books and records. If the restaurant doesn't have good books, then I value it based on sale of assets in place.

With liquor, hard to duplicate. Without liquor, much easier to open a restaurant.

It's all about leasing and location in pricing and marketing.

With the overreach of government regulation and the shrinking profit margins, success becomes a daunting task that is only attained with hard work, a competent staff, a good location, and hands-on management.

A significant portion of the restaurant/bar business is from cash sales. A buyer should verify that sales reported by the owner are accurate.

The restaurant business is a grueling one, and most sales are motivated by burnout of the owner after some period of years. Restaurants serving three meals, 7 days a week are most difficult to sell as they are burnout-prone operations. Primary traits of successful operators are drive, ability to multitask, human relations skills, ability to analyze a business and stay on top of costs. Everyone wants a restaurant because they think it is a dinner party every evening and don't realize the commitment a restaurant takes.

Costs of food and labor result in small profit margin. Very competitive, but industry overall has demand from consumers. Cost of entry can be very high relative to return on investment if doing a new build-out. Recommend second generation facility for this reason. Usually cost effective to buy an existing restaurant even if paying some goodwill and then changing the concept.

Sellers need to understand that if they are the ones who made the initial capital investment, they may not recoup their investment. I try to make them understand that when they opened it was based on returning the investment in the form of operating profits over the course of ownership (years). Market value based on cash flow may not justify a price that would equal the high cost of investment. Normally the reason for sale is something other than, or in addition to, simply making money from the sale. Buyers should ask the typical questions about reason for sale and what the seller would do if he or she were to stay longer. The landlord relationship should be discussed. Competitive changes in the area should be researched.

There is typically a very large capital investment to open a restaurant in compliance with building and health codes. Restaurants can usually be sold, whether profitable or not, mainly because of the high cost of build-out. Asset sales for conversion are common unless the restaurant is not viable, usually due to lease or location. Industry trend-there will always be a need for restaurants as people dine out for convenience or pleasure, but cost of goods, cost of labor, and regulatory environment continue to squeeze the profit margin which makes the business challenging and risky. Ease of replication-in relation to some other businesses I would say it is easy to create and open with the exception of the high cost of initial build-out and remodeling. It is not too difficult to open especially if the infrastructure is already in place, but it can be difficult to make a profit. Operational experience is important although many enter the business without the recommended experience, which then justifies the opinion that this is a high-risk category.

Experience is not required but preferred. Successful owners can run all aspects of their operation (including the kitchen); for restaurants performing $1MM or under this is a must, whereas larger operations (>$1MM) can allocate more payroll for specialists.

Make sure you have a busy location with a lease no more than 10% of the gross sales.

The buyer should first sit down with an expert and let the expert explain to them the pluses and minuses of buying a restaurant. Too many buyers function strictly on an emotional level. With the help of someone who knows that type of business, ask for actual food and beverage purchases. Get a list of the suppliers and call them to verify.

Normalize owner and/or manager salaries. Question how many hours the owner is working. Be very careful with lease options that are at market rent. If it is a triple net lease, check and see if the building is for sale. As an example; the current owner paid $800K 10 years ago. He wants to sell as an investment property. New landlord pays $1,600,000. Taxes that the tenant must pay just went from $15,000 annual to $30,000 or more. Nothing the buyer of the business can do but he should be prepared that it may happen in strong markets.

I will advise the buyer to make sure that he watches the activity during the busy times, to be ready to spend enough time in the business in order to manage it correctly, that this type of business needs a full time owner operator to be successful and grow the business, and to make sure that he hires a due diligence expert that is familiar with restaurants. I will advise the seller to price the business in a realistic way since most of the businesses on the market for sale are restaurants. I will show the seller sold comps in his area, and also tell him to keep all his records in order to prove the numbers during due diligence.

If the restaurant is leased, make sure that the lease is assumable and that renewal options exist so that similar rent going forward can be obtained.

Develop a good business plan and make your changes slowly. Don't spend all your money on leasehold improvements! Buy the real estate if you can.

The rental rate per the lease agreement is very important. Watch out for percentage rent clauses as well. A below-market lease with years to go is a big benefit. A short lease or above-market rent is a problem.

Barrier to entry can be restricted by number of pouring licenses in town or municipality.

Seller Financing

- Seller financing is common; however, buyers should consider that the seasoned business with financials which are healthy enough to secure third-party funding are probably worth the extra money.
- All cash, or seller financing, is more common than SBA financing. Many of the businesses cannot support an SBA loan due to the tax returns, plus many lenders avoid the industry. Seller financing terms might be in the range of 30 to 50 percent max financing, usually over two to five years, with amortization depending on what the business can afford in terms of cash flow. The interest rate is 5 to 7 percent or sometimes zero if less than two years.
- Seller financing is very common, especially if
  1) seller is unable to prove books/records,
  2) actual sales do not match sales tax reports or POS or income tax returns.
- Price less than $500,000: Typical financing is 1/3 cash down + 2/3 seller financing for five years.
- We are seeing more seller-financed deals unless a seller has fantastic books and records that show annual growth.
- Seller financing is common with at least 25 percent down.
- Usually a combination of outside and seller financing. Seller usually holds around 10 percent.
- Cash or some seller financing. I usually suggest at least 60 percent cash paid at the purchase.
- We see more than 70 percent of our deals with financing at this time; however, that was not always the case.
- 50 percent of deals owner financed and 50 percent of deals using SBA or conventional/equity financing.
- Typically seller financing at 6 percent interest over 60 months.
- Generally see seller financing for all or partial financing. Usually a 10- to 15-year payout. Recently all kinds of deals are being made such as no money down, low interest rate such as 4 percent. Sellers are doing anything to make a deal.
- Unless there is real estate included, most restaurants will have seller financing. Typically they will finance for three to five years at about 6 to 8 percent. Usually the seller will finance from 20 to 40 percent of the sales price.
- Of the buyers that receive funding, 70 percent are seller carry-backs and 30 percent are SBA lenders. We work very closely with local SBA lenders and often host office Q&A meetings with SBA reps to stay current with requirements

and terms and to cultivate relationships with them.

- For listings with strong cash flow, we will secure SBA approval prior to posting the advertising.
- 1. All cash 2. Cash down of 30% to 50% and owner carries rest as a loan 3. SBA financing with less than 10% of transactions 4. Don't waste your time with the big banks!
- For franchises bank financing, independents primarily cash or owner financing.
- Mom and pop units are difficult to finance; sellers will likely have to carry financing. National franchise affiliates can be financed if the seller reported all of the revenue and has good records.
- Old-line restaurants that are paid for tend to have sellers willing to finance. 3rd party lenders are very conservative in their lending practices.
- Owner finance ten years with a balloon after three years.
- Seeing many cash transactions on entry level businesses.

Resources

- Today's Restaurant News: http://www.trnusa.com
- Ohio Restaurant Association: http://www.ohiorestaurant.org
- Restaurant Hospitality: http://www.restaurant-hospitality.com
- Restaurant Business Magazine: http://www.restaurantbusinessonline.com/
- Muradian Business Opportunities: http://muradianbusiness.com
- Restaurant Finance Monitor: http://www.restfinance.com
- ServSafe: http://www.servsafe.com
- Nation's Restaurant News: http://www.nrn.com
- Massachusetts Restaurant Association (MRA): http://www.themassrest.org/
- National Restaurant Association: http://www.restaurant.org
- Food Service Technology Center: http://www.fishnick.com/
- Golden Gate Restaurant Association: http://ggra.org/
- RestaurantOwner.com: https://www.restaurantowner.com/
- IBISWorld, February 2017: http://ibisworld.com
- IBISWorld, August 2017: http://ibisworld.com
- Restaurant Startup and Growth: http://www.rsgmag.com
- We Sell Restaurants: http://www.wesellrestaurants.com

Restaurants—Limited Service		
SIC 5812-08	NAICS 722513	Number of Businesses/Units 306,858

Rules of Thumb

➢ 30–40% of annual sales for independents; 45–60% for many franchises—plus inventory

➢ 1.5–2.5 x SDE plus inventory

➢ 2–3 x EBIT

➢ 2.5–3.5 x EBITDA

➢ For a rule of thumb for many limited-service franchises see Franchised Food Businesses, Franchises, and the specific franchise listing, if available.

R

Pricing Tips

- Pricing is function of sales volume, profitability, concept, duration, need for renovation, lease, liquor license, grandfathered C.O. issues, build-out, owned vs. lease assets, scalability....
- For nonfranchise,
  - ✓ if CFO is $50–$100K, price is 1.5–2.5 x
  - ✓ if CFO is $100–$250K, price is 2.5–3.5 x
  - ✓ if CFO is $250–$500K, price is 3–4 x
  - ✓ if CFO is $500K–$1M, price is 3.5–4.5 x
- Most retail make 10% to 20% off the top if run properly. Coffee houses do a bit better.
- Location and lease will affect the sale price directly.
- Add liquor license cost & value of FF&E.
- Location and history are important. Independents are less attractive but often more profitable than franchises. The key is low overhead, and most franchises have high overhead. Considering owner financing is a must.
- Limited-service may be lower volume than a full-service restaurant allowing for some higher rent as a % of sales. Make sure that true profitability is over 20% (near 25%).
- Independent restaurants priced to sell should be around 1.5 to 2.0 times EBITDA (real estate not included) and owner must be willing to consider some sort of owner financing. Franchised limited-service restaurants may go for as high as 3 times EBITDA but be prepared to go through the franchise-transfer process. You will need patience.
- Price: twice the yearly net income
- You arrive at two sets of figures, based on profit and sales. Price tends to move towards higher figure when a new store, has length of lease, volume increasing, and favorable market placement. Price tends to go lower if short lease, declining volume, no franchise term, equipment old, store tired, dropping profitability.
- Gross revenue is the key, but if the SDE doesn't support the debt service requirements and a reasonable salary, then the % of gross will have to come down.
- Sales are a much better indicator of value than bottom-line numbers. Different operators can have a huge impact on food and labor costs running the same business.
- Limited menu a bonus; delivery and length of lease major considerations.
- Normal situation—I would take last year's net plus any adjustments such as cars, insurance for owner, depreciation and interest, and make it a multiple of .72 to 2 times that number depending upon location, growth or decline of sales, age of fixtures and condition of building, then add value of FF&E, liquor license and other assets for a good value number.
- Increase in upcoming rental amount; ease of menu; delivery and competition in the market

Benchmark Data

Statistics (Fast Food Restaurants)

Number of Establishments	306,858
Average Profit Margin	5.3%
Revenue per Employee	$55,100
Average Number of Employees	14.7
Average Wages per Employee	$13,728

Products and Services Segmentation

Burgers 42.0%
Sandwiches 14.0%
Asian 10.0%
Chicken 10.0%
Pizza and Pasta 9.0%
Mexican 8.0%
Other 7.0%

Industry Costs

Profit 5.3%
Wages 24.9%
Purchases 36.4%
Depreciation 2.9%
Marketing 2.8%
Rent & Utilities 13.1%
Other 14.6%

Market Share

McDonald's Corp. 15.2%
Yum! Brands Inc. 8.4%
Subway 4.6%

Statistics (Coffee & Snack Shops)

Number of Establishments 79,054
Average Profit Margin 7.0%
Revenue per Employee $55,400
Average Number of Employees 9.3
Average Wages per Employee $15,094

Products and Services Segmentation

Coffee beverages 51.0%
Food 36.0%
Other beverages 9.0%
Other 4.0%

Industry Costs

Profit 7.0%
Wages 27.0%
Purchases 38.5%
Depreciation 3.6%
Marketing 3.5%
Rent & Utilities 11.1%
Other 9.3%

Market Share

Starbucks Corporation 43.3%
Dunkin' Brands Inc. 22.1%

Expenses (% of Annual Sales)

Cost of Goods .... 28% to 33%
Occupancy Costs .... 08% to 12%
Payroll/Labor Costs .... 25% to 35%
Profit (pretax) .... 10% to 20%

R

- Food costs 28%–40%, depending on concept
- Rent including NNN, 6%–10%
- Direct labor (excluding owner), 15%–30%, depending on concept
- Seller's Discretionary Income, 10%
- Prime cost (cost of goods plus payroll costs divided by sales) must remain below 60%
- Lower quartile per seat is $5,115, median is $7,510, and $14,293 is upper. $10,000 per seat is a benchmark for a successful quick-service restaurant.
- Food usually maximum of 35%. Sandwich shops very popular today. Catering a plus, hard to prove without good reliable records.
- Good menu can add to success. Location, visibility, and parking key ingredients for profitable business.
- Ownership of real estate very desirable. Franchise stores more marketable than independents. Franchise presence in marketplace very important.

Questions

- Why selling? Are there any family members working in business? Who does the cooking? What is food/beverage percent split? How does that compare to liquor license and zoning requirements? Average ticket? Which is stronger: breakfast, lunch, dinner? Is there anything in the restaurant that you do not own, e.g., dishwasher, ice machine, POS, beer draft system? Franchise transfer fees? Other franchise fees?
- Would you do it again? Biggest challenges?
- What can be done to improve the business that you are not doing?
- Sales, purchase invoices, detail of expenses
- Who are your key people? How many hours per week do you work? How long have you been in business?
- Tax issues. Relationship with franchisor if applicable. Any mandatory remodeling in near future. Lease terms and length. CAM charges.
- When was the last time you had a menu change or price change?

Industry Trend

- Continued growth
- "The Fast Food Restaurants industry will continue to play an influential role in the US food services sector over the next five years. The industry's ability to provide convenient food at a low price will remain popular, especially with consumers seeking affordable food options. However, the industry will remain highly competitive, forcing fast food chains to compete on price and service, which will ultimately restrict the industry's revenue and profit growth. As a result, industry revenue growth is expected to be subdued, increasing at an annualized rate of just 1.6% to $265.7 billion over the five years to 2022."

Source: IBISWorld Industry Outlook

Expert Comments

Seller:

1) Maintain good books/records, especially 2 yrs before sale.

2) Report all income, especially 2 yrs before sale.

Buyer:

1) Do not buy if you don't have food service experience.

2) Must have adequate working capital.

3) Hold back 10% of purchase price for 30–90 days to ensure all bills are paid.

4) Is the concept scalable?

Operations closing, which will help the ones left as long as consumers keep spending. Expensive to equip and furnish without knowing if the concept will go. Takes a lot of money to find out. Controlling overhead is key.

Established independents often are better deals than the franchises as far as net cash flow.

Tough to compete against national chains and big franchises

Highly competitive; tied to economic outlook

Large capital investment in equipment required. Makes resales a bargain!

Increasing food costs squeezing profits

Easy to open, hard to master. Very difficult to run absentee; owner must be present.

Lots of competition. Risk factor: must give consistent product, with good quality.

Catering a plus for today's business environment. Many sandwich shops add catering. Some catering-only locations with delivery, in low-rent areas with little highway exposure.

Seller Financing
- Seller financing is very common, especially if
  1) seller is unable to prove books/records.
  2) actual sales do not match sales tax reports, POS, or income tax returns.
- Price < $500,000: Typical financing is 1/3 cash down + 2/3 seller financing for 5 yrs.
- Five years—8 percent
- 3 to 4 years
- 7 to 10 years with a 3- to 5-year stop
- Average of 5 years and prime plus 2 percent
- Depends on size and cash flow; 8 years is an average of our last 20 restaurant transactions.

Resources
- IBISWorld, March 2017: http://ibisworld.com
- IBISWorld, October 2017: http://ibisworld.com
- National Restaurant Association (NRA): http://www.restaurant.org/Home
- Texas Restaurant Association (TRA): https://www.txrestaurant.org/

R

Restaurants—Mexican

		Number of Businesses/Units 44,472

Rules of Thumb

➢ 30% of annual sales

Benchmark Data

Statistics (Mexican Restaurants)

Number of Establishments	44,472
Average Profit Margin	4.3%
Revenue per Employee	$43,500
Average Number of Employees	20.2
Average Wages per Employee	$13,170

Products and Services Segmentation

On-premises limited-service restaurants	22.9%
Drive-thru limited-service restaurants	26.9.0%
Full-service restaurants	27.3%
Off-premises (take out) limited-service restaurants	22.2%
Cafeterias and buffets	0.7%

Industry Costs

Profit	4.3%
Wages	34.5%
Purchases	35.5%
Depreciation	2.2%
Marketing	2.6%
Rent & Utilities	8.5%
Other	12.4%

Market Share

Taco Bell Corp.	23.7%
Chipotle Mexican Grill	9.4%

Industry Trend

- "The Mexican Restaurants industry stands to benefit from the continued improvement in consumer spending over the next five years. As more Americans return to work and household incomes improve, spending at restaurants will likely grow. The US economy is exhibiting consistent growth and Americans are forecast to increase their spending in the next five years. Therefore, Mexican restaurants will benefit from both greater foot traffic and higher average checks. Consequently, IBISWorld estimates that industry revenue will grow 1.8% per year on average through 2021 to total $42.0 billion."

Source: IBISWorld Industry Outlook

Expert Comments

- "Chains that specialize in Mexican food do well, but not at the expense of independent competitors that serve authentic fare and outnumber them by a wide margin."

Source: "Mom-and-pop model endures in the Mexican segment," by Brad Bloom restaurant-hospitality.com, June 23, 2015

R

Resources

- IBISWorld, October 2016: http://ibisworld.com

Retail Businesses (In General)

Rules of Thumb

➤ 10 x EBIT

➤ 12 x EBITDA

➤ 30–35% of annual sales plus inventory

➤ 1.5–3 x SDE plus inventory

Pricing Tips

- Sales per square foot, inventory turns, marketing campaign structure, leadership turnover, door swings, outdoor customer exposure, drive-by traffic, ease of visibility, Website sale
- Location, remodel, condition of the business/equipment, lease, stability of revenue and general market conditions are some of the factors which will have an effect on valuation.
- Excess Inventory or slow-moving inventory may have to be included in normal level of inventory.

Benchmark Data

Expenses (% of Annual Sales)

Cost of Goods	25% to 28%
Occupancy Costs	15% to 18%
Payroll/Labor Costs	20% to 25%
Profit (pretax)	28% to 30%

Questions

- What type of marketing is giving you the best return? What metrics are important to you on a daily/weekly/monthly basis? How long does it take to train a new employee? Where do you turn to study industry trends?
- Cash sales, stale inventory, inventory turnover compared to prior years, justification for a 3% annual growth when the business only grew 2% last year, employee turnover.
- How long in business; trend of sales; expected new competition; why selling, product mix and industry changes, industry trade shows. Will the seller help the new owner in buying?
- A buyer needs to look at more than just the P&L and balance sheet. Look hard at the inventory. Do they have excessive amounts of merchandise that haven't moved? Are the racks empty? Are the payables up to date? A retail company can be showing a profit and still go out of business because of poor cash management. Does the P&L have any shrinkage? All retail companies are subject to significant amount of theft. If they don't show any losses on the P&L, then they aren't properly inventorying the store and the inventory on the balance sheet can be way off. Don't buy inventory without going in and doing a physical count at cost. If the inventory is out of line with the balance sheet, be sure the selling price is adjusted at close to reflect the proper amount.

R

Industry Trend

- "We've all heard that retail is in trouble — even serious trouble, depending on who you listen to. It's true that some large, well-known brands are facing challenging times, just as in every industry. But the narrative that retail is struggling — or even dying — is significantly overblown.

  "Competition is tougher than ever. Foreign retailers are steadily increasing their presence in the United States, innovative new business models are being developed to appeal to the modern consumer and small businesses and startups can compete in niche markets in ways that would have been impossible just a decade ago. The challenges brought by technological innovation are impacting businesses across a range of industries—and when big companies start to struggle, people take notice.

  "Retail is generally misunderstood to be dominated by big businesses. The truth is that 91 percent of retail businesses have fewer than 20 employees — increasing that number to 100 employees captures 98 percent of all retail businesses. These companies that make up the backbone of America tend to be overlooked as the media naturally focuses on the handful of large companies closing stores.

  "There are over 1 million retail establishments across the U.S. and retail sales have been growing at almost 4 percent annually since 2010. According to the Commercial Real Estate Development Association, 2016 saw 86.8 milliion square feet of new retail construction, and retail rents were at their highest level since 2008 through the first quarter of 2017. What's more, availability rates have been steadily declining since the end of the recession.

  "Stores are still in vogue. Many online retailers recognize the value of a physical presence—businesses like Amazon, Warby Parker, Bonobos and Blue Nile are experimenting with bricks-and-mortar locations. All retailers, whether purely online or purely bricks-and -mortar, must adapt to how customers prefer to shop in a digital world.

  "Online sales are growing rapidly for store-based retailers as well as internet pureplays. But that's the problem, right? Soon everyone is going to be doing all their shopping online. Not according to the data. Online sales currently make up less than 10 percent of total retail sales. If you just focus on pureplay online sellers, this figure drops below 6 percent. While online is growing rapidly, it's only a small part of a much larger whole. People still shop in stores for reasons ranging from convenience to preference. In a recent study NRF conducted with IBM on Gen Z, we found that 98 percent of these young, digitally active consumers shop in stores."

  Source: "Retail's reinvention story is just getting started" by Mark Mathews, June 14, 2017, https://nrf.com/news/retails-reinvention-story-is-just-getting-started

- "About 14% of retailers tracked by Moody's Investors Service qualified as 'distressed' in February, reaching the highest point since the Great Recession. Physical store sales for companies in the sporting goods, hobby store, book and music sector tumbled 6.9% during the 2016 holiday shopping season, while online sales jumped 19%, according to payment technology company First Data, which has a data analytics arm. Unlike online sellers, stores have to pay for often costly leases, which hampers their ability to keep prices low."

  Source: "Why sporting goods stores are down for the count," USA Today, March 7, 2017, https://www.usatoday.com/story/money/2017/03/07/sporting-goods-stores-retail-bankruptcy/98682338/

- "Store closures have become a growing trend, with big boxes such as Walmart, J.C. Penney, Sears, Kmart and others shuttering or planning to close scores of locations. The reason is neither declining retail sales, nor entirely because of e-commerce, The Atlantic magazine reports. 'So what the heck is going on? The reality is that overall retail spending continues to grow steadily, if a little meagerly,' The Atlantic article says.

"Here are The Atlantic's suggestions for the reasons retail sales are growing but stores are rapidly closing:

- ✓ Shoppers are shopping online more, using mobile apps to make purchases more often and taking advantage of easier returns.
- ✓ The U.S. has more malls than it needs, and when a few important stores in a mall close, others follow.
- ✓ Americans are buying possessions less often and paying for more experiences, such as vacations and dining out."

Source: "3 Reasons Retail Stores Are Steadily Closing," by Kate Klein, April 15, 2017, http://www.hardwareretailing.com/3-reasons-retail-stores-are-steadily-closing/

- Optimistic. People are shopping more but are becoming more savvy with their dollars.
- "The 'Amazon Strangehold' report, authored by Stacy Mitchell, co-director of ILSR, and Olivia LaVecchia, a researcher with ILSR's Community-Scaled Economy Initiative, notes that Amazon is now capturing nearly $1 in every $2 that Americans spend online. The company sells more books, toys, and, by next year, apparel and consumer electronics than any retailer online or off. 'Amazon increasingly controls the underlying infrastructure of the economy,' the authors write.

"Amazon's market dominance 'comes with significant consequences,' the report stresses. 'It's eroding opportunity and fueling inequality, and it's concentrating power in ways that endanger competition, community life, and democracy. And yet these consequences have gone largely unnoticed thanks to Amazon's remarkable invisibility and the way its tentacles have quietly extended their reach.'

"The report concludes with an analysis of how Amazon has taken advantage of billions of dollars in tax subsidies to fuel further growth and how government should respond to Amazon in the same manner it responded in the last century to the market dominance of Standard Oil and A&P."

Source: "New Report Provides Analysis on Amazon's Negative Impact," by David Grogan, November 30, 2016 http://bookweb.org/news/new-report-provides-analysis-amazon%E2%80%99s-negative-impact-35046

Expert Comments

For the buyer, it's about identifying the important metrics and watching it daily. Owners need to mix with the customers on occasion and listen to their buying desires. Sellers, enjoy your long vacation after selling. I recommend Turks and Caicos!

The industry as a whole is experiencing sales and profit challenges as online sales continue to increase putting pressure on box stores. The economy overall is improving and wallets are opening more over 2016.

Seller Financing

- I'm seeing a lot of SBA activity as it's first-time buyers.
- Seller financing. 30 percent down, 70 percent financed over 5 years.
- Seller financing unless the property is also being sold.

R

Resources
- National Retail Federation: https://nrf.com/
- Stores Magazine: https://nrf.com/connect-us/stores-magazine

Retail Stores (Small Specialty)	
	Number of Businesses/Units 139,003

Rules of Thumb
➤ 15–20% of annual sales plus inventory
➤ 1.8–2.2 x SDE plus inventory

Pricing Tips
- IBISWorld includes such businesses in this category as tobacco stores, artists' materials, souvenirs and collectibles, coin and stamp shops, religious goods (not books), occupational supplies and other similar type businesses. Approximately 85 percent of them are single-owner/small family businesses. Eighty-eight percent of these businesses have 9 or fewer employees.

Benchmark Data

Statistics (Small Specialty Retail Stores)
Number of Establishments	139,003
Average Profit Margin	4.3%
Revenue per Employee	$135,300
Average Number of Employees	1.7
Average Wages per Employee	$16,897

Products and Services Segmentation
Tobacco product and smokers' accessories	31.2%
Collectibles and monuments	20.9%
Other	20.5%
Pools, pool chemicals, pool supplies and accessories	15.8%
Home goods	7.9%
Groceries and alcoholic beverages	3.7%

Industry Costs
Profit	4.3%
Wages	12.5%
Purchases	48.9%
Depreciation	0.9%
Marketing	1.7%
Rent & utilities	5.6%
Other	26.1%

Industry Trend
- "IBISWorld forecasts that the Small Specialty Retail Stores industry will continue to decline as external competition intensifies. Revenue is forecast to continue a downward trend as consumers trend toward other retail sources for

specialty goods. Beyond the pressure generated from external competition, the industry will experience market conditions unfavorable to niche and specialty items. Over the five years to 2022, revenue is expected to decrease at an annualized 0.3% to $31.0 billion. During the outlook period, consumer spending is forecast to continue steady growth, but consumer confidence will decline. Financial uncertainty and sluggish growth will drag on consumer's propensity to spend on discretionary items."

Source: IBISWorld Industry Outlook

Resources

- IBISWorld, April 2017: http://ibisworld.com

Rita's Italian Ice	Franchise
Approx. Total Investment	$140,500–$414,200
Estimated Annual Sales/Unit	$230,000
NAICS 722515	Number of Businesses/Units 600

Rules of Thumb

➢ 80–100 x annual sales plus inventory

Resources

- Rita's Italian Ice: http://www.ritasice.com

Rocky Mountain Chocolate Factory	Franchise
Approx. Total Investment	$126,300–$421.400
Estimated Annual Sales/Unit	$350,000
NAICS 311352	Number of Businesses/Units 235

Rules of Thumb

➢ 50–55% of annual sales plus inventory

Resources

- Rocky Mountain Chocolate Factory: https://www.rmcf.com/

Roly Poly Sandwiches	Franchise
Approx. Total Investment	$101,050–$220,200
NAICS 722211	Number of Businesses/Units 125

Rules of Thumb

➢ 35% of annual sales plus inventory

R

Benchmark Data
- For Benchmark Data see Sandwich Shops

Resources
- Roly Poly Franchise Systems: http://www.rolypoly.com

Route Distribution Businesses

Rules of Thumb

➤ 35–40% of annual sales plus inventory

➤ 1–4 x SDE plus inventory

➤ 3 x SDE plus inventory—3–4 x for name brands; 1–2 x for no-name brands

➤ 1–4 x EBIT

➤ 10–20 x weekly gross plus inventory

➤ 3–3.5 x EBITDA

Pricing Tips
- The majority of route businesses are priced at a multiple of two times a year's income, with a range going from 1.5–2.5. The most prestigious (like Pepperidge Farm) go for 4 x, with the least desirable (independent cake or bread distributor) selling for 1 x.
- The quality of the routes has a direct effect on pricing. If the routes all touch each other, pricing should be higher. If there is a combination of ground routes and home delivery routes in the same territory, that has a positive effect on pricing. If the trucks are newer vs. older trucks, the pricing is higher. Having debt free equipment must be taken into consideration when pricing. Another factor is the maintenance and repair of the equipment; some contractors have their own mechanic/shop. That would lead to higher pricing.
- Area route operates in; days & hours of route; distance from pickup to route area. Does one need to handle staples/returns from its customers?
- Quality of routes and condition and age of vehicles is critical. Good books and records attracts larger potential group of buyers and possible bank financing.
- "How much does a route cost? The net profit of the route is the main factor in determining its value. Other significant factors include the type of route, the gross, the area, days and hours, and the vehicle. A general rule to keep in mind for the purchase of a route is 'double net.' The amount that you net in one year will be the approximate down payment amount, and double that figure will be the total purchase price. (Example: route netting $1,000/wk would cost approximately $100,000 with $50,000 down.) As a rule of thumb, the bigger the name a brand route is, the more the route will cost. Independent routes and service routes, on the other hand, cost usually 1 to 1 ½ year's net as opposed to 2 years' net (double net)."

  Source: Mr. Route, www.mrrouteinc.com—a very informative website
- Actual SDE & EBIT ranges from 1–4 according to the type of distribution business.
- The larger transactions involve a multiple of sales. The multiple range is 1–2 x sales. 1 x sales—sometimes even less, depending on a number of factors—is common for the smaller transactions. The larger ones are clearly in the M & A field, as these can be $5 million to $50 million also involving land, bottling plants, spring sources and truck fleets.

- The sales that are in our ranges of $50,000 to about $2 million are in the multiple range of .75 to 1.5 x sales and usually include assets that are needed to run the business (office, warehouse, inventory, and trucks). The .75 range or even less is for the smallest of these under $200,000 with owners that are very anxious to sell. The higher multiple is generated when buyers are very anxious to buy for strategic regions and the sellers are not forced to sell.
- Profitability, EBITDA, etc. are not factors, because the buyer rolls the accounts into his own operation inheriting none of the overhead. Often there is not even an increase in the cost of delivery. This depends on how large an operation the buyer has and the size of the business he is buying. Therefore the sales less COGS drops to the bottom line and is extremely profitable for the buyer. COGS in the water industry is only 10%-20% of sales. In coffee, it would be 33%–50%.

Benchmark Data

- The newest FedEx requirement is to own 5 routes or deliver 500 stops a day in the exclusive delivery zone to be compliant with the Independent Service Provider (ISP) model. The average route produces gross revenue of $100,000 annually. If the business has at least 5 routes and a manager to handle the day-to-day operations, profit margins of 22% to 28% are possible. Drivers are usually paid a daily wage. Most do not receive any benefits. The drivers may get a one-week paid vacation after one year of employment.
- Any viable route should net (after all expenses) its operator between $200–$300 per day.
- Income is fairly stable. Dedicated routes sell for more than non-dedicated. Average annual revenue per route can vary from $325,000 to $460,000 per year.
- Bread, chip & provisions routes sometimes try to use a multiple of weekly sales. Beverage & juice routes usually use a price/case. Majority of routes, even those mentioned above, are priced at a multiple of annual net profit.
- Each category (bread, coffee, chips, candy & nut, cookie, dairy, juice, paper, pie & pastry, provisions, soda & beverage, vending, package delivery (FedEx, etc.) of route businesses is priced differently. Even within categories, such as soda & beverage, a Snapple route will go for a higher multiple then an independent beverage route.
- The route must net a minimum of $175 per day after all expenses. What are categorized as A routes are the most common in the market. They are one-man routes that operate out of a truck that does not require a CDL license; operate 4-5 days per week & net an income between $700-$1400 per week. The next larger category of routes is classified as B routes. They may require a helper; may operate out of a CDL truck & net a weekly income of $1400-$2500 per week. The largest routes are classified as C routes. They require the use of helper(s), operate out of CDL trucks & net a weekly income of more than $2500 per week.
- Most routes sell at a multiple of weekly sales from 12 to as high as 50:1 on each dollar of sales.

Expenses (% of Annual Sales)

Cost of Goods	35% to 40%
Occupancy Costs	0% to 10%
Payroll/Labor Costs	05% to 15%
Profit (pretax)	10% to 20%

R

Questions

- The buyer should ask the seller how long the seller will stay engaged and give advice and assist for peak season.
- Where is route? What type, size and age of truck used? Are returns taken and who is responsible for such? What are the operating hours? How far is pickup from accounts serviced? How do accounts pay?
- History of drivers and trucks
- Documentation of purchases, sales and expenses.
- Ask for the past full year's worth of purchase and/or sales records; copy of contract (if franchised) for review; permission to take truck in for inspection; list of active (& inactive) accounts.

Industry Trend

- The trend over the next 3 years is for the entire country to convert from the IC model to the ISP model.
- More of the "big boys" controlling most food (& non-food) industries, while the smaller manufacturers are scurrying around for the pieces of the market left!
- Increased package freight cross country should continue to increase for the foreseeable future.
- Over the years there has been much consolidation within the industry, with larger regional firms buying smaller regionals, the smaller regionals buying larger local firms, and the larger locals buying smaller (under $500,000) companies. Today super-large national companies such as Nestle (which controls 50% of the U.S. market and is worldwide) bought most of the regional brands, and DS Waters, another national water company, bought the rest. So virtually all of the mega-consolidation has already taken place. However there is still plenty of consolidation being done on a smaller basis, with transactions ranging from $50,000 to $5,000,000. There are still a number of smaller regional bottlers and distributors buying companies in this range.

Expert Comments

Use an educated and experienced intermediary. Not many buyers understand the FedEx model. It takes a lot of buyer education to get someone up to speed on the FedEx model.

With FedEx P&D routes, the contractor has an exclusive right to deliver in a designated area. There is no competition between contractors. They usually work together and assist one another as needed in times of high volume, when driver does not show up for work, truck breakdowns, etc.

The FedEx industry has been growing at an annual rate of 9% on average across most markets. The increase is due to the independent contractor model operated by FedEx. They are taking market share away from UPS and USPS because of the IC model.

Use a broker rather than yourself to market it! Selling a route business is a full-time job and you want to be sure to keep lots of customer and financial info confidential ...except to those buyers who have the interest to proceed forward.

Seller Financing

- In over 80 transactions that we have facilitated, cash at closing is the most popular method of payment. There are very few banks and lenders that will loan on FedEx. We have not had any sellers offer financing terms.

- 40–50% down and the remaining balance financed over enough years (@ 5%–6% rate) where the monthly payment will be—tops— one week's net income!
- Most deals are for cash. However with good books and records and a positive three-year trend this business is suitable for SBA financing. Some seller financing is seen but adequate security becomes an issue.
- Typically, when financing is available, it is through the seller with 5-year terms and interest rates currently averaging around 5-7%.
- Most routes are sold with owner financing. There are several big franchised routes (like Pepperidge Farm) which offer outside financing to buyers.
- 90% may be seller financed, with the exception of some companies (like Bimbo & Pepperidge Farm) that provide financing to buyers looking to come into their company with a route purchase.

Resources
- ROUTE BROKERS®, INC.: http://www.routebrokers.com
- MyGroundBiz: http://mygroundbiz.com

RV Dealerships

SIC 5561-03	NAICS 441210	Number of Businesses/Units 6,900

Rules of Thumb

➢ 15% of annual sales plus RV inventory & parts, etc.

Pricing Tips

- A good formula: ease of entry, big secular swings, keep the price in the 4x range for smaller, privately owned companies. Also, balance sheets generally are not critical.

Benchmark Data

Statistics (Recreational Vehicle Dealers)

Number of Establishments	6,900
Average Profit Margin	3.8%
Revenue per Employee	$412,400
Average Number of Employees	7.2
Average Wages per Employee	$54,040

Products and Services Segmentation

Travel trailers	64.0%
Fifth-wheel trailers	18.4%
Class A	4.6%
Class C	7.0%
Parts and services	2.4%
Folding trailers	1.9%
Truck campers	0.6%
Class B	1.1%

R

Industry Costs

Profit	3.8%
Wages	13.1%
Purchases	73.5%
Depreciation	0.3%
Marketing	1.3%
Rent & Utilities	2.6%
Other	5.4%

- High direct costs, low period costs, so when you go by breakeven, about 15% of sales drops to the bottom line. C.O.D. business, which also helps ease of entry and rapid growth.
- "By the Numbers
    - ✓ 8.9 million US households own an RV
    - ✓ There are 460 RV rental outlets across the country
    - ✓ The RV rental business is $350 million annual industry"

Source: Cruise America, Recreation Vehicle Industry Association, www.gorving.com

Questions
- Gross margin—it's really important to have that straight.

Industry Trend
- "RV shipments through February 2017 totaled 73,287 units, an increase of 8.6% from the same period in 2016. This continues seven consecutive years of shipments growth as the industry has bounced back from effects of the Great Recession. In 2016, RV shipments totaled 430,691 units, a gain of 15.1% over the previous year. This was the seventh consecutive annual increase."

Source: http://www.rvia.org/?ESID=indicators

- Very strong right now. Gas is cheap, credit is cheap; millions of families already own a vehicle.
- "The RV market continued to race ahead through the first half of 2016 with total RV wholesale shipments reaching 226,286 units, an 11.7% increase over this same period last year, according to RVIA's June survey of RV manufacturers. The monthly total for June was 40,072 units, rising 18.7% above June one year ago and marking the third monthly total in excess of 40,000 units this year. "Shipments through June were at a seasonally adjusted annualized rate of nearly 415,000 units and the six-month total this year was the best since 1977. Towable RV shipments led the way in volume total with shipments reaching 197,515 units through June, an 11% gain over the 177,939 units shipped during the same six-month time frame in 2015. Meanwhile, motorhome shipments showed the largest percentage gain with the market segment up 16.4% to 28,771 units compared to 24,714 units last year at the same point."

Source: http://rvia.org/?ESID=preleases&PRID=1769&SR=1 August 4, 2016

Expert Comments

Learn the business from the first company you buy-and a year or so later look for an add-on.

Elkhart has had 19% unemployment to 2% above full employment, back and forth. The last ten years have seen big consolidation moves and only a handful of companies dominate now, but new companies come along regularly. Basically an assembly business, not much capital required to start.

Seller Financing
- Outside financing and maybe some seller paper to keep the transaction kosher

Resources
- IBISWorld, October 2017: http://ibisworld.com
- Recreational Vehicle Industry Association, (RVIA)-A very informative site: http://www.rvia.org
- RV Pro: https://rv-pro.com

RV Parks		
SIC 7033-02	NAICS 721211	

Rules of Thumb

➤ 3.3% of annual sales plus inventory

➤ 8.5 x SDE plus inventory

Pricing Tips
- These businesses are based on cap rates starting at 4% for a 5-star manufactured home community up to 12% for an overnight campground.
- Cap rates range from 7% to 12%.
- "RV parks are a very high-yielding investment, with returns from 10% to 20%+ on your money. RV parks are among the highest yielding of all real estate asset classes. So if your goal is to maximize the return on your money, RV parks are not a bad starting spot."

  Source: http://www.rvparkuniversity.com/articles/is-buying-an-rv-park-worth-the-investment.php
- The industry is getting more sophisticated at marketing and pricing. Many hotel/motel pricing strategies are starting to work for campgrounds.

Benchmark Data
- See Campgrounds for additional Benchmark Data

Expenses as a percentage of sales

Marketing	10%
Utilities	14%
Payroll	25%
G&A	05%

- Gross income minus 30 to 40% in total expenses based on renting lots/sites and not homes/cottages.
- Below 5,000 camper nights per year is difficult to operate the business and make a profit.

Expenses (% of Annual Sales)

Cost of Goods	10%
Occupancy Costs	30% to 40%
Payroll/Labor Costs	10%
Profit (pretax)	40%

Questions

- Ask for a complete due diligence package and if they will sign a noncompete agreement.
- What would you do to maximize the income?

Industry Trend

- 3–4% increase in the net operating income based on inflation below 3%
- Increased revenues based on limited supply and high demand.
- Affordable travel that should grow. Retired baby boomers should keep the business strong for several years.

Expert Comments

Gather all the due diligence information available and consult an industry expert.

The retiree seasonal or yearly resident makes this business a very low risk profitable investment. The ability to duplicate these properties in similar locations at today's prices creates very low competition and a high demand for the existing businesses.

Have a business plan that is achievable based on improving all areas of opportunities that the current owner is not maximizing.

Seller Financing

- More typical for outside financing but when there is seller financing the cost is less. Outside financing 4–5% interest, 20- to 30-year terms, 5–10 balloons.
- Outside financing based on low interest rates.

Resources

- RV Life—an industry publication: http://www.rvlife.com
- Florida Association of RV Parks and Campgrounds: http://www.FARVC.org
- National Association of RV Parks and Campgrounds: http://www.arvc.org
- Appraising Manufactured (Mobile) Home Communities and RV Parks: http://www.appraisalinstitute.org/appraising-manufactured-mobile-home-communities-and-recreational-vehicle-parks-print-pdf-packa/
- Florida RV Trade Association: http://www.frvta.org/
- Good Sam Club: http://www.goodsamclub.com/
- rvjournal: http://www.rvjournal.com/
- Woodall's Campground Management: http://www.woodallscm.com/
- RV Business: http://www.rvbusiness.com/
- Recreation Vehicle Industry Association: http://www.rvia.org/

			Franchise
Safe Ship			
Approx. Total Investment			$39,900–$94,800
	NAICS 488991		Number of Businesses/Units 40

Rules of Thumb

➢ 40% of annual sales

Resources
- Safe Ship: http://www.safeship.com

Sales Businesses (In General)
Rules of Thumb
➢ 1–2 x SDE plus inventory

Pricing Tips
- In this industry, there is an abundance of owner benefits such as: high-end automobiles that are not necessary to conduct business, but are definitely a benefit, extensive travel throughout the world, dining out at five-star restaurants, etc.

Benchmark Data
- 40% of your gross commission should equate to your owner's benefit.

Questions
- Are all of your lines paying 5% or more? How long have you had each line? How many of your lines are industry leaders?

Seller Financing
- 36 months

Sales Consulting

SIC 8748-08	NAICS 541613	

Rules of Thumb
➢ 33% of annual sales includes inventory

Pricing Tips
- Price paid should be affected by current accounts surviving the exit of the owner.

Samurai Sam's Teriyaki Grill

		Franchise
Approx. Total Investment		$115,600–$427,050
	NAICS 722513	Number of Businesses/Units 29

Rules of Thumb
➢ 45% of annual sales
➢ 1.5 x SDE

Resources
- Samurai Sam's Teriyaki Grill: http://www.samuraisams.net

S

Sandwich Shops

SIC 5812-19	NAICS 722513	

Rules of Thumb

➢ 2 x SDE plus inventory

➢ 3 x EBIT

➢ 40–50% of annual sales plus inventory

Benchmark Data

Statistics (Sandwich & Sub Store Franchises)

Number of Establishments	39,912
Average Profit Margin	5.2%
Revenue per Employee	$52,300
Average Number of Employees	10.3
Average Wages per Employee	$12,814

Products and Services Segmentation

Limited-service restaurants	46.8%
Cafeteria restaurants	33.5%
Takeout restaurants	19.7%

Industry Costs

Profit	5.2%
Wages	24.5%
Purchases	36.4%
Depreciation	2.9%
Marketing	2.9%
Rent & Utilities	13.1%
Other	15.0%

Market Share

Subway	53.5%
Jimmy John's	11.0%

Expenses (% of Annual Sales)

Cost of Goods	28%
Occupancy Costs	10%
Payroll/Labor Costs	22%
Profit (pretax)	20%

Industry Trend

- "Over the five years to 2021, IBISWorld forecasts that industry revenue will increase at an annualized rate of 1.6% to $22.9 billion. The Sandwich and Sub Store Franchises industry will continue to benefit as the economy improves, unemployment rates decrease and consumers begin to spend money on luxuries, such as restaurant dining, more often. During this period, consumer spending is expected to increase at an annualized rate of 2.5%. Additionally, demand for sandwich and sub shops will increase as companies expand their healthy menu options. Aggressive international growth will also reinvigorate major franchises' overall revenue"

Source: IBISWorld Industry Outlook

Resources

- IBISWorld, December 2016: http://ibisworld.com

Sarpino's Pizzeria		Franchise
Approx. Total Investment		$246,995–$333,795
SIC 5812-22	NAICS 722513	Number of Businesses/Units 46

Rules of Thumb

➢ 50% of annual sales plus inventory

Resources

- Sarpino's Franchise Opportunities: http://www.sarpinosfranchise.com

Schools—Educational & Nonvocational		
	NAICS 61	

Rules of Thumb

➢ 3.5–4 x EBITDA

➢ 40%–50% of annual gross sales

➢ 2–3 x SDE

Pricing Tips

- 2.5 to 5 times adjusted EBITDA is a starting point for Title IV career colleges. EBITDA must be adjusted for the cost of a company or campus president. Where the school is on that range will depend on revenue trends, margins, program types, type of accreditation, etc.
- 40–50% staffing, 15–20% facility, 20–25% other
- Simple rule for schools: preschools 20% rent or bank loan, 20% other expenses, 40 to 45% staff, balance is yours. As for private schools up to 12th grade, staff is 50 to 55%.
- Sales can be based on the number of students in the school. Today's range is from $5,000 to $12,000 per student.
- For small schools (revenues < $5M 3 to 4 X Adjusted EBITDA. For medium schools (revenues between $5M and $20M) 4 to 5 X Adjusted EBITDA. For large schools (revenues > $20M) 5 to 6 X Adjusted EBITDA. Accreditation adds to value. Good regulatory metrics add to value.

Benchmark Data

Statistics (Business Certification & IT Schools)

Number of Establishments	16,770
Average Profit Margin	8.9%
Revenue per Employee	$82,900
Average Number of Employees	1.9
Average Wages per Employee	$35,876

S

Products and Services Segmentation

Professional development and management training	10.4%
Computer and information sciences	68.3%
Basic education and improvement courses	12.3%
Other	9.0%

Industry Costs

Profit	8.9%
Wages	43.5%
Purchases	17.2%
Depreciation	1.9%
Marketing	4.1%
Rent & Utilities	7.0%
Other	17.4%

- There are a number of postsecondary schools that provide training, and the sales and profits usually relate to the number of students and the tuition charged.
- Student roster and valuation per student enrolled

Expenses (% of Annual Sales)

Cost of Goods	10% to 20%
Occupancy Costs	15% to 20%
Payroll/Labor Costs	40% to 50%
Profit (pretax)	10% to 20%

Questions

- What to understand in the business from top to bottom: expense, staffing, care of the children, state requirements, and the list goes on.
- Please provide financial and compliance audits for the last three years.
- What are your gainful employment statistics?
- How much time is left on your accreditation?
- Any complaints filed with your accrediting agency, state licensing agency, or the U.S. Department of Education?
- How has the seller started and grown the business, and how can the buyer continue to grow the business?
- Financials and reason for selling.
- Look at the books, look at staff cost, look at student income and make sure your debt if you get a loan can service the loan and give you a profit.
- Do you have programs for kids? How is the establishment record with community care licensing? Do you provide snacks, lunch? What curriculum is being utilized and what is the average experience of the teachers? Do you have a director? What are his or her responsibilities?
- A buyer of a career school should ask all the questions that would be asked during any business transaction. In addition, of great importance for a career school acquisition, are:
  - ✓ Names and contact information of all regulatory bodies
  - ✓ Updates on past and current regulatory issues
  - ✓ Status of all approvals and dates of upcoming renewals
  - ✓ Enrollment trends

✓ Job saturation for programs and community served
✓ How long the owners will stay on.

Industry Trend

- It is a growing and needed business.
- The U.S. faces a severe shortage of skilled workers. As a result, the demand for skill-based career education is strong and will increase in the future. Due to heightened regulatory scrutiny, most of the poorly run schools have been closed down. As a result, the schools that are still standing will face less competition and should thrive.
- There will be increased demand for these types of graduates.
- Not many opening, but a lot will sell.
- As the population grows so does the business. Parents need care in preschool, and education leads to better jobs.
- The sale of schools is coming back. Buyers are looking for good investments that have a good track record.
- There are many trends that affect transactions:
  ✓ Currently baby-boomer school owners are ready for retirement. They have built great schools and want to divest to help support their retirement.
  ✓ Increased regulations are forcing some good as well as bad schools to sell. This creates opportunities for qualified and knowledgeable buyers.
  ✓ The international market is growing. International schools and investors are seeking U.S. acquisitions in international-friendly cities.

Expert Comments

Seek out the help of an investment banker, accountant, and regulatory attorney with experience in this industry.

The for-profit career college sector is highly regulated. Financial statements need to be audited. Schools need to go through regular compliance audits and re-accreditation. Failing to meet regulatory standards can cause a school to lose its accreditation and Title IV status, which can effectively put a school out of business.

Have good strong financials that show what the business is doing.

Look at books, enrollment numbers, staff expense. You do not have to go back far; look at more current data. You're buying today, not 3 years ago.

High school and college type schools are in big demand and there is a limited number of schools on the market. Trade school is a new area that is in demand.

Both school buyers and sellers should work with M&A intermediaries who are extremely knowledgeable in the industry. Because of the challenging regulatory environment, logic alone cannot be relied upon. Buyers and sellers need to know the right questions to ask and what information to request. Most importantly, they need to clearly understand the answers that are provided. Additionally, every transaction requires an industry-experienced attorney. There are many nuances in today's regulatory environment that require the knowledge that only experience can provide.

S

Seller Financing
- SBA financing and some seller notes sometimes
- In most cases, sellers should expect to finance between 20 and 30 percent of the purchase price.
- Most schools are sold with outside financing, and the terms vary.
- Smaller schools—seller financing; larger schools—outside financing

Resources
- Accrediting Commission of Career Schools and Colleges (ACCSC): http://www.accsc.org
- Accrediting Council for Continuing Education and Training (ACCET): http://www.accet.org
- IBISWorld, April 2017: http://ibisworld.com
- Accrediting Council for Independent Colleges and Schools (ACICS): http://www.acics.org
- Career Education Colleges and Universities: http://www.career.org
- The Higher Learning Commission: https://www.hlcommission.org/
- U.S. Department of Education: http://www.ed.gov
- Distance Education Accrediting Commission: http://www.deac.org/
- New England Association of Schools and Colleges (NEASC): http://www.neasc.org
- The Southern Association of Colleges and Schools Commission on Colleges: http://www.sacscoc.org
- Accrediting Bureau of Health Education Schools (ABHES): http://www.abhes.org

Schools—Tutoring & Driving Schools		
	NAICS 611691	Number of Businesses/Units 171,325

Rules of Thumb
➤ 1 x SDE + fair market value of fixed assets

➤ 40–45% of annual sales + fair market value of fixed assets

Pricing Tips
- High barrier to entry due to increasingly higher and stricter state regulations and standards.

Benchmark Data

Statistics (Tutoring & Driving Schools)
Number of Establishments	171,325
Average Profit Margin	8.4%
Revenue per Employee	$30,300
Average Number of Employees	1.9
Average Wages per Employee	$13,387

Products and Services Segmentation
Test preparation	41.0%
Tutoring	33.5%
Other schools	16.0%
Driving schools	9.5%

Industry Costs

Profit	8.4%
Wages	43.8%
Purchases	10.8%
Depreciation	3.1%
Marketing	2.9%
Rent & Utilities	7.1%
Other	23.9%

Resources

- IBISWorld, January 2017: http://ibisworld.com

Schools—Vocational & Training		
	NAICS 611210	

Rules of Thumb

➤ 1.5 x EBIT

➤ 75–100% of annual sales plus inventory

➤ 2–4 x SDE plus inventory

➤ 3–5 x EBITDA

Pricing Tips

- Home-based franchise sells for much higher multiple of 4 or above, if it's generating $300K+ in revenue. Educational franchise that allows office location contributes to higher SDE. Customer base of 4-14 years is highly preferred due to high demand.
- Accreditation and Title IV funding provides for higher pricing.
- Pricing is all over the board because of the size of a facility. The larger the school, the more the owners profit.
- Value is driven by type of program (longer, more expensive programs are more valuable), enrollment, and enrollment growth.

Benchmark Data

Statistics (Trade and Technical Schools)

Number of Establishments	9,018
Average Profit Margin	6.3%
Revenue per Employee	$103,100
Average Number of Employees	14.4
Average Wages per Employee	$40,860

Products and Services Segmentation

Other professional development programs	48.6%
Flight training programs	23.7%
Cosmetology and barber schools	16.9%
Apprenticeship training programs	10.8%

S

Industry Costs

Profit	6.3%
Wages	39..4%
Purchases	12.5%
Depreciation	3.3%
Marketing	3.8%
Rent & Utilities	10.8%
Other	23.9%

- No benchmarks; based on the cash flow of the business and type of program. Also Federal funding it you have it.

Expenses (% of Annual Sales)

Cost of Goods	10% to 20%
Occupancy Costs	10% to 20%
Payroll/Labor Costs	40% to 50%
Profit (pretax)	15% to 25%

Questions

- Financial questions and what needs to be done for the licensing and reporting
- Employee qualifications, turnaround and hiring process.
- Is the school accredited and what is the status?

Industry Trend

- "On its surface, the prospects for the job market look to be the victims of automation, with an estimated 282,100 jobs eliminated in production fields by 2024. Yet even with this massive shrinkage, there will still be approximately 9 million jobs in production, and for many jobs such as aircraft technicians, the lack of growth will not mean a lack of available jobs.

  "There will only be 1,600 more aircraft mechanics and service technicians in 2024 than there were in 2014, but with over 30,000 job openings over that time, schools like PIA (the Pittsburgh Institute of Aeronautics) are poised to hook students up with available and fine-paying jobs. This is the story across the industry: although hundreds of thousands of jobs will be cut, there will have been over 2.2 million job openings by 2024. Welders, cutters, solderers and brazers – jobs that are as technical as they get – alone will have experienced 128,500 job openings and 14,400 jobs created according to the BLS."

  Source: "The Top 30 Two-Year Trade Schools: Colleges that Fight the Nation's Skills Gap"
by Carter Coudriet, June 19, 2017, https://www.forbes.com/sites/cartercoudriet/2017/06/19/the-
top-30-two-year-trade-schools-colleges-that-fight-the-nations-skills-gap/#33b1a35e6675

- It is a hard business to enter into; there are many licensing requirements.

Expert Comments

Make sure you understand the business you are getting into.

Seller Financing

- SBA financing is the only place for financing unless they are coming into the country. Seller will do some financing.
- Most of the time seller finance due to lack of tangible assets

S

Resources
- Real Work Matters (RWM): www.rwm.org
- Schools for Sale: http://www.schoolsforsale.com
- IBISWorld, December 2016: http://ibisworld.com

Franchise
Sears Carpet and Upholstery Care & Home Services

Approx. Total Investment	$26,000–$192,000

	NAICS 561740	Number of Businesses/Units 138

Rules of Thumb
➤ 35% of annual sales includes inventory

Resources
- Own a Sears Home Services Franchise: http://www.ownasearsfranchise.com
- Sears Carpet and Air Duct Cleaning: http://www.searsclean.com

Security Services/Systems/Alarm Companies

SIC 7382-02	NAICS 561621	Number of Businesses/Units 81,593

Rules of Thumb
➤ 50% of annual sales includes inventory

➤ 3 x EBIT

➤ 4 x EBITDA

➤ 2–3 x SDE includes inventory

➤ 24–28 x monthly revenue based on an average $25 month per account plus inventory

Pricing Tips
- Security Alarm companies generally sell on a multiple of their Recurring Monthly Revenue. Currently, the multiple is 33 times, excluding assets. Monitoring contracts is key to the deal.

Benchmark Data

Statistics (Security Alarm Services)
Number of Establishments	66,300
Average Profit Margin	6.2%
Revenue per Employee	$116,200
Average Number of Employees	3.0
Average Wages per Employee	$37,974

Products and Services Segmentation
Residential security alarm system services with monitoring	43.6%
Nonresidential security alarm system services with monitoring	28.4%
Nonresidential security system and lock installation without monitoring	15.8%
Residential security system and lock installation without monitoring	6.7%
Other	5.5%

Major Market Segmentation

Residential clients.. 50.1%
Business and commercial clients.. 39.2%
Government and not-for-profit clients 10.7%

Industry Costs

Profit 6.2%
Wages... 32.6%
Purchases.. 34.2%
Depreciation... 0.7%
Marketing 2.2%
Rent & Utilities 4.3%
Other... 19.8%

Market Share

ADT LLC 17.7%

Statistics (Security Services)

Number of Establishments... 15,293
Average Profit Margin 6.5%
Revenue per Employee $41,400
Average Number of Employees 54.1
Average Wages per Employee $26,298

Products and Services Segmentation

Security guard services for buildings and grounds 68.1%
Investigation services 15.8%
Armored vehicle services... 7.2%
Other services... 5.5%
Security guard services for special events 3.4%

Major Market Segmentation

Corporations 33.0%
Residential and other... 24.0%
Financial institutions 16.0%
Government and clients.. 14.0%
Retail and leisure 13.0%

Industry Costs

Profit 6.5%
Wages... 63.3%
Purchases.. 8.6%
Depreciation... 1.2%
Marketing 1.0%
Rent & Utilities 2.5%
Other... 16.9%

Market Share

Allied Universal 9.3%
G4S PLC.. 6.8%
Securitas AB 5.0%

- Generally, there should be 500 paying monthly monitoring accounts for every one technician.

Dealers' Revenue Segmented by Business Services

Monitoring	49%
Sales/Installation	30%
Service contracts	09%
Non-contracted service	05%
Test & inspection	03%
Other	02%
Hosted & managed services	01%

Source: "Performance Remains Solid" by Laura Stepanek, sdmag.com, May 8, 2015

Enterprises by Employment Size

Number of Employees	Share
1–4	63.8%
10–19	9.4%
20–99	7.1%
100–499	1.1%

Expenses (% of Annual Sales)

Cost of Goods	40%
Occupancy Costs	05% to 10%
Payroll/Labor Costs	40%
Profit (pretax)	10%

Questions

- A buyer wants to see a seller's contracts and the terms of the contracts.
- 1. Do they own the central station? 2. If not, do they own the phone lines that connect to central station? 3. What % of their customers are contracted?
- Type of guard services and customer list. Most guard companies have one major client.

Industry Trend

- "The Security Service industry will benefit from a projected increase in corporate profit levels, which will lead to an increase in security budgets over the five years to 2022. In addition, the industry will continue to benefit from increased residential, commercial and public construction over the next five years, improving demand for industry operators to safeguard real estate and infrastructure development projects. Rising industrial activity and investments in new manufacturing facilities will also lead to an increase in demand for security services. The industrial production index, the Federal Reserve's measurement of output from mining, manufacturing, electric and gas sectors, is expected to increase at an annualized rate of 1.3% over the next five years. Private investment in manufacturing structures is also expected to increase at an annualized rate of 2.8% during this period. An increase in the total number of US factories will subsequently lead to rising demand for security services, as industry operators will be needed to protect manufacturing facilities, equipment and finished goods."

Source: IBISWorld Industry Outlook

S

Expert Comments

There are many barriers to entry, specifically having the licenses in place to run the business. A buyer with no experience would need 4 years just to obtain the licensing.

An alarm company can be run from any location because all work is completed at a customer's home or business. They are very marketable and are not easy to replicate. The hurdle is that a new owner needs to hold a Class C & D license for low-voltage wiring, which is a 3- to 5-year process to obtain.

Seller Financing

- Easily financed through SBA. In any deal, there will be a hold back of 10%–25% of the deal for a period of 13 months for any customer loss.
- There are industry specific financing companies that will hold contracted accounts as collateral. Also the SBA has gone 10 years because of the RMR.
- 3 to 5 years and an average of 20 to 50 percent of transaction value financed by seller

Resources

- National Burglar & Fire Alarm Association: http://www.alarm.org
- The American Society for Industrial Security (ASIS): http://www.asisonline.org
- Security Industry Association (SIA): http://www.siaonline.org
- IBISWorld, May 2017: http://ibisworld.com
- IBISWorld, June 2017: http://ibisworld.com

Self Storage (Mini Storage)		
	NAICS 531130	Number of Businesses/Units 60,128

Rules of Thumb

➢ 1 x EBITDA

Pricing Tips

- Very few buyers or appraisers will count revenues in excess of 90% of potential rents, except in very unusual circumstances.
- These are difficult because they are often a means of holding land until it reaches the point where it is more profitable to redevelop it for another use. Most buyers look for a cash on cash return of about 20% on the amount they must invest to purchase the property compared to the purchase price/financing that can be obtained.
- Key factors are vacancy and turnover of units. Buyers want to get at least a 20% cash-on-cash return.
- Most involve the real estate.
- Pricing is driven by capitalization rates and expense ratios.

Benchmark Data

Statistics (Storage and Warehouse Leasing)

Number of Establishments	60,128
Average Profit Margin	43.0%
Revenue per Employee	$264,000
Average Number of Employees	2.5
Average Wages per Employee	$29,105

Products and Services Segmentation

10-by-10-foot storage spaces	23.1%
10-by-20-foot storage spaces	20.6%
Other	15.6%
10-by-15-foot storage spaces	14.4%
Five-by-10-foot storage spaces	11.3%
10-by-30-foot storage spaces	6.2%
10-by-25-foot storage spaces	5.3%
Five-by-5-foot storage spaces	3.5%

Major Market Segmentation

Long-term residential customers	48.9%
Short-term residential customers	21.0%
Commercial firms	18.4%
Military	5.9%
Students	5.8%

Industry Costs

Profit	43.0%
Wages	11.1%
Purchases	6.6%
Depreciation	14.0%
Marketing	2.2%
Rent & Utilities	11.9%
Other	11.2%

Market Share

Public Storage Inc.	7.2%

- "Largest self-storage operators (publicly traded) in the U.S. (by revenue)
  - ✓ Public Storage: $2.56 billion (2016)
  - ✓ Extra Space Storage: $991.87 million (2016)
  - ✓ CubeSmart: $510 million (2016)
  - ✓ Life Storage: $462.6 million (2016)
  - ✓ U-Haul: $247.9 million (fiscal 2016 – self-storage revenue only)

  "Largest self-storage operators in the U.S. (by number of facilities, owned or managed)
  - ✓ Public Storage: 2,348 (December 31, 2016)
  - ✓ Extra Space Storage: 1,427 (December 31, 2016
  - ✓ U-Haul (AMERCO): 1,360 (as of March 31, 2016)
  - ✓ CubeSmart: 791 (as of December 31, 2016)
  - ✓ Life Storage: 659 (as of December 31, 2016)

S

"Average national cost by unit size:
- ✓ 5×10: $63 per month
- ✓ 10×10: $96.09 per month
- ✓ 5×5: $45.30 per month
- ✓ 10×20: $137.06 per month
- ✓ 10×15: $123.01 per month"

Source: "U.S. self-storage industry statistics" by Alexander Harris, August 23, 2017, https://www.sparefoot.com/self-storage/news/1432-self-storage-industry-statistics/

Sample facility

Size	40,000 SF
Average Rent	$71/month
Rent/SF	$8.52/yr.
Current Occupancy	88%
Market Occupancy	70%
Potential Rent	$341,000
Rents Collected @ 88%	$300,000/yr.
Expenses	$100,000
Net Operating Income	$200,000/yr.
Value @ 9.5	$2,100,000
Loan Amount @ 75%	$1,575,000
Debt Service @ 6.5%	$128,000/yr.

Expenses (% of Annual Sales)

Profit (pretax)	05%

Questions

- Who manages the site and are they willing to stay on? Can existing financing be assumed?
- Occupancy and waiting list
- Management turnover

Industry Trend

- "6 reasons why the Self-Storage Industry is on the rise:
  - ✓ Unprecedented Growth
  - ✓ Third-Generation Properties
  - ✓ New Amenities and Fancy Offerings
  - ✓ Ease of Use and Security
  - ✓ Repurposing Vacant Buildings
  - ✓ Location, Location, Location"

Source: "Trending Alert: 6 Reasons Why the Self Storage Industry is on the Rise" by Eric Carlson, August 17, 2016, https://www.lifestorage.com/blog/storage/self-storage-industry-trends/

- "They are popping up all over, these garages-for-rent. The Self Storage Association will proudly tell you that self storage has been the fastest growing segment of the commercial real estate industry over the last four decades, while Wall Street analysts consider the industry to be recession-proof. There are 59,500 self storage facilities worldwide. Of these, 48,500 are in the U.S."

Source: "Important Self Storage Industry Trends Moving Companies Shouldn't Miss," http://blog.hireahelper.com/self-storage-industry-trends-for-movers/

Expert Comments

Storage units are a great way to warehouse land until the highest and best use changes.

This is a real-estate purchase with a business element attached to it. The value of the underlying real estate controls a large part of the value of the property. Management is more important than most people realize.

Seller Financing
- 10 to 15 years

Resources
- Mini Storage Messenger—excellent resources: http://www.selfstoragenow.com
- Self Storage Association—an excellent site with lots of information: http://www.selfstorage.org
- Argus Self-Storage Sales Network: http://www.argusselfstorage.com
- IBISWorld, March 2017: http://ibisworld.com

		Franchise
Senior Helpers		
Approx. Total Investment		$89,000–$117,300
	NAICS 621610	Number of Businesses/Units 265

Rules of Thumb
➢ 40–45% of annual sales

Resources
- Senior Helpers: http://www.seniorhelpers.com

Service Businesses (In General)

Rules of Thumb
➢ 72% of annual sales plus inventory

➢ 35–50% percent of annual revenues [sales] plus inventory; however, it is not unusual for service businesses to sell for a much higher figure

➢ 2–2.8 x SDE

Pricing Tips
- The buyers only care about what they will make and how long it will take them to recoup their investment.
- One of the most important factors is determining how replaceable the owner is, and how much of the revenue the owner generates him/herself.
- Consider the last 3 to 5 years—is it an up or down trend? Is the business expandable or is it at its peak?

Expenses (% of Annual Sales)

Cost of Goods	30%
Occupancy Costs	05%
Payroll/Labor Costs	30%
Profit (pretax)	20%

S

Industry Trend

- Growth

Expert Comments

Competition and the industry trends (growing or constant) are important for calculating the ROI on the intangible part.

		Franchise
ServiceMaster Clean		
Approx. Total Investment		$51,000–$260,000
	NAICS 561720	Number of Businesses/Units 3,077

Rules of Thumb

➤ 55–60% of annual sales plus inventory

Resources

- The ServiceMaster Company: http://www.ownafranchise.com

		Franchise
Servpro		
	NAICS 561720	Number of Businesses/Units 1,000

Rules of Thumb

➤ 90–95% of annual sales plus inventory

Resources

- Servpro: http://www.servpro.com

Shoe Stores		
SIC 5661-01	NAICS 451110	Number of Businesses/Units 30,173

Rules of Thumb

➤ 15–20% of annual sales plus inventory

Benchmark Data

Statistics (Shoe Stores)

Number of Establishments	30,173
Average Profit Margin	2.3%
Revenue per Employee	$152,100
Average Number of Employees	7.9
Average Wages per Employee	$17,602

Products and Services Segmentation

Women's nonathletic shoes	29.7%
Men's athletic shoes	25.4%
Children's shoes	15.2%
Men's nonathletic shoes	13.1%
Women's athletic shoes	11.8%
Slippers and other shoes	4.8%

Industry Costs

Profit	2.3%
Wages	11.5%
Purchases	55.9%
Depreciation	0.9%
Marketing	2.4%
Rent & Utilities	10.7%
Other	16.3%

Market Share

Foot Locker Inc.	13.5%
Caleres Inc.	7.0%
Designer Shoe Warehouse Inc.	6.9%
Payless ShoeSource	6.0%

Industry Trend

- "Trends:
  - ✓ Higher wages
  - ✓ Declining sales prices
  - ✓ Rising import taxes
  - ✓ Lower synthetic and rubber costs"

  Source: "4 Big Trends Impacting Shoe Companies Right now" by Sheena Butler-Young, March 31, 2017, http://footwearnews.com/2017/business/retail/shoe-companies-footwear-trends-business-retail-332210/

- "IBISWorld expects the Shoe Stores industry to experience solid growth as consumers continue to regain confidence and purchasing power in the five years to 2020. During the five-year period, the Consumer Confidence Index is forecast to grow at an annualized rate of 0.9%, while disposable income is expected to increase at an annualized rate of 2.5%. Instead of simply purchasing necessities, shoppers will increasingly return to shopping for discretionary items. Recovering purchasing habits are expected to help boost industry revenue; IBISWorld projects revenue to grow at an annualized rate of 2.7% to $42.5 billion over the five years to 2020.

  "The U.S. market for athletic shoes is one of the strongest of the global markets. However, U.S.-based companies and their competitors have long been multi-national firms operating in diverse overseas markets selling footwear and also athletic apparel in increasingly competitive markets. The athletic footwear is highly dependent on fashion trends, customer preferences and other fashion-related factors. Many of the industry's highest-margin products are sold to young males between the ages of 12 and 25 and are subject to frequent shifts in fashion trends."

  Source: "Athletic Shoe Industry Analysis" by Robert Shaftoe, Demand Media
  http://smallbusiness.chron.com/athletic-shoe-industry-analysis-74098.html

Resources

- National Shoe Retailers Association: http://www.nsra.org
- Footwear News: http://footwearnews.com
- IBISWorld, June 2017: http://ibisworld.com

S

Short Line Railroads

	NAICS 482112	

Pricing Tips

- These are highly regulated businesses that, as businesses, tend to be basically real estate businesses. Many buyers tend to be hobby buyers. Historically, buyers have grossly overpaid to purchase these businesses, then not exploited the potential of the real estate business. Buyers are almost always industry related in some way. Sellers are mainly large operating corporations who cannot operate these units economically.

Industry Trend

- "America's short line railroads provide fuel savings and environmentally friendly shipping for small businesses and communities around the country. One freight rail car can carry a ton of cargo 436 miles on just one gallon of fuel. Short line railroads take the equivalent of nearly 33 million truck loads off the highways, saving the country over $1.4 billion annually in highway repair costs and improving highway safety and congestion."

Source: American Short Line and Regional Railroad System (ASLRRA)

Shuttle Services & Special Needs Transportation

	NAICS 485999	

Rules of Thumb

➢ 3 x EBITDA plus the value of the vehicles

Benchmark Data

Statistics (Airport Shuttle Operators)

Number of Establishments	619
Average Profit Margin	8.5%
Revenue per Employee	$64,900
Average Number of Employees	20.8
Average Wages per Employee	$26,389

Products and Services Segmentation

Local shuttle services for leisure	67.0%
Local shuttle services for business	30.5%
Other	1.9%
Long-distance shuttle services	0.6%

Industry Costs

Profit	8.5%
Wages	40.5%
Purchases	13.1%
Depreciation	6.1%
Marketing	0.5%
Rent & Utilities	3.2%
Other	28.1%

Resources

- IBISWorld, August 2016: http://ibisworld.com

Signarama	Franchise
Approx. Total Investment	$168,000–$172,000
NAICS 339950	Number of Businesses/Units 875

Rules of Thumb

➤ 55–60% of annual sales plus inventory

Resources

- Signarama: http://www.signarama.com

Sign Companies	
NAICS 339950	

Rules of Thumb

➤ 2.5 x SDE includes inventory

➤ 48–50% of annual sales includes inventory

➤ 3.5–5 x EBITDA

Pricing Tips

- Relative to annual revenue—critical to have a 3rd party certified valuation of the business and commercial real estate when optional.
- Businesses with gross sales of over $1M typically will get slightly higher #'s than the rule of thumb. Technology can have an impact on the sales price. Large format printers and flatbed printers have become more commonplace and are expected to be in-house by many buyers.
- Margins do vary significantly in this industry. The product is custom made, and there are a variety of products that can be produced, with margins varying within the product ranges. So, one company that is producing one product 'niche' within the category may be more profitable than another company focusing on a different product niche.
- Most sign companies are small independents-SDE is a better calculation than EBIT or EBITDA. Inventory is not usually an excessive number, and usually included as part of a 2.5–3 x multiple of SDE.

Benchmark Data

Statistics (Sign & Banner Manufacturing Franchises)

Number of Establishments	37
Average Profit Margin	4.8%
Revenue per Employee	$150,400
Average Number of Employees	7.2
Average Wages per Employee	$40,602

S

Products and Services Segmentation

Banners and flags	24.6%
Building signs	23.2%
Trade show exhibits	20.6%
Point-of-sale displays	13.6%
Electric signs	13.2%
Other	4.8%

Major Market Segmentation

Accommodation and food services	48.6%
Other retailers	21.1%
Car dealers and gas stations	16.5%
Professional services	8.8%
Other	5.0%

Industry Costs

Profit	4.8%
Wages	28.0%
Purchases	40.4%
Depreciation	1.6%
Marketing	1.5%
Rent & Utilities	0.8%
Other	21.2%

Market Share

Signarama	51.5%
Fastsigns International Inc.	33.9%
Image360	14.5%

Sales per employee—$150,000 to $180,000

Expenses (% of Annual Sales)

Cost of Goods	25% to 28%
Occupancy Costs	15% to 20%
Payroll/Labor Costs	20% to 25%
Profit (pretax)	20% to 25%

Questions

- Ensure that the customer database is diverse and that no one customer dominates the sales.
- How do they secure customers? What kind of repeat customer base do they have? How much of the business/sales depends on their personal relationship with customers?

Industry Trend

- "Market trends affecting sign franchises:
  - ✓ E-Commerce Is More Popular Than Ever
  - ✓ Market Demand For Printed Signage Persists
  - ✓ The Indoor Signage Market Continues To Overtake Outdoor Signage Demands
  - ✓ The Demand For Short-Lived Retail Signage Continues To Climb"

Source: "5 Market Trends Affecting Sign Franchises in 2017," May 27, 2017,
http://signworld.org/5-market-trends-affecting-sign-franchises-2017/

- "The digital signage market will reach $32.84 billion by 2023, and will grow at a compound annual growth rate of 7.4 percent between 2017 and 2023, according to a report by ReportsnReports. LED and LCD displays are expected to drive the market, although OLED displays will also experience high growth. However, the lack of standards of interoperability between devices is restricting growth.
  "Other key trends covered in the report include:
    - ✓ Cloud-based digital signage software and interactive signage systems continue to grow;
    - ✓ North America will hold the highest market share in the period; and
    - ✓ The Asia-Pacific region will experience the most growth during the forecasted period."

    Source: "Report: Digital signage market to reach $32 billion by 2023," August 3,2017, https://www.digitalsignagetoday.com/news/report-digital-signage-market-to-reach-32-billion-by-2023/

- "Digital signage is today used in numerous market verticals such as retail, healthcare, transportation, office and enterprise, education, foodservice and outdoor signage. At the end of 2014, there were approximately 25.4 million connected digital screens in use worldwide. Berg Insight forecasts that this number will grow at a CAGR of 20.2 percent to reach 63.8 million units by 2019."

    Source: "Shipments Of Connected Digital Signs Will Reach 17.2 Million In 2019," http://www.signs.org/Newsroom/IndustryNews/IndustryNewsItem.aspx?NewsID=3358

- Big transitions: outdoor signage going to digital wide-format printing, installation, even car wraps. Promotional, fragmented, small players, local. Very few regional, national players interested in operations; focus is on project management.

Expert Comments

Difficulty in selling operations-real estate is usually more valuable than the business.

There are many segments/areas of specialization within the industry that can affect margins and equipment needed. Additionally, some buyers will view the location as a critical element and others do not. The industry is a B2B service, so there are varying points of view on the issue of location.

Make sure that customer base is diverse—both in terms of types of industries served as well that one or two key customers aren't a huge percentage of the total revenue.

Seller Financing
- Cash; very few sellers have options to offer financing. Buyers are offering bargain prices.
- Outside financing is usually available, although we have seen some seller finance deals over the last few years.
- Typically use outside financing

Resources
- Specialty Graphic Imaging Association: http://www.sgia.org
- Sign & Digital Graphics Magazine: http://www.sdgmag.com
- International Sign Association: http://www.signs.org
- IBISWorld, July 2016: http://ibisworld.com
- Signs of the Times: https://www.signsofthetimes.com/

S

	Franchise
Sir Speedy Printing	
Approx. Total Investment	$275,000–$350,000
NAICS 323111	Number of Businesses/Units 250

Rules of Thumb

➢ 55–60% of annual sales plus inventory

Resources

▪ Sir Speedy Printing: http://www.sirspeedy.com

Ski Shops		
SIC 7011-10	NAICS 532292	Number of Businesses/Units 379

Rules of Thumb

➢ 40% of gross annual sales plus inventory

➢ 2.5–3.5 x SDE plus inventory

Pricing Tips

▪ It depends if the business is retail, service, rental, or some combination of all of these offerings. We find we are able to get good multiples because of the desirability of the businesses.

▪ Key is long-term lease, since location is so important in resort retail sales. If lease is less than 3 years, a heavy discount in percentage of gross sales is appropriate. The price goes down the higher the inventory-which is always in addition to price (calculated on Rules of Thumb). Every store is different. Be careful—the trend is for ski companies to get into the retail business and compete with independent shops.

▪ In resort businesses, location is key. Businesses must be in the tourist foot traffic areas.

▪ A strong lease securing such a location is the key in determining the multiple of cash flow. Since most areas have limited real estate, competition plays a large factor in determining price; e.g., how many ski shops are in your immediate area?

Benchmark Data

Statistics (Ski & Snow Board Resorts)

Number of Establishments	379
Average Profit Margin	8.1%
Revenue per Employee	$36,300
Average Number of Employees	199.8
Average Wages per Employee	$11,355

Products and Services Segmentation

Skiing facilities	53.7%
Equipment Rental	12.6%
Ski schools	12.5%
Food and beverages	8.3%
Merchandise	7.2%
Other	5.7%

Major Market Segmentation

Destination visitors	58.7%
Local visitors	41.3%

Industry Costs

Profit	8.1%
Wages	31.4%
Purchases	24.7%
Depreciation	9.1%
Utilities	4.2%
Rent	6.1%
Other	16.4%

Market Share

Vail Resorts Inc.	56.3%
Intrawest Corporation	9.2%
Boyne Resorts	8.1%
POWDR Corporation	5.3%

- Gross profit is the single biggest benchmark for success. After that, it's sales per square foot and inventory turns that matter.

Expenses (% of Annual Sales)

Cost of Goods	45% to 50%
Occupancy Costs	08% to 12%
Payroll/Labor Costs	22% to 28%

Industry Trend

- Positive, based upon an improving economy and increased discretionary income. Recreation is a perceived need rather than perceived want.

Expert Comments

Our market tends to be competitive and the bar is set high. The businesses are expected to be very knowledgeable and have a lot of inventory in stock. We have seen a trend in retailers having difficulty in maintaining margins in order to keep or increase market share. In certain industries, having the right brands or product lines is very important.

Seller Financing

- 3 years maximum

S

Resources

- IBISWorld, September 2017: http://ibisworld.com

Smartbox Portable Storage & Moving		Franchise
Approx. Total Investment		$365,900–$849,300
	NAICS 484210	Number of Businesses/Units 25

Rules of Thumb

➢ 45–50% of annual sales includes inventory

Resources

- Smartbox Portable Storage & Moving: http://smartboxmovingandstorage.com/

Smoothie King		Franchise
Approx. Total Investment		$176,300–$403,550
Estimated Annual Sales/Unit		$475,000
	NAICS 722515	Number of Businesses/Units 740

Rules of Thumb

➢ 40–45% of annual sales

Resources

- Smoothie King: http://www.smoothieking.com

Snap Fitness		Franchise
Approx. Total Investment		$109,525–$285,620
	NAICS 713940	Number of Businesses/Units 1,290

Rules of Thumb

➢ 40% of annual sales plus inventory

Resources

- Snap Fitness: http://www.snapfitness.com

Soft Drink Bottlers		
	NAICS 312111	Number of Businesses/Units 476

Rules of Thumb

➢ $10/case sold annually

Benchmark Data

Statistics (Soda Production)

Number of Establishments	476
Average Profit Margin	8.2%
Revenue per Employee	$865,100
Average Number of Employees	107.4
Average Wages per Employee	$55,641

Products and Services Segmentation

Regular carbonated soft drinks	51.4%
Energy and sports drinks	24.0%
Diet carbonated soft drinks and sparkling water	19.8%
Mixers	4.8%

Major Market Segmentation

Grocery Stores	41.1%
Gas stations and convenience stores	19.0%
Vending machines	12.7%
Warehouse clubs and supercenters	16.7%
Other	8.2%
Exports	2.3%

Industry Costs

Profit	8.2%
Wages	6.4%
Purchases	64.2%
Depreciation	2.1%
Marketing	4.2%
Rent & Utilities	1.3%
Other	13.6%

Market Share

The Coca-Cola Company	30.8%
PepsiCo Inc.	29.6%
Dr. Pepper Snapple Group Inc.	9.3%
Monster Beverage Corp.	6.7%

Industry Trend

- "The beverage industry is experiencing some major changes heading into the new year. Sugary sodas are under fire. Juice sales are slipping. Many of the brightest points are new brands and beverages that no one had heard of a few years ago.

  "Here are four key trends to watch out for in the industry in 2016, according to some of the biggest executives and experts in the business.
  - ✓ The growth of energy, water, and sports drinks brands
  - ✓ Reworking recipes
  - ✓ Smaller cans and bottles
  - ✓ Attempts at authenticity"

    Source: "The 4 biggest ways American beverage consumption will change in 2016," by Kate Taylor, January 2, 2016, http://www.businessinsider.com/4-big-beverage-industry-trends-in-2016-2015-12

S

Resources
- IBISWorld, September 2017: http://ibisworld.com
- Beverage Industry: http://www.bevindustry.com/

Software Companies		
	NAICS 511210	

Rules of Thumb
➤ 1–3 x revenue (trailing 12 months) plus inventory
➤ 5.5–7.5 x SDE
➤ 5–7 x EBITDA
➤ 6–7 x EBIT

Pricing Tips
- Enterprise value is a factor of:
  1. Recurring maintenance revenue (stable and adds more value)
  2. Recurring subscription revenue (increasing and adds more value)
  3. Legacy system license revenue (lessening and adds less value)
  4. Percentage of products engineered/re-engineered for SaaS
  5. Industry (stable)
  6. Client type (B2B, B2C, combo-value higher for B2B due to stickiness of base)
  7. Foundation (i.e., size of base and ability to influence demand of product type)
  8. Competitive inhibitors (can influence value dramatically, mostly to the negative)
  9. Organization (particularly engineering base-higher value for core engineering component and reasonable access to professionals, offshore use)
  10. Architecture (engineering platform-more generally accepted/current technology gets better value)
- SDE, EBIT, & EBITDA ratios are meaningless in this industry because of the great differences in product, market, and development stage from company to company. Businesses even without profits or negative net worth can command multiples of gross revenue. Values are more focused on revenues trending upward, consistency and sustainability of the existing customer base, and potential for growth.

Benchmark Data
- Typical models for revenue per employee is difficult unless you split pre-revenue/emerging companies from established ones. Also, in the software space, different types of software garner different KPI's. So ERP software development is different than consumer versus HR versus vertical software platforms.
- Gross profit is very high on software. Typically companies will sell software and related services. Software typically 70% of revenues, services 30% for B2B companies. For B2C, Support contracts help to define continued customer contracts assist in customer relations, marketing, social media comments, etc.

- Actual and replication costs per source code line is a significant measurement used by potential acquirers.
- For B2B look at average length of maintenance agreement-not the length of the contract, but the length of time the average client stays with the vendor. For B2C software companies, its more sales focused, so gauge their development life cycle, and their ability to keep innovating, and remain ahead of the marketplace. Remaining ahead of the marketplace also includes ability to provide products that consumers need and want. In a larger scale B2B, with mission-critical type systems, look for average length of contracts in excess of 5 years to achieve a higher multiple. In a B2C, look for scheduled and periodic releases, their contribution to revenue, and their future development lifecycle. B2C companies have had pressure to drop prices over the years, as the model for less expensive 'throw away' software becomes more mainstream. Brand effectiveness is key. SaaS offerings are required in most cases to be considered 'current', but legacy systems will be around for a long time.

Expenses (% of Annual Sales)

Cost of Goods	05% to 11%
Occupancy Costs	10% to 15%
Payroll/Labor Costs	60% to 65%
Profit (pretax)	25%

Questions

- Some key questions: a) Define the marketplace served by your software products. b) What is the life cycle for product development (SDLC). c) What percentage of your clients is on maintenance? (B2B). d) What percentage of your clients on maintenance has been on contracts for over 5 years? (B2B). e) What percentage of your total product income comes from maintenance? Over the last three years? (B2B). f) What do you sell your products for (MSRP)? (B2C). g) What is your policy for product updates (time and cost to consumer)? (B2C). h) Who is your competition? i) Explain your distribution model (B2B and B2C). j) Critique your development personnel, average longevity, and income patterns. k) Do you deploy a high percentage of your development or support offshore? l) Do you have an SaaS model? If not why not? If planned, when will it be released and what competition do you see in that marketplace? m) What is your revenue per employee over the last three years, and what has been your average tenure for engineers in your company? n) What is your average employee longevity? o) Explain in-house technical skill set. p) Explain benefit package and cost (remember, it will be different than average, and that is to be expected). q) What is unique about your business plan? r) Do you have a customer retention plan? s) How do you formulate your product/service pricing plan? t) Are you subject to any regulatory issues, especially if paving new ground with product introduction?
- Calculations of net cash flow, consistently applied, are good for historical analysis. Discounted cash flow models vary widely, but commonly use higher rates because of risk and uncertainty. Premiums for control, discounts for illiquidity are usually magnified from more stable industries. The broker/intermediary should inquire about capitalization policies of the software asset. Many companies will not capitalize their product; others will be based on cost accumulation. Niche software with an established client base will attract buyers because of the ongoing service revenues.

S

Industry Trend

- "Trends in the enterprise software market favor big guns, says Goldman Sachs, and another wave of mergers and acquisitions seems likely with smaller players getting swallowed by the likes of Oracle (ORCL), SAP, Salesforce.com (CRM), Workday (WDAY) and Ultimate Software Group (ULTI). Goldman Sachs says companies such as Cornerstone OnDemand (CSOD), Blackline (BL) and Zendesk (ZEN) could be takeover targets, though no deals seem imminent.

  "'Our view is that the wave of (mergers) is slowly beginning to build, and we would expect to continue to see a healthy dose of best-of-breed vendors consolidated into suites (both legacy software vendors like Oracle and SAP, as well as 'born in the cloud' vendors like Salesforce and Workday),' the note went on to say.

  "While software makers enjoy revenue growth above 30% and 40%, Goldman Sachs expects billings growth to slow for most. It expects suite vendors like Oracle, SAP and Microsoft (MSFT) to claw back market share.

  "'To sustain share gains, we believe that best-of-suites like Salesforce.com and Workday will continue to focus on building out their respective suites,' the report said. 'To a certain extent, we have already seen several rounds of acquisitions of best-of-breed vendors, and our view is that M&A activity will only intensify, especially as growth rates of best-of-breed providers start to decelerate.'"

  Source: "When Software Mergers Heat Up, These Companies Will Be Buyers" by Reinhardt Krause, July 17, 2017, http://www.investors.com/research/ibd-industry-themes/when-software-mergers-heat-up-these-companies-will-be-buyers/

- Further development in consumer based trends will transcend to other areas. For example, development in VR systems has multiple revenue channels including consumer, defense, and commercial (like driverless cars). Software companies are developing key AI components to provide to major software aggregators, whether through licensing or via acquisition.

- Companies that develop process and control systems, especially those that enhance regulatory concerns in key industries like Pharma, have a smaller market, but can produce better than average return when they are introduced in a critical number of industry players. Software companies will be continually looking to new extensions of areas that in the past would never have been considering digitally connected.

- The Internet of Things (IoT) promises to enhance the need for sophisticated technology in all aspects of life. From wearable tech like the Apple Watch, Fitbit, refrigerators, automotive, to clothing like Ralph Lauren shirts that measure various health factors through integrated threads that transmit wireless data, the confluence of everyday life and software systems to control them will give rise to many new companies. The key is to see who can generate an accepted marketplace and monetize it. Software companies will be continually looking to new extensions of areas that in the past would never have been considered digitally connected." "Accordingly, and in an attempt to gain traction, more companies specialize in segments they believe will become more commonplace in the future. Some companies develop software that are integral to future plans and offerings of larger entities and become competitive targets for acquisitions. That is where the true value is at.

Expert Comments

Software development and sales requires different cultures than typical brick, manufacturing, or other service-based companies. They tend to be younger, have complex requirements that cannot be easily learned, and have changing requirements that outpace many other industries.

Because the products are people-centric in use, the ability to generate demand is based upon functionality, usability, and fitness for a particular purpose. Cost issues place demands on companies such that without traction, it's not cost effective to create competitive offerings against well-established companies. Personnel costs for qualified engineers, business analysts, designers, and QA/QC professionals is, per capita, expensive. As the Internet of Things (IoT) becomes more prevalent, the need for technology solutions that incorporate more complex solutions is growing geometrically.

Software development is very difficult. The programming must be completed in view of superior user interface design, process modeling, and speed (response times). Because of the low cost as a barrier to entry, many individuals who gain education and skills don't fully understand that programming is not, in and of itself, a business. Getting product to market (i.e., in this case, deploying the software) is complex and costly, such as it is in many other industries.

Many companies with great software products never succeed because they lack first mover status, or the marketing prowess to gain mass customer adoption. Those are key to an enterprise value since the likelihood of continuous revenue when a customer has been acquired is high. The change from one software platform/program/application is difficult and costly. Cost-of-ownership models have been around for a long time, but the key metrics still exist and many companies will not make changes in their software very often accordingly.

Software companies must attract highly qualified individuals who work both in teams and on their own. Their experience is difficult to replicate, as software can be developed in many different platforms and require knowledge in a wide array of languages and development methodologies. Accordingly, companies that are valuable tend to have very liberal benefits and workplace accommodations to keep their staff. Employee acquisition costs are high.

Seller Financing
- It varies. There is no average, as many software companies are sold with equity participation vs. seller notes in order to value the upside of the future software adoption.
- Given the competitive landscape for this type of business, sales typically have significant cash or stock components. Sellers are requested to hold notes that vary in scale based upon the maturity of the product and customer base. When there is a large base of existing customers with a high probability of continuous maintenance or upgrade revenue to continue, the valuation will likely exceed normal/median valuation for an average company and have limited seller financing. If acquired by a public company, leverage using the company's public stock offering is used to sweeten the deal and lessen the need for outside or seller financing.

Resources
- Industry/Company Analysis and Trends (fee based): http://www.factset.com
- Software & Information Industry Association: http://www.siia.net
- How to evaluate a Software Company:

http://www.essensys.ro/whitepapers/How-to-Evaluate-a-Software-Company.pdf
- Association of Information Technology Professionals: http://www.aitp.org
- Association of Software Professionals: http://www.asp-software.org
- Association for Computing Machinery: http://www.acm.org

Sound Contractors		
SIC 5065-07	NAICS 238210	

Rules of Thumb

➤ 75% of annual sales includes inventory

➤ 5 x EBIT

➤ 3 x EBITDA

➤ 2–3 x SDE and/or 30–60 x monthly contract billing for music services includes inventory

Pricing Tips

- Most contractors in this industry supply some type of music service; if it is a recurring base and the contractors are on their paperwork, then this company will have more value to a buyer.
- Any inventory over 24 months is dead inventory and should not be part of sale.

Benchmark Data

- Recurring services are a key in value to this industry.

Expenses (% of Annual Sales)

Cost of Goods	35%
Occupancy Costs	10%
Payroll/Labor Costs	35%
Profit (pretax)	20%

Questions

- Inventory: how much is dead and on the books?
- Relationship to customers

Industry Trend

- 5% to 10% growth each year
- Business is stable.

Expert Comments

If company is a commercial contractor, the economy does not have much effect on industry. If they give good service and have experience in technical support, business will be stable.

There are few good sound contractors with a great customer list.

Seller Financing

- 5 to 8 years

Sporting Goods Stores

SIC 5941-13	NAICS 451110	Number of Businesses/Units 45,310

Rules of Thumb

➤ 25% of annual sales plus inventory

➤ 4 x EBIT

Pricing Tips

- Add or subtract based on nearby competition
- Inventory should be excluded due to rapid obsolescence.

Benchmark Data

Statistics (Sporting Goods Stores)

Number of Establishments	45,310
Average Profit Margin	3.0%
Revenue per Employee	$159,500
Average Number of Employees	6.9
Average Wages per Employee	$20,001

Products and Services Segmentation

Sporting equipment	61.5%
Athletic apparel	17.0%
Athletic footwear	10.8%
Other	10.7%

Industry Costs

Profit	3.0%
Wages	12.6%
Purchases	63.2%
Depreciation	0.8%
Marketing	2.1%
Rent & Utilities	6.2%
Other	12.1%

Market Share

Dick's Sporting Goods Inc.	16.7%
Academy Sports & Outdoor	9.9%
Bass Pro Shops, Inc.	9.1%
REI	5.4%

Expenses (% of Annual Sales)

Cost of Goods	45% to 55%
Occupancy Costs	15% to 20%
Payroll/Labor Costs	17%
Profit (pretax)	08%

Questions

- Are the sales personnel knowledgeable in their specific areas?

28th Edition

S

Industry Trend

- "Despite strong growth in US sportswear sales, sporting goods retailers are struggling as consumers change their purchasing habits, sportswear brands focus more on direct channels, and new players enter the market."

  Source: "Why U.S. Sporting Goods Retailers Are Struggling," April 22, 2017,
  http://blog.euromonitor.com/2017/04/us-sporting-goods-retailers-struggling.html

- "Sporting goods stores are down for the count. The scourge of insolvency is sweeping through the sector as online sellers gain the upper hand over yet another corner of retail just recently dominated by big-box chains, specialty stores and mom-and-pop shops.

  "Yet another general sporting goods retailer, MC Sports, filed for bankruptcy in February with plans to liquidate its 68 stores, as the fallout accelerates. Others have included:

  - ✓ Sports Authority
  - ✓ Golfsmith
  - ✓ Sport Chalet
  - ✓ Eastern Outfitters
  - ✓ Total Hockey

  "Amid the ruin, some see opportunity. Dick's Sporting Goods, the dominant remaining chain, is capitalizing on the fallout. It acquired dozens of stores from its bankrupt competitors, including converting 22 Sports Authority locations into its own stores. Dick's also purchased Sports Authority's intellectual property, including its website, which now redirects to Dick's."

  Source: "Why sporting goods stores are down for the count," USA Today, March 7, 2017,
  https://www.usatoday.com/story/money/2017/03/07/sporting-goods-stores-retail-bankruptcy/98682338/

Expert Comments

Increasing competition from online retailers

Resources

- IBISWorld, May 2017: http://ibisworld.com
- National Sporting Goods Association (NSGA): http://www.nsga.org

Staffing Services (Health Care)

Industry Trend

- "All four sub-segments of healthcare staffing — travel nurse, per diem nurse, locum tenens and allied health — are projected to continue growing through 2018, though the landscape has shifted dramatically in favor of travel over per diem assignments during the past few years."

  Source: "A mixed outlook for healthcare staffing" January 8, 2017, http://www2.staffingindustry.com/Editorial/
  Healthcare-Staffing-Report/Jan.-12-2017/A-mixed-outlook-for-healthcare-staffing

Resources

- Staffing Industry Analysts (SIA): http://www.staffingindustry.com

	Franchise

Subway

Approx. Total Investment	$116,000–$300,000
Estimated Annual Sales/Unit	$475,000

SIC 5812-06	NAICS 722513	Number of Businesses/Units 27,000

Rules of Thumb

➢ 2.5–3.5 x EBIT

➢ 3.5 x EBITDA

➢ 45–55% of annual sales includes inventory

➢ 3.3–3.8 x SDE includes inventory

➢ 35–40 x weekly sales

Pricing Tips

- From 2010–2015, locations through our brokerage were selling for about 55–60% of sales or 3 X SDE. The past few years have dramatically brought those averages down to about 40% of sales and 2–2.5 X SDE.
- Discount value for sales less than national average of $8,500 a week but compare with local average. Discount for remodeling required. Discount for short lease. Discount for rent over 10% of sales. Discount if SDE less than $50,000.
- Factor in costs of high rent (>12%), remodel costs, short lease, new store coming nearby.
- 70% of asking price minus remodel cost if any.

Benchmark Data

- For additional Benchmark Data see Sandwich Shops
- 29% food, 18% labor with owner working 40 hours and rents below 8%. That is a winner.
- True cost of goods is 30% in a well-run, owner-operated store. Rent should be less than 10% for real profitability. Valuation/pricing does range from 25% to 85% of sales, depending on the numbers and region.
- Most stores are 1,000 square feet, have approximately 20 seats and are owner operated. Food cost is controllable.

Expenses (% of Annual Sales)

Cost of Goods	30% to 35%
Occupancy Costs	10%
Payroll/Labor Costs	20% to 25%
Profit (pretax)	15% to 25%

Questions

- How involved are you in the business? How many hours do you spend at the store? How have you marketed and advertised the location?
- Are they going to open a new store nearby? Does it need a remodel?
- Is the DA support good?

S

- Lease length and terms, trend of gross sales, years established
- Remodel due? Rent and CAM? Combo report?

Industry Trend

- "Subway is planning to upgrade locations in the coming years. It will be a while before Subway will be able to get back to the unit growth that was once its birthright."

Source: "Why Subway is Shrinking" by Jonathan Maze, April 24, 2017, http://www.nrn.com/quick-service/why-subway-shrinking

- Subway has seen a downward trend in overall sales due to bad publicity, industry competition, internal competition, etc.
- I believe it will flat-line for a few years and then slowly gain as a much-needed franchise overhaul hopefully takes place.

Expert Comments

If investing in a low-middle volume store, you will definitely need to be an owner-operator, at least until you increase sales, for the right return.

60 hours a week to start, then 40. Must be hands-on owner operator for efficiencies. Buy a store with $350k plus price tag if you can find one, and sales about $550k plus. Always keep rent below 10%; mall stores not recommended.

Seller Financing

- Almost always bank financing. SBA lenders are very receptive of financing franchises, especially Subways.
- Seller financing best option, but financing not very difficult as the brand is favoured.

Resources

- Subway: http://www.subway.com/en-us

Sunroom and Awning Installation		
SIC 1521-22	NAICS 326199	

Rules of Thumb

➤ 35% of annual sales plus inventory

Pricing Tips

- Strong, knowledgeable managers who have been with this specialty business for a long time can add a lot of value to the company. This would also increase the buyer pool greatly. A buyer with no knowledge or experience in this business could purchase it and be successful.

Benchmark Data

- 30%+ net income based on gross sales

Expenses (% of Annual Sales)

Cost of Goods 15%
Occupancy Costs 15%
Payroll/Labor Costs .... 25% to 30%
Profit (pretax) 30%

Questions
- What contracts do you have with whom?

Industry Trend
- Growing due to housing boom in area

Expert Comments

Competition—this is a specialty business; risk—there is an abundance of work in this field; profit trend—sales have shown steady increases; location—a shop and a central location is all you need; marketability—there is a high demand for this type of work; industry trend—new housing boom and damages from hurricane have this business booked for years; replication—this being a specialty business, most construction workers don't have the necessary knowledge to do these jobs.

Resources
- National Sunroom Association (NSA): http://www.nationalsunroom.org

Supermarkets/Grocery Stores

SIC 5411-05	NAICS 445110	Number of Businesses/Units 66,639

Rules of Thumb

➤ 3 x EBIT

➤ 10–22% of annual sales plus inventory

➤ 2–3 x SDE; add fixtures, equipment plus inventory

➤ 3–3.5 x EBITDA

Pricing Tips
- There are different departments within a supermarket, with some departments having a gross profit of 30% or more and others having lower than 10% and even negative gross profit on sale items; so depending on the store customers' buying habits and how these departments are managed, the selling price will be adjusted.
- When we benchmarked the typical hard-discounter P&L versus traditional grocers, we found that the discounters turn a 12 percentage-point disadvantage in gross margin into a 3.5 percentage-point advantage in EBITDA. They do this with carefully designed operations that leverage deep sourcing expertise, massive sales intensity per SKU on a small number of 'bull's eye' lines, low-labor merchandising and very small-footprint stores. The result is a store that can be profitable with prices up to 20 percent below Walmart's, and in locations that are too densely populated to support a Walmart Supercenter.

S

- Since traditional grocers today run with 2 percent earnings before interest and tax (EBIT) and a 20 percent volume variable margin, a 10 percent market share to online would erase their aggregate profitability at current footprint.
- Gas & lottery sales should not be included in gross sales.
- EBITDA is most reliable. Gross sales are fairly irrelevant for smaller stores (sales under $5M).
- Location, demographics, and competition are the 3 biggest factors in pricing.
- Rent above 3% of sales, or a short-term lease will reduce value of business.

Benchmark Data

Statistics (Supermarkets and Grocery Stores)

Number of Establishments	66,639
Average Profit Margin	2.0%
Revenue per Employee	$227,600
Average Number of Employees	40.6
Average Wages per Employee	$22,815

Products and Services Segmentation

Other food items	35.0%
Beverages (Including alcohol)	18.1%
Dairy Products	12.8%
Other non-food items	9.4%
Fresh and frozen meat	9.1%
Frozen foods	6.4%
Drugs and health products	5.5%
Fruit and vegetables	3.7%

Industry Costs

Profit	2.0%
Wages	10.0%
Purchases	74.6%
Depreciation	0.9%
Marketing	0.8%
Rent & Utilities	4.3%
Other	7.4%

Market Share

The Kroger Co.	15.8%
Albertsons LLC	9.9%
Publix Super Markets Inc.	5.7%

- "As consumers adopt more healthy eating habits, organic and locally sourced products grow in importance. The study found that 48 percent prefer to buy organic products, when given a choice. Produce is by far the most popular organic item—90 percent said they had purchased it in the previous 30 days. Meat wasn't far behind with 55 percent, dairy was a close third with 54 percent, and packaged canned (soups, sauces, etc.) and dry products (cereal, pasta, etc.) were each cited by 29 percent to tie for fourth. On the flip side, only 6 percent of shoppers reported purchasing organic baby products."

Source: http://www.progressivegrocer.com/industry-news-trends/
trader-joes-leads-market-force-ranking-favorite-grocers

- Supermarket Facts

  Number of employees.. 3.4 million
  Source: Bureau of Labor Statistics

  Total supermarket sales—2016 ....$668.680 Billion

  Number of supermarkets—2016.. 38,441
  Source: Progressive Grocer Magazine

  Net profit after taxes—2016.. 1.1%

  Median total store size in square feet—2016 41,300

  Median weekly sales per supermarket—2016... $397,499

  Weekly sales per square foot of selling area—2016..$11.89

  Sales per customer transaction—2016.. $30.02

  Sales per labor hour—2016.. $137

  Average number items carried in supermarket in 2016 38,900
  Source: Food Marketing Institute, https://www.fmi.org/our-research/supermarket-facts

Expenses (% of Annual Sales)

Cost of Goods	70% to 75%
Occupancy Costs	05% to 05%
Payroll/Labor Costs	05% to 15%
Profit (pretax)	02% to 15%

Questions

- What are the prospects of new competition? How is pricing managed?
- Why are you selling? Check the store order history to determine what kind of clients are shopping the store. A store with high add ordering and low everyday items ordering is not a good store, and you have to examine the P&L very carefully.
- What additional incentives do your suppliers provide that may not show on the financial statements?
- Consider the possibility of a new competitor coming into the market and what effect it will have on the store location. It is also important to have effective security measures in place to minimize employee theft. Look at the ability to expand the square footage of the store in order to offer more variety and departments within the business.

Industry Trend

- "Amazon has the know-how to make shopping a better experience. They will absolutely revolutionize the way Whole Foods manages its logistics and inventory. The whole experience is going to be very different. Grocery stores are going to revolutionize the way people buy items, the way they pay for them, the way they handle inventory, the way they distribute to stores — all to compete with Amazon, they are going to have to find new ways to be efficient."
  Source: "How big can Amazon-Whole Foods get?"
  https://www.washingtonpost.com/news/get-there/wp/2017/08/30/the-man-who-sold-his-supermarket-to-whole-foods-talks-about-the-future-of-grocery-stores/?utm_term=.cccecbb569a
- "There is a fundamental shift afoot in the grocery world, one that promises to recreate the shopping experience in customers. Retailers, however, may not be so charmed and some will not survive the transition being driven by the following forces. The shift to healthier eating has already changed grocery retail. Retailers from Kroger to Walmart and Aldi have increased offerings in these categories, driving prices down and increasing access for U.S. consumers to healthy foods. Whole Foods has already felt the impact of this--posting six consecutive quarters of sales declines--and has ceded ground that used to be exclusively theirs."
  Source: "Grocery Shopping Is About t Change Dramatically" by Laura Heller, Forbes, March 21, 2017, https://www.forbes.com/sites/lauraheller/2017/03/21/grocery-shopping-is-about-to-change-dramatically/

S

Expert Comments

Check out the current competitive environment and ask about any anticipated new competition.

Competition is the most influential effect on a grocery store. There are many independent stores that thrive in areas that are too small or remote for a larger chain. However, the arrival of a new chain store, even if it is out of town, can drastically disrupt the business. Industry sales and profits are fairly steady. There is good buyer demand for well-located stores.

A good location is difficult to secure, but once you have established a strong business it can be very lucrative. The food business is a low margin business with nice cash flow but there is always new competition coming aboard. Walmart, drug stores, dollar stores, and convenience stores require store operators to constantly run a tight ship.

We see a high demand for established retail food stores. New or threatened competition can decrease value greatly and diminish buyer interest. Stores in smaller, rural areas have a reduced threat of larger operators and are in good demand.

Seller Financing

- In more rural areas, grocery stores own their real estate. This makes bank financing easier. For stores without real estate, subordinate seller financing is often necessary in addition to bank financing.
- Most larger stores are sold with outside financing. Smaller stores that do not include real estate usually require seller financing.
- Generally, we are seeing sellers financing a small portion, along with a primary lender.

Resources

- National Grocers Association (NGA): http://www.nationalgrocers.org
- Grocery Manufacturers of America (GMA): http://www.gmaonline.org
- New Hampshire Grocers Association (NHGA): http://www.grocers.org
- Progressive Grocer: http://www.progressivegrocer.com
- Food Marketing Institute (FMI): http://www.fmi.org
- Supermarket News: http://www.supermarketnews.com
- IBISWorld, October 2017: http://ibisworld.com
- FMI Foundation Supermarket Facts: http://www.fmi.org/research-resources/supermarket-facts

		Franchise
Swisher (Restroom Hygiene Service)		
Approx. Total Investment		$100,000—$150,000
	NAICS 561720	Number of Businesses/Units 110

Rules of Thumb

➤ 50% of annual sales plus inventory

Resources

- Swisher: http://www.swsh.com/

Franchise

Sylvan Learning Center

Approx. Total Investment		$70,980–$159,890
	NAICS 611691	Number of Businesses/Units 565

Rules of Thumb

➢ 1.7 x SDE plus inventory

Pricing Tips

- The multiples of SDE vary depending on the owner benefit. Higher owner benefits drive higher multiples.

Questions

- How much in prepaid revenues as of today?

Expert Comments

With the advent of SylvanSync, Sylvan has brought technology to the forefront and no other competitor has such a product to offer.

Seller Financing

- 2 years

Resources

- Sylvan Learning Center: http://sylvanfranchise.com

Franchise

Synergy HomeCare

Approx. Total Investment		$35,425–$149,400
	NAICS 621610	Number of Businesses/Units 338

Rules of Thumb

➢ 30–35% of annual sales includes inventory

Resources

- Synergy HomeCare: http://www.synergyhomecare.com

Franchise

Taco John's

Approx. Total Investment		$336,000–$1,094,000
Estimated Annual Sales/Unit		$935,000
	NAICS 722513	Number of Businesses/Units 387

Rules of Thumb

➢ 30% of annual sales plus inventory

T

Resources
- Taco John's: http://www.tacojohns.com

Tanning Salons		
SIC 7299-44	NAICS 812199	Number of Businesses/Units 13,829

Rules of Thumb
➢ 2 x EBITDA

➢ 2–2.5 x SDE includes inventory

➢ 50–60% of annual sales plus inventory

➢ 2 x EBIT

Pricing Tips
- Age of the equipment. Age of the tanning lamps. High-pressure tanning beds & tanning booths vs. low-pressure ones. High-pressure equipment has more value and brings in more revenue, but the lamp replacements cost more. They tend to be newer equipment. Variety & diversity of the equipment adds value, for example, having equipment that provides red light therapy for skin rejuvenation, equipment that senses skin sensitivity to prevent burning, having equipment with mostly UVA rays for very light skin or sensitive skin, having stand-up booths & lay-down beds, providing body wrap services, tooth whitening services.
- Pricing may vary based on the time of year the salon is sold, due to seasonality. Higher multiples will be achieved in the December to February time frames, as peak season is March until June. Buyers will seek to get in and implement changes prior to the busy season. Salon values are then depressed from June until November, as the salons are far less lucrative (or even operating in the red) during these months.

Benchmark Data

Statistics (Tanning Salons)
Number of Establishments	13,829
Average Profit Margin	9.4%
Revenue Per Employee	$66,600
Average Number of Employees	2.6
Average Wages per Employee	$24,401

Products and Services Segmentation
UV tanning	50.3%
Sunless tanning	37.5%
Merchandise sales	12.2%

Industry Costs
Profit	9.4%
Wages	36.6%
Purchases	23.7%
Depreciation	3.2%
Marketing	4.7%
Rent & Utilities	11.8%
Other	10.6%

- Average sales per tanner/client should be around $15 in addition to the membership fees.
- Rent, payroll, COGS, and utilities should account for approximately 90% of total expenses.
- It will be worthwhile to determine bed utilization, electrical power capacity utilization, sales per square foot, and percentage of sale percentages from monthly electronic fund transfers, recurring memberships or single sessions.

Expenses (% of Annual Sales)

Cost of Goods	10%
Occupancy Costs	15% to 25%
Payroll/Labor Costs	20% to 25%
Profit (pretax)	30%

Questions

- Seller to keep good books and records where the computer sales reports match the tax returns. Buyer should ask & verify the age of the equipment and age of the bulbs in each equipment. The good thing for a buyer is that a lot of information can be analysed, verified through the salon computer in terms of sales breakdown by demographics, age & gender of the clients, amount spent by each client, busy time of the day or busy time of the year and much more.
- Have any of your competitors gone out of business within the last 12 months? Who has opened up within the last 12 months? How old are each of the beds? How old are the bulbs in each bed?
- How many hours are truly worked by owner? Are there any new competitors?
- How many members have you lost in the last 12 months? What is your retention percentage? How old is each piece of equipment? Do you have every bed metered? How do you check on your employees to make sure they are not giving away free time?
- How old is the equipment? How often is maintenance performed? Is there an EFT system in place?

Industry Trend

- "The tanning industry found little to celebrate during Barack Obama's presidency, but it's starting to cheer up. Mr. Obama's signature health law, the Affordable Care Act, put a 10 percent excise tax on indoor tanning services, and during his two terms, the federal government and states sought to deter the use of tanning beds by young people in particular, citing evidence that it causes skin cancer.

  "The tanning industry says the tax has helped force thousands of salons out of business. But now, the bill Republicans proposed this week to repeal the A.C.A. would abolish the tanning tax, along with an array of other taxes imposed to help finance expanded health insurance coverage."
  Source: Tanning Industry, Taxed Under Obama, Cheers G.O.P. Health Bill" by Abby Goodnough, The New York Times, March 9, 2017, https://www.nytimes.com/2017/03/09/health/tanning-tax-repeal.html?mcubz=0
- "Lori Crane, a professor at the Colorado School of Public Health, who has studied the marketing techniques tanning salons use to court customers.: 'One thing we have seen is more ads for spray tans than ultraviolet tanning,' said Crane, who has studied the behavior of salon businesses."
  Source: "Twilight of the Tanning Salons: As Federal Health Regulations Close in and the Economy Struggles, Is the Sun Setting on the Tanning Industry?" by Patrick Clark, October 5, 2016, https://www.bloomberg.com/features/2016-tanning-salon-industry/

T

- "From its early beginnings in the 60s to the incredible, high-tech units of today, sunless tanning is deeply embedded in the everyday business of the tanning industry. When sunless tanning started, it was thought of as ancillary product to a UV tanning experience. Now, it plays a vital role in a salon's business plan. "Additionally, when public health officials and dermatologists started blaming the rise in skin cancer on UV tanning or excessive sun exposure, people began shying away from those options and seeking out alternate methods for achieving their desired tan. Further, there has been a substantial increase of governmental regulations on the tanning bed industry including the 'Tan Tax' and age restrictions that have caused the UV industry to suffer as a result, and therefore seek out other or additional services to offer their customers. Hence, the rise in sunless automated booths and custom airbrushing services."

  Source: "Industry Report: The State of Sunless" posted by Joe Schuster, March 1, 2016, http://www.istmagazine.com/industry-report-the-state-of-sunless/

- "The industry is shifting to more modern high-end salons versus the traditional mom and pop style locations. Gyms nail salons and beauty shops continue to add single tanning beds. This is perceived as a threat but novice entrants are rarely successful in tanning."

  Source: http://www.bizben.com/blog/posts/tanning-salons- should-you- consider-buying- one-6775.php

Expert Comments

Good equipment is very expensive, thus it is not easy to replicate. It will cost a minimum of $100,000.00 in equipment alone to set up a new & modern salon. All new equipment can go up much higher.

Locations are often difficult to replicate, but they are one of the most important factors in valuation. Adjacent anchor tenants, nearby gyms, or complementary neighbors such as hair and nail salons or day spas also influence value and provide a business a sustainable competitive advantage.

Resources
- The National Tanning Training Institute (NTTI): http://www.tanningtraining.com
- Smart Tan Magazine: http://www.smarttan.com
- ist Magazine: http://www.istmagazine.com
- IBISWorld, April 2017: http://ibisworld.com

Tattoo Parlors

SIC 7299-43	NAICS 812199	Number of Businesses/Units 41,362

Rules of Thumb

➤ 50% of annual sales includes inventory

Benchmark Data

Tattoo Statistics (Tattoo Artists)

Number of Establishments	41,362
Average Profit Margin	10.7%
Revenue per Employee	$22,300
Average Number of Employees	1.2
Average Wages per Employee	$12,009

Products and Services Segmentation

Custom-designed tattoos	59.5%
Predesigned tattoos	19.8%
Piercings	14.3%
Other	6.4%

Industry Costs

Profit	10.7%
Wages	54.2%
Purchases	10.7%
Depreciation	1.8%
Marketing	1.2%
Rent & Utilities	11.2%
Other	10.2%

Industry Trend

- "In the U.S., tattoos are estimated to be a $1 billion industry according to research house IBIS World. In 2016, there were about 38,879 tattoo businesses registered in the U.S., where the market grew 13 percent between 2011 and 2016.

  "'Tattoo studios haven't changed a huge amount since the late-1980s in this country,' Lodder [Matt Loder, lecturer who studies the tattoo industry] said. 'Most tattooists don't take credit cards; it's still very much a cash-in-hand business. So I'd be really surprised if anyone seized on this.'

  "The Internet has had a major effect on the tattoo industry though, he says. As brick and mortar stores increasingly vacate premises to sell online, opportunities for a physical presence have increased for businesses who simply cannot conduct business online, such as tattooists.

  "'It's the same reason we've got this influx of barber shops and hairdressers,' Lodder says. 'It's one of those things you can't buy on the internet. You'll find a lot of old shop spaces being taken up by tattoo artists because that's the sort of business that still needs premises. You can't send a tattoo over the Internet.'"

Source: "Now Everyone's Getting Tattooed, This Startup Is Digitizing the Industry" by Nate Lanxon, June 7, 2017, https://www.bloomberg.com/news/articles/2017-06-07/now-everyone-s-getting-tattooed-this-startup-is-digitizing-the-industry

Resources

- IBISWorld, September 2016: http://ibisworld.com

Taxicab Businesses		
SIC 4121-01	NAICS 485310	Number of Businesses/Units 356,616

Rules of Thumb

➢ 4 x EBITDA plus value of vehicles

Pricing Tips

- Selling price should be between 1 year and 2 years' net profit, depending upon the number of cabs and their respective ages.

T

Benchmark Data

Statistics (Taxi & Limousine Services)

Number of Establishments	356,616
Average Profit Margin	8.2%
Revenue per Employee	$45,500
Average Number of Employees	1.2
Average Wages per Employee	$32,730

Products and Services Segmentation

Taxi and taxi leasing services	36.7%
Stretch limousine services	23.8%
Luxury and corporate sedan services	20.3%
Hearse rentals and other funeral services	9.9%
SUV, large van and other services	9.3%

Industry Costs

Profit	8.2%
Wages	71.1%
Purchases	6.8%
Depreciation	6.1%
Marketing	0.7%
Rent & Utilities	3.7%
Other	3.4%

Industry Trend

- "More than 2,900 of Chicago's nearly 7,000 licensed taxis were inactive in March 2017 — meaning they had not picked up a fare in a month, according to the Cab Drivers United/AFSCME Local 2500 report. The average monthly income per active medallion — the permit that gives cabbies the exclusive right to pick up passengers who hail them on the street — has dipped from $5,276 in January 2014 to $3,206 this year. The number of riders in Chicago hailing cabs has also plummeted during that same period from 2.3 million monthly riders to about 1.1 million."

  Source: "Chicago cabbies say industry is teetering toward collapse" by Aamer Madhani, *USA TODAY*, June 5, 2017, https://www.usatoday.com/story/news/2017/06/05/chicago-cabbies-say-industry-teetering-toward-collapse/102524634/

- "The upending of the traditional taxi business across the United States and around the world by Uber, Lyft and other ride-hailing services has given consumers new and sometimes cheaper options and forced cities to re-examine their transportation policies. Uber, in some places, has employed aggressive techniques to evade regulatory limits, and prompted demonstrations by taxi drivers and owners in places like Paris, London and Brasília. And it has ignited an intense competition for drivers, nowhere more so than in New York.

  "Despite the conflicts, Uber is a relentless competitor, and the taxi and Uber centers that have opened in different sections of the same neighborhood in Queens are a visible manifestation of how the rival industries continue to take on each other out of view of their customers. Both have introduced amenities for drivers once unheard-of in a no-frills industry, but Uber's showstopping center and incentives underscore how the deep-pocketed newcomer has become the behemoth in a crowded field."

  Source: "As Uber Woos More Drivers, Taxis Hit Back" by Winnie Hu, *The New York Times*, March 18, 2017, https://www.nytimes.com/2017/03/18/nyregion/nyc-taxi-center-uber.html?mcubz=0

- "What's more, employment rose not just in self-employed drivers, but also in traditional taxi services. It's also noticeable that Uber drivers were found to earn more than those in traditional taxi services. This is largely due to the fact that the Uber software allows drivers to better optimize their time and services.
"'The higher hourly earnings among self-employed drivers suggest that capacity utilization, in terms of the time spent in the car with a passenger, has increased with Uber, as its platform allows for better matching between drivers and passengers. But for traditional taxi drivers the effect has been the opposite, with a decline in the amount of time they have a passenger in their vehicle,' Frey (Oxford Martin School's Carl Benedikt Frey) says.
"In much of the discourse around this issue, the suggestion seems to be that the market is of a fixed size, and therefore Uber drivers are taking income from licensed drivers. I suspect however, that the reality is that Uber et al have significantly increased the size of the market, especially in off-peak times where dissatisfaction with licensed drivers is at its peak."
Source: "Study Explores the Impact of Uber on the Taxi Industry," by Adi Gaskell, January 26, 2017, https://www.forbes.com/sites/adigaskell/2017/01/26/study-explores-the-impact-of-uber-on-the-taxi-industry/#3d923bfe16b0

Resources
- IBISWorld, January 2017: http://ibisworld.com

		Franchise
TCBY and Mrs. Fields		
Approx. Total Investment		$100,000–$450,000
	NAICS 722515	Number of Businesses/Units 880

Rules of Thumb
➢ 40–45% of annual sales plus inventory

Resources
- TCBY: http://www.tcby.com

Technology Companies—Information

Rules of Thumb
➢ 100% of annual sales plus inventory

➢ 3 x EBIT

➢ 3–3.5 x SDE plus inventory

➢ 3–4 x EBITDA

Pricing Tips
- The larger the technology company, the higher the multiple. We've sold some for 6 or 7x EBITDA.
- Recurring revenue is key to sales and key to higher valuation.
- "In fact, the best time to sell a technology company is when you are growing. Our rule of thumb is that while the company's revenues are growing greater than 20%, it is best to keep growing the company. When it starts teetering

around 20% or dropping below 20%, it is best to sell the company. The reason is that selling a company exhibiting growing forecasts is much easier than selling a company exhibiting flat or nominally increasing forecasts. Buyers are typically looking at the forecasts of your company to determine its value, so it is much better being in a position to offer strong, growing forecasts that a buyer can believe."

Source: Orion Capital Group

- Renewal rates are paramount, whether the business is advertiser supported or subscription supported.

Benchmark Data

- The sales ratio to employee expense should exceed 1.5 to 1.

Expenses (% of Annual Sales)

Cost of Goods	40%
Occupancy Costs	05% to 08%
Payroll/Labor Costs	22% to 25%
Profit (pretax)	20% to 25%

Questions

- Concentration of customers. Code for software. Other cross-sell opportunities. Who are the competitors?

Industry Trend

- "So-called 'exponential' technologies including robotics, virtual and augmented reality (VR) (AR), 3-D printing, and artificial intelligence (AI) are opening up significant areas of opportunity.

  Cognitive technologies such as machine learning, natural language processing, and speech and pattern recognition are being embedded in software applications, imbuing big data with superior capabilities.

  Blockchain, the foundation for the digital currency bitcoin, has enormous implications not only for the financial services industry, but for any company that manages a large amount of transaction data.

  The Internet of Things has only just begun to reveal its promise.

  'Anything as a service' offerings; ones that allow usage-based consumption are likely to emerge.

  Cybersecurity products and services are another area with a bright future."

Source: Paul Sallomi in "Deloitte's 2017 Technology Outlook," https://www2.deloitte.com/us/en/pages/
technology-media-and-telecommunications/articles/technology-industry-outlook.html

- It will continue to grow.
- High demand for tech business with recurring revenue, and technology in general

Expert Comments

Due diligence on the product and code is important as is the ability to offer the product in the cloud. If you can transition the product to a cloud-based product, there is an opportunity to sell to a wider base, although at a lower price point. Unique, niche software is a good option as long as the industry is wide enough.

1. Uniqueness of software is key. 2. Technicians and technical staff are important. 3. Difficult to duplicate due to writing of code

Seller Financing
- Usually a cash component, notes, and some sort of earnout based on realized revenue or signatures for contracts obtained from customers.

Technology Companies—Manufacturing		
	NAICS 334111	

Rules of Thumb
➤ Niche market—4.25 to 4.75 x adjusted net plus inventory

➤ PCB—4.65 to 5.0 x adjusted net plus inventory

➤ Software—4.50 to 6.0 x adjusted net plus inventory

➤ Non-niche—4.35 to 5.5 x adjusted net plus inventory

Pricing Tips
- The technology industry is very diverse and there are many subsegments. The asset-intensive sectors tend to be mostly in the 0.5 to 1.0 times sales, but the asset-light companies can go for several times sales. However, as the industries mature, many fall in to the 3 to 7 times EBITDA range.
- For specialty companies, there are no Rules of Thumb. Very high multiples are possible if the company has a very desirable product or technology.
- Adjusted net times [EBIT] 4 to 5.5 (depending on prior growth curves)

Expenses (% of Annual Sales)

Cost of Goods	60%
Occupancy Costs	10%
Payroll/Labor Costs	15%
Profit (pretax)	15%

Benchmark Data
- Revenue per employee is almost always in excess of $100,000. For some higher-knowledge companies, it can be $200,000 per employee or more.

Questions
- The most important things to find out are competition and the stickiness of customers.

Industry Trend
- Continued growth

Expert Comments
Buyers should not consider if they do not have the technical background.

Entry into the segment requires considerable technical expertise, and usually there is no space for people outside of the industry to enter. The customer relationships also tend to be deep, making it difficult for competition to take away business.

T

Seller Financing
- A lot of transactions are financed with cash and earnouts.

Technology Companies—Service		
	NAICS 541	

Rules of Thumb
➤ 3–7 x EBITDA

➤ Temporary Agencies—1.25 to 3.5 x EBITDA

➤ Test Services—2.75 to 3.35 x EBITDA

➤ Design Services—2.5 to 3.5 x EBITDA

➤ (Adjusted net for large companies is EBITDA, for smaller ones SDE is used as adjusted net)

Pricing Tips
- The multiples are not consistent since every company has its own gross profit percentage and cost of goods sold. In most manufacturing and distribution companies, the net income margins are very thin, thus the overall percentage of net profit to revenue is also small.
- Very specialized. Normal price or sales multiples are not normal at all. Sales multiples can go from 0.5 to 8, all depending on the scalability and profitability of the model. EBITDA multiples typically tend to be above par. 5–8 x is normal for good deals.
- Growth is very important; stagnating companies tend to be closer to 3 x SDE or 4–5x EBITDA. Growth companies can get 4–5 x SDE and 5–8 x EBITDA

Benchmark Data
- For small service business, there should be at least $150K per year per employees; for high value-added situations the number can be closer to $300K per year; net margins of high teens are common for successful companies.

Expenses (% of Annual Sales)
Cost of Goods	40% to 50%
Occupancy Costs	04% to 05%
Payroll/Labor Costs	20% to 22%
Profit (pretax)	15% to 20%

Questions
- 1. What are the staffing issues;
- 2. How consistent have the margins been for specific products;
- 3. What is your biggest challenge in operating the business;
- 4. What would you do to grow the business in the next 12–18 months.
- Typically margins tell the story. If the margins are not in high teens, then there may not be too many barriers to the business. Probe about competition. That is the key.
- Focus should be on strategic value of the business because most of the time the value has very little to do with current financials.

Industry Trend

- With shrinking margins, combinations are inevitable and occurring on a regular basis. The legacy owners of companies with less than $25M in volume are subject to takeover and acquisition due to the economies of scale. Larger companies can reduce the Cost of Goods Sold by 4–5%, savings which go to the bottom line.
- Technology is an increasing part of everyone's life. The growth trend is likely to continue.

Expert Comments

Understanding the upcoming changes in the industry and understanding competition is critical to success.

Competition for a lot of companies can come from anywhere in the world. Service companies tend to be more local. At the same, time customers tend to be sticky. The more value added, the more sticky.

Most companies in the industry have been around a while and have their own niche; lots of long-term customers; usually good downside protection.

Seller Financing

- Smaller companies (less than $10M) are seller financed while others may qualify for bank or outside financing depending on inventory levels, receivable levels and past banking relationships.
- SBA is difficult because most of the value is likely to be in goodwill. High cash component, seller carry and performance payouts are common.
- Combination of cash and seller financing; buyer may tap into existing lines of credit; typically no new SBA financing.
- Typically sellers get a good parity of value on earnouts, noncompetes, etc.

Tee Shirt Shops		
SIC 5699-17	NAICS 448190	
Rules of Thumb		

➤ 30% of annual sales plus inventory

Telecommunication Carriers (Wired)		
	NAICS 517311	
Rules of Thumb		

➤ 2.5 x SDE includes inventory

Pricing Tips

- Need to understand how the carrier commission structure will impact the current client base and future sales. Trained, knowledgeable and professional sales staff is critical-this is not an order-taking environment.

Benchmark Data

- Sales per employee

Expenses (% of Annual Sales)

Cost of Goods	40%
Occupancy Costs	12%
Payroll/Labor Costs	24%
Profit (pretax)	17%

Questions
- Trends for client counts. Cancellation rates and velocity.

Industry Trend
- "Ever since Donald Trump's presidential victory, the stock prices of most of the major telecom stocks have enjoyed a bullish run in the market through the end of the first quarter of 2017. . . the less restrictive nature of the FCC will aid mergers and acquisitions which will likely spur growth in 2017.
  "Key attributes for 2017:
    - ✓ The telecommunications industry is essentially characterized by high barriers to entry.
    - ✓ A major characteristic of the telecommunications industry is that it is immune to international geo-political disturbances, even when these lead to economic fluctuations.
    - ✓ Wireless network strength is the key to future growth of the overall telecom industry.
    - ✓ Telecom companies offer one of the highest dividend yields in the U.S. economy.
    - ✓ Mergers and acquisitions (M&A) are not uncommon in the U.S. telecom industry. In order to stay ahead of competition, existing players need to be constantly on their toes to introduce innovative products or merge with other companies. In the near future, the U.S. telecom industry is likely to witness further mergers and acquisitions along with product diversifications."

  Source:"U.S. Telecommunications Industry Outlook-April 2017" by Zacks Equity Research, http://www.nasdaq.com/article/us-telecommunications-industry-outlook-april-2017-cm769297

- "The Wired Telecommunications Carriers industry is anticipated to experience declining revenue over the next five years. The move away from copper infrastructure will underpin the gradual transition from traditional telephony to VoIP. Telecommunications providers are increasingly competing to be a one-stop shop for consumers, offering an array of services over the same infrastructure. Consequently, it is unlikely that carriers will continue to use copper infrastructure to provide voice services in areas where fiber-optic networks are available. By offering voice, data and video services through the same infrastructure, telecommunications carriers are able to spread their fixed costs not only across their subscriber base, but also across three different markets. Operators will likely choose to offer VoIP technology over this infrastructure because of its price attractiveness to consumers and the lower maintenance associated with sending voice transmission the same way data is already transmitted."

  Source: http://clients1.ibisworld.com/reports/us/industry/industryoutlook.aspx?entid=1268

Expert Comments
Very robust, competitive landscape, but a savvy operator can carve out a healthy market share.

Telecommunications

| | NAICS 517110 | |

Rules of Thumb

➤ 3 x SDE includes inventory

➤ 5 x EBITDA

Pricing Tips

- Depends on the amount of equipment involved as well as the quality. Differentiate from fiber optic splicers and diggers.
- Three variables—$1,000 to $2,000 per installed port; 20 to 40 percent of annual revenues, depending upon sales mix and earnings; earnings impact selling price, but on a case by case basis relating to the first two variables plus cash flow analysis. This industry is far from exact, as market share, client base revenues, product line exclusivity, market potential (saturation) and earnings all impact market value. The old adage "beauty is in the eye of the beholder" definitely applies to the telecom industry. Client (installed) base revenue mix and profit margin? New system sales product mix? Competition? Service reputation? Customer retention rate? Inventory obsolescence factor? Overall pretax profit?

Questions

- Where do your customers come from?
- Are there any Competitive Local Exchange Carriers (CLECs) operational in market area? Do they have their own facilities or are they reselling?

Industry Trend

- "A report from Ovum details the situation's stakes: telecom firms are projected to grow to over $297 billion just by 2020, with new information and communications technology (ICT) revenues kicking in the largest share of that growth, around $173 billion total. That represents a compound annual growth rate (CAGR) of 9.9 percent between 2015 and 2020, and that means a huge number of competitors eager to claim a slice of that rapidly-growing market."

  Source: "With Managed Services on the Rise, How Can Telcos Stay Ahead?" by Steve Anderson, August 2, 2016, http://www.msptoday.com/topics/msp-today/articles/ 423765-with-managed-services-the-rise-how-telcos-stay.htm

- "Major telecommunications companies include AT&T, Verizon and ComCast, but the bright future painted by our economy is not limited to these industry conglomerates. Small businesses in the telecommunications sector can expect a year of growth and advancement, making it an excellent time to start planning for their future."

  Source: http://www.vikingmergers.com/blog/2016/determining-the-value-of-a-telecom-company/

Seller Financing

- 3 to 5 years

Resources

- Telephony Magazine: http://www.tmcnet.com

T

Television Stations		
SIC 4833-01	NAICS 515120	

Rules of Thumb

➢ 9–12 x EBITDA

Industry Trend

- "So Much TV—On average, American adults are watching five hours and four minutes of television per day. The bulk of that — about four and a half hours of it — is live television, which is television watched when originally broadcast. Thirty minutes more comes via DVR.

  "The Young Flee Live TV—Let's break this into groups. People over the age of 50 watch the most TV, somewhere in the range of 50 hours a week, according to Nielsen. In fact, people over the age of 50 are watching more TV per week this year than last. But that's where that trend ends. People 24 and under are watching, roughly, two fewer hours of live TV and DVR programming per week than last year. And 25- to 34-year-olds (roughly speaking, millennials)? They're watching an hour less per week, down from 27 and a half hours to 26 and a half hours. People between 35 and 49 mostly held steady and are watching about 22 minutes less television per week: 36 and a half hours from nearly 37 hours a week.

  "Streaming Services Roar—About 50 percent of Americans now have subscription services like Netflix, Amazon Prime and Hulu in their homes, Nielsen said. That is up from 42 percent last year. And that figure of 50 percent for the paid services equals for the first time the proportion of homes with DVR players. The DVR numbers have held steady for the past year.

  "Tablets and Phones Rule—Tablets are now in 58 percent of American homes, a jump of 17 percent from last year (for comparison, HD TVs are in 94 percent of American homes, an increase of about 4 percent). And time spent consuming media on tablets has increased 63 percent — to 31 minutes from 19 minutes a day (in 2014, the average was 12 minutes a day). Likewise, people are spending one hour and 39 minutes a day consuming media on their phones this year, versus an hour and two minutes last year — a 60 percent jump.

  "Wired All The Time—The amount of time you spend consuming media — watching TV, surfing the web on a computer, using an app on your phone, listening to the radio and so forth — continues to go up. Nielsen said that in 2015, Americans spent about nine and a half hours each day consuming content this way. This year? The average is 10 hours and 39 minutes."

  Source: "How Much Do We Love TV? Let Us Count the Ways" by John Koblin, June 30, 2016, https://www.nytimes.com/2016/07/01/business/media/nielsen-survey-media-viewing.html

		Franchise
The Maids		
Approx. Total Investment		$93,000–$125,000
	NAICS 561720	Number of Businesses/Units 1,092

Rules of Thumb

➢ 40–45% of annual sales plus inventory

Resources
- The Maids: http://www.maids.com

Therapists—Offices of Occupational, Physical, Speech and Audiologists

Rules of Thumb
➢ 63% of annual sales plus inventory
➢ 2.6 x SDE plus inventory
➢ 4.5 x EBIT
➢ 4.8 x EBITDA

Benchmark Data

Expenses (% of Annual Sales)
Cost of Goods	22%
Payroll/Labor Costs	04%
Profit (pretax)	10%

Questions
- Payor mix, market share, patient demographic data

Industry Trend
- Competition is steady, growth is expected for the next 5 years, fragmentation should remain constant.

Seller Financing
- Outside financing

		Franchise
The Zoo Health Club		
Approx. Total Investment	$73,899–$278,499 (equipment purchased);	
$48,399–$189,249 (equipment leased)		
	NAICS 713940	Number of Businesses/Units 25

Rules of Thumb
➢ 20% of annual sales

Resources
- The Zoo Health Club: http://www.zoogym.co

Ticket Services		
SIC 7999-73	NAICS 561599	

Rules of Thumb
➢ 2 x SDE

T

Pricing Tips
- Due to StubHub, RazorGator and private equity shops, multiple has increased.

Questions
- Number of corporate clients?
- Length of time in business? Stability of earnings? How do they get tickets? Average markup? Repeat business?

Industry Trend
- "'Ticketing, to put it bluntly, is a fixed game,' said a report Schneiderman's [New York Attorney General Eric Schneiderman] office released Thursday. Part of the problem is so-called computer bots, which are programs that ticket brokers use to quickly buy a large number of tickets the minute they go on sale. Schneiderman's report cites examples such as a U2 tour last year in which a single bot bought 15,000 tickets in one day and Beyonce's 2013 concert at the Barclay's Center in Brooklyn, which sold 520 tickets in 3 minutes."

  Source: "Event ticket sales are rigged says attorney general" by Chris Isidore, January 28, 2016, CNN, http://money.cnn.com/2016/01/28/news/companies/unfair-ticket-sales/index.html

Resources
- National Association of Ticket Brokers: http://www.natb.org

---

Tire Stores

SIC 5531-23	NAICS 441320	Number of Businesses/Units 35,675

Rules of Thumb
- ➤ 25% of annual gross sales
- ➤ 1–3 x SDE plus inventory
- ➤ 3–4 x EBIT
- ➤ 2.5–3 x EBITDA

Pricing Tips
- Tire Centers with some aftermarket services (minimum 5 bays, the average tire store has 6 to 8 bays), non-franchise multiples shown below. For franchises like Big O Tire, Goodyear, Firestone, etc. you would add an additional .20 to the multiple. Index Owner's Cash Flow (SDE) 1.5 x to $50K + inv. 2.0 x to $75K + inv. 2.5 x to $100K + (sales normally exceed $800K) 3.0 x from $125k to $250k (sales exceed $1MM+)
- Tire stores grossing over $1 million are very desirable, despite low margins, and are fetching a 3–3.5 multiple.
- The buyer needs to know what percentage of the revenues are tires vs. auto repair. A good mix is 50/50, tires to auto repair.

Benchmark Data

Statistics (Tire Dealers)

Number of Establishments	35,675
Average Profit Margin	1.7%
Revenue per Employee	$201,500
Average Number of Employees	5.5
Average Wages per Employee	$36,864

Products and Services Segmentation

Automotive services... 49.3%
Passenger car and light-truck tires 39.5%
Medium- and heavy-duty truck tires.. 8.4%
Off-road tires... 2.1%
Farm tires... 0.7%

Industry Costs

Profit 1.7%
Wages.. 18.3%
Purchases.. 61.7%
Depreciation... 1.1%
Marketing 1.1%
Rent & Utilities 4.2%
Other..11.9%

Market Share

Discount Tire Co. 11.5%
Sumitomo Corporation.. 8.5%

- Most common trend to look for in this industry is number of service bays as each service bay should produce at least $25k per month in sales if the shop is a top producer. Tires are a high price commodity and the average vehicle that purchases four tires with mounting and balancing will cost over $550; with some higher priced vehicles the cost will be over $1000.
- Some trends to look for when you are analyzing a tire store value or their success are the revenues; if they exceed $900,000 annually you can feel good about the fact it's making a six-figure adjusted net.
- Benchmark in this industry is determined by daily car count vs. the average price per invoice per vehicle. This is an integral factor for each customer who walks through the door.

Expenses (% of Annual Sales)

Cost of Goods..36% to 43%
Occupancy Costs..09% to 15%
Payroll/Labor Costs ....20% to 28%
Profit (pretax).. 13% to 20%

Questions

- Ask the owner what is their percentage of revenues on tires vs. aftermarket services. The split for a good store would be 50% tires to 50% services; however, the average normally comes in at 70% tires to 30% services. You may also ask what is their vehicle count and average ticket on a monthly basis. Do they have a manager and key techs, the tenure of each one, are all employees W-2, and what are their benefits?
- Where do they obtain their tires from (suppliers) and what is their delivery process timewise?
- Reason for selling. What he/she does on a daily basis. Worker's comp mode rate. Upside potential.

T

Industry Trend

- "Light trucks, SUVs and CUVs are continuing to grow in popularity in the U.S., prompting a surge in larger-sized aftermarket wheel demand."

  Source: "Tire Business" by Kathy McCarron, June 26, 2017,
  http://www.tirebusiness.com/article/20170626/NEWS/170629959/lt-wheels-get-bigger-in-size-and-popularity

- "The buzzword when it comes to tires is 'Low Rolling Resistance' (LRR). Every tire company in the world has jumped onto the low rolling resistance bandwagon and is marketing at least one tire that they claim is more fuel-efficient than the rest."

  Source: "Low Rolling Resistance Tires: What You Need to Know" by Sean Phillips, May 2, 2017,
  https://www.thoughtco.com/low-rolling-resistance-tires-3234470

- "However, as a company, Bridgestone Americas Inc. accounts for the greatest share of not only the replacement passenger tire market, but also the consumer (passenger and light truck) tire market. Its three main brands represent 38.1 million tires, ahead of Michelin North America Inc. (37.9 million) and Goodyear Tire & Rubber Co. (36.2 million). The three companies combined account for 48% of the replacement consumer tire market."

  Source: http://www.moderntiredealer.com/uploads/stats/facts-section16.pdf

Expert Comments

For a buyer-you want to do your books and records check along with the staff in place, who are their suppliers and their proximity to the store. Are there any commercial accounts that attribute more than 20% of the revenues and the number of customers in their database.

For a seller-you need to have your books and tax returns in order, an operations manual, mgt. in place, all employees on a W-2, good monthly records showing average ticket and number of vehicles for the same period. Keep your shop very clean and upgrade the customer area annually.

This business has shown some growth but has been affected by the competition from the big box stores and major discount stores. Tire prices have gone up as well as the other normal business expenses, i.e., rent, utilities, parts and labor costs have increased and these are four main variables. As such the owner needs to increase his car count their hourly labor rate and product costs to offset growing expenses, like labor and rent factors.

Seller Financing

- When the revenues exceed $1MM you will generally see outside financing, for the smaller producing stores you will generally see seller financing.
- Normally five years, note of 30 to 35% of the total price, at 6% interest.

Resources

- Modern Tire Dealer—a great website, one of the best: http://www.moderntiredealer.com
- Tire Business: http://www.tirebusiness.com
- Tire Review: http://www.tirereview.com
- IBISWorld, October 2017: http://ibisworld.com

Title Abstract and Settlement Offices

SIC 6541-02	NAICS 541191	

Rules of Thumb

➤ 60% of annual sales

➤ 3 x SDE

➤ 5 x EBIT

➤ 4.5 x EBITDA

Pricing Tips

- 'Affiliated Business Arrangements' (ABAs) are in vogue. Make sure the ABA is transferable upon sale. Title agencies will command higher prices in states with higher filed premiums.
- Criteria include the sales history and trends. Title companies' revenues are affected by interest rates, but the stronger ones will maintain profits through the ups and downs by adjustments of variable expenses.

Benchmark Data

Statistics (Conveyancing Services)

Number of Establishments	37,729
Average Profit Margin	12.0%
Revenue per Employee	$146,200
Average Number of Employees	2.9
Average Wages per Employee	$46,229

Products and Services Segmentation

Conveyancing and title abstract services	43.6%
Settlement and closing services	24.1%
Title search and other document filing services	12.7%
Other legal services	12.1%
Process services	5.3%
Patent copyright and other intellectual property document servi	2.2%

Major Market Segmentation   s

Businesses	61.4%
Individuals	35.8%
Government and nonprofit organizations	2.8%

Industry Costs

Profit	12.0%
Wages	31.8%
Purchases	6.3
Depreciation	1.0%
Marketing	2.3%
Rent & Utilities	8.6%
Other	38.0%

T

Market Share

Fidelity National Financial, Inc.	11.2%
First American Financial Corporation	9.2%
Stewart Information Services Corporation	6.2%

- Title companies typically retain 70% of the premium on title insurance policies issued, with remaining 30% going to the underwriter.
- Labor/Gross Revenues = <35% for metropolitan markets. Labor/Gross Revenues = <30% for rural markets

Expenses (% of Annual Sales)

Cost of Goods	30%
Occupancy Costs	07%
Payroll/Labor Costs	20%
Profit (pretax)	35%

Questions
- How many referral sources does the company have solid relationships with?

Expert Comments

Although there is significant competition, this is a highly profitable industry with relatively low barriers to entry.

Buyers for title agencies have increased due to legislative changes.

Resources
- IBISWorld, January 2017: http://ibisworld.com

Tobacco Stores		
SIC 5993-01	NAICS 453991	

Rules of Thumb

➢ 15–20% of annual sales plus inventory

Industry Trend
- "Tax increases — especially California's recently approved $2-per-pack levy increase — are among the issues convenience store retailers expect to have the biggest impact on tobacco this year. Less usage, fewer smokers and an increase in vapor users are also expected to hit cigarette numbers, according to the findings of the 15th annual Convenience Store News Forecast Study."

Source: "The 2017 Forecast for Tobacco" by Melissa Kress, January 17, 2017, https://csnews.com/2017-forecast-tobacco

Resources
- Tobacco Merchants Association (TMA): http://www.tma.org

Togo's Eatery

	Franchise
Approx. Total Investment	$257,813–$419,796
Estimated Annual Sales/Unit	$655,000

	NAICS 722513	Number of Businesses/Units 250

Rules of Thumb

> ➤ 60% of annual sales includes inventory

Resources

- Togo's Eateries: http://www.togos.com

Tour Operators

SIC 4725-01	NAICS 561520	Number of Businesses/Units 7,765

Rules of Thumb

> ➤ 2 x SDE for small companies
> ➤ 2–4 x SDE
> ➤ 3–5 x EBITDA—multiple expands as profits go up

Pricing Tips

- Upscale or mid-grade?
- Average mark up? Wholesale or direct?
- Length of time in business? Single destination operators warrant a bit higher; type of travel (golf, ski, scuba, etc.), specialist vs. generalist. Wholesale via agents or direct business? Inbound or outbound?

Benchmark Data

Statistics (Tour Operators)

Number of Establishments	7,765
Average Profit Margin	6.6%
Revenue per Employee	$203,200
Average Number of Employees	4.2
Average Wages per Employee	$39,797

Products and Services Segmentation

International packaged tours	33.5%
Domestic packaged tours	28.8%
International customized tours	12.2%
Domestic customized tours	11.0%
Reservation services	7.9%
Reselling tours	4.2%
Other	2.4%

Major Market Segmentation

Individuals	52.4%
Travel agencies	32.6%
Businesses	9.0%
Other	6.0%

Industry Costs

Profit	6.6%
Wages	19.7%
Purchases	66.3%
Depreciation	1.6%
Utilities	2.5%
Rent	2.8%
Other	0.5%

Market Share

The Travel Corporation	12.4%
The Mark Travel Corporation	9.4%
Flight Centre Ltd.	5.8%

Expenses (% of Annual Sales)

Cost of Goods	80%
Occupancy Costs	15% (after COG)
Payroll/Labor Costs	55% (after COG)
Profit (pretax)	20%

Questions

- Which key employees stay post-sale? Are wholesale contracts transferable?

Industry Trend

- "7 travel trends for 2017 that will drive the global tourism industry
    - ✓ Millennials
    - ✓ Active and Adventure Trips
    - ✓ Female Solo Travel
    - ✓ Food Tourism
    - ✓ Responsible Tourism
    - ✓ Mobile Photography
    - ✓ Business and Leisure Travel

Source: "7 Travel Trends for 2017 that will drive the global tourism industry,"
Posted by Sara Napier Burkhard on Dec 5, 2016,
https://www.trekksoft.com/en/blog/7-travel-trends-for-2017-that-will-drive-the-global-tourism-industry

Expert Comments

Travel & tourism is universal. World is shrinking. Huge inheritance in USA to fuel 20-year boom.

Resources

- National Tour Association: http://www.ntaonline.com
- IBISWorld, December 2016: http://ibisworld.com

Towing Companies

SIC 7549-01	NAICS 488410	Number of Businesses/Units 45,217

Rules of Thumb

➤ 70% of annual revenues plus inventory

➤ 2.75 x EBITDA

Pricing Tips

- Extreme care with adding back depreciation, and/or allowance to replace trucks. Define which segment of industry, and check to see if the insurance premium is fair market value. Small companies and those in non-consent business are hard to sell.
- The last of the consolidators has liquidated its acquisitions at a loss. The implication is that there are negative economies of scale at both ends of the scale, large and small, i.e., above some size these businesses based on revenue, etc. have a declining value, and that optimal values are found within the span of control of one person. Ease of entry has been increasing, so going-concern values have been declining.

Benchmark Data

Statistics (Automobile Towing)

Number of Establishments	45,217
Average Profit Margin	8.3%
Revenue per Employee	$69,600
Average Number of Employees	2.2
Average Wages per Employee	$25,382

Products and Services Segmentation

Light-duty truck towing	43.3%
Passenger car towing	35.6%
Roadside assistance	21.1%

Major Market Segmentation

Individuals	46.6%
Commercial customers	26.5%
State and local government	26.9%

Industry Costs

Profit	8.3%
Wages	36.3%
Purchases	34.4%
Depreciation	5.5%
Marketing	1.2%
Rent & Utilities	6.3%
Other	8.0%

Expenses (% of Annual Sales)

Cost of Goods	30%
Occupancy Costs	08%
Payroll/Labor Costs	30%
Profit (pretax)	20%

T

Industry Trend

- Trend is positive, but competition is fierce. Many companies come and go.
- "More than 85 percent of all tows in the U.S. involve passenger cars and light trucks. The majority of these tows are provided by small, family-owned towing businesses."

Source: Towing and Recovery Association of America (TRAA)

Expert Comments

These businesses vary widely. Hands-on management is almost always a critical element. Control of operating real estate is usually a major element in profitability.

Seller Financing

- 5 years

Resources

- Tow Times Magazine: http://www.towtimes.com
- IBISWorld, September 2017: http://ibisworld.com

Toy Stores		
SIC 5945-17	NAICS 451120	

Rules of Thumb

➢ 20–25% of annual sales plus inventory

Benchmark Data

- For Benchmark Data see Hobby Shops

Industry Trend

- "Toys 'R' US Inc., the ultimate toyland for a generation of postwar baby boomers, filed for bankruptcy thanks to a crushing debt load from a buyout and relentless competition from warehouse and online retailers. The retailer, which has 1,600 stores in 38 countries, said its hand was forced after an attempt to restructure out of court sparked a press report about a potential bankruptcy, spooking critical vendors and credit insurers. But it intends to make the best of the situation and revive its business in time for the holiday shopping season.

"'Chapter 11 was certainly not the company's preferred outcome,' Chief Executive David Brandon said in a court filing. 'The timing of all of this could not have been worse.' He cited the immediate need to build inventory for the holiday season, which accounts for 40 percent of annual revenue. Thanks to a new $3.1 billion operating loan, the company plans to stabilize operations and reopen supply channels while in bankruptcy, he said.

"The filing is the latest blow to a brick-and-mortar retail industry, which has seen a string of bankruptcies from Payless Inc. and Gymboree Corp. to Perfumania Holdings Inc. Chains are reeling from store closures, sluggish mall traffic and the gravitational pull of Amazon.com Inc.'s lower costs and global home delivery. More than 10 percent of U.S. retail space, or nearly 1 billion square feet, may need to close, convert to other uses or renegotiate rent, according to data from CoStar Group."

Source: "Toys 'R' Us Collapses Into Bankruptcy Thanks to Crushing Debt" By Dawn McCarty, Tiffany Kary, and Daniela Wei, September 18, 2017, https://www.bloomberg.com/news/articles/2017-09-19/toys-r-us-files-for-bankruptcy-crushed-by-online-competition

- 2017 Trends
  - ✓ Collectibles 2.0
  - ✓ Up & Active
  - ✓ Technology Trends
  - ✓ Oh So Classic!
  - ✓ Movie Mania
  - ✓ From STEAM to STREAM

Source: http://www.toyassociation.org/trends

Resources

- The Toy Association: http://www.toyassociation.org

Translation and Interpretation Services

SIC 7389-20	NAICS 541930	Number of Businesses/Units 58,380

Rules of Thumb

➢ 40–45% of annual sales plus inventory

Benchmark Data

Statistics (Translation Services)

Number of Establishments	58,380
Average Profit Margin	7.8%
Revenue per Employee	$59,600
Average Number of Employees	1.5
Average Wages per Employee	$22,906

Products and Services Segmentation

Interpretation services	47.9%
Written translation services	37.4%
Other	14.7%

Major Market Segmentation

Technology, finance, and retail	46.4%
State and local governments	55.7%
Business firms and farms	37.7%
Not-for-profit organizations	5.0%
Other	1.6%

Industry Costs

Profit	7.8%
Wages	38.4%
Purchases	9.0%
Depreciation	0.7%
Marketing	1.2%
Rent & Utilities	3.6%
Other	39.3%

Market Share

TelePerformance	9.3%
Lionbridge Technologies Inc.	5.2%

T

- "It's all about supply and demand and since the U.S. became involved in Afghanistan after the Sept. 11 attacks, there has been demand for linguists or interpreters of the two main Afghan languages, Dari and Pashto. The average salary for a linguist or interpreter who speaks Dari is $187,000 and it's $193,000 for those who speak Pashto, according to Indeed.com. The jobs range from an interpreter for military personnel to a media desk officer who would translate Afghan news stories and communicate with Afghan media."

  Source: http://www.salary.com

Industry Trend

- "It is a fact that the translation market is not heavily affected by recessions. However, it is a very fragmented market, with spot number 1 claimed by military contractors and the Top 100 firms ranging from $427M down to $4M according to studies by Common Sense Advisory, a translation industry think tank which estimated the size of the industry to be $33.5 billion in 2012. According to a report by IBISWorld, translation services are expected keep on growing and reach $37 billion in 2018. The United States represents the largest single market for translation services. Europe is a close second and Asia is the largest growth area. Currently, business is generated from the government and private industries alike. According to the U.S. Bureau of Statistics, the translation industry is expected to grow by 42% between 2010–2020."

  Source: http://www.pangeanic.com/knowledge_center/size-of-the-translation-industry/

Resources

- IBISWorld, April 2017: http://ibisworld.com

Travel Agencies		
SIC 4724-02	NAICS 561510	Number of Businesses/Units 24,343

Rules of Thumb

➢ 45% of annual gross profit

➢ 2–3 x EBIT for small to mid-size agencies

➢ 3–5 x EBITDA for larger agencies

➢ 1.8–3 x SDE plus inventory

➢ Small operations, $1 to $3 million—35 percent of annual commissions and fees; $4 to $8 million—40 percent; $9 to $20 million—45 percent; 3.5 x EBITDA above $20 million in volume; 5 x EBITDA for shops earning over $1 million net profit.

➢ For agencies with $1 to $4 million in sales, 1.5–2.0 x SDE is customary. If $5 to $10 million, then 2.0–2.5 x SDE

Pricing Tips

- The most important factors are gross profits, diversity, how long established, steady goodwill, staff expertise, seller's covenant not to compete.
- The higher the EBITDA, the higher the multiple. Is there management in place? Cost for keeping owner on during transition has an impact on add-backs, etc. Does the business wholesale to travel agencies? Direct to the public? Unique

website, booking engine in place?

- 1. Goodwill is the most important; inside vs. independent employees is another factor.
  2. Quality & diversity of the client base
  3. ARC & IATAN appointments
  4. How long in business
  5. Seller's Covenant not to Compete
- "There is no Inventory in this business as it is service; the travel agent is only an agent of the airlines, hotels, cruise companies and the tour company. "There are no hard and fast rules on pricing, he explained, but the more profitable an agency, the higher the multiple. For instance:
  - ✓ An agency that generates up to $150,000 in free cash flow each year will likely sell for 2.5 to three times earnings.
  - ✓ An agency that generates between $150,000 and $500,000 in free cash flow each year will likely sell for 4.5 times earnings.
  - ✓ An agency that generates between $500,000 and $1 million in free cash flow each year will likely sell for about 5.5 times earnings.

  "The typical purchase price is around five times EBITDA, according to Adams. There is always room for adjustments based on specific situations such as less productive family members on the payroll or particularly valuable accounts tied to specific agents."

  Source: http://www.travelmarketreport.com/articles/How-Much-Is-Your-Agency-Worth
- It is important to have good clean financials, e.g., a P & L that has a breakdown of the expenses that would go away after the sale. Having 2–3 years' worth of financials to start is important; don't buy new office equipment, sign a new building lease, or other long-term contracts prior to listing your business. Net profit and excess owner's compensation, potential replacement cost of an owner to stay on all contribute to the valuation. Multiple of EBITDA typically average 2–4 times, and 2–3 for SDE.
- Multiples expand as profit level rises...anywhere between 2 to 5 x is the range of earnings paid.
- Top importance is: 1. The gross income not gross sales 2. In-house income not independent agent income. Income verification is easy in this business as there is a paper trail for all transactions.
- Profitability? Agency more than 3 years old? Agency does not depend on more than one account for more than 10 percent of gross? Agency does not rebate? Manager stays on?
- Always include service charges, fees and markups to the gross sales. These are becoming a more and more important part of agencies' income.

Benchmark Data

Statistics (Travel Agencies)

Number of Establishments	24,343
Average Profit Margin	2.6%
Revenue per Employee	$175,400
Average Number of Employees	9.7
Average Wages per Employee	$52,400

T

Products and Services Segmentation

Tours and packaged travel bookings 32.0%
Cruise bookings 26.0%
International and domestic airline bookings.. 23.0%
Accommodation bookings... 11.0%
Other services.. 5.0%
Car rental 3.0%

Major Market Segmentation

Leisure-international travel 52.0%
Leisure-domestic travel.. 25.0%
Corporate-unmanaged.. 11.0%
Corporate-managed... 8.0%
Other... 4.0%

Industry Costs

Profit 2.6%
Wages.. 30.0%
Purchases.. 20.0%
Depreciation.. 0.5%
Marketing 4.4%
Rent & Utilities 6.0%
Other... 36.5%

Market Share

Expedia Inc. 13.8%
The Priceline Group Inc. 5.1%

- Excellent owner goodwill relationships with high commissions from the vendors, like airlines, tour, and cruise company and staff; at least $1 million sales per employee
- Corporate agent should produce $120K in fees. Leisure agent should produce $70K in fees.
- Over 15% net
- Going virtual is best.
- Please note that travel agents do not buy any tickets and/or goods; they provide service and get a commission. The average commission income is 10% for the gross sales. Major expense is the employees. Rental space can be small or average; the appointments, insurance & utilities are low.
- Good leisure agent should book $59k in commission fee income, good corporate agent over $1 million
- Each agent should produce 2.5x their salary.
- Sales per employee should be high. Most important factor: the ratio between inside(salaried) or outside (independent contractor) employees. On sale of the business independent employees can leave and goodwill will be lost.
- Higher net commissions due to special contracts. Service fee income. Overall control on expenses.
- Look for preferred supplier and override agreements, written contractual agreements with corporate customers, relationships with wholesalers on airline tickets. GDS (airline computer system) contract situation is a key factor.

Expenses (% of Annual Sales)

Cost of Goods	10% to 20%
Occupancy Costs	10% to 20%
Payroll/Labor Costs	50% to 60%
Profit (pretax)	05% to 15%

Questions

- Resources of steady income; client's base; reason for sale
- Let's check last quarter ARC report. How much business under deposit vs. same time last year? Can the business run without you?
- What are areas you know are keys to growth that you've not gone after? What are the slow months? How is cash flow; any debt? What creates lean times in your experiences?
- Any marketing data to show what clients are interested in? Are you marketing to them? Do you have a list of detailed owner expenses? Do you have a solid database?

Industry Trend

- Going up, getting better, more buyers than sellers
- "Technology has led to exponential advancements in all spheres of life, travel included. It's shaping the way we want to travel, how travel agencies interact with us and the places we want to go to. Millennials constitute the age group that is most exposed to technology, they have an immense travel spending potential, higher tendencies to travel, and also dictate to a great extent the future of travel and the trends to expect in 2017."

  Source: "Trends to Expect in the Travel Industry in 2017," January 4, 2017, https://www.hospitalitynet.org/news/4080188.html

- "Though travel agencies' business isn't expected to return to pre-internet levels, online booking has, even as it has flourished, shown travelers the frustrations that can come with booking travel themselves—and that outsourcing the stress of arranging travel can be worthwhile."

  Source: "Who Uses a Travel Agent in This Day and Age?" by Bourree Lam, June 22, 2016, https://www.theatlantic.com/business/archive/2016/06/travel-agent/488282/

- Luxury to grow as huge transfer of wealth inheritance will be very positive for years to come. The world is shrinking; experimental trips. Multigenerational family trips growing.
- Going higher; people are traveling more and love to share with their friends and family. Lots of inheritance monies coming in and more trips are being taken with skilled travel consultants.
- People are traveling more than ever. The travel industry is overall healthy. It is the second biggest industry in the world next to food.
- More and more travel related businesses will be selling as the age of the owners, on average, is high amongst a large percentage of travel companies.

Expert Comments

Great happy business for life, be prepared to learn all the time as business changes happen all the time. It is second biggest industry in the world.

Travel volume is up and the travel agents are again in the demand, especially with high volume. Travel agents, tour operators and wholesale consolidators.

Easy to learn business as well as international and overseas buyers.

Be prepared to be on a huge learning curve; but once informed, start to learn how to market, use social media, and hire good sales agents.

Tour operators and niche travel companies do get impacted by many threats. Most owners have lost the passion to market, but this can be a bonus to young, tech savvy buyers to really turn it around. Portability of the Internet-based business is a plus. The traveling public is coming back to working with experienced travel counselors.

For outside the industry, do your homework; it is a tough business to slide into and think you will now own a sexy travel company. For inside the industry already, by acquiring the assets of another travel company, you can greatly enhance your bottom line, increase destinations, gain new agents, increase profits with suppliers and expand your client database.

Seller Financing
- Typical is all cash or seller financing, as outside financing is not available.
- Seller financing, half cash balance over 30 monthly payments
- Seller financing, 1/3 down and balance over 2 years

Resources
- TravelMole: http://www.travelmole.com
- Tnooz: http://www.tnooz.com
- U.S. Travel Association: http://www.ustravel.org
- American Society of Travel Agents (ASTA): http://www.asta.org
- Travel Weekly: http://www.travelweekly.com
- IBISWorld, September 2017: http://ibisworld.com
- National Tour Association: http://www.ntaonline.com
- Travel Agent Magazine: http://www.travelagentcentral.com
- TravelAge West: http://www.travelagewest.com

Travel Wholesalers/Consolidators		
	NAICS 561520	

Rules of Thumb
➤ 3–5 x EBITDA

Pricing Tips
- Airlines not giving out as many contracts as they have in the past due to 90 percent of all airline seats being filled as number of aircraft has decreased. Airlines pushing more direct channels to their own Websites. Value of wholesaler is under some pressure.

Questions
- Are the contracts owned or are they subcontracted?
- Length of time in business? Salary vs. commission? Who controls the business? How long are contracts valid?

Trophy Studios

	NAICS 453998	

Rules of Thumb

➤ 40–45% of annual sales plus inventory

Industry Trend

- Should be about the same as it has been, but technology is changing the business.

		Franchise

Tropical Smoothie Café

Approx. Total Investment	$198,050–$478,550
Estimated Annual Sales/Unit	$625,000

	NAICS 722515	Number of Businesses/Units 540

Rules of Thumb

➤ 50–55% of annual sales plus inventory

Resources

- Tropical Smoothie Café : https://www.tropicalsmoothiecafe.com/

Trucking Companies

	NAICS 484230	Number of Businesses/Units 616,891

Rules of Thumb

➤ 50% of annual sales

➤ 5 x EBIT

➤ 2–3 x EBITDA

➤ 2–3 x SDE + market value of assets

➤ $4,000 to $6,000 per driver

Pricing Tips

- The quality of the earnings (contracts, longevity, size, concentration), the condition of the trucks and trailers, and the workforce are all-important and potential deal breakers if the information is not detailed and accurate.
- Focus should be on strategic value of the business because most of the time the value has very little to do with current financials.
- Gross Sales important of course; understand all costs involved from licensing, broker (trucking brokers) fees, fuel surcharges, trailer and truck parking and driver salaries; all are important to understand. Understand the length of contracts; some contracts are not for actual work, but allow for bids to do the work/deliveries.

T

Benchmark Data

Statistics (Long-Distance Freight Trucking)

Number of Establishments	398,131
Average Profit Margin	7.0%
Revenue per Employee	$167,000
Average Number of Employees	2.8
Average Wages per Employee	$42,787

Products and Services Segmentation

Other transportation services	38.1%
Truckload carriers	37.4%
Less-than-truckload carriers	24.5%

Major Market Segmentation

Manufacturing sector	62.1%
Retail and wholesale sector	32.9%
Other	5.0%

Industry Costs

Profit	7.0%
Wages	25.6%
Purchases	41.3%
Depreciation	2.2%
Marketing	3.7%
Rent & Utilities	11.0%
Other	9.2%

Statistics (Local Freight Trucking)

Number of Establishments	218,760
Average Profit Margin	6.7%
Revenue per Employee	$114,600
Average Number of Employees	1.8
Average Wages per Employee	$36,577

Products and Services Segmentation

Truckload transportation	46.8%
Less-than-truckload transportation	24.5%
Other Services	11.9%
Intermodal transportation	9.9%
Dry bulk transportation	6.9%

Major Market Segmentation

Other wholesalers and manufacturers	30.1%
Petroleum product wholesalers	17.9%
Petroleum and coal products manufacturing	13.8%
Farm product wholesalers	10.0%
Nonmetallic mineral product manufacturing	8.7%
Food and beverage manufacturing	8.0%
Chemical manufacturing	6.2%
Grocer wholesalers	5.3%

Industry Costs

Profit 6.7%
Wages.. 32.1%
Purchases... 25.4%
Depreciation.. 4.1%
Marketing 0.9%
Rent & Utilities 13.7%
Other... 17.1%

Expenses (% of Annual Sales)

Payroll/Labor Costs .... 40% to 60%
Profit (pretax)... 08% to 15%

Questions

- Equipment—payoffs or leasing; the fine details are critical. Driver history—be sure to interview each driver and employee. It's important to be sure no after-sale promises have been made by the seller, i.e., pay increase, vacation time, profit sharing and the like.
- How old are the trucks? Who owns the trailers? Where do you park and do you offer warehousing?

Industry Trend

- "Six 2017 Trucking Industry Trends to Watch
  1. Increased Interdependence
  2. Increased Efficiencies
  3. Changes in Government Regulations
  4. Self-Driving Vehicles
  5. Increased Automation
  6. Workforce Evolution"

  Source: https://www.dbsquaredinc.com/2017-trucking-industry-trends/

- Seems to be growing and fuel costs are trending downward.
- "The 10 most critical issues facing trucking companies:
  1. Hours of Service
  2. CSA
  3. Driver Shortage
  4. Driver Retention
  5. Truck Parking
  6. ELD Mandate
  7. Driver Health/Wellness
  8. Economy
  9. Infrastructure/Congestion/Funding
  10. Driver Distraction"

  Source: American Transportation Research Institute survey

- Trucking is becoming even more important as Internet sales and the need for packages to be moved from place to place increase.

Expert Comments

Listen closely to the seller about why he has or has not grown revenues—beyond that of "he kept it at a level he was comfortable with."

T

- It can be easy to open a trucking company; the challenge seems to be the operations side—gaining customers, keeping drivers, providing quality customer service and on-time deliveries at a fair price.
- This is difficult because of the variations in different types of motor carriers.

Seller Financing

- Seller financing is pretty common. Very important to know about the truck and trailer financing—leased or owned. Find out at the beginning if those contracts are assignable and if there are any early payoff fees. That is really important to know for a broker taking a listing; those fees can be thousands of dollars.
- 2 years, up to 50%. Earnouts can work in this industry.

Resources

- IBISWorld, January 2017: http://ibisworld.com
- America's Independent Truckers' Association, Inc.: http://www.aitaonline.com
- IBISWorld, February 2017: http://ibisworld.com

Truck Stops		
SIC 5541-03	NAICS 447190	

Rules of Thumb

➤ 75% of annual sales

➤ 5 x SDE plus inventory, may deduct cost of cosmetic update.

➤ 5 x EBITDA

Pricing Tips

- The rule of thumb for truck stops is going to be 5–6 times EBITDA with the factors coming into play like the quality of the assets, and are there any environmental issues that will need to be deducted from the value of the truck stop. However, to arrive at an EBITDA one must add up all of the different profit centers that comprise the truck stop such as: income from the scales, truck wash, video games, gift shop, restaurant income or restaurant lease income if the unit is leased out, and sometimes there are other ancillary forms of income that will all need to be added together to get to the EBITDA of the truck stop.
- A lot of people will try to pump up the value of a truck stop by stating how much property is comprised by the truck stop, because it takes several acres to make a truck stop, but anything beyond the basic amount of property needed that is being used to support the business should not be included as additional value. For example, there may be a truck stop that sits on a 10-acre tract of ground and the seller has another 5 acres that he thinks add additional value to the truck stop, but it doesn't. Only the property that is being used at the present time.
- Be sure to check to see if they have any additional profit centers such as scales and if the scales are leased or owned. Other profit centers such as gambling machines (video poker, etc.) sometimes are not included in the P & L's due to skimming.
- Due to the multiple streams at one location the goodwill can go for a premium.
- Limited buyers who buy this kind of business, due to the large number of employees and size of operation.

Benchmark Data

- To be a profitable truck stop it seems inevitable that there is a restaurant connected to the facility. Many of the truck stops are now partnering with Hardee's, Wendy's, McDonald's, Arby's etc., while the others have a sit-down restaurant.
- Convenience/Retail combined is approximately $500 per sq. ft.
- Typical Full-Service Travel Plaza Statistics
  At a typical full-service travel plaza you will find:
  - ✓ Convenience or retail stores (97%)
  - ✓ Check cashing (98%)
  - ✓ Private showers (89%)
  - ✓ Free parking (93%)
  - ✓ Buses welcome (82%)
  - ✓ Public fax machines (81%)
  - ✓ Restaurants or delis (77%)
  - ✓ Platform scales (59%)
  - ✓ Laundry facilities (58%)
  - ✓ Truck repair (50%)
  - ✓ Emergency road service (63%)
  - ✓ ATM machines (91%)
  - ✓ Security/local police patrol (54%)
  - ✓ Load boards (75%)
  - ✓ Postal service (53%)
  - ✓ Truck washes (28%)
  - ✓ Hotels or motels (28%)
  - ✓ Driver lounges (48%)
  - ✓ Recreational vehicle facilities (23%)
  - ✓ On-site fast food (51%)
  - ✓ Church services (38%)
  - ✓ Food court (15%)
  - ✓ Internet services (39%)

Expenses (% of Annual Sales)

Cost of Goods	63%
Occupancy Costs	02% to 03%
Payroll/Labor Costs	08%
Profit (pretax)	04%

Questions

- Do they own the restaurant or lease it out? What is the environmental situation?
- Does it have any fuel agreements with any trucking lines? Does he have Fuel Man or similar fuel agreements that would be in place to draw regional or national trucking companies to him? Any hidden income, i.e., video machines, laundry, showers etc.?
- As much paperwork as possible including tax returns.
- When valuing the business be sure to question the Seller about all of the sources of income. Most units have income from video games which is very

T

lucrative, but that doesn't make it to the P & L; scale income and do they own the scales or lease them, any contracts with carriers, do they have Mr. Fuel or other recognized fuel discount programs, shower income etc.? The money is still made on the inside so the higher the fuel volume, the more people that visit the facility, the more money they will spend inside. Is the unit branded with Shell, BO, TA etc.? If so how much time is left on the contract with them and what are their costs to them? Who do they buy their fuel from? To purchase fuel, you must have a fuel purchase agreement with your supplier and what is the length of the term and the charge for the fuel? Most agreements are for 7–10 years and if it is a branded unit you will be required to pay them back if you do not fulfill the length of the agreement, and this can be very costly. Are there any rebates coming back from the fuel supplier? How much over rack are they charging you? Very important that you know what the cost to buy fuel is. If you are doing 400,000 gallons of fuel per month and you are paying 1 cent over the posted rack price, that is $4,000 per month plus freight to bring it to your facility. The seller will know this and the buyer should know it too.

Industry Trend

- "Each year, more than 2 billion gallons of diesel are wasted by overnight idling, according to a study from Argonne National Labs. Idling is the industry standard method of providing overnight comfort to the more than 1 million drivers who sleep in their trucks each night."

  Source: http://www.prnewswire.com/news-releases/fuel-savings-and-improved-air-quality-highlight-duke-energys-truck-stop-effort-in-nc-300456034.html

- There are not many independent truck stops left in the country with Pilot acquiring Flying J and making deals with other operators like Road Ranger to sell their Pilot fuel. It has been said that Pilot alone controls almost 60% of the diesel fuel sales in the United States.
- Large chains will survive and mom and pops will have to specialize or get out.
- Very slow growth due to the nature of the business. Large lots of 10+ acres required, and investments upwards of $10+ million per site make the field of players very limited.

Expert Comments

The truck stop industry has taken a severe beating lately due to the increased diesel fuel prices. Plus added to that the fact that the major truck stop operators such as Love's, Petro, Flying J, and Pilot are ruthless on their competition and have decreased the fuel margins considerably. Plus the majors that I just mentioned have made it a point to have fueling agreements with most of the major truck carriers across the country leaving only the independent truckers who will stop at the independent truck stops.

Very expensive to replicate and build, few buyers, due to the heavy labor involvement and the 24X365 days business, yet very profitable.

Even though the travel plazas are profitable, the size of operation and management acumen required can be daunting. Also, the upfront monies required are pretty hefty as compared to most small businesses.

The average return on investment for a truck stop is 6 to 8 percent. The high profit return on investment for a truck stop is 16 to 17 percent. In order for a buyer to determine a good deal-12 to 15 percent ROI for a truck stop should provide a good rule of thumb.

Seller Financing
- Property and land included: 10 to 15 years (8% to 11%); business only: 3 to 8 years (8% to 10%)

Resources
- America's Independent Truckers' Association, Inc.: http://www.aitaonline.com
- National Association of Truck Stop Operators: http://www.natso.com
- Fuel Oil News: http://www.fueloilnews.com

		Franchise
Two Men and a Truck		
Approx. Total Investment		$75,000–$590,500
	NAICS 48412	Number of Businesses/Units 268

Rules of Thumb
➤ 40–45% of annual sales plus inventory

Resources
- Two Men and a Truck: http://www.twomenandatruck.com

Uniform Rental		
	NAICS 812331	Number of Businesses/Units 4,407

Rules of Thumb
➤ 40–45 x weekly sales plus inventory

Pricing Tips
- An industry expert says that if there are contracts with the accounts serviced, the rule of thumb will be 70 percent of gross annual sales.

Benchmark Data

Statistics (Industrial Laundry & Linen Supply)
Number of Establishments	4,407
Average Profit Margin	8.8%
Revenue per Employee	$138,700
Average Number of Employees	26.5
Average Wages per Employee	$41,662

Products and Services Segmentation
Work uniform rental and cleaning	30.6%
Flat linens rental and cleaning	20.5%
Linen garments rental and cleaning	15.3%
Other	14.1%
Industrial mats rental and cleaning	11.5%
Industrial wiping cloths rental and cleaning	4.8%
Industrial mops and related products	3.2%

U

Major Market Segmentation

Healthcare	24.8%
Food service	19.3%
Retail and service	18.8%
Hospitality and lodging	16.0%
Manufacturing and distribution	12.4%
Other	8.7%

Industry Costs

Profit	8.8%
Wages	30.0%
Purchases	34.8%
Depreciation	4.7%
Marketing	0.9%
Rent & Utilities	4.4%
Other	16.4%

Market Share

Cintas Corporation	25.3%
Aramark Corporation	10.3%
UniFirst Corporation	8.9%
G&K Services Inc.	5.4%

Resources
- IBISWorld, January 2017: http://ibisworld.com

	Franchise
UPS Store	
Approx. Total Investment	$139,673–$353,580
NAICS 561431	Number of Businesses/Units 4,700

Rules of Thumb

➢ 35–40% of annual sales plus inventory

➢ 2–3 x SDE plus inventory

Resources
- The UPS Store: http://www.theupsstore.com

Urgent Care Centers	
NAICS 621493	Number of Businesses/Units 7,546

Benchmark Data

Statistics (Urgent Care Centers)

Number of Establishments	7,546
Average Profit Margin	23.0%
Revenue per Employee	$174,700
Average Number of Employees	19.3
Average Wages per Employee	$51,458

Products and Services Segmentation

All other patient care	24.6%
Digestive system diseases	20.5%
Musculoskeletal system and connective tissue diseases	20.0%
Nervous system and sense organs diseases	11.7%
Injury and poisoning	7.7%
Symptoms, signs and ill-defined conditions	6.3%
Respiratory system diseases	5.6%
Infectious and parasitic diseases	3.6%

Major Market Segmentation

Private insurers	56.4%
Government insurers	26.4%
Patient out-of-pocket	10.1%
Other patient care revenue	7.1%

Industry Costs

Profit	23.0%
Wages	29.0%
Purchases	10.1%
Depreciation	3.7%
Marketing	1.7%
Rent & Utilities	7.4%
Other	25.1%

Resources
- IBISWorld, February 2017: http://ibisworld.com

	Franchise
U-Save Car & Truck Rental	
Approx. Total Investment	$60,000–$681,300
NAICS 532111	Number of Businesses/Units 170

Rules of Thumb

➢ 10% of annual sales

Resources
- U-Save Car & Truck Rental: http://www.usave.com/

Used Goods	
NAICS 45331	Number of Businesses/Units 84,352

Rules of Thumb

➢ 20–25% of annual sales includes inventory unless it is on consignment

---

28th Edition

V

Benchmark Data

Statistics (Used Goods Stores)

Number of Establishments	84,352
Average Profit Margin	3.6%
Revenue per Employee	$75,600
Average Number of Employees	3.2
Average Wages per Employee	$16,705

Products and Services Segmentation

Clothing, footwear and accessories	47.6%
Furniture, appliances and home furnishings	16.9%
Other	14.9%
Antiques and collectables	12.6%
Entertainment, recreation and culture product	8.0%

Industry Costs

Profit	3.6%
Wages	22.0%
Purchases	40.4%
Depreciation	1.0%
Marketing	2.5%
Rent & Utilities	11.9%
Other	18.6%

Market Share

Goodwill Industries International Inc.	17.0%
Savers Inc.	5.3%
Winmark Corporation	4.9%

Industry Trend

- "Over the five years to 2022, Used Goods Stores industry revenue is expected to continue its upward climb, despite rising incomes and falling unemployment. Although many consumers will opt for new items from big-box stores, many young consumers will continue shopping at used goods stores to find unique items not offered by traditional retailers. Despite this, rising external competition from online retailers and positive economic conditions will make industry growth more subdued. Over the next five years, industry revenue is expected to rise at an annualized rate of 1.4% to reach $21.7 billion in 2022."

Source: IBISWorld Industry Outlook

Resources

- The Association of Resale Professionals: https://www.narts.org
- IBISWorld, September 2017: http://ibisworld.com

		Franchise
Valpak Direct Marketing Systems		
Approx. Total Investment		$$32,500–$2,000,000
	NAICS 541870	Number of Businesses/Units 160

Rules of Thumb

> ➤ 2 x SDE plus inventory
> ➤ 40–45% of annual sales plus inventory

Resources

- Valpak: http://www.valpak.com

Valvoline Instant Oil Change	Franchise
Approx. Total Investment	$200,000–$2,000,000
NAICS 811191	Number of Businesses/Units 900

Rules of Thumb

> ➤ 50% of annual sales

Resources

- Valvoline Instant Oil Change Franchising: http://www.viocfranchise.com

Vending Machine Industry		
SIC 2599-02	NAICS 454210	Number of Businesses/Units 21,178

Rules of Thumb

> ➤ 2–3 x SDE plus inventory
> ➤ 3–4 x EBIT
> ➤ 3–5 x EBITDA
> ➤ 65–75% of annual sales plus inventory

Pricing Tips

- Pricing will vary considerably based on customer contracts, age of equipment, and technology utilized within the business.
- One must know if machines are owned outright, if there are E-ports on machines, how to access the accounts to be serviced, age of equipment, commissions paid, vend prices attained at each location, and age of accounts.
- Prices for coffee service will typically be on the higher end of the spectrum. Values for vending businesses very dependent on the age and quality of equipment.
- Inventory in machines on location & coins in coin machines are included in the price-estimate at $100 per machine. Inventory in trucks and warehouse is not included. Most machines should be MDB capable—this allows machines to be fitted for credit cards and inventory control software.
- These factors will also influence price determination: ownership status of the machines coming with the sale; are they leased, owned, financed; the type of machines that the route consists of and the service schedule that they would need to have the machines produce income (sandwiches need daily servicing … soda/snacks many need weekly servicing); the locale of the machines … inside, outside, 24-hour access, limited access; is the commission paid to accounts above the normal 10% to 15%?
- Ratios of investment dollars (borrowed or asset) and estimated length of return

V

Benchmark Data

Statistics (Vending Machine Operators)

Number of Establishments... 21,178
Average Profit Margin 5.0%
Revenue per Employee $134,100
Average Number of Employees... 2.4
Average Wages per Employee $23,660

Products and Services Segmentation

Food.. 33.1%
Beverages.. 31.8%
Movies and games... 29.1%
Other products 6.0%

Major Market Segmentation

Retail sites 35.4%
Manufacturing sites and offices 22.3%
Other... 17.8%
Schools and colleges..11.7%
Hospitals and nursing homes 7.1%
Restaurants, bars and clubs 5.7%

Industry Costs

Profit 5.0%
Wages... 18.0%
Purchases... 50.7%
Depreciation... 4.5%
Marketing 0.6%
Rent & Utilities 3.9%
Other... 17.3%

Market Share

Outerwall Inc... 22.1%
Compass Group PLC.. 12.4%
Aramark Corporation 7.3%

- Cost of goods sold: <50%; labor: <20%
- Food cost on product sold should not be higher than 55%. Accounts should have an in-house head count of a minimum of 75 ...with hopefully transient/ walk-by traffic as well.
- Profit depends on volume and percentage paid to customer providing space & power.

Expenses (% of Annual Sales)

Cost of Goods...35% to 50%
Occupancy Costs..02% to 10%
Payroll/Labor Costs ....20% to 30%
Profit (pretax)..10% to 15%

Questions

- 1. Age of equipment and trucks
  2. Customer contracts
  3. Commission rates paid to customers
  4. Technology and software utilized
  5. Compensation system for route personnel
- Do you have contracts in place with your major customer? What cash controls do you have in the business? When did you last raise selling prices? Is any of your business controlled by third parties?
- Seller: 1) Get your books and records in order, 2) Make sure you have clean financial statements, 3) Have a professional valuation completed. Buyer: 1) Fully grasp the capital requirements for both new business and the maintenance of existing business, 2) Be prepared to invest in technology.
- Are machines owned or leased? How old is equipment? Is any equipment supplied with E-Ports? Commissions paid? How geographically far apart are the accounts located? Access to machines? 24/7?
- Are your machines DEX capable? What controls do you have on the cash in the machines? Is all the money going into the bank? If no, they have to hold paper.
- Head count at the particular location & permissible servicing time for each account.
- Do you have contracts?
- How many people work at a location? How close are accounts? Are commissions paid to all or some customers? Do you pay commissions to accounts; do machines carry perishable food stuffs?

Industry Trend

- The industry will continue to consolidate as the larger firms become more efficient and profitable through the use of technology.
- "With a history that dates back to ancient times, vending machines are likely to remain a part (and perhaps a growing part) of the world's diet in the future. But several current trends have left the vending machine industry at a crossroads.

  "Current Trend 1: The obesity epidemic. In case you've been hiding in a vending machine for the past decade, there's an ongoing obesity epidemic, including an obesity epidemic among children, which has motivated a closer look at where people, especially children, get their food and drink. More and more states and municipalities have been considering policies that more strongly regulate what is available in vending machines that fall under their jurisdiction.

  "Current Trend 2: Busy schedules and laziness. . . .the demand for ready-to eat- food seems to be growing.

  "Current Trend 3: Online ordering and mobile applications. As turnaround and delivery times get faster, the convenience of online ordering could eventually begin to rival the convenience of vending machines.

  "So what does this mean for the future of vending machines? Well, these are likely to lead to several future trends in vending machines:

  "Future Trend 1: Vending machines that provide healthy food.

  "Future Trend 2: Vending machines that provide nutritional and health education. The Food and Drug Administration (FDA) already requires operators who own or operate 20 or more vending machines to disclose calorie information for food sold from vending machines, subject to certain exemptions.

"Future Trend 3: Vending machines that can customize, cook, and prepare food.

"Future Trend 4: Vending machines that provide other products related to food.

"Future Trend 5: Online vending machines. This doesn't mean purchasing vending machines over the Internet, which you can already do. This means vending machines that are connected to the Internet to allow ordering or purchasing over the web or a smartphone app.

"Future Trend 6: Vending machines in new locations.

"Future Trend 7: More interactive vending machines."

Source: "Current and Future Trends in Vending Machines," by Bruce Y. Lee, Forbes, April 22, 2016

- Lot less small players...with the big guys getting bigger!
- The industry is becoming much more technology driven as operators implement remote monitoring of the machines at customer locations. A higher degree of owner sophistication will be required in order to successfully deploy the technology to drive efficiencies.
- A majority, 82.7 percent, of operators report having locations request healthier products be placed in the machines. This is a trend that is not receding.
- Both margins and operating results should steadily improve as technology makes the operators more efficient and able to better manage their businesses.
- Profits are up due to price increases by operators. Replication difficult as purchase price is usually near asset value which does not take into account the marketing and effort to locate the machines.

Expert Comments

Utilize an industry expert to handle the transaction. There are numerous landmines within these businesses that require experience and knowledge.

The business is changing dramatically with the introduction of remote monitoring and dynamic scheduling. This requires that an owner/operator has the resources to successfully implement and manage a more sophisticated business.

It seems to be a very easy business to enter, which is the reason it is highly plagued by scam artists who promise one 'the stars,' but usually deliver nothing!! The problem of securing good producing accounts-ones that make the cost of the equipment needed to properly serve that account worthwhile-is the problem that most of the time can only be circumvented by buying established routes with a track record!

Buyer: Recognize the maintenance capital requirement to replace worn/obsolete equipment and trucks. Seller: Begin preparing to sell three years ahead of the target date. Get financials up-to-date and in good order. Pay down debt. Obtain customer contracts whenever possible.

"'The vending industry and atmosphere is not the same as it was ten, or even five years ago,' said Rosset (Marc Rosset, CEO of Professional Vending Consultants). 'It is a different industry in many ways, and that includes buying and selling.' According to Rosset, there are four things every operator should consider when thinking about selling.

"One: The region your company serves—'Within the last few years there has been so much consolidation in the industry that there are only a handful of vending operations in each state that are looking to buy,' said Rosset.

"Two: Technology investment history—When it comes to investing to make a vending company look more desirable, many operators look towards technology. Rosset says this is a good idea for some, but not all. 'Sometimes it is not appropriate to invest in technology,' he said.

"Three: Life outside of the industry—Rosset recommends that operators think about life outside of vending. 'For many, the vending company has been their life. It's an emotional process and once it's sold, you don't get it back. It's life changing, so really be sure that you're ready to let go.'

"Four: Obtain professional help—Obtaining professional help, such as that of an acquisitions consultant, may also ease the process."

Source: "4 Things to Consider When Selling Your Vending Business," Marc Rosset, contributor
www.vendingmarketwatch.com

The industry is experiencing consolidation as baby boomer owners are retiring. Further, the implementation of technology is narrowing the ranks as less sophisticated owners are leaving the industry.

Seller Financing

- Outside financing can be difficult to obtain, particularly for someone new to the industry. More often than not, seller financing is required to bridge the gap. Terms vary depending on the deal and creditworthiness of the buyer.
- Seller financing for 35–50% of price is usually obtainable, and many times the equipment can be used as a source of collateral for purchasing the route.
- Seller financing is typical in the vending industry. Normally in the 30–40% of purchase price range. Bank financing can be difficult to obtain as the hard collateral (vending machines) are scattered at customer locations.
- We see both outside and seller financing. The recent trend has been for an increased willingness of the banking/lending sector to loan into the industry reducing the need for seller financing.

Resources

- Vending Times: http://www.vendingtimes.com
- National Automatic Merchandising Association (NAMA)—good site: https://namanow.org/
- Amusement & Music Operators Association (AMOA): http://www.amoa.com
- IBISWorld, January 2017: http://ibisworld.com
- VendingMarketWatch.com: http://www.vendingmarketwatch.com
- 2017 State of the Vending Industry Report: http://media.cygnus.com/files/base/AUTM/document/2017/06/autm_SOI_noads_Spread.pdf

Veterinary Hospitals		
	NAICS 541940	

Rules of Thumb

➢ 65–70% of annual revenues plus inventory

V

Pricing Tips

- "A veterinary hospital is worth, as a rule of thumb, about one year's gross sales."

Source: https://www.bloomberg.com/news/features/2017-01-05/
when-big-business-happens-to-your-pet January 5, 2017

Industry Trend

- "Veterinary hospital growth—Active patients, patient visits, and overall practice revenue continue to grow.
  - ✓ Active patients in 2015 grew 2.6% relative to 2014
  - ✓ Patient visits in 2015 grew 3.2% relative to 2014
  - ✓ Overall practice revenue in 2015 grew by 6.4% relative to 2014
  - ✓ Outgrowers exhibit 8.7% growth in active patients
  - ✓ Growers exhibit .9% growth in active patients
  - ✓ Decliners exhibit a 7.1% decrease in active patients
  - ✓ Outgrowers now make up 35% of veterinary hospitals"

Source:https://www.aaha.org/public_documents/professional/resources/
aaha_2016_state_of_the_industry_fact_sheet.pdf

Resources

- American Animal Hospital Association (AAHA): https://www.aaha.org/default.aspx

Veterinary Practices		
SIC 0742-01	NAICS 541940	Number of Businesses/Units 53,972

Rules of Thumb

➤ 70–75% of annual sales includes inventory

➤ 2–3 x SDE for small-animal practices includes inventory

➤ 2–5.2 x EBIT

➤ 3–5 x EBITDA

Pricing Tips

- For solo-doctor veterinary practices, SDE multiple derives a very accurate estimate of practice value. For multidoctor practices, EBITDA multiple is preferred for an accurate estimate of practice value.
- On average veterinary practices sell for about 70% of annual gross income. However, the range is quite wide. It is not uncommon for the price range to be between 40% to 100% on annual gross income. Many factors come into play: type of practice (e.g., small-animal vs. equine vs. ER vs. specialty referral), number of veterinarians, number of hours worked by the veterinarians, amount and type of furniture and equipment, drug inventory, etc. These and other factors can skew price above or below the average price by significant amounts.
- Small-animal practices (dogs/cats) are most common type. Most veterinarian buyers are looking for this type of practice. Goodwill tends to transfer well with small-animal practices. Still a very fragmented market with many independent practices. There are a number of corporate nationals with large numbers of

practices nationwide who buy practices. However, they usually want larger, multidoctor practices, with gross income of over $1 million.

- Good financing for doctor/veterinarian buyers...up to 100% financing provided there is sufficient cash flow.
- Typically, a practice needs 1400–1500 active clients to support each full-time veterinarian.
- Demographic trend for veterinarians is strongly skewed to female doctors. Most new graduates are female.
- For highly profitable practices (profit greater than 20%) most traditional lenders don't want to lend more than 100% of the annual revenues, so seller financing would usually be required for such transactions involving high-value practices.
- Mixed-animal, large-animal and rural practices typically sell for lower multiples.
- There is a wide variation in sales price for veterinary practice sales. The most common range for percent of gross sales is 65% to 80%, however, very profitable practices will sell for 90% or more. Almost all sales are asset sales, not stock. For companies with revenues greater than $2,000,000, there are several national corporate purchasers, who will pay 5 times or greater than 5 times EBITDA. Using SDE is very accurate for single-owner practices, but it becomes less helpful in multi-doctor practices.
- Pricing is strongly associated with a multiple of EBITDA, after adjustments for non-operating, non-recurring and discretionary expenses. The largest factors affecting the size of the selected multiple are location, local demographics, local competition, curb appeal and growth or decline in earnings. Multiples of gross sales have declined over the past 20 years because of increased costs of labor and supplies. The major factors affecting profitability are COGS, staff wages and rent expense. Poor management of these expenses leads to poor profitability and decreased value.
- In regard to financial analysis, the gross multiple has declined over the past 30 years because of increased cost for labor, outside services and products. It should not be relied upon for a sales valuation, but can be used as a test for reasonableness of pricing. The most reliable multiples are for SDE (solo doctor practice, only) and EBITDA (solo and multi-doctor practice), both based on a normalized income statement or tax return. Fundamental factors, such as location, curb appeal, practice growth, quality of equipment, average transaction fee and competition are all very important to buyers. Large animal practices will have lower multiples. Rural and remote small animal practices are difficult sales.
- Inventory included in the sale is usually a working level or 30-day supply. Most sales are asset sales and include equipment, furniture, removable fixtures, working levels of consumable inventory, and intangibles (goodwill).

Benchmark Data

Statistics (Veterinary Services)

Number of Establishments	53,972
Average Profit Margin	13.2%
Revenue per Employee	$105,100
Average Number of Employees	7.1
Average Wages per Employee	$36,911

V

Products and Services Segmentation

Nonsurgical treatments	26.8%
Routine examinations	23.2%
Laboratory services	16.4%
Surgical treatments	14.9%
Merchandise sales	11.0%
Other	3.4%
Boarding services	2.9%
Pet grooming services	1.4%

Major Market Segmentation

Companion animal exclusive practices	65.7%
Companion animal predominate practices	9.1%
Food animal exclusive practices/predominate practices	6.8%
Mixed animal practices	6.3%
Other	6.3%
Equine	5.8%

Industry Costs

Profit	13.2%
Wages	35.0%
Purchases	20.7%
Depreciation	2.3%
Marketing	1.5%
Rent & Utilities	5.3%
Other	22.0%

Market Share

VCA Antech Inc.	6.5%

- Productivity of employed small-animal veterinarians should be about $600,000 in revenues on a full-time basis. Nonveterinarian staff should average, as a fraction of revenues, about $175,000 to $200,000 each. An employed small-animal veterinarian should be paid about 20% of his or her production.
- Per the AAHA's most recent "Financial & Productivity Pulsepoints," the Average Client Transaction (ACT) was $137. Per AAHA, the average annual revenue/ veterinarian is $516,000.
- Sales per support staff of $150,000 to $180,000 indicate average to above average productivity. Cost of supplies, including drugs and diet foods of 20% of revenues or less is positive. However, many practices have COGS much greater, but it the practice sells a lot of product, then the impact on profitability can be lessened because many product sales contribute to ancillary income. The three major expenses that cut into profitability are staff wages (not including doctors) greater than 20% of revenues, COGS greater than 20% of revenues and facility rents greater than 8% of revenues. Shopping center practices often have high rents that can affect the practice earnings.
- The expenses above are the most common benchmarks used for expenses. Revenues per full-time veterinarian—$525,000 to $600,000. Revenues per full-time employee (non-veterinarian)—$130,000 to $170,000 (median about $150,000). Ancillary income (grooming, boarding, diet food and retail sales) of 14% to 16% of revenues is desirable because higher ancillary income tends to increase the productivity of the doctors.

Business Reference Guide **2018**

- Average annual gross income per DVM is about $500K, of which about $450K is professional services (as opposed to retail, prescription refills, grooming, etc.). Average transaction charge is $114. Income per square foot is $338. Should have about 4 support staff for every full-time veterinarian.

Expenses (% of Annual Sales)

Cost of Goods	15% to 20%
Occupancy Costs	05% to 11%
Payroll/Labor Costs	20% to 30%
Profit (pretax)	20% to 30%

Questions

- The buyer needs to ask for everything related to the practice—tax returns, practice computer reports, employee information, equipment lists—and learn the local economics, including competition, of the community. Then the buyer must perform extensive due diligence.
- Type of practice; hours worked per week; number of client transactions per day; ancillary services; percent of revenue (grooming, boarding, retail); types of procedures performed; types of species treated; drug inventory levels; in-house lab and equipment capabilities
- What is the value of the procedures currently being referred out of the office? Do you have agreements with suppliers of practice services, such as laboratory services and are those agreements transferable to a buyer? What are the demographics in the area and what are the demographics of the clients in this practice?
- Learn their practice philosophy and see if it is compatible with yours. Next, ask for three years of tax returns, supporting documents, practice performance reports, equipment list and information on the staff.
- Gross hours worked, type of patients seen, and percentage mix; ancillary profit centers support staff info; number active clients in last 2 years
- What is the turnover rate, large vs. small animal, surgery vs. treatment, retail sales, inventory size, payroll costs?
- Ask what medical services they do not provide that could be added.
- Are they willing to sign a covenant not to compete? Can they work in the practice after the sale? How was price arrived at and justified? What is the value of the real estate and how was the price arrived at? What is being sold for the asked price? How many hours per week are worked by the owner/doctor? How are emergencies calls covered?
- Standard recasting info for sellers. Types of surgery performed? 1 or 3 vaccination schedule? Relationship with local shelters/humane societies? How are emergencies handled?

Industry Trend

- As a percentage of revenues, anesthesia and surgery income has declined, while revenues from diagnostic procedures (radiology, ultrasound, etc.) and laboratory fees have increased. In general, small-animal practices have developed more income from internal medicine and less from surgical procedures income. Recent graduates tend to refer many surgical procedures to board-certified specialists.
- "When pet owners carry pet health insurance, it is a win for them, their pets

and veterinarian caretakers; pet insurance can be a hard sell but veterinarians can prove the difference, according to John Volk, senior consultant, Brakke Consulting, a Dallas-based animal health and veterinary practice management consulting firm. When people have pet health insurance, they are more likely to follow through with veterinarian recommendations, optimize veterinary medical services for their pet and spend more on their pet's health according to those who Volk and the NAPHIA interviewed."

Source: "Veterinary Survey Says Pet Insurance is a Practice Boon," May 13, 2017, http://www.veterinarypracticenews.com/veterinary-survey-says-pet-insurance-is-a-practice-boon/

- Plenty of buyers for good practices. Good growth for pet industry and veterinary medicine services.
- More and more baby boomer owner-operator veterinarians will be selling their practices.
- Larger practices (>$2,000,000) are increasingly selling to consolidators (larger corporate companies). Smaller practices still hold their own because clients feel that they are receiving more personalized services. There is a concern in the industry that there may an over-supply of veterinarians leading to increased competition in the future. The current market is still favorable to sellers because of the large number of buyers.
- For practice acquisitions, there may be a change in supply and demand. Boomers, who have been holding on to their practices, may be forced to sell because of age and health reasons. As the economy rebounds, the aging Boomers may feel more comfortable retiring because their real estate holdings and investment accounts have returned to pre-recession levels. Many veterinary practice analysts expect far more practices to become available in the coming years.

Expert Comments

For a seller preparing to retire, maintaining the practice revenues is very important. Sometimes an owner will begin to reduce the hours working, which leads to declining revenues. This is a negative selling factor for buyers and lenders. For a buyer, the process can be very complex. Be sure to have expert advice from someone in the field of veterinary practice transitions.

Competition was high during the past recession, but it is more moderate in the current economy. The risk is low because many practice lenders are available and willing to provide up to 100% practice financing. Lenders have typically had very few loan defaults with licensed veterinarians. Profits have been increasing with the current economy. Most small-animal facilities have very good locations and must appear attractive and clean because clients visit these facilities on a regular basis. Replication of the business requires a veterinary license, which requires several years of education to obtain. The industry trend has changed remarkably in the past few years. There are many corporate buyers now; these are companies that own many practices and are currently in a strong acquisition mode. This trend has been favorable to practices that have revenues greater than $1,000,000. However, most corporate buyers will require the selling practitioner to remain at the practice for up to three to five years, post-sale. The expansion of corporate acquisitions has created a negative effect on single-facility practices. Many practices are having difficulty in hiring veterinarians because most of the corporate practices offer excellent pay and benefits packages to employed veterinarians.

"The culture and relationships within a veterinary practice may have a significant impact on the success of a veterinary hospital, according to survey data revealed during the American Animal Hospital Association 2016 State of the Industry presentation. The AAHA 2016 State of the Industry, which was presented during the AAHA Austin 2016 Yearly Conference, examined data from a fall 2015 survey AAHA conducted with the Daniels College of Business at the University of Denver that studied organizational culture in veterinary practices.

"The culture study surveyed over 1,000 veterinary hospitals to study the qualities of organizational culture in veterinary practices, evaluate the overall and specific subcultures in veterinary hospitals, and determine how culture affects veterinary practice metrics.

"On the economic front, data from the 2016 State of the Industry indicated that more practices have moved into the 'Outgrower' category of practices that demonstrate growth of more than 10 percent year-over-year. Thirty-five percent of practices are now considered Outgrowers, compared to 24 percent from the 2015 State of the Industry.

"Other key points from the economic data revealed:

"'We know that successful veterinary practices such as Outgrowers focus on strengthening bonds and building relationships,' Cavanaugh said. 'We'll see that category continue to grow as more and more practices focus on strengthening the bonds and improving culture within their own practices.'"

Source: AAHA 2016 State of the Industry, http://www.aaha.org/blog/NewStat/post/2016/04/04/102724/
Culture-can-impact-veterinary-practice-success-AAHA-2016-State-of-the-Industry-reveals.aspx

The market is mostly vets selling to other vets. Very few non-veterinarian buyers/sellers outside of large corporate nationals.

Competition varies city by city. Some locations can be saturated. Risk is typically very low. This is reflected by excellent financing terms. Strong industry. Very good projected growth nationwide. Most facilities are good. Most practices in suburban locations. Can be in leased space/strip malls or standalone buildings. Marketability is good for practices with good cash flow. Replication is fairly easy in that startup financing is plentiful for veterinarians.

A buyer should study each aspect about the available practices, from location to financial performance, and determine whether a specific practice will meet his/her needs. Have a building inspection done, if acquiring the real estate. A seller needs to be prepared to provide a smooth transition. Typically, the seller should be prepared to work in the practice for at least a couple months after the sale, and normally the seller is compensated.

The veterinary world is changing. Single-doctor practices are becoming a thing of the past. There are a lot of corporate buyers like VCA Antech Inc. who are acquiring practices.

For buyers, be sure to have experts on your side-consultants, accountants and attorneys. Then perform your due diligence. For sellers, keep working hard and do not let the revenues decline. Practices that are declining are red flags to both buyers and lenders.

V

Since the great recession, most practices have been steadily growing. The amount of risk with new ownership is low because the goodwill transferability remains high. The clients and the support staff are basically the buyer's to lose. Most transitions are successful. The larger risks are related to practices that have very high average transaction fees. It takes are very confident buyer to purchase a high-end practice. Marketability tends to be good. Practices in more rural locations take much longer to sell because of the limited amount of buyers for rural practices. Curb appeal of the facility and modern equipment add to marketability. Practices with low revenues or low profitability are more difficult sales. It requires a confident buyer, who knows that he or she can grow the practice.

Competition can be quite variable, tending to moderate to heavy in desirable places to live. The risk is low, as evidenced by the ease of lender financing up to 100% of the acquisition price. Trends in historical profit have been variable through the economic downturn. High fee practices have suffered declines in revenues, while moderate fee practices have actually grown during the past few years. Location and facilities are variable. Most practices are located in accessible sites within a community, but some communities, mainly rural locations, have a limited number of potential buyers making sales difficult. Marketability is good because there is currently strong demand for practices by potential buyers. Trends are good because pet-owning clients will take care of their animals, even in difficult economic times. Replication is hard because of the extensive education, training and licensing requirements.

The practice transition process is so complex that both seller and buyer should utilize consultants who are knowledgeable in veterinary practice sales transactions.

Competition has been growing because of many new veterinary colleges that have opened in the past 20 years, producing more graduates. Risk is low because lenders have a very low default rate with licensed veterinarians, indicating most acquisitions are successful. Profitability has been difficult to maintain because of the economic downturn, competition from human and online pharmacies, animal shelters providing vaccinations and spays and neuters. Small-animal practices are giving up lower cost margin income sources because many procedures and treatments are referred to specialty centers. Facilities are generally good because practice clients expect a clean and presentable clinic/hospital. Urban/suburban locations are the best. Marketability has been good because there are many buyers and few sellers. Many boomers, who should retire, are holding on to their practices because their revenues have declined, and their real estate holdings and retirement accounts took a big hit during the recession. Industry trends are positive because animal owners will still spend money on their pets and sacrifice discretionary income for other types spending. Ease of replication is very dependent on the buyer's ability to replace the seller's skill level and communication abilities (bedside manner). Most buyers are quite competent in the practice of veterinary medicine, but the change in the practice's culture and perceived quality of care, whether better or worse, can be a challenge to a new owner. Typically, it is best for a new buyer to change the acquired practice's culture and the fees gradually.

Competition varies by region. The typical small-animal vet needs about 1,500 active clients to make a decent living. Small-animal fixed base practices sell best. Mobile practices usually have little value other than asset value.

V

Seller Financing

- Complete seller financing is rare now. There are many lenders willing to completely finance a practice asset sale. Down payments can be minimal; terms may be from 10 to 15 years for a practice loan. Rates have been increasing. Currently loans are averaging 4% to 5% annual interest.
- Outside financing very common. 10 years, 5%–6%. Both commercial and SBA loans.
- Veterinarians are a preferred business type for SBA lenders. It is possible to obtain 100% loan to value financing with a 25-year amortization when purchasing an existing, profitable practice and building. Sometimes this requires the vet selling the practice/building to take back a second mortgage of 10–25%.
- A financially sound buyer (good credit score and personal liquidity) can typically borrow most of the sale price. Weaker buyers will require some form of seller participation. The typical seller may not have to finance greater than 10% of the sale price. There are both conventional lenders and SBA lenders. Interest rates for both are quite low now. Many conventional loans have fixed interest rates between 4.0% to 4.5%. SBA loans are around 5%, but they are variable quarterly.
- Many lenders, both conventional and SBA, are ready to lend 100% of the acquisition price. Seller financing tends to be minimal.
- For qualified buyers, greater than 90% of practices sold are completed with outside financing. Sellers typically receive all cash or contribute minimally (<20%) to buyer financing.

Resources

- American Animal Hospital Association: http://www.aahanet.org
- Veterinary Economics: http://veterinarybusiness.dvm360.com/
- Vet Quest Classifieds: http://www.vetquest.com
- Veterinary Information Network: http://www.vin.com
- Veterinary Practice News: http://www.veterinarypracticenews.com/
- American Veterinary Medical Association: http://www.avma.org
- VetPartners: http://www.vetpartners.org
- IBISWorld, August 2017: http://ibisworld.com
- DVM360: http://www.dvm360.com

Video Stores

SIC 7841-02	NAICS 532230	Number of Businesses/Units 2,705

Rules of Thumb

➢ .65–1.0 x annual sales includes inventory

➢ Most buyers want to recover their investment within 24 months, so 2 x SDE is a safe bet, including inventory.

➢ It used to be one year's SDE plus the fair market value of the tapes and games, but inventory drops in value too dramatically after the new release prime period (90 days) has passed.\1 to 2 times SDE to a working owner plus fair market value for videos, games & DVDs

V

Pricing Tips

- The inventory price of the videos and games drops drastically from its original retail.Unit prices can be as low as $5.00 or less.
- If the current owner can computer-generate a video rental report that shows you how many times each video in inventory has been rented and the income associated with it, you will see how much 'dead inventory' could be replaced to increase revenues. Special- interest videos and games like Nintendo and PlayStation 2, etc. would be good profit generators.

Benchmark Data

Statistics (DVD, Game & Video Rental)

Number of Establishments	2,705
Average Profit Margin	2.7%
Revenue per Employee	$218,300
Average Number of Employees	4.9
Average Wages per Employee	$25,196

Products and Services Segmentation

Nonsubscription rental	62.3%
Subscription rental	32.0%
Other	5.7%

Industry Costs

Profit	2.7%
Wages	12.0%
Purchases	42.0%
Depreciation	5.7%
Marketing	1.9%
Rent & Utilities	10.4%
Other	25.3%

Expenses (% of Annual Sales)

Cost of Goods	33%
Occupancy Costs	15%
Payroll/Labor Costs	27%
Profit (pretax)	25%

Industry Trend

- "The pivot to streaming Video on Demand (VOD) is expected to continue diminishing demand for the DVD, Game and Video Rental industry over the next five years. Moreover, many automated machines have replaced brick-and-mortar locations to provide convenience without the costs of operating a store. Due to declining sales, intense price competition and higher operational costs, many industry players will be forced to close their brick-and-mortar operations. Overall, revenue is expected to decline at an annualized rate of 4.9% to $2.4 billion during the five-year period to 2022."

  Source: IBISWorld Industry Outlook

- "The Entertainment Merchants Association's recently released 2016 D2: Disc to Digital annual report on the home entertainment industry demonstrates that the DVD and Blu-ray Disc market is not dead or dying; rather it remains a significant and important segment of our evolving industry.

"While the physical goods market has slowly declined since its heyday in 2004, it remains strong. Citing figures released by DEG, the report notes that spending on rental and purchases accounted for half of the overall home video market in 2015, and is expected to still represent 30% of the market in 2019. Both disc rental and disc retail spending currently far exceed their digital equivalents.

"Discs contribute significantly to the bottom lines of the studios, as disc sales and rentals are almost equal to theatrical box office. They continue to be an integral part of the economics of the motion picture industry."

Source: "The Disc is not Dead," by Mark Fisher, President and CEO of EMA (Entertainment Merchants Association), May 2016, http://entmerch.org/press-room/marks-remarks/the-disc-is-not-dead.html

- "Almost half of all U.S. households subscribe to Amazon Prime, Hulu Plus, Netflix or a combination of these services. UltraViolet has over 21 million users with 110 million movies and TV shows in their libraries."

Source: http://entmerch.org/industry/facts-home-video-mkt.html

Expert Comments

The industry has changed with the switch to games.

Seller Financing

- 12 to 24 months
- 3 years

Resources

- Entertainment Merchants Association: http://www.entmerch.org/
- IBISWorld, August 2017: http://ibisworld.com

Visa/Passport Companies

Rules of Thumb

➤ 3–5 x EBITDA

Pricing Tips

- Immigration is rising.
- Total number of applications processed year over year (up or down?)
- Due to new U.S. Government requirements, this industry multiple has increased.

Questions

- How do they execute quick turnaround? How long does it take them to fulfill applications?

Expert Comments

This industry deals as expeditors of government travel documents.

W

Waste/Garbage/Trash Collection

	NAICS 56211	Number of Businesses/Units 11,362

Rules of Thumb

➤ 95% of annual sales

➤ 3 x SDE

➤ 5 x EBIT

➤ 4 x EBITDA

Pricing Tips

- For a company with predictable repeat earnings with service contracts, eleven times the last twelve months' revenue. For a company involved in the construction industry, there may be a holdback of an amount multiple to adjust for homebuilder risk. The most valued are ongoing commercial accounts, which might have an adjustment or an earnout up or down. The best buyers are the "big boys" in waste management.

Benchmark Data

Statistics (Waste Collection Services)

Number of Establishments	11,362
Average Profit Margin	8.4%
Revenue per Employee	$280,800
Average Number of Employees	14.9
Average Wages per Employee	$52,870

Products and Services Segmentation

Residential waste collection	39.8%
Nonresidential waste collection	22.3%
Other	18.0%
Transfer and storage facility	7.7%
Hazardous waste collection	5.6%
Recyclable material collection	4.0%
C&D site waste collection	2.6%

Major Market Segmentation

Individuals and households	28.9%
Commercial	27.9%
Industrial	22.9%
Construction and demolition	10.2%
Government and nonprofit	10.1%

Industry Costs

Profit	8.4%
Wages	18.8%
Purchases	24.2%
Depreciation	7.3%
Marketing	1.2%
Rent & Utilities	6.4%
Other	33.7%

Market Share

Waste Management Inc.	21.9%
Republic Services Inc.	18.6%
Waste Connections Inc.	7.4%

Expenses (% of Annual Sales)

Cost of Goods	20%
Occupancy Costs	05%
Payroll/Labor Costs	50%
Profit (pretax)	25%

Industry Trend

- "6 waste and recycling trends to watch in 2017:
  - ✓ Commodity prices likely to make a comeback
  - ✓ Recyclers to move away from weight-based
  - ✓ Flexible packaging to continue growing (and presenting challenges)
  - ✓ Shifts in politics to create more division
  - ✓ Increased infrastructure spending to present competitive opportunities
  - ✓ Technology to transform operations — whether or not the industry is ready"

  Source: http://www.wastedive.com/news/6-waste-and-recycling-trends-to-watch-in-2017/433337/

- "The US waste management industry includes about 24,000 establishments (single-location companies and units of multi-location companies) with combined annual revenue of about $60 billion."

  Source: www.firstresearch.com

- "The top two companies, Waste Management and Republic Services accounted for 39 percent of total industry revenue. All of the publicly traded companies together comprised 61 percent of total revenues. All told, the private sector represents 78 percent of the industry while the municipal sector controls the remaining 22 percent. This is a sharp contrast to 1992 when municipalities controlled 35 percent of industry revenue.

  "Recent mergers, including that of Veolia's U.S. waste business by Advanced Disposal, promise a reshaped industry much further along its path of privatization. The companies understand that one way to deal with turbulent economic times amidst rising fuel, labor and equipment costs is to streamline operations and vertically integrate their markets.

  "Rising costs have focused company managers on disciplined price increases especially now that the industry is more consolidated, more attentive to return on invested capital, more rational about valuing existing landfill capacity and mindful of lessons in the past when pricing was sacrificed."

  Source: "New Report Details the $55 Billion U.S. Waste Industry,"
  http://www.wastebusinessjournal.com/overview.htm

Expert Comments

This has been a very difficult business dominated by a few large companies.

Resources

- Waste 360: http://www.waste360.com
- IBISWorld, July 2017: http://ibisworld.com

W

Web Hosting

	NAICS 518210	

Rules of Thumb
➤ 3–4 x EBITDA

Pricing Tips
- Prices are down from 2 years ago.

Benchmark Data
- Most are netting between 33% and 44% of gross income.

Expenses (% of Annual Sales)

Cost of Goods	n/a
Occupancy Costs	n/a
Payroll/Labor Costs	n/a
Profit (pretax)	33%

Industry Trend
- "The Internet Hosting Services industry is expected to experience strong growth over the five years to 2022, as maintaining an attractive web presence becomes increasingly important for businesses. The desire to improve the customer experience online, coupled with the continued shift to online services, will drive demand for industry services. Growing corporate profit will incentivize businesses to invest in their digital property. As a result, IBISWorld expects industry revenue to grow at an annualized rate of 8.0% to $30.0 billion during the five-year period."

  Source: IBISWorld Industry Outlook

- Massive growth

Expert Comments
Industry was growing by 50% per year prior to the economic downturn. Still growth in the industry.

Resources
- IBISWorld, June 2017: http://ibisworld.com

Weight Loss Services/Centers

SIC 7299-34	NAICS 812191	Number of Businesses/Units 39,563

Rules of Thumb
➤ 50–55% of annual sales

Benchmark Data

Statistics (Weight Loss Services)

Number of Establishments	39,563
Average Profit Margin	8.4%
Revenue per Employee	$33,000
Average Number of Employees	1.7
Average Wages per Employee	$9,706

Products and Services Segmentation

Meeting fees	81.5%
In-meeting product sales	10.8%
Other fees	7.7%

Industry Costs

Profit	8.4%
Wages	29.2%
Purchases	15.1%
Depreciation	2.8%
Marketing	3.0%
Rent & Utilities	13.8%
Other	27.7%

Market Share

Weight Watchers International Inc.	28.0%
Nutrisystem Inc.	27.3%
MediFast Inc.	10.7%

Industry Trend

- "Should you consider a weight loss franchise? The weight loss industry as a whole is still adapting to changing consumer sentiments about health. Some of the industry stalwarts are struggling - but they are still profitable in many cases and are figuring out how to steer in these new waters. Smaller or new companies are more nimble and can more quickly embrace a more holistic viewpoint of health."

Source: "Weight Loss Industry Analysis 2017—Cost & Trends,"
https://www.franchisehelp.com/industry-reports/weight-loss-industry-report/

- "A new study by Transparency Market Research (TMR), titled 'Weight Loss Services Market—Global Industry Analysis, Size, Share, Growth, Trends and Forecast 2016–2023,' states that the global weight loss services market is poised to grow in the coming years, thanks to increasing awareness among people about their health and well-being. The huge consumer base is a key market driver for the growth of global weight loss services market and will continue to remain due to increasing global population, particularly in the Asia Pacific and rest of the world."

Source: July 11, 2016,
https://globenewswire.com/news-release/2016/07/11/854979/0/en/Weight-Loss-Services-Market-set-to-Grow-in-Coming-Years-Driven-by-Huge-Consumer-Base-Transparency-Market-Research.html

Resources

- IBISWorld, April 2017: http://ibisworld.com

	Franchise
Wienerschnitzel	
Approx. Total Investment	$350,000–$1,000,000
Estimated Annual Sales/Unit	$790,000

	NAICS 722513	Number of Businesses/Units 320

Rules of Thumb
➤ 30–35% of annual sales plus inventory

	Franchise
Wild Birds Unlimited	
Approx. Total Investment	$146,692–$228,405

	NAICS 453910	Number of Businesses/Units 308

Rules of Thumb
➤ 30–35% of annual sales plus inventory

Resources
- Wild Birds Unlimited: http://www.wbu.com

Wind Farms (Energy)		
	NAICS 333611	

Rules of Thumb
➤ 10 x EBITDA

Pricing Tips
- Use a cap rate, similar to pricing commercial real estate.

Benchmark Data
- Revenue per kilowatt hour, capacity factor, PPA rate

Industry Trend
- "America's wind power workforce installed 908 utility-scale turbines in the first quarter of 2017, totaling 2,000 megawatts (MW) of capacity. This is the wind industry's strongest start in eight years, according to a new report released today by the American Wind Energy Association (AWEA)."

  Source: http://www.awea.org/1Q2017MarketReportRelease May 2, 2017

- "The leading 25 owners of wind assets have seen their share of global installed capacity fall from 47% to 41% over the past three years, according to a report by Make Consulting."

  Source: August 10, 2016, http://www.windpowermonthly.com/article/1405306/top-asset-owners-losing-market-share

Expert Comments

This industry is, for a number of reasons, going to grow dramatically over the next decade. The economic model is very similar to that of commercial real estate-high upfront capital costs followed by extremely consistent cash flows, with upside appreciation potential. The smart money will get in early and ride the wave.

Resources

- Windpower Monthly: http://www.windpowermonthly.com
- American Wind Energy Association: http://www.awea.org/

Window Cleaning		
	NAICS 561720	

Rules of Thumb

➢ 60% of annual sales

Resources

- International Window Cleaning Association—a site with a lot of valuable information: http://www.iwca.org

Window Treatment/Draperies		
	NAICS 442291	

Rules of Thumb

➢ 35–40% of annual sales plus inventory

Industry Trend

- "Revenue for the Window Treatment Stores industry is forecast to decline at a slower rate over the next five years, dropping an annualized 0.3% through 2021 to $919.1 million. The improving economy will support a rise in discretionary income for most households, but the anticipated expansion of less-expensive retailers will result in more low-price product offerings, deterring more customers from paying high prices for premium products sold by this industry's operators. The coming years will be further shaped by changing demographics and innovation in window treatments, forcing many operators to change their marketing tactics through rebranding and new product lines. The number of businesses in the industry is anticipated to fall significantly in the coming years, as many stores will feel more pressure from competitors to lower prices, despite generally offering products of higher quality."

Source: IBISWorld Industry Outlook

Resources

- Window Coverings Association of America (WCAA): http://www.wcaa.org
- Window Fashion Vision: https://www.wf-vision.com
- IBISWorld, September, 2016: http://ibisworld.com

W

	Franchise

Wine Kitz (Canada)

Approx. Total Investment	$106,000–$135,000

	NAICS 312130	Number of Businesses/Units 95

Rules of Thumb

➤ 55% of annual sales plus inventory

Wineries

SIC 2084-01	NAICS 312130	Number of Businesses/Units 7,155

Rules of Thumb

➤ 25% of annual sales (does include real estate)

➤ 10 x SDE

➤ 60 x EBIT (does include real estate)

➤ 89 x EBITDA (does include real estate)

Benchmark Data

Statistics (Wineries)

Number of Establishments	7,155
Average Profit Margin	11.7%
Revenue per Employee	$465,900
Average Number of Employees	6.4
Average Wages per Employee	$56,886

Products and Services Segmentation

Chardonnay	26.4%
Zinfandel, Riesling and other blends	19.8%
Cabernet Sauvignon	19.4%
Merlot	10.8%
Pinot Grigio	10.3%
Pinot Noir	7.6%
Sauvignon Blanc	5.7%

Industry Costs

Profit	11.7%
Wages	12.1%
Purchases	39.2%
Depreciation	5.4%
Marketing	1.0%
Rent & Utilities	2.4%
Other	28.2%

Market Share

E. & J. Gallo Winery	22.2%
Constellation Brands Inc.	12.4%
The Wine Group, Inc.	8.8%

Expenses (% of Annual Sales)

Cost of Goods	59%
Occupancy Costs	20%
Payroll/Labor Costs	20%
Profit (pretax)	10%

Questions

- Will you [the seller] stay on as a consultant?

Industry Trend

- "Optimism is high that 2017 will continue to see the small but steady growth pattern of previous years, at around 1 to 3% volume and 2 to 4% in value. According to Wines & Vines (2017), total US wine sales approached $60 billion in 2016, with an estimated $39.8 billion in sales from domestic wine and the remainder from imports.
  "Growth of US Wineries and Exports
  - ✓ Number of US Wineries in 2017 = 9,091 (Fisher, 2017), up 4% from 8702 wineries in 2016.
  - ✓ Five Largest Wine States by # of Wineries: California 4202, Washington = 747, Oregon, 713, NY = 385, Texas = 287
  - ✓ US Exports – $1.62 billion in 2016, up from 1% from 2015. Volume = 412.7 million liters or 45.9 million cases. (Wine Institute, 2017)"

  Source: "The Future is Bright for U.S. Wine in 2017: Statistics from 2016 Paint Rosy Picture," January 31, 2017, https://lizthachmw.com

- "It is expected an increase in properties will go up for sale, especially if adult children do not share mom & dad's dream. But selling even a marginally profitable business is a challenge. Typically, it takes three years or more to find a qualified buyer."

  Source: http://www.hagarty-on-wine.com/OnWineBlog/?p=7130

Expert Comments

Wineries take 1–2 years to sell if they are priced well.

Resources

- American Society for Enology and Viticulture: http://www.asev.org
- Wine Business Monthly: http://www.winebusiness.com
- Family Winemakers of California: http://www.familywinemakers.org
- California Wineland: http://www.winesandvines.com
- IBISWorld, April 2017: http://ibisworld.com
- New York Wines: https://www.newyorkwines.org
- American Winery Guide: http://www.americanwineryguide.com

Wingstop Restaurants	Franchise
Approx. Total Investment	$242,787–$569,528
Estimated Annual Sales/Unit	$1,104,000
NAICS 722513	Number of Businesses/Units 537

Rules of Thumb

➢ 30–35% of annual sales plus inventory

Resources

- Wingstop: http://www.wingstop.com

Wireless Communications		
(Carriers, dealers & resellers of cellular, PCs, & paging)		
SIC 5999-02	NAICS 517210	

Rules of Thumb

➢ 30% of annual gross sales

➢ 2–3 x SDE plus inventory

➢ 2.5–5 x EBITDA includes inventory

➢ $50 to $130 per pop for operational market—less if naked license

Pricing Tips

- It is important to consider revenue per customer.
- Strong employee technical base/tenure desirable along with non-competes for key personnel
- Trend upward in volume and downward in service income is not abnormal
- Subscribers, physical plant capacity, client retention and gross margins
- Calculating furniture, fixtures and equipment value along with any real estate involved

Benchmark Data

- 3 x SDE is a good place to begin. Inventory/chargebacks and deactivations can be an issue if not clearly discussed.
- 35%–40% gross profit
- COGS 25%, payroll 20%, profit 28%, occupancy cost 18%
- Sales per employee
- Number of years owner has operated the business, along with how long they will stay and train. Are the employees staying or leaving? Location of the business and any customer lists they may have are all similar factors.

Expenses (% of Annual Sales)

Cost of Goods	60%
Occupancy Costs	05% to 10%
Payroll/Labor Costs	20%
Profit (pretax)	10%

Questions

- Seller Financing? Lease issues? Any problems with the carrier transferring the business to a buyer and what are those exact requirements? Timing.
- Ask if market is built out (to what percentage of population and geography) and if it is operational (how long).

- Number of activations per month currently doing? How many deactivations per month?
- What is advertising budget? How long at this location? Are employees on commission or salary or both? Number of locations?
- Pricing strategy and debt owed
- How will inventory be paid for and when? Period of time post-close that seller will be responsible for chargebacks and de-activations for pre-sale customers.

Industry Trend

- "What should businesses be mindful of as they plan for growth? Carriers should continue to focus on providing data and voice services that are high quality, reliable, and affordable. The challenge in 2017 will continue to be the focus on capital allocation. Carriers will need to make upgrades to their core connectivity infrastructure, which in the case of the coming shift to fifth generation (5G) mobile networks may run well into the billions of dollars. And, they will also require significant capital resources to fund such areas as the IoT, autonomous vehicles, industry verticals, M&A, and international expansion. Carriers will need both a clearly articulated strategy and an efficient approach to capital spending to maximize their investments."

  Source: https://www2.deloitte.com/us/en/pages/technology-media-and-telecommunications/
  articles/telecommunications-industry-outlook.html

- Trend toward commodity-based marketing and addition of synergistic product lines in an effort to offset eroding equipment profits

Expert Comments

Multi-store operators with strong sales and net earnings are in demand.

Difficult to replicate due to technical nature of business as well as myriad supplier relationships required

Expanding into synergistic product lines is becoming the norm.

Seller Financing

- 1–2 years
- Depends on size and complexity of transaction.

Resources

- Wireless Week: http://www.wirelessweek.com
- RCR Wireless News: http://www.rcrwireless.com
- Wireless Dealer Magazine: http://www.wirelessdealermag.com

Wireless Toyz		Franchise
Approx. Total Investment		$219,000–$648,000
Estimated Annual Sales/Unit		$650,000
	NAICS 443142	Number of Businesses/Units 187

Rules of Thumb

➢ 45–50% of annual sales plus inventory

W

Resources

- Wireless Toyz: http://www.wirelesstoyz.com

Women's Clothing		
SIC 5621-01	NAICS 448120	Number of Businesses/Units 58,189

Rules of Thumb

➤ 20% of annual sales plus inventory

➤ 2 x monthly sales plus inventory

Benchmark Data

Statistics (Women's Clothing Stores)

Number of Establishments	58,189
Average Profit Margin	4.7%
Revenue per Employee	$112,600
Average Number of Employees	6.4
Average Wages per Employee	$15,573

Products and Services Segmentation

Tops	27.6%
Other apparel and accessories	19.7%
Bottoms	18.4%
Outerwear	16.8%
Dresses	13.6%
Underwear	3.9%

Industry Costs

Profit	4.7%
Wages	13.8%
Purchases	54.5%
Depreciation	1.1%
Marketing	3.7%
Rent & Utilities	12.7%
Other	9.5%

Market Share

Ascena Retail Group Inc.	12.4%

Industry Trend

- "Over the five years to 2022, the Women's Clothing Stores industry is expected to benefit from a rise in the number of high-income households that demand premium-clothing items. The fashion-forward nature of stores that specialize in only women's clothing convinces customers that the value of specialized products justifies the cost. Still, bargain shopping is popular in any clothing industry and many stores are expected to continue using competitive pricing and sales to lure customers as competition heats up. Competition from online retailers is expected to be particularly intense over the next five years, largely hampering industry revenue growth. IBISWorld projects industry revenue to decline slightly at an annualized rate of 0.4% to $41.4 billion over the five years to 2022."

Source: IBISWorld Industry Outlook

Resources

- IBISWorld, January 2017: http://ibisworld.com

Worldwide Express	Franchise
Approx. Total Investment	$25,000–$150,000

	NAICS 561431	Number of Businesses/Units 138

Rules of Thumb

➢ 50–55% of annual sales plus inventory

Resources

- Worldwide Express: http://www.wwex.com

YourOffice	Franchise
Approx. Total Investment	$200,000–$500,000

	NAICS 531120	Number of Businesses/Units 7

Rules of Thumb

➢ 60% of annual sales plus inventory

Resources

- YourOffice: http://www.youroffice.com

You've Got Maids	Franchise
Approx. Total Investment	$40,000–$104,000

SIC 7349-23	NAICS 561720	Number of Businesses/Units 63

Rules of Thumb

➢ 60% of annual sales plus inventory

Resources

- You 've Got Maids: http://www.youvegotmaids.com

Ziebart International (Auto Services)	Franchise
Approx. Total Investment	$167,000–$326,000

NAICS 8111		Number of Businesses/Units 400

Rules of Thumb

➢ 42% of annual sales plus inventory

Resources

- Ziebart: http://www.ziebart.com

We are grateful to the following
Industry Experts who help
make this book possible.

Their experiences and insights provide
invaluable information for anyone buying,
selling or valuing a business.

More information about the
Industry Experts is available online at
http://industryexpert.net/expert-directory

Accounting Firms/CPAs

Ryan Gipple
Berkshire Business Sales &
Acquisitions
1763 W Coconino Drive
Chandler, AZ 85248
Work: 602-614-3583
ryan@ryangipple.com
http://www.berkshirebsa.com

Robert Fremder
Accounting Practice Sold, LLC
Work: 412-322-8843
rfremder@sbcglobal.net
http://www.AccountingPracticeSold.com

Chuck Hayes
ABA Advisors, LLC
5829 N. Post Road
Indianapolis, IN 46216
Work: 317-546-7720
Mobile: 317-431-3899
ch@acctsales.com
http://www.acctsales.com/

Brian Naab
Naab Consulting
5511 E 82nd Street, Suite H
Indianapolis, IN 46250
Work: 888-726-6282
brian@naabconsulting.com
http://www.naabconsulting.com/

David Sweeten
Business Brokers of Texas
8632 Fredericksburg Rd.
San Antonio, TX 78240
Work: (210) 697-8760 x 202
david@brokersoftexas.com
http://www.brokersoftexas.com

Accounting Firms/Practices

David Sweeten
Business Brokers of Texas
8632 Fredericksburg Rd.
San Antonio, TX 78240
Work: (210) 697-8760 x 202
david@brokersoftexas.com
http://www.brokersoftexas.com

Brian Naab
Naab Consulting
5511 E 82nd Street, Suite H
Indianapolis, IN 46250
Work: 888-726-6282
brian@naabconsulting.com
http://www.naabconsulting.com/

Chuck Hayes
ABA Advisors, LLC
5829 N. Post Road
Indianapolis, IN 46216
Work: 317-546-7720
Mobile: 317-431-3899
ch@acctsales.com
http://www.acctsales.com/

Robert Fremder
Accounting Practice Sold, LLC
Work: 412-322-8843
rfremder@sbcglobal.net
http://www.AccountingPracticeSold.com

Accounting/Tax Practices

Brian Naab
Naab Consulting
5511 E 82nd Street, Suite H
Indianapolis, IN 46250
Work: 888-726-6282
brian@naabconsulting.com
http://www.naabconsulting.com/

INDUSTRY EXPERTS

Chuck Hayes
ABA Advisors, LLC
5829 N. Post Road
Indianapolis, IN 46216
Work: 317-546-7720
Mobile: 317-431-3899
ch@acctsales.com
http://www.acctsales.com/

Robert Fremder
Accounting Practice Sold, LLC
Work: 412-322-8843
rfremder@sbcglobal.net
http://www.AccountingPracticeSold.com

Airport Operations

Michael Petridis
Axios Ventures, LLC
304 S. Cockrell Hill Road, Suite 201
Dallas, TX 75154
Work: (877) 538-4847
info@axiosadv.com
http://www.axiosadv.com

Ambulance Services

Reed Law
Southeast Business Exchange
9605 Caldwell Commons Circle, Ste A
Cornelius, NC 28031
Work: (704) 439-2510
reed@ambulancedeals.com
http://www.ambulancedeals.com

Robert Cimasi
Health Capital Consultants, LLC
2127 Innerbelt Business Center Drive,
Suite 107
St. Louis, MO 63114-5700
Work: 314-994-7641
rcimasi@healthcapital.com
https://www.healthcapital.com/

Ambulatory Surgery Centers

Robert Cimasi
Health Capital Consultants, LLC
2127 Innerbelt Business Center Drive,
Suite 107
St. Louis, MO 63114-5700
Work: 314-994-7641
rcimasi@healthcapital.com
https://www.healthcapital.com/

Assisted Living Facilities

Robert Cimasi
Health Capital Consultants, LLC
2127 Innerbelt Business Center Drive,
Suite 107
St. Louis, MO 63114-5700
Work: 314-994-7641
rcimasi@healthcapital.com
https://www.healthcapital.com/

Auto Body Repair

Bob McDowell
McDowell Business Associates
4130 Proton Drive Bldg 45D
Addison, TX 75001
Work: (214) 404-9133
Bobmcdowell58@gmail.com
http://mcdowellbb.com

Auto Dealers—New Cars

Scott Krause
AutoBizBrokers
3217 S. Cherokee Ln, Suite 730
Woodstock, GA 30188
Work: 404-406-3005
Scott@AutoBizBrokers.com
http://AutoBizBrokers.com

Auto Repair
(Auto Service Centers)

Bob McDowell
McDowell Business Associates
4130 Proton Drive Bldg 45D
Addison, TX 75001
Work: (214) 404-9133
Bobmcdowell58@gmail.com
http://mcdowellbb.com

Joseph Harrel
Sunbelt Montreal West Island
352 Dorval Ave, Bureau 207
Dorval, QC H9S3H8
Mobile: 514-927-3585
jharrel@sunbeltnetwork.com
http://sunbeltwestisland.com

Harold Janke
Sunbelt Business Intermediaries and
Omega Franchise Advisors
Work: 760-612-7018
halj@omegabusinessadvisors.com
http://sdcoast.sunbeltnetwork.com

Auto Transmission Centers

Bob McDowell
McDowell Business Associates
4130 Proton Drive Bldg 45D
Addison, TX 75001
Work: (214) 404-9133
Bobmcdowell58@gmail.com
http://mcdowellbb.com

Aviation and Aerospace

Michael Petridis
Axios Ventures, LLC
304 S. Cockrell Hill Road, Suite 201
Dallas, TX 75154
Work: (877) 538-4847
info@axiosadv.com
http://www.axiosadv.com

Jacques Bouzoubaa
Synergen Advisors, Inc
3425 Lebon Drive
San Diego, CA 92122
Work: 619-867-3758
jbouzoubaa@gmail.com

Bakeries—Commercial

Kenny Leif
Route World Brokers, Inc.
99 W Hawthorne Ave
Valley Stream, NY 11580
Work: (516) 825-6050
Mobile: (914) 337-2357
RWBKRS@GMAIL.COM
http://Routeworldbrokers.com

Bars

Rick Maerkle
American Investment Brokers/
Jacksonville Business Brokers
4600 Touchton Rd., Bld. 100, STE
150
Jacksonville, FL 32216
Work: 828-989-1858
Brokerrick@gmail.com
http://americaninvestmentbrokers.com/

Terri Sokoloff
Specialty Tavern & Restaurant
Brokers
3205 McKnight E Dr
Pittsburgh, PA 15237
Work: 412-656-4227
terri@specialtygroup.com
http://Specialtygroup.com

Bars—Adult Only
(Adult Clubs/Nightclubs)

H. Hines
HWH Properties
1099 E Oconee St
Chesnee, SC 29323
Work: (864) 580-3826
updaze@aol.com

INDUSTRY EXPERTS

Bars—Nightclubs

Jeff Adam
Megabite Restaurant Brokers, LLC/
Adam Noble Group, LLC
2000 E. Lamar Blvd. Suite 600
Arlington, TX 76006
Work: 817-467-2161
jeff@megabite-rb.com
http://www.megabite-rb.com

Rick Maerkle
American Investment Brokers/
Jacksonville Business Brokers
4600 Touchton Rd., Bld. 100, STE 150
Jacksonville, FL 32216
Work: 828-989-1858
Brokerrick@gmail.com
http://americaninvestmentbrokers.com/

Bed & Breakfasts

Bob Fuehr
The Inn Broker, Inc.
11368 E. Indian Lake Dr.
Vicksburg, MI 49097-9101
Work: 269-649-5556
fuehr@innbroker.com
http://innbroker.com

Blood and Organ Banks

Robert Cimasi
Health Capital Consultants, LLC
2127 Innerbelt Business Center Drive,
Suite 107
St. Louis, MO 63114-5700
Work: 314-994-7641
rcimasi@healthcapital.com
https://www.healthcapital.com/

Bowling Centers

Sandy Hansell
Sandy Hansell & Associates
28200 Southfield Rd
Lathrup Village, MI 48076
Work: (800) 222-9131
sandyhansell@aol.com
http://www.sandyhansell.com

Camps

Nick Gugliuzza
Empire Business Brokers
2821 Riverside Dr.
Ottawa, ON K1V 8N4
Work: 613-731-9140
gregkells@sunbeltcanada.com
http://www.sunbeltcanada.com

Canadian Business Sales and Acquisitions

Greg Kells
Sunbelt Business Brokers Canada
928 Fronch Rd
Buffalo, NY 14227
Work: 716-240-2544
Nick@Empirebb.com
http://www.Empirebb.com

Car Washes— Full Service/Exterior

Harold Janke
Sunbelt Business Intermediaries and
Omega Franchise Advisors
Work: 760-612-7018
halj@omegabusinessadvisors.com
http://sdcoast.sunbeltnetwork.com

Card Shops

Ed Pendarvis
Sunbelt Network
571 Savannah Hwy
Charleston, SC 29407
Work: 843-819-7842
etp@sunbeltnetwork.com
http://www.sunbeltnetwork.com

Chiropractic Practices

Keith Borglum
Professional Management and
Marketing
3468 Piner Road
Santa Rosa, CA 95401-3954
Work: (707) 546-4433
KBorglum@MedicalPracticeAppraisal.com
http://www.MedicalPracticeAppraisal.com

Robert Cimasi
Health Capital Consultants, LLC
2127 Innerbelt Business Center Drive,
Suite 107
St. Louis, MO 63114-5700
Work: 314-994-7641
rcimasi@healthcapital.com
https://www.healthcapital.com/

Collection Agencies

Edward Valaitis
Edison Avenue Capital LLC.
Work: 1-800-975-2114
info@EdisonAvenue.com
http://www.EdisonAvenue.com

Construction—In General

David Sweeten
Business Brokers of Texas
8632 Fredericksburg Rd.
San Antonio, TX 78240
Work: (210) 697-8760 x 202
david@brokersoftexas.com
http://www.brokersoftexas.com

Bill Scott
Front Range Business, Inc.
4816 Chippendale Drive
Fort Collins, CO 80526
Work: 970-215-2293
bscott@frontrangebusiness.com
https://frontrangebusiness.com/

Rhett Kniep
Centurion 7 Business Advisors
PO Box 2065
Rocklin, CA 95677
Work: 916-741-7390
rhett@centurion7.com
http://centurion7.com/

Enrique Lara
7 Development Group LLC
Work: 786-334-7532
eblara52@gmail.com

Construction— Specialty Trades

Chris Bond
Murphy Business & Financial
Corporation
15 E. Central St
Franklin, MA 2038
Work: (508) 440-5670
Mobile: (508) 380-7997
c.bond@murphybusiness.com
http://timesupllc.com

Rhett Kniep
Centurion 7 Business Advisors
PO Box 2065
Rocklin, CA 95677
Work: 916-741-7390
rhett@centurion7.com
http://centurion7.com/

INDUSTRY EXPERTS

Contract Manufacturing

Greg Carpenter
BTI Group/California Equity Advisors
4 North 2nd Street, Suite 560
San Jose, CA 95113
Work: 408-385-6658
Mobile: 408-898-0393
gregcarpenter@business-team.com
http://www.ca-equity.com

Day Care Centers/Children

David Sweeten
Business Brokers of Texas
8632 Fredericksburg Rd.
San Antonio, TX 78240
Work: (210) 697-8760 x 202
david@brokersoftexas.com
http://www.brokersoftexas.com

Jacques Bouzoubaa
Synergen Advisors, Inc
3425 Lebon Drive
San Diego, CA 92122
Work: 619-867-3758
jbouzoubaa@gmail.com

Henry Tiberi
Front Range Business, Inc.
5353 Manhattan Circle, Suite 101
Boulder, CO 80303
Work: 303-271-1010
htiberi@frontrangebusiness.com
http://www.frontrangebusiness.com

Dennis Mope
Schools For Sale, Inc.
8409 Tibet Butler Dr.
Windermere, FL 34786
Work: 407-865-4385
schoolsforsale@aol.com
http://www.schoolsforsale.com

Shep Campbell
CBI+Team
11601 Pleasant Ridge Road, Suite 101
Little Rock, AR 72212
Work: 870-450-3734
shep.campbell@cbiteam.com

Delivery Services (Courier Services)

Dawn Obarowski
Total Business Service Solutions, Inc.
Work: 980-245-7515
Mobile: 954-614-6211
dawn.e.obie@gmail.com
http://www.routeexperts.com

Dental Practices

Anthony Citrolo
New York Business Brokerage Inc.
7600 Jericho Turnpike, Suite 403
Woodbury, NY 11797
Work: (631) 390-9650
anthony@nybbinc.com
http://www.nybbinc.com

Cindy Collier
Healthcare Valuation Solutions
100 Highland Park Village, Suite 200
Dallas, TX 75205
Work: 214-295-3295
Mobile: 614-783-1671
cindycollier@cindycollier.com
http://www.cindycollier.com

Robert Cimasi
Health Capital Consultants, LLC
2127 Innerbelt Business Center Drive, Suite 107
St. Louis, MO 63114-5700
Work: 314-994-7641
rcimasi@healthcapital.com
https://www.healthcapital.com/

Rod Johnston
Omni Dental Practice Group
6513 132nd Ave NE #200
Kirkland, WA 98033
Work: 206-979-2660
rod@omni-pg.com
http://www.omni-pg.com

Diagnostic Imaging Centers

Robert Cimasi
Health Capital Consultants, LLC
2127 Innerbelt Business Center Drive,
Suite 107
St. Louis, MO 63114-5700
Work: 314-994-7641
rcimasi@healthcapital.com
https://www.healthcapital.com/

Dialysis Centers

Robert Cimasi
Health Capital Consultants, LLC
2127 Innerbelt Business Center Drive,
Suite 107
St. Louis, MO 63114-5700
Work: 314-994-7641
rcimasi@healthcapital.com
https://www.healthcapital.com/

Disability Facilities

Robert Cimasi
Health Capital Consultants, LLC
2127 Innerbelt Business Center Drive,
Suite 107
St. Louis, MO 63114-5700
Work: 314-994-7641
rcimasi@healthcapital.com
https://www.healthcapital.com/

INDUSTRY EXPERTS

Distribution/Wholesale—Durable Goods

Chris Bond
Murphy Business & Financial
Corporation
15 E. Central St
Franklin, MA 2038
Work: (508) 440-5670
Mobile: (508) 380-7997
c.bond@murphybusiness.com
http://timesupllc.com

Distribution/Wholesale—Grocery Products

Kenny Leif
Route World Brokers, Inc.
99 W Hawthorne Ave
Valley Stream, NY 11580
Work: (516) 825-6050
Mobile: (914) 337-2357
RWBKRS@GMAIL.COM
http://Routeworldbrokers.com

Distribution/Wholesale—In General

Chris Bond
Murphy Business & Financial
Corporation
15 E. Central St
Franklin, MA 2038
Work: (508) 440-5670
Mobile: (508) 380-7997
c.bond@murphybusiness.com
http://timesupllc.com

Anthony Citrolo
New York Business Brokerage Inc.
7600 Jericho Turnpike, Suite 403
Woodbury, NY 11797
Work: (631) 390-9650
anthony@nybbinc.com
http://www.nybbinc.com

INDUSTRY EXPERTS

John Henberger
Henberger Group Inc.
11622 El Camino Real, Suite 100
San Diego, CA 92130
Work: 760-271-5541
john@henberger.com
http://www.henberger.com

David Sweeten
Business Brokers of Texas
8632 Fredericksburg Rd.
San Antonio, TX 78240
Work: (210) 697-8760 x 202
david@brokersoftexas.com
http://www.brokersoftexas.com

Steve Ferber
The Wheatley Group
14358 North Frank Lloyd Wright,
Suite 1
Scottsdale, AZ 85260-8844
Work: 480-477-6305
steve@steveferber.com
http://www.steveferber.com

Darrow Graham
Transworld Business Advisors of
Grapevine
1701 West Northwest Highway,
Suite 100
Grapevine, TX 76051
Work: 214-729-2033
dgraham@tworld.com
http://www.tworld.com/grapevine

Distribution/Wholesale—Medical Equipment & Supplies

Alan Horwitz
Sunbelt Business Brokers of Las
Vegas
2300 W Sahara Suite 841
Las Vegas, NV 89102
Work: 702-714-0229
Mobile: 702-997-5453
lvbusinessbroker@gmail.com
http://vegasbusinessbroker.com

Dog Kennels

Teija Heikkila
National Kennel Sales & Appraisals
Work: 970-632-2075
teija@nationalkennelsales.com
http://nationalkennelsales.com

Dry Cleaners

Liliane Tietjen
Patriot Business Advisors
4387 Swamp Rd. #255
Doylestown, PA 18902
Work: (267) 391-7642
tietjen@patriotbusinessadvisors.com
http://www.patriotbusinessadvisors.com

Vic Kharadjian
Business Team
Work: 818-571-5628
vic@business-team.com
http://www.business-team.com

Peter Picciano
Premier Business Brokers
1654 Farmington Circle
Wellington, FL 33414
Work: 888-999-5603
peter@premierbusinessbrokers.com
http://www.premierbusinessbrokers.com

E-Cigarette Stores/ Vapor Stores

Kimberly Deas
Murphy Business Services
841 Prudential Drive, 12th Floor
Jacksonville, FL 32207
Work: 904-683-6655
Mobile: 904-571-9580
k.deas@murphybusiness.com
http://SellYourBusinessFlorida.com

Chris Williams
Work: 602-377-8790
media.ivgroup@gmail.com
http://www.infinitevapor.com

E-Commerce (Internet Sales)

Michael Ballas
Self Employed
Mobile: (805) 341-3361
michael.ballas@yahoo.com
http://mballas.com

Environmental Sciences

Craig Jones
Integral Consulting Inc.
Work: 831-334-8466
cjones@integral-corp.com
http://www.integral-corp.com

Fertility Clinics

Robert Cimasi
Health Capital Consultants, LLC
2127 Innerbelt Business Center Drive,
Suite 107
St. Louis, MO 63114-5700
Work: 314-994-7641
rcimasi@healthcapital.com
https://www.healthcapital.com/

Fitness Centers

Matthew Bradbury
Business Acquisition and Merger
Associates
3111-B Springbank Ln
Charlotte, NC 28226
Work: 704-295-0102
matt@buysellyourbusiness.com
http://www.buysellyourbusiness.com

Kevin Berson
Seapoint Business Advisors
2535 Townsgate Road Suite 301
Westlake Village, CA 91361
Work: 310-985-0250
kevin@seapointadvisors.com
http://www.seapointadvisors.com

Michael Hickey
Royalty Group Realty
Work: 604-762-6429
michael@yourbusinessbroker.ca
http://www.yourbusinessbroker.ca

Bob Fariss
Murphy Business & Financial
Corporation
5604 Poplar Court West
Colleyville, TX 76034
Work: 214-751-3921
Mobile: 817-471-9961
b.fariss@murphybusiness.com
http://www.tarrantbusinessbroker-fariss-murphy.com/

Don Owens
Work: 317-606-5417
don.owens96@comcast.net

Food Service Contractors

Jeff Adam
Megabite Restaurant Brokers, LLC/
Adam Noble Group, LLC
2000 E. Lamar Blvd. Suite 600
Arlington, TX 76006
Work: 817-467-2161
jeff@megabite-rb.com
http://www.megabite-rb.com

Joe Vagnone
Enlign Business Brokers
2009 Caminos Street
Raleigh, NC 27607
Work: 704-577-8030
joe@jvagnone.com
http://JVagnone.com

Franchise Food Businesses

Eric Gagnon
We Sell Restaurants
101 Centennial Olympic Park Drive SW
Atlanta, GA 30313
Work: (404) 800-6704
eric@wesellrestaurants.com
http://wesellrestaurants.com

INDUSTRY EXPERTS

Barney Greenbaum
FranNet/The Franchise Connection
5005 PIne Creek Drive
Westerville, OH 43081-4849
Work: (614) 882-7777
bgreenbaum@frannet.com

Franchises

Robin Gagnon
We Sell Restaurants
P.O. Box 387
Flagler Beach, FL 32136
Work: 404-513-5378
robin@wesellrestaurants.com
http://wesellrestaurants.com

Stacy Swift
FranNet Mountain West
1873 S. Bellaire Street, #620
Denver, CO 80222
Work: 303-715-0397
Mobile: 303-887-8887
sswift@frannet.com
http://www.frannet.com/sswift

Ed Teixeira
FranchiseKnowHow &
FranchiseGrade.com
76 Manchester Lane
Stony Brook, NY 11790
Work: 631-246-5782
ed.teixeira@franchisegrade.com
http://www.franchisegrade.com

Alan Horwitz
Sunbelt Business Brokers of Las
Vegas
2300 W Sahara Suite 841
Las Vegas, NV 89102
Work: 702-714-0229
Mobile: 702-997-5453
lvbusinessbroker@gmail.com
http://vegasbusinessbroker.com

Neal Patel
AGR Business Brokers
1 Station Plaza
Ridgefield Park, NJ 7660
Work: 800-845-2121
neal@agrbrokers.com
http://agrbrokers.com/

Fruits and Vegetables (Wholesale)

Kenny Leif
Route World Brokers, Inc.
99 W Hawthorne Ave
Valley Stream, NY 11580
Work: (516) 825-6050
Mobile: (914) 337-2357
RWBKRS@GMAIL.COM
http://Routeworldbrokers.com

Funeral Homes/Services

David Deighton
Mainstreet Business Brokers
6365 Acorn Way
Linden, MI 48451
Mobile: 810-835-1845
david.deighton@gmail.com
http://www.mainstreetbusinessbrokers.com

Gas Stations W/ Convenience Stores/ Minimarts

Harold Janke
Sunbelt Business Intermediaries and
Omega Franchise Advisors
Work: 760-612-7018
halj@omegabusinessadvisors.com
http://sdcoast.sunbeltnetwork.com

Tony Amato
Avison Young
3993 Howard Hughes Parkway Suite 350
Las Vegas, NV 89169
Work: 702-472-7979
tony.amato@avisonyoung.com
http://www.avisonyoung.com

Mark Habib
Royal Crown Group
3780 Miramontes Cir
Wellington, FL 33414
Work: 561-244-2575
mhabib@theroyalcrowngroup.com
http://www.theroyalcrowngroup.com

Gift Shops

Ed Pendarvis
Sunbelt Network
571 Savannah Hwy
Charleston, SC 29407
Work: 843-819-7842
etp@sunbeltnetwork.com
http://www.sunbeltnetwork.com

Golf Courses

Chris George
George & Company
65 James Street
Worcester, MA 1603
Work: 508-753-1400
cgeorge@georgeandco.com

Green Businesses

Matthew Bradbury
Business Acquisition and Merger
Associates
3111-B Springbank Ln
Charlotte, NC 28226
Work: 704-295-0102
matt@buysellyourbusiness.com
http://www.buysellyourbusiness.com

Home Centers

David Sweeten
Business Brokers of Texas
8632 Fredericksburg Rd.
San Antonio, TX 78240
Work: (210) 697-8760 x 202
david@brokersoftexas.com
http://www.brokersoftexas.com

Home Health Care/Home Nursing Agencies

Lilia Berezkina
VR Business Brokers Boca Raton/
Palm Beaches, FL
4722 NW Boca Raton Blvd.
Suite C-105
Boca Raton, FL 33431
Work: 561-756-9222
marketing@vrbocaraton.com
http://www.vrbocaraton.com

Robert Cimasi
Health Capital Consultants, LLC
2127 Innerbelt Business Center Drive,
Suite 107
St. Louis, MO 63114-5700
Work: 314-994-7641
rcimasi@healthcapital.com
https://www.healthcapital.com/

Ed Teixeira
FranchiseKnowHow &
FranchiseGrade.com
76 Manchester Lane
Stony Brook, NY 11790
Work: 631-246-5782
ed.teixeira@franchisegrade.com
http://www.franchisegrade.com

Vasilis Georgiou
CrossRoads Business Brokers, Inc.
700 Irvine Center Drive, Suite 800
Irvine, CA 92618
Work: 949-753-2825
Mobile: 949-462-9543
georgiouv@crossroadsbusiness.com
http://www.CrossRoadsBusiness.com

Penny Papaioannou
Atlantic Business Brokers, LLC
Work: 856-524-5178
atlanticbusinessbrokers@comcast.net

INDUSTRY EXPERTS

Chak Reddy
Elite Mergers & Acquisitions
2260 E Bidwell St #1114
Folsom, CA 95630
Work: 916-220-3052
creddy@tm.caks.net
http://www.EliteMandA.com

Hospitals—
Medical and Surgical

Robert Cimasi
Health Capital Consultants, LLC
2127 Innerbelt Business Center Drive,
Suite 107
St. Louis, MO 63114-5700
Work: 314-994-7641
rcimasi@healthcapital.com
https://www.healthcapital.com/

Hospitals—Psychiatric and
Substance Abuse

Robert Cimasi
Health Capital Consultants, LLC
2127 Innerbelt Business Center Drive,
Suite 107
St. Louis, MO 63114-5700
Work: 314-994-7641
rcimasi@healthcapital.com
https://www.healthcapital.com/

Hospitals—Specialty

Robert Cimasi
Health Capital Consultants, LLC
2127 Innerbelt Business Center Drive,
Suite 107
St. Louis, MO 63114-5700
Work: 314-994-7641
rcimasi@healthcapital.com
https://www.healthcapital.com/

Hotels & Motels

Barney Greenbaum
FranNet/The Franchise Connection
5005 PIne Creek Drive
Westerville, OH 43081-4849
Work: (614) 882-7777
bgreenbaum@frannet.com

Dennis Serpone
New England Restaurant Brokers
580 Salem St., Ste. 32
Wakefield, MA 1880
Work: 617-721-9655
DSerpone@comcast.net
http://NERestaurantBrokers.com

Neal Patel
AGR Business Brokers
1 Station Plaza
Ridgefield Park, NJ 7660
Work: 800-845-2121
neal@agrbrokers.com
http://agrbrokers.com/

Tim Blais
Gateway Business Brokers
Work: 902-441-9589
tim@gatewaybusinessbrokers.ca
http://www.gatewaybusinessbrokers.ca

HVAC—Heating, Ventilating
& Air Conditioning

Mike Lohbeck
MGL Business Solutions
6665 Taylor Road
Cincinnati, OH 45248-2124
Work: 513-200-0247
Mike@MGLBusinesssolutions.com
http://www.MGLBusinesssolutions.com

Inns

Bob Fuehr
The Inn Broker, Inc.
11368 E. Indian Lake Dr.
Vicksburg, MI 49097-9101
Work: 269-649-5556
fuehr@innbroker.com
http://innbroker.com

Insurance Agencies/ Brokerages

Kimberly Deas
Murphy Business Services
841 Prudential Drive, 12th Floor
Jacksonville, FL 32207
Work: 904-683-6655
Mobile: 904-571-9580
k.deas@murphybusiness.com
http://SellYourBusinessFlorida.com

Jeremy Hovater
Sunset Insurance Group
PO Box 1163
Montrose, AL 36559
Work: 251-751-4744
jch@sunsetig.com
http://www.sunsetig.com

Larry Morrison
BTN
Work: 866-475-9992
Larry.Morrison@comcast.net

Kathryn Christ
JMJ Brokers, Inc.
Work: 904-451-7604
kathy@jmjbrokers.com
http://www.jmjbrokers.com

David Ballou
Transworld Business Advisors
1962 SE Port St Lucie Blvd
Port St Lucie, FL 34952
Work: 772-207-3499
DBallou@TWorld.com
http://www.tworld.com/davidballou/

Stuart Ganis
Ganis Consulting
3655 Torrance Blvd, Ste 210
Torrance, CA 90503
Work: 310-937-6200
stuart@ganisco.com
http://www.GanisCo.com

Insurance Companies— Property & Casualty

Kimberly Deas
Murphy Business Services
841 Prudential Drive, 12th Floor
Jacksonville, FL 32207
Work: 904-683-6655
Mobile: 904-571-9580
k.deas@murphybusiness.com
http://SellYourBusinessFlorida.com

David Ballou
Transworld Business Advisors
1962 SE Port St Lucie Blvd
Port St Lucie, FL 34952
Work: 772-207-3499
DBallou@TWorld.com
http://www.tworld.com/davidballou/

Janitorial Services

Thomas Milana
Transworld Business Advisors
5101 NW 21st Avenue Suite 300
Fort Lauderdale, FL 33309
Work: 754-224-3118
Mobile: 561-702-6867
tom@tworld.com
http://www.tworldadvisor.com

INDUSTRY EXPERTS

Liquefied Petroleum Gas

Tony Amato
Avison Young
3993 Howard Hughes Parkway
Suite 350
Las Vegas, NV 89169
Work: 702-472-7979
tony.amato@avisonyoung.com
http://www.avisonyoung.com

Reed Law
Southeast Business Exchange
9605 Caldwell Commons Circle, Suite A
Cornelius, NC 28031
Work: (704) 439-2510
reed@ambulancedeals.com
http://www.ambulancedeals.com

Liquor Stores/Package Stores (Beer, Wine & Liquor Stores)

Stephen Atkins
Atkins Business Solutions
1830 Ritchie Hwy.
Annapolis, MD 21409
Work: 443-618-3213
steveatkins1830@gmail.com
http://www.atkinsrealtygroup.com

Adam Bauer
The Business Exchange LLC.
712 Main St.
Hyannis, MA 2601
Work: 508-790-4500
Mobile: 508-737-3613
abauer@tbxllc.com
http://www.tbxllc.com

Lumberyards

David Sweeten
Business Brokers of Texas
8632 Fredericksburg Rd.
San Antonio, TX 78240
Work: (210) 697-8760 x 202
david@brokersoftexas.com
http://www.brokersoftexas.com

Machine Shops

Chris George
George & Company
65 James Street
Worcester, MA 1603
Work: 508-753-1400
cgeorge@georgeandco.com

Julian Solomons
Solomons Strategic Advisors
Work: 949-861-1544
julian@solomonsadvisors.com
http://www.solomonsadvisors.com

Mail and Parcel Centers

Jeff Adam
Megabite Restaurant Brokers, LLC/
Adam Noble Group, LLC
2000 E. Lamar Blvd. Suite 600
Arlington, TX 76006
Work: 817-467-2161
jeff@megabite-rb.com
http://www.megabite-rb.com

Rodd Feingold
My Eye Media, LLC
2211 N. Hollywood Way
Burbank, CA 91505
Work: 818-674-2889
cabizexpert@yahoo.com
https://www.linkedin.com/in/
roddfeingold/

Manufacturing—General

Chris Bond
Murphy Business & Financial
Corporation
15 E. Central St
Franklin, MA 2038
Work: (508) 440-5670
Mobile: (508) 380-7997
c.bond@murphybusiness.com
http://timesupllc.com

Michael Ballas
Self Employed
Mobile: (805) 341-3361
michael.ballas@yahoo.com
http://mballas.com

Brenda Bernhard
Strong Business Advisors
3500 West Olive Avenue, Suite 300
Burbank, CA 91505
Work: (818) 321-6456
brenda@brendathebroker.com
http://Brendathebroker.com

Cal Heseman
Gateway Business Advisors
324 Sixth Avenue North
Jacksonville Beach, FL 32250
Work: 904-521-3602
cal@gatewaybusinessadvisors.com
http://www.gatewaybusinessadvisors.com

John Henberger
Henberger Group Inc.
11622 El Camino Real, Suite 100
San Diego, CA 92130
Work: 760-271-5541
john@henberger.com
http://www.henberger.com

David Kochendorfer
Wisconsin Small Business
Development Center
Work: 715-415-0300
koke@brucetel.net

Frances Brunelle
Accelerated Manufacturing Brokers
75 Frontage Rd
Asbury, NJ 8802
Work: 908-387-1000
Fran@AcceleratedMfgBrokers.com
http://www.AcceleratedMfgBrokers.com

Manufacturing— Metal Fabrication

Steve Bragg
Calhoun Companies
7600 Parklawn Ave., Suite 225
Minneapolis, MN 55435
Work: 218-663-7682
sbragg@boreal.org
http://www.calhouncompanies.com

Matthew Bradbury
Business Acquisition and Merger
Associates
3111-B Springbank Ln
Charlotte, NC 28226
Work: 704-295-0102
matt@buysellyourbusiness.com
http://www.buysellyourbusiness.com

Manufacturing— Plastic Products

Chak Reddy
Elite Mergers & Acquisitions
2260 E Bidwell St #1114
Folsom, CA 95630
Work: 916-220-3052
creddy@tm.caks.net
http://www.EliteMandA.com

INDUSTRY EXPERTS

Manufacturing—Powder Metallurgy Processing

Richard Mowrey
Management Services & Development, Ltd.
103 Carmalt Avenue
Punxsutawney, PA 15767
Work: 814-938-5463
rdm@MergerMentor.com
http://www.Biz-Hub.com

Manufacturing—Proprietary Products

Thomas Poyser
American Business Investors, Inc.
2711 E. 96th Street
Indianapolis, IN 46240
Work: 317-513-2898
TomAmericanBusiness@gmail.com
http://www.ABI-Broker.com

Manufacturing—Tactical Military Equipment

Jeff Snell
ENLIGN Business Brokers
2009 Caminos Street
Raleigh, NC 27607
Work: 919-624-1124
jsnell@enlign.com

Manufacturing—Wood Office Furniture

William Thomas
Florida Business Brokers
8641 Lake Worth Rd
Lake Worth, FL 33467
Work: 561-914-1182
William@Floridabizmls.com
http://www.FloridaBizMLS.com

Medical and Diagnostic Laboratories

Robert Cimasi
Health Capital Consultants, LLC
2127 Innerbelt Business Center Drive, Suite 107
St. Louis, MO 63114-5700
Work: 314-994-7641
rcimasi@healthcapital.com
https://www.healthcapital.com/

Medical Billing

Sean Seaman
First Choice Business Brokers
9899 Hibert St., Suite B
San Diego, CA 92131
Work: 858-472-3297
sean@fcbb.com
http://www.sdhotlist.com

Medical Practices

Keith Borglum
Professional Management and Marketing
3468 Piner Road
Santa Rosa, CA 95401-3954
Work: (707) 546-4433
KBorglum@MedicalPracticeAppraisal.com
http://www.MedicalPracticeAppraisal.com

Cindy Collier
Healthcare Valuation Solutions
100 Highland Park Village, Suite 200
Dallas, TX 75205
Work: 214-295-3295
Mobile: 614-783-1671
cindycollier@cindycollier.com
http://www.cindycollier.com

Robert Cimasi
Health Capital Consultants, LLC
2127 Innerbelt Business Center Drive,
Suite 107
St. Louis, MO 63114-5700
Work: 314-994-7641
rcimasi@healthcapital.com
https://www.healthcapital.com/

Kathryn Christ
JMJ Brokers, Inc.
Work: 904-451-7604
kathy@jmjbrokers.com
http://www.jmjbrokers.com

David Greene
Medical Practice Brokers
15847 Woodmeadow Ct.
Colorado Springs, CO 80921
Work: 719-487-9973
david@practicebrokers.com
http://www.practicebrokers.com

Alan Horwitz
Sunbelt Business Brokers of Las Vegas
2300 W Sahara Suite 841
Las Vegas, NV 89102
Work: 702-714-0229
Mobile: 702-997-5453
lvbusinessbroker@gmail.com
http://vegasbusinessbroker.com

Audra Padilla
Medical Practice Brokers, LLC
7680 Goddard St., Suite 100
Colorado Springs, CO 80920
Work: 719-644-2200
audra@practicebrokers.com
http://www.practicebrokers.com

Andrew Rogerson
Rogerson Business Services
5150 Fair Oaks Blvd, #101-198
Carmichael, CA 95608-5788
Work: 916-570-2674
andrew@rogersonbusinessservices.com
https://www.
rogersonbusinessservices.com/

Mental Health and Substance Abuse Centers

Robert Cimasi
Health Capital Consultants, LLC
2127 Innerbelt Business Center Drive,
Suite 107
St. Louis, MO 63114-5700
Work: 314-994-7641
rcimasi@healthcapital.com
https://www.healthcapital.com/

Mental Health Physicians

Robert Cimasi
Health Capital Consultants, LLC
2127 Innerbelt Business Center Drive,
Suite 107
St. Louis, MO 63114-5700
Work: 314-994-7641
rcimasi@healthcapital.com
https://www.healthcapital.com/

Mental Health Practitioners (Except Physicians)

Robert Cimasi
Health Capital Consultants, LLC
2127 Innerbelt Business Center Drive,
Suite 107
St. Louis, MO 63114-5700
Work: 314-994-7641
rcimasi@healthcapital.com
https://www.healthcapital.com/

Mining—Metals

Chuck Berg
Coldwell Banker Commercial Advisors
6550 South Millrock Drive, Suite 200
Salt Lake City, UT 84121
Work: 801-947-8308
chuck.berg@cbcadvisors.com
http://www.cbcadvisors.com

INDUSTRY EXPERTS

Nursing Homes/Skilled Nursing Facilities

Ronald Ekstrom
Sunbelt Business Sales & Acquisitions
800 West Cummings, Suite 2000
Woburn, MA 1801
Work: 781-503-9040
rekstrom@sunbeltne.com
http://www.sunbeltnemergers.com

Robert Cimasi
Health Capital Consultants, LLC
2127 Innerbelt Business Center Drive,
Suite 107
St. Louis, MO 63114-5700
Work: 314-994-7641
rcimasi@healthcapital.com
https://www.healthcapital.com/

Office Staffing & Temporary Agencies

Robert Flynn
United Brokers Group LLC
110 Pheasant Drive
East Greenwich, RI 2818
Work: 401-744-0320
unitedbrokersgroup@gmail.com
http://www.unitedbrokersgrp.com

Oil & Gas Related Businesses

John Johnson
BluestemUSA, IBG Business & The
Oil & Gas Advisor
5800 East Skelly Drive Suite 125
Tulsa, OK 74135
Work: 918-749-6016
jjohnson@IBGBusiness.com
http://oilgasadvisor.com/

Larry Hughes
The Hughes Group
9301 Cedar Lake Ave. Suite 203
Oklahoma City, OK 73114
Work: 405-478-3800
larry@thehughes-group.com
http://www.thehughes-group.com

Optometry Practices

Robert Cimasi
Health Capital Consultants, LLC
2127 Innerbelt Business Center Drive,
Suite 107
St. Louis, MO 63114-5700
Work: 314-994-7641
rcimasi@healthcapital.com
https://www.healthcapital.com/

Don Schwaderer
Professional Practice Acquisitions
1338 Wren Lane
Powell, OH 43065
Work: 614-888-7616
don@ProfessionalPracticeAcquisitions.com
http://professionalpracticeacquisitions.com/

Kathryn Christ
JMJ Brokers, Inc.
Work: 904-451-7604
kathy@jmjbrokers.com
http://www.jmjbrokers.com

Randy Krivo
Sunbelt Business Brokers
1300 Godward St NE, Suite 6000
Minneapolis, MN 55413
Work: 651-288-3791
rkrivo@sunbeltmidwest.com
http://www.sunbeltmidwest.com

Gary Ware
Practice Consultants
11 Canary Court
Danville, CA 94526-4963
Work: 800-576-6935
gary@PracticeConsultants.com
http://www.PracticeConsultants.com

Pawn Shops

Rod Triplett
Murphy Business & Financial Corp
3259 E Sunshine Suite H
Springfield, MO 65804
Work: 417-883-7758
Mobile: 417-827-2249
r.triplett@murphybusiness.com

Pest Control

Al Woodward
A+ Business Brokers, Inc.
17193 NW 242nd Street
High Springs, FL 32643-9122
Work: 386-454-3333
alwoodward@pestcontrolbiz.com
http://pestcontrolbiz.com

Pet Grooming

Teija Heikkila
National Kennel Sales & Appraisals
Work: 970-632-2075
teija@nationalkennelsales.com
http://nationalkennelsales.com

Pharmacies and Drug Stores

Hitesh Patel
TRANSWORLD Business Advisors of
Capital Region
Work: 717-909-1652
hpatel@tworld.com
http://www.tworld.com/capitalregion/
agents/hiteshpatel/

Terrell Coe
Exit Equity
777 108th Avenue NE Suite 2100
Bellevue, WA 98004
Work: 206-851-0993
terrellcoe@gmail.com
https://www.linkedin.com/in/terrellcoe/

Physical Therapy

Keith Borglum
Professional Management and
Marketing
3468 Piner Road
Santa Rosa, CA 95401-3954
Work: (707) 546-4433
KBorglum@MedicalPracticeAppraisal.com
http://www.MedicalPracticeAppraisal.com

Anthony Citrolo
New York Business Brokerage Inc.
7600 Jericho Turnpike, Suite 403
Woodbury, NY 11797
Work: (631) 390-9650
anthony@nybbinc.com
http://www.nybbinc.com

Pizza Shops

Paul McNally
Central Florida Business Brokerage
498 Palm Springs Drive, Suite 100
Altamonte Springs, FL 32701
Work: 407-403-4455
Paul@cfbb.biz
http://www.CFBB.biz

Rick Maerkle
American Investment Brokers/
Jacksonville Business Brokers
4600 Touchton Rd., Bld. 100, STE
150
Jacksonville, FL 32216
Work: 828-989-1858
Brokerrick@gmail.com
http://americaninvestmentbrokers.com/

Podiatrists

Keith Borglum
Professional Management and
Marketing
3468 Piner Road
Santa Rosa, CA 95401-3954
Work: (707) 546-4433
KBorglum@MedicalPracticeAppraisal.com
http://www.MedicalPracticeAppraisal.com

INDUSTRY EXPERTS

Robert Cimasi
Health Capital Consultants, LLC
2127 Innerbelt Business Center Drive,
Suite 107
St. Louis, MO 63114-5700
Work: 314-994-7641
rcimasi@healthcapital.com
https://www.healthcapital.com/

Don Schwaderer
Professional Practice Acquisitions
1338 Wren Lane
Powell, OH 43065
Work: 614-888-7616
don@ProfessionalPracticeAcquisitions.com
http://professionalpracticeacquisitions.com/

Pool Service (Swimming)

John Hawke
SpringBoard Pool Route Brokers
2795 E. Bidwell Street, Suite 100-243
Folsom, CA 95630
Work: 888-998-7665
john@sbpoolroutes.com
http://www.sbpoolroutes.com

Printing: Flexographic, Label, Silk Screen

Rock LaManna
LaManna Alliance
804 East Windward Way, Suite 618
West Palm Beach, FL 33462-8035
Work: 561-543-2323
rock@rocklamanna.com
http://www.rocklamanna.com

Print Shops/Commercial Printers

David Sweeten
Business Brokers of Texas
8632 Fredericksburg Rd.
San Antonio, TX 78240
Work: (210) 697-8760 x 202
david@brokersoftexas.com
http://www.brokersoftexas.com

Rock LaManna
LaManna Alliance
804 East Windward Way, Suite 618
West Palm Beach, FL 33462-8035
Work: 561-543-2323
rock@rocklamanna.com
http://www.rocklamanna.com

Property Management Companies

David Sweeten
Business Brokers of Texas
8632 Fredericksburg Rd.
San Antonio, TX 78240
Work: (210) 697-8760 x 202
david@brokersoftexas.com
http://www.brokersoftexas.com

Bill Scott
Front Range Business, Inc.
4816 Chippendale Drive
Fort Collins, CO 80526
Work: 970-215-2293
bscott@frontrangebusiness.com
https://frontrangebusiness.com/

Publishers—In General

Ronald Hoxter
Mill Creek Partners
715 Periwinkle Lane
Wynnewood, PA 19096
Work: 610-247-0922
Rhoxter@millcreekpartners.com
http://www.millcreekpartners.com

Rental Centers

Brenda Bernhard
Strong Business Advisors
3500 West Olive Avenue, Suite 300
Burbank, CA 91505
Work: (818) 321-6456
brenda@brendathebroker.com
http://Brendathebroker.com

Restaurants—Full Service

David Sweeten
Business Brokers of Texas
8632 Fredericksburg Rd.
San Antonio, TX 78240
Work: (210) 697-8760 x 202
david@brokersoftexas.com
http://www.brokersoftexas.com

Eric Gagnon
We Sell Restaurants
101 Centennial Olympic Park Drive SW
Atlanta, GA 30313
Work: (404) 800-6704
eric@wesellrestaurants.com
http://wesellrestaurants.com

Robin Gagnon
We Sell Restaurants
P.O. Box 387
Flagler Beach, FL 32136
Work: 404-513-5378
robin@wesellrestaurants.com
http://wesellrestaurants.com

Richard Chinappi
Read Commercial Properties, Inc.
Six Manhattan Square Suite 102
Hampton, VA 23666
Work: 757-865-6600
Mobile: 757-617-3237
rac@readcompanies.com
http://www.readcompanies.com

Vic Kharadjian
Business Team
Work: 818-571-5628
vic@business-team.com
http://www.business-team.com

Peter Picciano
Premier Business Brokers
1654 Farmington Circle
Wellington, FL 33414
Work: 888-999-5603
peter@premierbusinessbrokers.com
http://www.premierbusinessbrokers.com

Steve Bragg
Calhoun Companies
7600 Parklawn Ave., Suite 225
Minneapolis, MN 55435
Work: 218-663-7682
sbragg@boreal.org
http://www.calhouncompanies.com

Terri Sokoloff
Specialty Tavern & Restaurant
Brokers
3205 McKnight E Dr
Pittsburgh, PA 15237
Work: 412-656-4227
terri@specialtygroup.com
http://Specialtygroup.com

Paul Hyde
Hyde Valuations, Inc.
504 Grove Ave
Parma, ID 83660-0009
Work: 208-722-7272
prh@hydevaluations.com
http://www.hydevaluations.com

Michael Pfeffer
Murphy Business & Financial
Corporation
27499 Riverview Center Blvd., Suite 102
Bonita Springs, FL 34134
Work: 239-793-0431
Mobile: 239-877-9911
http://www.murphyofswfl.com

Adam Bauer
The Business Exchange LLC.
712 Main St.
Hyannis, MA 2601
Work: 508-790-4500
Mobile: 508-737-3613
abauer@tbxllc.com
http://www.tbxllc.com

Paul McNally
Central Florida Business Brokerage
498 Palm Springs Drive, Suite 100
Altamonte Springs, FL 32701
Work: 407-403-4455
Paul@cfbb.biz
http://www.CFBB.biz

INDUSTRY EXPERTS

Ron Niesmertelny
Restaurant Realty Associates
30 Maple Street
Somerville, NJ 8876
Work: 732-968-0001
rnies76408@aol.com

Dennis Serpone
New England Restaurant Brokers
580 Salem St., Ste. 32
Wakefield, MA 1880
Work: 617-721-9655
DSerpone@comcast.net
http://NERestaurantBrokers.com

Tricia Bernhardt
Restaurant eXchange
725 30th Street Suite 202
Sacramento, CA 95816
Work: 916-482-7979
tricia@restx.com
http://www.restx.com

Pablo Langesfeld
Transworld Business Brokers
8260 NW 27 Street
Miami, FL 33122
Work: 305-405-8142
Mobile: 786-290-1091
pablo@tworld.com
http://www.BizBarSell.com

Franco Ferrari
Sunbelt Orlando
1073 Willa Springs Drive, Suite 1005
Orlando, FL 32708
Work: 407-339-3101
info@fbba.com

Rick Maerkle
American Investment Brokers/
Jacksonville Business Brokers
4600 Touchton Rd., Bld. 100, STE 150
Jacksonville, FL 32216
Work: 828-989-1858
Brokerrick@gmail.com
http://americaninvestmentbrokers.com/

Julie Lazecki
Beach State Brokers
6975 A1A South Suite 3
St. Augustine, FL 32080
Work: 904-501-6011
julie@beachstatebrokers.com
http://www.beachstatebrokers.com

M Kathryn (Ryn) Longmaid
Santa Rosa Business & Commercial
318 Mendocino Avenue
Santa Rosa, CA 95401
Work: 707-526-1050
Ryn@Longmaid.com

Robert Leone
Acquisition Experts
Work: 772-621-0528
bobtbb@gmail.com
http://www.sellmybusinessportstlucie.com/

Greg Hrabcak
HER Commercial
Work: 614-906-2227
greg.hrabcak@herrealtors.com
http://www.greghrabcak.com

Michael Steinberg
Empire Business Management
Work: 516-835-4383
empirebusinessmgmt@gmail.com
http://www.
empirebusinessmanagement.com

Steve Josowitz
The Shumacher Group
Atlanta, GA
Work: 770-840-2121
steven@shumacher.com
http://www.shumacher.com

Charles Perkins
The Boston Restaurant Group, Inc.
PO Box 327
Boxford, MA 01921-9907
Work: 978-887-9895
cperkins@bostonrestaurantgroup.com
http://bostonrestaurantgroup.com

Restaurants—
Limited Service

Jeff Adam
Megabite Restaurant Brokers, LLC/
Adam Noble Group, LLC
2000 E. Lamar Blvd. Suite 600
Arlington, TX 76006
Work: 817-467-2161
jeff@megabite-rb.com
http://www.megabite-rb.com

David Sweeten
Business Brokers of Texas
8632 Fredericksburg Rd.
San Antonio, TX 78240
Work: (210) 697-8760 x 202
david@brokersoftexas.com
http://www.brokersoftexas.com

Barney Greenbaum
FranNet/The Franchise Connection
5005 Pine Creek Drive
Westerville, OH 43081-4849
Work: (614) 882-7777
bgreenbaum@frannet.com

Retail Businesses
(In General)

David Abbott
HPX Advisors
331 Shoshone Pl
Murfreesboro, TN 37128
Work: 615-631-5564
david@HPXadvisors.com
http://www.hpxadvisors.com

Route Distribution
Businesses

Kenny Leif
Route World Brokers, Inc.
99 W Hawthorne Ave
Valley Stream, NY 11580
Work: (516) 825-6050
Mobile: (914) 337-2357
RWBKRS@GMAIL.COM
http://Routeworldbrokers.com

Marshall Pollock
Transworld Business Advisors Of San
Diego North
701 Palomar Airport Road Suite # 125
Carlsbad, CA 92011
Work: 760-607-0641
mpollock@tworld.com
http://www.tworld.com/
sandiegonorthcounty

Patrick Gagliardi
Capital Business Solutions
1525 NW 3rd St Suite #9
Deerfield Beach, FL 33442
Work: 954-633-7278
pgagliardi@capitalbbw.com
http://www.capitalbbw.com

RV Parks

Rob Smith
Fortune Real Estate
4301 32nd St W, #EV8
Bradenton, FL 34205
Work: 941-812-6001
info@fortunerealestate.com

Schools—Educational &
Non-Vocational

Jacques Bouzoubaa
Synergen Advisors, Inc
3425 Lebon Drive
San Diego, CA 92122
Work: 619-867-3758
jbouzoubaa@gmail.com

Dennis Mope
Schools For Sale, Inc.
8409 Tibet Butler Dr.
Windermere, FL 34786
Work: 407-865-4385
schoolsforsale@aol.com
http://www.schoolsforsale.com

INDUSTRY EXPERTS

Charles Faherty
Charles Faherty & Associates, LLC
Work: 800-371-1159
cpfaherty@aol.com
http://www.c-f-associates.com

Richard Jackim
Jackim Woods & Co.
14961 Imperial Drive
Libertyville, IL 60048
Work: 224-513-5142
rjackim@jackimwoods.com
http://www.jackimwoods.com

Schools—
Vocational & Training

Dennis Mope
Schools For Sale, Inc.
8409 Tibet Butler Dr.
Windermere, FL 34786
Work: 407-865-4385
schoolsforsale@aol.com
http://www.schoolsforsale.com

Service Businesses (In General)

Randy Marshall
Doberstein Lemburg Commercial, Inc.
1401 Riverside Ave, Suite A
Fort Collins, CO 80524
Work: 970-691-7446
randy@dlcco.com

Sign Companies

Rock LaManna
LaManna Alliance
804 East Windward Way, Suite 618
West Palm Beach, FL 33462-8035
Work: 561-543-2323
rock@rocklamanna.com
http://www.rocklamanna.com

Software Companies

Blake Taylor
Synergy Business Brokers
7 Schuyler Street
New Rochelle, NY 10801
Work: 914-738-9350
btaylor@synergybb.com
http://www.synergybb.com

Subway

Lou Bellanca
AMD Business Brokers
2269 Lyell Ave, #201
Rochester, NY 14606
Work: 585-247-4750
lbellanca@amdbizbrokers.com
http://www.amdbizbrokers.com

Tanning Salons

Nick Modares
Neighborhood Business Brokers
285 Boulder Dr., Suite 100
Roswell, GA 30075
Work: 770-640-0010
nick@nbb-web.com
http://www.bizbrokersinc.com

Technology Companies—
Information

Anthony Citrolo
New York Business Brokerage Inc.
7600 Jericho Turnpike, Suite 403
Woodbury, NY 11797
Work: (631) 390-9650
anthony@nybbinc.com
http://www.nybbinc.com

Blake Taylor
Synergy Business Brokers
7 Schuyler Street
New Rochelle, NY 10801
Work: 914-738-9350
btaylor@synergybb.com
http://www.synergybb.com

Technology Companies— Manufacturing

Anthony Citrolo
New York Business Brokerage Inc.
7600 Jericho Turnpike, Suite 403
Woodbury, NY 11797
Work: (631) 390-9650
anthony@nybbinc.com
http://www.nybbinc.com

Chak Reddy
Elite Mergers & Acquisitions
2260 E Bidwell St #1114
Folsom, CA 95630
Work: 916-220-3052
creddy@tm.caks.net
http://www.EliteMandA.com

Technology Companies— Service

Chak Reddy
Elite Mergers & Acquisitions
2260 E Bidwell St #1114
Folsom, CA 95630
Work: 916-220-3052
creddy@tm.caks.net
http://www.EliteMandA.com

Blake Taylor
Synergy Business Brokers
7 Schuyler Street
New Rochelle, NY 10801
Work: 914-738-9350
btaylor@synergybb.com
http://www.synergybb.com

Therapists—Offices of Occupational, Physical, Speech and Audiologists

Robert Cimasi
Health Capital Consultants, LLC
2127 Innerbelt Business Center Drive,
Suite 107
St. Louis, MO 63114-5700
Work: 314-994-7641
rcimasi@healthcapital.com
https://www.healthcapital.com/

Tire Stores

Harold Janke
Sunbelt Business Intermediaries and
Omega Franchise Advisors
Work: 760-612-7018
halj@omegabusinessadvisors.com
http://sdcoast.sunbeltnetwork.com

Travel Agencies

Veena Sadana
Veena Lana Business Brokers,Inc.
801 Ocean Ave Ste 405
Santa Monica, CA 90403
Work: 310-963-1428
veenalana@gmail.com

Bob Sweeney
Innovative Travel Acquisitions, Inc.
1015 Clairborne Drive
Alpharetta, GA 30009
Work: 800-619-0185 *1
bob@tvlacq.com
http://www.tvlacq.com

Doug Haugen
Innovative Travel Acquisitions
1015 Clairborne Drive
Alpharetta, GA 30009
Work: 800-619-0185
Doug@tvlacq.com
http://www.tvlacq.com/

INDUSTRY EXPERTS

Trucking Companies

Brenda Bernhard
Strong Business Advisors
3500 West Olive Avenue, Suite 300
Burbank, CA 91505
Work: (818) 321-6456
brenda@brendathebroker.com
http://Brendathebroker.com

Vending Machine Industry

Kenny Leif
Route World Brokers, Inc.
99 W Hawthorne Ave
Valley Stream, NY 11580
Work: (516) 825-6050
Mobile: (914) 337-2357
RWBKRS@GMAIL.COM
http://Routeworldbrokers.com

Michael Kelner
Vending Biz Broker, LLC
Work: 704-942-4621
m.kelner@me.com
http://www.vbbadvisors.com

Veterinary Practices

Don Schwaderer
Professional Practice Acquisitions
1338 Wren Lane
Powell, OH 43065
Work: 614-888-7616
don@ProfessionalPracticeAcquisitions.com
http://professionalpracticeacquisitions.com/

David Greene
Medical Practice Brokers
15847 Woodmeadow Ct.
Colorado Springs, CO 80921
Work: 719-487-9973
david@practicebrokers.com
http://www.practicebrokers.com

Richard Wattles
Pacific Professionals, Inc
545 Sespe Avenue
Fillmore, CA 93015
Work: 805-524-3195
pacproinc@gmail.com
http://www.pacificproinc.com

Cal Heseman
Gateway Business Advisors
324 Sixth Avenue North
Jacksonville Beach, FL 32250
Work: 904-521-3602
cal@gatewaybusinessadvisors.com
http://www.gatewaybusinessadvisors.com

Wireless Communications

Brenda Bernhard
Strong Business Advisors
3500 West Olive Avenue, Suite 300
Burbank, CA 91505
Work: (818) 321-6456
brenda@brendathebroker.com
http://Brendathebroker.com

Tamer Shoukry
Mr. Wireless Ohio
Work: 614-226-2723
mrwirless@gmail.com

Notes

Notes

Notes

Notes

Notes

Notes